Teacher's Manual
Level Four

Elena Steele
K–12 Foreign Language Specialist
Clark County, Nevada, Public Schools

Holly Johnson
Español para ti Video Teacher

National Textbook Company
a division of NTC/Contemporary Publishing Group, Inc.
Lincolnwood, Illinois USA

Editorial and Production Management: Elm Street Publications, Wellesley, MA
Composition: William J. Cataldi, Ewing Systems, New York, NY
Illustrations: Don Wilson, Len Shalansky

ISBN: 0-8442-0315-7

Published by National Textbook Company,
a division of NTC/Contemporary Publishing Group, Inc.
4255 West Touhy Avenue
Lincolnwood (Chicago), Illinois 60646-1975 U.S.A.

Manufactured in the United States of America.

09 08 07 06 05 M L 0 9 8 7 6 5 4 3 2

Table of Contents 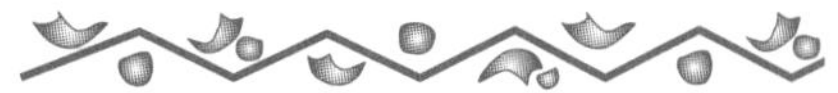

A Message from the Authors

Bienvenidos a *Español para ti.* (*Welcome to* ***Español para ti.***)

We are happy to welcome you to a new language adventure! It is our hope that you are excited about giving your students the gift of learning a second language. Relax and enjoy the experience! You don't need to speak Spanish in order to use ***Español para ti.*** The program offers you an abundance of support so that you can successfully join with your students in learning the language and the cultures of the Spanish-speaking world.

As experienced Spanish teachers, we have designed an interactive program offering you, our colleagues, the very best and easiest approach to teaching Spanish through the rich medium of video in a fun, exciting, and non-threatening way. Everything you need to facilitate instruction is provided for you in convenient kits. You and your students will enjoy the puppet characters, music, mimes, excursions, activities, and games that make learning Spanish through ***Español para ti*** a real treat.

For us, the creation of ***Español para ti*** has been a labor of love and a dream come true, and you are our partners in the realization of this dream. With your help, we can bring Spanish instruction to every child at the elementary school level. Your enthusiastic implementation of ***Español para ti*** will make your students successful language learners, and you will experience that Spanish truly is **para ti** (*for you*) and for everyone!

Our best wishes for a wonderful experience with ***Español para ti.***

Mil gracias y muy buena suerte. (*Many thanks and best wishes.*)

Elena Steele

Doña Elena
Elena Steele

Holly Johnson

La maestra
Holly Johnson

Español para ti Components 

Materials Center

Videocassettes

The videos serve as the core of instruction. The programs for Levels 1 and 2 consist of 17 videocassettes containing 66 fifteen-minute video lessons. The programs for Levels 3–5 consist of 20 videocassettes containing 60 twenty-minute video lessons. With the help of human-like puppets, a mime, and a dancer, the vivacious video teacher (**la maestra** in Spanish) introduces and practices Spanish. The interaction between the teacher and the other characters is lively and often results in humorous situations.

Teacher's Manual

The Teacher's Manual makes no assumptions that teachers speak Spanish, so any teacher can easily follow the step-by-step directions for presenting each lesson of ***Español para ti*** and coordinating the use of the many support materials. The Teacher's Manual for Level 4 provides a self-contained lesson plan for each of the 60 lessons. Each lesson plan includes:

- learning objectives for the lesson
- key vocabulary items with English translations, teaching tips, and cultural information
- an outline of what takes place on the video lesson
- activities and games that reinforce the language presented on the video
- miniature reproductions of the Blackline Masters used in the lesson

In addition, there are guidelines for formal and informal assessments and audiovisual techniques.

Teacher's Resource Book

This valuable resource contains:

- a course completion certificate, which can be duplicated for each child
- four letters to send home to parents, which explain the program and suggest ways that families can help and encourage children
- formal assessments to be used at the end of the semester and at the end of the year, and a rubric for holistic evaluations
- large Number Cards for 1–20 and 10–100 by tens
- Month and Season pictures
- 66 Blackline Masters to use in a variety of ways—for vocabulary practice, in games, and as aids to remembering songs

Activity Cassettes 1 and 2

These two cassettes provide listening and speaking activities that coordinate with the video lessons and reinforce them. These activities either practice what was taught in the related video lesson or review previously learned vocabulary.

Song Cassette

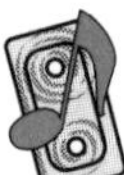

All the songs taught by the video teacher are included on Side A of this cassette. These songs are lively and fun, but are also instructional and teach vocabulary. Lyrics and translations for the songs appear in the lesson of the Teacher's Manual where a song is first introduced, as well as in the Song Appendix at the end of this book. Side B of the Song Cassette contains the Fredo stories.

Assessment Cassette

The audio portions of the Midyear Assessment are on Side A and the End-of-year Assessment on Side B.

Visuals Package

Puppets

Español para ti includes hand puppets for the two characters who appear most frequently on the videos for Levels 1, 2, and 3—the adorable but sometimes outrageous Rosco, a wolf, and the ever-lovable Dora, a cow. The video teacher talks to the puppets to model words, questions, and answers, and the puppets frequently provide further modeling by talking to one another. Sometimes the puppets ask the children questions or answer the video teacher's questions along with the children. Classroom teachers might find the puppets useful for the children to practice language. Some children may find speaking through or to the puppets less threatening than talking as themselves.

Flashcards

Two sets of Flashcards (Gold and Red) are provided for use in activities and for vocabulary reinforcement. The video teacher introduces vocabulary and expressions with the same large, colorful Flashcards, providing continuity between the videos and the classroom. Since they are on heavy paper and are large enough to be seen from a distance, they are ideal for use in classroom activities.

Posters

There are two large posters—the classroom and the animals' party. The classroom poster shows examples of the classroom vocabulary presented in the lessons. The colorful poster of the animals' party shows the animals for which the children learn Spanish names. The posters are featured in Levels 1, 2, and 3.

Las aventuras de Fredo (*Fredo's Adventures*)

New to the Level 4 ***Español para ti*** program is the storybook, ***Las aventuras de Fredo***, which consists of five short stories featured on various segments of the video. The five stories feature the lovable character Fredo and his adventures in a music store, at a magic café, in the city, at the zoo, and looking for his feline friend Mimi. Created for reading practice and vocabulary reinforcement, these original stories reuse concepts and themes introduced in the video lessons.

The stories are read on the video by doña Elena and they are also recorded on audiotape, on Side B of the Song Cassette. The 64-page storybooks are available for purchase so that the children can read the books themselves.

Teachers can do the Fredo activities with the class in two ways. Teachers can recue the video segment in which doña Elena reads the story, as suggested in the Activity Lesson. Or, teachers with a classroom set of the storybooks can substitute the "Fredo Book Activity" described in the margin of the Activity Lesson. Either way, teachers can use the audiotape recording of the stories for additional listening practice.

Introduction to the Program 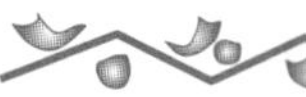

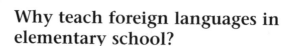

Why teach foreign languages in elementary school?

Improved academic performance

> "Children who have studied a foreign language in elementary school achieve expected gains and score higher on standardized tests of reading, language arts, and mathematics than children who have not studied a foreign language."
>
> –U.S. Congress

There are many benefits to early foreign language learning. It's been shown that children who have studied a foreign language in the elementary grades achieve higher scores on standardized testing. Learning a second language also improves children's understanding of their native language. In addition, children who study a foreign language show greater cognitive development than many of their peers. Finally, as educator Gladys Lipton points out in her book *Practical Handbook to Elementary Foreign Language Programs,*[1] "children who have studied a foreign language have an improved self-concept and sense of achievement in school."

Ease of learning

Research shows that children are most receptive and more able to learn a language before the age of ten. In a *Time Magazine* article about brain research, J. Madeleine Nash[2] wrote:

> There appears to be a series of windows for developing language. The window for acquiring syntax may close as early as five or six years of age, while the window for adding new words may never close. The ability to learn a second language is highest between birth and the age of six, then undergoes a steady and inexorable decline. . . .

Young children learn languages with great enthusiasm. They are willing to imitate the new sounds in a foreign language, to sing and play with it, unlike older students who may be more self-conscious about such efforts.

Young children also have time to master a second language. Think about the young children you know, and how many years of extended practice they need to learn English. These resources—a long period of time and repeated practice—are required to learn any language. This is particularly true if fluency—speaking, reading, and writing like or almost like a native speaker—is the goal. Starting language learning in the early grades enables children to achieve that fluency.

> "I wish I had had the chance to take Spanish in elementary school. As it was, it wasn't until high school; and I think if we can start our children earlier, they'll have a better grasp [of a foreign language] and they'll be much more competitive in today's society."
>
> –A parent

A jump on the future

Learning a foreign language fosters tolerance and appreciation of different cultures. When Americans of different cultural backgrounds live and work together amicably, society's efforts can be directed toward creativity and productivity.

---

[1] Gladys Lipton, *Practical Handbook to Elementary Foreign Language Programs,* Lincolnwood, IL: NTC/Contemporary Publishing Group, 1998.

[2] J. Madeleine Nash, "Fertile Minds" (*Time Magazine,* February 3, 1997; pages 55–56).

In addition, businesses in the United States are now involved in increased competition with foreign companies on the one hand and in more cooperative ventures in foreign countries on the other. American workers in areas such as manufacturing, marketing, product development, and engineering, for example, find themselves interacting increasingly with representatives of foreign subsidiaries or holding companies. The ability to speak the language of these representatives gives those workers both a personal and an economic advantage.

"Four out of five new jobs in the United States are created from foreign trade."
–U.S. Congress

How does *Español para ti* work?

The videos are the heart of the program. You, the classroom teacher, are the facilitator who watches the video with the children and responds along with them. And don't worry if you don't speak Spanish. The on-screen video teacher (**la maestra** in Spanish) introduces small amounts of information at a time, and she explains in English what is happening or what is going to happen. She frequently uses a gesture, a picture, or an object to help the children, and you, understand what is being said. She repeatedly models any language that the children are supposed to say or react to. And, when **la maestra** asks a question, she or one of the puppet characters always models the answer. Watch and listen with the class. Before long, you'll discover one of the great benefits of ***Español para ti***. You'll be learning Spanish along with your students!

"The age of ten is a crucial time in the development of attitudes toward nations and groups perceived as 'other' . . . The awareness of a global community can be enhanced when children have the opportunity to experience involvement with another culture through a foreign language."
–Barbara Wing, Educator[3]

Teaching techniques

Español para ti employs a "spiral" method of teaching. Material is usually introduced in one lesson, practiced in several succeeding lessons, dropped for a while, and then practiced again. New material is always introduced in the context of known vocabulary. Explanations are always given in English so no one is ever lost.

Throughout the program, the video teacher uses a technique called Total Physical Response (TPR) in which children respond physically to a command or direction to help them learn vocabulary and concepts. First, she states a command and models the accompanying activity several times. Second, she repeats the command and has the children respond as a group. Then she gives commands to individuals who respond, and finally, children give commands to classmates. As facilitator, you may enjoy following the commands along with the children.

Support materials

Vocabulary and language concepts are reinforced with Flashcards, Blackline Masters, the Fredo books, the Song Cassette, and the activities on the Activity Cassettes. The audio teacher (**la**

[3] Barbara H. Wing, "Starting Early: Foreign Languages in the Elementary and Middle Schools," in Barbara H. Wing, ed., *Northeast Conference Reports: Foreign Languages for All, Challenges and Choices*, copyright 1996, Lincolnwood, IL: National Textbook Company, p. 41.

> "I speak a little bit of Spanish and I've learned a lot more with the children. We've both learned a lot from this experience with ***Español para ti***. I've been using it now for four years and it's wonderful. The program is just wonderful."
>
> –Tracy Wright, Second grade teacher

> "Learning a foreign language at a very young age can clearly benefit children's reading abilities, and hopefully parents and educators can help to provide resources for this to happen."
>
> –Ellen Bialystok, Psychologist

maestra again or her friend doña Elena) explains each activity in English and provides all the necessary Spanish. She also supplies responses. During the video, she often uses songs to provide a framework for learning vocabulary. These songs also appear on the Song Cassette, so that **la maestra** can continue to practice singing them with the children in your class.

Think of the video teacher as someone with whom you are team teaching. Her job is to model, teach, and practice Spanish whether on the videotape, the Activity Cassette, or the Song Cassette. Your job is to facilitate what she is choreographing. So relax and have fun. Seeing that you are participating and learning will make your students even more eager to master their new language.

What are the goals of *Español para ti?*

By the end of Level 4, children will be able to

- understand more basic vocabulary and structures that are essential for everyday communication
- respond to simple questions and commands using words, phrases, and in some instances short sentences
- read and write simple sentences
- describe or demonstrate more customs from Spanish-speaking countries

For a complete list of the language and vocabulary taught at this level, see Topics and Language Covered on pages xxxvii–xlvii of this Teacher's Manual.

In Level 4, the scope of ***Español para ti*** widens from just listening and speaking skills to reading and writing in Spanish.

Introduction to a Lesson 

How do I use the materials provided?

The Teacher's Manual is your guide to the program. In it is a self-contained lesson plan for each of the video segments or lessons in ***Español para ti.*** Lesson plans are made up of six pages.

The Lesson Opener

The first two pages of each lesson plan contain:

- a list of *Objectives* outlining the language, culture, and vocabulary that will be presented by the video teacher
- a list of *Materials to gather* that you will want to collect prior to watching the video or doing the activities with the children
- simple *Warm-up* and *Review* activities that you can do with the class to prepare them to watch the video
- a brief *Introduction to the video*

The Video Lesson

The next two pages of each lesson plan contain an outline of what occurs on the video. The interactions among the video teacher, the puppets, and their guests are described. The vocabulary, expressions, songs, stories, and cultural items with which children work are listed, explained, and translated into English.

The Activity Lesson

The final two pages of each lesson plan contain the Activity Lesson. Each Activity Lesson includes at least three activities that practice the content of the Video Lesson or review materials from earlier lessons. Many of the activities require the use of one of the Activity Cassettes and/or the Song Cassette and are intended to provide additional opportunity for the children to practice listening, speaking, or singing in Spanish. Other materials required for doing an activity, such as an overhead projector, crayons, pencils, or the optional Fredo storybooks, are listed at the beginning of the activity. The Blackline Masters, Number Cards, and Month and Seasons pictures used in certain activities are located in the Teacher's Resource Book and may be duplicated or made into overhead transparencies. Miniature reproductions of the Blackline Masters appear in the margin next to the activity where they are needed, so you always know exactly what to have on hand.

What do I do when?

Day 1: A Video Lesson

To prepare for a lesson, you might glance through the lesson plan for the Video Lesson. This will give you a quick overview of the content of the video. In addition, the notes in the margins give information and suggestions to help you introduce and follow up on the video more effectively.

Remember, in ***Español para ti*** you and the video teacher are team teaching. She teaches, models, and practices Spanish with the class. You facilitate instruction. In that role, it is important that you cue the videotape before gathering children to watch it. Have the class seated and quiet before beginning the video. Be sure everyone can see and hear. You may want to introduce a special seating arrangement for video watching to make the Spanish class a special experience.

View the video segment or lesson with the class and participate if possible. Repeat after the video teacher and have patience with your mistakes. These modeled behaviors show children that learning a language requires practice and that making mistakes is all right and a natural part of learning.

> "The materials for ***Español para ti*** are excellent. I don't have to be a Spanish teacher to teach the program. All I need to do is to facilitate. All the materials are there for you. It's very, very good . . . very teacher friendly."
>
> –Yumi Arai,
> Fourth grade teacher

Monitor class reaction to the video. Is the class paying attention to **la maestra**? Are children following directions by repeating after her, answering questions, raising their hands? If most children do not seem to understand what is happening, stop the tape, discuss the problem, and then continue with the lesson.

Do some shy children seem hesitant to participate? Keep an eye on them to see if the problem persists. Sometimes a child is willing to speak if he or she uses a puppet. Also bear in mind that some children need to listen for a longer time before they start talking. Do not force a child to speak Spanish.

After viewing the video, you and the children may choose to discuss a particular part of the lesson. Perhaps it relates to something that they are learning in another content area. Perhaps a heritage speaker has something to share. The notes in the margins of the lesson plan offer cultural and cross-curricular information you may want to share with the class.

Day 2: An Activity Lesson

Each Activity Lesson contains at least three activities, numbered according to the lesson. The instruction for each activity contains:

- a list of materials needed to do the activity—Activity Cassette, Song Cassette, Blackline Master, Flashcards, crayons, etc.
- an explanation of any preparation that needs to be done in advance, such as duplicating a Blackline Master or distributing crayons

Some activities are structured as games, others require the use of the Activity Cassette or Song Cassette, while still others are craft activities. Note that all materials related to an activity have the same number as the activity. For example, for Activity 1B, you will use Activity 1B on the Activity Cassette and Blackline Master 1B. When a Blackline Master is reused later in the level, it will be labeled with its original number. The songs as they appear on the Song Cassette can be found in the Song Appendix.

To prepare for an Activity Lesson, read over the descriptions of the activities and gather any materials you need. You may want to preview the activities on the Activity Cassette before playing them for the children. (They are very short!) Describe the activity to the class before starting the tape. In this way, you can be sure that children understand the directions. The audio teacher will explain the activity in English, work through the activity in Spanish, and usually supply answers. Answers are provided as needed in the Teacher's Manual.

These activities practice vocabulary or concepts that have already been taught. By reading an activity's description and listening to the audio teacher, you can identify what is being practiced, even if you don't understand Spanish. Monitor the class's responses to the tape. Are children holding up the correct picture? Are they responding appropriately to commands? On the basis of your observations, decide if the class would benefit from repeating the activity or going on to another activity.

When choosing among the other activities, keep your observations in mind. What did the class do well? What might children need more practice with? What kinds of activities did your class particularly like to do? Learning is easier when the process is enjoyable!

Most Activity Lessons also include an optional activity called *If you have time . . .* if, indeed, you do have time left over in Spanish class. This activity follows the same format as the others.

A series of optional *Dictionary* activities provide children with the opportunity to create their own visual Spanish-language dictionary. Following the format of the other activities, this activity appears in a number of Activity Lessons, beginning in Lesson 6 and culminating in Lesson 59.

If your school has purchased the readers, ***Las aventuras de Fredo,*** you will want to look for the Fredo Book Activity in the margin. These optional activities, which are recorded on Side B of the Song Cassette, integrate the use of the storybooks into your Activity Lesson.

Annotated sample lesson pages follow. These pages are from Levels 1 and 4 and are taken from a variety of lessons.

Lesson plans are numbered and consist of six pages. The first two pages list the *Objectives* and the *Materials to gather*, and contain the *Warm-up, Review,* and *Introduce the video* activities.

The *Objectives* list goals of the lesson.

Language—student behaviors that indicate comprehension of the language.

Materials to gather

- VCR and Video Lesson 5 on Tape 2
- Cassette player
- Activity Cassette 1
- Song Cassette
- Hand puppet Rosco
- World map or globe
- Gold Flashcards 1 and 2
- Poster **"El salón de clase"** (*The classroom*)
- Blackline Master 5A (things/people found in the classroom)
- Blackline Master 5B (José and Rosita)
- Scissors, one pair per student
- Crayons
- Glue
- ***Optional materials:*** paper cutter

Objectives

Language

- Match the correct pictures to the words **maestra** (*female teacher*), **maestro** (*male teacher*), and **calendario** (*calendar*)
- Respond to the command **Toca** _____ (*Touch* _____)

Culture—customs, body language, stories, and songs that are native to Spanish-speaking countries.

Culture

- Sing "The Finger Play Song"

Review

- Sing **"Buenos días a ti"** (*"Good Morning to You"*) and **"Buenas tardes a ti"** (*"Good Afternoon to You"*)
- Ask and respond to the questions **¿Cómo te llamas tú?** (*What is your name?*) and **¿Cómo se llama?** (*What is his/her name?*)
- Recall that **la maestra** means *female teacher* and **el maestro** means *male teacher*
- Review the meaning of **Muéstrame** _____ (*Show me* _____), using classroom objects

Vocabulary

José es el amigo.	*José is the (male) friend.*
Rosita es la amiga.	*Rosita is the (female) friend.*
el calendario	*calendar*
Toca _____.	*Touch* _____.
el escritorio	*desk*

Review—previously learned language and culture concepts that are practiced again.

Vocabulary—new words and expressions that are presented in the lesson. Vocabulary from Levels 1, 2, and 3 is reintroduced in Level 4.

The list always begins with audiovisual materials. The part labeled *Optional materials* names materials needed for the *If you have time . . .* activity, or lists materials that are not essential for an activity but would make it more enjoyable, such as a small bell or laminating machine.

In Levels 3 and 4, this Warm-up includes practice with greetings, farewells, the opening conversation, songs, and questions and answers on various topics.

The puppets icon means that one or both of the hand puppets may be used in this activity. The puppets are optional in Level 4.

Warm-up

Greet the hand puppet Rosco with **Hola, Rosco** (*Hello, Rosco*). Have him respond to you with **Hola** and then to the class with **Hola, clase.** Encourage the children to say **Hola, Rosco.**

Review

Review some of the classroom objects by pointing to the objects in your classroom and asking the children what they are called in Spanish. Vocabulary practiced: **el calendario** (*calendar*), **el escritorio** (*desk*), **el globo** (*globe*), **el lápiz** (*pencil*), **la mesa** (*table*), **la pizarra** (*chalkboard*), **la regla** (*ruler*), **el reloj** (*clock*), **la silla** (*chair*), **la tiza** (*chalk*).

Introduce the video

Remind the children that in the last lesson they learned the names of some colors in Spanish. Introduce Video Lesson 16 by inviting children to listen, watch, and take part as **la maestra** and Ñico teach them the names of more colors.

FYI Although **rosado** is the standard word for *pink* in Spanish-speaking countries, **rosita** is an accepted regionalism in many parts of Mexico. There are many words for brown, but **café** is understood everywhere. If heritage speakers question the usage or pronunciation of a word taught in these lessons, tell them that they are fortunate to now know two ways of saying the same thing. The Spanish taught in these lessons is standard American Spanish—the vocabulary and pronunciation of all the Spanish-speaking countries except Spain.

This activity is a quick review of a topic or vocabulary from a previous lesson. The selected items are often used in the video for this lesson.

This section explains the focus of the upcoming Video Lesson. If relevant, there is also a description of how topics in this lesson are connected to material learned in previous lessons.

The letters *FYI* mean *For Your Information.* FYIs include additional information on the Spanish language or a cultural topic. These are included primarily for your own information. You may wish to share the information with the class.

The Video Lesson is an outline of the video segment. The Video Lesson describes what occurs on the videotape and what is taught.

In the first activity, the video teacher and the puppet characters or the class usually say the opening conversation.

VIDEO LESSON

Numbers 1 to 20:

1	uno	*11*	once
2	dos	*12*	doce
3	tres	*13*	trece
4	cuatro	*14*	catorce
5	cinco	*15*	quince
6	seis	*16*	dieciséis
7	siete	*17*	diecisiete
8	ocho	*18*	dieciocho
9	nueve	*19*	diecinueve
10	diez	*20*	veinte

HERITAGE SPEAKERS

If heritage speakers have brought in pictures of the flags of their countries, display them for the class and ask the heritage speakers to tell the class what country they come from and to name in Spanish the colors in their flags.

The flags of the U.S. and Cuba have the colors **rojo** (*red*), **blanco** (*white*), and **azul** (*blue*). The flag of Mexico is **rojo** (*red*), **blanco** (*white*), and **verde** (*green*). The flag of Ecuador is **amarillo** (*yellow*), **azul** (*blue*), and **rojo** (*red*).

In the words **México** (*Mexico*) and **mexicano/mexicana** (*Mexican*), the letter **x** has the sound that is similar to the English *h*.

1. Greeting the children

La maestra has the opening conversation with Rosco, tl with the children (**M** = Maestra, **R** = Rosco, **C** = class):

M: Buenos días, Rosco/clase.	*Good morning, Rosco/*
R/C: Buenos días, Maestra.	*Good morning, Teache*
M: ¿Cómo estás tú?	*How are you?*
R/C: Muy bien, gracias. ¿Y usted?	*Very well/Fine, thank And you?*
M: Muy bien, gracias.	*Very well/Fine, thank*

The Spanish and English for previously taught vocabulary is provided in different ways, sometimes in the description of the segment and other times in a sidebar. In some instances, a cross-reference to such vocabulary may be made.

2. Reviewing numbers

La maestra and Rosco review the numbers 1 to 20.

3. Discussing the number 20

La maestra and Rosco discuss different combinations of numbers: **diez y diez son veinte** (*ten and ten are twenty*); **cinco y cinco son diez** (*five and five are ten*); **diez y cinco son quince** (*ten and five are fifteen*); **quince y cinco son veinte** (*fifteen and five are twenty*).

4. Comparing *las banderas* (*flags*)

La maestra reminds the children that there are 20 Spanish-speaking countries. She and Rosco compare the colors of **la bandera de los Estados Unidos de América** (*the flag of the United States of America*) with those of **la bandera de Cuba** (*the flag of Cuba*), **la bandera de México** (*the flag of Mexico*), and **la bandera de Ecuador** (*the flag of Ecuador*).

5. Reviewing questions

La maestra reviews two useful questions and responses for making friends:

¿Cómo te llamas tú?	*What is your nar*
Me llamo ______.	*My name is* ___
¿Cómo se llama?	*What is his/her n*
Se llama ______.	*His/Her name is* ___

The video teacher presents and reviews several topics during a video. These changes in topic correspond to the numbered sections.

6. Playing a game

La maestra shows pictures of puppet characters (Rosco, Dora, Ñico, and Jorge) and asks the children **¿Cómo se llama?** (*What is his/her name?*). Children respond with **Se llama** ______.

These sections contain suggestions for how to use to advantage the expertise of students who are native Spanish speakers. There are also suggestions for dealing with regional varieties of Spanish.

CROSS-CULTURAL CONNECTIONS

The information in *Cross-cultural connections* points out how people are alike and different. They offer opportunities to explore similarities and differences based upon what was learned on the video.

A description of the context within which an activity is taking place is provided for your convenience in previewing and reviewing the lesson.

Both Spanish and English are provided for the reviewed vocabulary.

The checkmark icon points out a way to informally assess children's progress.

9. Introducing new words

La maestra introduces two new words for the classroom: **la regla** (*ruler*) and **la silla** (*chair*).

10. Playing *Muéstrame* _____ (*Show me* _____)

La maestra again plays **Muéstrame** _____ with the children, this time occasionally pointing to a picture and waiting for the children to name it. **La maestra** reviews the following vocabulary in the order given: **el calendario** (*calendar*), **la maestra** (*female teacher*), **el maestro** (*male teacher*), **el escritorio** (*desk*), **la mesa** (*table*), **el globo** (*globe*), **el lápiz** (*pencil*), **la pizarra** (*chalkboard*), **la silla** (*chair*), **la bandera** (*flag*), **la tiza** (*chalk*), **el libro** (*book*), **el reloj** (*clock*), **el mapa** (*map*), **la regla** (*ruler*), **la tiza** (*chalk*). (*Chalk* was mentioned twice.) After the game, Rosco says he feels **Muy bien** (*Very well*).

Because in this activity the children are sometimes expected to reply without prompting, you have an ideal opportunity to gauge their progress in learning the classroom vocabulary.

11. Reviewing numbers 1 to 10

¡Vamos a contar! (*Let's count!*), says Rosco before helping **la maestra** count blocks forward and backward.

LANGUAGE ACROSS THE CURRICULUM

Include counting in Spanish in physical education classes. For example, children can count the number of players on a team, the number of hops or jumps, the number of sit-ups, and so on.

These sections suggest ways to use Spanish in other subject areas and vice versa. The lessons in ***Español para ti*** are tied directly into many content areas, such as health, math, science, social studies, and career awareness. (See the list called Content-Based Topics on pages xxxv–xxxvi of the Teacher's Manual for Level 4.)

12. Singing a song

Rosco says eagerly, **¡Vamos a cantar!** (*Let's sing!*). **La maestra** leads the children in singing both verses of **"Uno, dos, tres niñitos"** (*"One, Two, Three Little Children"*).

Uno, dos, tres niñitos,	*One, two, three little children,*
Cuatro, cinco, seis niñitos,	*Four, five, six little children,*
Siete, ocho, nueve niñitos,	*Seven, eight, nine little children,*
Diez niñitos son.	*There are ten little children.*
Diez, nueve, ocho niñitos,	*Ten, nine, eight little children,*
Siete, seis, cinco niñitos,	*Seven, six, five little children,*
Cuatro, tres, dos niñitos,	*Four, three, two little children,*
Un niñito es.	*There is one little child.*

Song lyrics are given in both Spanish and English.

13. Reviewing expressions for feelings

Using the face masks, **la maestra** and Rosco review the expressions **Muy bien** (*Very well*); **Así, así** (*So-so*); and **Muy ma** (*Very bad*).

14. Closing

La maestra and Rosco bid the children **Adiós** (*Good-bye*) and **Hasta luego** (*See you later*).

After viewing the video, praise the children for their good listening and watching skills.

Lesson Twelve

The Closing section describes how the video teacher sums up the lesson and brings closure. Sometimes the summary includes the entire lesson. At other times the video teacher and the puppets just use various expressions to say good-bye. You may wish to end your own lesson in a similar manner.

Tipped boxes offer you teaching "tips" and instructional techniques for Spanish class.

Blackline Masters are located in the Teacher's Resource Book. The number of the activity and the Blackline Master are usually the same. For example, Blackline Master 38A is to be used with Activity 38A. When a Blackline Master is used in a later activity, it retains the original number.

The Activity Lesson includes at least three activities and a closing. The activities mainly practice what was taught in the Video Lesson and often review topics from previous lessons. Sometimes activities are based on the Activity Cassettes and/or the Song Cassette. Sometimes there are art activities and optional activities called *If you have time . . . .*

228

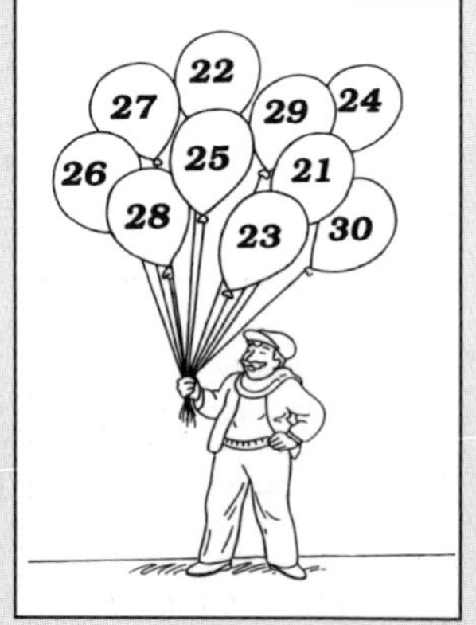

Blackline Master 38A

Answers to Activity 38A:

(21) pink	(22) yellow
(23) red	(24) orange
(25) black	(26) brown
(27) blue	(28) purple
(29) black	(30) green

When the children talk about the answers to this activity, a colored overhead transparency of this page would make the discussion easier.

EN ESPAÑOL

In several lessons, you have heard **la maestra** say, **Te toca a ti** (*It's your turn*) to Rosco or Dora. Rosco often excitedly insists, **Me toca a mí** (*It's my turn*). If you feel comfortable with these expressions, try to incorporate them into daily activities and games.

LEVEL ONE

Activity Lesson

Activity 38A: Make a balloon bouquet

Materials: Cassette player; Activity Cassette 2, Side A; Blackline Master 38A, one per child; pink, yellow, red, orange, brown, blue, purple, black, and green crayons for each child.

Preparation: Give each child a copy of Blackline Master 38A and the nine crayons.

Point out that each balloon on Blackline Master 38A has a number on it. **La maestra** will say a number and a color twice. The children should color the balloons according to these directions. Assure the children that they simply need to color part of the balloon in the time given. They can color the rest of the balloons after the tape has stopped.

All the materials needed for an activity are listed. If any advance preparation is required, it is also explained.

Activity 38B: Act out feelings

Materials: Cassette player; Activity Cassette 2,

You may want to have children sit in a circle for this Tell the children that they are going to pretend to fe ways. When **la maestra** states a feeling, they should The feelings are stated in the following order: **Tengo** (*I'm hungry*), **Tengo sed** (*I'm thirsty*), **Tengo calor** (*I'r* **Tengo frío** (*I'm cold*).

There is a summary of the activity on the Activity Cassette.

The activity number in the Teacher's Manual matches the number of the activity on the tape. Activity 38B uses audio Activity 38B, which is on Activity Cassette 2, Side A.

Activity 38C: Sing about the ranc

Materials: Cassette player; **"Vengan a ver** (*"Come See My Ranch"*) on the Song Cassette; Go 20-22 and 24-27.

Turn the Gold Flashcards facedown. Explain to t that they are going to sing **"Vengan a ver mi ra** *See My Ranch"*) with **la maestra.** Ask for seven v the volunteers to each take a Flashcard and to keep the picture hidden. Ask them to line up in front of the class. In the song, the animals are named in this order: cat, dog, cow, chicken, rooster, horse, pig. When the class comes to the part of the song that names an animal, the child with that Flashcard should step forward and show it to everyone.

A cassette player and the Song Cassette are used with this activity. Song lyrics with translations can be found in the Song Appendix.

The video teacher and the puppets sometimes say Spanish words and expressions that are frequently used in daily life but are not part of the core vocabulary. **En español** sidebars point out these expressions so that you may use them yourself if you feel comfortable doing so.

This kind of activity may include ideas for practicing a song or for using a song in a different way.

The audio teacher usually supplies answers for the Activity Cassettes directly on the cassettes. Occasionally she does not. In such cases, the answers are provided in the lesson plan of the Teacher's Manual.

The cassette icon indicates that a cassette player and an Activity Cassette are needed for this activity.

This section helps you bring closure to the lesson. It also provides you with information to preview the next lesson for the class. There may also be a short activity, such as the closing conversation.

7

Closing

Tell the children that Spanish class is finished for today. In the next lesson they will review the locations and names of the countries where Spanish is spoken and play a game with numbers.

The hourglass points out that *If you have time . . .* is an optional activity.

If You Have Time . . .

Lead the children in a discussion about careers and school subjects. Ask what careers interest them and what subjects will help them prepare for these careers. How might the knowledge of another language be helpful in their career(s)?

These optional activities always practice and/or review previously introduced materials.

Family Connection

To foster a friendly link between home and school, you may wish to send out Family Letter 1 (found in the Teacher's Resource Book). The letter informs family members about what the children will be learning in Spanish this year and suggests ways they can support their child's efforts.

There are four Family Connection letters. This section reminds you to send them home after Lessons 1, 20, 40, and 60, if you wish to do so. The letters are located in the Teacher's Resource Book.

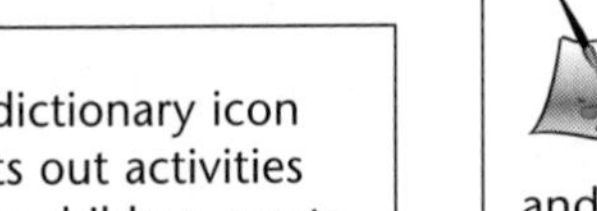

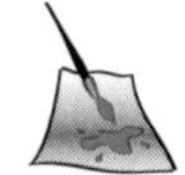

The craft icon points out activities in which children make and use art to learn Spanish.

The dictionary icon points out activities where children create their own visual Spanish-language dictionaries. These activities begin in Lesson 6 and culminate in Lesson 59.

In Level 4, the children read several stories about the adventures of a character named Fredo. ***Las aventuras de Fredo*** consists of five stories that are featured on various segments of the video. Teachers can use the video segment in their Activity Lesson. Alternatively, teachers with a classroom set of the Fredo books can substitute the "Fredo Book Activity" described in the margin of the lesson. The stories are recorded on Side B of the Song Cassette.

Lesson One

AUDIOVISUAL TECHNIQUES 

Video Viewing Strategies

For the teacher:

- Before watching a video segment or lesson with the class, we encourage you to read through the corresponding lesson in the Teacher's Manual (that is, the *Objectives,* the *Video Lesson,* and the *Activity Lesson*). This preview will provide you with the goals and content of the lesson.
- Cue the video lesson before seating the class in front of the television.
- During the video lesson, take an active part along with your class. Your example encourages children to participate.
- Once in a while, the video teacher is going to ask you to facilitate an activity for her by choosing a child to participate. **La maestra** moves quickly through the lesson, and you don't want to be left behind!
- The video teacher often directs questions directly to the children. Encourage the students to answer. However, try to train the children not to speak while **la maestra** is talking because they will miss important information.
- In some lessons, doña Elena reads stories from ***Las aventuras de Fredo*** to the children. The stories are intentionally a mixture of known and unknown vocabulary, and both the text and pictures are visible on the screen. Before children hear a story, reassure them by telling them they won't understand everything. Explain that every story is repeated later in the year and they'll be surprised at how much more they understand and can read then.

  Listen to the story along with the class. Your reaction is important since children may take their cue from you. If you are learning Spanish, you are going to experience some frustration. Show some, but try not to overreact. Be pleased at what you do understand. After the video, do some sharing and mutual "wondering" with the class.
- Congratulate the children on their good watching, listening, and participatory skills.

For the children:

- Tell the children that the video takes fifteen to twenty minutes.
- Ask them if they are seated so that they can see and hear the video clearly.
- Tell them to listen and watch closely, imitating and responding to the video teacher as she indicates. Tell them they will discover they can mimic new sounds and use them and that they may want to use Spanish in real-life situations.

Activity Cassette Strategies

For the teacher:

- The cassette activities are extremely important because they provide needed practice in hearing and speaking Spanish. The tapes practice material that has already been introduced. Spanish, like math and writing, requires practice for mastery. Please use each activity at least once. If possible, repeat it so that many children have the opportunity to participate.
- Read the description of the activity before playing the cassette for the class. This description lists all needed materials and any required advance preparations. It also includes the goals and content of the activity.
- If possible, listen to cassette activities before your class does. They are very short.
- Have all the needed/prepared materials at hand before gathering the class to take part in an activity. Sometimes the audio teacher is going to ask you to facilitate an activity for her. Be prepared to move quickly.
- Cue the Activity Cassette to the appropriate activity before gathering the class to take part in it.
- Describe the tape activity to your class before turning on the tape. With this preview, children are prepared for the audio teacher's description. She will practice the activity with the class before asking them to participate.
- During the tape activity, you may want to take an active part. By all means do so, especially if you are learning Spanish along with the class. Your example encourages children to participate. At other times, you may simply want to observe. Watching the children's physical and verbal reactions provides you with valuable information about how well they understand and can perform the relevant skills.
- If children are having difficulty doing an exercise, stop the tape and discuss what the problem is. Sometimes the class may not understand the directions or may not understand the concept in English. Giving children a point of reference, such as where the class/the video teacher did the same kind of activity on the video, is often helpful. Be sure to explain that the tape activities are for practice. Children are not expected to get everything right the first time nor all the time.
- In some cassette activities, the audio teacher may make a request or ask a question and a harp-like sound will follow. Please pause the tape at the sound of the harp to allow children time to respond. Then continue the activity. Children may enjoy playing this role once they understand the harp's function.
- Usually the audio teacher provides an immediate reply to each exercise. Emphasize that children should pay attention to her answers. Once in a while you are going to give them the answers. They are provided for you in the Teacher's

Manual, and you may wish to make them into an overhead transparency.

- Congratulate the children on using the relevant skills for a particular activity—watching, listening, speaking, and/or writing.
- For activities that require the children to color objects in specific colors, have them color only a piece of the object (puppet, piece of furniture, or part of a house) while the tape is running. Afterwards they can finish coloring their activity sheet.

For the children:

- Tell the children to follow the directions.
- Let them know that sometimes the audio teacher is going to ask them a question followed by a short musical sound. They need to say their answer then.
- Usually they are going to hear the correct answers on the tape. It is very, very important to listen carefully and check their answers against the audio teacher's. This checking is an extra chance to practice their Spanish.

Song Cassette Strategies

For the teacher:

- Before having children do an activity that includes the Song Cassette, read the description in the Activity Lesson. This description lists all needed materials and any required advance preparations. It also includes the goals and content of the activity.
- Have all the needed/prepared materials on hand before gathering the class to take part in the song activity.
- Cue the cassette to the appropriate song before gathering the class to sing it. In a few instances this is only partly possible because there is more than one song in an activity. The songs as they appear on the Song Cassette can be found in the Song Appendix.
- Children will have heard, and usually practiced, all or part of a song before they practice it with the cassette. Depending on the length of a song or the portion that you are practicing, play it at least once or twice before inviting the children to join in.
- As you know, children love to sing, and these songs are fun. Initially children may be able to sing only a few words here and there. Let them know that's all right. The more often the children hear the tape and watch the videos, the more they are going to pick up.
- Depending on the length and complexity of a song, you may want to practice a few lines or a stanza with the tape until the class can sing most of it so they have a sense of accomplishment. Then go on to the next part. The songs are lively and fun and singing them should always be fun.

- Sing along with the class. Your example encourages children to participate. It doesn't matter if you make a mistake or two. At other times, you may simply want to observe. Watching and listening provides you with valuable information about how well children know and understand the song.

For the children:

- Tell the children to sing as much of a song as they can. Practicing helps them learn more.
- Have them act out the words as they are singing or listening to the tape. That will help them remember the words.
- Have them ask you to replay the particular parts of a song, so they learn the words or music better.
- Have the children read along with song lyrics projected on overhead transparencies.

Song Cassette Contents:

SIDE A (SONGS)

"Español para ti" (*"Spanish Is for You, and for Me"*)

"La canción de geografía" (*"The Geography Song"*)

"Alphabet Rap"

"Months Rap"

"Las estaciones" (*"The Seasons"*)

"Las vocales" (*"The Vowel Tree Song"*)

"De diez en diez" (*"Ten by Ten"*)

"¿Cómo está Lorena?" (*"How Is Lorena?"*)

"Calendar Rap"

"¿Adónde vas?" (*"Where Are You Going?"*)

"En los Estados Unidos" (*"In the United States"*)

"De colores" (*"Colors"*)

"¿Dónde está Mimi?" (*"Where Is Mimi?"*)

"Dulce canta el burro" (*"Sweetly Sings the Donkey"*)

SIDE B (FREDO STORIES)

Las aventuras de Fredo (*Fredo's Adventures*)

Book 1: La tienda de música (*The Music Store*)

Book 2: El café mágico (*The Magic Café*)

Book 3: En la ciudad (*In the City*)

Book 4: En el jardín zoológico (*At the Zoo*)

Book 5: ¿Dónde está Mimi? (*Where is Mimi?*)

TIMING, PACING, AND ARTICULATION

> "I really enjoy the videos. They're very organized . . . structured well, so it's easy to put them in a video machine and get them started. I really love the music tapes. They're wonderful. The children enjoy singing the music. And the interactive activity sheets are delightful. The children do a lot with them."
>
> –Jeffrey Hybarger, First grade teacher

> "As a first generation Hispanic who does not speak my native language, Spanish, I am glad to know that my children have the opportunity to learn a foreign language in the elementary school."
>
> –A parent

How much time does it take?

The ***Español para ti*** program consists of five levels—one level per school year. Levels 1 and 2 have 66 lessons each and Levels 3 to 5 have 60 lessons each. Level 4 provides for two 20-minute Video Lessons and two 20-minute Activity Lessons per week. It is possible to teach two complete lessons in less than an hour and a half!

The Video Lessons are imaginative and fun and have a variety of activities and experiences that will appeal to every learning style. Depending on the interests of the children in your class, you may not wish to do all of the activities provided in an Activity Lesson. When working through an Activity Lesson, however, the exercises on the Activity Cassette should take priority so that the children are given as much opportunity as possible to hear and react to the language.

As you would expect, the instruction at each level builds on what was taught in earlier levels. For example, children learn the numbers 1 to 50 in Level 1. In Level 2, children review the numbers 1 to 50 and then learn 51 to 100. In Levels 3 and 4, children review numbers 1 to 100 and practice doing addition and subtraction with those numbers in Spanish. But since learning a language, like math, requires much repeated practice, instruction within each level is also spiraled—topics are repeatedly reviewed and integrated with new content. Consider the vocabulary for animals: through the Video Lessons of Levels 1–3, children learned the names of many domestic or farm animals, such as cat, dog, cow, and horse. In Level 4, children review the names of the domestic and farm animals and expand their animal vocabulary to include wild or zoo animals—zebra, giraffe, bear. The new vocabulary is split into small groups and presented in Lessons 50, 51, and 52 with familiar vocabulary reviewed each time new vocabulary is introduced. The vocabulary is reinforced on the video through repeated showings of a trip to the San Diego Zoo in Lessons 51, 52, 53, and 59 and in the Fredo adventure story that the children hear and read in Lessons 52, 53, and 59. In these segments the animals are described by their size and color, thus connecting the animal vocabulary to previously introduced describing words. The vocabulary is also practiced in many Warm-up and Review sections, and in lesson activities beginning with Lesson 51.

What do I do with children who join the class later in the year?

Spiraling helps the entire class learn Spanish, but it also addresses another issue—what to do with children who join the class later in the year. Such a child may have some difficulty at first, but spiraling, with its continual reviewing, helps a great deal. ***Español para ti*** provides many opportunities for children to catch up. In addition, the video teacher (**la maestra**) uses pictures, objects, and body language to demonstrate and reinforce the meaning of Spanish words and expressions as she reviews. Whether the videos and Activity Cassettes are in the classroom or in the media center, they provide a team teacher who can present any part of the program before school, after school, during recess, or during those times when children self-select activities. In addition, parents can check out videos from the classroom or media center and help children to catch up at home. Since the video teacher employs the same Flashcards as are provided for you in the Visuals Package, newcomers may use them to practice vocabulary with classmates.

Where do children go after *Español para ti?*

The programs ***¡Hola!*** (*Hello!*), ***¿Qué tal?*** (*What's Happening?*), and ***¡Adelante!*** (*Onward!*) lead students from ***Español para ti*** through to a first year high-school proficiency in Spanish. ***¡Hola!*** provides a multi-level approach to Spanish. It may be used both with students who have completed ***Español para ti*** and with those who have no knowledge of Spanish. ***¡Hola!*** begins with the world of the student at school and spirals out to the family. While using ***¿Qué tal?*** and ***¡Adelante!,*** students continue to extend their Spanish listening, speaking, reading, and writing skills. In ***¿Qué tal?*** students focus first on home life and gradually expand their focus to the community. ***¡Adelante!*** explores the world in general. The use of ***¿Qué tal?*** and ***¡Adelante!*** over a two-year period provides students with the opportunity for repeated language practice in a variety of situations, a critical factor in language acquisition.

Integrating Spanish with the Curriculum

Why should I spend precious time teaching Spanish?

As was pointed out earlier, ***Español para ti*** requires only one hour of instruction a week. Moreover, the program is not an add-on to your curriculum; the lessons are tied in directly to other content areas. Spanish becomes an integral part of the curriculum, reinforcing and adding new dimensions to what is already being taught. Math, science, social studies, health, and career awareness are all woven into the lessons of ***Español para ti.*** During the course of the year, for example, your class is going to practice the numbers 1 to 100 in Spanish which were presented in Levels 1 and 2. Among other mathematical strategies, the video teacher is going to use children's knowledge of how to count; how to add and subtract; and how to count by tens to reinforce numbers from 1 to 100. As a result the class is going to have more practice in number order, addition, and subtraction in Spanish class.

Before the children actually write Spanish in Level 4 of ***Español para ti***, they are going to hear, read, and discuss stories told in Spanish. Since the tales are in picture-book format and involve both known and unknown vocabulary, children will use context and pictures to help determine meaning—strategies they also employ while learning to read in English. (For specifics regarding the correlation between Spanish and other content areas, see the Content-Based Topics listed on pages xxxiv–xxxv.)

Since the Video Lesson and Activity Lesson take only 20 minutes each and provide review in each lesson, ***Español para ti*** is also suitable for use in Spanish language enrichment courses that meet before or after school as infrequently as once per week.

"Children, by starting second language study early, advance in the development of an intelligent understanding of language concepts, which will help in learning additional languages."
–Gladys C. Lipton, Educator

How much preparation time does *Español para ti* require?

Very little. The Teacher's Resource Book has all the reproducible Blackline Masters that teachers need for the student activities, as well as assessment pages. Prior to showing Lesson 1, we suggest that you laminate frequently handled items such as the Month and Seasons pictures (found in the Teacher's Resource Book), so that they have a longer life. The Teacher's Manual points out other useful items to laminate throughout the course.

Since the *Warm-up* and *Review* are done prior to the Video Lesson, you may sometimes need to gather program components, such as Flashcards, for these activities. It is also helpful to cue the videotape before it is time for the lesson.

The Activity Lessons often require gathering one or more program components, such as an Activity Cassette and/or the

"The *Español para ti* materials are very easy to use. They are all laid out for you. Where you leave off one day, you pick up the next day. And it's ready to go every day."
–Tracy Wright, Second grade teacher

Song Cassette, cueing an audiovisual component before class begins, copying Blackline Masters for the class, and making overhead transparencies of Blackline Masters. Occasionally an activity may need additional craft supplies. Materials you need to assemble prior to doing an activity are outlined in the "Materials" and "Preparation" sections of the activity and in the "Prepare ahead" section in some of the lessons.

> "I tell them all the time, 'This is new to me too, so I'm learning right with you.'"
> –Laura Schumacher, First grade teacher

> "When we first started the program, I think teachers were a bit nervous because they did not speak Spanish. But as they were in-serviced into the program, they saw the ease of working with the videos that were already done for them and when they actually used them in the classroom with the children and saw the enthusiasm of the children, I felt that they became quite confident."
> –Nadine Nielsen, Principal

Assessment

How can I tell how my class is doing when I don't speak Spanish?

For a start, you're watching the same video as your class. If most children are watching the video, repeating when asked, and answering questions without hesitation, you can assume that everything is going all right. Perhaps it's the other times you're wondering about, and for those, we offer the following suggestions.

- Whenever the video teacher asks the children a question, she allows time for them to respond, and then she or one of the puppets answers it. She wants children to know what the right answer is. Compare her answer with theirs.
- What if most children do not answer a question or answer incorrectly? Frequently the same question is immediately asked again or within a couple of minutes. Watch if more children attempt to answer or answer correctly the next time. Learning a language, like learning math facts, requires practice. Watch for cumulative improvement rather than perfection.
- Follow the video teacher's lead. If something is difficult, she often reassures children that they are going to have many opportunities to practice it. Don't worry.
- It is just as possible to have a bad Spanish day as it is to have a bad hair day. If most children are not involved in a video or a cassette activity, stop the tape and find out what the problem is. Sometimes children are not paying attention at the beginning, and as the lesson becomes more complicated, they cannot continue because they've missed a key element. Perhaps the children are having difficulty with a concept instead of the language. Pinpointing the problem enables the class to finish the lesson.
- If the class is singing, notice if the children have learned more of the lyrics or melody than the last time they sang the song.
- Ask small groups or pairs to sing a song or demonstrate an activity.
- As children play games, check that they are following directions and using Spanish words or phrases.
- After the video teacher has taught multiple answers to a question, check if children are using any of the newer responses.
- Note individual and/or group responses to cassette activities.
- When the video teacher stresses similarities or differences between pairs of words, listen for the accuracy of children's responses.
- From time to time, ask children to explain why their answers are correct.

- Make a copy of the rubric for holistic assessment (in the Teacher's Resource Book) for each child. You might want to complete the rubric for each child while they are watching a Video Lesson, or you may wish to observe them while they watch a Video Lesson and take part in an Activity Lesson and complete the rubric at a later time. The rubric is designed to be used at any time and as often as you feel necessary throughout the year.

What can I use for formal assessments?

Español para ti, Level 4, provides two formal assessments—one for the midyear and one for the end of the year. The directions and questions for each exam are located on the Assessment Cassette, Side A and B, and the reproducible student assessment pages are in the Teacher's Resource Book. Children are going to follow doña Elena's directions and mark their answers on the Blackline Masters. You can give the first exam after Lesson 30 and the final exam after Lesson 60.

If you need frequent formal assessments so that you can give grades, reuse activities on Activity Cassettes 1 and 2 with their accompanying Blackline Masters.

FAMILY AND COMMUNITY 

Parents, guardians, and other members of the community can play a vital role in motivating children to learn and use Spanish, and in reinforcing the value of learning about and understanding other cultures.

Laying the groundwork for support and participation starts with communication. It is very important to begin the school year by sharing the goals of the Spanish program with parents and guardians and by explaining how parents and guardians may assist their children. Use the Introduction to the Program (pages ix–xi) and Video Lessons as resources to explain to families the reasons for teaching Spanish at this grade and the methods that are being used.

> "The children go home and speak Spanish with their parents. The parents love the fact that their children are learning a second language."
>
> –Tracy Wright, Second grade teacher

In the Teacher's Resource Book, there are four letters that you may want to send home during the school year. Family Letter 1 introduces the year, what children will do, and encourages caretakers to ask—but not pressure—children to share with them what they're learning. Family Letter 2 updates families on what children have been learning and will be doing next. Family Letter 3 suggests ways in which families can encourage their children's learning of Spanish. Family Letter 4 stresses the large amount of Spanish that children have learned over the year and suggests ways to help them maintain their language skills over the summer.

Within the school, parents can also do many things to encourage interest in Spanish.

- Talk to the class about experiences (trips and/or jobs) in Spanish-speaking cultures.
- Speak to the children in Spanish.
- Share foods, videos or audiotapes, and souvenirs or gifts from Spanish-speaking countries.
- Help with the decorations, food, or clean-up during a Spanish-related event.

Many people are willing to visit classes and/or participate in school events. Drawing on Spanish speakers from the community unites all participants in a shared experience. Consider the following possibilities:

- Community service: paramedic, librarian, police officer, firefighter, postal worker
- Recreation: athlete, disc jockey, travel agent
- Health: exercise instructor, nurse or nurse's aide, physician, dietitian, pharmacist
- Science: florist, conservationist, programmer, scientist
- Labor: construction worker, custodian, mechanic, painter
- Other: baker, banker, cook, musician, photographer, secretary, television or radio personality, reporter, restaurant owner, waiter/waitress

Which of these people might be volunteers for your children as they investigate topics such as "What do our community workers do?"; "What do plants need in order to live?"; and "How do you make bread?" What is fascinating is that language does not live in a vacuum! Language is always being used by someone for something. Any of these individuals may also be native speakers of Spanish who would be willing to talk to your children about what they do, how they use Spanish on the job, or even about non-work-related topics, such as family life and schools in other countries. An enthusiastic class-written thank-you note, and perhaps some drawings of the event, earns goodwill for the school and the program.

So far the discussion has centered on people and events in the classroom, but don't forget field trips, which are valuable experiences in the real world. Does your class want to see what happens behind the scenes at a television station or to know how a gift shop owner knows what to order? Anywhere you take your class—to a bank, a hospital, or a grocery store—you or someone else may possibly make a connection to a language other than English. Each time this connection occurs, it shows the value of learning another language.

HERITAGE SPEAKERS

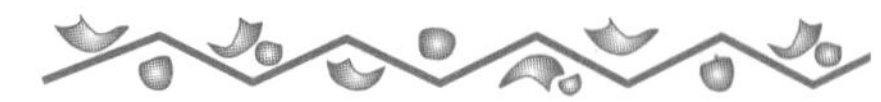

This section contains ideas for enriching the course with the experiences of children whose native language is Spanish. The language and customs of Spanish speakers are particularly relevant to this course, but heritage speakers of other languages offer children unique opportunities to hear about how various cultural groups deal with daily needs, relationships, and important events. If speakers of Spanish question the usage or pronunciation of a word or expression, tell them that they are fortunate to now know two ways of saying the same thing. The Spanish taught here is standard American Spanish—the vocabulary and pronunciation of all the Spanish-speaking countries except Spain. The following list suggests guidelines for drawing on the expertise of heritage speakers in your class.

- Some children are proud of their non-English background and are glad to share information about their birth countries and native languages. Other children may feel sensitive about "being different." Invite children to share their experiences, but don't single them out too often.
- Ask for help with pronunciation, as needed. Keep in mind that children from different countries may have slightly different pronunciations.
- During the year, the children are going to discuss some specific areas where Spanish is spoken. Children from these locations might tell what they know about them. If necessary, point out that these comments only partly describe what these places are like.
- ***Español para ti*** treats many topics related to daily life—family members, colors, greetings, clothing, seasons, weather, numbers, animals, traffic and transportation, and so forth. The course also includes vocabulary and scenes related to appliances, food, and furniture—but all within an American context. Encourage non-English speakers to compare these topics and locations with those in their birth countries.
- Songs and stories are an integral part of ***Español para ti.*** Invite heritage speakers to share the same or comparable ones from their cultures.
- In the lessons that involve reading stories, allow heritage speakers to explain maybe one or two parts that everyone is curious about. Perhaps they might teach the class a couple of words or expressions. Do *not* have them translate the whole story!

Try to include adult heritage speakers as classroom visitors. They bring a wider perspective and often have surprising experiences in the United States that point out cultural similarities and differences with their countries of origin. While it's not likely that you'll have bullfighters or **vaqueros** (*cowboys*) as guests, children also enjoy learning about the kinds of work adults have done and are doing. In addition, children simply enjoy hearing stories about when adults were themselves young children.

> "***Español para ti*** has, I think, brought cultural joy into the classroom. It's given the children an opportunity to see another culture, to hear the language, to hear the celebrations."
> –Jeffrey Hybarger, First grade teacher

Content-Based Topics 

Art

Cut and paste
Draw with various media
Match pictures and vocabulary

Computers

Define computer terms
Describe technologies in society
Identify parts of a computer system

Health and nutrition

Determine the need for food
Discuss the importance of expressing feelings
Explore foods of the Spanish-speaking world

Language arts

Activate prior knowledge
Classify words
Communicate in complete sentences
Compare and contrast information
Compare and contrast sounds
Create a dictionary
Demonstrate critical listening skills
Describe and classify objects
Differentiate between a question, statement, command, and exclamation
Expand vocabulary
Follow multiple-step directions
Identify and compose an interrogative sentence
Identify a purpose for listening
Identify a speaker's purpose
Interact verbally in informal situations
Link new information to prior knowledge
Listen to different types of literature
Make introductions
Obtain information by asking questions
Participate in various forms of oral communication
Read for a variety of purposes
Recall presented materials
Take notes from dictation
Use the alphabet
Use knowledge of words to construct meaning (adjectives)
Use relationship between letters and sounds

Mathematics

Relate patterns
Represent number relationships

Music

Perform a repertoire of songs
Recognize various culture-specific rhythms
Sing songs in a limited range

Science

Construct criteria for classifying matter
Explore the effects of a force on an object
Explore the effects of weather
Investigate the geographical relationships between the hemispheres
Investigate liquids
Investigate matter and its properties
Observe the habitats of animals
Observe the interaction between living things and their environment
Observe weather conditions

Social studies

Be aware of the United States and its people
Be introduced to people and places in other parts of the world
Demonstrate an understanding of the concept of a rule
Describe characteristics that make each human unique
Describe the colonization of North America
Describe how training prepares people for work
Describe how work can be specialized
Describe the relationship of the U.S. to some other countries
Discuss how people from various cultures migrated to the American West
Explore the different cultures represented in a community
Give examples of how immigration affected American life
Identify self by name and place of residence
Locate hemispheres, continents, and oceans on maps and globes
Locate places on a map
Name the twenty Spanish-speaking countries and locate them on a world map
Name types of occupations
Observe different types of communities
Recognize geographical features on maps and globes
Recognize that people from many different cultures settled in the U.S.
Respect individual and cultural differences
Use positional words to describe location of a person, place, or thing

Topics and Language Covered

These lists show only those items that the children practice, plus a few others that the video teacher (**la maestra**) introduces as enrichment and to develop children's listening and comprehension skills. The English equivalents are what an English-speaking person would ordinarily say in a comparable situation. They are not word-for-word translations.

The topics listed below are introduced in Level 4. Within each topic, words and expressions are usually in alphabetical order. Some sections are divided into vocabulary items and functional expressions in the form of questions and answers.

Greetings, farewells, introductions

Vocabulary

Adiós.	*Good-bye.*
Buenas noches.	*Good evening.*
Buenas tardes.	*Good afternoon.*
Buenos días.	*Good morning.*
Hasta la vista.	*Until we meet again.*
Hasta luego.	*See you later.*
Hola.	*Hello!/Hi!*
¿Qué tal?	*How's it going?*
¿Qué pasa?	*What's happening? What's going on?*
Nada.	*Nothing.*

Asking about names and ages

¿Cómo te llamas (tú)?	*What is your name? (informal)*
¿Cómo se llama (usted)?	*What is your name? (formal)*
Me llamo ___.	*My name is ___.*
Mucho gusto.	*It's nice to meet you.*
¿Cómo se llama?	*What is his/her name?*
Se llama ___.	*His/Her name is ___.*

Expressions of feeling

Vocabulary

Así, así.	*So-so.*
Muy bien.	*Very good; Fine/Very well.*
Muy mal.	*Very bad.*

Asking about feelings

¿Cómo está usted?	*How are you? (formal)*
¿Cómo estás (tú)?	*How are you? (informal)*
Estoy aburrido/aburrida.	*I'm bored.*
Estoy cansado/cansada.	*I'm tired.*
Estoy (muy) contento/contenta.	*I am (very) happy.*
Estoy enojado/enojada.	*I am angry.*
Estoy triste.	*I am sad.*
Tengo ___ años.	*I'm ___ years old.*
Tengo calor.	*I'm hot.*
Tengo catarro.	*I have a cold.*
Tengo dolor.	*I'm hurt.*
Tengo frío.	*I'm cold.*
Tengo hambre.	*I'm hungry.*
Tengo miedo.	*I'm afraid.*
Tengo sed.	*I'm thirsty.*
Tengo sueño.	*I'm sleepy.*

School subjects

Vocabulary

el arte	*art*
las ciencias	*science*
las computadoras	*computers*
el drama	*theater, drama*
el español	*Spanish*
la escritura	*writing*
la geografía	*geography*
la historia	*history*
la hora de recreo	*recess*
el inglés	*English*
la lectura	*reading*
las matemáticas	*math*
la música	*music*

Asking and talking about school subjects

¿Qué haces en la clase de ___?	*What do you do in ___ class?*
Estudio ___.	*I study ___.*
Borro.	*I erase.*
Canto en ___.	*I sing in ___.*
Coloreo.	*I color.*
Dibujo.	*I draw.*
Flota.	*It floats.*
No flota.	*It doesn't float.*
Hablo ___.	*I speak ___.*
Juego.	*I play.*
¿Qué clase es?	*What class is it?*
Es la clase de ___.	*It's ___ class.*
Vamos a leer.	*Let's read.*

Professions and work

Vocabulary

el camarero/la camarera	*waiter/waitress*
el cocinero/la cocinera	*male/female cook*
el director/la directora	*male/female school principal*
el doctor/la doctora	*male/female doctor*
el dueño/la dueña	*male/female owner*
el enfermero/la enfermera	*male/female nurse*
el jefe de la policía	*police chief*
el maestro/la maestra	*male/female teacher*
el payaso/la payasa	*clown*
el policía/la policía	*policeman/policewoman*
el secretario/la secretaria	*male/female secretary*
el trabajo	*job, work*

Asking and talking about work

¿Qué quieres ser?	*What do you want to be?*
Quiero ser ___.	*I want to be ___.*
Trabajo.	*I work.*
Trabaja.	*He/She works.*

Countries

Argentina	*Argentina*
Bolivia	*Bolivia*
Chile	*Chile*
Colombia	*Colombia*
Costa Rica	*Costa Rica*
Cuba	*Cuba*
Ecuador	*Ecuador*
EE.UU.	*abbrev. for* los Estados Unidos (*United States of America*)
El Salvador	*El Salvador*
España	*Spain*
los Estados Unidos	*United States of America*
Guatemala	*Guatemala*
Honduras	*Honduras*
México	*Mexico*
Nicaragua	*Nicaragua*
Panamá	*Panama*
Paraguay	*Paraguay*
Perú	*Peru*
Puerto Rico	*Puerto Rico*
La República Dominicana	*Dominican Republic*
Uruguay	*Uruguay*
Venezuela	*Venezuela*

Continents

Norteamérica	*North America*
Sudamérica	*South America*

Geography

el campo	*countryside*
el centro	*center*
la ciudad	*city*
las ciudades	*cities*
el pueblo	*town*
los pueblos	*towns*
el norte	*north*
el este	*east*
el sur	*south*
el oeste	*west*

Colors

Vocabulary

amarillo	*yellow*
anaranjado	*orange*
azul	*blue*
blanco	*white*
café	*brown*
gris	*gray*
morado	*purple*
negro	*black*
rojo	*red*
rosado	*pink*
verde	*green*

Asking about colors

¿De qué color es ___?	*What color is ___?*
___ es de color ___.	*___ is the color ___.*
Es ___.	*It is ___.*
¿De qué color son ___?	*What color are ___?*
Son (de color) ___.	*They are ___.*

Positive commands

Anda.	*Walk.*
Borra.	*Erase.*
Busca ___.	*Look for ___.*
Canta.	*Sing.*
Colorea.	*Color.*
Corre.	*Run.*
Dame ___.	*Give me ___.*
Dibuja.	*Draw.*
Juega.	*Play.*
Muéstrame ___.	*Show me ___.*
Párate.	*Stand up.*
Ponte ___.	*Put on ___.*
Quítate ___.	*Take off ___.*
Siéntate.	*Sit down.*
Toca ___.	*Touch ___. Play (a musical instrument) ___.*
Toma.	*Drink.*

Classroom objects

Vocabulary

el bolígrafo (el boli)	*pen*
los bolígrafos (los bolis)	*pens*
los colores	*crayons*
el cuaderno	*notebook*
la goma	*eraser*
las gomas	*erasers*
el globo	*globe*
el lápiz	*pencil*
los lápices	*pencils*
el libro	*book*
el papel	*paper*
la regla	*ruler*
las reglas	*rulers*
el sacapuntas	*pencil sharpener*
las tijeras	*scissors*

Asking about a person or object

¿Quién es?	*Who is it?*
Es ___.	*It is ___.*
¿Qué necesitas?	*What do you need?*
Necesito ___.	*I need ___.*
Necesitas ___.	*You need ___.*
¿Qué más necesitas?	*What else do you need?*
¿Es ___ o es ___?	*Is it ___ or is it ___?*
Es ___.	*It is ___.*
¿Son ___ o son ___?	*Are they ___ or are they ___?*
¿Qué es esto?	*What is this?*
¿Cuál falta?	*What's missing?*
¿Dónde está ___?	*Where is ___?*
En ___.	*In ___.*

Days of the week[4]

lunes	*Monday*	jueves	*Thursday*
martes	*Tuesday*	viernes	*Friday*
miércoles	*Wednesday*	sábado	*Saturday*
		domingo	*Sunday*

Months

Vocabulary

el mes	*month*
los meses	*months*
enero	*January*
febrero	*February*
marzo	*March*
abril	*April*
mayo	*May*
junio	*June*
julio	*July*
agosto	*August*
septiembre	*September*
octubre	*October*
noviembre	*November*
diciembre	*December*

Asking about the date, month, and day of the week

¿Cuál es la fecha?	*What is the date?*
Es el [*number*] de [*month*].	*It is the [number] of [month].*
¿Qué mes es?	*What month is it?*
Es ___.	*It is ___.*
¿Qué día es?	*What day of the week is it?*
¿Qué día (de la semana) es hoy?	*What day (of the week) is today?*
(Hoy) (Mañana) es ___.	*(Today) (Tomorrow) is ___.*

Seasons of the year

Vocabulary

las estaciones	*seasons*
el invierno	*winter*
la primavera	*spring*
el verano	*summer*
el otoño	*fall*

Asking about the seasons

¿Qué estación te gusta?	*What season do you like?*
Me gusta ___.	*I like ___.*
¿Qué estación es?	*What season is it?*
Es ___.	*It is ___.*
En + (*season*) + hace (*kind of weather*).	*In (season)* + it's *(the kind of weather).*

[4] Given in calendar order for Spanish-speaking countries.

Weather expressions

Vocabulary

Hace buen tiempo.	*It's good weather.*
Hace mal tiempo.	*It's bad weather.*
Hace calor.	*It's hot.*
Hace frío.	*It's cold.*
Hace sol.	*It's sunny.*
Hace viento.	*It's windy.*
Llueve.	*It's raining.*
Nieva.	*It's snowing.*

Talking about the weather

En ___ hace ___.	*In ___ it is ___.*
Hace ___.	*It's ___.*

Articles of clothing

Vocabulary

el abrigo	*coat*
la blusa	*blouse*
los calcetines	*socks*
la camisa	*shirt*
la chaqueta	*jacket*
la falda	*skirt*
las gafas de sol	*sunglasses*
los pantalones	*pants*
los pantalones cortos	*shorts*
el pijama	*pajamas*
la ropa	*clothing*
las sandalias	*sandals*
el sombrero	*hat*
los sombreros	*hats*
el suéter	*sweater*
el traje de baño	*bathing suit*
el vestido	*dress*
los zapatos	*shoes*

Talking about clothing

El vestido es rojo.	*The dress is red.*
La falda es roja.	*The skirt is red.*
Los vestidos son rojos.	*The dresses are red.*
Las faldas son rojas.	*The skirts are red.*

Musical instruments

Vocabulary

el clarinete	*clarinet*
los clarinetes	*clarinets*
la flauta	*flute*
las flautas	*flutes*
la guitarra	*guitar*
las guitarras	*guitars*
los instrumentos musicales	*musical instruments*
la pandereta	*tambourine*
las panderetas	*tambourines*
el piano	*piano*
los pianos	*pianos*
el tambor	*drum*
los tambores	*drums*
la trompeta	*trumpet*
las trompetas	*trumpets*
el violín	*violin*
los violines	*violins*

Asking about musical instruments

¿Qué instrumento (musical) es?	*What (musical) instrument is it?*
Es ___.	*It's ___.*
Toca ___.	*Play ___.*
¿Qué toca?	*What is he/she playing?*
¿Cuál es tu instrumento musical favorito?	*Which is your favorite musical instrument?*
Mi instrumento musical favorito es ___.	*My favorite musical instrument is ___.*

Stereo and entertainment equipment

Vocabulary

la cinta	*cassette*
el disco CD	*compact disc (CD)*
la grabadora	*cassette player*
el radio	*radio*
la televisión	*television*
el tocadiscos CD	*CD player*

Describing words

Vocabulary

alto/alta	*tall*
bajo/baja	*short*
bonito/bonita	*pretty*
delgado/delgada	*thin*
duro/dura	*hard*
feo/fea	*ugly*
gordo/gorda	*fat*
grande	*large*
limpio/limpia	*clean*
mediano/mediana	*medium (in size)*
pequeño/pequeña	*small*
simpático/simpática	*friendly; nice*
suave	*soft*
sucio/sucia	*dirty*

Describing people and objects

El payaso es gordo.	*The male clown is fat.*
Los payasos son pequeños.	*The male clowns are small.*
La payasa es gorda.	*The female clown is fat.*
Las payasas son pequeñas.	*The female clowns are small.*
El apartamento es grande.	*The apartment is large.*
Los apartamentos son grandes.	*The apartments are large.*
La casa es grande.	*The house is large.*
Las casas son grandes.	*The houses are large.*

Buildings

Vocabulary

el apartamento	*apartment*
los apartamentos	*apartments*
la biblioteca	*library*
la cafetería	*cafeteria*
la casa	*house*
el edificio	*building, edifice*
el edificio de apartamentos	*apartment building*
la escuela	*school*
el hospital	*hospital*
el hotel	*hotel*
la oficina	*office*
el rascacielos	*skyscraper*
el restaurante	*restaurant*
el supermercado	*supermarket*
la tienda (de ropa)	*(clothing) store*

Parts of a building

Vocabulary

la chimenea	*chimney*
la entrada	*entrance*
la oficina	*office*
la puerta	*door*
la salida	*exit*
el techo	*roof*
la ventana	*window*
las ventanas	*windows*

Asking where one lives

¿Dónde vives tú?	*Where do you live?*
Vivo en ___.	*I live in ___.*

Rooms and parts of the house

Vocabulary

el baño	*bathroom*
la casa	*house*
la cocina	*kitchen*
el comedor	*dining room*
el cuarto	*room; bedroom*
los cuartos	*rooms; bedrooms*
el dormitorio	*bedroom*
el garaje	*garage*
el jardín	*garden*
el patio	*patio*
el portal	*porch*
la sala	*living room*

Asking about a house

¿Qué tiene la casa?	*What does the house have?*
La casa tiene ___.	*The house has ___.*
¿Qué cuarto es?	*What room is it?*
Mi casa es tu casa.	*My house is your house.*

Furniture

Vocabulary

la cama	*bed*
las camas	*beds*
la mesa	*table*
las mesas	*tables*
la silla	*chair*
las sillas	*chairs*

Asking about furniture

¿Cuántas ___ hay en ___?	*How many ___ are there in ___?*
Hay ___.	*There are ___.*

Places to go

Vocabulary

el café	*café, coffee shop*
el cine	*movie theater*
el museo	*museum*
el parque	*park*
la playa	*beach*
el supermercado	*supermarket*

Asking and talking about going places

¿Adónde vas (tú)?	*Where are you going?*
Voy a ___.	*I'm going (to) ___.*
Vamos a ___.	*We're going to ___./ Let's go to ___.*
¿Cómo vas (tú)?	*How are you going?*
Voy en ___.	*I'm going by ___.*
Voy a ___ en ___.	*I'm going to ___ by ___.*
Hago un viaje.	*I'm taking a trip.*

Money

Vocabulary

alto	*high (price)*
bajo	*low (price)*
los dólares	*dollars*
el precio	*price*
los precios	*prices*

Asking about the price of something

¿Cuánto es?	*How much is it?*
Es ___ dólares.	*It's ___.*
¿Cuánto cuesta?	*How much does it cost?*
¿Cuánto cuestan?	*How much do they cost?*
___ dólares.	*___ dollars.*

Foods and meals

Vocabulary

el almuerzo	*lunch*
el arroz	*rice*
el café	*coffee*
la cena	*dinner*
el cereal	*cereal*
comer	*to eat*
el desayuno	*breakfast*
la fresa	*strawberry*
las fresas	*strawberries*
la fruta	*fruit*
las frutas	*fruits*
el jugo	*juice*
los jugos	*juices*
el jugo de naranja	*orange juice*
la leche	*milk*
un vaso de leche	*a glass of milk*
la manzana	*apple*
las manzanas	*apples*
el menú	*menu*
el pan	*bread*
el pan tostado	*toast*
la papa	*potato*
las papas	*potatoes*
el plátano	*banana*
los plátanos	*bananas*
el pollo	*chicken*
el refresco	*soft drink*
el sándwich	*sandwich*
la sopa	*soup*
la uva	*grape*
las uvas	*grapes*
las zanahorias	*carrots*

Talking about food

Come ___.	*He/She/It eats ___.*
Tiene ___.	*He/She/It has ___.*
Toma ___.	*He/She/It drinks ___.*
por la mañana	*in the morning*
por la tarde	*in the afternoon*
por la noche	*in the evening; at night*
¿Qué haces?	*What are you doing?*
Como.	*I'm eating./I eat.*
Tomo.	*I'm drinking./I drink.*
Buen provecho.	*Enjoy your meal.*
¿Hay ___?	*Is there/Are there ___?*
Sí, hay ___.	*Yes, there is/there are ___.*
No, no hay ___.	*No there isn't/there aren't ___.*

Modes of transportation and traffic

Vocabulary

el autobús	*bus*
los autobuses	*buses*
el avión	*plane*
los aviones	*planes*
el bote	*boat*
los botes	*boats*
el camión	*truck*
los camiones	*trucks*
el coche	*car*
los coches	*cars*
despacio	*slowly*
las luces del tráfico	*traffic lights*
la moto	*motorcycle*
las motos	*motorcycles*
rápido	*rapidly*
el taxi	*taxi*
los taxis	*taxis*
el tren	*train*
los trenes	*trains*
el yipi	*jeep*
los yipis	*jeeps*

Talking about street-crossing safety

Amarillo: ¡Espera!	*Yellow: Wait!, Caution!*
Rojo: ¡Alto!	*Red: Stop!*
Verde: ¡Sigue!	*Green: Go!*
Miro a la derecha.	*I look to the right.*
Miro a la izquierda.	*I look to the left.*
Cruzo la calle.	*I cross the street.*

Animals and their habitats

Vocabulary

el burro	*donkey*
los burros	*donkeys*
el caballo	*horse*
la cabra	*goat*
la cebra	*zebra*
las cebras	*zebras*
el cerdo	*pig*
el conejo	*rabbit*
el elefante	*elephant*
los elefantes	*elephants*
la foca	*seal*
las focas	*seals*
la gallina	*chicken, hen*
el gallo	*rooster*
el gato	*male cat*
la gata	*female cat*
el guardián	*zookeeper*
el jardín zoológico	*zoo*
la jirafa	*giraffe*
las jirafas	*giraffes*
la llama	*llama*
el león	*lion*
los leones	*lions*
el oso	*bear*
los osos	*bears*
el pájaro	*bird*
los pájaros	*birds*
el pato	*duck*
los patos	*ducks*
el perro	*dog*
el pez	*fish (singular)*
los peces	*fish (plural)*
el rancho	*farm*
el tigre	*tiger*
los tigres	*tigers*
la vaca	*cow*

Asking and talking about animals

¿Qué animal es?	*What animal is it?*
¿Qué animal te gusta?	*What animal do you like?*
Me gusta ___.	*I like ___.*
¿Dónde vive ___?	*Where does the ___ live?*
En ___.	In/*On ___.*

Words indicating location or position

Vocabulary

abajo de	*under, underneath, below*
arriba de	*on top of, over, above*
cerca de	*close to*
debajo de	*under, underneath, below*
delante de	*in front of*
dentro de	*inside of*
detrás de	*behind, in back of*
fuera de	*outside of*
lejos de	*far from*

Asking where someone is

¿Dónde está ___?	*Where is ___?*
___ está debajo de la mesa.	*___ is underneath the table.*
___ está fuera de la casa.	*___ is outside the house.*
Está aquí.	*He/She/It is here.*

Miscellaneous

ahora	*now*
¡Bravo!	*Terrific!; Very, very good!*
¡Buena suerte!	*Good luck!*
la concha	*shell*
de habla hispana	*Spanish-speaking*
en	*in*
¡Excelente!	*Excellent!*
¡Fabuloso!	*Fabulous!*
Gracias.	*Thank you.*
hispano	*of Hispanic origin*
No.	*No.*
¿Necesitas ___?	*Do you need ___?*
Necesito ___.	*I need ___.*
No necesito ___.	*I don't need ___.*
¡Olé!	*Hurray!*
¡Perfecto!	*Perfect!*
por favor	*please*
¿Por qué?	*Why?*
Porque ___.	*Because ___.*
¡Qué extraño!	*How strange!*
¡Qué lástima!	*What a pity!*
¿Qué necesitas?	*What do you need?*
la siesta	*nap*
Sí.	*Yes.*
¡Silencio!	*Silence!*
tengo	*I have*
tiene	*he/she/it has*
un/una	*a, an*

Numbers 1–100

uno	*one*
dos	*two*
tres	*three*
cuatro	*four*
cinco	*five*
seis	*six*
siete	*seven*
ocho	*eight*
nueve	*nine*
diez	*ten*
once	*eleven*
doce	*twelve*
trece	*thirteen*
catorce	*fourteen*
quince	*fifteen*
dieciséis	*sixteen*
diecisiete	*seventeen*
dieciocho	*eighteen*
diecinueve	*nineteen*
veinte	*twenty*
veintiuno	*twenty-one*
veintidós	*twenty-two*
veintitrés	*twenty-three*
veinticuatro	*twenty-four*
veinticinco	*twenty-five*
veintiséis	*twenty-six*
veintisiete	*twenty-seven*
veintiocho	*twenty-eight*
veintinueve	*twenty-nine*
treinta	*thirty*
treinta y uno	*thirty-one*
treinta y dos	*thirty-two*
treinta y tres	*thirty-three*
treinta y cuatro	*thirty-four*
treinta y cinco	*thirty-five*
treinta y seis	*thirty-six*

treinta y siete	*thirty-seven*	sesenta y nueve	*sixty-nine*
treinta y ocho	*thirty-eight*	setenta	*seventy*
treinta y nueve	*thirty-nine*	setenta y uno	*seventy-one*
cuarenta	*forty*	setenta y dos	*seventy-two*
cuarenta y uno	*forty-one*	setenta y tres	*seventy-three*
cuarenta y dos	*forty-two*	setenta y cuatro	*seventy-four*
cuarenta y tres	*forty-three*	setenta y cinco	*seventy-five*
cuarenta y cuatro	*forty-four*	setenta y seis	*seventy-six*
cuarenta y cinco	*forty-five*	setenta y siete	*seventy-seven*
cuarenta y seis	*forty-six*	setenta y ocho	*seventy-eight*
cuarenta y siete	*forty-seven*	setenta y nueve	*seventy-nine*
cuarenta y ocho	*forty-eight*	ochenta	*eighty*
cuarenta y nueve	*forty-nine*	ochenta y uno	*eighty-one*
cincuenta	*fifty*	ochenta y dos	*eighty-two*
cincuenta y uno	*fifty-one*	ochenta y tres	*eighty-three*
cincuenta y dos	*fifty-two*	ochenta y cuatro	*eighty-four*
cincuenta y tres	*fifty-three*	ochenta y cinco	*eighty-five*
cincuenta y cuatro	*fifty-four*	ochenta y seis	*eighty-six*
cincuenta y cinco	*fifty-five*	ochenta y siete	*eighty-seven*
cincuenta y seis	*fifty-six*	ochenta y ocho	*eighty-eight*
cincuenta y siete	*fifty-seven*	ochenta y nueve	*eighty-nine*
cincuenta y ocho	*fifty-eight*	noventa	*ninety*
cincuenta y nueve	*fifty-nine*	noventa y uno	*ninety-one*
sesenta	*sixty*	noventa y dos	*ninety-two*
sesenta y uno	*sixty-one*	noventa y tres	*ninety-three*
sesenta y dos	*sixty-two*	noventa y cuatro	*ninety-four*
sesenta y tres	*sixty-three*	noventa y cinco	*ninety-five*
sesenta y cuatro	*sixty-four*	noventa y seis	*ninety-six*
sesenta y cinco	*sixty-five*	noventa y siete	*ninety-seven*
sesenta y seis	*sixty-six*	noventa y ocho	*ninety-eight*
sesenta y siete	*sixty-seven*	noventa y nueve	*ninety-nine*
sesenta y ocho	*sixty-eight*	cien	*one hundred*

Asking about numbers and letters

¿Qué número es?	*What number is it?*
Es ___.	*It's ___.*
¿Cuántos son?	*How many are there?*
Son ___.	*There are ___.*
más	*plus*
menos	*minus*
son	*equal*
¿Qué letra es?	*What letter is it?*

Lessons 1 – 60

Song Appendix

LESSON 1

Materials to gather

- VCR and Video Lesson 1 on Tape 1
- Cassette player
- Song Cassette
- Blackline Master 1A (song "**Español para ti**")
- Blackline Master 1B (question **¿Cómo te llamas tú?**)
- A blank transparency
- Overhead projector

OBJECTIVES

Language

- Sing **"Español para ti"** (*"Spanish Is for You, and for Me"*)
- Say one's name
- Ask someone for his or her name
- Learn the names of school subjects
- Understand the exchanges during a visit with a police chief and a doctor

Culture

- Understand that many teachers in Spanish-speaking countries wear smocks
- Hear a polite phrase used when one is introduced to someone
- Learn to be helpful to newcomers in class
- Learn that Spanish is important in many careers

Vocabulary

Buenos días.	*Good morning.*
¿Cómo estás tú?	*How are you?*
Muy bien, gracias.	*Very well, thank you.*
¿Y usted?	*And you?*
Muy contento/contenta.	*Very happy.*
Mucho gusto.	*It's nice to meet you.*
¿Quién es?	*Who is it?*
Es ___.	*It is ___.*
¿Cómo te llamas (tú)?	*What is your name?*
Me llamo ___.	*My name is ___.*
¿Cómo se llama?	*What is his/her name?*
Se llama ___.	*His/Her name is ___.*
Hola.	*Hello.*

¡Perfecto!	*Perfect!*
¡Fabuloso!	*Fabulous!*
la lectura	*reading*
la escritura	*writing*
las computadoras	*computers*
la geografía	*geography*
el drama	*theater, drama*
la música	*music*
la historia	*history*
las matemáticas	*math*
las ciencias	*science*
el arte	*art*
el jefe de la policía	*police chief*
el doctor	*doctor*
Adiós.	*Good-bye.*

Warm-up

Remind children how much they learned in Spanish last year—say hello and good-bye, give their name, ask someone for his or her name, say how they feel, say the numbers 1 to 100, and say where someone is in the house. They also learned many songs, including one about elephants balancing on the thread of a spider's web! Now they are going to use what they already know to learn more Spanish.

Introduce the video

Point out that the children are going to hear many words and expressions that they learned last year, as well as new ones. In this lesson, they are going to play the familiar game of *Who is it?* (**¿Quién es?**) with **la maestra** (the video teacher) and their disguised puppet friends Rosco, Dora, Jorge, and Ñico. In addition, they are going to meet some new friends and visit with a police chief and a doctor.

Video Lesson

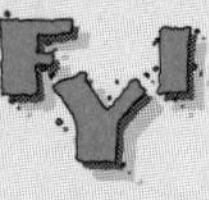

Escuchen la música. (*Listen to the music.*)
Vamos a cantar. (*Let's sing.*)

1. Starting another year of Spanish

La maestra greets the children with **Bienvenidos todos a la clase de español** (*Welcome everyone to Spanish class*). Like teachers in many Spanish-speaking countries, she is wearing a smock. She sings **"Español para ti"** (*"Spanish Is for You, and for Me"*) with the children.

Español para ti.	*Spanish for you.*
Español para mí.	*Spanish for me.*
Para ti, para mí.	*For you, for me.*
Y así todos sentir	*And so, everyone feels*
Una nueva sensación.	*A new sensation.*

EN ESPAÑOL

La maestra often exclaims **¡Muy bien, clase!** (*Very good, class!*) when working with the children. Use the expression with your class if you wish.

2. Recalling old friends

La maestra asks **¿Quién es?** (*Who is it?*) and says **Vamos a mirar** (*Let's watch*). The children guess the names of their disguised old friends Jorge the giraffe, Dora the cow, Ñico the toucan, and Rosco the wolf by saying **Es** (*It's*) and the name of the puppet.

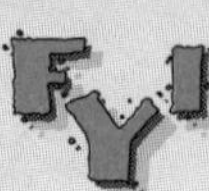

Maestra (*female teacher*) is a title of respect.

3. Introducing new friends

La maestra greets LeeAnn and has the opening conversation with her. She introduces the polite thing to say when meeting someone new (**M** = Maestra, **L** = LeeAnn):

M: Buenos días.	*Good morning.*
L: Buenos días, Maestra.	*Good morning, Teacher.*
M: ¿Cómo estás tú?	*How are you?*
L: Muy bien, gracias. ¿Y usted?	*Very well, thank you. And you?*
M: Muy bien. Estoy muy bien.	*Very well. I am very well.*
Muy contenta. ¿Cómo te llamas tú?	*I am very happy. What is your name?*
L: Me llamo LeeAnn.	*My name is LeeAnn.*
M: Clase, se llama LeeAnn.	*Class, her name is LeeAnn.*
Mucho gusto, LeeAnn.	*It's nice to meet you, LeeAnn.*
L: Mucho gusto.	*It's nice to meet you.*

When **la maestra** holds her hand to her ear, she is indicating that the children should listen. When her arm is outstretched, the children should respond.

4. Practicing questions and answers about names

La maestra practices the following questions and answers with the children.

¿Cómo te llamas tú?	*What is your name?*
Me llamo ___.	*My name is ___.*
¿Cómo se llama?	*What is his/her name?*
Se llama ___.	*His/Her name is ___.*

5. Introducing more new friends

La maestra greets Kipper with **Hola** (*Hello*) and asks him how he is. Kipper tells **la maestra** there is one more new **amigo** (*friend*) to meet. She talks about the importance of being friendly to newcomers. She greets Winston and introduces him to the class. They practice the new phrase **Mucho gusto** (*It's nice to meet you*).

6. Talking about careers

Standing in front of **las manos muy grandes** (*very large hands*), **la maestra** tells the children that with the big hands they can **toca el futuro** (*touch the future*). She reviews the concept of cognates and talks about subjects the children will be studying in school that will help them in their futures: **la lectura** (*reading*), **la escritura** (*writing*), **las computadoras** (*computers*), **la geografía** (*geography*), **el drama** (*theater*), **la música** (*music*), **la historia** (*history*), **las matemáticas** (*math*), **las ciencias** (*science*), and **el arte** (*art*).

7. Visiting the police station

La maestra greets **el jefe de la policía** (*the police chief*). LeeAnn, who wants to be a police officer, talks to the chief. They exchange names and LeeAnn asks him if girls can be police officers and also where he learned Spanish. They talk about what a good idea it is to learn Spanish if you want to be a police officer.

8. Visiting the doctor's office

La maestra points out that no matter what career you choose, knowing Spanish will be helpful. In the doctor's office, **la maestra** tells the children that **el doctor habla español y la enfermera habla español también** (*the doctor speaks Spanish and the nurse speaks Spanish also*). She greets the doctor, asks him if he has many patients, and if Spanish is important in his work.

9. Closing

With Winston, Kipper, and LeeAnn, **la maestra** says **Adiós** (*Good-bye*) to the children.

In the doctor's office:

¿El doctor está aquí?
(*Is the doctor here?*)

Sí, pase.
(*Yes, go on in.*)

Buenas tardes.
(*Good afternoon.*)

¿Está usted mal?
(*Are you feeling sick/badly?*)

No, no estoy mal.
(*No, I'm not feeling sick.*)

¿Por qué está aquí entonces?
(*Then why are you here?*)

Estoy aquí para visitarle.
(*I'm here to visit you.*)

El español es importante en su trabajo, ¿no?
(*Spanish is important in your work, isn't it?*)

EN ESPAÑOL

Remind children to say farewell—**Adiós** (*Good-bye*), **Hasta luego** (*See you later*), or **Hasta la vista** (*Until we meet again*)—to **la maestra** and their new friends.

After viewing the video, praise the children for their good listening and watching skills.

Español para ti
(Spanish Is for You, and for Me)
Español para ti
Español para mí.
Para ti, para mí.
Y así todos sentir
Una nueva sensación.

Blackline Master 1A

¿Cómo te llamas tú?

Blackline Master 1B

Activity Lesson

Activity 1A: Sing a song

Materials: Cassette player; Song Cassette, Side A; Blackline Master 1A (found in the Teacher's Resource Book); a blank transparency; and an overhead projector.

Preparation: Make a transparency of Blackline Master 1A.

Display the transparency. Tell the children they are going to practice the song "**Español para ti**" (*"Spanish Is for You, and for Me"*). Ask for a volunteer to point to the words on the transparency while singing the song. You may find it helpful to play the activity several times to allow children to refamiliarize themselves with the song. For children new to ***Español para ti*** this year, assure them that they will learn the song over time.

Activity 1B: What's different?

Materials: Blackline Master 1B.

Display Blackline Master 1B. Point to the question on the Blackline Master: **¿Cómo te llamas tú?** (*What is your name?*). Ask the children how the use of question marks is different in Spanish as compared to English. Emphasize that every question in Spanish has an upside-down question mark at the beginning and a right-side-up question mark at the end.

Activity 1C: Introduce yourself

Ask volunteers to introduce themselves to the class as they did to **la maestra**, LeeAnn, Kipper, and Winston, by saying **Me llamo** ___ (*My name is* ___). Instruct the class to practice saying the polite Spanish expression for *It's nice to meet you* (**Mucho gusto**).

Closing

Tell the children that Spanish class is finished for today. In the next lesson they will review the locations and names of the countries where Spanish is spoken and play a game with numbers.

Family Connection

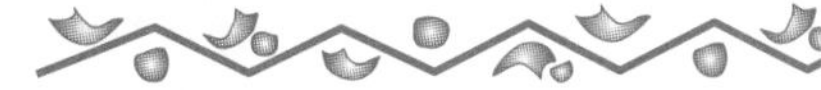

To foster a friendly link between home and school, you may wish to send out Family Letter 1 (found in the Teacher's Resource Book). The letter informs family members about what the children will be learning in Spanish this year and suggests ways they can support their child's efforts.

If You Have Time . . .

Lead the children in a discussion about careers and school subjects. Ask what careers interest them and what subjects will help them prepare for these careers. How might the knowledge of another language be helpful in their career(s)?

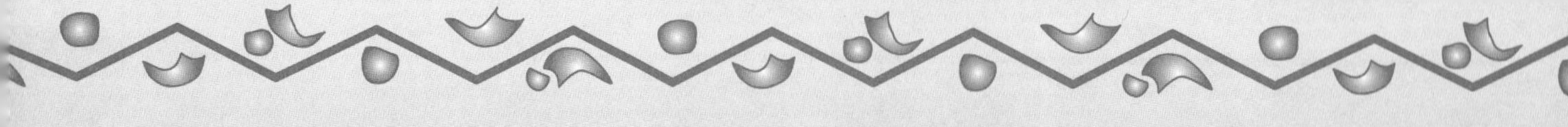

Lesson 2

Materials to gather

- VCR and Video Lesson 2 on Tape 1
- Cassette player
- Activity Cassette 1
- Song Cassette
- Blackline Master 2A (2 skiers)
- Blackline Master 2B (Spanish-speaking countries)
- A blank transparency
- Overhead projector
- A map of the world

Objectives

Language

- Sing **"La canción de geografía"** (*"The Geography Song"*)
- Count from 1 to 20
- Answer the question **¿Qué número es?** (*What number is it?*)
- Learn the names of the twenty Spanish-speaking countries

Culture

- Learn how the Spanish language came to North and South America
- Understand that children all over the world are learning similar subjects in school

Review

- Practice the opening conversation
- Answer the question **¿Cómo se llama?** (*What is his/her name?*)
- Review the names of school subjects

Vocabulary

Así, así.	*So-so.*	Panamá	*Panama*
Muy mal.	*Very bad.*	Cuba	*Cuba*
Tengo frío.	*I'm cold.*	La República Dominicana	*Dominican Republic*
Tengo calor.	*I'm hot.*	Puerto Rico	*Puerto Rico*
España	*Spain*	Venezuela	*Venezuela*
México	*Mexico*	Colombia	*Colombia*
Guatemala	*Guatemala*	Ecuador	*Ecuador*
Honduras	*Honduras*	Perú	*Peru*
El Salvador	*El Salvador*	Bolivia	*Bolivia*
Nicaragua	*Nicaragua*	Chile	*Chile*
Costa Rica	*Costa Rica*		

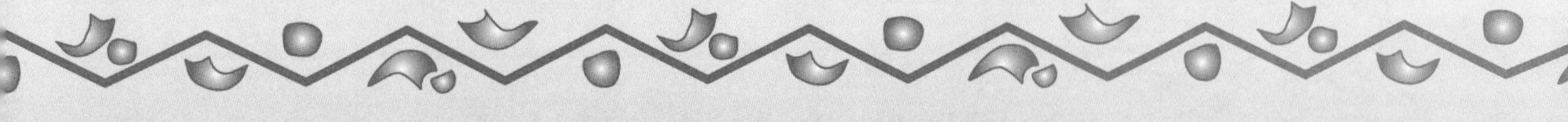

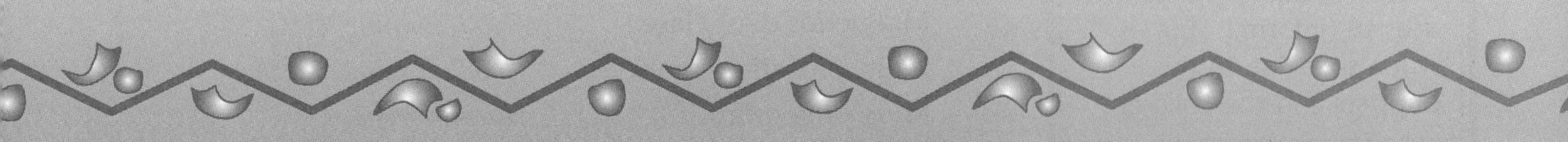

Argentina	*Argentina*	hispano	*of Hispanic origin*
Paraguay	*Paraguay*	de habla hispana	*Spanish-speaking*
Uruguay	*Uruguay*	¿Qué número es?	*What number is it?*

uno	*one*	ocho	*eight*	quince	*fifteen*
dos	*two*	nueve	*nine*	dieciséis	*sixteen*
tres	*three*	diez	*ten*	diecisiete	*seventeen*
cuatro	*four*	once	*eleven*	dieciocho	*eighteen*
cinco	*five*	doce	*twelve*	diecinueve	*nineteen*
seis	*six*	trece	*thirteen*	veinte	*twenty*
siete	*seven*	catorce	*fourteen*		

Warm-up

Pretend the sun is just coming up and ask the children how they would greet you in Spanish (**Buenos días**—*Good morning*).

Review

Ask the children if they recall the names of the three newcomers **la maestra** introduced in the last lesson (LeeAnn, Kipper, and Winston). How would they ask one of them for his or her name in Spanish? (**¿Cómo te llamas tú?**—*What is your name?*) Divide the class into pairs and have them practice asking each other for their names and stating their names. Remind the children to use the polite phrase **Mucho gusto** (*It's nice to meet you*) that they learned in the last lesson.

¿Cómo te llamas (tú)?	*What is your name?*
Me llamo ___.	*My name is ___.*
Mucho gusto.	*It's nice to meet you.*

Introduce the video

Invite the children to listen and watch as **la maestra** sings a new song that includes the names of all the Spanish-speaking countries.

EN ESPAÑOL

If you feel comfortable, greet the children with **Hola** (*Hello*) and tell them it is time for **la clase de español** (*Spanish class*).

VIDEO LESSON

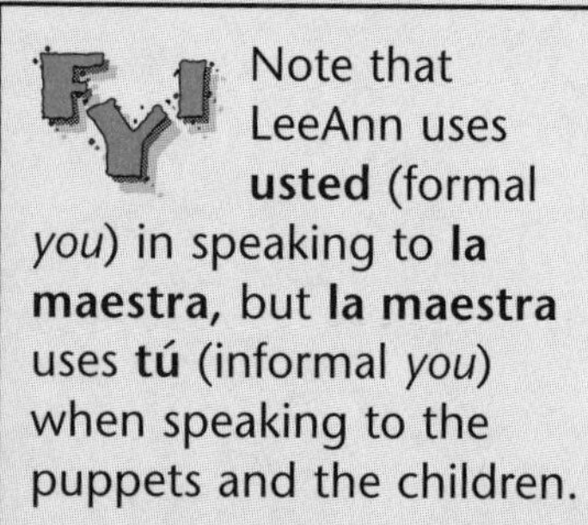

Note that LeeAnn uses **usted** (formal *you*) in speaking to **la maestra,** but **la maestra** uses **tú** (informal *you*) when speaking to the puppets and the children.

1. Greeting the children

La maestra greets the puppets LeeAnn, Kipper, and Winston and tells the children **Bienvenidos a la clase de español** (*Welcome to Spanish class*). She holds the opening conversation with LeeAnn and then with the children (**M** = Maestra, **L/C** = LeeAnn/class):

M: Buenos días, clase. — *Good morning, class.*
L/C: Buenos días, Maestra. — *Good morning, Teacher.*
M: ¿Cómo estás tú? — *How are you?*
L/C: Muy bien, gracias. ¿Y usted? — *Very well, thank you. And you?*
M: Muy bien, gracias. — *Very well, thank you.*

La maestra reviews additional answers to **¿Cómo estás tú?** (*How are you?*).

Así, así. — *So-so.*
Muy mal. — *Very bad.*
Estoy bien. — *I'm well.*
Estoy contento/contenta. — *I'm happy.*
Tengo frío. — *I'm cold.*
Tengo calor. — *I'm hot.*

Note that boys say **contento**; girls say **contenta**.

2. Practicing the question *¿Cómo se llama?* (*What is his/her name?*)

Pointing to each of the puppets, **la maestra** asks the children **¿Cómo se llama?** (*What's his/her name?*) and the children respond **Se llama** ___ (*His/Her name is* ___).

3. Singing "Español para ti" (*"Spanish Is for You, and for Me"*)

Everyone sings the song.

Español para ti. — *Spanish for you.*
Español para mí. — *Spanish for me.*
Para ti, para mí. — *For you, for me.*
Y así todos sentir — *And so, everyone feels*
Una nueva sensación. — *A new sensation.*

4. Presenting the origin of Spanish in North and South America

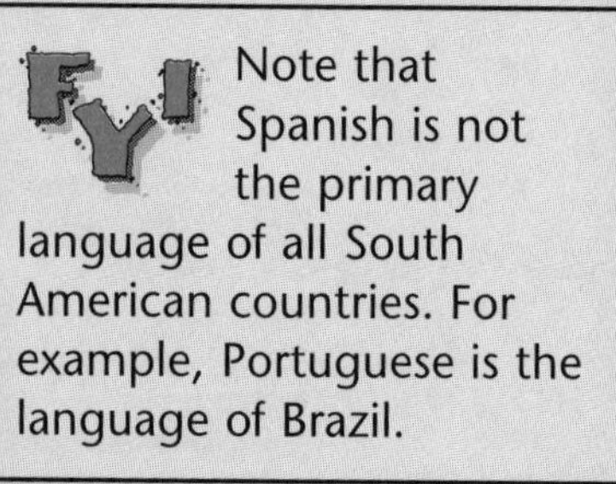

Note that Spanish is not the primary language of all South American countries. For example, Portuguese is the language of Brazil.

La maestra points out that North America (**Norte América**) consists of Canada, the United States, Mexico, the countries of Central America, and the countries of the Caribbean, and that South America (**Sudamérica**) consists of all the countries south of Panama. She emphasizes that when one talks about Americans, one is referring to all the people of North and South America. Describing the settlement of the Americas by Christopher

Columbus sailing from Spain (**España**) and the sailors, explorers, soldiers, and priests following him, she explains how so many Americans in twenty countries came to speak Spanish.

5. Explaining new terms

La maestra explains that if one is **hispano**, one or one's family is *from a Spanish-speaking country* and that if one speaks Spanish, one is **de habla hispana** (*Spanish-speaking*).

6. Presenting the new song "La canción de geografía" (*"The Geography Song"*)

La maestra sings the new song about the twenty Spanish-speaking countries. For song lyrics, see Activity 2B in this lesson.

1. España (*Spain*)
2. México
3. Guatemala
4. Honduras
5. El Salvador
6. Nicaragua
7. Costa Rica
8. Panamá
9. Cuba
10. La República Dominicana
11. Puerto Rico
12. Venezuela
13. Colombia
14. Ecuador
15. Perú
16. Bolivia
17. Chile
18. Argentina
19. Paraguay
20. Uruguay

7. Presenting the numbers 1–20

La maestra, Winston, and the children count from 1 to 20. **La maestra** and the children count from 11 to 20. Then she plays a number game by pointing to a number and asking the children **¿Qué número es?** (*What number is it?*). For numbers 1–20, see the Vocabulary section in this lesson.

8. Reviewing the names of school subjects

La maestra mentions that children in the Spanish-speaking countries and all over the world are studying many of the same subjects the children are studying in preparation to **toca el futuro** (*touch the future*). She shows pictures representing the various school subjects and reviews the names of the subjects with the children.

la música	*music*	el drama	*theater, drama*
la historia	*history*	la geografía	*geography*
las matemáticas	*math*	las computadoras	*computers*
las ciencias	*science*	la escritura	*writing*
el arte	*art*	la lectura	*reading*

9. Closing

The children and **la maestra** sing **"Español para ti"** (*"Spanish Is for You, and for Me"*). For song lyrics, see section 3 above.

LANGUAGE ACROSS THE CURRICULUM

Many words in English and Spanish sound alike and have similar meanings. These words are called cognates. Being aware of such similarities helps children remember the meaning of Spanish words. Tell the children that many of the names of the Spanish-speaking countries sound the same in both Spanish and English.

After viewing the video, praise the children for their good listening and watching skills.

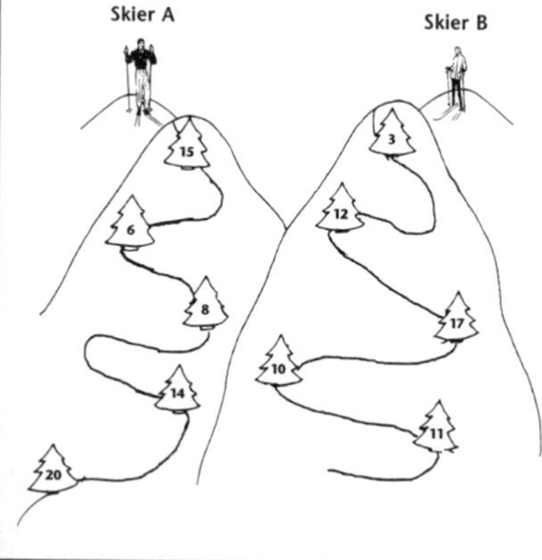

Here is a racing game to play with a partner. See who can ski down the mountain first and without falling down. There are different numbers in the trees at each turn. Decide who will be Skier A and Skier B. Start at the top and take turns saying the numbers in the trees as you go down. If you say the correct number, you may go to the next tree. If you say the wrong number, you "fall down" and must stay at that tree until you say the correct number. Good luck!

Blackline Master 2A

Children familiar with ***Español para ti*** will recognize doña Elena. Doña Elena is from Cuba and came to the United States as a girl. **Doña** is a title of respect usually used with a woman to whom the speaker is not related.

Los países de habla hispana
(Spanish-Speaking Countries)

1. España
2. México
3. Guatemala
4. Honduras
5. El Salvador
6. Nicaragua
7. Costa Rica
8. Panamá
9. Cuba
10. La República Dominicana
11. Puerto Rico
12. Venezuela
13. Colombia
14. Ecuador
15. Perú
16. Bolivia
17. Chile
18. Argentina
19. Uruguay
20. Paraguay

Blackline Master 2B

Activity Lesson

Activity 2A: Racing and numbers

Materials: Cassette player; Activity Cassette 1, Side A; and Blackline Master 2A, one per child.

Preparation: Make one copy of Blackline Master 2A for each child.

Divide the class into pairs. Tell the children to decide who in each pair will be skier A and who will be skier B. Give each child a copy of Blackline Master 2A. Point out that at the top is a place for them to write in their names—**Me llamo** ___ (*My name is* ___).

Tell the children that doña Elena is going to show skier A the way down the mountain by saying each of the numbers along the ski trail. She will do the same for skier B. The skiers should follow the trail as doña Elena reads the numbers because afterward they are going to say the numbers on their trail to their partners. Once doña Elena has finished, turn off the tape and read the instructions at the top of Blackline Master 2A aloud to the class. Then have them play the racing game together.

Skier A:		***Skier B:***	
15	quince	*3*	tres
6	seis	*12*	doce
8	ocho	*17*	diecisiete
14	catorce	*10*	diez
20	veinte	*11*	once

Activity 2B: Sing the new song

Materials: Cassette player; Song Cassette, Side A; Blackline Master 2B; a blank transparency; and an overhead projector.

Preparation: Make a transparency of Blackline Master 2B. Display the transparency.

Tell the children they are going to sing **"La canción de geografía"** (*"The Geography Song"*) about the Spanish-speaking countries. Point to each of the country names on the transparency and encourage the children to sing them. Reassure them that with time they will learn the entire song, but for now they should just concentrate on the names of the countries.

Los países de habla hispana	*The Spanish-speaking countries*
Todos vamos a contar.	*Let's count them all.*
Veinte naciones de habla hispana	*Twenty Spanish-speaking nations*
Vamos todos a pronunciar.	*Let's pronounce them all.*
España, México, Guatemala,	*Spain, Mexico, Guatemala,*
Honduras, El Salvador, Nicaragua,	*Honduras, El Salvador, Nicaragua,*

Costa Rica, Panamá.	*Costa Rica, Panama.*
En el Caribe tres países	*In the Caribbean three countries*
Todas islas de sol y mar	*All islands of sun and sea*
Cuba, La República Dominicana,	*Cuba, Dominican Republic,*
Puerto Rico allí están.	*Puerto Rico are there.*
Venezuela, Colombia, Ecuador,	*Venezuela, Colombia, Ecuador,*
Perú, Bolivia, Chile,	*Peru, Bolivia, Chile,*
Argentina, Uruguay y Paraguay.	*Argentina, Uruguay, and Paraguay.*
Todos los países de habla hispana	*All the Spanish-speaking countries*
Veinte.	*Twenty.*

Activity 2C: Who went where?

Materials: A map of the world.

Lead children in a discussion about how English came to the United States. Talk about the Pilgrims coming from England to the northeast coast of the U.S. and settling in Plymouth, Massachusetts. Talk about the similarities between the spread of English in the U.S. and the spread of Spanish in the Americas.

Closing

Tell the children that Spanish class is finished for today. In the next lesson **la maestra** will talk about colors and take a trip to an elementary school.

Language Across the Curriculum

On a map or globe of the world, point out the Andes mountain range that extends from Venezuela to Tierra del Fuego in Argentina. The highest peak in the Andes is in Argentina and is over 22,000 feet high. In Spain, point out the Pyrenees on the border with France, as well as other mountain ranges, e.g., Sierra de Guadarrama near Madrid and Sierra Nevada near Granada in southeastern Spain. Mention that skiing is popular in Spain and in some South American countries. **Sierra** means *mountain range.*

If You Have Time . . .

Materials: Cassette player; Song Cassette, Side A; a map of the world; your overhead transparency from Activity 2B; and an overhead projector.

Have the children sing **"La canción de geografía"** (*"The Geography Song"*) while a volunteer points to each of the countries on the overhead transparency and you point to the countries on the world map. Then have the children count the 20 Spanish-speaking countries in Spanish as you point to them on the map.

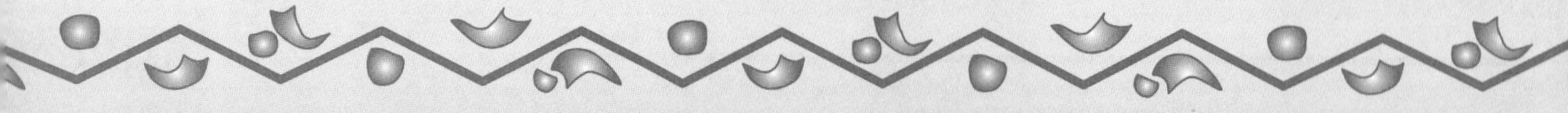

Lesson 3

Materials to gather

- VCR and Video Lesson 3 on Tape 1
- Cassette player
- Song Cassette
- Number Cards 1–20
- Overhead transparency of Blackline Master 2B (20 Spanish-speaking countries)
- Overhead projector
- Blackline Master 3B (four paintbrushes)
- One red, blue, orange, and purple crayon per child
- Scissors, one pair per child
- ***Optional materials:*** Video Lesson 2 on Tape 1; a map of the world; Rosco (the wolf) hand puppet

Objectives

Language

- Answer the question **¿De qué color es?** (*What color is it?*) with **rojo** (*red*), **azul** (*blue*), **morado** (*purple*), and **anaranjado** (*orange*)
- Listen to an extended conversation about school classes
- Answer the question **¿Qué haces en la clase de ___?** (*What do you do in ___ class?*)

Culture

- Understand that non-English speakers are learning English just as the class is learning Spanish

Review

- Practice the greeting **Buenos días** (*Good morning*)
- Practice stating how one is
- Answer the questions **¿Cómo te llamas tú?** (*What is your name?*) and **¿Cómo se llama?** (*What is his/her name?*)
- Review the names of school subjects
- Sing **"Español para ti"** (*"Spanish Is for You, and for Me"*)

Vocabulary

¡Excelente!	*Excellent!*
Estoy enojado/enojada.	*I'm angry.*
¿De qué color es?	*What color is it?*
rojo	*red*
azul	*blue*
morado	*purple*
anaranjado	*orange*
el español	*Spanish*
el inglés	*English*
¿Qué haces en la clase de ___?	*What do you do in ___ class?*
Estudio ___.	*I study ___.*

Warm-up

Materials: Rosco (the wolf) hand puppet (if available).

Display the Rosco hand puppet, telling the children that an old friend has come to visit today's Spanish class. Ask for a volunteer to "play" Rosco and lead the class in the opening conversation (**R** = Rosco, **C** = class):

R: Buenos días/Hola, clase.	*Good morning/Hello, class.*
C: Buenos días/Hola, Rosco.	*Good morning/Hello, Rosco.*
R: ¿Cómo estás tú?	*How are you?*
C: Muy bien, gracias. ¿Y tú?	*Very well, thank you. And you?*
R: Muy bien, gracias.	*Very well, thank you.*

If you do not have a Rosco puppet, ask for a volunteer to hold this conversation with the class and to play himself or herself.

Review

Materials: Number Cards 1–20 (found in the Teacher's Resource Book); *optional:* VCR and Video Lesson 2 on Tape 1.

Hold up the Number Cards in order one at a time and have the children count from 1 to 20. Do this several times, going faster each time. If the children are having difficulty, play section 7 from Lesson 2, in which **la maestra** models these numbers. Once the children appear confident, hold up the Number Cards in order and have them name the numbers again.

1	uno	*6*	seis	*11*	once	*16*	dieciséis
2	dos	*7*	siete	*12*	doce	*17*	diecisiete
3	tres	*8*	ocho	*13*	trece	*18*	dieciocho
4	cuatro	*9*	nueve	*14*	catorce	*19*	diecinueve
5	cinco	*10*	diez	*15*	quince	*20*	veinte

Introduce the video

Invite the children to listen and watch as **la maestra** greets LeeAnn and Winston, and visits a Spanish-speaking elementary school.

Some children may answer **¿Cómo estás tú?** (*How are you?*) with **Muy mal** (*Very bad*); **Así, así** (*So-so*); **Estoy contento/contenta** (*I'm happy*); **Tengo frío** (*I'm cold*); **Tengo calor** (*I'm hot*); **Tengo sed** (*I'm thirsty*); **Tengo miedo** (*I'm afraid*); **Tengo sueño** (*I'm sleepy*); **Estoy enojado/enojada** (*I'm angry*); or with Rosco's favorite reply, **Tengo hambre** (*I'm hungry*).

Many activities specify using volunteers, so that children who are ready to speak Spanish individually may do so. Children who are more hesitant, on the other hand, have more opportunities to listen and to speak with the whole class and in groups before talking as individuals.

Video Lesson

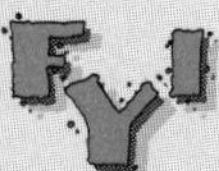

In answering the question **¿Cómo estás tú?** (*How are you?*), one may say **Muy bien** (*Very well*) or **Estoy muy bien** (*I am very well*).

1. Greeting the children

La maestra greets the children with **Buenos días** (*Good morning*) and asks them how they are (**M** = Maestra, **C** = class):

M: Buenos días, clase.	*Good morning, class.*
C: Buenos días, Maestra.	*Good morning, Teacher.*
M: ¿Cómo estás tú?	*How are you?*
C: Estoy muy bien, gracias. ¿Y usted?	*I am very well, thank you. And you?*
M: Muy bien, gracias. ¡Excelente!	*Very well, thank you. Excellent!*

Te toca a ti. (*It's your turn.*)

2. Answering questions

La maestra asks the puppets and the children **¿Cómo te llamas tú?** (*What's your name?*). Each puppet and child answer **Me llamo** ___ (*My name is* ___). She reviews the question **¿Cómo se llama?** (*What is his/her name?*) and its answer **Se llama** ___ (*His/Her name is* ___), and presents the question **¿Quién es?** (*Who is it?*) and its answer **Es** ___ (*It's* ___) as another way of finding out someone's name.

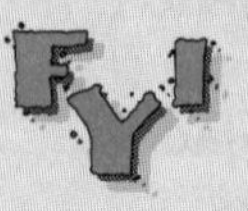

Colores can mean both *colors* and *crayons*. Context will clarify the meaning.

3. Asking the puppets how they are

La maestra holds the opening conversation with each of the puppets. LeeAnn says **Estoy contenta** (*I'm happy*), but Winston says **Estoy enojado** (*I'm angry*). When **la maestra** asks him **¿Por qué?** (*Why?*), he responds **No tengo colores** (*I don't have any crayons*).

4. Practicing color names

La maestra and the puppets say **Me gustan los colores** (*I like colors*). The mime reviews the colors. **La maestra** shows the children colored **sombreros** (*hats*) and asks **¿De qué color es?** (*What color is it?*). She tells the children **¡Repite, por favor!** (*Repeat, please!*).

rojo	*red*	morado	*purple*
azul	*blue*	anaranjado	*orange*

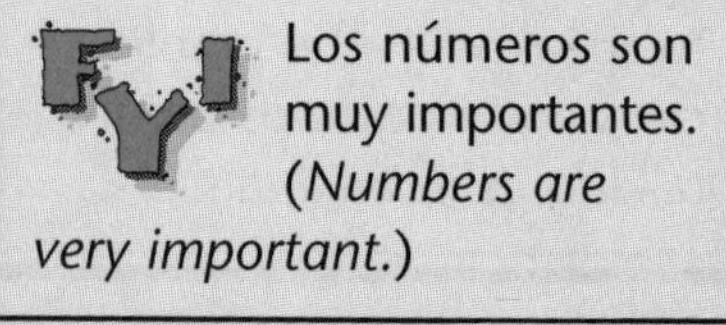

Los números son muy importantes. (*Numbers are very important.*)

5. Reviewing the words for school subjects

Pointing to each word, **la maestra** reviews the names of the subjects and mentions the importance or content of each subject.

el arte	*art*	la geografía	*geography*
las ciencias	*science*	las computadoras	*computers*
la historia	*history*	la escritura	*writing*
la música	*music*	la lectura	*reading*
el drama	*theater, drama*		

6. Visiting an elementary school

La maestra visits an elementary school. Some of her statements are as follows.

Estamos en una escuela.	*We are at a school.*
Vamos a una clase de música, una clase de arte y una clase de inglés.	*We are going to a music class, an art class, and an English class.*
Y vamos a jugar en la hora de recreo.	*And we are going to play during recess.*
En la clase de música estudiamos música.	*In music class we study music.*
Me gusta la música.	*I like music.*
Carlos es alumno en la clase de arte.	*Carlos is a pupil in the art class.*
¿Qué haces en la clase?	*What do you do in class?*
¿Te gusta la clase?	*Do you like the class?*
Me gusta mucho.	*I like it a lot.*
En la clase de inglés los alumnos leen en inglés, escriben en inglés y hablan todo en inglés.	*In English class, the pupils read in English, write in English, and speak all the time (only) in English.*

7. Introducing a new question and answer

La maestra asks LeeAnn and the children what they do in English, art, and music class.

¿Qué haces en la clase de ___?	*What do you do in ___ class?*
Estudio ___.	*I study ___.*

8. Singing *"Español para ti"* (*"Spanish Is for You, and for Me"*)

Everyone sings the song. For song lyrics, see Song 1 in the Song Appendix.

9. Closing

La maestra says **A mí me gustan todas las clases** (*I like all the classes*). LeeAnn says **Me gusta cantar** (*I like to sing*). They bid the children **Adiós, amigos** (*Good-bye, friends*).

After viewing the video, praise the children for their good listening and watching skills.

Activity Lesson

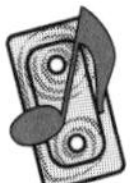

If You Have Time . . .

Materials: Cassette player; Song Cassette, Side A; a map of the world; the overhead transparency you made of Blackline Master 2B.

Have the children sing along to **"La canción de geografía"** (*"The Geography Song"*) while one volunteer points to the country names on the transparency and another volunteer points to the countries on the world map.

Activity 3A: Sing the song about the Spanish-speaking countries

Materials: Cassette player; Song Cassette, Side A; overhead projector; and the overhead transparency you made of Blackline Master 2B in Lesson 2.

Display the overhead transparency with the country names. Tell the children to sing along with **la maestra** as she sings **"La canción de geografía"** (*"The Geography Song"*). Reassure them that they only need to sing the country names. Point to each country name as it is sung.

Los países de habla hispana	*The Spanish-speaking countries*
Todos vamos a contar.	*Let's count them all.*
Veinte naciones de habla hispana	*Twenty Spanish-speaking nations*
Vamos todos a pronunciar.	*Let's pronounce them all.*
España, México, Guatemala,	*Spain, Mexico, Guatemala,*
Honduras, El Salvador, Nicaragua,	*Honduras, El Salvador, Nicaragua,*
Costa Rica, Panamá.	*Costa Rica, Panama.*
En el Caribe tres países	*In the Caribbean three countries*
Todas islas de sol y mar	*All islands of sun and sea*
Cuba, La República Dominicana,	*Cuba, Dominican Republic,*
Puerto Rico allí están.	*Puerto Rico are there.*
Venezuela, Colombia, Ecuador,	*Venezuela, Colombia, Ecuador,*
Perú, Bolivia, Chile,	*Peru, Bolivia, Chile,*
Argentina, Uruguay y Paraguay.	*Argentina, Uruguay, and Paraguay.*
Todos los países de habla hispana	*All the Spanish-speaking countries*
Veinte.	*Twenty.*

Activity 3B: Read the color names

Materials: Blackline Master 3B (found in the Teacher's Resource Book); one red, orange, purple, and blue crayon per child.

Preparation: Duplicate and distribute Blackline Master 3B, one copy per child. Make sure everyone has the four crayons.

Point out that on each paintbrush is the Spanish word for a color. Children should read each word to themselves and color the paintbrush the appropriate color. Once they have finished coloring, divide the class into pairs. Children should compare their worksheet with a partner's, reading the Spanish words aloud to each other as they do so. Colors: **rojo** (*red*), **anaranjado** (*orange*), **morado** (*purple*), **azul** (*blue*).

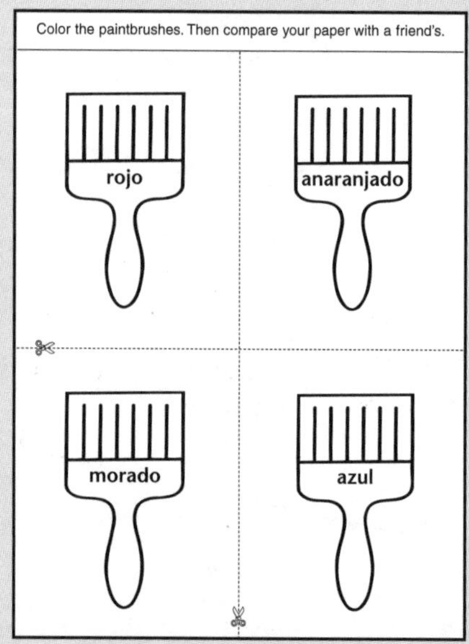
Color the paintbrushes. Then compare your paper with a friend's.
rojo
anaranjado
morado
azul

Blackline Master 3B

Activity 3C: Cooperative learning—Make up a rap about colors

Materials: Children's colored paintbrushes from Activity 3B; scissors, one pair per child.

Have the children cut out the paintbrushes by cutting along the dotted lines. Then divide the class into small groups. Have each group work together to make up the first verse of a "colors rap," using the color names **rojo** (*red*), **anaranjado** (*orange*), **morado** (*purple*), and **azul** (*blue*). Let them know that they will be adding verses as more colors are presented in the videos. Suggest they use their colored paintbrushes for emphasis in the song. Encourage them to include movement in their raps. Raps can be very simple, e.g., just the color names said in rhythm. Allow them a few minutes to come up with their raps. Then ask volunteers from each group to perform their rap for the class.

LANGUAGE ACROSS THE CURRICULUM

During music class, ask the children to sing their Spanish raps about the colors. If you don't teach the children music, mention to the music teacher that the children have written the first verse of a rap. If appropriate, suggest that children play or add music to their raps.

CLOSING

Tell the children that Spanish class is finished for today. In the next lesson they will practice more answers to the question **¿Cómo estás tú?** (*How are you?*) and review more color names.

Lesson 4

Materials to gather

- VCR and Video Lesson 4 on Tape 2
- Cassette player
- Activity Cassette 1
- Song Cassette
- Number Cards 1–20
- Overhead transparency of Blackline Master 2B (20 Spanish-speaking countries)
- Overhead projector
- Blackline Masters 4C-1, 4C-2, 4C-3, 4C-4 (11 paintbrushes)
- Blackline Master 4C-5 (rainbow)
- Crayons or colored pencils (see the Review section)
- ***Optional materials:*** laminating machine
- ***Prepare ahead:*** 11 paintbrushes (see the Review section)

Objectives

Language

- Practice the feeling expression **Estoy triste** (*I'm sad*)
- Practice additional colors: **verde** (*green*), **amarillo** (*yellow*), **rosado** (*pink*), and **blanco** (*white*)
- Review the commands **¡Dibuja!** (*Draw!*), **¡Borra!** (*Erase!*), and **¡Colorea!** (*Color!*)
- Learn what one does in art, music, and English classes, and during recess
- Learn the commands **¡Canta!** (*Sing!*) and **¡Juega!** (*Play!*)

Culture

- Review that while some children learn Spanish, others are learning English
- Sing **"Español para ti"** (*"Spanish Is for You, and for Me"*)

Review

- Review feeling expressions **Estoy enojado/enojada** (*I'm angry*) and **Estoy contento/contenta** (*I'm happy*)
- Practice the colors **rojo** (*red*), **azul** (*blue*), **morado** (*purple*), and **anaranjado** (*orange*)

Vocabulary

Estoy triste.	*I'm sad.*
verde	*green*
amarillo	*yellow*
rosado	*pink*
blanco	*white*
¿Qué clase es?	*What class is it?*
la clase de arte	*art class*
¡Dibuja!/Dibujo.	*Draw!/I draw.*
¡Borra!/Borro.	*Erase!/I erase.*
¡Colorea!/Coloreo.	*Color!/I color.*
la clase de música	*music class*
Estudio música.	*I study music.*
¡Canta!/Canto.	*Sing!/I sing.*
la clase de inglés	*English class*
Hablo inglés.	*I speak English.*
Canto en inglés.	*I sing in English.*

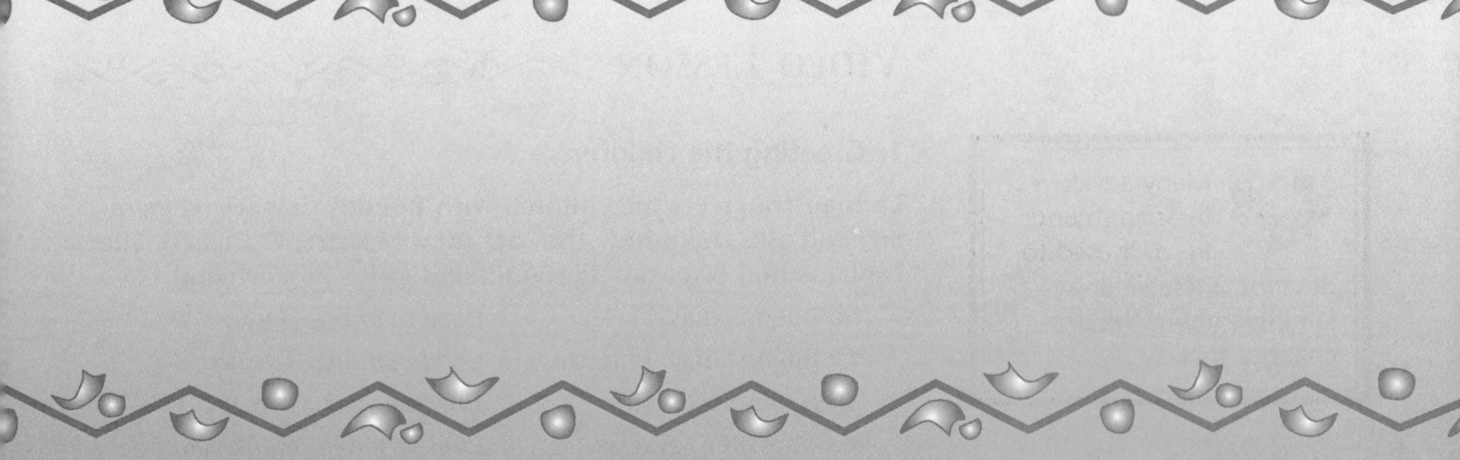

la hora de recreo	*recess*
¡Juega!/Juego.	*Go play!/I play.*
Hasta la vista.	*Until we meet again.*
Hasta luego.	*See you later.*

Warm-up

Materials: Number Cards 1–20 (found in the Teacher's Resource Book).

Tell the children you are going to hold up some numbers from 1 to 20 out of order and they should say the number in Spanish. Hold up the following numbers in this order:

15	quince	8	ocho	19	diecinueve
6	seis	12	doce	3	tres
10	diez	14	catorce	20	veinte

For numbers 1–20, see the Review section in Lesson 3.

Review

Materials: Blackline Masters 4C-1, 4C-2, 4C-3, and 4C-4; crayons: red, blue, gray, purple, orange, brown, green, yellow, black, pink, and white; *optional*: laminating machine.

Preparation: Color the paintbrushes in the following colors:

4C-1: **rojo** (*red*), **azul** (*blue*), **gris** (*gray*)

4C-2: **morado** (*purple*), **anaranjado** (*orange*), **café** (*brown*)

4C-3: **verde** (*green*), **amarillo** (*yellow*), **negro** (*black*)

4C-4: **rosado** (*pink*), **blanco** (*white*)

Hold up the red, blue, purple, and orange paintbrushes one at a time and ask the children to name the color in Spanish. If you feel comfortable, ask **¿De qué color es**? *(What color is it?*). Then ask children which of the four colors they like the best.

Introduce the video

Invite the children to listen and watch as **la maestra** reviews more color names.

If you feel comfortable, ask **¿Qué número es?** (*What number is it?*). You may also ask for a volunteer who knows the numbers well to lead the class in the Warm-up activity.

We suggest not coloring over the Spanish word on each paintbrush so that children start to associate the written word with the spoken language. Laminate the sheets, if possible, and then cut the eleven paint-brushes apart. Set all but the blue, red, purple, and orange paintbrushes aside for future use.

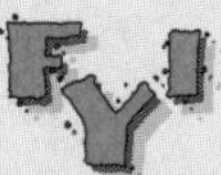

Many adjectives in Spanish end in **-o**. If used to describe a female or a feminine noun, the **o** changes to **a**.

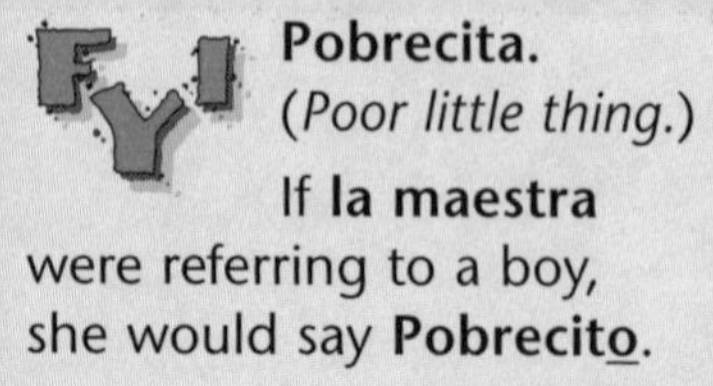

Pobrecita. (*Poor little thing.*) If **la maestra** were referring to a boy, she would say **Pobrecito**.

Colors:

Section 4:

azul	*blue*
rojo	*red*
morado	*purple*
anaranjado	*orange*

Section 5:

verde	*green*
amarillo	*yellow*
rosado	*pink*
blanco	*white*

VIDEO LESSON

1. Greeting the children

La maestra greets the children with **Buenos días** (*Good morning*) and asks them how they are (**M** = Maestra, **C** = class). She explains that boys say **¡Perfecto!** and girls say **¡Perfecta!**

M: Buenos días, clase.	*Good morning, class.*
C: Buenos días, Maestra.	*Good morning, Teacher.*
M: ¿Cómo estás tú?	*How are you?*
C: Muy bien, gracias. ¿Y usted?	*I am very well, thank you.* *And you?*
M: Muy bien. ¡Perfecta!	*Very well. Perfect!*

2. Practicing other ways of expressing how one feels

La maestra holds the opening conversation with each of the puppets. Kipper says **Estoy contento** (*I'm happy*). **La maestra** explains that girls say **Estoy contenta** but that boys say **Estoy contento.** LeeAnn says **Estoy triste** (*I'm sad*). **La maestra** reviews the feeling expressions **Muy bien** (*Very well*); **Así, así** (*So-so*); **Muy mal** (*Very bad*), and **Estoy enojado/enojada** (*I'm angry*).

3. Saying how someone else feels

A new friend—Lorena—demonstrates how she feels when **la maestra** asks **¿Cómo está Lorena?** (*How is Lorena?*): **Está enojada** (*She's angry*); **Está contenta** (*She's happy*); **Está triste** (*She's sad*).

4. Reviewing color names

LeeAnn tells **la maestra Voy a la clase de arte** (*I'm going to art class*). **La maestra** asks her **¿Te gusta la clase de arte?** (*Do you like art class?*) and LeeAnn responds **Sí, me gusta** (*Yes, I like it*). Holding up colored **sombreros** (*hats*), **la maestra** asks LeeAnn and the children **¿De qué color es?** (*What color is it?*).

5. Practicing additional color names

After LeeAnn asks **¿Hay más colores?** (*Are there more colors?*), **la maestra** and the mime present more colors. **La maestra** asks LeeAnn and the children **¿De qué color es?** (*What color is it?*).

6. Practicing commands

La maestra asks LeeAnn **¿Qué haces en la clase de arte?** (*What do you do in art class?*) and LeeAnn tells her **Dibujo** (*I draw*), **Borro** (*I erase*) and **Coloreo** (*I color*). Doña Elena tells the mime to draw and erase. **La maestra** reviews the commands **¡Dibuja!** (*Draw!*), **¡Borra!** (*Erase!*), and **¡Colorea!** (*Color!*).

7. Talking about music class

Kipper appears with his trumpet. **La maestra** talks to Kipper about where he's going.

¿Adónde vas?	*Where are you going?*
Voy a la clase de música.	*I'm going to music class.*
¿Qué haces en la clase de música?	*What do you do in music class?*
Toco la trompeta y canto.	*I play the trumpet and I sing.*

8. Presenting a new command

La maestra tells the mime **¡Canta!** (*Sing!*). He follows her instructions.

9. Singing "*Español para ti*" ("*Spanish Is for You, and for Me*")

Kipper, **la maestra**, and the children sing the song. For song lyrics, see Song 1 in the Song Appendix. **La maestra** explains the difference between commanding someone to sing (**¡Canta!**) and saying *I sing* (**Canto**).

10. Talking about English class and recess

La maestra asks Kipper **¿Qué más haces en la escuela?** (*What else do you do in school?*). He says **Voy a la clase de inglés** (*I go to English class*), and they discuss what he does there: **Estudio inglés** (*I study English*), **Canto en inglés** (*I sing in English*), and **Hablo inglés** (*I speak English*).

Then Kipper and **la maestra** talk about **la hora de recreo** (*recess*). Kipper tells her, **Juego en la hora de recreo** (*I play during recess*). Finally, **la maestra** makes the distinction between **Juego** (*I play*) and the command **¡Juega!** (*Go play!*).

11. Reviewing phrases

Using pictures, **la maestra** reviews the phrases they've learned.

12. Closing

La maestra mentions all the things the children have done in today's class. She and Kipper say **Adiós** (*Good-bye*), **Hasta la vista, amigos** (*Until we meet again, friends*), and **Hasta luego** (*See you later*).

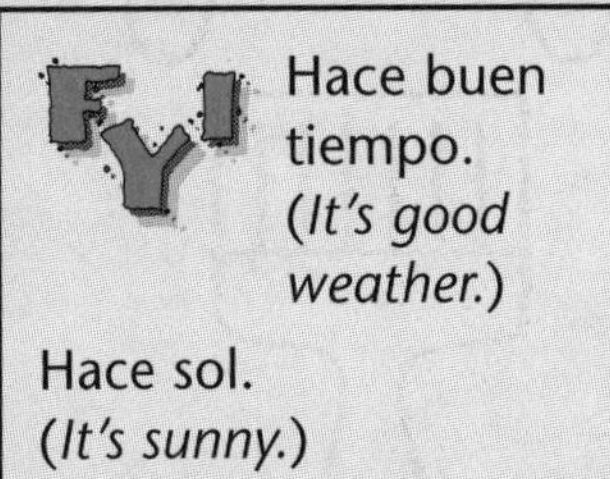

Hace buen tiempo. (*It's good weather.*)

Hace sol. (*It's sunny.*)

After viewing the video, praise the children for their good listening and watching skills.

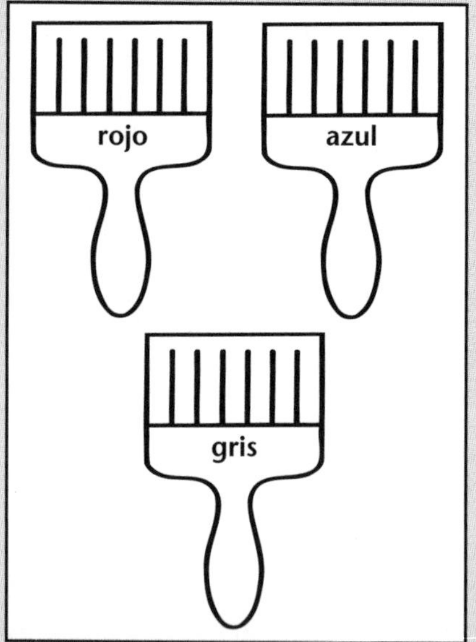

Blackline Master 4C-1

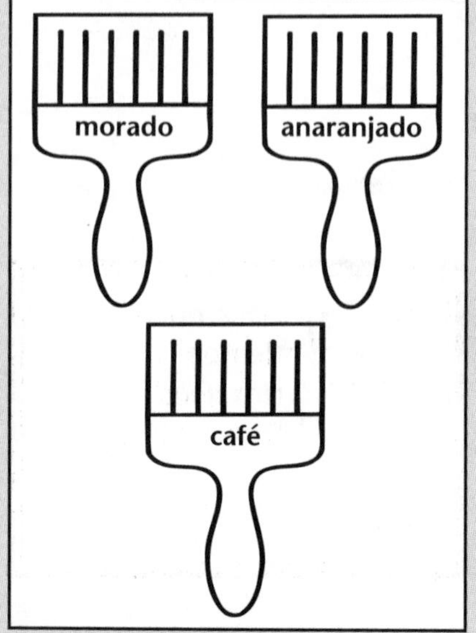

Blackline Master 4C-2

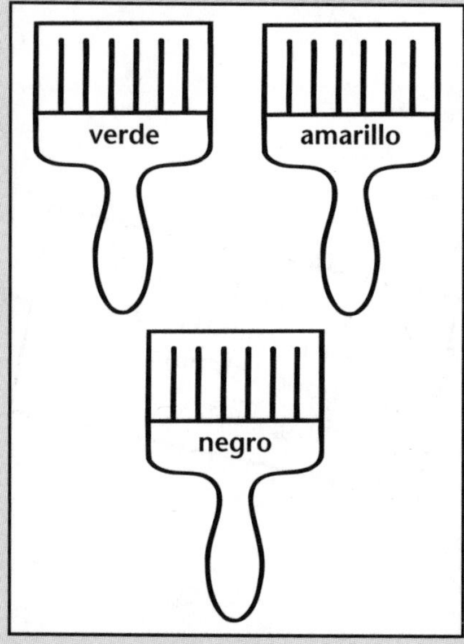

Blackline Master 4C-3

Activity Lesson

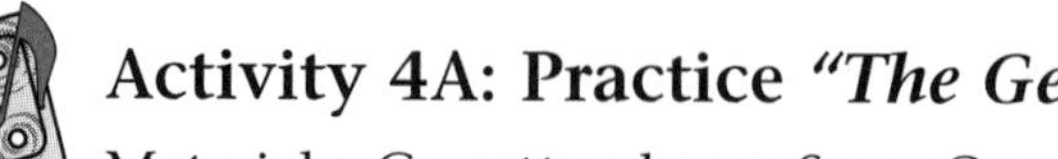

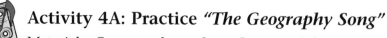

Activity 4A: Practice *"The Geography Song"*

Materials: Cassette player; Song Cassette, Side A; overhead projector; and your transparency of Blackline Master 2B.

Display the transparency of Blackline Master 2B. Tell the children they are going to sing the song about the twenty Spanish-speaking countries and encourage them to sing along. Point to the names of the countries as they are sung. For song lyrics, see Song 2 in the Song Appendix.

Activity 4B: Act out emotions

Materials: Cassette player; Activity Cassette 1, Side A.

Review the feeling phrases with the children. Smile and tell the children you are happy. Ask them how they would say *I'm happy* in Spanish (**Estoy contento/contenta**). Make an angry face and ask the children how to say *I'm angry* in Spanish (**Estoy enojado/enojada**). Make a sad face and follow the same procedure (*I'm sad*—**Estoy triste**). Tell the children to take Lorena's place and mime the emotions as she did while doña Elena says how Lorena is feeling. Children should mime the emotions in this order: **Está contenta** (*She's happy*), **Está enojada** (*She's angry*), **Está triste** (*She's sad*).

Check that the boys are saying **contento** and **enojado** and that the girls are saying **contenta** and **enojada.**

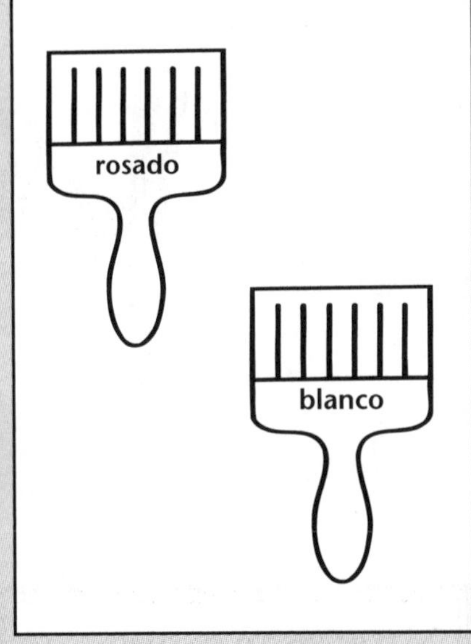

Blackline Master 4C-4

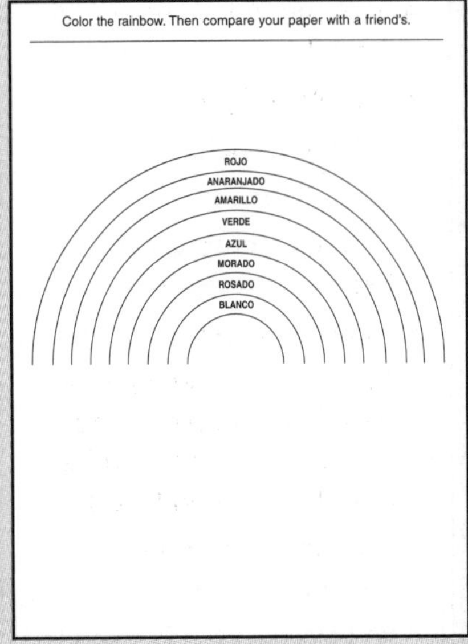

Blackline Master 4C-5

Activity 4C: Color the rainbow

Materials: The laminated paintbrushes prepared in the Review section in these colors: red, blue, purple, orange, green, yellow, pink, white; crayons or colored pencils in the same colors; and Blackline Master 4C-5.

Preparation: Duplicate and distribute Blackline Master 4C-5, one copy per child. Be sure each child has his/her crayons or colored pencils ready.

Review the color names by holding up each of your colored paintbrushes and asking the children to call out the name of the color.

rojo	*red*	azul	*blue*
anaranjado	*orange*	morado	*purple*
amarillo	*yellow*	rosado	*pink*
verde	*green*	blanco	*white*

Ask the children what the shape of the drawing in Blackline Master 4C-5 is (a rainbow). Tell them to color in the arches of the rainbow, using the Spanish words for colors as a guide. Once they've completed their coloring, divide the class into small groups and have the children compare their rainbows, pointing to each arch and saying in Spanish the color they colored it.

Closing

Tell the children that Spanish class is finished for today. In the next lesson, children will practice the rest of the colors and talk about science and math classes.

En español

As you review the color names using the paint-brushes, ask the children **¿De qué color es?** (*What color is it?*) if you feel comfortable.

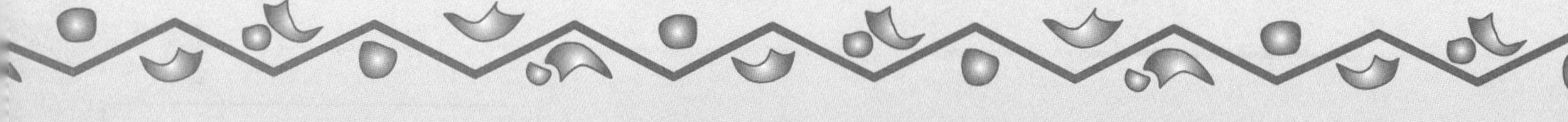

Lesson 5

Materials to gather

- VCR and Video Lesson 5 on Tape 2
- Cassette player
- Activity Cassette 1
- Song Cassette
- Colored paintbrushes from Lesson 4 (Review)
- Plain white paper
- Crayons or colored pencils (red, blue, purple, orange, green, yellow, pink, white, gray, brown, and black)
- Blackline Master 5B ("Alphabet Rap")
- Red Flashcards 45–47 and 49
- ***Optional materials:*** Rosco hand puppet

Objectives

Language

- Practice the colors **café** (*brown*), **gris** (*gray*), and **negro** (*black*)
- Count by tens to 100
- Understand more of the extended conversation at the elementary school
- Learn the names for three additional classes
- Understand the greetings **Buenas tardes** (*Good afternoon*) and **Buenas noches** (*Good evening*)
- Play **¿Cuál falta?** (*What's missing?*)

Culture

- Sing the "Alphabet Rap"

Review

- Practice the opening conversation
- Review the questions about names
- Answer the questions **¿Qué clase es?** (*What class is it?*) and **¿Qué es?** (*What is it?*)
- Review colors

Vocabulary

Buenas tardes.	*Good afternoon.*
Buenas noches.	*Good evening.*
café	*brown*
gris	*gray*
negro	*black*
¿Cuál falta?	*What's missing?*
la clase de ciencia(s)	*science class*
la clase de matemática(s)	*math/mathematics class*
la clase de computadora(s)	*computer class*

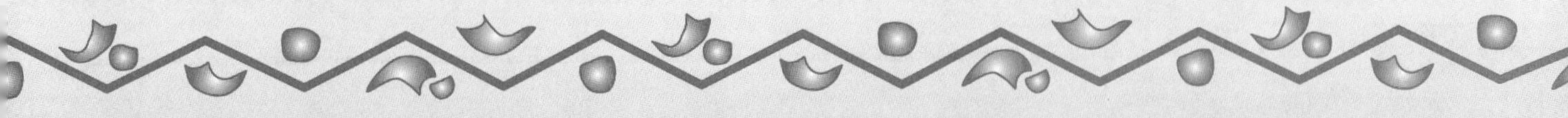

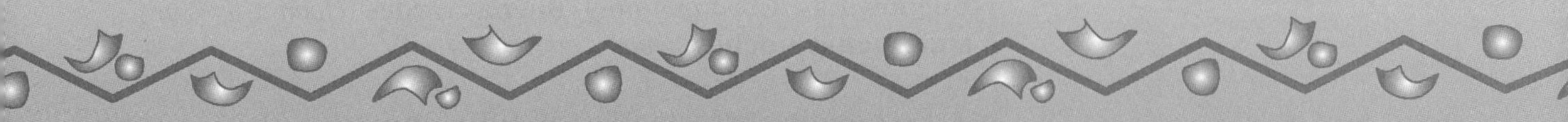

treinta	*thirty*	setenta	*seventy*
cuarenta	*forty*	ochenta	*eighty*
cincuenta	*fifty*	noventa	*ninety*
sesenta	*sixty*	cien	*one hundred*

Warm-up

Holding the Rosco hand puppet (if you have one), ask children what class they think it's time for (**la clase de español**—*Spanish class*). Tell them to greet Rosco. Ask them what class and subject names they've been learning in Spanish this year. Cue the children if necessary by humming or pretending to paint or throw a ball. Possible responses are:

la clase de arte	*art class*	el arte	*art*
la clase de música	*music class*	la música	*music*
la clase de inglés	*English class*	el inglés	*English*
la hora de recreo	*recess*		

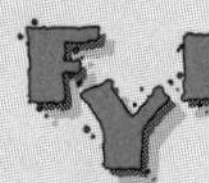

In Spanish, language names are preceded by the definite article **el** (*the*) and they are not capitalized.

Review

Materials: Colored paintbrushes from Lesson 4 (Review section), except for the brown, black, and gray ones.

Review the colors below with the children. Hold up one paintbrush at a time and ask them to name the color in Spanish. Point to objects in the classroom and ask the children what color the things are.

blue	azul	*purple*	morado
green	verde	*red*	rojo
orange	anaranjado	*white*	blanco
pink	rosado	*yellow*	amarillo

EN ESPAÑOL

If you feel comfortable, ask **¿De qué color es?** (*What color is it?*). Reinforce correct answers with **Sí, muy bien** (*Yes, very good*).

Introduce the video

Invite the children to listen and watch as **la maestra** and Winston sing the "Alphabet Rap" and Lorena dances to it.

Video Lesson

1. Greeting the children

La maestra holds the opening conversation with Winston and the children, using **Hola** (*Hello*) as the greeting. Winston answers **Estoy contento** (*I'm happy*) to the question **¿Cómo estás tú?** (*How are you?*). **La maestra** mentions the greetings **Buenos días** (*Good morning*), **Buenas tardes** (*Good afternoon*), and **Buenas noches** (*Good evening*).

2. Exchanging information about names

La maestra reviews the questions and answers involving names: **¿Cómo te llamas tú?** (*What is your name?*)—**Me llamo** ___ (*My name is* ___) and **¿Cómo se llama?** (*What is his/her name?*)—**Se llama** ___ (*His/Her name is* ___).

3. Reviewing school subjects

La maestra reviews the names of various classes.

¿Qué clase es?	*What class is it?*
la clase de arte	*art class*
la clase de música	*music class*
la clase de inglés	*English class*
¿Qué es?	*What is it?*
la hora de recreo	*recess*

4. Visiting the elementary school

Once again the children accompany **la maestra** on her visit to the Spanish-speaking elementary school. For additional comments, see Lesson 3, Video Lesson, section 6.

Es una escuela primaria.	*It is an elementary school.*
Ésta es una clase de música.	*This is a music class.*
Cantamos y hay instrumentos musicales en la clase de música.	*We sing and there are musical instruments in music class.*
Carlos, ¿qué haces en la clase?	*Carlos, what do you do in the class?*
Yo coloreo, pinto y hago diferentes fotos.	*I draw, I color, and I make different pictures.*
Ésta es la clase de inglés.	*This is the English class.*
Aquí está la maestra de inglés.	*Here is the English teacher.*
Es la hora de recreo.	*It's recess.*
Tenemos muchos amigos y nosotros jugamos en la hora de recreo con todos nuestros amigos.	*We have many friends and we play during recess with all our friends.*

5. Working with colors

La maestra asks Winston **¿Qué clase te gusta más?** (*Which class do you like the most?*). Winston answers **la clase de arte** (*art class*). Holding up colored **sombreros** (*hats*), **la maestra** asks **¿De qué color es?** (*What color is it?*)—**amarillo** (*yellow*), **rosado** (*pink*), **blanco** (*white*). She and the mime introduce the colors **café** (*brown*), **negro** (*black*), and **gris** (*gray*).

6. Playing *¿Cuál falta?* (*What's missing?*)

From the four displayed colored **sombreros** (*hats*), **la maestra** removes one at a time and asks the children **¿Cuál falta?** (*What's missing?*). The children respond with the color of the missing hat. She plays the same game with colored fish.

7. Presenting new classes

La maestra shows Winston and the children pictures representing **la clase de ciencia**(s) (*science class*) and **la clase de matemática**(s) (*math class*) as she asks **¿Qué clase es?** (*What class is it?*).

8. Practicing *los números grandes* (*big numbers*)

Everyone counts to 100 by tens as Lorena dances to the numbers. Then Winston comments **Me gusta Lorena** (*I like Lorena*) and **la maestra** responds, **Lorena es muy bonita y baila muy bien** (*Lorena is very pretty and she dances very well*).

diez	*ten*	sesenta	*sixty*
veinte	*twenty*	setenta	*seventy*
treinta	*thirty*	ochenta	*eighty*
cuarenta	*forty*	noventa	*ninety*
cincuenta	*fifty*	cien	*one hundred*

9. Presenting the term for *computer class*

Showing another class picture, **la maestra** presents the term **la clase de computadora**(s) (*computer class*). She points out that on the computer keyboard, one finds **el alfabeto** (*the alphabet*).

10. Singing and dancing the "Alphabet Rap"

As **la maestra** sings the rap, Lorena dances to it. For lyrics to the rap, see Activity 5B.

11. Closing

La maestra states **La clase de español es muy buena con amigos como Lorena y como Winston** (*Spanish class is very good with friends like Lorena and Winston*). She and Winston say **Adiós** (*Good-bye*) and **Hasta luego** (*See you later*) to the children.

Colors:

amarillo	*yellow*
anaranjado	*orange*
azul	*blue*
blanco	*white*
café	*brown*
gris	*gray*
morado	*purple*
negro	*black*
rojo	*red*
rosado	*pink*
verde	*green*

Reassure the children if they identify the *yellow* fish as *green* (**verde**), the *red* fish as *orange* (**anaranjado**), or the *orange* fish as *yellow* (**amarillo**) that sometimes it is difficult to tell the color of things on video.

Praise the children if they point out that the picture **la maestra** shows has **matemática** instead of **matemáticas** and **ciencia** instead of **ciencias**. Both sets of words are often interchanged in Spanish.

In section 8, encourage the children to repeat the numbers after Winston.

After viewing the video, praise the children for their good listening and watching skills.

ACTIVITY LESSON

Activity 5A: Color the numbers

Materials: Cassette player; Activity Cassette 1, Side A; plain white paper; red, blue, purple, orange, green, yellow, pink, white, gray, brown, and black crayons or colored pencils—one of each color per child.

Give each of the children a piece of paper and be sure they have their crayons or colored pencils ready. Instruct the children to write the numerals 10 to 100 by tens (10, 20, 30, etc.) on their paper. Doña Elena is going to say a number and a color. They are to draw a line over (or circle) each number she says with the color she specifies. Once you've played the activity, divide the class into pairs and have them compare their work by telling each other in Spanish what color they used for each number, e.g., **diez rojo** (*ten red*). Children should have used the following colors with each number: 10 red, 20 blue, 30 purple, 40 orange, 50 green, 60 yellow, 70 pink, 80 black, 90 brown, 100 gray. For colors, see section 6 of this Video Lesson and for numbers, see section 8.

Activity 5B: Sing the "Alphabet Rap"

Materials: Cassette player; Song Cassette, Side A; and Blackline Master 5B.

Preparation: Duplicate and distribute Blackline Master 5B, one copy per child.

Have the children write their names on the blank line after **Me llamo** (*My name is*). Tell them **la maestra** is going to sing the "Alphabet Rap." The first time you play the tape, they should just point to each letter as **la maestra** sings it. The second time, the children should sing along and point to the letters. Then rewind the tape and play the activity again.

a	b	c	n	ñ	o
ch	d	e	p	q	
f	g		r	s	
h	i		t	u	
j	k		v	w	x
l	ll	m	y	z	

Collect the "Alphabet Rap" pages for later use.

Alphabet Rap
El alfabeto

a	b	c
ch	d	e
f	g	
h	i	
j	k	
l	ll	m
n	ñ	o
p	q	
r	s	
t	u	
v	w	x
y	z	

Blackline Master 5B

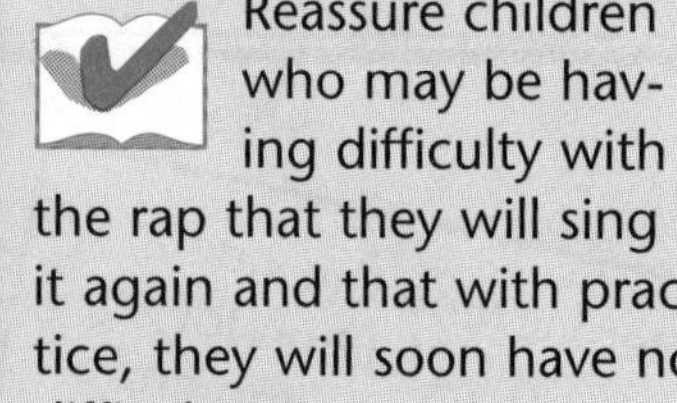

Reassure children who may be having difficulty with the rap that they will sing it again and that with practice, they will soon have no difficulty singing it.

Activity 5C: What class is it?

Materials: Red Flashcards 45–47 and 49.

Display the Flashcards where children can see them. Review the names of each class and subject with the children. Point to the top picture on Red Flashcard 45 and ask the children to tell you in Spanish what class the picture represents (**la clase de ciencia[s]**—*science class*). Ask them what the subject area is called (**las ciencias**—*sciences*). Follow the same procedure with the other pictures.

Red Flashcard:	Class:	Subject Area:
#45 (top)	la clase de ciencia(s) (*science class*)	las ciencias (*sciences*)
#45 (bottom)	la clase de arte (*art class*)	el arte (*art*)
#46 (top)	la clase de matemáticas (*math class*)	las matemáticas (*math/mathematics*)
#46 (bottom)	la clase de computadoras (*computer class*)	las computadoras (*computers*)
#47 (top)	la clase de música (*music class*)	la música (*music*)
#47 (bottom)	la hora de recreo (*recess*)	
#49 (top)	la clase de inglés (*English class*)	el inglés (*English*)

EN ESPAÑOL

If you feel comfortable, ask **¿Qué clase es?** (*What class is it?*). For the picture of recess (Flashcard 47, bottom) ask **¿Qué es?** (*What is it?*).

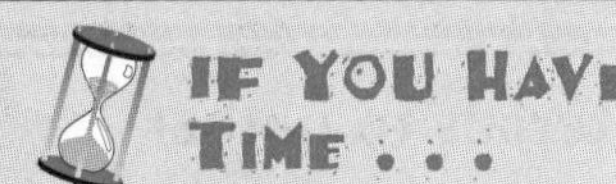

IF YOU HAVE TIME . . .

Materials: Red Flashcards 45–47 and 49.

Hold up one Red Flashcard at a time and ask the children which class they like better. If you feel comfortable, ask **¿Qué clase te gusta más?** (*Which class do you like more?*).

CLOSING

Tell the children that Spanish class is finished for today. In the next lesson they will observe a science experiment.

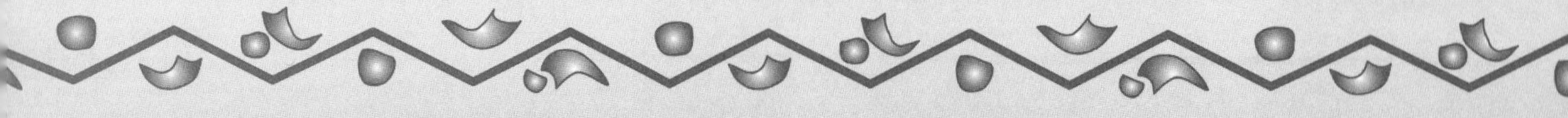

Lesson 6

Materials to gather

- VCR and Video Lesson 6 on Tape 2
- Cassette player
- Activity Cassette 1
- Colored paintbrushes from Lesson 4
- ***Optional materials:*** a Hundred Chart; children's "Alphabet Rap" pages (from Activity 5B); blank paper; and Song Cassette

Objectives

Language

- Comprehend a science experiment
- Understand an extended conversation about science, math, and computer classes

Culture

- Understand that math, science, and computer classes are important for one's future
- Sing the "Alphabet Rap"

Review

- Review several feeling expressions
- Count from 10 to 100 by tens
- Review the names for *science class, math class,* and *computer class*

Vocabulary

Flota.	*It floats.*
No flota.	*It doesn't float.*

Warm-up

Greet the children, using **Hola** (*Hello*) or **Buenos días** (*Good morning*), if you feel comfortable. Ask for two volunteers to greet each other and ask each other for their names. Encourage them to use the polite phrase **Mucho gusto** (*It's nice to meet you*) (**V1** = volunteer 1, **V2** = volunteer 2):

V1: Buenos días.	*Good morning.*
V2: Buenos días.	*Good morning.*
V1: ¿Cómo te llamas tú?	*What is your name?*
V2: Me llamo ___.	*My name is ___.*
¿Cómo te llamas tú?	*What is your name?*
V1: Me llamo ___.	*My name is ___.*
V2: Mucho gusto.	*It's nice to meet you.*

Review

Materials: The eleven colored paintbrushes from Lesson 4.

Give each child (or pair of children, depending on the size of your class) a paintbrush. Ask for a volunteer to call out one color at a time in Spanish. The child (or children) with the color should stand up until the volunteer calls out the next color.

black	negro	*pink*	rosado
blue	azul	*purple*	morado
brown	café	*red*	rojo
gray	gris	*yellow*	amarillo
green	verde	*white*	blanco
orange	anaranjado		

To reinforce the spelling of the color names in Spanish, put the paintbrushes on permanent display in your classroom.

Introduce the video

Invite the children to listen and watch as **la maestra** and Winston work on a scientific experiment.

VIDEO LESSON

1. Greeting the children

La maestra greets the children using **Buenas tardes** (*Good afternoon*) and holds the opening conversation with them (**M** = Maestra, **C** = class):

M: Buenas tardes, clase.	*Good afternoon, class.*
C: Buenas tardes, Maestra.	*Good afternoon, Teacher.*
M: ¿Cómo estás tú?	*How are you?*
C: Muy bien, gracias. ¿Y usted?	*Very well, thank you. And you?*
M: Muy bien, gracias.	*Very well, thank you.*

She points out that one says **Buenos días** (*Good morning*) but **Buenas tardes** (*Good afternoon*).

2. Reviewing the questions and answers about names

La maestra reviews questions and answers: **¿Cómo te llamas tú?** (*What is your name?*) —**Me llamo** ___ (*My name is* ___) and **¿Cómo se llama?** (*What is his/her name?*) —**Se llama** ___ (*His/Her name is* ___).

3. Replying to the question *¿Cómo estás tú?* (*How are you?*)

Winston and **la maestra** have the opening conversation. Winston says **Estoy contento** (*I'm happy*) and **la maestra** says **Estoy contenta** (*I'm happy*). They review **Así, así** (*So-so*); **Estoy enojado/enojada** (*I'm angry*); and **Estoy triste** (*I'm sad*). **La maestra** asks **¿Cómo está Lorena?** (*How is Lorena?*) and describes how Lorena feels based on her dancing: **Está enojada** (*She's angry*), **Está contenta** (*She's happy*), and **Está triste** (*She's sad*). **La maestra** explains that when talking about oneself, one says **Estoy** ___ (*I am* ___), but when talking about someone else, one uses **Está** ___ (*She/He is* ___).

4. Doing a science experiment

Winston says **Me gustan las ciencias** (*I like science*) and **Estudio ciencia** (*I study science*). He and **la maestra** do **un experimento** (*an experiment*). Winston's hypothesis is that big things don't float and little things float. **La maestra** asks **¿Flota o no flota?** (*Does it float or not?*) as she puts a large apple (**una manzana grande**), a small coin (**una moneda pequeña**), an orange, and a key in the water. Winston determines that whether something floats has nothing to do with size.

5. Practicing *los números grandes* (*the big numbers*)

La maestra and the children count by tens to one hundred as Lorena dances. Lorena dances again to the numbers and **la maestra** asks **¿Qué número es?** (*What number is it?*).

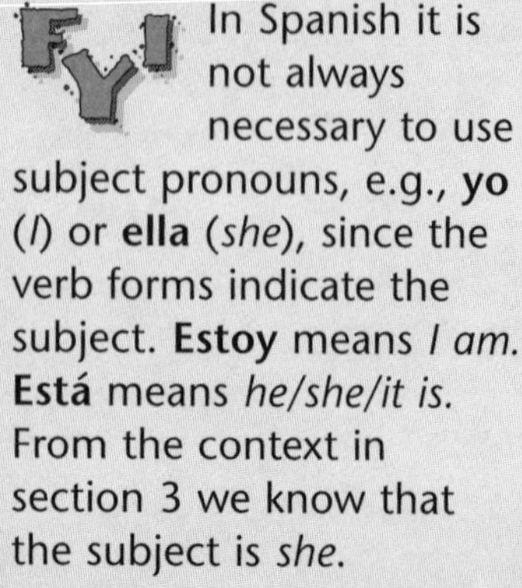

FYI: In Spanish it is not always necessary to use subject pronouns, e.g., **yo** (*I*) or **ella** (*she*), since the verb forms indicate the subject. **Estoy** means *I am.* **Está** means *he/she/it is.* From the context in section 3 we know that the subject is *she*.

LANGUAGE ACROSS THE CURRICULUM

After watching the video, have a brief science lesson with the children by doing the experiment using different objects.

10–100 by tens:

diez	*10*
veinte	*20*
treinta	*30*
cuarenta	*40*
cincuenta	*50*
sesenta	*60*
setenta	*70*
ochenta	*80*
noventa	*90*
cien	*100*

6. Reviewing *las letras del alfabeto* (*the letters of the alphabet*)

Holding up the picture of **la computadora** (*computer*), **la maestra** points out that **en la computadora hay unas letras del alfabeto** (*on the computer there are the letters of the alphabet*). Lorena dances to the "Alphabet Rap" as **la maestra** sings.

7. Reviewing the names of three classes

Winston wants to be a doctor. **La maestra** shows him pictures of three classes that will be important for him. She asks **¿Qué clase es?** (*What class is it?*) and **¿Qué haces en la clase de ___?** (*What do you do in ___ class?*).

la clase de ciencias	*science class*
Estudio ciencias y hago experimentos.	*I study science and I do experiments.*
la clase de computadoras	*computer class*
Estudio computadoras.	*I study computers.*
la clase de matemáticas	*math class*
Estudio matemáticas.	*I study math.*

8. Visiting a high school for science, computers, and math

La maestra attends classes with Kurt and Samantha at the special **colegio** (*high school*) for science, math, and computers.

Aquí está la clase de ciencias.	*Here is science class.*
En la clase de ciencias estudio ciencias.	*In science class I study science.*
¿Qué es esto?	*What is this?*
Es un microscopio.	*It's a microscope.*
Hacemos experimentos y estudiamos científicos famosos.	*We do experiments and we study famous scientists.*
¿Qué son estos?	*What are these?*
Son las formas geométricas.	*They are geometric shapes.*
¿Te gusta la clase de matemáticas?	*Do you like math class?*
Sí, me gusta muchísimo.	*Yes, I like it very, very much.*
Puedes escribir mucho en la computadora, ¿no?	*You can write a lot on the computer, can't you?*
¡Muy rápido!	*Very fast!*

9. Closing

La maestra reviews how important math, science, and computer classes are in getting ready to *touch the future* (**toca el futuro**). She and Winston bid the children **Adiós** (*Good-bye*).

Encourage the children to listen carefully as **la maestra** sings the "Alphabet Rap." Each time they hear the song, they will remember a little bit more.

EN ESPAÑOL

La maestra often introduces tasks with the following phrases. Use them if you feel comfortable.

Vamos a contar.
(*Let's count.*)

Vamos a jugar.
(*Let's play.*)

Vamos a cantar.
(*Let's sing.*)

Vamos a mirar.
(*Let's watch.*)

After viewing the video, praise the children for their good listening and watching skills.

ACTIVITY LESSON

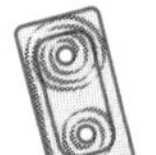

Activity 6A: Count by tens to 100

Materials: Cassette player; Activity Cassette 1, Side A; *optional:* a Hundred Chart.

Write the numbers from 10 to 100 by tens on the chalkboard or use a Hundred Chart for this exercise. Tell the children they are going to count from 10 to 100 by tens with doña Elena. Point to the numbers as the children count. Stop the tape and ask for volunteers to count again from 10 to 100 by tens.

diez	*10*	sesenta	*60*
veinte	*20*	setenta	*70*
treinta	*30*	ochenta	*80*
cuarenta	*40*	noventa	*90*
cincuenta	*50*	cien	*100*

FYI On the tape, doña Elena says **de diez en diez hasta el cien,** which means *ten by ten to one hundred.* **Y ahora te toca a ti** means *And now it's your turn.* She also wishes the children **Buena suerte** (*Good luck*).

Activity 6B: Scientific experiments

Talk with the children about the value of scientific experiments. Why was Winston's experiment valuable? (It proved to him that if something floats, it has nothing to do with its size; he learned something new.) Have children describe the process and results of experiments they have performed. Suggest they interview scientists or researchers they or their families may know and report back to the class. For whom do the scientists or researchers work and what are they working on?

Activity 6C: Are science, math, or computers for you?

Ask children to share their impressions of the visit to the math, science, and computer classes at the special high school. Do they like math? Can they say why? Do they have an opportunity to use a computer at school or home?

What do they use it for? Which of those subjects is their favorite?

Closing

Tell the children that Spanish class is finished for today. In the next lesson they will talk about more school subjects and sing **"La canción de geografía"** (*"The Geography Song"*).

Materials: Cassette player; "Alphabet Rap" on the Song Cassette, Side A; children's "Alphabet Rap" pages (Blackline Master 5B); and a blank sheet of paper for each child.

Play the song and have children sing and follow along on their papers. Tell them they are going to create their own Spanish dictionary. Distribute one sheet of blank paper to each child. On the paper children should write the first letter of the Spanish alphabet: **A**. Ask them to think of words they know in Spanish that begin with **A** (**amarillo**—*yellow,* **azul**—*blue,* **amigo/amiga**—*friend,* **adiós**—*good-bye*). Tell them to begin looking at home for pictures that show some of the words they have chosen, e.g., something in the colors yellow or blue, a picture of a friend or of someone waving good-bye). They should bring the pictures to class, since they will be pasting the pictures on their **A** page and writing the Spanish word next to each picture.

Lesson 7

> **Materials to gather**
> - VCR and Video Lesson 7 on Tape 3
> - Cassette player
> - Activity Cassette 1
> - Song Cassette
> - Overhead projector
> - Overhead transparency of Blackline Master 1A (song "**Español para ti**")
> - Overhead transparency of Blackline Master 2B (20 Spanish-speaking countries)
> - A map of the world
> - Red Flashcards 45–49
> - ***Optional materials:*** children's "Alphabet Rap" pages (from Activity 5B); children's letter **A** pages (from Dictionary activity in Lesson 6); paste or tape

Objectives

Language

- Learn the names for the subjects history, geography, and Spanish
- Answer the question **¿Qué clase es?** (*What class is it?*)
- Understand an extended conversation about history, geography, and Spanish classes

Culture

- Recall that there are twenty Spanish-speaking countries
- Sing **"La canción de geografía"** (*"The Geography Song"*)

Review

- Understand that boys say **Estoy contento** (*I'm happy*) and **Estoy enojado** (*I'm angry*) and that girls say **Estoy contenta** (*I'm happy*) and **Estoy enojada** (*I'm angry*)
- Practice the feeling expression **Estoy triste** (*I'm sad*)
- Review how to say how someone else feels
- Practice the names of the school subjects

Vocabulary

la clase de historia	*history class*
la clase de geografía	*geography class*
la clase de español	*Spanish class*
Es la clase de ___.	*It's ___ class.*

Warm-up

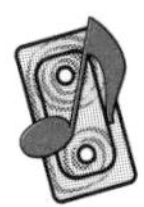

Materials: Cassette player; Song Cassette, Side A; overhead projector; and the overhead transparency of Blackline Master 1A.

Display the overhead transparency of the lyrics to **"Español para ti"** (*"Spanish Is for You, and for Me"*). Tell the children they are going to sing a song they haven't sung in a few lessons. Play the song, pointing to each line on the transparency as it is sung. Encourage children to read the lyrics as they sing so they become familiar with the spelling of the words.

Review

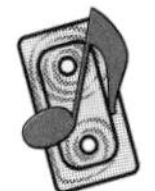

Materials: Cassette player; **"La canción de geografía"** (*"The Geography Song"*) on the Song Cassette, Side A; map of the world; overhead projector; and the transparency of Blackline Master 2B.

Display the map and the overhead transparency listing the twenty Spanish-speaking countries. Ask for two volunteers, one to point to the names of the countries on the overhead and one to point to the countries on the map as the class sings the *"The Geography Song"* (**"La canción de geografía"**). For song lyrics, see Song 2 in the Song Appendix.

Introduce the video

Invite the children to listen and watch as **la maestra** reviews the names of the Spanish-speaking countries and introduces the names of three more school subjects.

VIDEO LESSON

1. Greeting the children

La maestra holds the opening conversation with LeeAnn and the children (**M** = Maestra, **L** = LeeAnn, **C** = class):

M:	Buenos días, clase.	*Good morning, class.*
L/C:	Buenos días, Maestra.	*Good morning, Teacher.*
M:	¿Cómo estás tú?	*How are you?*
L/C:	Muy bien, gracias. ¿Y usted?	*Very well, thank you. And you?*
M:	Estoy muy bien. Estoy contenta.	*I'm very well. I'm happy.*

La maestra and LeeAnn review that to say *I'm happy*, boys say **Estoy contento** and girls say **Estoy contenta**.

2. Saying how someone else feels

Antonito mimes the feelings **Estoy contento** (*I'm happy*), **Estoy triste** (*I'm sad*), and **Estoy enojado** (*I'm angry*). **La maestra** asks LeeAnn **¿Cómo está Antonito?** (*How is Antonito?*).

3. Presenting the subjects history and geography

LeeAnn and **la maestra** discuss what one learns in history and geography classes. She mentions that in history class one learns about George Washington—**el primer presidente de los Estados Unidos** (*the first president of the United States*), who is also referred to as **el padre del país** (*the father of the country*). **La maestra** mentions that in geography class **usamos los mapas** (*we use maps*).

la clase de historia	*history class*
la clase de geografía	*geography class*
Estudio la historia y leo.	*I study history and I read.*

4. Singing *"La canción de geografía"* (*"The Geography Song"*)

La maestra sings the song about the twenty Spanish-speaking countries. For song lyrics, see Song 2 in the Song Appendix.

5. Introducing the term for Spanish class

La maestra reviews the terms **de habla hispana** (*Spanish-speaking*), **hispano** (*male of Hispanic origin*), and **hispana** (*female of Hispanic origin*). She also introduces the term **la clase de español** (*Spanish class*). LeeAnn says **Yo no soy hispana pero me gusta el español** (*I'm not Hispanic, but I like Spanish*).

Sabemos una canción de geografía.
(*We know a song about geography.*)
Hay veinte países de habla hispana.
(*There are 20 Spanish-speaking countries.*)

HERITAGE SPEAKERS

You may wish to ask native Spanish-speaking children to tell the class in Spanish if they are of Hispanic origin and from what country or region they or their families come.

6. Visiting a high school

La maestra visits history, geography, and Spanish classes at a high school.

Aquí está mi clase de historia.	*Here is my history class.*
¿Qué haces en la clase de historia?	*What do you do in history class?*
En la clase de historia estudio historia.	*In history class I study history.*
Aquí está la clase de geografía.	*Here is geography class.*
¿Qué haces en la clase de geografía?	*What do you do in geography class?*
En la clase de geografía estudio la geografía del mundo.	*In geography class I study the geography of the world.*
Aquí está la clase de español.	*Here is Spanish class.*
¿Qué haces en la clase de español?	*What do you do in Spanish class?*
En la clase de español estudio español, canto en español y estudio los colores.	*In Spanish class I study Spanish, sing in Spanish, and I study colors.*
¿Quién sabe de qué color es ___?	*Who knows what color the ___ is?*

7. Reviewing all school subjects

La maestra reviews the names of the new subjects and plays **¿Qué clase es?** (*What class is it?*) and **¿Sí o no?** (*Yes or no?*).

Historia / Español / Geografía / Música	*History / Spanish / Geography / Music*
La clase de inglés.	*English class.*
La clase de arte.	*Art class.*
Ésta no es una clase. Es la hora de recreo.	*This is not a class. It's recess.*
La clase de matemáticas.	*Math class.*
La clase de ciencias.	*Science class.*
La clase de computadoras.	*Computer class.*
¿Es la clase de ___?	*Is it ___ class?*
No, no es la clase de ___. Es la clase de ___.	*No, it isn't ___ class. It's ___ class.*

8. Closing

After reviewing all the children have done in Spanish class today, **la maestra** bids the children **Hasta luego** (*See you later*).

FYI Colors mentioned in the Spanish class in section 6:

amarillo	*yellow*
blanco	*white*
negro	*black*
verde	*green*
rojo	*red*

Note that the **-o** or **-a** ending on a color name, like that of other adjectives, matches the gender and number of the noun the color is describing. For example, in answering the first question about the colors on the flag of Spain, the student answers **amarilla y roja** because the word for flag is **la bandera,** a feminine singular noun.

After viewing the video, praise the children for their good listening and watching skills.

Los países de habla hispana
(*Spanish-Speaking Countries*)

1. España
2. México
3. Guatemala
4. Honduras
5. El Salvador
6. Nicaragua
7. Costa Rica
8. Panamá
9. Cuba
10. La República Dominicana
11. Puerto Rico
12. Venezuela
13. Colombia
14. Ecuador
15. Perú
16. Bolivia
17. Chile
18. Argentina
19. Uruguay
20. Paraguay

Blackline Master 2B

Encourage the children to sing along in Activity 7A. Are the children better able to sing the song now that they have heard it several times?

EN ESPAÑOL

If you feel comfortable, ask **¿Qué clase es?** (*What class it is?*) as you point to each picture.

ACTIVITY LESSON

Activity 7A: Sing *"The Geography Song"*

Materials: Cassette player; Song Cassette, Side A; overhead projector; and the overhead transparency of Blackline Master 2B.

Display the overhead transparency of Blackline Master 2B. Tell the children they are going to practice the song about the twenty Spanish-speaking countries. Ask for a volunteer to point to the names of the countries as the class sings the song. For song lyrics, see Song 2 in the Song Appendix.

Activity 7B: What subject is it? What class is it?

Materials: Red Flashcards 45–49.

Display Red Flashcards 45–49 where the children can see them. Have volunteers call out the Spanish name of the subject or class as you point to each picture.

Red Flashcards:	Subjects:	Classes:
#45 (top)	las ciencias (*science*)	la clase de ciencias (*science class*)
(bottom)	el arte (*art*)	la clase de arte (*art class*)
#46 (top)	las matemáticas (*math*)	la clase de matemáticas (*math class*)
(bottom)	las computadoras (*computers*)	la clase de computadoras (*computer class*)
#47 (top)	la música (*music*)	la clase de música (*music class*)
(bottom)		la hora de recreo (*recess*)
#48 (top)	la historia (*history*)	la clase de historia (*history class*)
(bottom)	la geografía (*geography*)	la clase de geografía (*geography class*)
#49 (top)	el inglés (*English*)	la clase de inglés (*English class*)
(bottom)	el español (*Spanish*)	la clase de español (*Spanish class*)

Activity 7C: Communicative learning—How are you?

Divide the class into pairs—child A and child B. Direct child A to ask child B *How are you?* (**¿Cómo estás tú?**). Direct child B to answer with one of the phrases **la maestra** practiced in the video—*I'm happy, I'm sad,* or *I'm angry.*

	Boy:	**Girl:**
I'm happy.	Estoy contento.	Estoy contenta.
I'm angry.	Estoy enojado.	Estoy enojada.
I'm sad.	Estoy triste.	Estoy triste.

Closing

Tell the children that Spanish class is finished for today. In the next lesson **la maestra** will talk about items the children need for the various classes.

Listen to the children as they work on Activity 7C. Are boys using **contento** and **enojado**? Are girls using **contenta** and **enojada**?

DICTIONARY

Materials: Paste or tape; children's dictionary pages for **A** and the pictures of items that begin with **A** that they were to collect (per Dictionary activity in Lesson 6); and children's "Alphabet Rap" pages (Activity 5B).

Have the children tape or paste their pictures onto their **A** page and write the name in Spanish of each item pictured. Ask volunteers to describe their **A** page to the class.

Next ask a volunteer to tell you the Spanish name for his/her favorite school subject. Have children write the Spanish name of their favorite school subject next to the appropriate letter on their "Alphabet Rap" paper. For a list of subjects, see Activity 7B, above. (When alphabetizing, do not include the definite articles **el, la, los,** or **las.**) Tell children to start collecting or making pictures that represent that subject. Be sure children save their "Alphabet Rap" and dictionary pages for future use.

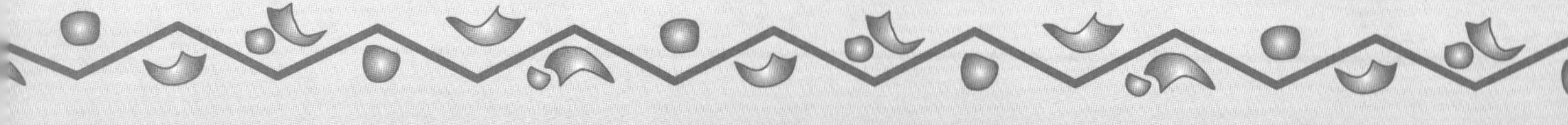

Lesson 8

Materials to gather

- VCR and Video Lesson 8 on Tape 3
- Cassette player
- Activity Cassette 1
- Song Cassette
- Children's "Alphabet Rap" pages from Activity 5B
- Blackline Master 8A (6 school subject drawings)
- Scissors
- A ball for bouncing
- 11 colored paintbrushes from Lesson 4

Objectives

Language

- Comprehend more of the visit to classes at an elementary school
- Understand more of the visit to a high school and the classes

Culture

- Hear that Albert Einstein was a famous scientist and that Abraham Lincoln was a president of the United States

Review

- Greet the teacher and say how one feels
- Sing **"Español para ti"** (*"Spanish Is for You, and for Me"*)
- Review the names of school subjects

Vocabulary

Tengo catarro.	*I have a cold.*

Warm-up

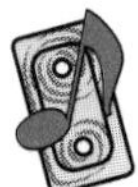

Materials: Cassette player; "Alphabet Rap" on the Song Cassette, Side A; and children's "Alphabet Rap" pages from Activity 5B.

Play the "Alphabet Rap" and have the children sing along.

Review

Write the words **azul, amarillo,** and **anaranjado** on the chalkboard. Ask the children what the words have in common (they are color names; they all begin with the letter **a**). Point to each word and have children read the word and then point to something in the classroom that is that color.

azul	*blue*	amarillo	*yellow*
anaranjado	*orange*		

If you have the colored paintbrushes displayed in your classroom, you may wish to turn the blue, yellow, and orange ones over before doing the Review.

Introduce the video

Invite the children to listen and watch as **la maestra** visits an elementary school and a high school.

Video Lesson

Are children using the many phrases they have reviewed thus far?

Muy bien.
(*Very well.*)

Muy mal.
(*Very bad.*)

Así, así.
(*So-so.*)

Muy contento/contenta.
(*Very happy.*)

Tengo frío.
(*I'm cold.*)

Tengo calor.
(*I'm hot.*)

Estoy triste.
(*I'm sad.*)

Tenemos (*we have*) and **jugamos** (*we play*) are first person plural present tense forms of the verbs **tener** (*to have*) and **jugar** (*to play*). In Spanish it is not necessary to use the subject pronoun (**nosotros**—*we*) as the verb form (**tenemos** or **jugamos**) indicates the subject. Subject pronouns can be used for emphasis as is the case with **<u>nosotros</u> jugamos en la hora de recreo.**

1. Greeting the children

La maestra holds the opening conversation with the children and Kipper (**M** = Maestra, **C/K** = class/Kipper). Kipper says he feels **muy mal porque tengo catarro** (*very bad because I have a cold*).

M: Buenos días, clase.	*Good morning, class.*
C/K: Buenos días, Maestra.	*Good morning, Teacher.*
M: ¿Cómo estás tú?	*How are you?*
C/K: Muy bien, gracias. ¿Y usted?	*Very well, thank you. And you?*
M: Yo estoy muy bien, gracias.	*I'm very well, thank you.*

2. Singing *"Español para ti"* (*"Spanish Is for You, and for Me"*)

La maestra says **Vamos a cantar** (*Let's sing*) to the children but tells Kipper **No cantes** (*Don't sing*) because he's sick. For song lyrics, see Song 1 in the Song Appendix.

3. Practicing the names of some school subjects

Before reviewing several school subjects, **la maestra** suggests that Kipper go to **la oficina de la enfermera** (*the nurse's office*), but Kipper wants to go to class.

la clase de inglés	*English class*
la clase de arte	*art class*
la clase de música	*music class*
la hora de recreo	*recess*

4. Visiting an elementary school

La maestra visits several classes in an elementary school. See also Lesson 3, Video Lesson, section 6 and Lesson 5, Video Lesson, section 4.

En la clase de inglés hay muchos alumnos y hay una maestra de inglés.	*In English class there are many pupils and there is an English teacher (female).*
Estos alumnos estudian inglés, leen inglés y hablan inglés.	*These pupils study English, read English, and speak English.*
Tenemos muchos amigos y nosotros jugamos en la hora de recreo con todos nuestros amigos.	*We have many friends and we play during recess with all our friends.*
Hace sol y hace buen tiempo.	*It's sunny and it's good weather.*
¡Juguemos!	*Let's play!*

5. Reviewing more school subjects

La maestra asks Kipper **¿Qué clase te gusta más?** (*Which class do you like most?*). Kipper says **la clase de música** (*music class*).

la clase de computadoras	*computer class*
la clase de historia	*history class*
la clase de matemáticas	*math class*
la clase de geografía	*geography class*
la clase de ciencias	*science class*
la clase de español	*Spanish class*

6. Visiting high school classes

La maestra visits several high school classes. See also Lesson 6, Video Lesson, section 8 and Lesson 7, Video Lesson, section 6.

A Samantha le gusta la clase de matemáticas.	*Samantha likes math class.*
Es una buena estudiante.	*She is a good student.*
Aquí viene un amigo de Samantha.	*Here comes a friend of Samantha's.*
A Kurt le gusta la clase de computadoras.	*Kurt likes computer class.*
Miro por el microscopio.	*I look through the microscope.*
En el microscopio es muy grande pero es pequeño.	*In the microscope it looks very large but it's small.*
Es verdad, es muy grande.	*That's true, it's very large.*
Albert Einstein es un cientifico muy famoso.	*Albert Einstein is a very famous scientist.*
¡Qué interesante!	*How interesting!*
¿Qué es esto?	*What is this?*
Aquí está el alfabeto.	*Here is the alphabet.*
¿Que haces en la clase historia?	*What do you do in history class?*
¿Quién es?	*Who is it?*
Es Abraham Lincoln, un presidente de los Estados Unidos.	*It's Abraham Lincoln, a president of the United States.*

7. Playing a game of *¿Qué clase es?* (*What class is it?*)

La maestra points to pictures of several classes and asks the children **¿Qué clase es?** (*What class is it?*).

8. Closing

La maestra says **Adiós** (*Good-bye*) to Kipper and the children.

After viewing the video, praise the children for their good listening and watching skills.

Separate the picture of Carlos. Listen to Activity 8A and place Carlos in the appropriate classes.

1. la música
2. las computadoras
3. las matemáticas
4. la geografía
5. el arte
6. las ciencias

Blackline Master 8A

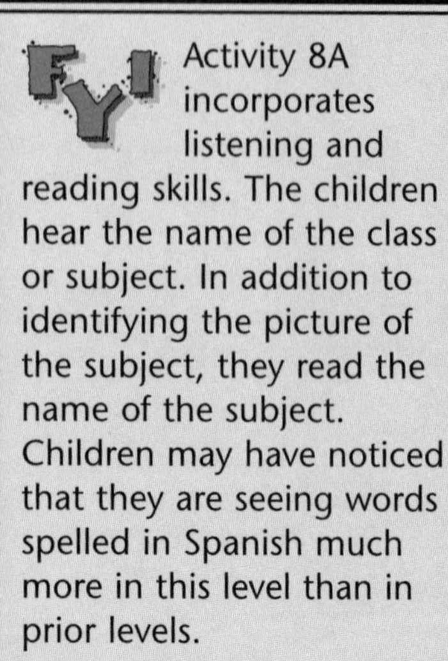

Activity 8A incorporates listening and reading skills. The children hear the name of the class or subject. In addition to identifying the picture of the subject, they read the name of the subject. Children may have noticed that they are seeing words spelled in Spanish much more in this level than in prior levels.

Activity Lesson

Activity 8A: Where is Carlos?

Materials: Cassette player; Activity Cassette 1, Side A; Blackline Master 8A; and scissors, one pair per child.

Preparation: Duplicate and distribute Blackline Master 8A, one copy per child. Have the children cut out the figure of Carlos at the bottom of the page.

Have children fill in their names at the top of their pages. Point out that on the page are pictures representing each of the school subjects the children have learned. Tell them that doña Elena is going to ask **¿Dónde está Carlos?** (*Where is Carlos?*) two times and then say what class Carlos is in (**Carlos está en la clase de ___**). They are to place Carlos on top of the picture that represents the class she said Carlos is in.

Activity 8B: What class is it?

Materials: Cassette player; Activity Cassette 1, Side A; and Blackline Master 8A.

Make sure children have their copies of Blackline Master 8A in front of them. Tell them that for each of the numbered pictures doña Elena is going to say the number and then ask two times **¿Qué clase es?** (*What class is it?*). They are to say the name of the class in Spanish. Children should name the classes as follows:

1. la clase de música (*music class*)
2. la clase de computadoras (*computer class*)
3. la clase de matemáticas (*math class*)
4. la clase de geografía (*geography class*)
5. la clase de arte (*art class*)
6. la clase de ciencias (*science class*)

Activity 8C: Play ball!

Materials: Your eleven colored paintbrushes from Lesson 4; a bouncing ball.

Review color names in Spanish with the children, by holding up one paintbrush at a time and having the children say the color. Then have the children stand in a circle. Give one child the ball. He or she is to say a color and bounce the ball to a child in the circle wearing that color. Children should continue bouncing the ball to one another and identifying a color worn by the child to whom they bounce the ball.

black	negro	*pink*	rosado
blue	azul	*purple*	morado
brown	café	*red*	rojo
gray	gris	*yellow*	amarillo
green	verde	*white*	blanco
orange	anaranjado		

If your school wears uniforms, give each child a piece of colored paper. Or punch a tiny hole in the tip of each laminated paintbrush and wind a piece of string through it so that each child can wear a paintbrush.

CLOSING

Tell the children that Spanish class is finished for today. In the next lesson children review the names of classroom objects.

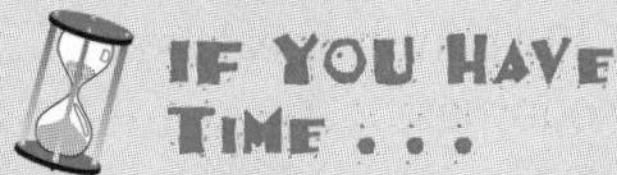

Divide the class into pairs and have them point to various items they are wearing or that are near them and ask each other **¿Qué color es?** (*What color is it?*).

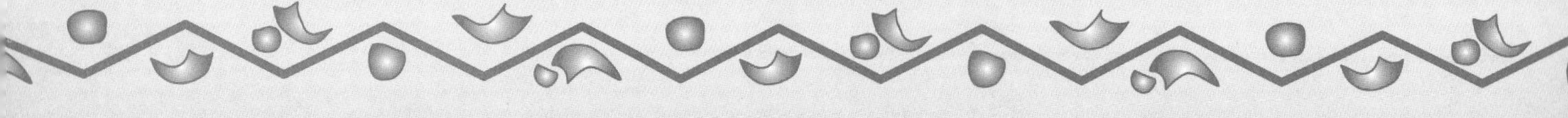

Lesson 9

> **Materials to gather**
> - VCR and Video Lesson 9 on Tape 3
> - Cassette player
> - Activity Cassette 1
> - Song Cassette
> - Overhead projector
> - Overhead transparency of Blackline Master 2B (20 Spanish-speaking countries)
> - Blackline Master 9B (Central and South America)
> - Pencils, one per child
> - Yellow, blue, green, red, orange, and purple crayons, one per child
> - ***Optional materials:*** blank paper; crayons, colored pencils, or markers

Objectives

Language

- Practice vocabulary for classroom items
- Learn to say what you need

Culture

- Learn that people all over the world feel differently at different times

Review

- Sing **"La canción de geografía"** (*"The Geography Song"*)
- Review the names of school subjects
- Practice the names of colors

Vocabulary

¿Qué necesitas?	*What do you need?*
Necesito ___.	*I need ___.*
Necesitas ___.	*You need ___.*
¿Qué más necesitas?	*What else do you need?*
el papel	*paper*
el libro	*book*
la regla	*ruler*
el lápiz	*pencil*
el boli (bolígrafo)	*pen*
los colores	*crayons*

Warm-up

Materials: Cassette player; **"La canción de geografía"** (*"The Geography Song"*) on the Song Cassette, Side A; an overhead projector; and the overhead transparency of Blackline Master 2B.

Play the song, encouraging the children to sing along. Ask for a volunteer to point to the names of the countries on the overhead transparency as you sing. Singing the song repeatedly helps the children remember it. For song lyrics, see Song 2 in the Song Appendix.

Review

Be sure the overhead projector (used in the Warm-up) is turned off and the overhead transparency is not visible to children. Ask volunteers to call out the names of Spanish-speaking countries. Accept answers in English and Spanish. Can the class name all twenty?

Introduce the video

Invite the children to listen and watch as **la maestra** and Winston talk about what things Winston needs for his various classes.

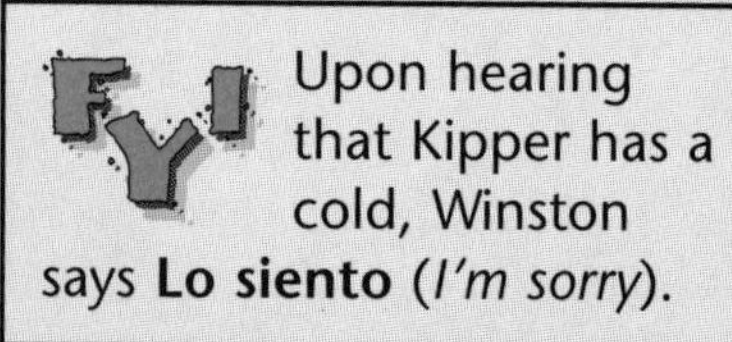
Upon hearing that Kipper has a cold, Winston says **Lo siento** (*I'm sorry*).

School subjects:

la clase de inglés (*English class*)

la clase de matemáticas (*math class*)

la clase de historia (*history class*)

la clase de computadoras (*computer class*)

la clase de geografía (*geography class*)

la clase de español (*Spanish class*)

la hora de recreo (*recess*)

la clase de arte (*art class*)

la clase de música (*music class*)

la clase de ciencias (*science class*)

VIDEO LESSON

1. Greeting the children

La maestra greets the children and Winston with **Hola** (*Hello*) and asks them how they are (**M** = Maestra, **W** = Winston, C = class):

M: Hola, clase.	*Hello, class.*
C/W: Buenos días, Maestra.	*Good morning, Teacher.*
M: ¿Cómo estás tú?	*How are you?*
C/W: Muy bien, gracias. ¿Y usted?	*Very well, thank you. And you?*
M: Muy bien, gracias.	*Very well, thank you.*

She reviews the phrases **Tengo catarro** (*I have a cold*), **Estoy contento/contenta** (*I'm happy*), **Estoy enojado/enojada** (*I'm angry*), and **Estoy triste** (*I'm sad*).

2. Singing *"La canción de geografía"* ("*The Geography Song*")

Everyone sings the song about the twenty Spanish-speaking countries. For song lyrics, see Song 2 in the Song Appendix.

3. Reviewing the names of school subjects

La maestra shows Winston and the children pictures representing the school subjects and asks the following questions.

¿Qué clase es?	*What class is it?*
¿Qué haces en la clase de ___?	*What do you do in ___ class?*
Estudio ___.	*I study ___.*

4. Playing *¿Qué clase es?* (*What class is it?*)

Pointing to pictures of the school subjects, **la maestra** plays **¿Qué clase es?** (*What class is it?*) with the children.

5. Presenting vocabulary for classroom items

La maestra asks Winston what classroom item he needs.

¿Qué necesitas?	*What do you need?*
Necesito ___.	*I need ___.*
Necesitas ___.	*You need ___.*
¿Qué más necesitas?	*What else do you need?*
el papel	*paper*
el libro	*book*
la regla	*ruler*
el lápiz	*pencil*
el boli	*pen*
los colores	*crayons*

6. Practicing the names of colors

La maestra says **Vamos a jugar** (*Let's play*) and then asks the children **¿De qué color es?** (*What color is it?*) as she points to various shapes. She reviews the colors **rojo** (*red*), **azul** (*blue*), **morado** (*purple*), **anaranjado** (*orange*), **verde** (*green*), **amarillo** (*yellow*), **rosado** (*pink*), **blanco** (*white*), **negro** (*black*), **café** (*brown*), and **gris** (*gray*).

La maestra points to the words on the screen so that children will see how the words are spelled as she says them.

7. Reviewing the names of the school subjects

La maestra reviews the school subjects again by pointing to the drawings on the **Toca el futuro** (*Touch the future*) board. She mentions classes children may like, e.g., **la clase de drama** (*drama class*).

8. Closing

She bids the children **Adiós** (*Good-bye*) and **Hasta luego** (*See you later*).

After viewing the video, praise the children for their good listening and watching skills.

Activity Lesson

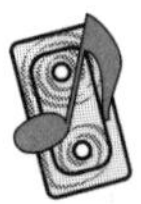

Activity 9A: Sing about the 20 Spanish-speaking countries

Materials: Cassette player; Song Cassette, Side A; an overhead projector; and the overhead transparency of Blackline Master 2B.

Tell the children they are going to sing along with **la maestra** as she sings the song about the twenty Spanish-speaking countries—**"La canción de geografía"** (*"The Geography Song"*). As they sing, point to the names of the countries on the transparency. For song lyrics, see Song 2 in the Song Appendix.

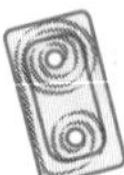

Activity 9B: Read the names of six Spanish-speaking countries

Materials: Cassette player; Activity Cassette 1, Side A; Blackline Master 9B; and pencils, one per child.

Preparation: Duplicate and distribute Blackline Master 9B, one copy per child. Give each child a pencil.

Have children fill in their names at the top of their pages. Point out to the children that the names of six of the Spanish-speaking countries appear on the left side of the page and that their locations in Central America and South America are indicated by the numbers on the map. Tell them that doña Elena is going to read each name two times. They are to read each name aloud after her. Then have the children draw a line from the country name to the country location on the map.

Listen to Activity 9B and repeat the names of these six Spanish-speaking countries. Then draw a line to match the name of each country with its location.

Spanish-Speaking Countries

1. México
2. Cuba
3. Panamá
4. Colombia
5. Chile
6. Argentina

Blackline Master 9B

Activity 9C: Color the countries

Materials: Cassette player; Activity Cassette 1, Side A; Blackline Master 9B; and one yellow, blue, green, red, orange, and purple crayon per child.

Be sure the children have their copies of Blackline Master 9B from Activity 9B and their crayons ready. Tell them that doña Elena is going to direct them to color each of the six Spanish-speaking countries a different color. Play Activity 9B. Children should not try to color the entire country during the activity. Allow a bit of time at the end for children to finish coloring the countries.

CLOSING

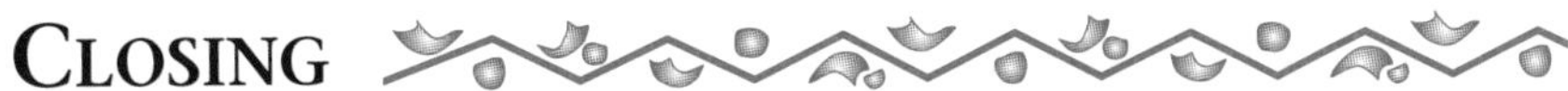

Tell the children that Spanish class is finished for today. In the next lesson they'll learn about schools in the Spanish-speaking countries.

DICTIONARY

Materials: Blank paper, one sheet per child; colored pencils, markers, or crayons.

Give each child a blank paper. Tell the children they are going to make the next page in their Spanish dictionaries. Have them write the letter **B** on the paper. Ask them what class-room object **la maestra** showed in today's lesson begins with a **B** (**boli**—*pen*). Tell them to draw a picture of a pen on their **B** page and then put the page with their "Alphabet Rap" and letter **A** pages.

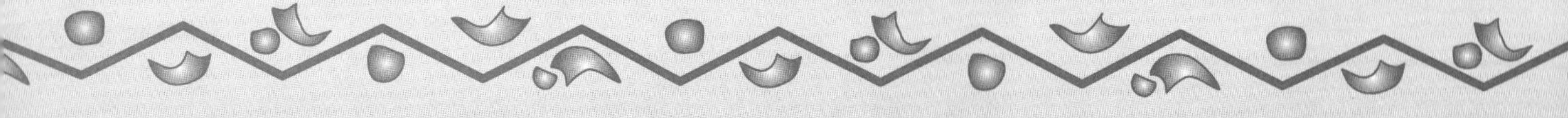

Lesson 10

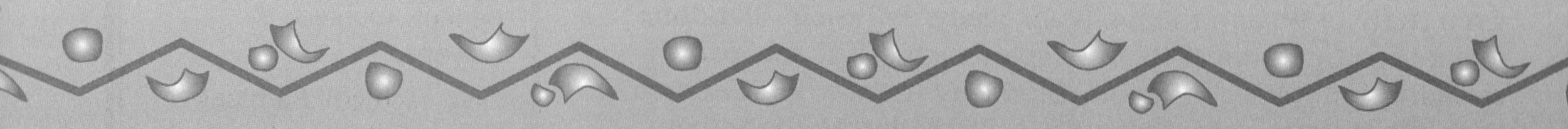

Materials to gather

- VCR and Video Lesson 10 on Tape 4
- Cassette player
- Song Cassette
- Classroom objects: paper, a book, a ruler, a pencil, a pen, and crayons
- Blackline Master 10A-1 ("Months Rap")
- Blackline Master 10A-2 ("**Las estaciones**")
- Blackline Master 10B (crossword puzzle)
- Pencils, one per child
- ***Optional materials:*** blank paper or children's dictionary letter **A** pages; markers or colored pencils

Objectives

Language

- Practice vocabulary for classroom objects
- Review the names of the four seasons
- Recite the months of the year
- Sing "**Las estaciones**" (*"The Seasons"*) and the "Months Rap"
- Express the date

Culture

- Learn that the weather is different north and south of the equator
- Hear how schools in Spanish-speaking countries vary from schools in the United States

Review

- Greet the teacher and state how you feel
- Review the words for some classroom objects

Vocabulary

los bolis	*pens*
el cuaderno	*notebook*
el globo	*globe*
las gomas	*erasers*
los lápices	*pencils*
el sacapuntas	*pencil sharpener*
las tijeras	*scissors*
¿Es ___ o es ___?	*Is it ___ or is it ___?*
Es ___.	*It's ___.*
¿Son ___ o son ___?	*Are they ___ or are they ___?*
¿Qué es esto?	*What is this?*
las estaciones	*seasons*

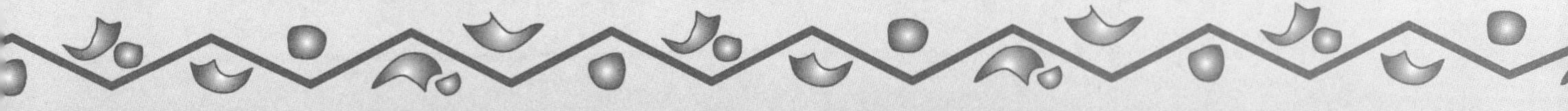

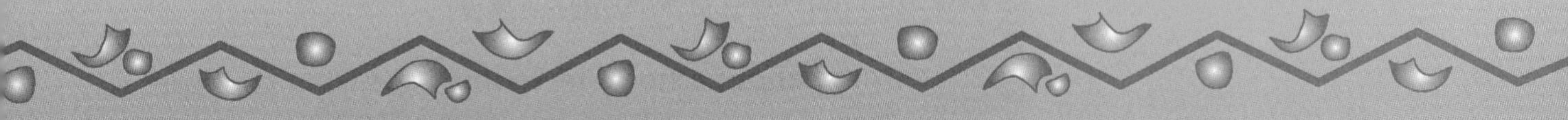

el invierno	*winter*	abril	*April*
la primavera	*spring*	mayo	*May*
el verano	*summer*	junio	*June*
el otoño	*fall*	julio	*July*
el mes	*month*	agosto	*August*
los meses	*months*	septiembre	*September*
enero	*January*	octubre	*October*
febrero	*February*	noviembre	*November*
marzo	*March*	diciembre	*December*

¿Cuál es la fecha?	*What is the date?*
Es el [*number*] de [*month*].	*It's the* [*number*] *of* [*month*].

Warm-up

Materials: Paper; a book; a ruler; a pencil; a pen; and crayons.

Display the items where children can see them. Tell the children it's time for Spanish class. Mention that in the last lesson they practiced some of the words for classroom objects. Point to the items displayed and have them call out the names: *paper* (**el papel**); *pencil* (**el lápiz**); *book* (**el libro**); *pen* (**el boli**); *ruler* (**la regla**); *crayons* (**los colores**).

EN ESPAÑOL

If you feel comfortable, say **la clase de español** (*Spanish class*).

Review

Ask the children if they remember the term for words that sound similar and have the same meaning in Spanish and English (cognates). Ask them to name the words they've learned this year that are cognates (e.g., **el drama**—*theater, drama*; **la geografía**—*geography*; **la historia**—*history*; **las computadoras**—*computers*; **el arte**—*art*; **la música**—*music*).

Introduce the Video

Invite the children to listen and watch as **la maestra** practices more classroom objects and sings songs that use many cognates.

Video Lesson

1. Greeting the children

La maestra greets Winston and the children with **Buenos días** (*Good morning*) and asks them how they are. Winston replies **Estoy muy contento** (*I am very happy*). **La maestra** asks him **¿Por qué? ¿Qué haces?** (*Why? What are you doing?*). He tells her **Estudio ciencias** (*I'm studying science*).

2. Learning about schools in Spanish-speaking countries

La maestra explains that in the schools in many Spanish-speaking countries children wear uniforms, that there are many separate schools for boys and girls, and that for grades 1–6 one attends **la escuela primaria** (*elementary school*) and for grades 7–12 **la escuela secundaria** (*high school*). In Latin American countries, the teachers—not the children—change classrooms for each class. After high school, many students attend a school that specializes in their chosen fields of interest, e.g., an art school or a school specializing in sciences.

3. Presenting additional classroom objects

La maestra plays a choosing game with classroom objects.

¿Es ___ o es ___?	*Is it ___ or is it ___?*
Es ___.	*It's ___.*
¿Son ___ o son ___?	*Are they ___ or are they ___?*
Son ___.	*They are ___.*

los bolis	*pens*	las gomas	*erasers*
la(s) regla(s)	*ruler(s)*	los colores	*crayons*
los lápices	*pencils*	el sacapuntas	*pencil sharpener*
el cuaderno	*notebook*	el libro	*book*
las tijeras	*scissors*	el globo	*globe*
el papel	*paper*		

4. Playing *¿Qué es esto?* (*What is this?*)

La maestra plays **¿Qué es esto?** with various classroom objects. After the children have answered, the name of the object appears on the screen so the children can see how it is spelled.

5. Presenting the names of the seasons

La maestra explains that when it is winter north of the equator, it is summer south of it.

el invierno	*winter*	la primavera	*spring*
el verano	*summer*	el otoño	*fall*

6. Singing *"Las estaciones"* ("The Seasons")

La maestra sings **"Las estaciones"** (*"The Seasons"*).

En el invierno, en el invierno,	*In the winter, in the winter,*
diciembre, enero, febrero.	*December, January, February.*
La primavera, la primavera,	*The spring, the spring,*
marzo, abril y mayo.	*March, April, and May.*
En el verano, en el verano,	*In the summer, in the summer,*
junio y julio y agosto.	*June and July and August.*
Viene septiembre, octubre,	*Come September, October,*
noviembre,	*November,*
para el otoño.	*for the fall.*

7. Practicing the months of the year

Using Gold Flashcards, **la maestra** practices the names of the months with the children.

enero	*January*	mayo	*May*	septiembre	*September*
febrero	*February*	junio	*June*	octubre	*October*
marzo	*March*	julio	*July*	noviembre	*November*
abril	*April*	agosto	*August*	diciembre	*December*

8. Singing the "Months Rap"

La maestra sings the rap. For rap lyrics, see Activity 10A in this lesson.

9. Explaining how to say the date

Using **el calendario del mes de septiembre** (*the calendar of the month of September*), **la maestra** asks what the date is and explains that one uses a number plus the month to say the date.

¿Cuál es la fecha?	*What is the date?*
el dos de septiembre	*September 2*

10. Expressing the date

La maestra shows the children a number and a month and asks **¿Cuál es la fecha?** (*What is the date?*): **el veinte de enero** (*January 20*), **el trece de febrero** (*February 13*), **el diez de marzo** (*March 10*), **el doce de septiembre** (*September 12*), **el treinta de diciembre** (*December 30*), and **el quince de agosto** (*August 15*).

11. Closing

La maestra tells the children that they have been **fabuloso** (*fabulous*) and bids them **Adiós** (*Good-bye*).

In Spanish, the names of the months are not capitalized.

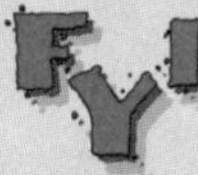

In English the date may be expressed two ways—as September 2 or the second of September, for example. In Spanish the date may only be expressed as the [number] of [month], as in **el dos de septiembre**.

For a list of numbers 1–100, see the Topics and Language Covered section in the Front Matter of this Teacher's Manual. Students have learned these numbers in Levels 2 and 3 and should remember them.

After viewing the video, praise the children for their good listening and watching skills.

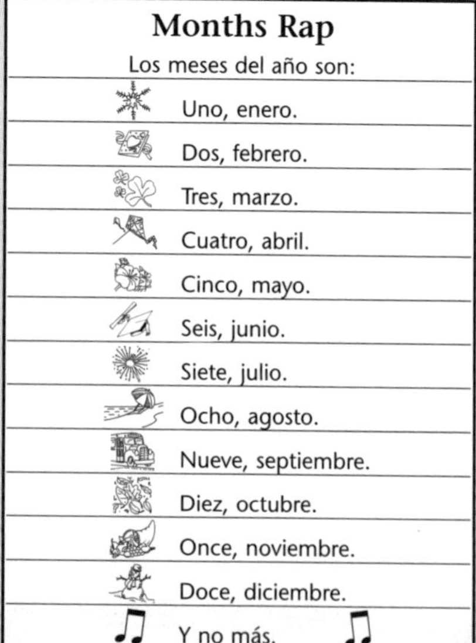

Months Rap

Los meses del año son:

Uno, enero.

Dos, febrero.

Tres, marzo.

Cuatro, abril.

Cinco, mayo.

Seis, junio.

Siete, julio.

Ocho, agosto.

Nueve, septiembre.

Diez, octubre.

Once, noviembre.

Doce, diciembre.

Y no más.

Blackline Master 10A-1

Las estaciones

(*The Seasons*)

En el invierno, en el invierno, diciembre, enero, febrero.

INVIERNO

La primavera, la primavera, marzo, abril y mayo.

PRIMAVERA

En el verano, en el verano, junio y julio y agosto.

VERANO

Viene septiembre, octubre, noviembre, para el otoño.

OTOÑO

Blackline Master 10A-2

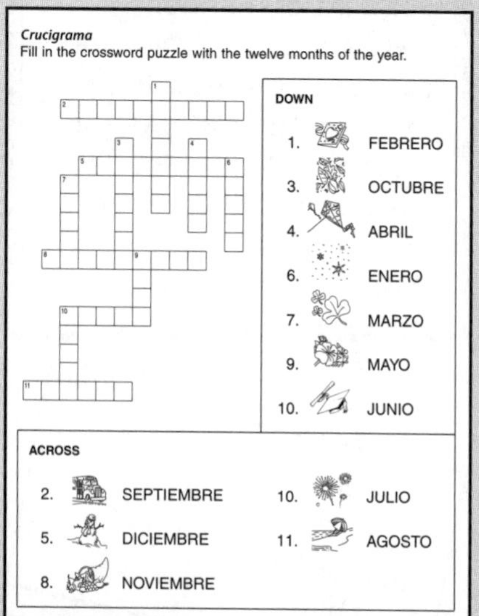

Crucigrama

Fill in the crossword puzzle with the twelve months of the year.

DOWN

1. FEBRERO
3. OCTUBRE
4. ABRIL
6. ENERO
7. MARZO
9. MAYO
10. JUNIO

ACROSS

2. SEPTIEMBRE
5. DICIEMBRE
8. NOVIEMBRE
10. JULIO
11. AGOSTO

Blackline Master 10B

Activity Lesson

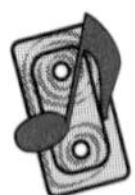

Activity 10A: Sing the songs about the months and seasons

Materials: Cassette player; Song Cassette, Side A; Blackline Masters 10A-1 and 10A-2; two blank overhead transparencies; and an overhead projector.

Preparation: Make an overhead transparency of each Blackline Master. Display the transparency for the "Months Rap."

Tell the children that you've displayed the lyrics to the "Months Rap." Have the class read the lyrics aloud as you point to each line.

Los meses del año son:	*The months of the year are:*
Uno, enero.	*1, January.*
Dos, febrero.	*2, February.*
Tres, marzo.	*3, March.*
Cuatro, abril.	*4, April.*
Cinco, mayo.	*5, May.*
Seis, junio.	*6, June.*
Siete, julio.	*7, July.*
Ocho, agosto.	*8, August.*
Nueve, septiembre.	*9, September.*
Diez, octubre.	*10, October.*
Once, noviembre.	*11, November.*
Doce, diciembre.	*12, December.*
Y no más.	*And no more.*

Ask the children which month names sound alike in English and Spanish. Then have them sing the rap with **la maestra**. Ask for a volunteer to point to each line as the class sings. Stop the tape after the rap.

Next, display your overhead transparency of Blackline Master 10A-2 and tell the children they are going to sing the song about the seasons. Ask for a volunteer to point to the lines of the song as the children sing with **la maestra**. Restart the tape, continuing Activity 10A.

Activity 10B: Complete the crossword puzzle

Materials: Blackline Master 10B; one pencil for each child.

Preparation: Duplicate and distribute Blackline Master 10B, one copy per child. Give each child a pencil.

Have the children fill in their names on the top left side of the paper. Then pointing to the right side of the paper, tell them to fill in today's date by using the number of the day and the name of the month. The names of the month appear on the paper (although they aren't in order from January to

December) so the children can see how to spell them. Once they've written in the date, have the children complete the puzzle by spelling the names of the months as indicated by the down and across clues.

Activity 10C: Pros and cons

Ask the children what they learned in the video lesson about schools in Spanish-speaking countries (children wear uniforms, boys and girls go to separate schools, teachers rather than children move from classroom to classroom). Lead the children in a discussion of the pros and cons of wearing uniforms to school or of boys and girls going to separate schools.

CLOSING

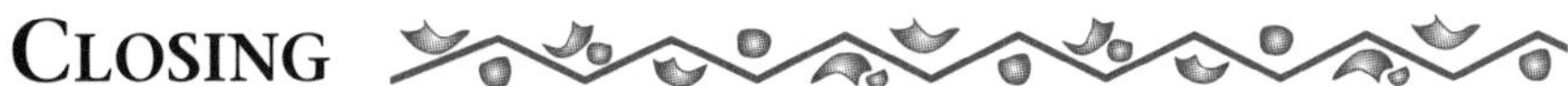

Tell the children that Spanish class (**la clase de español**) is finished for today. In the next lesson they will practice weather expressions.

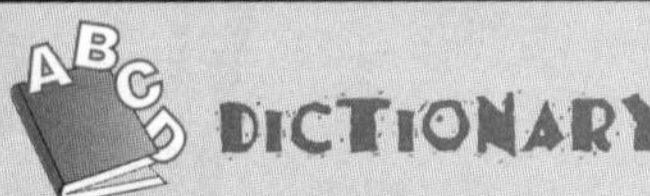

Materials: Children's copies of Blackline Master 10B; a blank piece of paper or the children's letter **A** pages; and markers or colored pencils.

Have the children make a dictionary page on which to write the Spanish name of the current month. Tell them to write the first letter of the name of the month on the top of the paper and then write the name of the month somewhere on the paper. Have them refer to the names of the months on Blackline Master 10B in order to correctly spell the name of the month. If it is August, children should add **agosto** to their **A** page.

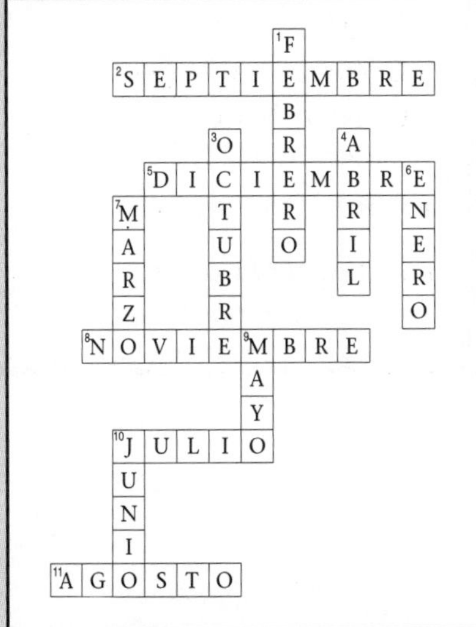

Answers to Activity 10B

Lesson 11

Materials to gather

- VCR and Video Lesson 11 on Tape 4
- Cassette player
- Activity Cassette 1
- Song Cassette
- Month and Season Pictures
- Tape
- Overhead transparency of Blackline Master 10A-2 (**"Las estaciones"**)
- Overhead projector
- Blackline Master 11B (**Ponte** and **Quítate**)
- Gold Flashcards 41–47 and 51–61
- Overhead transparency of Blackline Master 10A-1 ("Months Rap")
- Pencils (one per child)
- ***Optional Materials:*** Laminating machine

Objectives

Language

- Practice weather expressions
- Match seasons and weather expressions
- Review the commands **Ponte** ___ (*Put on* ___) and **Quítate** ___ (*Take off* ___)
- Practice vocabulary for clothing items

Culture

- Learn that the names of the months coordinate with different seasons south of the equator

Review

- Express the date
- Sing the "Months Rap"
- Review the names of the seasons

Vocabulary

Hace calor.	*It's hot.*	Hace sol.	*It's sunny.*
Hace frío.	*It's cold.*	Llueve.	*It's raining.*
Nieva.	*It's snowing.*	Hace viento.	*It's windy.*

Hace buen tiempo.	*It's good weather.*
Hace mal tiempo.	*It's bad weather.*
En el invierno hace frío.	*In winter it's cold.*
En la primavera hace buen tiempo.	*In spring it's good weather.*
En el verano hace calor.	*In summer it's hot.*
En el otoño hace viento.	*In fall it's windy.*
Quítate ___.	*Take off* ___.
Ponte ___.	*Put on* ___.

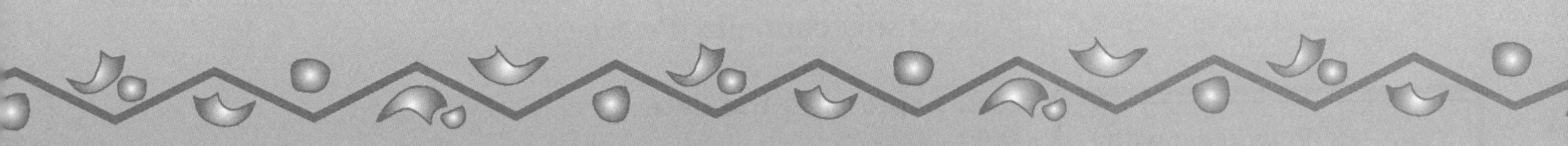

la ropa	*clothing*	el sombrero	*hat*
las gafas de sol	*sunglasses*	los sombreros	*hats*
los pantalones	*pants*	la camisa	*shirt*
los calcetines	*socks*	los zapatos	*shoes*
la blusa	*blouse*	el suéter	*sweater*
el vestido	*dress*	la falda	*skirt*
la chaqueta	*jacket*	el pijama	*pajamas*
el traje de baño	*bathing suit*	el abrigo	*coat*

Warm-up

Greet the children and let them know it's time for Spanish class (**la clase de español**). Ask them what the date is (**¿Cuál es la fecha?**): **el** [*number*] **de** [*month*]. For the months, see Lesson 10, Video Lesson, section 7.

Review

Materials: Month and Season Pictures (found in the Teacher's Resource Book); tape; *optional:* laminating machine.

Preparation: Cut the Month Pictures apart. You may wish to laminate each Month and Season Picture for durability. Tape the four Season Pictures to the chalkboard.

Hold up the Month Pictures one at a time and have the children recite the months in Spanish from January to December. Distribute the Month Pictures among the children. Then have them tape their pictures under the season in which their months fall. Let them work simultaneously. Encourage them to help each other.

Introduce the video

Invite the children to listen and watch as **la maestra** reviews expressions for talking about the weather.

Seasons and months:

el invierno (*winter*): diciembre (*December*), enero (*January*), febrero (*February*)

la primavera (*spring*): marzo (*March*), abril (*April*), mayo (*May*)

el verano (*summer*): junio (*June*), julio (*July*), agosto (*August*)

el otoño (*fall*): septiembre (*September*), octubre (*October*), noviembre (*November*)

Explain that your pictures for May and June are different from those of **la maestra**. Your pictures make the months easier to remember. The Flashcard of open flowers represents May. Then discuss the significance of the graduation cap and diploma for June.

Video Lesson

In working with Kipper on dates, **la maestra** says **uno más**, which means *one more.*

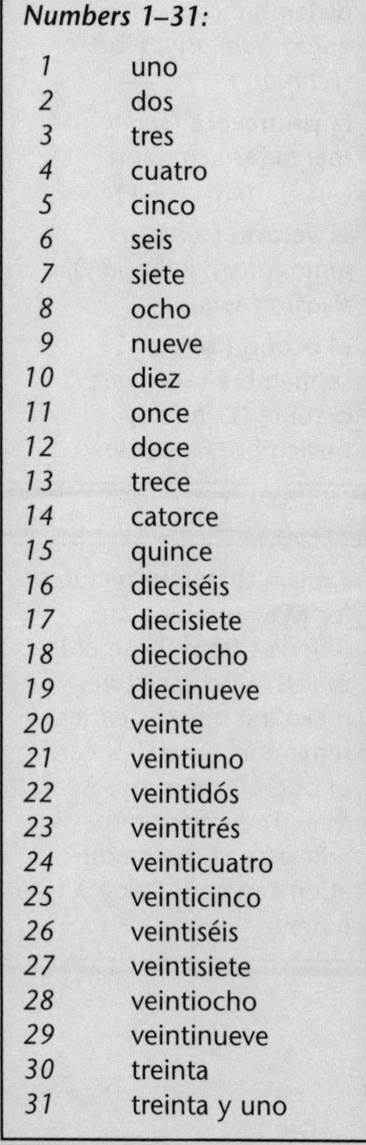

Numbers 1–31:

1	uno
2	dos
3	tres
4	cuatro
5	cinco
6	seis
7	siete
8	ocho
9	nueve
10	diez
11	once
12	doce
13	trece
14	catorce
15	quince
16	dieciséis
17	diecisiete
18	dieciocho
19	diecinueve
20	veinte
21	veintiuno
22	veintidós
23	veintitrés
24	veinticuatro
25	veinticinco
26	veintiséis
27	veintisiete
28	veintiocho
29	veintinueve
30	treinta
31	treinta y uno

1. Greeting the children

La maestra greets the children and Kipper with **Buenos días** (*Good morning*) and asks them how they are. In response to **¿Cómo estás tú?** (*How are you?*), Kipper says **Muy bien, gracias. ¿Y usted?** (*Very well, thank you. And you?*). **La maestra** says **Estoy contenta** (*I'm happy*).

2. Expressing the date

Showing Kipper and the children Gold Flashcards representing the months and number cards, **la maestra** asks **¿Cuál es la fecha?** (*What is the date?*). She reviews the dates **el cuatro de marzo** (*March 4*), **el veintitrés de febrero** (*February 23*), and **el doce de abril** (*April 12*).

3. Singing the "Months Rap"

La maestra sings the song. For rap lyrics, see Song 4 in the Song Appendix.

4. Reviewing the names of the seasons

La maestra reminds Kipper that the months fit into the **cuatro estaciones** (*four seasons*): **el invierno** (*winter*), **la primavera** (*spring*), **el verano** (*summer*), and **el otoño** (*fall*). She sings **"Las estaciones"** (*"The Seasons"*).

En el invierno, en el invierno,	*In the winter, in the winter,*
diciembre, enero, febrero.	*December, January, February.*
La primavera, la primavera,	*The spring, the spring,*
marzo, abril y mayo.	*March, April, and May.*
En el verano, en el verano,	*In the summer, in the summer,*
junio y julio y agosto.	*June and July and August.*
Viene septiembre, octubre,	*Come September, October,*
noviembre,	*November,*
para el otoño.	*for the fall.*

5. Practicing weather expressions

Using Gold Flashcards, **la maestra** and Kipper review weather expressions.

¿Qué tiempo hace?	*What's the weather like?*
Hace sol.	*It's sunny.*
Hace buen tiempo.	*It's good weather.*
Hace frío.	*It's cold.*
Llueve.	*It's raining.*
Nieva.	*It's snowing.*

6. Matching seasons and weather

La maestra asks the children what season it is and what the weather is like based on pictures.

¿Qué estación es?	*What season is it?*
Es el invierno.	*It's winter.*
¿Qué tiempo hace?	*What's the weather?*
Hace frío.	*It's cold.*
En el invierno hace frío.	*In winter it's cold.*
En la primavera hace buen tiempo.	*In spring it's good weather.*
En el verano hace calor.	*In summer it's hot.*
En el otoño hace viento.	*In fall it's windy.*

7. Reviewing two commands

Kipper asks **la maestra ¿Llevas gafas de sol?** (*Are you wearing sunglasses?*). She responds **Sí, llevo gafas de sol** (*Yes, I am wearing sunglasses*). When Kipper asks her **¿Por qué?** (*Why?*), she tells him **Porque hace sol** (*Because it's sunny*). Doña Elena tells Toño to take off and put on various clothing items.

Quítate ___.	*Take off ___.*
Ponte ___.	*Put on ___.*

8. Practicing vocabulary for clothing

La maestra asks the children **¿Qué es esto?** (*What is this?*) with items of clothing.

la ropa	*clothing*	el vestido	*dress*
el sombrero	*hat*	el suéter	*sweater*
la camisa	*shirt*	los zapatos	*shoes*
los pantalones	*pants*	la blusa	*blouse*
los calcetines	*socks*		

9. Closing

La maestra praises the children for their participation and says **Hasta luego** (*See you later*).

Are children recalling the vocabulary easily? If they are having difficulty or are new to ***Español para ti,*** reassure them that they will practice the words again and with time they will remember them.

While reviewing the clothing items, **la maestra** says:

La ropa es muy importante. (*Clothing is very important.*)

Cuando hace frío llevo el suéter. (*When it's cold, I wear a sweater.*)

Note that in English and Spanish, pants are considered plural—*pants* and **los pantalones**.

After viewing the video, praise the children for their good listening and watching skills.

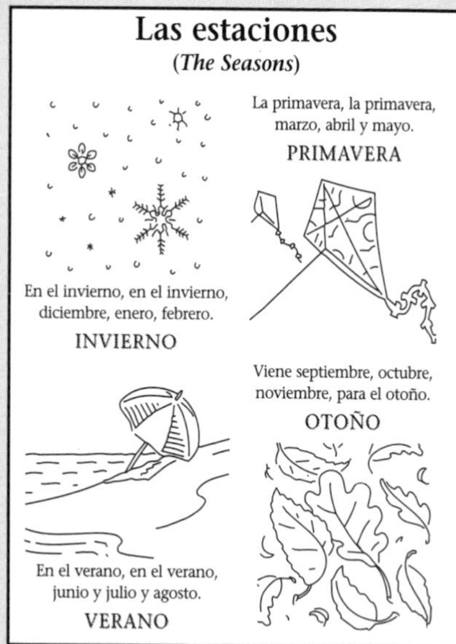

Las estaciones
(The Seasons)
La primavera, la primavera,
marzo, abril y mayo.
PRIMAVERA
En el invierno, en el invierno,
diciembre, enero, febrero.
INVIERNO
Viene septiembre, octubre,
noviembre, para el otoño.
OTOÑO
En el verano, en el verano,
junio y julio y agosto.
VERANO

Blackline Master 10A-2

FYI
In English *pajamas* is plural, but in Spanish **el pijama** is singular.

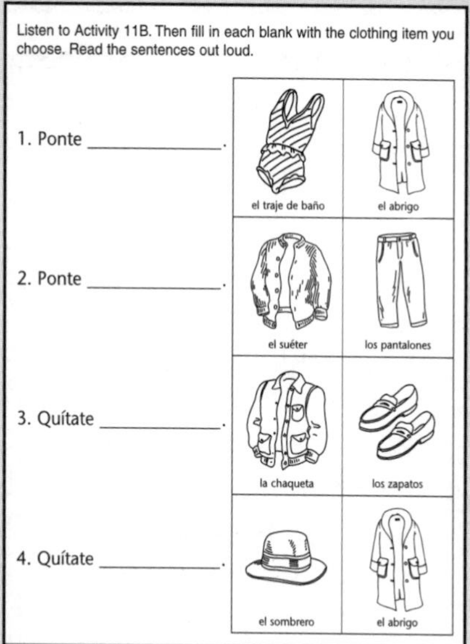
Listen to Activity 11B. Then fill in each blank with the clothing item you choose. Read the sentences out loud.

1. Ponte ____________. (el traje de baño / el abrigo)

2. Ponte ____________. (el suéter / los pantalones)

3. Quítate ____________. (la chaqueta / los zapatos)

4. Quítate ____________. (el sombrero / el abrigo)

Blackline Master 11B

ACTIVITY LESSON

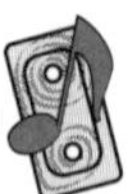

Activity 11A: Sing the song about the seasons

Materials: Cassette player; Song Cassette, Side A; the overhead transparency of Blackline Master 10A-2; and an overhead projector.

Tell the children to sing along with **la maestra** as she sings **"Las estaciones,"** the song that matches the months to the seasons—at least north of the equator.

Activity 11B: Practice commands and clothing words

Materials: Cassette player; Activity Cassette 1, Side A; Blackline Master 11B; Gold Flashcards 51–61; the overhead transparency of Blackline Master 10A-1; an overhead projector; and pencils.

Preparation: Make a copy of Blackline Master 11B for each child, but do not distribute it yet. Display Gold Flashcards 51–61.

Review the names of clothing items by pointing to each Flashcard and having the children identify them. If you feel comfortable, say **¿Qué es esto?** (*What is this?*) as you review the words.

Gold Flashcards:

#51:	el sombrero/los sombreros	*hat/hats*
#52:	los pantalones	*pants*
#53:	la camisa	*shirt*
#54 (top):	los calcetines	*socks*
#54 (bottom):	los zapatos	*shoes*
#55:	la blusa	*blouse*
#56:	el suéter	*sweater*
#57:	el vestido	*dress*
#58:	la falda	*skirt*
#59:	la chaqueta	*jacket*
#60:	el pijama	*pajamas*
#61:	el traje de baño	*bathing suit*

Now distribute the copies of Blackline Master 11B and the pencils and display your transparency of Blackline Master 10A-1 ("Months Rap") on the overhead projector. Have the children fill in their names after **Me llamo** (*My name is*) and today's date after **Fecha** (*date*). To complete the date they will use the number of the day and the name of the month. Have them refer to the transparency for how to spell the name of the month. Once they have completed that step, turn off the overhead projector.

Next point out that in row 1 there is a picture of a *coat* (**el abrigo**), which is a new word for them. Remind the children that in the video lesson, they heard doña Elena tell Antonio to *put on* (**Ponte**) and *take off* (**Quítate**) various items of clothing. Now **la maestra** is going to lead them in telling someone to take off or put on one of the pieces of clothing shown for each row. For now they should just say the sentences aloud. Play Activity 11B. Once it's finished, have the children complete the written commands on their papers, by writing in the words for the clothing items they said should be put on or taken off.

Answers:

1. Ponte el traje de baño. (*Put on the bathing suit.*) or:
   Ponte el abrigo. (*Put on the coat.*)
2. Ponte el suéter. (*Put on the sweater.*) or:
   Ponte los pantalones. (*Put on the pants.*)
3. Quítate la chaqueta. (*Take off the jacket.*) or:
   Quítate los zapatos. (*Take off the shoes.*)
4. Quítate el sombrero. (*Take off the hat.*) or:
   Quítate el abrigo. (*Take off the coat.*)

Activity 11C: What's the weather like?

Materials: Gold Flashcards 41–47.

Hold up one Gold Flashcard at a time and ask volunteers to say what the weather is like in the picture. If you feel comfortable, ask **¿Qué tiempo hace?** (*What's the weather like?*) for each Flashcard.

Accept all reasonable answers. For example, **Hace sol** (*It's sunny*) for Gold Flashcards #42 and #43. Children new to ***Español para ti*** will not recognize the picture on Gold Flashcard #47 and its expression **Hace mal tiempo** (*It's bad weather*).

Gold Flashcards:

#41:	Hace calor. *or* Hace sol.	*It's hot.* or *It's sunny.*
#42:	Hace frío.	*It's cold.*
#43:	Hace buen tiempo.	*It's good weather.*
#44:	Llueve.	*It's raining.*
#45:	Nieva.	*It's snowing.*
#46:	Hace viento.	*It's windy.*
#47:	Hace mal tiempo.	*It's bad weather.*

IF YOU HAVE TIME . . .

Materials: Gold Flashcards 41–47.

As you hold up each Flashcard, ask the children what season it is. If you feel comfortable, ask **¿Qué estación es?** (*What season is it?*):

Gold Flashcards:

#41 **el verano** (*summer*)
#42 **el invierno** (*winter*)
#43 **el verano** (*summer*)
#44 **la primavera** (*spring*) or **el verano** (*summer*)
#45 **el invierno** (*winter*)
#46 **el otoño** (*fall*)
#47 **la primavera** (*spring*), **el verano** (*summer*), or **el otoño** (*fall*)

CLOSING

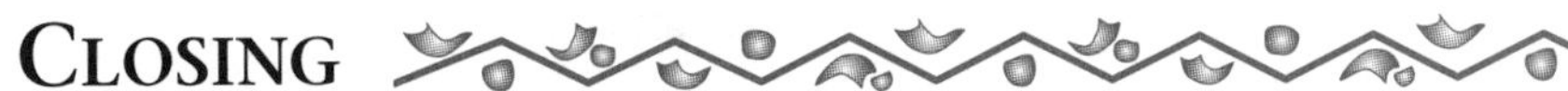

Tell the children that Spanish class is finished for today. In the next lesson the children will learn about the names of several musical instruments.

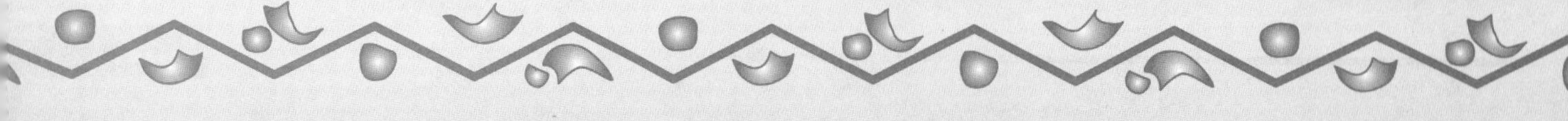

Lesson 12

Materials to gather

- VCR and Video Lesson 12 on Tape 4
- Cassette player
- Activity Cassette 1
- Blackline Master 12A (season and weather pictures)
- Red Flashcards 50 and 51
- Several rulers and pens
- Pencils

Objectives

Language

- Hear how to express what season one likes
- Practice the names of four musical instruments
- Understand that the word **toca** can mean *touch* and also *play* (*an instrument*)

Culture

- Sing **"Las estaciones"** (*"The Seasons"*)

Review

- Practice weather expressions
- Combine information about the season and the weather into one sentence

Vocabulary

¿Qué estación te gusta?	*What season do you like?*
Me gusta ___.	*I like ___.*
los instrumentos musicales	*musical instruments*
¿Qué instrumento es?	*What instrument is it?*
el tambor/los tambores	*drum/drums*
la guitarra/las guitarras	*guitar/guitars*
la trompeta/las trompetas	*trumpet/trumpets*
el piano/los pianos	*piano/pianos*
Toca ___.	*Touch ___; Play* (*musical instrument*).

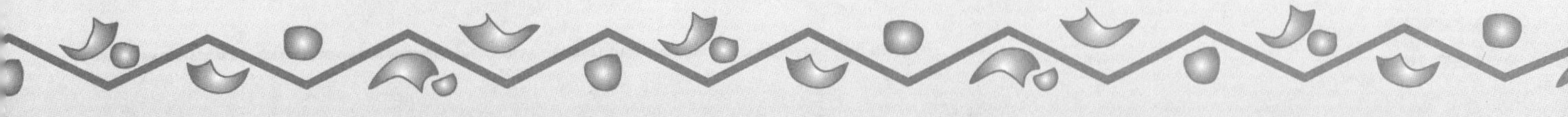

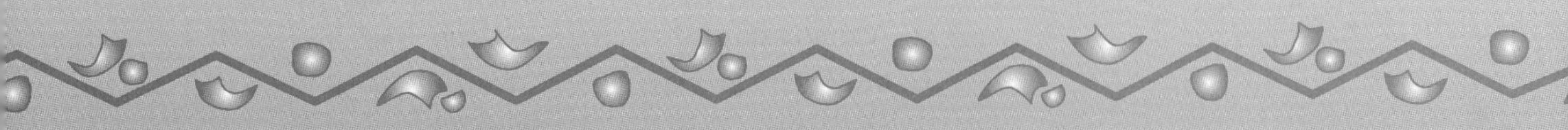

Warm-up

Greet the children and ask them what the date is. Ask them what the weather is like today. Ask for volunteers to say the date—**el** [*number*] **de** [*month*]—and what the weather is like in Spanish.

Months:

enero	*January*	julio	*July*
febrero	*February*	agosto	*August*
marzo	*March*	septiembre	*September*
abril	*April*	octubre	*October*
mayo	*May*	noviembre	*November*
junio	*June*	diciembre	*December*

Weather expressions:

Hace frío.	*It's cold.*	Llueve.	*It's raining.*
Hace calor.	*It's hot.*	Nieva.	*It's snowing.*
Hace sol.	*It's sunny.*	Hace viento.	*It's windy.*

Hace buen tiempo.	*It's good weather.*
Hace mal tiempo.	*It's bad weather.*

Review

Walk around the room briefly touching various classroom objects, e.g., your desk, a chair, a book, the chalkboard, a wall, a window. Ask the children what you are doing (touching). Ask them if they recall how to say *touch* in Spanish (**toca**).

Introduce the video

Invite the children to listen and watch as **la maestra** introduces the words for four musical instruments and a new meaning for the word **toca**.

Numbers 1–31:

1	uno
2	dos
3	tres
4	cuatro
5	cinco
6	seis
7	siete
8	ocho
9	nueve
10	diez
11	once
12	doce
13	trece
14	catorce
15	quince
16	dieciséis
17	diecisiete
18	dieciocho
19	diecinueve
20	veinte
21	veintiuno
22	veintidós
23	veintitrés
24	veinticuatro
25	veinticinco
26	veintiséis
27	veintisiete
28	veintiocho
29	veintinueve
30	treinta
31	treinta y uno

Video Lesson

1. Greeting the children

La maestra greets the children with **Buenos días** (*Good morning*) and asks them how they are (**M** = Maestra, **C** = class):

M: Buenos días, clase.	*Good morning, class.*
C: Buenos días, Maestra.	*Good morning, Teacher.*
M: ¿Cómo estás tú?	*How are you?*
C: Muy bien, gracias. ¿Y usted?	*Very well, thank you. And you?*
M: Muy bien. Estoy contenta.	*Very well. I'm very happy.*

She says **Hola** (*Hello*) to Kipper and asks him how he is. He says **Estoy contento** (*I'm happy*). **La maestra** says **Estoy contenta; Kipper está contento** (*I'm happy; Kipper is happy*) to reinforce the use of **estoy** and **está** (*I am* and *he/she is*) and **contento/contenta** (*happy*).

Las estaciones (*the seasons*):

el invierno	*winter*
la primavera	*spring*
el verano	*summer*
el otoño	*fall*

2. Reviewing the names of the seasons

La maestra reviews the names of the seasons and then asks Kipper which season he likes and what the weather is like. Kipper then asks **la maestra** the same questions.

¿Qué estación te gusta?	*What season do you like?*
Me gusta ___.	*I like ___.*
¿Qué tiempo hace en ___?	*What's the weather like in ___?*
En el verano hace calor y hace sol.	*In summer it's hot and it's sunny.*
En el otoño hace viento.	*In fall it's windy.*

3. Singing *"Las estaciones"* (*"The Seasons"*)

La maestra sings the song about the seasons and the months.

En el invierno, en el invierno,	*In the winter, in the winter,*
diciembre, enero, febrero.	*December, January, February.*
La primavera, la primavera,	*The spring, the spring,*
marzo, abril y mayo.	*March, April, and May.*
En el verano, en el verano,	*In the summer, in the summer,*
junio y julio y agosto.	*June and July and August.*
Viene septiembre, octubre,	*Come September, October,*
noviembre,	*November,*
para el otoño.	*for the fall.*

4. Practicing the weather expressions

Holding up Gold Flashcards, **la maestra** reviews the weather expressions with the children. She asks **¿Qué tiempo hace?** (*What's the weather like?*).

Hace frío y nieva.	*It's cold and it's snowing.*
Hace buen tiempo y hace sol.	*It's good weather and it's sunny.*
Llueve.	*It's raining.*
Hace viento.	*It's windy.*
Hace sol y hace calor.	*It's sunny and it's hot.*

5. Matching the weather and seasons

La maestra asks the children **¿Qué estación es?** (*What season is it?*) and **¿Qué tiempo hace?** (*What's the weather like?*). Children put the two pieces of information together to form one sentence.

En el invierno hace frío.	*In winter it's cold.*
En la primavera hace buen tiempo.	*In spring it's good weather.*
En el verano hace calor.	*In summer it's hot.*
En el otoño hace viento.	*In fall it's windy.*

6. Introducing the names of musical instruments

Kipper wants to be **un músico** (*a musician*). **La maestra** introduces the words for four musical instruments by pointing to a picture of each instrument on the Red Flashcards and saying the word. The children repeat the words after her.

los instrumentos musicales	*musical instruments*
el tambor	*drum*
la guitarra	*guitar*
la trompeta	*trumpet*
el piano	*piano*

7. Presenting the command *Toca* with musical instruments

Antonio plays each instrument when he's told **Toca** (*Play*) and the name of the instrument. **La maestra** points out that **el tambor** means *drum* and **los tambores** means *drums*. She explains that **toca** means *touch* and in the case of musical instruments it also means *play*.

8. Practicing musical instruments vocabulary

La maestra asks Kipper and the children to identify the musical instruments. She asks **¿Qué instrumento es?** (*What instrument is it?*).

9. Closing

La maestra bids the children **Hasta luego** (*See you later*).

After viewing the video, praise the children for their good listening and watching skills.

Listen to Activity 12A. Match the pictures of the seasons with weather pictures.
Hace calor.
Hace buen tiempo.
Hace frío.
Hace viento.

Blackline Master 12A

Activity Lesson

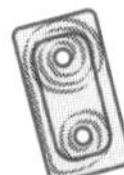

Activity 12A: Match the seasons and the weather

Materials: Cassette player; Activity Cassette 1, Side B; Blackline Master 12A; and pencils, one per child.

Preparation: Duplicate and distribute Blackline Master 12A, one copy per child.

Holding up Blackline Master 12A, tell the children that on the left side of the paper are pictures representing various seasons. Review the seasons represented by each picture: snowflakes—*winter* (**el invierno**); kites—*spring* (**la primavera**); beach scene—*summer* (**el verano**); and falling leaves—*fall* (**el otoño**). On the right side of the paper are weather expressions. Tell the children to listen carefully as **la maestra** describes the weather in a particular season. They are to match the season with the weather expression. Children should match the snowflakes with **Hace frío** (*It's cold*); the kites with **Hace buen tiempo** (*It's good weather*); the beach scene with **Hace calor** (*It's hot*); and the falling leaves with **Hace viento** (*It's windy*). Children may also match the kites with **Hace viento** (*It's windy*).

Activity 12B: Cooperative learning—What instrument am I playing?

Materials: Red Flashcards 50 and 51.

Display the Flashcards. Review the name of each instrument with the children by pointing to it and asking them to tell you what it is called in Spanish. If you feel comfortable, ask **¿Qué instrumento es?** (*What instrument is it?*). Then divide the class into pairs. One child in each pair mimes playing one of the instruments shown on the Flashcards. The other child names the instrument his/her partner is miming. Children then reverse roles, continuing the game until each pair has mimed all four instruments.

Red Flashcards:

#50 (top)	el tambor (*drum*)
#50 (bottom)	la guitarra (*guitar*)
#51 (top)	la trompeta (*trumpet*)
#51 (bottom)	el piano (*piano*)

IF YOU HAVE TIME . . .

Talk to the children about what it takes to be a musician (many years of lessons and practice). Ask who plays an instrument and which instrument he/she plays. How long has the child played? Is the child taking lessons? Does he/she practice every day? How long? Does he/she like to play the instrument? Would he/she like to learn another instrument?

Activity 12C: The plurals of nouns in Spanish

Materials: Several rulers and pens.

Preparation: Write the following words on the chalkboard in two columns (Spanish only):

la regla	las reglas (*rulers*)
el boli	los bolis (*pens*)
la guitarra	las guitarras (*guitars*)
el piano	los pianos (*pianos*)
el tambor	los tambores (*drums*)
la trompeta	las trompetas (*trumpets*)

Hold up one ruler and ask the children what it is called in Spanish (**la regla**). Hold up several rulers and ask what they are called (**las reglas**). Follow the same procedure with the pens. Point out that on the left column on the board are the singular forms of the words for two classroom objects and for the four musical instruments they've learned. On the right is the plural form for each word. Ask the children to analyze the differences between the plural forms. Give them a hint: Look at the last letter of each word in its singular form and then look at the plural form. Words whose singular form ends in a vowel form their plural by adding an **-s**. Words whose singular form ends in a consonant form their plural by adding **-es**. **La** (*the*) becomes **las** (*the*); **el** (*the*) becomes **los** (*the*).

Closing

Tell the children that Spanish class is finished for today. In the next lesson they will learn the names of four more musical instruments.

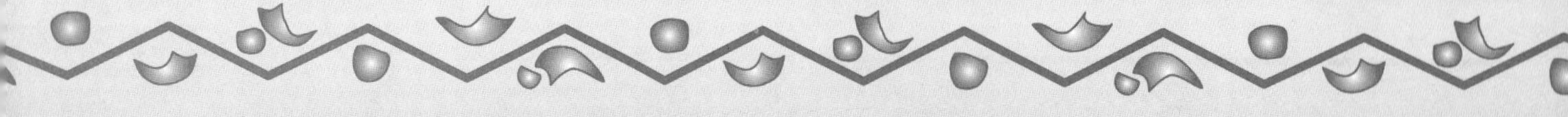

Lesson 13

Materials to gather

- VCR and Video Lesson 13 on Tape 5
- Cassette player
- Activity Cassette 1
- Song Cassette
- Red Flashcards 50 and 51
- Overhead transparency of Blackline Master 10A-1 ("Months Rap")
- Overhead projector
- ***Optional materials:*** Red Flashcards 50–53; blank paper; colored markers or crayons; children's dictionary pages

Objectives

Language

- Use the greeting **Buenas tardes** (*Good afternoon*)
- Answer the question **¿Qué mes es?** (*What month is it?*)
- Learn the names of additional musical instruments

Culture

- Learn that the guitar, trumpet, and maracas are commonly used in Latin American music

Review

- Say the names of the months
- Sing the "Months Rap"
- Express dates
- Recognize the names of several musical instruments

Vocabulary

¿Qué mes es?	*What month is it?*
¿Qué instrumento musical es?	*What musical instrument is it?*
la flauta/las flautas	*flute/flutes*
el violín/los violines	*violin/violins*
el clarinete/los clarinetes	*clarinet/clarinets*
la pandereta/las panderetas	*tambourine/tambourines*

Warm-up

Greet the children and ask them to tell you today's date in Spanish. Write the following on the chalkboard, underlining the words "number" and "month."

el [*number*] **de** [*month*]

For a list of the months, see Activity 13B in this lesson. For the numbers 1–31, see the sidebar to the Warm-up section in Lesson 12.

Review

Materials: Red Flashcards 50 and 51.

Display Red Flashcards 50 and 51. Point to each instrument and ask the children what it is called in Spanish.

Red Flashcards:

#50 (top)	el tambor (*drum*)
#50 (bottom)	la guitarra (*guitar*)
#51 (top)	la trompeta (*trumpet*)
#51 (bottom)	el piano (*piano*)

Introduce the video

Invite the children to listen and watch as **la maestra** introduces the names of more musical instruments.

Video Lesson

1. Greeting the children

La maestra greets the children with **Buenas tardes** (*Good afternoon*) and asks them how they are (**M** = Maestra, **C** = class):

M: Buenas tardes, clase.	*Good afternoon, class.*
C: Buenas tardes, Maestra.	*Good afternoon, Teacher.*
M: ¿Cómo estás tú?	*How are you?*
C: Muy bien, gracias. ¿Y usted?	*Very well, thank you. And you?*
M: Muy bien, gracias.	*Very well, thank you.*

She says she heard a boy say **Estoy contento** (*I'm happy*) and a girl say **Estoy enojada** (*I'm angry*).

2. Reviewing the months of the year

La maestra and the children recite **los doce meses del año** (*the twelve months of the year*).

enero	*January*	julio	*July*
febrero	*February*	agosto	*August*
marzo	*March*	septiembre	*September*
abril	*April*	octubre	*October*
mayo	*May*	noviembre	*November*
junio	*June*	diciembre	*December*

3. Singing the "Months Rap"

La maestra and the children sing the rap. For song lyrics, see Song 4 in the Song Appendix.

4. Recognizing the month symbols

La maestra asks the children **¿Qué mes es?** (*What month is it?*) as she points to each of the month symbols.

5. Answering the question *¿Cuál es la fecha?* (What is the date?)

La maestra explains that one uses the number and the name of the month to state the date—**los números con los meses del año** *(the numbers with the months of the year)*. She asks the children **¿Cuál es la fecha?** *(What is the date?)* as she shows them numbers and month symbols.

el veinte de enero	*January 20*
el doce de septiembre	*September 12*
el trece de febrero	*February 13*
el treinta de diciembre	*December 30*
el diez de marzo	*March 10*
el quince de agosto	*August 15*

Heritage Speakers

Point out that the pictures for the months of February, March, July, and November represent the holidays Valentine's Day, St. Patrick's Day, the Fourth of July, and Thanksgiving, respectively. Encourage heritage speakers to describe some holidays associated with certain months in their culture.

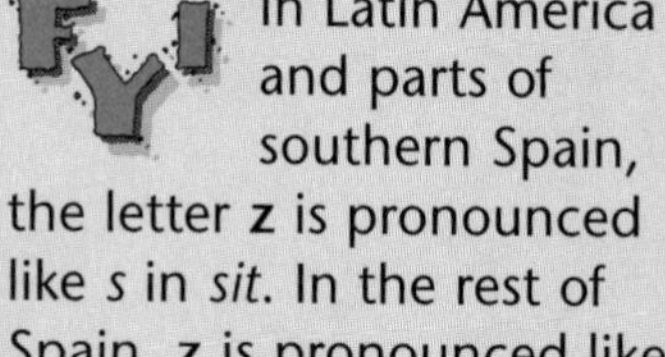

In Latin America and parts of southern Spain, the letter **z** is pronounced like *s* in *sit*. In the rest of Spain, **z** is pronounced like the *th* in *think*.

6. Reviewing the names of musical instruments

La maestra shows Kipper and the children Red Flashcards of the four musical instruments they have learned and asks **¿Qué instrumento musical es?** (*What musical instrument is it?*).

el tambor	*drum*	la trompeta	*trumpet*
los tambores	*drums*	el piano	*piano*
la guitarra	*guitar*		

7. Presenting more musical instruments

Showing pictures of four more musical instruments, **la maestra** introduces the words to Kipper and the children. She asks Toño **¿Qué tienes?** (*What do you have?*) and tells him to play (**Toca**) each of the instruments.

el clarinete	*clarinet*	el violín	*violin*
la flauta	*flute*	la pandereta	*tambourine*

8. Reviewing the names of all the musical instruments

The children and Kipper repeat the word for each instrument after **la maestra**. She mentions that **la guitarra** (*guitar*), **la trompeta** (*trompet*), and **las maracas** (*maracas*) are commonly used in Latin American music.

9. Closing

She and Kipper say **Adiós** (*Good-bye*) to the children.

CROSS-CULTURAL CONNECTIONS

The guitar was introduced into Spain by the Moors and was brought to North and South America from Spain hundreds of years ago. The first guitars, however, were not electric.

After viewing the video, praise the children for their good listening and watching skills.

Months Rap

Los meses del año son:

Uno, enero.
Dos, febrero.
Tres, marzo.
Cuatro, abril.
Cinco, mayo.
Seis, junio.
Siete, julio.
Ocho, agosto.
Nueve, septiembre.
Diez, octubre.
Once, noviembre.
Doce, diciembre.
Y no más.

Blackline Master 10A-1

The numbers 16–19 and 21–29 can also be spelled as three words, e.g., **diez y seis** (*16*), **diez y siete** (*17*), **veinte y uno** (*21*), **veinte y dos** (*22*), **veinte y tres** (*23*).

Activity Lesson

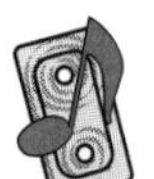

Activity 13A: Rap along to the "Months Rap"

Materials: Cassette player; Song Cassette, Side A; an overhead projector; and the overhead transparency of Blackline Master 10A-1.

Display your overhead transparency of Blackline Master 10A-1. Tell the children they are going to practice the months of the year by "rapping" with **la maestra**. Have the children stand up and prepare to clap at the appropriate places in the rap. Suggest that following the words on the transparency will help them remember how the months and numbers are spelled in Spanish.

Activity 13B: Say when your birthday is

Materials: Cassette player; Activity Cassette 1, Side B.

Preparation: On the chalkboard, write "**Mi cumpleaños es el veintiuno de enero.**"

Point to the sentence on the board and ask the children if they can tell you what the words mean (*My birthday is January 21*). Tell them to listen as **la maestra** talks about a date that is of particular importance to her. Play Activity 13B, stopping the tape at the harp sound and ask the children what **la maestra** said: **Mi cumpleaños es el veintiuno de enero. Sí, me gusta mi cumpleaños. Es el veintiuno de enero.** (*My birthday is January 21. Yes, I like my birthday. It's January 21.*)

Play the activity to the end. Then ask volunteers to tell you in Spanish when their birthdays are. Remind them that to say the date in Spanish, they need the number and the month. Encourage them to use a full sentence: **Mi cumpleaños es el** [*number*] **de** [*month*]. If you feel comfortable, replace **veintiuno** and **enero** in the statement on the chalkboard with the number and the month of the volunteers' birthdays. For numbers 1–31, see the sidebar to the Warm-up section in Lesson 12.

January	enero	*July*	julio
February	Febrero	*August*	agosto
March	marzo	*September*	septiembre
April	abril	*October*	octubre
May	mayo	*November*	noviembre
June	junio	*December*	diciembre

Activity 13C: The plurals of nouns

Preparation: Write the following words, except those in parentheses, on the chalkboard.

el violín	los violines	la flauta	las flautas
el clarinete	(los clarinetes)		
el tambor	(los tambores)		
la pandereta	(las panderetas)		

Ask the children to read each word as you point to it. Then ask them to analyze the difference between the plural of **violín** (*violin*) and **flauta** (*flute*): **Flauta** ends in a vowel and thus forms its plural by adding **-s**. **La** (*the*) becomes **las** (*the*). **Violín** ends in a consonant and forms its plural by adding **-es**. **El** (*the*) becomes **los** (*the*). Ask children to guess the plurals of the other musical instruments: *clarinet, drum,* and *tambourine*. Write the correct plural forms on the board (see the words in parentheses). Have children restate the rule for pluralization of Spanish nouns: Words ending in a vowel, add **-s**. Words ending in a consonant, add **-es**.

CLOSING

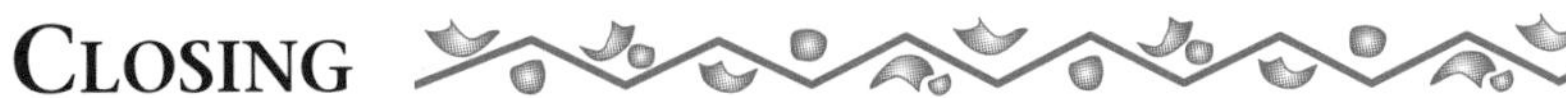

Tell the children that Spanish class is finished for today. In the next lesson they will visit a music store.

DICTIONARY

Materials: Red Flashcards 50–53; a blank page for each child; colored markers or crayons; children's dictionary pages.

Display Red Flashcards 50–53 and give each child a blank page. Direct the children to make a dictionary page for their favorite musical instrument of those displayed. They should write the first letter of the word on the top of their blank papers, draw a picture of the instrument on the paper, and then write the name of the instrument underneath the picture. For example, for drum, they would write **T** on the top of the paper, draw a drum, and write **el tambor**. Remind children to alphabetize words without the definite article **el** or **la** (*the*), thus the word for *drum* (**el tambor**) appears under **t** in the dictionary, not **e**. Children may need help spelling the words: **el tambor** (*drum*), **la guitarra** (*guitar*), **la trompeta** (*trumpet*), **el piano** (*piano*), **la flauta** (*flute*), **el violín** (*violin*), **el clarinete** (*clarinet*), **la pandereta** (*tambourine*).

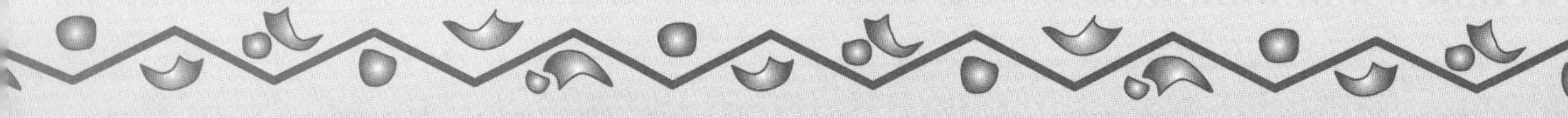

Lesson 14

Materials to gather

- VCR and Video Lesson 14 on Tape 5
- Cassette player
- Activity Cassette 1
- A world map
- Red Flashcards 50–53
- *Optional materials:* cassette with **merengue** music

Objectives

Language

- Answer the question **¿Qué toca?** (*What is he/she playing?*)
- Understand an extended conversation about musical instruments

Culture

- Learn about instruments typical in Latin American music

Review

- Greet the teacher with **Buenas tardes** (*Good afternoon*)
- Review the names of musical instruments

Vocabulary

¡Buena suerte!	*Good luck!*
¿Qué toca?	*What is he/she playing?*

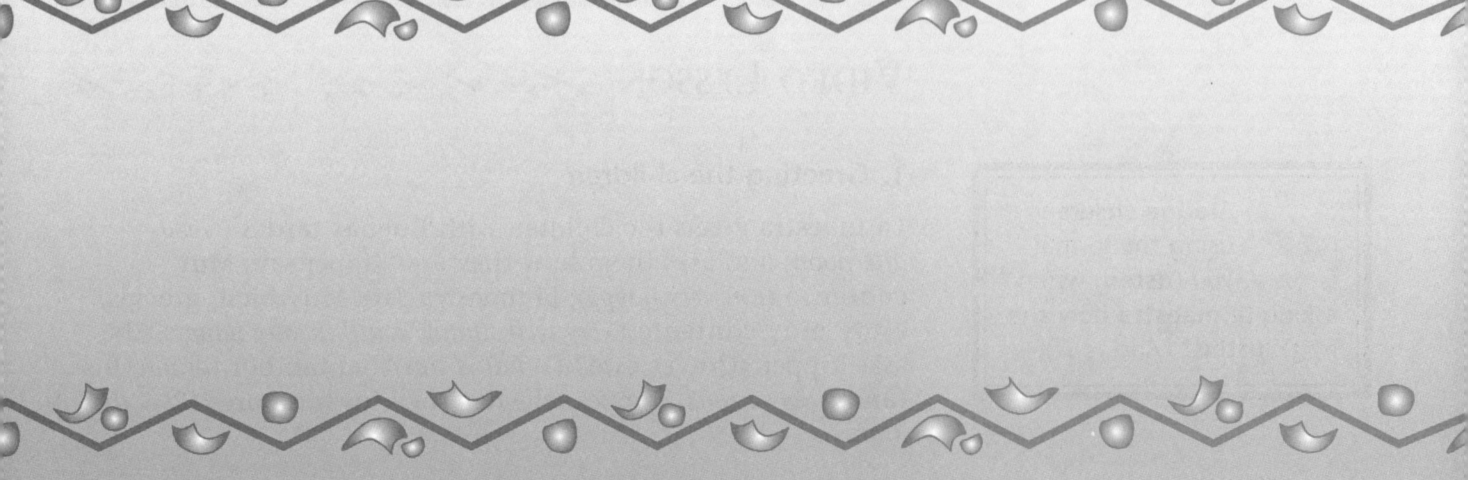

Warm-up

Greet the children and tell them it's time for Spanish class (**la clase de español**). Ask them how they'd say today's date in Spanish: **el** [*number*] **de** [*month*]. For the months, see Activity 13B. For numbers 1–31, see the sidebar to the Warm-up section in Lesson 12. Then ask them what the weather is like, saying **¿Qué tiempo hace?** if you feel comfortable.

Weather expressions:

Hace frío.	*It's cold.*	Llueve.	*It's raining.*
Hace calor.	*It's hot.*	Nieva.	*It's snowing.*
Hace sol.	*It's sunny.*	Hace viento.	*It's windy.*

Hace buen tiempo.	*It's good weather.*
Hace mal tiempo.	*It's bad weather.*

Review

Materials: Red Flashcards 50–53.

Display Red Flashcards 50–53. Review the names of the instruments by pointing to each picture and asking the children what the instrument is called in Spanish. If you feel comfortable, ask **¿Qué instrumento es?** (*What instrument is it?*).

Red Flashcards:

#50 (top)	el tambor (*drum*)
#50 (bottom)	la guitarra (*guitar*)
#51 (top)	la trompeta (*trumpet*)
#51 (bottom)	el piano (*piano*)
#52 (top)	la flauta (*flute*)
#52 (bottom)	el violín (*violin*)
#53 (top)	el clarinete (*clarinet*)
#53 (bottom)	la pandereta (*tambourine*)

Introduce the video

Invite the children to listen and watch as **la maestra** visits a music store.

VIDEO LESSON 

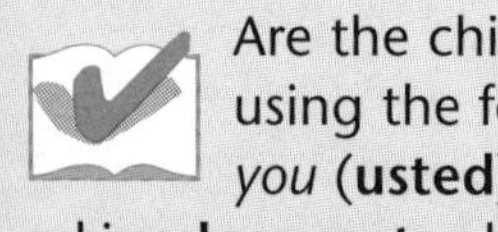

Are the children using the formal *you* (**usted**) when asking **la maestra** how she is: **¿Y usted?** (*And you?*).

1. Greeting the children

La maestra greets the children with **Buenas tardes** (*Good afternoon*) and asks them how they are. Kipper says **Muy contento** (*I'm very happy*); **la maestra** says **Muy bien, gracias, estoy muy contenta** (*Very well, thank you, I'm very happy*). She asks Kipper **¿Qué es esto?** (*What is this?*): **el tambor** (*drum*), **los tambores** (*drums*). Kipper tells her **Toca los tambores** (*Play the drums*).

2. Reviewing the names of the musical instruments

La maestra shows Kipper and the children Red Flashcards of **los instrumentos musicales** and asks **¿Qué instrumento es?** (*What instrument is it?*). She reviews the words **la trompeta** (*trumpet*), **el piano** (*piano*), **el tambor** (*drum*), **la guitarra** (*guitar*), **el clarinete** (*clarinet*), **la pandereta** (*tambourine*), **la flauta** (*flute*), and **el violín** (*violin*).

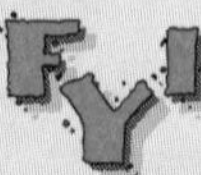

In section 4, Kipper asks **¿Qué son?** (*What are they?*). **La maestra** tells him they are **maracas** (*maracas*) and says **Me gustan las maracas** (*I like the maracas*).

3. Answering the question *¿Qué toca?* (*What is he/she playing?*)

Antonio plays each instrument; **la maestra** asks the children **¿Qué toca?** (*What is he playing?*) and reinforces the children's statement: **Toca** ___ (*He's playing* ___).

4. Playing Latin American instruments

La maestra plays **las maracas** (*maracas*). She explains that many countries have a particular instrument that goes with music typical of the country. Many countries in **Latinoamérica** (*Latin America*), including those in the Caribbean, South America, and Mexico, use **las maracas** (*maracas*). Kipper and LeeAnn dance as Antonio plays **los instrumentos latinos** (*Latin instruments*): **las maracas** (*maracas*), **la pandereta** (*tambourine*), and **las claves** (*a percussion instrument that looks like two sticks*).

LANGUAGE ACROSS THE CURRICULUM

Mention to the children that **la guitarra** came to the Latin American countries from Spain. Other instruments and rhythms in Latin America, particularly in the Caribbean countries, stem from Africa because the Caribbean was a destination for many Africans who were enslaved. The marimba, the steel drum, and maracas are all instruments resulting from the unique combinations of cultures in the Caribbean.

5. Visiting a music store

La maestra visits a music store and talks with musicians about each instrument. Some of the conversation follows.

Aquí estoy en una tienda.	*Here we are in a store.*
Es una tienda de música con muchos instrumentos musicales.	*It's a music store with many musical instruments.*
Me gusta la música y me gustan los instrumentos musicales.	*I like music and I like musical instruments.*
Me gustan los tambores.	*I like the drums.*
Me gusta la guitarra.	*I like the guitar.*
Me gusta escuchar la música de la guitarra.	*I like to listen to guitar music.*
Me gusta tocar el piano.	*I like to play the piano.*
Me gusta la trompeta/ el violín/la flauta/ la pandereta.	*I like the trumpet/ the violin/the flute/ the tambourine.*

6. Playing *¿Qué instrumento es?* (*What instrument is it?*)

La maestra reviews each instrument that Antonio plays and then asks the children **¿Qué instrumento es?** (*What instrument is it?*) as she points to pictures of Antonio playing an instrument.

Los instrumentos musicales:

el clarinete	*clarinet*	el tambor	*drum*
la flauta	*flute*	los tambores	*drums*
el piano	*piano*	la trompeta	*trumpet*
la guitarra	*guitar*	el violín	*violin*
la pandereta	*tambourine*		

7. Closing

Kipper plans to be a musician. He says **Voy a ser músico** (*I'm going to be a musician*). **La maestra** wishes everyone **¡Buena suerte!** (*Good luck!*). She and Kipper say **Adiós** (*Good-bye*).

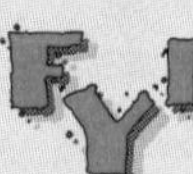

Me gusta and **Me gustan** mean *I like.* **Me gusta** is used when speaking about one thing, e.g., **Me gusta la guitarra** (*I like the guitar* or literally, *the guitar is pleasing to me*). **Me gustan** is used when speaking about more than one thing, e.g., **Me gustan los tambores** (*I like the drums* or literally, *the drums are pleasing to me*).

La maestra describes some of the instruments. **El violín es muy bonito.** (*The violin is very pretty.*) **La flauta es muy bonita.** (*The flute is very pretty.*) Note that if an adjective ends in an **-o**, the **o** changes to **a** if used to describe a feminine noun.

In saying good-bye to the children, Kipper uses the diminutive of **amigos** (*friends*) when he says **Adiós amiguitos** (*Good-bye little friends*). The diminutive is formed by adding **-ito(s)** or **-ita(s)**. It is used with names or nouns to indicate affection or to address a young child.

After viewing the video, praise the children for their good listening and watching skills.

Activity Lesson

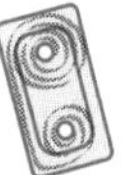

Activity 14A: What instruments do you hear?

Materials: Cassette player; Activity Cassette 1, Side B.

Tell the children they are going to listen to some music. They should listen carefully and try to name what instruments they heard. Possible instruments:

las claves	(*a percussion instrument much like small sticks*)
la guitarra	*guitar*
las maracas	*maracas*
la pandereta	*tambourine*
el piano	*piano*
la trompeta	*trumpet*

Activity 14B: Which instrument is that?

Materials: Cassette player; Activity Cassette 1, Side B.

Preparation: Write the names of the musical instruments on the board in the following order:

la trompeta	___
el piano	___
la flauta	___
los tambores	___
la guitarra	___
el violín	___

Tell the children **la maestra** is going to say *musical instrument* plus a number from one to six, e.g., **instrumento musical número uno** (*musical instrument number one*). Then the children will hear one of the six instruments listed on the board being played. You will stop the tape when directed by **la maestra** and children should tell you what number to write on the board next to the word for the musical instrument they just heard. The instruments will not be played in the order listed on the board.

Answers for Activity 14B:

la trompeta	3
el piano	6
la flauta	5
los tambores	1
la guitarra	4
el violín	2

Activity 14C: Make connections

Materials: A map of the world.

Lead the class in a discussion of the connection between Africa and the Caribbean. Begin by locating on the world map Africa, the Caribbean Sea, and the Caribbean countries (Mexico, Guatemala, Honduras, Nicaragua, Costa Rica, Panama, Colombia, Venezuela, Cuba, Dominican Republic, Puerto Rico). Talk about the slave trade and its cultural influence on the Caribbean countries, which brought over different types of music and dances. The children may find it interesting that percussion instruments such as **las claves** (sticks), **la conga**, and **los bongós** (types of drums) are originally from Africa. You may also wish to mention the many Spanish-speaking Afro-Caribbean natives residing there today.

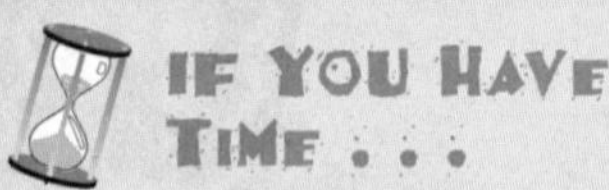

Materials: A cassette with **merengue** music of the Caribbean; cassette player.

Play the tape and explain that **merengue** music comes from the Dominican Republic and that it is played in the Caribbean islands as well as in northern parts of South America. Ask the children what instruments they hear in the music (drums, saxophones, big metal scrapers).

CLOSING

Tell the children that Spanish class is finished for today. In the next lesson they will review the words for entertainment appliances.

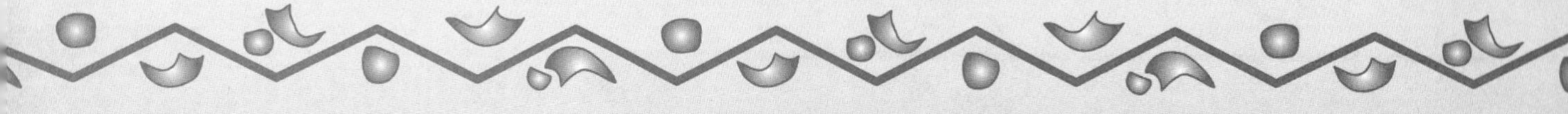

Lesson 15

Materials to gather

- VCR and Video Lesson 15 on Tape 5
- Cassette player
- Song Cassette
- Overhead projector
- Pictures of a CD player and CDs from newspaper or magazine ads
- Laminating machine
- Red Flashcards 25, 26, 30
- Two blank transparencies
- Blackline Master 15A (musical instruments)
- Two fly swatters
- Blackline Master 15B ("The Vowel Tree Song")

Objectives

Language

- Comprehend an extended conversation about entertainment appliances
- Hear the names of several entertainment appliances
- Understand a conversation about musical instruments
- Listen to descriptions of several musical instruments

Culture

- Notice that friends in Spanish-speaking countries often greet by kissing each other on both cheeks

Review

- Greet the teacher and ask him or her how he or she is
- Recognize and name the musical instruments

Vocabulary

Tengo hambre.	*I'm hungry.*
la televisión	*television*
el radio	*radio*
la grabadora	*cassette player*
la cinta	*cassette*
el tocadiscos CD	*compact disc (CD) player*
el disco CD	*CD*

Warm-up

Greet the children and ask them how they are. Divide the class into pairs and tell them to greet each other and ask each other how they are—this time in Spanish. Tell them to be sure to use the greeting appropriate to the time of day and to use the familiar form of *you* (**tú**) in talking to one another (**P1** = Partner 1, **P2** = Partner 2):

P1: Buenos días (Buenas tardes), ___.	*Good morning (Good afternoon), ___.*
P2: Buenos días (Buenas tardes), ___.	*Good morning (Good afternoon), ___.*
P1: ¿Cómo estás tú?	*How are you?*
P2: Muy bien, gracias. ¿Y tú?	*Very well, thank you. And you?*
P1: Muy bien, gracias.	*Very well, thank you.*

Feeling expressions:

Muy mal.
Very bad.

Así, así.
So-so.

Estoy contento/a.
I'm happy.

Tengo calor.
I'm hot.

Tengo frío.
I'm cold.

Tengo hambre.
I'm hungry.

Tengo miedo.
I'm afraid.

Tengo sed.
I'm thirsty.

Tengo sueño.
I'm sleepy.

Review

Materials: Red Flashcards 25, 26, and 30; your pictures of CD player and CDs; a laminating machine.

Preparations: Paste your pictures of a CD player and CDs to a piece of paper and laminate the picture for use as a Flashcard. Display your Flashcard along with Red Flashcards 25, 26, and 30.

Ask the children what the machines in the Flashcards have in common (one can listen to music on all of them, even the television). Point to the picture of the television and radio and ask the children if they can recall their names in Spanish. Give them a hint that the words are cognates, i.e., they sound similar in English and Spanish—**la televisión** (*television*) and **el radio** (*radio*).

Introduce the video

Invite the children to listen and watch as **la maestra** visits a store with lots of televisions and stereo equipment.

VIDEO LESSON 

1. Greeting the children

La maestra greets the children with **Buenos días** (*Good morning*) and asks them how they are. Kipper says **Estoy contento** (*I'm happy*) and **la maestra** says **Estoy muy contenta** (*I'm very happy*). She reviews **Tengo hambre** (*I'm hungry*) and **Tengo calor** (*I'm hot*) as answers to **¿Cómo estás tú?** (*How are you?*). She asks Kipper **¿Qué tienes?** (*What do you have?*). He responds **Tengo un radio** (*I have a radio*). **La maestra** points out **Es un radio y es una grabadora para la música** (*It's a radio and a cassette player for music*).

2. Visiting an entertainment appliance store

In an appliance store, **la maestra** explains the parts of a stereo system.

la televisión	*television*
el radio	*radio*
la grabadora	*cassette player*
la cinta	*cassette*
el tocadiscos CD	*compact disc (CD) player*
el disco CD	*CD*

Some of her statements follow.

Aquí estoy en la tienda de televisiones.	*Here I am in the television store.*
Hay televisiones pequeñas y hay televisiones grandes.	*There are small televisions and there are large televisions.*
Es una máquina muy interesante porque tiene muchas cosas.	*It's a very interesting appliance because it has many things.*
Escucho la música en el radio.	*I listen to music on the radio.*

3. Visiting a music store

Kipper asks **¿Dónde hay instrumentos musicales?** (*Where are there musical instruments?*). **La maestra** visits a music store. For additional statements, see Lesson 14, Video Lesson, section 5.

Toco el piano.	*I play the piano.*
¡Toca la trompeta!	*Play the trumpet!*
¡Toca el violín!	*Play the violin!*
No es fácil tocar el violín.	*It isn't easy to play the violin.*
¡Toca la flauta!	*Play the flute!*

CROSS-CULTURAL CONNECTIONS

Notice that doña Elena and **la maestra** greet by kissing each other on both cheeks. In Spanish-speaking countries, it is typical for friends (two women or a man and a woman) to greet each other in this manner. In business situations, a handshake is the appropriate greeting.

¡Qué bonita es la flauta! — *How pretty the flute is [sounds]!*

Es un instrumento negro y largo. ¿Qué es? — *It's a long black instrument. What is it?*

¡El clarinete! — *The clarinet!*

¡Qué bonito es el clarinete! — *How pretty the clarinet is [sounds]!*

Vamos a tocar. — *Let's play.*

4. Naming four musical instruments

As Antonio plays **el tambor/los tambores** (*drum/drums*), **la guitarra** (*guitar*), **el piano** (*piano*), and **la trompeta** (*trumpet*), **la maestra** asks **Niños, ¿qué toca?** (*Children, what's he playing?*). She reviews the name of each instrument and then plays a game of **¿Qué instrumento es?** (*What instrument is it?*). She confirms the children's responses by saying **Antonio toca** (*Antonio plays*) and the name of the instrument.

5. Practicing four more musical instrument names

La maestra asks the children **¿Qué toca?** (*What's he playing?*) as Antonio plays **el violín** (*violin*), **la flauta** (*flute*), **el clarinete** (*clarinet*), and **la pandereta** (*tambourine*). She plays another game of **¿Qué instrumento es?** (*What instrument is it?*) and describes some of the instruments.

¿Te gustan los instrumentos musicales? — *Do you like the musical instruments?*

El violín es de color café. — *The violin is brown.*

La flauta es muy larga y muy bonita. — *The flute is very long and very pretty.*

¿De qué color es el clarinete? — *What color is the clarinet?*

El clarinete es negro. — *The clarinet is black.*

Es un instrumento muy bonito y muy importante. — *It is a very pretty and very important instrument.*

Los instrumentos musicales son muy bonitos y muy importantes. — *The musical instruments are very pretty and very important.*

6. Closing

La maestra and Kipper bid the children **Adiós** (*Good-bye*).

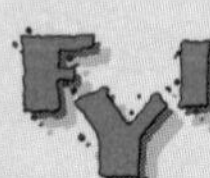

Note that the ending on the adjective **bonito** (*pretty*) is **-a** when the word describes a feminine singular noun, e.g., **la flauta** (*flute*) and **-o** when it describes a masculine singular noun, e.g., **el clarinete** (*clarinet*).

FYI In describing the instruments in section 5, **la maestra** uses forms of the adjectives **bonito** (*pretty*) and **importante** (*important*) with masculine (**el clarinete**) and feminine (**la flauta**) nouns and with the masculine plural noun **los instrumentos musicales** (*musical instruments*). By hearing such sentences over and over, the children will internalize the grammatical pattern without actually learning the rule that the adjective endings change to match the gender and number of the noun.

After viewing the video, praise the children for their good listening and watching skills.

Los instrumentos musicales

Blackline Master 15A

Activity Lesson

Activity 15A: Swat that instrument!

Materials: Blackline Master 15A; a blank overhead transparency; an overhead projector; and two fly swatters.

Preparation: Make an overhead transparency of Blackline Master 15A and project it on a screen or wall.

Tell the children they are going to play a game to see who can recognize the musical instruments the fastest. Ask one child to be the moderator and to read the names of the instruments out loud and clear. Divide the class into two teams and give one child in each team a fly swatter. As the moderator says the name of each instrument, the children with the fly swatters should swat at the instrument projected on the screen or board. The first child to hit the proper picture earns a point for his/her team. Children should take turns being the swatter. Encourage the moderator to call out the instruments in random order.

Musical instruments on Blackline Master 15A:

el violín (*violin*)
la pandereta (*tambourine*)
la trompeta (*trumpet*)
la flauta (*flute*)
el tambor (*drum*)
la guitarra (*guitar*)
el clarinete (*clarinet*)
el piano (*piano*)

Las vocales
(The Vowel Tree Song)
i
e
o
a
u
A, E, I, O, U.
A, mapa.
E, Pepe.
I, Lili.
O, rojo.
U, cucú.
A, E, I, O, U.

Blackline Master 15B

Activity 15B: The vowels in Spanish

Materials: Cassette player; Song Cassette, Side A; Blackline Master 15B; a blank overhead transparency; and an overhead projector.

Preparation: Make a transparency of Blackline Master 15B and project it.

Tell the children they are going to sing **"Las vocales"** (*"The Vowel Tree Song"*), which they learned last year. The lyrics are displayed so that they can follow along. It may be necessary to play the song several times to refamiliarize the children with it or for children new to the program this year to learn it. After singing the song, ask volunteers to pronounce the five words in the song.

Pronunciation of vowels:

A—[ah] E—[eh] I—[ee] O—[oh] U—[oo]

Lyrics:

A, E, I, O, U (4x)
A, mapa.
E, Pepe.
I, Lili.
O, rojo.
U, cucú.
A, E, I, O, U (2x)

Activity 15C: Complete the "mystery words"

Preparation: Write the following words on the chalkboard with blanks for the missing vowels as indicated.

la tr_mpeta	el viol_n
los t_mbor_s	la t_l_visión
la gr_bad_ra	el r_dio

Point to the each word and ask the children what vowel(s) is (are) missing. When you hear the missing vowel, fill it in. Once all words are complete, ask volunteers to pronounce each one.

Answers:

la trompeta (*trumpet*)	el violín (*violin*)
los tambores (*drums*)	la televisión (*television*)
la grabadora (*cassette player*)	el radio (*radio*)

Point out that the letter missing in the word for *violin* is the **i** with an accent. Tell children that the accent is necessary in order to pronounce the word correctly.

CLOSING

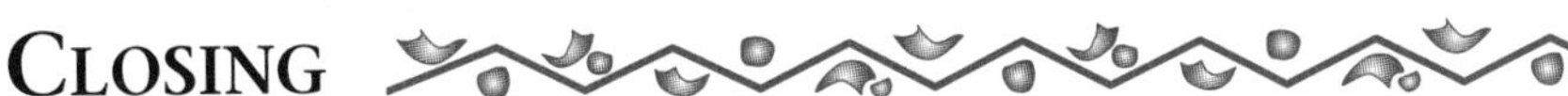

Tell the children that Spanish class is finished for today. In the next lesson they will work on math problems with **la maestra**.

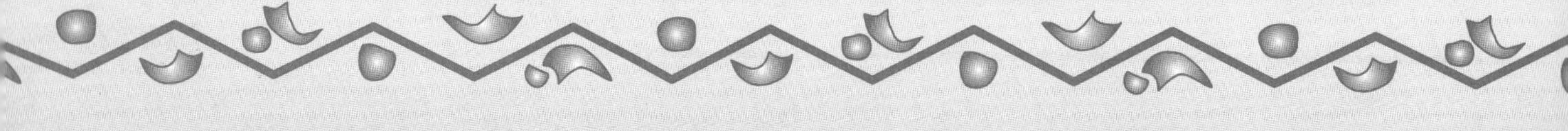

Lesson 16

Materials to gather

- VCR and Video Lesson 16 on Tape 6
- Cassette player
- Activity Cassette 1
- Blackline Master 16A (classroom scene)
- Pencils (one per child)
- Red Flashcards 25, 26, and 30
- Your Flashcard of a CD player and CDs (from Lesson 15, Review)

Objectives

Language

- Comprehend a conversation about entertainment appliances and musical instruments
- Learn the words needed to do addition and subtraction problems
- Answer the question **¿Cuál es tu instrumento musical favorito?** (*Which is your favorite musical instrument?*)

Culture

- Understand that one's voice is a musical instrument

Review

- Identify musical instruments
- Name entertainment appliances
- Count from 10 to 100 by tens
- Answer the question **¿Qué número es?** (*What number is it?*)

Vocabulary

más	*plus*
menos	*minus*
son	*equals*
¿Cuál es tu instrumento musical favorito?	*Which is your favorite musical instrument?*
Mi instrumento musical favorito es ___.	*My favorite musical instrument is ___.*

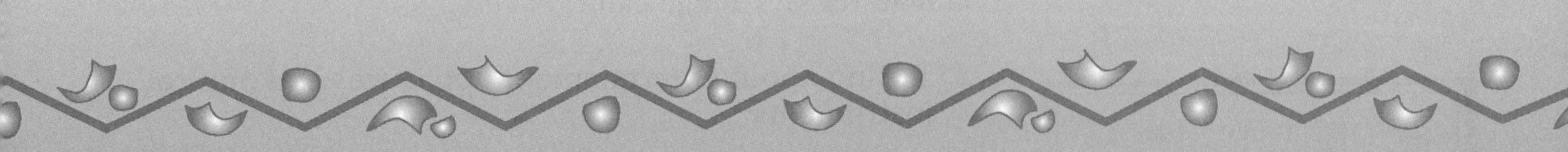

Warm-up

Greet the children and tell them it's time for Spanish class (**la clase de español**). Ask for a volunteer to lead the class in the opening conversation. Suggest the volunteer expand the conversation by asking the class what the date is and what the weather is like. For the months, see Activity 13B. For numbers 1–31, see the sidebar to the Warm-up in Lesson 12. (**V** = volunteer, **C** = class):

V: Buenos días (Buenas tardes), clase.	*Good morning (Good afternoon), class.*
C: Buenos días (Buenas tardes), ___.	*Good morning (Good afternoon), ___.*
V: ¿Cómo estás tú?	*How are you?*
C: Muy bien, gracias. ¿Y tú?	*Very well, thank you. And you?*
V: Muy bien, gracias. ¿Cuál es la la fecha?	*Very well, thank you. What is the date?*
C: El [*number*] de [*month*].	(*Answer will vary*).
V: ¿Qué tiempo hace?	*What's the weather like?*
C: (*Answers will vary.*)	

For weather expressions, see the Warm-up section for Lesson 14.

Review

Materials: Red Flashcards 25, 26, 30; your Flashcard of a CD player and CDs.

As you point to each entertainment appliance, ask children to tell you what it is called in Spanish. If you feel comfortable, ask **¿Qué es esto?** (*What is this?*).

Introduce the video

Invite the children to listen and watch as **la maestra** and Kipper talk about Kipper's stereo system and solve math problems.

Red Flashcards:

#25	la televisión (*television*)
#26	el radio (*radio*)
#30 (top)	la grabadora (*cassette recorder*)
#30 (bottom)	la cinta (*cassette*)

Your Flashcard:

el tocadiscos CD (*CD player*)

el disco CD/los discos CD (*CD/CDs*)

Heritage Speakers

Heritage speakers may use other words for some of the appliances, e.g., rather than **la cinta**, they may use **el cassette** for *cassette*. Tell them how fortunate they are to know more than one word for the same thing.

Video Lesson

1. Greeting the children

La maestra greets the children and Kipper with **Buenas tardes** (*Good afternoon*). She asks them how they are. Kipper answers **¿Cómo estás tú?** (*How are you?*) with **Tengo frío** (*I'm cold*), but **la maestra** says **Tengo calor** (*I'm hot*).

2. Talking about entertainment appliances and musical instruments

La maestra and Kipper look at Kipper's stereo system and listen to music on the radio.

Hay un radio.	*There is a radio.*
Hay una grabadora.	*There is a cassette player.*
La cinta está aquí.	*The cassette is here.*
Vamos a escuchar la música.	*Let's listen to music.*
Son los tambores.	*They are the drums.*
Vamos a escuchar la música del radio.	*Let's listen to the music on the radio.*
Es el piano.	*It's a piano.*
No es la trompeta.	*It's not a trumpet.*

3. Visiting an entertainment appliance store

La maestra shows the children the parts of a stereo system. For some of her statements, see Lesson 15, Video Lesson, section 2. Additional statements follow below.

Mira esta máquina.	*Look at this machine.*
Tiene el radio.	*It has the radio.*
Y también tiene una grabadora.	*And it also has a cassette player.*
En la grabadora uso la cinta.	*In the cassette player I use a tape.*
Tiene el tocadiscos CD.	*It has a CD player.*
El tocadiscos CD usa el disco CD.	*The CD player uses a CD.*
Pongo el disco CD en el tocadiscos CD.	*I put the CD in the CD player.*

4. Identifying musical instruments and entertainment appliances

La maestra points to pictures of Antonio playing various instruments and to pictures of entertainment appliances and asks the children to identify the instruments and appliances.

¿Qué es?	*What is it?*
Es ___.	*It's ___.*

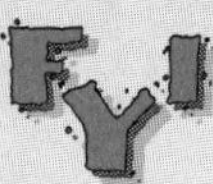

In Level 4 **la maestra** and the puppets carry on lengthier conversations than in earlier levels. If the children are having difficulty following the conversations, replay the video once or twice. Remind them that looking for props and body language as well as listening for familiar vocabulary will help them understand what is being said.

Entertainment appliances:

la cinta	*cassette*
la grabadora	*cassette player*
el radio	*radio*
el televisión	*television*
el tocadiscos CD	*CD player*
el disco CD	*CD*

Musical instruments:

la flauta	*flute*
la guitarra	*guitar*
el clarinete	*clarinet*
la pandereta	*tambourine*
el piano	*piano*
el tambor	*drum*
la trompeta	*trumpet*
el violín	*violin*

5. Practicing the command *Canta* (*Sing*)

La maestra explains that each child possesses a musical instrument, his/her voice (**la voz**), and she tells Lorena **Canta** (*Sing*).

6. Counting by tens to 100

Lorena dances as **la maestra** counts by tens from 10 to 100.

diez	*10*	sesenta	*60*
veinte	*20*	setenta	*70*
treinta	*30*	ochenta	*80*
cuarenta	*40*	noventa	*90*
cincuenta	*50*	cien	*100*

7. Solving math problems

La maestra shows Kipper and the children an addition problem and a subtraction problem and reviews the words for *plus* (**más**), *minus* (**menos**), and *equals* (**son**).

doce	12	cincuenta y cuatro	54
más veinte	+ 20	menos once	– 11
son treinta y dos	32	son cuarenta y tres	43

8. Answering the question *¿Qué número es?* (*What number is it?*)

As Lorena *dances* (**baila**), **la maestra** asks the children to say what number is on the screen, thus counting by tens from 10 to 100.

9. Closing

La maestra asks Kipper **¿Cuál es tu instrumento musical favorito?** (*Which is your favorite musical instrument?*). He replies **la trompeta** (*trumpet*). **La maestra** says **Mi instrumento musical favorito es el piano** (*My favorite musical instrument is the piano*). She asks the children what their favorite instrument is. She reminds children that one can also play music **en la grabadora** (*on the cassette player*) and **en el radio** (*on the radio*). She and Kipper say **Adiós** (*Good-bye*), **Hasta luego** (*See you later*), and **Hasta la vista** (*Until we meet again*).

LANGUAGE ACROSS THE CURRICULUM

When working with addition and subtraction problems with numbers from 1 to 100, encourage the children to say the problems to themselves in Spanish as a way of reinforcing what they have been learning in Spanish class. You may even wish to have them say the problems aloud in Spanish as a group during math lessons.

After viewing the video, praise the children for their good listening and watching skills.

These students and their teacher just heard a concert. They are all thinking about music. What does each person like? Look at the picture and write the name of the instrument or entertainment appliance each person likes. Use the word bank (Palabras) to help you. The first sentence has been done for you.

La maestra Aventura dice: Me gusta el tocadiscos CD.

Pepe dice: ____________

Ana dice: ____________

José dice: ____________

Rita dice: ____________

Luis dice: ____________

Berta dice: ____________

Paco dice: ____________

PALABRAS
la televisión
el piano
la trompeta
el radio
el clarinete
la flauta
el tocadiscos CD
la pandereta
la grabadora
el tambor

Blackline Master 16A

The months:

enero	*January*
febrero	*February*
marzo	*March*
abril	*April*
mayo	*May*
junio	*June*
julio	*July*
agosto	*August*
septiembre	*September*
octubre	*October*
noviembre	*November*
diciembre	*December*

Answers to Activity 16B:

1. 46: cuarenta y seis
2. 25: veinticinco
3. 10: diez
4. 38: treinta y ocho
5. 19: diecinueve
6. 15: quince

ACTIVITY LESSON

Activity 16A: Who likes what?

Materials: Blackline Master 16A; pencils (one per child).

Preparation: Copy and distribute Blackline Master 16A so that each child has one.

Have the children fill in their names and the current date on the top of the page. If necessary, remind them that the months are not capitalized in Spanish. Read the paragraph at the top of the page aloud. Point out that **Maestra Aventura** (*Teacher Aventura*) is thinking about a CD player and that below the picture on the line next to her name it says **Me gusta el tocadiscos CD** (*I like the CD player*). Tell the children to write on the lines what each child likes. Point out that the words for the musical instruments and entertainment appliances appear in the box labeled **Palabras** (*Words*). There are two extra words on the list. Review the answers by asking volunteers to write their responses on the board. Answers (with translations in parentheses) are as follows:

Pepe dice: Me gusta el tambor. (*I like the drum.*)
Ana dice: Me gusta la trompeta. (*I like the trumpet.*)
José dice: Me gusta el piano. (*I like the piano.*)
Rita dice: Me gusta el radio. (*I like the radio.*)
Accept also:
Me gusta la grabadora. (*I like the cassette player.*)
and
Me gusta el tocadiscos CD. (*I like the CD player.*)
Luis dice: Me gusta la grabadora. (*I like the cassette player.*)
Berta dice: Me gusta la pandereta. (*I like the tambourine.*)
Paco dice: Me gusta la televisión. (*I like the television.*)

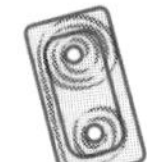

Activity 16B: What number is it?

Materials: Cassette player; Activity Cassette 1, Side B.

Preparation: Write the following numbers on the board in the order listed.

1. 46
2. 25
3. 10
4. 38
5. 19
6. 15

Tell the children that **la maestra** is going to ask them what each of the six numbers is. Choose six volunteers—one for each number. Play Activity 16B, pausing the tape at the harp sound to allow the volunteer time to answer the question **¿Qué número es?** (*What number is it?*). For numbers 1–100, see the Topics and Language Covered section in the Front Matter of this book.

Activity 16C: Cooperative learning—Solve math problems

Preparation: Write the following math problems on the board.

48 + 12 = 60	(Cuarenta y ocho más doce son sesenta.)
29 – 13 = 16	(Veintinueve menos trece son dieciséis.)

Ask the children to guess which word means *plus* (**más**), which word means *minus* (**menos**), and which word means *equals* (**son**). Leave the problems above on the board and write the following ones on the board.

10 + 25 =	10 – 4 =
19 + 15 =	38 – 9 =

Break the class into pairs or small groups. Direct the children to solve the problems and then to take turns saying the problems and their solutions in Spanish.

Answers:

10 + 25 = 35	(Diez más veinticinco son treinta y cinco.)
19 + 15 = 34	(Diecinueve más quince son treinta y cuatro.)
10 – 4 = 6	(Diez menos cuatro son seis.)
38 – 9 = 29	(Treinta y ocho menos nueve son veintinueve.)

CLOSING

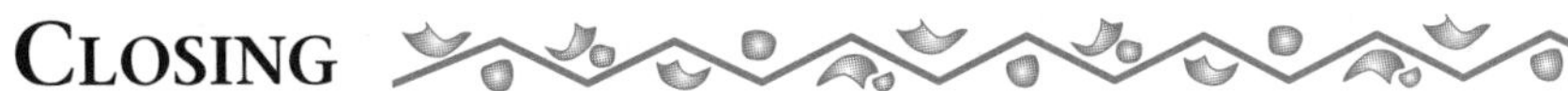

Tell the children that Spanish class is finished for today. In the next lesson they will sing some familiar songs.

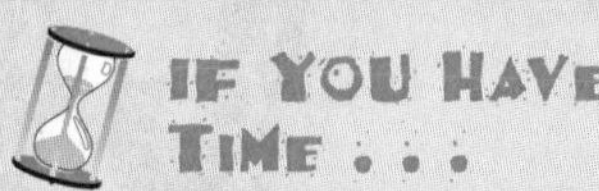

IF YOU HAVE TIME . . .

Allow three or four volunteers each to write a math problem on the board. Have the class solve each problem and then recite the problem in Spanish after it has been solved. Remind the children that they can only use numbers from 1 to 100 and that no problem can have an answer higher than 100.

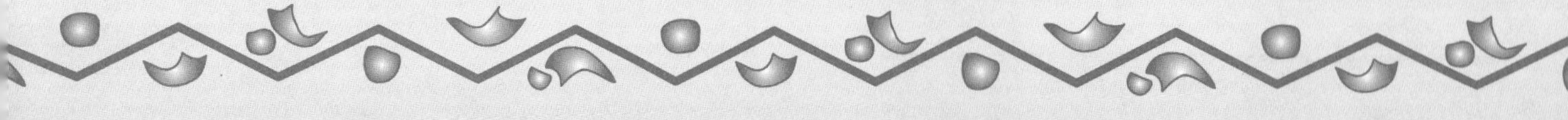

Lesson 17

Materials to gather

- VCR and Video Lesson 17 on Tape 6
- Cassette player
- Song Cassette
- Overhead projector
- Transparency of Blackline Master 2B (20 Spanish-speaking countries)
- Blackline Master 17C (seasons in the Northern and Southern Hemispheres)
- A blank transparency
- A world map

Objectives

Language

- Practice feeling expressions

Culture

- Review how Spanish came to the Americas
- Understand that when Columbus arrived there were people already living in the Americas
- Recall the difference in climate between countries north and south of the equator

Review

- Sing **"La canción de geografía"** (*"The Geography Song"*)
- Sing the "Alphabet Rap"
- Sing **"Las estaciones"** (*"The Seasons"*)
- Express several dates

Vocabulary

Tengo dolor.	*I'm hurt.*
Tengo miedo.	*I'm afraid.*
Tengo sed.	*I'm thirsty.*
Tengo sueño.	*I'm sleepy.*

Warm-up

Tell the children it is time for Spanish class (**la clase de español**). Ask them what the name of the current season is in Spanish. Have them describe the weather typical for the current season by miming the weather: winter—shiver for *it's cold;* spring—smile for *it's good weather;* summer—wipe hand across brow for *it's hot;* fall—make a rushing wind sound for *it's windy.*

Desired responses:

En el invierno hace frío y nieva.	*In winter it's cold and it snows.*
En la primavera hace buen tiempo.	*In spring it's good weather.*
En el verano hace calor.	*In summer it's hot.*
En el otoño hace viento.	*In fall it's windy.*

Review

Materials: The transparency of Blackline Master 2B; overhead projector; a world map.

Project the transparency. Ask for volunteers to go to the map and point out a Spanish-speaking country. If children need help in remembering the names of the countries, mention that they are all listed on the transparency.

Introduce the video

Invite the children to listen and watch as **la maestra** and LeeAnn review many expressions and songs as well as historical and geographical information about the Spanish-speaking countries.

Video Lesson

In this Video Lesson, **la maestra** reviews songs the children have sung this year. Encourage them to sing along with her.

In some areas, seasons are distinguished more by weather characteristics, e.g., "the rainy season" or "the dry season" rather than by our nomenclature of winter, spring, summer, and fall.

HERITAGE SPEAKERS

Ask heritage speakers to talk about the different seasons and months in their countries of origin. Ask them what the geography is like. Is the country mountainous? Are there any big rivers? What are their names? What kind of vegetation grows? What is the weather like during the various seasons?

1. Greeting LeeAnn and the children

La maestra greets LeeAnn and the children with **Buenos días** (*Good morning*) and asks them how they are. LeeAnn says **Estoy contenta** (*I'm happy*).

2. Reviewing feeling expressions

Antonio, **la maestra**, and LeeAnn demonstrate the feeling expressions.

Tengo calor.	*I'm hot.*	Tengo miedo.	*I'm afraid.*
Tengo frío.	*I'm cold.*	Tengo sueño.	*I'm sleepy.*
Tengo hambre.	*I'm hungry.*	Tengo dolor.	*I'm hurt.*
Tengo sed.	*I'm thirsty.*		

3. Explaining the spread of Spanish to the Americas

Using a map of the world, **la maestra** reviews how the Spanish language and culture came to the Americas.

4. Singing the song about the Spanish-speaking countries

La maestra and the children sing **"La canción de geografía"** (*"The Geography Song"*). For song lyrics, see Song 2 in the Song Appendix.

5. Singing the "Alphabet Rap"

LeeAnn tells **la maestra** that the letter **ñ** doesn't exist in the English alphabet. Lorena dances to the "Alphabet Rap," which **la maestra** and the children sing.

6. Reviewing geography and climate differences

La maestra points out that **Norteamérica** (*North America*) is above the equator in the Northern Hemisphere and that **Sudamérica** (*South America*) is below the equator in the Southern Hemisphere and that when it's winter in North America it is summer in South America and vice versa.

7. Singing about the seasons

La maestra and the children sing **"Las estaciones"** (*"The Seasons"*). For song lyrics, see Song 4 in the Song Appendix.

8. Stating the date

Using Gold Flashcards and Number Cards, **la maestra** reviews how the date is stated. She asks LeeAnn **¿Cuál es la fecha?** (*What is the date?*): **el 4 de marzo** (*March 4*) and **el 23 de mayo** (*May 23*).

9. Playing *¿Cuál es la fecha?* (*What is the date?*)

La maestra plays a game of **¿Cuál es la fecha?** (*What is the date?*) with the children. She shows them the following combinations of number cards and month pictures:

el cinco de abril	*April 5*
el diecisiete de mayo	*May 17*
el veintiuno de junio	*June 21*
el treinta y uno de octubre	*October 31*
el once de noviembre	*November 11*
el cuatro de julio	*July 4*

10. Closing

La maestra mentions all the things covered in today's lesson. She and LeeAnn say **Adiós** (*Good-bye*) to the children.

Students may need to be reminded that on **la maestra's** Flashcards the flower bud represents May and the blooming flower represents June.

In the closing, **la maestra** mentions **los países de habla hispana,** which means *the Spanish-speaking countries.*

After viewing the video, praise the children for their good listening and watching skills.

Activity Lesson

Divide the class into groups of 3–4 children. Have each group pick one of the Spanish-speaking countries to "explore." Plan a time for the class to visit your school library or tell the children to visit your local public library to look up the country in encyclopedias. Tell them to find out the number of people that live in the country, the name of the capital city, and one other geographical fact about the country, e.g., highest mountain, longest river, ocean it borders. Perhaps your school subscribes to an online encyclopedia. If so, suggest that children access the encyclopedia on the World Wide Web. You may find the following address useful for this activity: http://www.atlapedia.com/index.html

Allow time in your next Spanish class for the groups to report their findings. Provide a world map for their use.

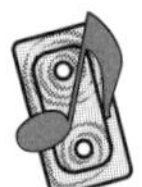

Activity 17A: Sing about the Spanish-speaking countries

Materials: Cassette player; **"La canción de geografía"** (*"The Geography Song"*) on the Song Cassette, Side A; a world map; the overhead transparency of Blackline Master 2B; and an overhead projector.

Project the transparency of Blackline Master 2B and display the world map. Tell the children they are going to review the names and locations of the twenty Spanish-speaking countries by singing *"The Geography Song"* (**"La canción de geografía"**). Ask for two volunteers—one to point to the names of the countries on the transparency and another to point to the countries on the map. For song lyrics, see Song 2 in the Song Appendix.

Activity 17B: The "New World"

Materials: A world map.

Display the world map. Lead the children in a discussion of what the exploration for new lands meant to the explorers and to the native peoples of the land explored. Locate Spain on the map and review how Columbus and his three ships (Niña, Pinta, and Santa María) traveled from Spain to the New World starting in 1492 (over 500 years ago), exploring North and South America and the Caribbean. Mention that they were followed by additional explorers from Spain and other European countries such as England and the Netherlands. Ask the children to identify the "New World" and why the explorers referred to the lands as the "New World" (people in Europe didn't know the lands existed, the lands were "new" to them). Explain that there were native people living in the lands (Aztecs, Incas, etc.). Brainstorm a list of reactions and feelings the native people experienced as the European explorers and then colonists entered their world. Create a second list of the reasons why the explorers undertook the explorations, why the colonists then followed, and what feelings the colonists had as they settled in the "New World."

Activity 17C: Seasons in the two hemispheres

Materials: An overhead projector; a blank transparency; Blackline Master 17C; and a world map.

Preparation: Make a transparency of Blackline Master 17C. Project the transparency and display the world map.

On the world map, point out the equator. Explain to the children that it is an imaginary circle around the earth's surface. It is equidistant from the North and South Poles and perpendicular to the earth's axis of rotation. The area above the equator is called the Northern Hemisphere; the area below it is called the Southern Hemisphere. Have the children point out the countries that are above and below the equator. Using the transparency, point out that our winter months (December, January, and February) are the summer months in the Southern Hemisphere. Do this for each season.

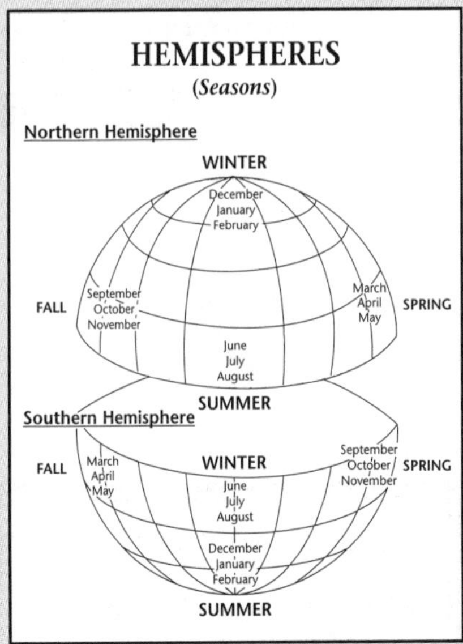

Blackline Master 17C

CLOSING

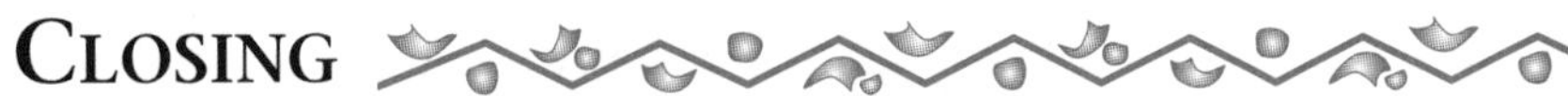

Tell the children that Spanish class is finished for today. In the next lesson the children will view the game show **"Super Repaso"** (*"Super Review"*).

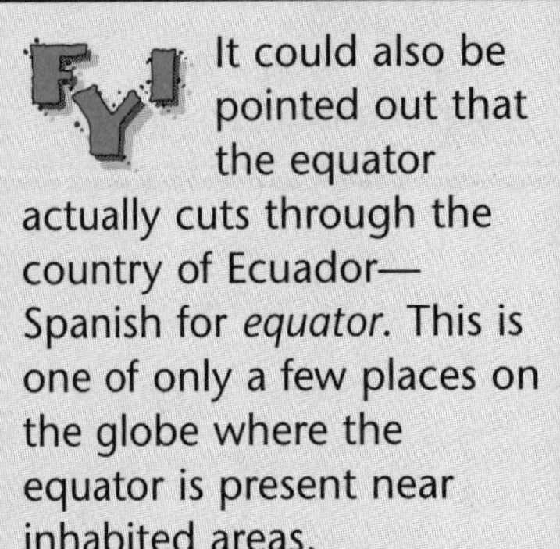

FYI It could also be pointed out that the equator actually cuts through the country of Ecuador—Spanish for *equator*. This is one of only a few places on the globe where the equator is present near inhabited areas.

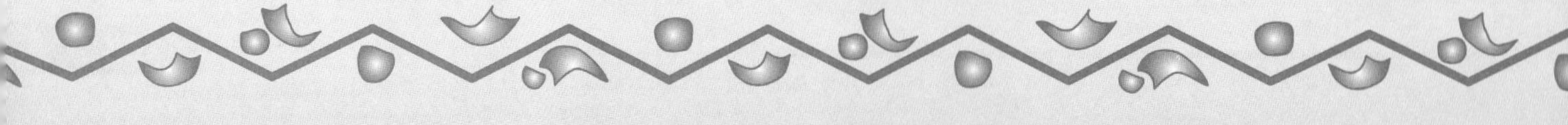

Lesson 18

Materials to gather

- VCR and Video Lesson 18 on Tape 6
- Laminated pink paintbrush from Lesson 4, Review
- Red Flashcards 48 and 53
- Month Picture of **septiembre** (*September*)

Objectives

Language

- Comprehend sustained conversation during a game show

Culture

- Recall the names of two Spanish-speaking countries
- Name a Spanish-speaking country that is an island
- Remember the name of the original Spanish-speaking country

Review

- Answer questions such as **¿Qué clase es?** (*What class is it?*), **¿Qué instrumento es?** (*What instrument is it?*), **¿Cuál es la fecha?** (*What is the date?*), **¿Qué estación es?** (*What season is it?*), **¿De qué color es?** (*What color is it?*), **¿Qué tiempo hace?** (*What's the weather like?*), and **¿Cómo estás tú?** (*How are you?*)

Vocabulary

No new vocabulary is introduced in this lesson.

Warm-up

Greet the children and ask them if they recall the name of the game show Rosco (the wolf), Dora (the cow), Jorge (the giraffe), and Ñico (the toucan) participated in last year (**"Repaso"**—*"Review"*). Tell them that today they are going to watch their new friend Winston play **"Super Repaso"** (*"Super Review"*) with some other contestants.

Review

In preparation for the game show, have the children brainstorm questions that are likely to be asked on the show. If necessary, give them hints, e.g., write a number on the chalkboard and ask them how they would ask what number it is in Spanish, or hold up one of the colored paintbrushes and ask how they would ask what color something is. Possible questions follow.

¿Qué número es?	*What number is it?*
¿De qué color es?	*What color is it?*
¿Cómo estás tú?	*How are you?*
¿Cómo te llamas tú?	*What is your name?*
¿Cómo se llama?	*What's his/her name?*
¿Qué es esto?	*What is this?*
¿Qué mes es?	*What month is it?*
¿Qué estación es?	*What season is it?*
¿Cuál es la fecha?	*What is the date?*
¿Qué clase es?	*What class is it?*
¿Qué instrumento [musical] es?	*What [musical] instrument is it?*

Introduce the video

Invite the children to listen and watch as Winston plays **"Super Repaso"** (*"Super Review"*).

VIDEO LESSON

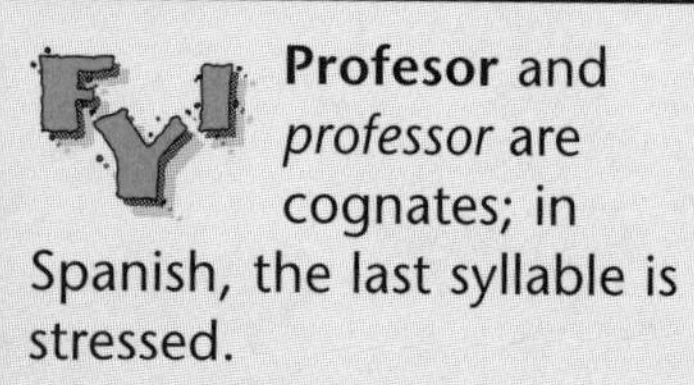

Profesor and *professor* are cognates; in Spanish, the last syllable is stressed.

1. Welcoming everyone to *"Super Repaso"* (*"Super Review"*)

Profesor Correctísimo (*Professor Most Correct*), the host of the game show **"Super Repaso,"** greets everyone—**Buenos días a todos y bienvenidos** (*Good morning everyone and welcome*). He introduces the teams—**el equipo Rojo** (*team Red*) and **el equipo Verde** (*team Green*) and explains that in the game there will be two questions per category.

2. Playing Round One of *"Super Repaso"*

	Questions	Answers
1.	¿Qué clase es? (*What class is it?*)	la geografía (*geography*) las matemáticas (*math*)
2.	¿Qué instrumento es? (*What instrument is it?*)	la trompeta (*trumpet*) el piano (*piano*)
3.	¿Cuál es la fecha? (*What is the date?*)	el catorce de febrero (*Feb. 14*) el veintiuno de enero (*Jan. 21*)
4.	¿Qué tiempo hace? (*What is the weather like?*)	Hace frío. (*It's cold.*) Hace viento. (*It's windy.*)
5.	¿Cómo estás tú? (*How are you?*)	Estoy enojada. (*I'm angry.*) Estoy contento. (*I'm happy.*)

Profesor Correctísimo (*Professor Most Correct*) shows each team's points: **el equipo Verde tiene treinta** (*team Green has thirty points*) **y el equipo Rojo tiene sesenta** (*and team Red has sixty points*).

6.	Name two countries **de habla hispana** (*Spanish-speaking countries*).	Venezuela y Cuba Puerto Rico y México
7.	¿Qué número es? (*What number is it?*)	setenta y ocho (*68*) cuarenta y dos (*42*)
8.	¿De qué color es? (*What color is it?*)	anaranjado (*orange*) azul (*blue*)
9.	¿Qué estación es?—diciembre, enero y febrero. (*What season is it?—December, January, and February.*)	el invierno (*winter*)
	¿Qué estación es?—junio, julio y agosto. (*What season is it?—June, July, and August.*)	el verano (*summer*)
10.	Name a home appliance for listening to music.	un radio (*radio*) la televisión (*television*)

Profesor Correctísimo shows the final scores of Round One and declares **el equipo Rojo gana** (*team Red wins*) by a score of 140 to 50.

3. Playing Round Two of *"Super Repaso"*

Profesor Correctísimo welcomes viewers to the short round of **"Super Repaso."** After he introduces a new player on **el equipo Verde** (*team Green*), the game begins. (In Round Two, there is only one question per category.)

	Questions	Answers
1.	¿Qué instrumento toca? (*What instrument is he/she playing?*)	los tambores (*drums*)
2.	¿De qué color es? (*What color is it?*)	café (*brown*)
3.	¿Qué es esto? (*What is this?*)	el papel (*paper*)
4.	Name the original Spanish-speaking country.	España (*Spain*)
5.	¿Cuál es la fecha? (*What is the date?*)	el cinco de diciembre (*December 5*)
6.	¿Qué tiempo hace? (*What is the weather like?*)	Hace calor. (*It's hot.*)
7.	¿Qué estación es?—septiembre, octubre, noviembre. (*What season is it?—September, October, November.*)	el otoño (*fall*)
8.	¿Qué número es? (*What number is it?*)	veintinueve (*29*)
9.	¿Cómo estás tú? (*How are you?*)	Tengo hambre. (*I'm hungry.*)
10.	Name a Spanish-speaking country that is an island in the Caribbean.	Cuba

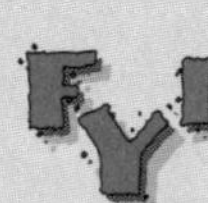

At the end of the game, the host says **Gracias a todos por jugar *"Super Repaso,"*** which means *Thanks to everyone for playing **"Super Repaso."***

Profesor Correctísimo totals up the points: **el equipo Rojo—treinta** (*team Red—thirty*); **el equipo Verde—setenta** (*team Green—seventy*).

4. Closing

La maestra expresses her delight in the game: **¡Qué divertido fue!** (*What fun that was!*). ***"Super Repaso"* es un programa de televisión que es muy divertido.** (*"Super Review" is a television show that is a lot of fun.*) **Me gusta mucho *"Super Repaso"*.** (*I like "Super Review" a lot.*) She bids the children **Adiós** (*Good-bye*).

After viewing the video, praise the children for their good listening and watching skills.

Depending on the size of your class, you may wish to divide the class into four teams, adding team Blue (**el equipo Azul**) and team Red (**el equipo Rojo**). You may also wish to let each team select its own team color name.

Numbers for totaling points:

5	cinco
10	diez
15	quince
20	veinte
25	veinticinco
30	treinta
35	treinta y cinco
40	cuarenta
45	cuarenta y cinco
50	cincuenta

Answers:

1. Tengo hambre. (*I'm hungry.*)
2. ¿Cómo te llamas tú? (*What is your name?*)
3. cincuenta y cinco (*55*)
4. rosado (*pink*)
5. el globo (*globe*) *or* el mapa (*map*)
6. el lápiz (*pencil*) *or* el boli (*pen*)
7. el arte (*art*)
8. las matemáticas (*math*)
9. el verano (*summer*)
10. marzo, abril, mayo (*March, April, May*)

Activity Lesson

Activity 18A: Play *"Super Repaso"* (*"Super Review"*)

Materials: The laminated pink paintbrush from Lesson 4.

Preparation: Write the number 55 on the board but cover it so that the children can't see it. Keep the pink paintbrush out of the children's sight.

Divide the class into two teams—team Purple (**el equipo Morado**) and team Green (**el equipo Verde**). Ask for a volunteer from each team to keep score on the chalkboard for his/her team. Each team should choose a spokesperson. Tell the children you will ask a question. Team members should consult and once they have an answer, the spokesperson will raise his/her hand. You will call on the spokesperson whose hand was raised first. If the answer given is incorrect, you will allow the spokesperson for the opposing team to answer the question. Each correct answer is worth 5 points (**cinco puntos**).

	Questions
1.	What would you say if you had eaten only a banana for breakfast and it is now 6:00 P.M.?
2.	How would you ask someone what his/her name is?
3.	(Uncover the number 55 on the board and ask:) What number is it?
4.	(Hold up the pink paintbrush and ask:) What color is it?
5.	What classroom object would you use to show where Argentina is located?
6.	What classroom object would you use to write?
7.	Which school subject uses paints, brushes, paper, scissors, paste, glue, etc.?
8.	Which school subject uses numbers?
9.	When it is winter in the Northern Hemisphere, what season is it in the Southern Hemisphere?
10.	Name the months of spring (**la primavera**) in the U.S.

Tell the children that Round One of "**Super Repaso**" has ended. Have the scorekeepers total up the points and announce the number of points for his/her team in Spanish. Announce which team is ahead after Round One.

Activity 18B: The final round of *"Super Repaso"* (*"Super Review"*)

Materials: Red Flashcards 48 and 53; Month Picture of **septiembre**.

Preparation: Cover up the top picture on Red Flashcard 48. Keep both Red Flashcards out of sight. On the Month Picture **septiembre**, cover up the word **septiembre**. Write the number 11 on the chalkboard and cover it so the children can't see it.

Tell the class it's time for the final round of "**Super Repaso**" (*"Super Review"*). Ask a different child from each team to be the scorekeeper for this round. Let the children know that in this round, you will be asking only 5 questions and each question is worth 10 points (**diez puntos**). Remind them to choose a spokesperson for their team, to confer about the answer, and then have the spokesperson raise his/her hand to indicate the team is ready to respond. You will call on the child who raised his/her hand first. If the first team's answer is incorrect, the opposing team will have an opportunity to answer.

	Questions
1.	Name an entertainment appliance that you can watch and listen to at the same time.
2.	(Hold up Red Flashcard 48, point to the bottom picture, and ask:) What school subject is this?
3.	(Hold up Red Flashcard 53 and ask:) Name these two instruments.
4.	(Hold the September Month Picture next to the uncovered number 11 on the chalkboard and ask:) What is the date?
	Bonus question:
5.	Name Kipper's favorite musical instrument.

Answers:

1. la televisión (*television*)
2. la geografía (*geography*)
3. el clarinete (*clarinet*) la pandereta (*tambourine*)
4. el once de septiembre (*September 11*)
5. la trompeta (*trumpet*)

Have the scorekeepers total up the points from Round Two and add them to their team's score for Round One. Announce the winning team and write the team's name and members' names on the chalkboard.

Activity 18C: What do you like about Spanish class?

Lead the children in a discussion of what they like about learning Spanish. Do they like learning new ways of saying things? Have they used Spanish outside the classroom—among themselves or with other Spanish speakers? What have they learned new this year in Spanish class (e.g., names of musical instruments and school subjects; names of the 20 Spanish-speaking countries; how Spanish came to the Americas)?

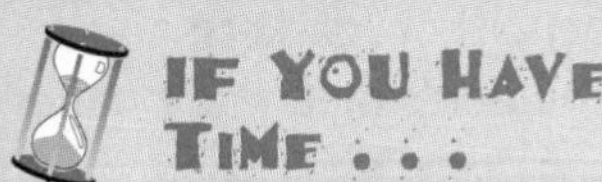

If you had children "explore" a Spanish-speaking country as suggested in the **If you have time . . .** Activity in Lesson 17, have the groups report on their findings.

CLOSING

Tell the children that Spanish class is finished for today. In the next lesson they will learn more words for describing things.

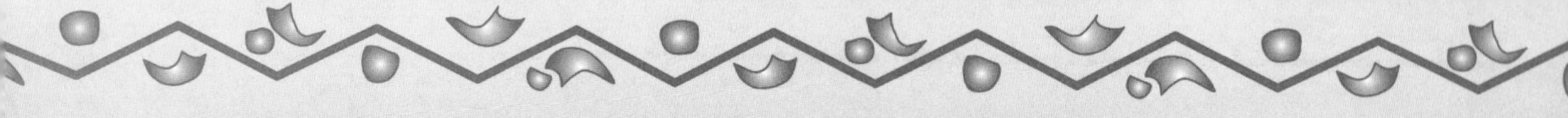

Lesson 19

Materials to gather

- VCR and Video Lesson 19 on Tape 7
- Cassette player
- Activity Cassette 1
- Blackline Master 19A (house and shoe pictures)
- Month Pictures
- Pencils (one per child)
- 11 colored paintbrushes from Lesson 4 Review
- A picture of a flag, a shoe, and a house (or actual items)
- ***Optional materials:*** blank paper; colored pencils or markers; children's dictionary pages

Objectives

Language

- Listen for the different endings on color words
- Learn the adjectives **grande** (*big*), **mediano/mediana** (*medium*), and **pequeño/pequeña** (*small*)
- Understand that the sound at the end of an adjective may change depending on the sound at the end of the word it describes

Culture

- Understand that there is much to learn for the future

Review

- Exchange greetings with **la maestra**
- Review the names of school subjects
- Recall the names of four colors

Vocabulary

grande	*large*
mediano/mediana	*medium (in size)*
pequeño/pequeña	*small*
el payaso	(*male*) *clown*
la payasa	(*female*) *clown*

Warm-up

Materials: The 11 colored paintbrushes from Lesson 4 Review.

Review the color names. Hold up each paintbrush with the color name covered up and have the children say the color. Make it fun by going faster and faster and repeating colors.

amarillo	*yellow*	morado	*purple*
anaranjado	*orange*	negro	*black*
azul	*blue*	rojo	*red*
blanco	*white*	rosado	*pink*
café	*brown*	verde	*green*
gris	*gray*		

Review

Have the children describe various classroom objects in English using the adjectives *big* and *small* and the color words.

Introduce the video

Invite the children to listen and watch as **la maestra** introduces them to some adjectives and explains how these words can change in Spanish.

EN ESPAÑOL

If you feel comfortable, ask **¿De qué color es?** (*What color is it?*) as you review the colors in the Warm-up.

Color names will come up frequently over the next several lessons, so you may wish to put your colored paintbrushes on more permanent display for a few weeks.

You may find it helpful to display the Month Picture that represents the current month, changing it as the months change. Children will often need to fill in the date on a Blackline Master; having the Month Picture with the month's name displayed will help them in spelling the name of the month.

VIDEO LESSON

1. Greeting the children

La maestra greets the children with **Buenos días** (*Good morning*) and asks them how they are. She reviews the feeling expressions **Estoy contento/contenta** (*I'm happy*), **Tengo hambre** (*I'm hungry*); **Estoy enojado/enojada** (*I'm angry*), and **Muy bien, gracias** (*Very well, thank you*).

2. Reviewing school subjects

Pointing to the school subjects on the **Toca el Futuro** (*Touch the Future*) board, **la maestra** reviews vocabulary and mentions what one needs for each subject.

la lectura	*reading*	la música	*music*
la escritura	*writing*	la historia	*history*
las computadoras	*computers*	las matemáticas	*math*
la geografía	*geography*	las ciencias	*science*
el drama	*theater, drama*	el arte	*art*

3. Reviewing four color names

Antonio juggles or plays with items of four colors. The name of each color appears on the screen: **rojo** (*red*), **azul** (*blue*), **morado** (*purple*), and **anaranjado** (*orange*).

4. Using color words to describe objects

La maestra asks Winston **¿De qué color es la camisa?** (*What color is the shirt?*). He responds **Es blanca, roja y azul** (*It's white, red, and blue*). **La maestra** explains that the endings on some of the color words change. They revisit the Spanish class at the high school, where they review colors.

¿De qué color es la bandera española?	*What color is the Spanish flag?*
Amarilla y roja.	*Yellow and red.*
¿Quién sabe de qué color son las letras?	*Who knows what color the letters are?*
Verdes.	*Green.*
¿De qué color es el pizarrón?	*What color is the chalkboard?*
Blanco.	*White.*
¿De qué color son mis zapatos?	*What color are my shoes?*
Negros.	*Black.*
¿De qué color es la puerta?	*What color is the door?*
Amarilla.	*Yellow.*

FYI In talking about the school subjects, **la maestra** uses the following vocabulary:

Para ___ necesito ___.
(*For ___ I need ___.*)

los libros
(*books*)

las letras del alfabeto
(*letters of the alphabet*)

papeles
(*paper*)

lápices
(*pencils*)

bolis
(*pens*)

los países de habla hispana
(*Spanish-speaking countries*)

Estoy triste.
(*I'm sad.*)

colores
(*colors*)

formas
(*forms*)

La maestra emphasizes that **la puerta** (*door*) ends in an **a** sound, so the word for *yellow* ends in an **a** sound instead of an **o** sound (**amarilla**, not **amarillo**): **La puerta es amarilla** (*The door is yellow*). **Zapatos** (*shoes*) ends in an **os** sound, so the word for *black* ends in an **os** sound instead of an **o** sound (**negros**, not **negro**): **Los zapatos son negros** (*The shoes are black*).

5. Introducing new characters

La maestra introduces two clowns and then asks the children the clowns' names.

el payaso Roberto	*(male) clown Roberto*
la payasa Roberta	*(female) clown Roberta*
¿Cómo se llama el payaso/la payasa?	*What is the (male/female) clown's name?*
El payaso/La payasa se llama ___.	*The (male/female) clown's name is ___.*

6. Presenting three new adjectives

Using visuals of different size shoes and houses, **la maestra** introduces three new adjectives and demonstrates how the endings on two of the adjectives change: **mediano** (*medium*) and **pequeño** (*small*) end in the same sound as **zapato** (*shoe*); **mediana** and **pequeña** end in the same sound as **casa** (*house*). **Grande** (*big*) doesn't change when describing a singular noun. She asks the children to describe the shoes and the houses.

grande	*big*
mediano/mediana	*medium*
pequeño/pequeña	*small*
¿Cómo es el zapato?	*What is this shoe like?*
Es grande. / El zapato es grande.	*It's large. / The shoe is large.*
Es mediano. / El zapato es mediano.	*It's medium. / The shoe is medium.*
Es pequeño. / El zapato es pequeño.	*It's small. / The shoe is small.*
Todos los zapatos son diferentes.	*All the shoes are different.*
¿Cómo es la casa?	*What is the house like?*
La casa es grande.	*The house is large.*
La casa es mediana.	*The house is medium.*
La casa es pequeña.	*The house is small.*

7. Closing

La maestra says **Adiós** (*Good-bye*) to the children.

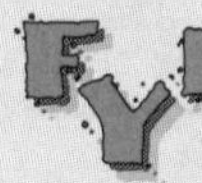

In explaining the agreement of nouns and adjectives, **la maestra** does not mention the gender of nouns in Spanish. Her approach is simply to show the children how to change the endings of the adjectives to match the endings of the nouns. Masculine singular nouns generally end in –**o**, as do adjectives describing them. Masculine plural nouns generally end in **-os** and adjectives describing them also end in **-os**. Feminine singular nouns and adjectives describing them end in **-a**; feminine plural nouns and their adjectives end in **-as**. Adjectives ending in **-e**, e.g., **grande** (*big*), **verde** (*green*), do not have distinct masculine or feminine forms; with plural nouns they add an **-s**—**las letras son verdes** (*the letters are green*) or **los zapatos grandes** (*the big shoes*).

After viewing the video, praise the children for their good listening and watching skills.

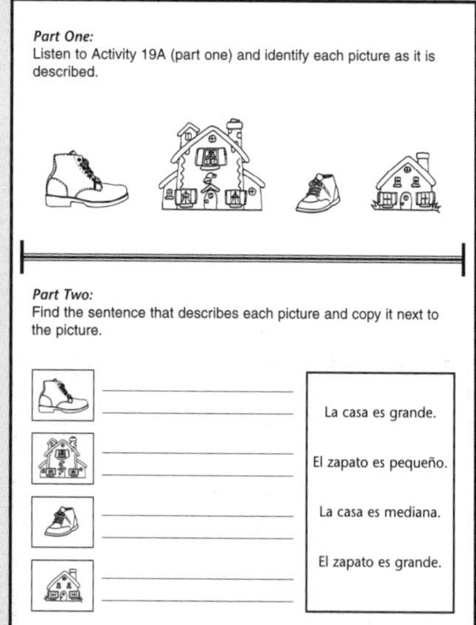

Part One:
Listen to Activity 19A (part one) and identify each picture as it is described.

Part Two:
Find the sentence that describes each picture and copy it next to the picture.

La casa es grande.
El zapato es pequeño.
La casa es mediana.
El zapato es grande.

Blackline Master 19A

19A: Part Two Answers
(in order of drawings):

large shoe: El zapato es grande.
large house: La casa es grande.
small shoe: El zapato es pequeño.
medium house: La casa es mediana.

Activity Lesson

Activity 19A: Match the picture to the sentence

Materials: Cassette player; Activity Cassette 1, Side B; Blackline Master 19A; Month Pictures; and pencils (one per child).

Preparation: Duplicate and distribute Blackline Master 19A, one copy per child. Display the Month Pictures.

Have the children write their names and the date on their copies of Blackline Master 19A. If they need help spelling the month, refer them to the Month Pictures you have displayed. Refer the children to Part One of Blackline Master 19A. Point to the large shoe and ask them what it is (a shoe). Ask them how it differs from the other shoe in Part One (it's big, the other is small). Tell them **la maestra** is going to describe each picture in Part One. They are to locate the picture she is describing and point to it. She will say each statement twice. Children should point first to the small shoe, then the large house, the large shoe, and finally the medium house.

After **la maestra** has described the four pictures in Part One, turn off the tape and refer the children to Part Two. Tell them to find the sentence in the box at the lower right corner and write it on the line next to the picture that it describes.

Activity 19B: Make comparisons

Preparation: Write the following pairs of English phrases and their Spanish equivalents on the board:

red shoe	zapato rojo
big house	casa grande
orange cat	gato anaranjado
small shirt	camisa pequeña

Ask the children to identify the adjectives and the nouns. Have them compare the position of the adjectives and nouns in English versus Spanish (in English the adjectives precede the nouns; in Spanish the adjectives follow the nouns). Encourage the children to look at these language differences in a positive manner. If you have speakers of other languages in your class, ask them how they would say *red shoe* or *orange cat* in their languages and whether the adjective comes before or after the noun or is combined with the noun.

Activity 19C: Which adjective goes with the noun?

Materials: A picture of a flag, a shoe, and a house (or actual items).

Preparation: Write the following words and adjectives on the board.

la bandera	rojo amarilla	la casa	grande pequeño
el zapato	negro blanca		

Review the meanings of the nouns with the children by pointing to the item or a picture of the item in the classroom: **la bandera** (*flag*), **el zapato** (*shoe*), **la casa** (*house*). Review the names of the colors by pointing to each word and asking volunteers to point to something in the room that is the color: **rojo** (*red*), **amarilla** (*yellow*), **negro** (*black*), **blanca** (*white*). Point to the word **grande** (*big*) and ask them what the word means. Demonstrate it by spreading your arms wide. Point to the word **pequeño** (*small*) and ask them what the word means. Demonstrate it by holding your hands close together.

Tell the children to choose from each pair of colors the one that appropriately describes the noun. Remind them that if the noun ends in an **a** sound, the adjective will end in an **a** sound; and that if the noun ends in an **o** sound, the adjective will end in an **o** sound. Tell them too that if the adjective ends in an **e**, it does not change. Children should have chosen: **la bandera amarilla** (*the yellow flag*), **el zapato negro** (*the black shoe*), and **la casa grande** (*the large house*). If necessary, explain that the word for *small* (**pequeño**) here can't be right because it ends in an **o** sound and can't be used to describe the word for house (**casa**), which ends in an **a** sound. The word for *big* (**grande**) ends in an **-e**, which doesn't change so it can go with the word for *house* (**casa**).

DICTIONARY

Materials: The eleven colored paintbrushes from Lesson 4; paper (one or more sheets per child); markers or colored pencils; and children's dictionary pages.

Display the colored paintbrushes. Have the children choose three of their favorite colors and make dictionary pages for them by writing the first letter of the color word on the top of the paper and the color name underneath it—all in the appropriate color. Some children may already have a page on which to write their favorite color names, e.g., an **A** page for **azul** (*blue*). If the children need help spelling the color names, refer them to the colored paintbrushes. Have them order the new pages within their other pages.

CLOSING

Tell the children that Spanish class is finished for today. In the next lesson they will see more of the clowns.

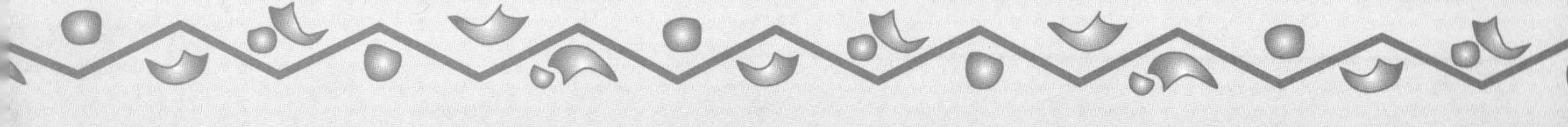

Lesson 20

Materials to gather

- VCR and Video Lesson 20 on Tape 7
- Cassette player
- Activity Cassette 1
- Song Cassette
- Transparency of Blackline Master 1A (song **"Español para ti"**)
- Overhead projector
- Blackline Master 20B (draw a house)
- Month Pictures
- Pencils
- Markers or colored pencils

Objectives

Language

- Learn additional adjectives—**alto/alta** (*tall*) and **bajo/baja** (*short*)
- Demonstrate understanding of the changes in adjective endings depending on the ending of the nouns

Culture

- Remember that boys say **estoy enojado** and girls say **estoy enojada**

Review

- Exchange greetings with **la maestra**
- Answer the question **¿Qué es?** (*What is it?*)
- Use the adjectives **grande** (*big*), **mediano/mediana** (*medium*), and **pequeño/pequeña** (*small*) to describe shoes and houses
- Answer the question **¿Cómo es?** (*What's it like?*)

Vocabulary

alto/alta	*tall*
bajo/baja	*short*

Warm-up

Greet the children and ask them how they are. Hold your arm and moan a bit and ask them how you would say in Spanish how you are feeling (**Tengo dolor**—*I'm hurt*).

Feeling expressions:

Muy mal.	*Very bad.*	Tengo dolor.	*I'm hurt.*
Así, así.	*So-so.*	Tengo hambre.	*I'm hungry.*
Estoy contento/a.	*I'm happy.*	Tengo miedo.	*I'm afraid.*
Tengo calor.	*I'm hot.*	Tengo sed.	*I'm thirsty.*
Tengo frío.	*I'm cold.*	Tengo sueño.	*I'm sleepy.*

Review

Preparation: Make three simple drawings of a house on the chalkboard—one large house, one medium-sized house, and one very small house.

Ask the children what you've drawn (**la casa**—*house*, **tres casas**—*three houses*, **las casas**—*houses*). Then pointing to the large house, ask what new word they would use to describe the house (**grande**). Do the same for the medium-sized house (**mediana**) and the small house (**pequeña**).

Introduce the video

Invite the children to listen and watch as **la maestra** introduces two more words used to describe.

EN ESPAÑOL

If you feel comfortable, use **Buenos días, niños** (*Good morning, children*) or **Buenas tardes, niños** (*Good afternoon, children*), **¿Cómo estás tú?** (*How are you?*).

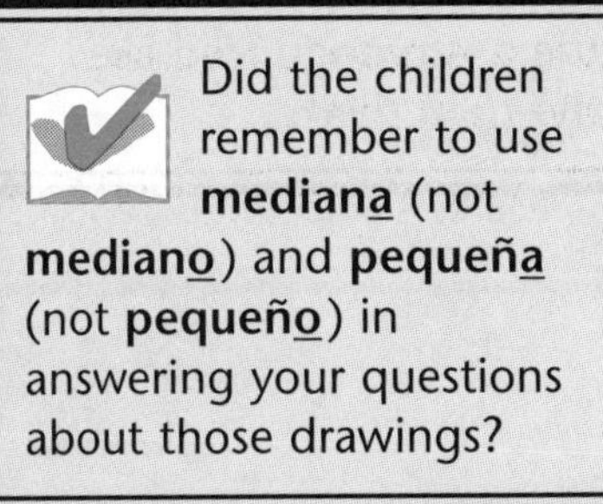

Did the children remember to use **mediana** (not **mediano**) and **pequeña** (not **pequeño**) in answering your questions about those drawings?

Video Lesson

1. Greeting Winston and the children

La maestra greets the children with **Buenos días** (*Good morning*) and asks them how they are. Winston says **Estoy enojado porque tengo hambre** (*I'm angry because I'm hungry*). **La maestra** mentions that Winston said **enojado** because he is a boy.

2. Reviewing feeling expressions

La maestra tells the children to listen carefully to the endings on the words **contento** (*happy*), **enojado** (*angry*), and **triste** (*sad*). Lorena dances as **la maestra** asks **¿Cómo está Lorena?** (*How is Lorena?*) and describes how Lorena is feeling: **Está enojada** (*She is angry*), **Está contenta** (*She is happy*), **Está triste** (*She is sad*). **La maestra** reviews the fact that **triste** (*sad*) doesn't end in an **a** or **o** sound so it doesn't change, but **contento** changes to **contenta** for a girl.

FYI In most Spanish-speaking countries, the letter **z** is pronounced like a soft English *s* in the word *saddle*—this is how **la maestra** pronounces it. In most of Spain, however, the **z** is pronounced like the *th* in *think*.

3. Describing the shoe and the house

Using visuals to cue the children's answers, **la maestra** asks them to describe the shoe and the house. She reminds them that **rojo** ends in an **o** sound so its ending will change to an **-a** if the noun ends in an **a** sound but that **verde** (*green*) and **azul** (*blue*) don't change.

¿Qué es?	*What is it?*
Es el zapato.	*It's the shoe.*
¿Cómo es el zapato?	*What is the shoe like?*
Es pequeño.	*It's small.*
¿De qué color es?	*What color is it?*
Es azul.	*It's blue.*
Es la casa.	*It's the house.*
¿Cómo es la casa?	*What's the house like?*
Es pequeña.	*It's small.*

4. Reviewing two commands

La maestra tells the children **Dibuja una casa grande** (*Draw a big house*). Antonio follows the commands when doña Elena tells him **Dibuja** (*Draw*) and **Borra** (*Erase*).

La maestra tells the children **Dibuja un zapato pequeño** (*Draw a small shoe*). She reviews the descriptions of the shoes: **¿Cómo es el zapato?** (*What is the shoe like?*), **Es grande** (*It's big*), **Es mediano** (*It's medium*), and **Es pequeño** (*It's small*). She asks the children **¿Tienes un zapato pequeño, grande o mediano?** (*Do you have a small, large, or medium shoe?*).

5. Introducing two more adjectives

La maestra reintroduces **el payaso Roberto** (*the* [*male*] *clown Roberto*) and **la payasa Roberta** (*the* [*female*] *clown Roberta*). She presents the adjectives **alto/alta** (*tall*) and **bajo/baja** (*short*).

El payaso es alto.	*The (male) clown is tall.*
Roberto es alto.	*Roberto is tall.*
La payasa es alta.	*The (female) clown is tall.*
Roberta es alta.	*Roberta is tall.*
El payaso es bajo.	*The (male) clown is short.*
La payasa es baja.	*The (female) clown is short.*
Los payasos son bajos.	*The clowns are short.*

6. Asking the children to describe the clowns

La maestra shows the children pictures of clowns and asks them questions.

¿Cómo es el payaso?	*What is the (male) clown like?*
Es bajo.	*He's short.*
Es alto.	*He's tall.*
¿Cómo es la payasa?	*What is the (female) clown like?*
Es baja.	*She is short.*
Es alta.	*She is tall.*

7. Reviewing the adjectives

Describing the shoes, houses, and clowns, **la maestra** reviews the adjectives.

La payasa es baja.	*The (female) clown is short.*
El payaso es alto.	*The (male) clown is tall.*
La casa es grande.	*The house is large.*
La casa es mediana.	*The house is medium.*
La casa es pequeña.	*The house is small.*
El zapato es grande.	*The shoe is large.*
El zapato es mediano.	*The shoe is medium.*
El zapato es pequeño.	*The shoe is small.*

8. Closing

La maestra and Winston say **Adiós** (*Good-bye*) and **Hasta luego** (*See you later*) to the children.

FYI When both male and female clowns are meant, the masculine plural form of the noun is used and the ending on the adjective changes to match it: **Los payasos son bajos** (*The clowns* [*both male and female*] *are short*). Context will make it clear whether just males or a combination of males and females are meant.

After viewing the video, praise the children for their good listening and watching skills.

EN ESPAÑOL

At the end of the song, **la maestra** says **¡Viva! ¡Viva! ¡Viva! Español para ti. ¡Viva!** is a cheer much like *Hurray!* Explain this to the children and then use it when the children have done something well in a class, a school event, or on the playground.

Part One:
Listen to Activity 20B. Draw a house. Then choose a word from the word bank that describes your house and complete the sentence. Read your sentence out loud.

PALABRAS: grande, mediana, pequeña

Mi casa es ________________.

Part Two:
Find the word that describes each picture and complete the sentences. Read your sentences out loud.

Los payasos son ________________.
La payasa es ________________.
El zapato es ________________.
Las casas son ________________.
Las payasas son ________________.

PALABRAS: pequeño, bajas, grandes, alta, bajos

Blackline Master 20B

ACTIVITY LESSON

Activity 20A: Sing a familiar song

Materials: Cassette player; Song Cassette, Side A; the overhead transparency of Blackline Master 1A ("**Español para ti**"); and an overhead projector.

Project the overhead transparency of Blackline Master 1A. Tell the children they are going to sing a familiar song. Play the song, drawing their attention to the lyrics projected on the screen or wall if they are having difficulty remembering them. Encourage the children to make the trilling **r** sound that **la maestra** makes between verses. Play the song through two times.

Activity 20B: Follow the instructions

Materials: Cassette player; Activity Cassette 1, Side B; Blackline Master 20B; the Month Pictures; and pencils.

Preparation: Copy and distribute Blackline Master 20B to each child. Display the Month Pictures.

Have the children fill in their names and the date on the top of their copies of Blackline Master 20B. Refer them to the displayed Month Pictures if they need assistance in spelling the name of the month. Tell the children to use Part One of their sheet and follow the instructions **la maestra** gives them. **La maestra** tells the children **Dibuja una casa** (*Draw a house*). Stop the tape and allow the children time to complete their drawings. Then have the children complete the sentence underneath their drawings with the appropriate adjective in the word bank (**Palabras**). Ask volunteers to describe their houses by reading their sentences.

Next have the children complete the descriptions of each picture in Part Two of their papers by choosing the correct adjective from the word bank (**Palabras**). Ask volunteers to read their answers aloud.

Part Two Answers (top to bottom):

Los payasos son bajos.	*The clowns are short.*
La payasa es alta.	*The [female] clown is tall.*
El zapato es pequeño.	*The shoe is small.*
Las casas son grandes.	*The houses are large.*
Las payasas son bajas.	*The [female] clowns are short.*

Activity 20C: What color is your house?

Materials: Children's copies of Blackline Master 20B; markers or colored pencils.

Have the children color their houses in Part One of Blackline Master 20B. While they are coloring, write the sentence and color words below on the chalkboard. The English is provided for your information only. Then ask volunteers to describe the color of their houses, using the sentence and color words you've put on the board as a help.

Mi casa es de color ___.

azul	*blue*	gris	*gray*
amarilla	*yellow*	morada	*purple*
anaranjada	*orange*	negra	*black*
blanca	*white*	roja	*red*
café	*brown*	rosada	*pink*
verde	*green*		

CLOSING

Tell the children that Spanish class is finished for today. In the next lesson children will learn more adjectives.

FAMILY CONNECTION

To foster a friendly link between home and school, you may wish to send out Family Letter 2 (found in the Teacher's Resource Book). This letter mentions what the children have learned thus far and what they will be learning in upcoming lessons.

LANGUAGE ACROSS THE CURRICULUM

Use the introduction of the clowns in the Video Lesson to talk with the children about the circus as a kind of theater. Ask them to describe clowns they've seen—how they looked, what they did, what props they used. Have the children be "clowns." A volunteer should say a feeling and the "clowns" should perform it: **Estoy triste** (*I'm sad*), **Estoy enojado/enojada** (*I'm angry*), **Estoy contento/ contenta** (*I'm happy*). Remind the volunteer to call out both the boy and girl forms of the words *angry* and *happy*.

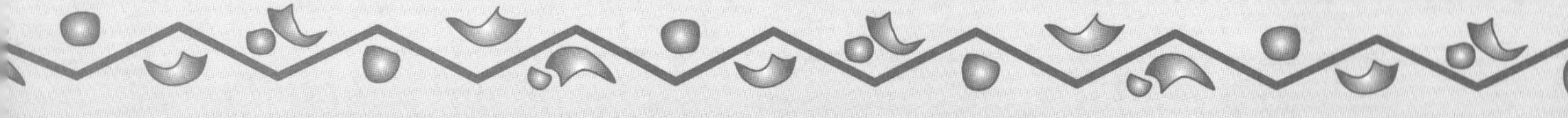

Lesson 21

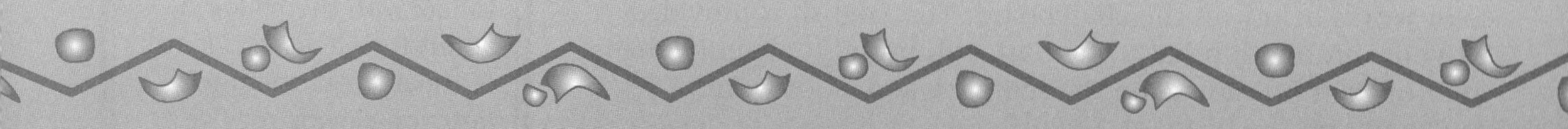

Materials to gather

- VCR and Video Lesson 21 on Tape 7
- Cassette player
- Activity Cassette 1
- Song Cassette
- Blackline Master 21A (6 sentences and clothing items)
- Blackline Master 21C (6 clown pictures and sentences)
- Pencils
- Overhead transparency of Blackline Master 1A (song **"Español para ti"**)
- Overhead projector
- 11 colored paintbrushes from Lesson 4 Review
- Month Pictures
- Crayons, markers, or pencils in these colors: brown, yellow, blue, red, pink, and orange
- ***Optional materials:*** blank paper

Objectives

Language

- Learn two new adjectives—**gordo/gorda** (*fat*) and **delgado/delgada** (*thin*)
- Understand a new exclamatory word—**¡Bravo!** (*Terrific!*)

Culture

- Sing **"Español para ti"** (*"Spanish Is for You, and for Me"*)

Review

- Exchange greetings with **la maestra** with **Buenas tardes** (*Good afternoon*)
- Review the names of four colors
- Use color words to describe clothing
- Answer the question **¿Cómo es ___?** (*What is ___ like?*)
- Use the adjectives **grande** (*big*), **mediano/mediana** (*medium*), and **pequeño/pequeña** (*small*) to describe houses and shoes

Vocabulary

¡Bravo!	*Terrific; Very, very good!*
¡Olé!	*Hurray!*
gordo/gorda	*fat*
delgado/delgada	*thin*

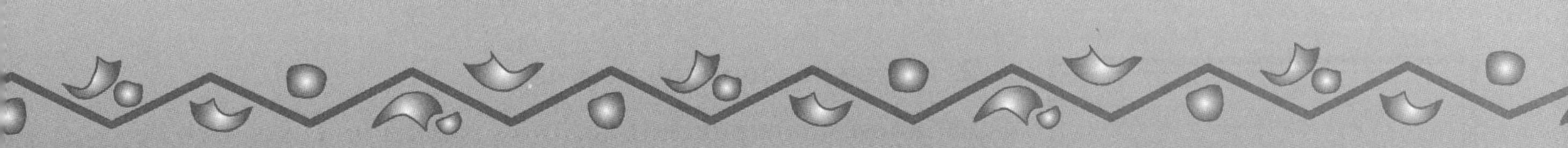

Warm-up

Materials: Month Pictures.

Display the Month Pictures. Greet the children and ask them what the date is in Spanish. If you feel comfortable, say **Hola, niños** (*Hello, children*) and ask **¿Cuál es la fecha?** (*What is the date?*).

el [*number*] de [*month*]

Review

Mime the adjective *short* (**bajo/baja**) by crouching down and ask the children what word they would use to describe your height. Some children may be able to say a full sentence: **El maestro es bajo/La maestra es baja** (*The* [*male*] *teacher/the* [*female*] *teacher is short*). Stand on your tiptoes and ask what word describes your height now—**alto/alta** (*tall*). Some children may be able to make a full sentence: **El maestro es alto/La maestra es alta** (*The teacher is tall*).

Introduce the video

Invite the children to listen and watch as **la maestra** presents more words for describing.

LANGUAGE ACROSS THE CURRICULUM

You may wish to make asking what the date is in Spanish a part of your daily classroom routine. For numbers 1–31, see the Topics and Language Covered section in the Front Matter of this Teacher's Manual.

VIDEO LESSON

1. Greeting the children

La maestra greets the children with **Buenas tardes** (*Good afternoon*) and asks them how they are. She says **Hola** (*Hello*) to LeeAnn. LeeAnn responds to **¿Cómo estás tú?** (*How are you?*) with **Estoy muy contenta** (*I am very happy*).

2. Reviewing four color names

La maestra compliments LeeAnn's sweater and asks her **¿De qué color es el suéter?** (*What color is your sweater?*): **El suéter es rojo** (*red*). Antonio plays with items in **verde** (*green*), **amarillo** (*yellow*), **rosado** (*pink*), and **blanco** (*white*).

3. Describing the colors of clothing

La maestra asks LeeAnn questions about the clowns' clothing. She explains that when describing **el suéter** (*sweater*), **rojo** (*red*) ends in an **-o** because there is only one sweater, but when describing **los zapatos** (*shoes*), **rojos** ends in **-s** because there is more than one shoe. Adjectives that end in **-e** (rather than **-o** or **-a**) don't change when the noun is singular, but if the noun is plural an **-s** is added.

¿De qué color son los zapatos del payaso?	*What color are the (male) clown's shoes?*
Son rojos.	*They are red.*
los zapatos rojos	*red shoes*
¿De qué color es el sombrero de la payasa?	*What color is the (female) clown's hat?*
Es verde.	*It's green.*
¿De qué color son los zapatos?	*What color are the shoes?*
Son verdes.	*They are green.*
¡Bravo!	*Terrific!*
¡Olé!	*Hurray!*

4. Practicing the adjectives *tall* and *short*

La maestra reviews adjectives and how they change their endings to match the sound at the end of the noun they describe. She asks the children to describe the clowns:

El payas<u>o</u> es alt<u>o</u>.	*The (male) clown is tall.*
La payas<u>a</u> es alt<u>a</u>.	*The (female) clown is tall.*
¿Roberto/Roberta es ___?	*Is Roberto /Roberta ___?*
Los payaso<u>s</u> son alto<u>s</u>.	*The clowns are tall.*
El payas<u>o</u> es baj<u>o</u>.	*The (male) clown is short.*
La payas<u>a</u> es baj<u>a</u>.	*The (female) clown is short.*
Los payaso<u>s</u> son bajo<u>s</u>.	*The clowns are short.*

LANGUAGE ACROSS THE CURRICULUM

As children are working in other subject areas—art, science, geography, reading—ask them to identify the color of things in Spanish. For example, ask them to tell you the Spanish word for the color they are going to paint a particular object or the Spanish word for the color of a body of water.

Possession in Spanish is expressed with the preposition **de** (*of*). When the preposition **de** is followed by the masculine definite article **el** (*the*), the two words contract to **del**: **los zapatos <u>del</u> payaso.** The feminine definite article **la** (*the*) does not contract: **el sombrero <u>de</u> <u>la</u> payasa.**

5. Presenting the adjective for *fat*

La maestra introduces the adjective **gordo/gorda** (*fat*). She asks the children to describe the clowns.

¿Cómo es Roberto/Roberta?	*What is Roberto/Roberta like?*
Roberto es gordo.	*Roberto is fat.*
Roberta es gorda.	*Roberta is fat.*
Los payasos son gordos.	*The clowns are fat.*

6. Introducing the adjective for *thin*

La maestra plays a game of **¿Sí o no?** (*Yes or no?*) and introduces the adjective **delgado/delgada** (*thin*).

¿Es gordo el payaso?	*Is the (male) clown fat?*
Sí, el payaso es gordo.	*Yes, the (male) clown is fat.*
No, no es gordo.	*No, he's not fat.*
Es delgado.	*He's thin.*
¿Es gorda la payasa?	*Is the (female) clown fat?*
No, no es gorda.	*No, she is not fat.*
Es delgada.	*She is thin.*

7. Practicing the adjectives for *big, medium,* and *small*

Showing the children pictures, **la maestra** asks them to describe the houses and shoes.

La casa es grande.	*The house is big.*
Es pequeña.	*It is small.*
¿Cómo es el zapato?	*What is the shoe like?*
Es grande.	*It's big.*
Es mediano.	*It's medium.*

8. Singing *"Español para ti"* (*"Spanish Is for You, and for Me"*)

LeeAnn, **la maestra**, and the children sing the song. For song lyrics, see Song 1 in the Song Appendix.

9. Closing

La maestra reviews the adjectives—**alto/alta** (*tall*), **bajo/baja** (*short*), **gordo/gorda** (*fat*), **delgado/delgada** (*thin*), **grande** (*big*), **mediano/mediana** (*medium*), and **pequeño/pequeña** (*small*). She and LeeAnn say **Adiós** (*Good-bye*) and **Hasta luego** (*See you later*) to the children.

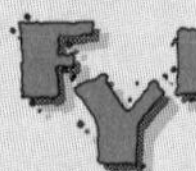

Spanish has two verbs that mean *to be*—**ser** and **estar**—which are used in different situations. **Es** in **¿Cómo es el payaso?** (*What is the clown like?*) is from the verb **ser**. **Está** in **¿Cómo está Lorena?** (*How is Lorena?*) is from the verb **estar**. You needn't concern yourself with when to use one or the other. Throughout ***Español para ti*** you and the children will use them automatically, without having to think about which one to use.

After viewing the video, praise the children for their good listening and watching skills.

Color the clothing items and complete the sentences. Read your sentences out loud and compare your paper with a friend's.

café
1. El sombrero es ________

amarillas
2. Las faldas son ________

verdes
3. Los vestidos son ________

roja
4. La blusa es ________

rosada
5. La camisa es ________

anaranjada
6. La chaqueta es ________

Blackline Master 21A

Activity Lesson

Activity 21A: Color the clothing items

Materials: The 11 colored paintbrushes; Month Pictures; crayons, markers, or pencils in these colors: brown, yellow, blue, red, pink, and orange (one set for each child); and Blackline Master 21A.

Preparation: Display the colored paintbrushes and Month Pictures where the children can see them. Copy and distribute Blackline Master 21A so that each child has a copy.

After the children have filled in their names and the date, have them color each clothing item in the color indicated. If they need help reading the color names, refer them to the color names on the paintbrushes you have displayed. Then have them complete the sentences describing the clothing items by writing in the name of the color as it appears in the drawing of the clothing item. Children may not be able to read the clothing names yet, so feel free to show them that each sentence is aligned opposite the picture of the clothing item being described. Encourage children to read their sentences aloud. Children should have colored the clothing items and completed the sentences as follows:

1. El sombrero es café. (*The hat is brown.*)
2. Las faldas son amarillas. (*The skirts are yellow.*)
3. Los vestidos son verdes. (*The dresses are green.*)
4. La blusa es roja. (*The blouse is red.*)
5. La camisa es rosada. (*The shirt is pink.*)
6. La chaqueta es anaranjada. (*The jacket is orange.*)

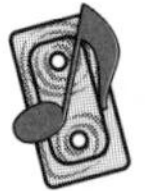

Activity 21B: Sing *"Español para ti"* (*"Spanish Is for You, and for Me"*)

Materials: Cassette player; Song Cassette, Side A; the overhead transparency of Blackline Master 1A; and an overhead projector.

Display the overhead transparency of Blackline Master 1A. Ask for a volunteer to point to the lyrics of the song *"Spanish Is for You, and for Me"* as the class sings it. **La maestra** sings the song through two times. After they have sung with **la maestra**, have them sing without the tape. Maybe they'd like to try singing the song in a round. Divide the class into two groups. Group 1 begins and Group 2 comes in at the end of the second line.

Activity 21C: Match the sentence with the picture

Materials: Cassette player; Activity Cassette 1, Side B; Month Pictures; Blackline Master 21C; pencils (one per child).

Preparation: Copy and distribute Blackline Master 21C so that each child has a copy.

Have the children write their names and the date on the top of their papers, referring to the Month Pictures if they need help spelling the name of the month. Read the instructions at the top of the paper aloud to the children, who are to describe the clown or clowns in each picture by choosing the correct sentence from those at the bottom of the paper. Review with the children which clown pictured is the *male clown* (**el payaso**) and which clown is the *female clown* (**la payasa**). Play Activity 21C, turning the tape off at the harp sound and allowing children time to complete the activity. Then turn the tape back on and tell the children to follow along as doña Elena reads each of the sentences on the bottom of the paper. Finally, check that children matched up the pictures and sentences as follows:

Top row:

left:	6. Los payasos son altos.	(*The clowns are tall.*)
middle:	3. La payasa es baja.	(*The female clown is short.*)
right:	1. La payasa es alta.	(*The female clown is tall.*)

Bottom row:

left:	2. El payaso es bajo.	(*The male clown is short.*)
middle:	5. El payaso es delgado.	(*The male clown is thin.*)
right:	4. La payasa es gorda.	(*The female clown is fat.*)

CLOSING

Tell the children that Spanish class is finished for today. In the next lesson **la maestra** will introduce even more adjectives.

Listen to Activity 21C. These clowns are lined up hoping to get jobs at the circus. The ringmaster must look them over. Look at each clown or pair of clowns and decide which sentence at the bottom of the page best describes each picture. Rewrite the correct sentence under each picture.

1. La payasa as alta.
2. El payaso es bajo.
3. La payasa es baja.
4. La payasa es gorda.
5. El payaso es delgado.
6. Los payasos son altos.

Blackline Master 21C

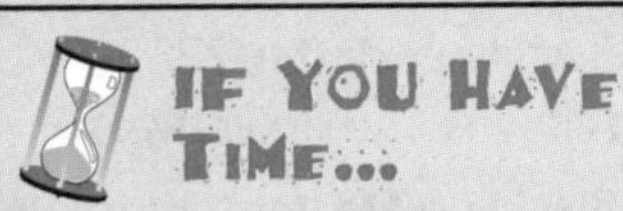

Materials: Blank paper; colored pencils or markers.

Have children draw their own picture of a clown or clowns based on one of the descriptions on Blackline Master 21C. They should write the appropriate description underneath their drawing. Ask volunteers to show the class their drawings and describe them. Perhaps they would like to add the picture to their dictionary under the letter **P** for **el payaso/la payasa** (*clown*).

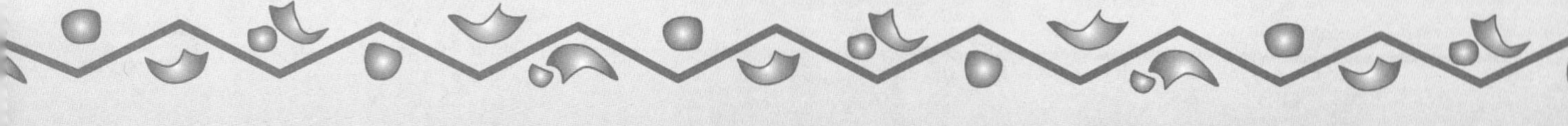

Lesson 22

Materials to gather

- VCR and Video Lesson 22 on Tape 8
- Cassette player
- Activity Cassette 1
- Blackline Master 22A (clowns and adjectives)
- Blackline Master 22B (male clown for coloring)
- Pencils
- Crayons, colored pencils, or markers
- ***Optional materials:*** current Month Picture; blank paper; children's dictionary pages

Objectives

Language

- Learn the adjectives **bonito/bonita** (*pretty*) and **feo/fea** (*ugly*)
- Become reacquainted with **el señor Papa** (*Mr. Potato Head*)
- Use colors in describing three body parts

Culture

- Recall that the sound at the end of some color words changes depending on the noun being modified

Review

- Exchange greetings with **la maestra**
- Review the color names **negro** (*black*), **café** (*brown*), and **gris** (*gray*)
- Review the adjectives **alto** (*tall*), **bajo** (*short*), **delgado** (*thin*), and **gordo** (*fat*)

Vocabulary

bonito/bonita	*pretty*
feo/fea	*ugly*

Warm-up

Greet the children. Ask them what words they've been using in Spanish class to describe things and people: color words, *big* (**grande**), *medium* (**mediano/mediana**), *small* (**pequeño/pequeña**), *tall* (**alto/alta**), *short* (**bajo/baja**), *thin* (**delgado/delgada**), and *fat* (**gordo/gorda**). Allow them to answer with just the English words. Ask them what they have learned about the endings of adjectives in Spanish (the ending changes to match the word being described).

Review

Preparation: Draw two simple stick figures of a male figure on the board—one tall and thin, one tall and fat—and label the figures Roberto 1 and Roberto 2, respectively. Draw two simple stick figures of a female figure—one short and thin, one short and fat—and label them Roberta 1 and Roberta 2, respectively.

Point to each picture and ask the children how they would describe them—Roberto 1: **alto** (*tall*), **delgado** (*thin*); Roberto 2: **alto** (*tall*), **gordo** (*fat*); Roberta 1: **baja** (*short*), **delgada** (*thin*); Roberta 2: **baja** (*short*), **gorda** (*fat*).

Introduce the video

Invite the children to listen and watch as **la maestra** and Winston greet an old friend and describe parts of his body.

Video Lesson

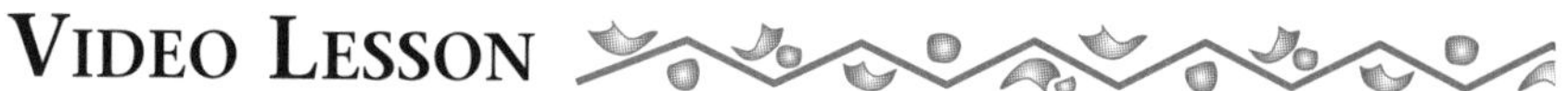

1. Greeting the children

La maestra greets the children with **Buenos días** (*Good morning*) and asks them how they are. She also greets Winston and he says **Estoy contento** (*I'm happy*).

2. Reviewing the adjectives *short* and *tall*

Showing Winston pictures of the clowns, **la maestra** asks him questions about them.

¿Quién es?	*Who is it?*
Es el payaso/la payasa.	*It is the (male) clown/the (female) clown.*
¿Cómo es el payaso?	*What is the (male) clown like?*
Es bajo/alto.	*He's short/tall.*
¿Cómo es la payasa?	*What is the (female) clown like?*
Es baja/alta.	*She's short/tall.*

3. Reviewing the names of three colors

Antonio demonstrates the colors **negro** (*black*), **café** (*brown*), **gris** (*gray*).

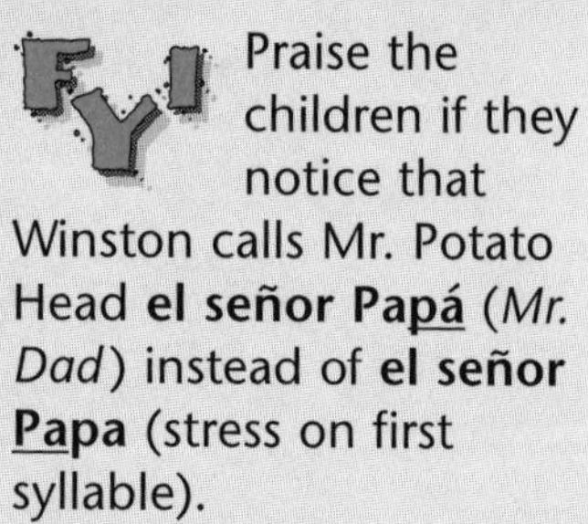

Praise the children if they notice that Winston calls Mr. Potato Head **el señor Papá** (*Mr. Dad*) instead of **el señor Papa** (stress on first syllable).

4. Describing body parts

La maestra asks Winston and the children the color of various body parts of **el señor Papa** (*Mr. Potato Head*).

¿De qué color es/son ___?	*What color is/are ___?*
El pelo es anaranjado.	*The hair is orange.*
Las orejas son amarillas.	*The ears are yellow.*
La boca es roja.	*The mouth is red.*

5. Explaining the pattern of adjectives matching the nouns they modify

The children identify the colors **negro** (*black*), **café** (*brown*), and **gris** (*gray*). **La maestra** explains that if colors are not describing something, the endings don't change. If, however, colors are describing nouns, those color names ending in **-o**, e.g., **amarillo** (*yellow*), change to match the sound on the end of the noun. **Gris** (*gray*) doesn't change because it doesn't end in an **o** sound. **La maestra** reviews the colors of **el señor Papa's** (*Mr. Potato Head's*) body parts.

6. Practicing the adjectives *thin* and *fat*

La maestra reviews the adjectives **delgado** (*thin*) and **gordo** (*fat*) with the children and then asks them questions about the clowns.

¿Cómo es el payaso?	*What is the (male) clown like?*
El payaso es delgado.	*The (male) clown is thin.*
El payaso es gordo.	*The (male) clown is fat.*
¿Cómo es la payasa?	*What is the (female) clown like?*
La payasa es delgada.	*The (female) clown is thin.*
La payasa es gorda.	*The (female) clown is fat.*

7. Introducing two more adjectives

La maestra introduces the adjectives **bonito/bonita** (*pretty*) and **feo/fea** (*ugly*) and asks the children to describe the clowns.

El payaso es bonito.	*The (male) clown is pretty.*
El payaso es feo.	*The (male) clown is ugly.*
La payasa es bonita.	*The (female) clown is pretty.*
La payasa es fea.	*The (female) clown is ugly.*

8. Reviewing all the adjectives

La maestra and Winston review the adjectives **bonito/bonita** (*pretty*), **feo/fea** (*ugly*), **alto/alta** (*tall*), **bajo/baja** (*short*), **gordo/gorda** (*fat*), and **delgado/delgada** (*thin*).

9. Closing

Winston and **la maestra** say **Adiós** (*Good-bye*) to the children.

LANGUAGE ACROSS THE CURRICULUM

In reading class ask the children to describe characters using the adjectives **alto/alta** (*tall*), **bajo/baja** (*short*), **delgado/delgada** (*thin*), and **gordo/gorda** (*fat*). If necessary remind the children that if describing a male character, the adjective ends in an **o** sound; if describing a female, the adjective ends in an **a** sound.

After viewing the video, praise the children for their good listening and watching skills.

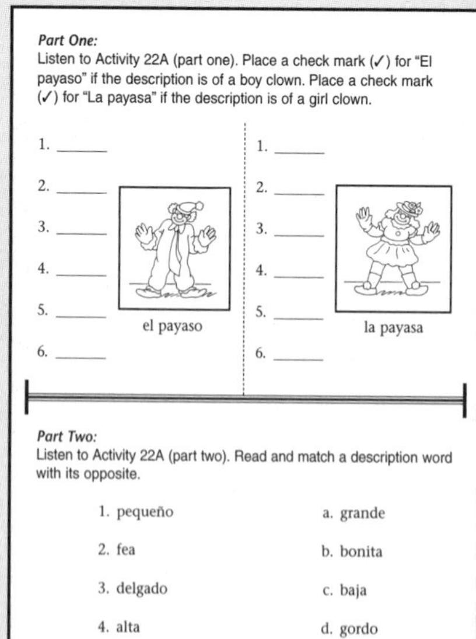

Part One:
Listen to Activity 22A (part one). Place a check mark (✓) for "El payaso" if the description is of a boy clown. Place a check mark (✓) for "La payasa" if the description is of a girl clown.

el payaso	la payasa
1. ____	1. ____
2. ____	2. ____
3. ____	3. ____
4. ____	4. ____
5. ____	5. ____
6. ____	6. ____

Part Two:
Listen to Activity 22A (part two). Read and match a description word with its opposite.

1. pequeño	a. grande
2. fea	b. bonita
3. delgado	c. baja
4. alta	d. gordo

Blackline Master 22A

On the tape, doña Elena tells the children **¡Cuidado!** (*Be careful!*).

Activity Lesson

Activity 22A, Part One: Who is being described?

Materials: Cassette player; Activity Cassette 1, Side B; Blackline Master 22A; pencils (one per child); *optional:* current Month Picture.

Preparation: Copy and distribute Blackline Master 22A so that each child has one.

Have the children fill in their names and the date at the top of the page. If necessary, display the current Month Picture to help them spell the name of the current month.

Tell them to look at Part One of their papers. Doña Elena is going to say six words describing the clowns. They are to listen carefully to each word. If the word describes the male clown Roberto, they are to place a check mark on the blank next to the corresponding number on the left side (the male clown side) of the paper. If the word describes the female clown Roberta, they are to place a check mark next to the corresponding number on the right side (the female clown side) of the paper. They will hear each word twice. Play Activity 22A Part One, stopping after doña Elena has checked the last answer with the children and said **¡Qué inteligentes son!** (*How intelligent you are!*). Children should have checked numbers 1, 5, and 6 on the left side and numbers 2, 3, and 4 on the right side.

Activity 22A, Part Two: Find the opposite

Materials: The same as in Activity 22A, Part One.

Be sure the children have Blackline Master 22A and a pencil ready. Point out that in Part Two of their papers there are many adjectives. They are to match each adjective in the left column with the adjective that means the opposite in the right column. Play Part Two of Activity 22A, stopping the tape at the sound of the harp to allow children time to complete the task. Children should have matched item 1 with A, 2 with B, 3 with D, and 4 with C.

Color by number. Compare your picture with a friend's.
1. amarillo
2. rojo
3. azul
4. verde
5. anaranjado
6. rosado
7. café
8. negro
9. morado
10. gris
11. blanco
el payaso

Blackline Master 22B

Activity 22B: Color the clown

Materials: Blackline Master 22B; crayons, pencils, or markers in these colors: black, blue, brown, gray, green, orange, pink, purple, red, white, and yellow (one set for each child); *optional:* current Month Picture.

Preparation: Copy and distribute Blackline Master 22B so that each child has a copy. Be sure each child has a set of crayons, pencils, or markers in the colors indicated.

Have the children fill in their names and the date at the top of the page. If necessary, display the current Month Picture to help them spell the name of the current month. Ask the children if the clown pictured is a boy or girl clown (boy clown). Ask them what sound the word clown on the bottom of the page ends in (**o**). Point out that at the top of the page are the names of the colors. Ask what sound the word for yellow ends in (**o**, **amarillo**). Do the same for *red* (**rojo**), *pink* (**rosado**), *black* (**negro**). Point out that **gris** (*gray*), **azul** (*blue*), and **verde** (*green*) don't change since they don't end in an **o** sound.

Next have them follow the numbers to color in the clown. Ask them what color they would color the clown's hair, which has the number 2 on it (**rojo**—*red*). Once they have finished, have them compare their pictures. Are all their pictures colored the same?

1. amarillo	*yellow*	7. café	*brown*
2. rojo	*red*	8. negro	*black*
3. azul	*blue*	9. morado	*purple*
4. verde	*green*	10. gris	*gray*
5. anaranjado	*orange*	11. blanco	*white*
6. rosado	*pink*		

Closing

Tell the children that Spanish class is finished for today. In the next lesson **la maestra** will introduce even more adjectives.

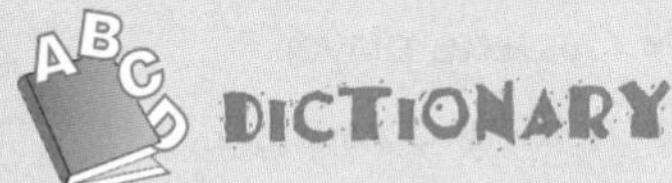

Materials: Blank paper; crayons, colored pencils, or markers; and children's dictionary pages.

Have the children choose one of the following adjectives and make a dictionary page for it: **grande** (*big*); **mediano/mediana** (*medium*); **pequeño/pequeña** (*small*); **alto/alta** (*tall*); **bajo/baja** (*short*); **delgado/delgada** (*thin*); **gordo/gorda** (*fat*); **bonito/bonita** (*pretty*); **feo/fea** (*ugly*). Remind them to write the first letter of the word on the top of the page. Suggest they draw a picture to illustrate the meaning of the word and then write the word beneath the picture. Have them add the page to their other dictionary pages.

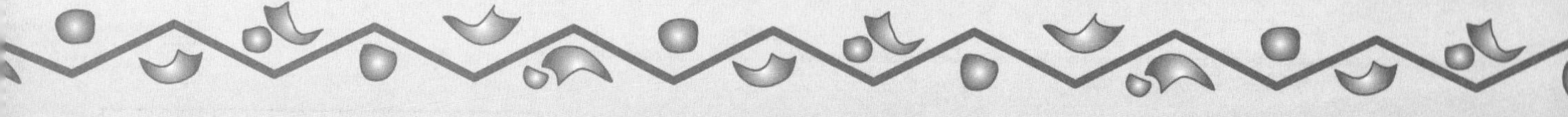

Lesson 23

Materials to gather

- VCR and Video Lesson 23 on Tape 8
- Cassette player
- Activity Cassette 2
- Current Month Picture
- Current calendar
- Blackline Master 19A
- Green, red, and purple paintbrushes from Lesson 4
- Blackline Master 23A (soft/hard)
- Pencils
- Crayons, colored pencils, or markers
- Blank paper

Objectives

Language

- Learn the adjectives **suave** (*soft*) and **duro/dura** (*hard*)
- Hear how to describe more than one thing
- Use two adjectives to describe something or someone

Culture

- Talk about terms of endearment

Review

- Exchange greetings with **la maestra**
- Review the adjectives **alto** (*tall*), **bajo** (*short*), **delgado** (*thin*), **gordo** (*fat*), **feo** (*ugly*), and **bonito** (*pretty*)
- Review the names of four colors

Vocabulary

suave	*soft*
duro/dura	*hard*

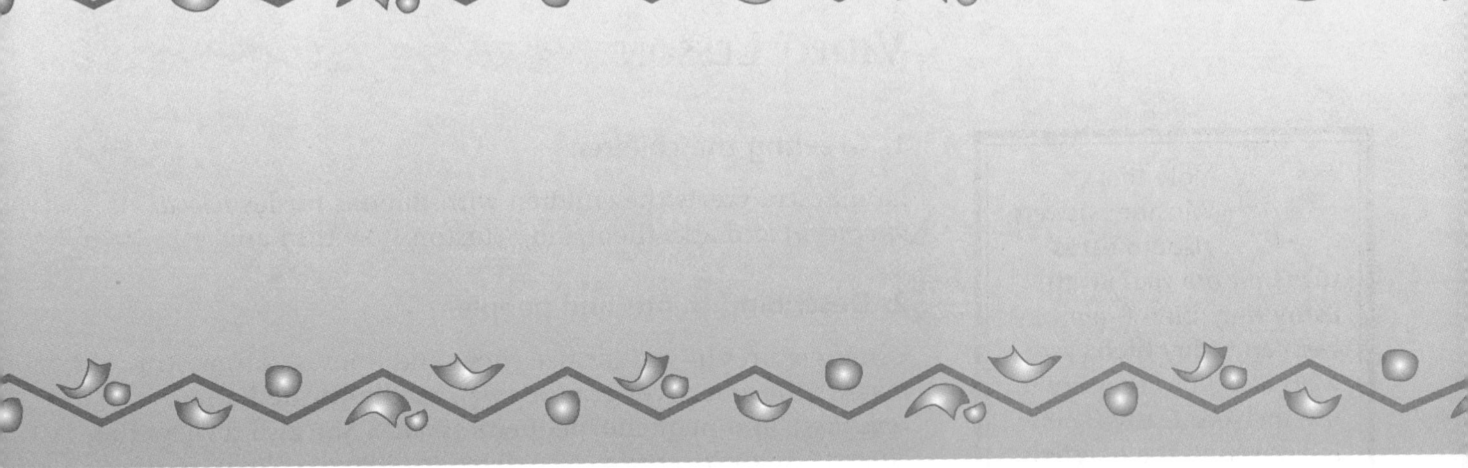

Warm-up

Materials: Current Month Picture; a current calendar.

Display the Month Picture that represents the current month. Greet the children and let them know it's time for Spanish class (**la clase de español**). Ask the children what the date is. If children need help identifying what day of the month it is, point to it on the calendar.

> **EN ESPAÑOL**
>
> If you feel comfortable, ask:
>
> **¿Cuál es la fecha?** (*What is the date?*).
>
> el [*number*] de [*month*]

Review

Materials: Blackline Master 19A; the green, red, and purple paintbrushes from Lesson 4.

Cover up Part Two of Blackline Master 19A. Point to each picture in Part One of Blackline Master 19A and ask the children to describe it in Spanish.

El zapato es grande (*or* mediano).	*The shoe is big (or medium).*
La casa es grande (*or* mediana).	*The house is big (or medium).*
El zapato es pequeño (*or* mediano).	*The shoe is small (or medium).*
La casa es pequeña (*or* mediana).	*The house is small (or medium).*

Next hold up one paintbrush at a time next to the large shoe and ask the children to tell you the color of the shoe:

El zapato es verde/ rojo/morado.	*The shoe is green/ red/purple.*

Finally, hold up one paintbrush at a time next to the large house and ask the children to tell you the color of the house.

La casa es verde/ roja/morada.	*The house is green/ red/purple.*

> **EN ESPAÑOL**
>
> When asking about the sizes and colors, you could ask **¿Cómo es el zapato?** (*What is the shoe like?*), **¿Cómo es la casa?** (*What is the house like?*), **¿De qué color es el zapato?** (*What color is the shoe?*), and **¿De qué color es la casa?** (*What color is the house?*).

Introduce the video

Invite the children to listen and watch as **la maestra** introduces two more adjectives.

Video Lesson

Note that Winston answers **¿Cómo estás tú?** (*How are you?*) with **Estoy muy bien** (*I am very well*) and **Muy bien** (*Very well*). It is not necessary to use the verb **Estoy** (*I am*) in answering the question.

1. Greeting the children

La maestra greets the children with **Buenas tardes** (*Good afternoon*) and asks them and Winston how they are.

2. Describing things and people

Using pictures of various size shoes and houses, **la maestra** reviews the adjectives **grande** (*big*), **mediano/mediana** (*medium*), and **pequeño/pequeña** (*small*). She also reviews the adjectives **gordo/gorda** (*fat*), **delgado/delgada** (*thin*), **feo/fea** (*ugly*), **bonito/bonita** (*pretty*), **alto/alta** (*tall*), and **bajo/baja** (*short*) using pictures of clowns.

¿Cómo es el zapato?	*What is the shoe like?*
Es grande/mediano/ pequeño.	*It is big/medium/ small.*
¿Cómo es la casa?	*What is the house like?*
Es grande/mediana/ pequeña.	*It's big/medium/ small.*
¿Cómo es el payaso?	*What is the (male) clown like?*
Es gordo.	*He's fat.*
¿Es gorda la payasa?	*Is the (female) clown fat?*
No. Es delgada.	*No. She's thin.*
Es delgada y alta.	*She's thin and tall.*

3. Describing more than one thing

Winston reads the adjectives **gordo** (*fat*), **alto** (*tall*), and **delgado** (*thin*). **La maestra** explains that if one were talking about a lot of male clowns, one would say **delgados**, not **delgado**, i.e., an **-s** is added.

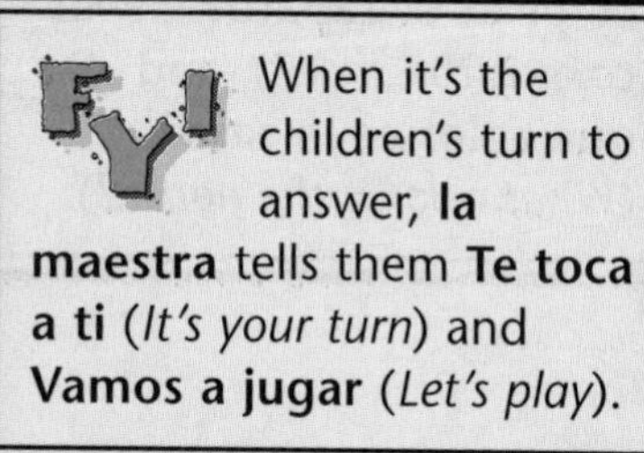

When it's the children's turn to answer, **la maestra** tells them **Te toca a ti** (*It's your turn*) and **Vamos a jugar** (*Let's play*).

4. Practicing describing the male and female clowns

La maestra asks the children **¿Cómo es la payasa?** (*What is the [female] clown like?*) and **¿Cómo es el payaso?** (*What is the [male] clown like?*). The children describe the clowns.

5. Introducing the adjectives *soft* and *hard*

Doña Elena and Antonio introduce the adjectives **suave** (*soft*) and **duro** (*hard*). Doña Elena tells Antonio **¡Siéntate!** (*Sit!*). **La maestra** asks Winston and then the children about various objects: **¿Es suave o es duro?** (*Is it soft or is it hard?*).

6. Reviewing the names of several colors

La maestra plays **¿De qué color es?** (*What color is it?*) with the children. She reviews the colors **verde** (*green*), **amarillo** (*yellow*), **rosado** (*pink*), and **blanco** (*white*).

7. Using two adjectives to describe something or someone

Winston describes a house, a shoe, an armchair, and clowns. **La maestra** reminds the children that the word **verde** (*green*) changes to **verdes** when used to describe more than one thing.

La casa es mediana. La casa es café.	*The house is medium.* *The house is brown.*
El zapato es azul y el zapato es pequeño.	*The shoe is blue and* *the shoe is small.*
El sillón es grande y es suave.	*The armchair is big and* *it's soft.*
Los zapatos son verdes.	*The shoes are green.*

8. Closing

La maestra mentions all the things the children have practiced and learned today. She and Winston say **Adiós** (*Good-bye*) to the children.

In this level, words being reviewed appear on the screen so that the children can see how they are spelled. Point this out to the children and tell them to look at the words and to read them as **la maestra** says them. Seeing the words over and over again will help some children remember how to write and spell them.

When saying good-bye, Winston often says **Adiós, Maestros** (*Good-bye, Teachers*), referring to the classroom teachers watching the video.

After viewing the video, praise the children for their good listening and watching skills.

Part One:
Listen to Activity 23A (part one). Place a check mark (✓) for "suave" if the item is soft. Place a check mark (✓) for "duro" if the item is hard.

	Suave	Duro
1.	______	______
2.	______	______
3.	______	______
4.	______	______
5.	______	______

Part Two:
Listen to Activity 23A (part two). Each numbered item could be described by only *one* of the words in the box. Draw a line from the numbered item to the correct word describing it.

1. los zapatos	azules blanca	4. la casa	mediana gordo
2. los payasos	feo altos	5. los libros	grandes interesante
3. la blusa	rosada rojo		

Blackline Master 23A

Some children may remember words by sounds they associate with them. On the tape, **suave** (*soft*) is indicated by a slow harp sound, while **duro** (*hard*) is related to a clash of cymbals. If children are having difficulty remembering which word means what as they do the activity, replay the activity directions so they can hear the sounds again.

Doña Elena wishes the children **Buena suerte** (*Good luck*).

Activity Lesson

Activity 23A: Practice the adjectives

Materials: Cassette player; Activity Cassette 2, Side A; Blackline Master 23A; pencils; *optional:* current Month Picture.

Preparation: Copy and distribute Blackline Master 23A so that each child has a copy. Make sure each child has a pencil.

Have the children fill in their names and the date at the top of the page. If necessary, display the current Month Picture to help them spell the name of the current month. Review the pictures in Part One of the paper so that the children know what each item is: 1. a straight-backed chair, 2. a cloud, 3. two feathers, 4. a pillow, and 5. a table or desk. Play Activity 23A, stopping at the harp sound so that children can mark each item as **suave** (*soft*) or **duro** (*hard*). Children should have marked the items as follows: 1. **duro**, 2. **suave**, 3. **suave**, 4. **suave**, and 5. **duro**.

Next draw the children's attention to Part Two of their pages. Point out that on the left are the words for various items and on the right are boxes with two describing words in each box. Children are to match the word on the left with the word in the box directly opposite it that correctly describes the word on the left. Mention that one of the words in each box can't be used to describe the item because it doesn't have the correct sound at the end. Play Activity 23A, stopping the tape at the harp sound to allow children time to complete the activity. Restart the tape so children can check their answers as doña Elena describes each item. Children should have matched the items as follows: 1. **los zapatos azules**, 2. **los payasos altos**, 3. **la blusa roja**, 4. **la casa mediana**, 5. **los libros grandes**.

Activity 23B: Cooperative learning—Let's draw!

Materials: Children's copies of Blackline Master 23A from Activity 23A; blank paper; crayons, colored pencils, or markers (be sure red and blue are included).

Divide the class into pairs. Distribute paper and crayons to each child. Have the children in each pair tell each other (in Spanish) to draw one of the items from Part Two of Blackline Master 23A. Children will tell each other:

1. Dibuja los zapatos azules. — *Draw the blue shoes.*
2. Dibuja los payasos altos. — *Draw the tall clowns.*
3. Dibuja la blusa roja. — *Draw the red blouse.*
4. Dibuja la casa mediana. — *Draw the medium house.*
5. Dibuja los libros grandes. — *Draw the large books.*

Then ask volunteers to show the class their pictures and describe them briefly.

Activity 23C: Cross-cultural connections

Explain that among many Spanish speakers, **gordo/gorda** (*fat*) or **gordito/gordita** (*little fat one*) is used as a term of endearment. The term is usually used by mothers when talking to their children, between husbands and wives, and among friends. An English speaker may be offended when called **gordo** or **gordito**, but a Spanish speaker will feel the intimacy of friendship and family. The term would never be used outside one's circle of friends or family. Ask the children what terms of endearment they use with friends or are used in their families, e.g., dear, honey, slugger, bug, princess, honey bunny, sweetie. If you have children in your class whose families speak other languages, ask them if their families or friends refer to them with special words of endearment. Have them share and define the words with the class.

Closing

Tell the children that Spanish class is finished for today. In the next lesson **la maestra** will introduce more adjectives.

En español

If children don't remember the command *draw* (**dibuja**), it is pronounced *dee-boo-ha*.

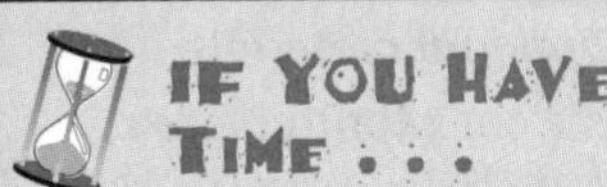

If you have time . . .

Point to various things in the classroom and ask the children if they are *hard* (**duro**) or *soft* (**suave**). If you feel comfortable, ask **¿Es duro o es suave?** (*Is it hard or is it soft?*). Children should say **duro** or **suave**. Try to point to things that are either hard or soft, e.g., the wall or chalkboard, the flag, the door, a tissue.

Lesson 24

Materials to gather

- VCR and Video Lesson 24 on Tape 8
- Cassette player
- Activity Cassette 2
- Blackline Master 24A (two paragraphs)
- Pencils
- ***Optional materials:*** current Month Picture; Red Flashcards 50–53

Objectives

Language

- Learn the adjectives **sucio/sucia** (*dirty*) and **limpio/limpia** (*clean*)

Culture

- Use greetings that are appropriate for the time of the day

Review

- Exchange greetings with **la maestra**
- Practice describing people and things
- Read sentences in Spanish

Vocabulary

sucio/sucia	*dirty*
limpio/limpia	*clean*

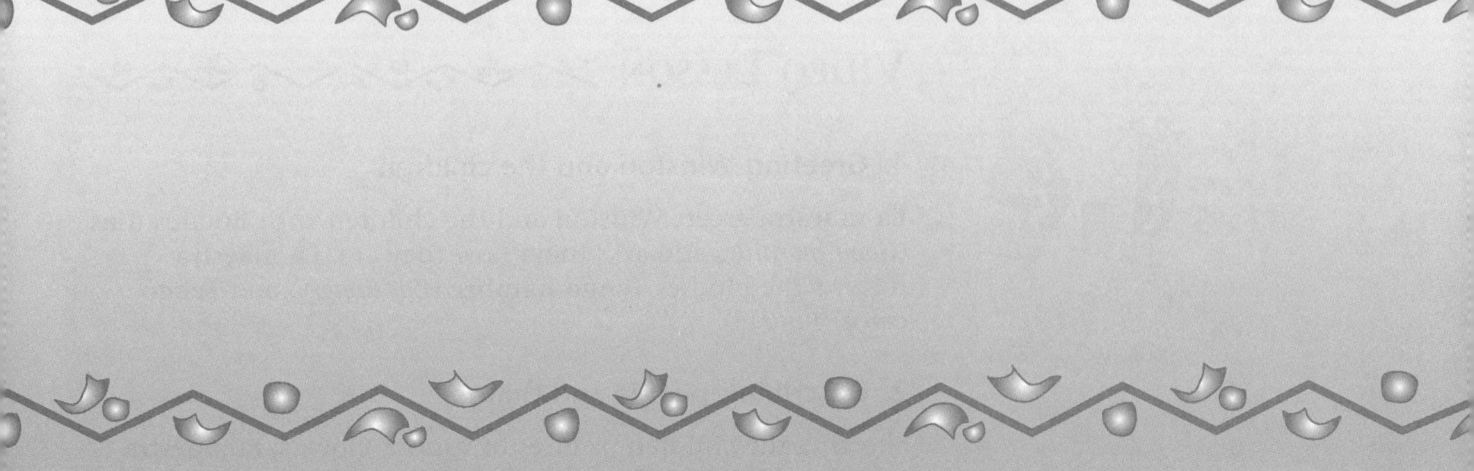

Warm-up

Greet the children. Let them know it's time for Spanish class (**la clase de español**). If you feel comfortable, ask **¿Están listos?** (*Are you ready?*). Tell them to have the opening conversation with a classmate sitting nearby. Encourage them to use the greeting appropriate to the time of day (**C1** = child 1, **C2** = child 2):

C1: Buenos días (Buenas tardes), ___.	*Good morning* (*Good afternoon*), ___.
C2: Buenos días (Buenas tardes), ___.	*Good morning* (*Good afternoon*), ___.
C1: ¿Cómo estás tú?	*How are you?*
C2: Muy bien, gracias. ¿Y tú?	*Very well, thank you. And you?*
C1: Muy bien, gracias.	*Very well, thank you.*

Review

Review the adjectives **alto/alta** (*tall*), **bajo/baja** (*short*), **gordo/gorda** (*fat*), **delgado/delgada** (*thin*), **feo/fea** (*ugly*), and **bonito/bonita** (*pretty*) by asking for volunteers to draw pictures of clowns on the chalkboard. Assign each volunteer one of the describing words and tell him/her to draw either a male or female clown. For example, have one child draw a tall male clown. When the drawings are finished, have the volunteers describe their clowns in Spanish for the class:

El payaso es alto/bajo/gordo/delgado.	*The* (*male*) *clown is tall/short/fat/thin.*
La payasa es alta/baja/gorda/delgada.	*The* (*female*) *clown is tall/short/fat/thin.*

Introduce the video

Invite the children to listen and watch as **la maestra** reviews all the adjectives and introduces two more.

Feeling expressions:

(Estoy) Muy mal.
(*I am*) *Very bad.*

(Estoy) Así, así.
(*I am*) So-so.

(Estoy) Contento/a.
(*I am*) Happy.

Tengo calor.
I'm hot.

Tengo frío.
I'm cold.

Tengo dolor.
I'm hurt.

Tengo hambre.
I'm hungry.

Tengo miedo.
I'm afraid.

Tengo sed.
I'm thirsty.

Tengo sueño.
I'm sleepy.

Video Lesson

Are children remembering the adjectives? Are they using the correct endings? If they are having difficulty, reassure them that they will continue to practice using the describing words and with time they will have no difficulty describing the pictures.

Children may notice that **está** (*is*) rather than **es** (*is*) is used with the adjectives **limpio** (*dirty*) and **sucio** (*dirty*). **Está** is from the verb **estar** (*to be*). **Estar** is used with adjectives to indicate a temporary state or condition, e.g., a state of health, a state of cleanliness. **Es** is from the verb **ser** (*to be*). **Ser** is used with adjectives to indicate inherent qualities or characteristics, e.g., color, physical attributes (height), personality (intelligence).

1. Greeting Winston and the children

La maestra greets Winston and the children with **Buenos días** (*Good morning*) and asks them how they are. **La maestra** reviews the phrases **Tengo hambre** (*I'm hungry*) and **Tengo calor** (*I'm hot*).

2. Describing people and things

Showing the children pictures of various clowns, **la maestra** asks the children **¿Cómo es?** (*What's he/she like?*) and the children respond using the adjectives **alto/alta** (*tall*), **bonito/bonita** (*pretty*), and **delgado/delgada** (*thin*). She also reviews the adjectives **duro/dura** (*hard*) and **suave** (*soft*).

¿Cómo es la silla?	*What is the chair like?*
Es dura.	*It's hard.*
¿Cómo es el sillón?	*What is the armchair like?*
Es suave.	*It's soft.*

3. Working with more adjectives

La maestra reviews that if the children are describing **la payasa Roberta** (*the female clown Roberta*), they will use words that end in an **a** sound; if they are describing **el payaso Roberto** (*the male clown Roberto*), they will use words that end in an **o** sound. She plays a game of **¿Cómo es el payaso/la payasa?** (*What's the clown like?*) with the children. They use the adjectives **feo/fea** (*ugly*), **gordo/gorda** (*fat*), **bajo/baja** (*short*), **bonito/bonita** (*pretty*), and **alto/alta** (*tall*).

4. Introducing the adjectives *clean* and *dirty*

With a picture of **el sombrero** (*hat*), **la maestra** introduces two new adjectives.

limpio/limpia	*clean*
El sombrero está limpio.	*The hat is clean.*
sucio/sucia	*dirty*
El sombrero está sucio.	*The hat is dirty.*

La maestra comments that in the sentence **La cara de Winston está limpia** (*Winston's face is clean*), the adjective ends in an **-a** because it agrees with **la cara** (*face*).

5. Reviewing three color names

La maestra plays a game of **¿De qué color es?** (*What color is it?*) with the children. Children identify the colors **negro** (*black*), **café** (*brown*), and **gris** (*gray*).

6. Completing and reading sentences

La maestra asks Winston to complete sentences with color words. He, **la maestra,** and the children read the sentences. **La maestra** plays games of **¿Cómo es ___?** (*What's ___ like?*) with the children. The children describe the houses and shoes using the adjectives **grande** (*big*), **mediano/mediana** (*medium*), and **pequeño/pequeña** (*small*).

La casa es roja.	*The house is red.*
La casa es grande/ mediana/pequeña.	*The house is big/ medium/small.*
El zapato es negro.	*The shoe is black.*
El zapato es grande/ mediano/pequeño.	*The shoe is big/ medium/small.*

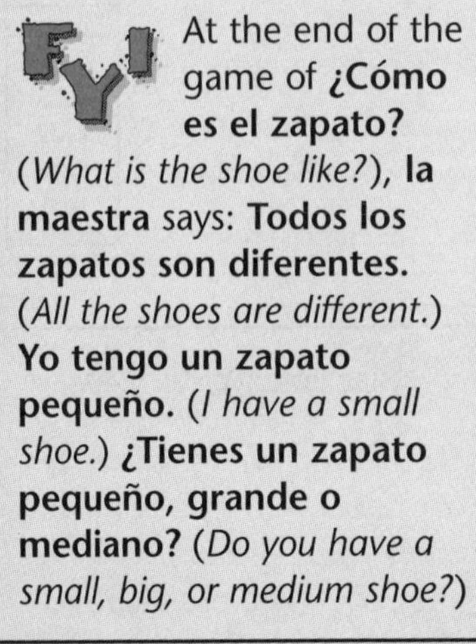

FYI
At the end of the game of **¿Cómo es el zapato?** (*What is the shoe like?*), **la maestra** says: **Todos los zapatos son diferentes.** (*All the shoes are different.*) **Yo tengo un zapato pequeño.** (*I have a small shoe.*) **¿Tienes un zapato pequeño, grande o mediano?** (*Do you have a small, big, or medium shoe?*)

7. Using the new adjectives

La maestra shows Winston and the children the word **sucio** (*dirty*) and describes the hat. She asks them what they would say to indicate that the house is dirty. She works with **limpio/limpia** (*clean*) in the same fashion.

El sombrero está sucio.	*The hat is dirty.*
La casa está sucia.	*The house is dirty.*
El sombrero está limpio.	*The hat is clean.*
La casa está limpia.	*The house is clean.*

8. Closing

The children and Winston say the adjective describing each picture. **La maestra** bids the children **Adiós** (*Good-bye*) and Winston says **Adiós a todos** (*Good-bye to everyone*).

After viewing the video, praise the children for their good listening and watching skills.

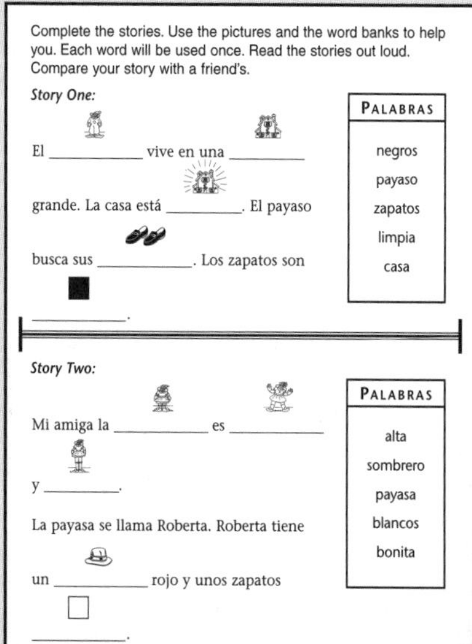

Complete the stories. Use the pictures and the word banks to help you. Each word will be used once. Read the stories out loud. Compare your story with a friend's.

Story One:

El ________ vive en una ________ grande. La casa está ________. El payaso busca sus ________. Los zapatos son ________.

PALABRAS
negros
payaso
zapatos
limpia
casa

Story Two:

Mi amiga la ________ es ________ y ________.

La payasa se llama Roberta. Roberta tiene un ________ rojo y unos zapatos ________.

PALABRAS
alta
sombrero
payasa
blancos
bonita

Blackline Master 24A

ACTIVITY LESSON

Activity 24A: Complete the paragraphs

Materials: Cassette player; Activity Cassette 2, Side A; Blackline Master 24A; pencils; *optional:* current Month Picture.

Preparation: Copy and distribute Blackline Master 24A so that each child has a copy. Make sure each child has a pencil.

Have the children fill in their names and the date at the top of the page. If necessary, display the current Month Picture to help them spell the name of the current month. Tell the children they are going to complete each paragraph by using the pictures above each blank and the words in the word bank (**Palabras**). Play Activity 24A, stopping the tape at the sound of the harp to allow children time to do Paragraph One. Once they have finished, restart the tape so they can check their answers and hear the directions for Paragraph Two. Again, stop the tape at the harp sound, restarting it again after children have filled in the blanks in Paragraph Two so that they can check their answers.

Paragraph One Answers:

El payaso vive en una casa grande.	*The (male) clown lives in a big house.*
La casa está limpia.	*The house is clean.*
El payaso busca sus zapatos.	*The (male) clown is looking for his shoes.*
Los zapatos son negros.	*His shoes are black.*

Paragraph Two Answers:

Mi amiga la payasa es bonita y alta.	*My friend the (female) clown is pretty and tall.*
La payasa se llama Roberta.	*The (female) clown's name is Roberta.*
Roberta tiene un sombrero rojo y unos zapatos blancos.	*Roberta has a red hat and white shoes.*

Activity 24B: What are the paragraphs about?

Materials: Children's copies of Blackline Master 24A.

Check the children's understanding of the stories in the two paragraphs by asking the following questions. Children may answer in English.

Paragraph One:

1. Is the clown's house big, small, or medium sized? (**grande**—*big*)
2. What other word is used to describe the house? (**limpia**—*clean*)
3. What is the clown looking for? (**los zapatos**—*the shoes*)
4. What color are his shoes? (**negros**—*black*)
5. Is the story about a boy clown or a girl clown? How do you know? (a boy because the story is about **el payaso**, not **la payasa**)

Paragraph Two:

1. What two words describe the clown? (**bonita**—*pretty*, **alta**—*tall*)
2. What is the clown's name? (Roberta)
3. What does the clown have? (**un sombrero**—*a hat*, **zapatos**—*shoes*)
4. What color is the clown's hat? (**rojo**—*red*)
5. What color are the clown's shoes? (**blancos**—*white*)
6. Is the story about a boy clown or a girl clown? How do you know? (a girl clown, because the story is about **la payasa**, not **el payaso**)

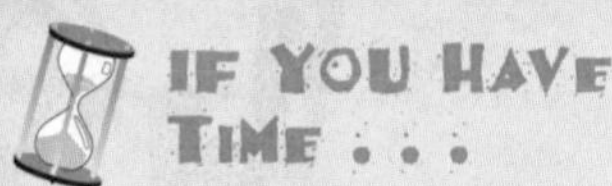

IF YOU HAVE TIME . . .

Materials: Red Flashcards 50–53.

Review the names of the musical instruments by pointing to each picture on the Red Flashcards and asking the children what the instrument is called in Spanish. If you feel comfortable, ask **¿Qué instrumento es?** (*What instrument is it?*).

Red Flashcards:

#50: el tambor (*drum*)/ la guitarra (*guitar*)

#51: la trompeta (*trumpet*)/ el piano (*piano*)

#52: la flauta (*flute*)/ el violín (*violin*)

#53: el clarinete (*clarinet*)/ la pandereta (*tambourine*)

Activity 24C: Read your paragraph

Materials: Children's copies of Blackline Master 24A.

Ask volunteers to read their paragraphs aloud in Spanish and then to re-tell them in English. Don't pressure children to read in Spanish.

CLOSING

Tell the children that Spanish class is finished for today. In the next video children will hear a story about a new character—Fredo—and his adventures in a music store!

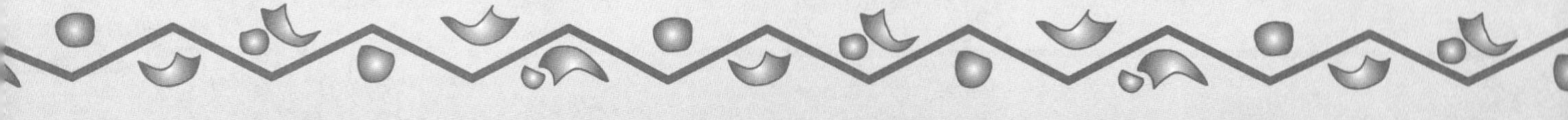

Lesson 25

Materials to gather

- VCR and Video Lesson 25 on Tape 9
- Cassette player
- Song Cassette
- Overhead projector
- A blank transparency
- Blackline Master 5B ("Alphabet Rap")
- Red Flashcards 50–53
- Blank ruled paper
- Pencils or pens
- ***Optional materials:*** *"Las aventuras de Fredo"* (*"Fredo's Adventures"*) books; musical instruments or toys: trumpet, drum, flute, violin, tambourine, piano, clarinet, guitar; a video camera

Objectives

Language

- Understand a story about a visit to a music store
- Recognize cognates
- Learn a new word in English—*edifice*
- Hear new words for types of buildings

Culture

- Understand that people live in houses and apartment buildings, not skyscrapers

Review

- Review the names of school subjects and classes
- Sing the "Alphabet Rap"
- Read familiar words

Vocabulary

la tienda	*store*
el edificio	*building, edifice*
el rascacielos	*skyscraper*
el edificio de apartamentos	*apartment building*
el apartamento	*apartment*
los apartamentos	*apartments*
el supermercado	*supermarket*
la escuela	*school*
la biblioteca	*library*
el restaurante	*restaurant*

Warm-up

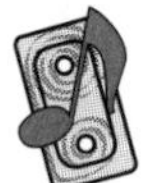

Materials: Cassette player; "Alphabet Rap" on the Song Cassette, Side A; a blank transparency; and Blackline Master 5B.

Preparation: Make an overhead transparency of Blackline Master 5B. Project the transparency.

Ask the children what they were able to start doing once they knew the English alphabet (sound out words, spell words, write words, read words and sentences). Tell them they are learning to do the same things in Spanish and to help them remember the Spanish alphabet, they are going to sing the "Alphabet Rap." Play the rap, pointing to each letter as it is sung.

Alphabet Rap
El alfabeto

a	b	c
ch	d	e
f	g	
h	i	
j	k	
l	ll	m
n	ñ	o
p	q	
r	s	
t	u	
v	w	x
y	z	

Blackline Master 5B

Review

Materials: Red Flashcards 50–53 or musical instruments.

Ask the children what musical instruments they have learned to name in Spanish. If they need help remembering the instruments, show them the Red Flashcards or the instruments you brought, and if you feel comfortable, ask **¿Qué instrumento es?** (*What instrument is it?*). Ask them how they would tell someone *play the drum* (**toca el tambor**). If they need help remembering the word *play*, give them a hint: the word also means *touch*.

Red Flashcards:

#50 el tambor (*drum*)/la guitarra (*guitar*)

#51 la trompeta (*trumpet*)/el piano (*piano*)

#52 la flauta (*flute*)/el violín (*violin*)

#53 el clarinete (*clarinet*)/la pandereta (*tambourine*)

Introduce the video

Invite the children to listen and watch as **la maestra** introduces a new friend—Fredo—and as doña Elena reads a story about one of Fredo's many adventures.

VIDEO LESSON

School subjects:

la lectura	*reading*
la escritura	*writing*
las computa-doras	*computers*
la geografía	*geography*
el drama	*theater, drama*
la música	*music*
la historia	*history*
las matemáticas	*math*
las ciencias	*science*
el arte	*art*

Are children watching when **la maestra** says the answers in section 3? Point out that after they have responded to the question, the name of each class appears on the screen so they can see how the words are spelled. Tell them to read the words to themselves as **la maestra** says them, thus working on their reading ability in Spanish.

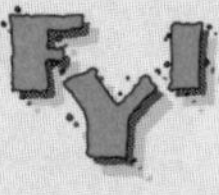

Before singing the "Alphabet Rap," **la maestra** talks about the importance of reading: **Una cosa muy muy importante es la lectura.** (*One very important thing is reading.*) **Me gustan mucho los libros.** (*I love books.*)

1. Greeting the children

La maestra greets the children with **Buenos días** (*Good morning*) and asks them **¿Cómo estás tú?** (*How are you?*). She says **Estoy muy contenta** (*I'm very happy*).

2. Reviewing the names of school subjects

Using the **Toca el Futuro** (*Touch the Future*) board, **la maestra** reviews the names of the school subjects.

3. Playing *¿Qué clase es?* (*What class is it?*)

La maestra plays **¿Qué clase es?** (*What class is it?*) with the children. Children respond with **la clase de** + the name of the subject. For example, **la clase de música** (*music class*).

4. Singing the "Alphabet Rap"

After explaining the process of learning the alphabet, learning to spell words, reading sentences, then paragraphs, and finally whole books, **la maestra** says the "Alphabet Rap" while Lorena dances to it.

5. Introducing a new friend—Fredo

La maestra shows LeeAnn a sentence. LeeAnn reads the sentence **Me gustan los libros** (*I like books*). **La maestra** introduces a new friend, Fredo. LeeAnn asks **¿Vamos a leer?** (*Are we going to read?*).

6. Reading about the adventures of Fredo

Doña Elena reads **"La tienda de música"** (*"The Music Store"*) as the children read along on the screen. Some of the sentences are as follows.

Mi amigo Fredo va a una tienda de música.	*My friend Fredo goes to a music store.*
Busca un instrumento musical.	*He is looking for a musical instrument.*
Aquí hay una trompeta.	*Here is a trumpet.*
¿Toca Fredo la trompeta?	*Does Fredo play the trumpet?*
No, no toca la trompeta.	*No, he doesn't play the trumpet.*
¿Y qué es esto?	*And what is this?*
A Fredo le gusta la guitarra.	*Fredo likes the guitar.*
Ahora Fredo está contento y va a casa con su guitarra.	*Now Fredo is happy, and he goes home with his guitar.*

7. Reviewing the concept of cognates

LeeAnn and the children read the names of two musical instruments—**la trompeta** (*trumpet*) and **el violín** (*violin*). **La maestra** explains that the words are cognates, i.e., they look and sound similar in Spanish and English. She shows them the English word *edifice* and shows them its Spanish cognate **edificio**.

8. Introducing the names of various types of structures

La maestra introduces the word for *skyscraper* (**el rascacielos**) and explains that **rasca** means *scratch* and **cielos** means *sky*, which indicates what the skyscraper does—it scratches the sky. She also introduces the word for *apartment building* (**el edificio de apartamentos**) and asks LeeAnn what kind of building she lives in. She and LeeAnn name other kinds of buildings: **la casa** (*house*), **la escuela** (*school*), **el supermercado** (*supermarket*), and **la biblioteca** (*library*).

El rascacielos es un edificio muy alto.	*The skyscraper is a very tall building.*
Es el edificio de apartamentos.	*It's the apartment building.*
Es muy alto y hay muchos apartamentos.	*It is very tall and there are many apartments.*
¿Dónde vives tú—en una casa o en un edificio de apartamentos?	*Where do you live—in a house or in an apartment building?*
Vivo en un edificio de apartamentos.	*I live in an apartment building.*
Yo vivo en una casa.	*I live in a house.*

As she introduces *skyscraper* and *apartment building*, **la maestra** says: **Estoy en el centro.** (*I'm in the center [of the city].*) **Y en el centro hay edificios muy grandes y muy altos.** (*And in the center there are very large and very tall buildings.*)

9. Closing

La maestra mentions several words that are cognates in Spanish and English. She tells LeeAnn that **escuela** and *school* are not cognates. She and LeeAnn say **Adiós** (*Good-bye*) and **Hasta luego** (*See you later*).

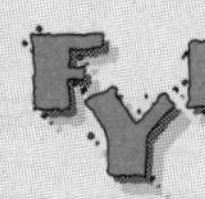

Children may remember the words **el supermercado** (*supermarket*), **el restaurante** (*restaurant*), **la biblioteca** (*library*), and **la escuela** (*school*) from Levels 2 and 3 of ***Español para ti.***

After viewing the video, praise the children for their good listening and watching skills.

Activity Lesson

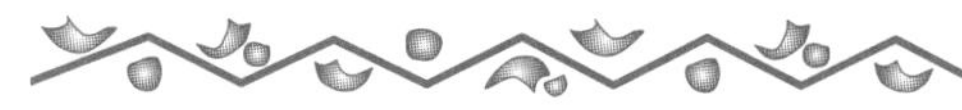

Activity 25A: Read *"La tienda de música"* (*"The Music Store"*)

Note: If your school has ***"Las aventuras de Fredo"*** (*"Fredo's Adventures"*) books available for the children, substitute the Fredo Book Activity in the margin for this activity.

Materials: VCR; Video Lesson 25 on Tape 9.

Preparation: Recue Video Lesson 25 to section 6, in which doña Elena reads the story **"La tienda de música."**

Explain to the children that they will be reading several stories about the adventures of Fredo and that *"The Music Store"* (**"La tienda de música"**) is the first one. Play section 6 of the video with the sound and tell the children to read along with doña Elena. Then rewind the video and replay the story without the sound. Pause the video to give the children time to read each line of the story to themselves.

Activity 25B: Talk about *"La tienda de música"* (*"The Music Store"*)

Ask the children questions to check their understanding of the story. Sample questions and their answers follow. Allow the children to answer in English.

1. What kind of store does Fredo visit? (**una tienda de música**—*a music store*)
2. What is Fredo looking for? (**un instrumento musical**—*a musical instrument*)
3. What instrument does Fredo play? (**la guitarra**—*guitar*)
4. What instruments does Fredo not play? (**la trompeta**—*trumpet*; **el tambor**—*drum*; **la flauta**—*flute*; **el violín**—*violin*; **la pandereta**—*tambourine*; **el piano**—*piano*; **el clarinete**—*clarinet*)
5. How is Fredo feeling when he leaves the store? (**Fredo está contento.**—*Fredo is happy.*)
6. Where does Fredo go when he leaves the store? (**Fredo va a casa.**—*Fredo goes home.*)

Activity 25C: Cooperative learning—Lights, camera, action!

Materials: Blank ruled paper; pencils or pens; *optional:* trumpet, drum, flute, violin, tambourine, piano, clarinet, guitar; a video camera; VCR and Video Lesson 25 on Tape 9.

Have the children prepare a production of Fredo's adventure *"The Music Store"* (**"La tienda de música"**). Ask several children to be the scriptwriters and to write the script for the narrator, using the sentences below as a guide. If necessary, have them

Fredo Book Activity

Materials: Cassette player; ***"Las aventuras de Fredo"*** (*"Fredo's Adventures"*), Book 1: **"La tienda de música"** (*"The Music Store"*) on Song Cassette, Side B; classroom copies of the book ***"Las aventuras de Fredo"*** (*"Fredo's Adventures"*).

Explain to the children that they will be reading several stories about the adventures of Fredo and that *"The Music Store"* (**"La tienda de música"**) is the first one. Distribute the copies of ***"Las aventuras de Fredo."*** Tell the children they are going to read the first story in the book—*"The Music Store"* (**"La tienda de música"**)—silently as doña Elena reads it. Play the audio tape. Then allow children time to re-read the story on their own.

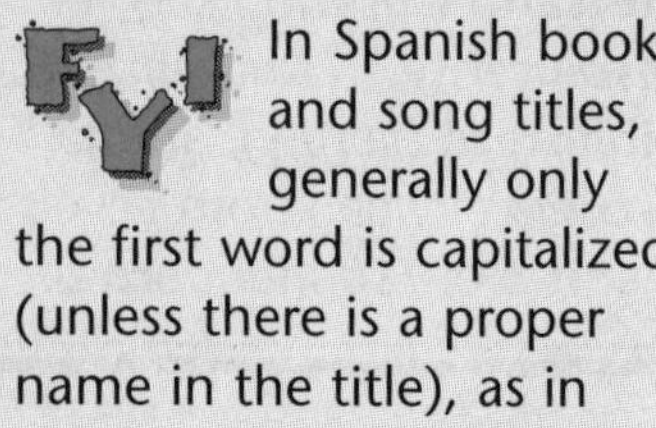

In Spanish book and song titles, generally only the first word is capitalized (unless there is a proper name in the title), as in ***Las aventuras de Fredo.***

watch section 6 of the Video Lesson several times. They will substitute other instrument names for **trompeta** and **tambor**, until they get to **guitarra**.

Mi amigo Fredo va a una tienda de música.	*My friend Fredo is going to a music store.*
Busca un instrumento musical.	*He is looking for a musical instrument.*
Aquí hay una trompeta/ un tambor.	*Here is a trumpet/ a drum.*
¿Toca Fredo la trompeta/ el tambor?	*Does Fredo play the trumpet/ the drum?*
No, no toca la trompeta/ el tambor.	*No, he doesn't play the trumpet/the drum.*
¿Toca Fredo la guitarra?	*Does Fredo play the guitar?*
Sí, toca la guitarra.	*Yes, he plays the guitar.*
A Fredo le gusta la guitarra.	*Fredo likes the guitar.*
Ahora Fredo está contento y va a casa con su guitarra.	*Now Fredo is happy, and he goes home with his guitar.*

While the writers are working, have children try out for the role of Fredo. If you feel comfortable, say **Toca** + the name of the instrument (e.g., Kristen, **toca el tambor**) to each child and have him or her act out a scene of the story. Assign the role of Fredo to eight children—one for each of the instrument-playing scenes (in this order: trumpet, drum, flute, violin, tambourine, piano, clarinet, and guitar). In the actual production, each "Fredo" acts out his or her scene as the narrator reads the corresponding text. "Trumpet Fredo" will also act out going into the music store and "Guitar Fredo" will also act out leaving the store with the guitar.

Allow the "Fredos" time to practice, giving them suggestions on how they could improve their performances. Have the narrators and actors rehearse together, using the actual instruments if they are available. When you feel they are ready, have them perform their production. Videotape it if possible. If appropriate, allow them to do it for a school assembly or show the videotape at a parent/teacher evening.

Activity 25C:

This activity will take several class sessions to prepare and should involve the entire class. Additional ways to involve children: (1) Casting: Choose casting assistants to help you supervise the tryouts and assign roles. (2) Props: Have a group of children assemble musical instruments or toy instruments, or make instruments out of cardboard and paper.
(3) Musical score: Have a group put together background music for the production, e.g., an audiotape of each instrument played. Select a child to start and stop the tape during the performance.
(4) Decor: Have children create a large **La tienda de música** sign to hang over the door to the music store.

CLOSING

Tell the children that Spanish class is finished for today. In the next lesson **la maestra** will visit a department store.

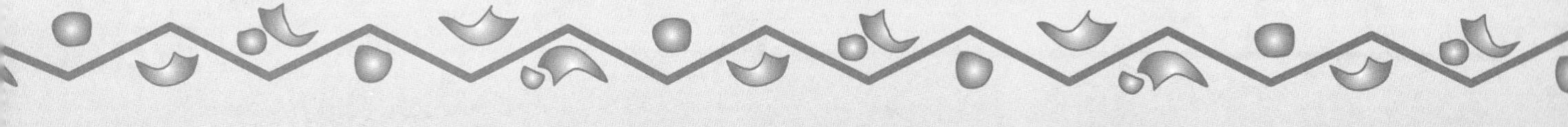

Lesson 26

Materials to gather

- VCR and Video Lesson 26 on Tape 9
- Cassette player
- Activity Cassette 2
- Current Month Picture
- A calendar
- Red Flashcards 54 and 56
- Blackline Master 26A (house and **sí/no**)
- Pencils
- ***Optional materials:*** crayons, colored pencils, or markers; blank paper; children's dictionary pages

Objectives

Language

- Review vocabulary for parts of the building
- Comprehend a trip to the department store

Culture

- Hear the polite phrase of hospitality **Mi casa es tu casa** (*My house is your house*)

Review

- Read **"La tienda de música"** (*"The Music Store"*)
- Review cognates
- Visit a skyscraper and an apartment building

Vocabulary

Vamos a leer.	*Let's read.*
el portal	*porch*
la puerta	*door*
el techo	*roof*
la ventana/las ventanas	*window/windows*
la chimenea	*chimney*
la tienda (de ropa)	*(clothing) store*
Mi casa es tu casa.	*My house is your house.*
¿Qué tiene la casa?	*What does the house have?*
La casa tiene ___.	*The house has ___.*

Warm-up

Materials: Month Picture for the current month; a calendar.

Display the Month Picture. Let the children know it is time for Spanish class (**la clase de español**). Ask them to tell you what the date is in Spanish: **el** [*number*] **de** [*month*]. If necessary, point out the day on the calendar and point to the current Month Picture to cue the name of the month. For a list of the months, see the Topics and Language Covered section in the Front Matter of this Teacher's Manual.

Review

Materials: Red Flashcards 54 and 56.

Remind the children that in the last lesson, they learned a new English word—*edifice*. Ask them what an edifice is (a building). State that they also learned the names of two buildings. Hold up Red Flashcard 54 and ask what they would call such a building in English (*a skyscraper*). Can they remember the Spanish word (**el rascacielos**)? What does that word mean literally (*scratch the sky*)? Show them Red Flashcard 56 and ask what it is called in English (*apartment building*). Can they recall the Spanish word for *apartment building* (**el edificio de apartamentos**)?

Introduce the video

Invite the children to listen, read along, and watch. In this video **la maestra** talks about what all buildings have in common, and she travels to another building—a department store.

EN ESPAÑOL

If you feel comfortable, use **Hola** (*Hello*), **Buenos días** (*Good morning*), or **Buenas tardes** (*Good afternoon*) when greeting the children.

Video Lesson

1. Greeting the children

La maestra greets Winston and the children with **Buenos días** (*Good morning*) and asks them how they are. Winston says **Tengo frío** (*I'm cold*).

2. Reading about Fredo's adventure in the music store

La maestra says **Vamos a leer** (*Let's read*). Everyone reads "**La tienda de música**" (*"The Music Store"*). See Lesson 25, Video Lesson, section 6 for additional sentences.

Aquí hay un tambor.	*Here is a drum.*
¿Toca Fredo el tambor?	*Does Fredo play the drum?*
No, no toca el tambor.	*No, he doesn't play the drum.*

La maestra reminds the children that **toca** means *touch* and with musical instruments it means *play*.

3. Recognizing cognates

Winston remembers cognates from the story about Fredo—**la flauta** (*flute*), **la trompeta** (*trumpet*)—and reads **el clarinete** (*clarinet*) and **el piano** (*piano*). He reads *edifice*, which means building in English, and then reads its Spanish cognate **el edificio**.

4. Visiting a skyscraper and an apartment building

La maestra reviews the words **el rascacielos** (*skyscraper*) and **los apartamentos** (*apartments*). She visits **el rascacielos** (*skyscraper*) and **el edificio de apartamentos** (*apartment building*). She talks with Winston about the type of building he lives in.

Estoy en el centro.	*I'm in the center* [*of the city*].
En el centro hay edificios muy grandes y muy altos.	*In the center there are very big and very tall buildings.*
¿Qué edificio es?	*What building is it?*
Winston, ¿dónde vives tú? ¿En una casa o en un apartamento?	*Winston, where do you live? In a house or in an apartment?*
Vivo en una casa.	*I live in a house.*

5. Reviewing vocabulary for parts of the house

La maestra asks Winston what every building has. The children read the following words: **el techo** (*roof*), **la puerta** (*door*), **la ventana** (*window*). She mentions the function of these parts of the building.

6. Visiting *la maestra*'s house

La maestra takes the children on a tour of the outside of her house.

Bienvenidos a mi casa.	*Welcome to my house.*
Mi casa es su casa.	*My house is your house.*
¿Qué tiene la casa?	*What does the house have?*
¿Cuántas ventanas hay en la casa?	*How many windows are there in the house?*
La casa tiene el portal.	*The house has a porch.*
Entramos por la puerta.	*We go in through the door.*

7. Recognizing buildings

La maestra asks Winston to locate the door, window, and roof on a model of **una casa pequeña** (*a small house*). She talks about what constitutes a building, introduces the word **la chimenea** (*chimney*), and visits a model city.

Muchos edificios tienen tres cosas.	*Many buildings have three things.*
¿Dónde está ___?	*Where is ___?*
Está aquí.	*It's here.*
En una ciudad hay muchos edificios.	*In a city there are many buildings.*
¿Es un edificio?	*Is this a building?*
Sí, es un edificio./No, no es un edificio.	*Yes, it's a building./No, it's not a building.*

8. Going to the clothing store

La maestra and Winston name various types of buildings including **la tienda** (*store*). **La maestra** asks Winston **¿Vamos a la tienda?** (*Shall we go to the store?*) She visits a clothing store.

Clase, ¿qué edificio es?	*Class, what building is it?*
Es la tienda.	*It's the store.*
El taxi va a la tienda.	*The taxi goes to the store.*
¿Y quién está en el taxi? ¿Quién es?	*And who is in the taxi? Who is it?*
Es la maestra.	*It's the teacher.*
Ella va a la tienda de ropa.	*She is going to the clothing store.*
Le gusta ir a la tienda de ropa.	*She likes to go to the clothing store.*

9. Closing

Winston and **la maestra** review building types and bid the children **Adiós** (*Good-bye*).

CROSS-CULTURAL CONNECTIONS

Mi casa es tu casa (*My house is your house*) is an expression of hospitality. Gracious hospitality is a priority in Spanish-speaking cultures. Guests are often greeted with **Estás en tu casa** (*You are in your home*) and they may depart with gifts from their hosts.

Los edificios y las tiendas (*Buildings and stores*):

los apartamentos	*apartments*
la biblioteca	*library*
la casa	*house*
el edificio de apartamentos	*apartment building*
la escuela	*school*
el restaurante	*restaurant*
el supermercado	*supermarket*
la tienda	*store*
la tienda de ropa	*clothing store*

After viewing the video, praise the children for their good listening and watching skills.

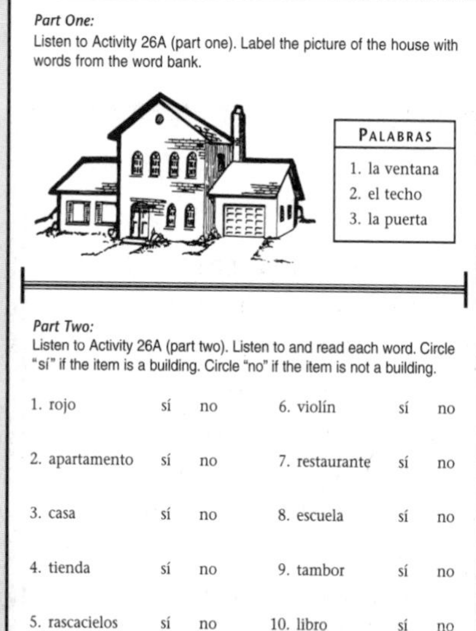

Part One:
Listen to Activity 26A (part one). Label the picture of the house with words from the word bank.

PALABRAS
1. la ventana
2. el techo
3. la puerta

Part Two:
Listen to Activity 26A (part two). Listen to and read each word. Circle "sí" if the item is a building. Circle "no" if the item is not a building.

1. rojo	sí	no	6. violín	sí	no
2. apartamento	sí	no	7. restaurante	sí	no
3. casa	sí	no	8. escuela	sí	no
4. tienda	sí	no	9. tambor	sí	no
5. rascacielos	sí	no	10. libro	sí	no

Blackline Master 26A

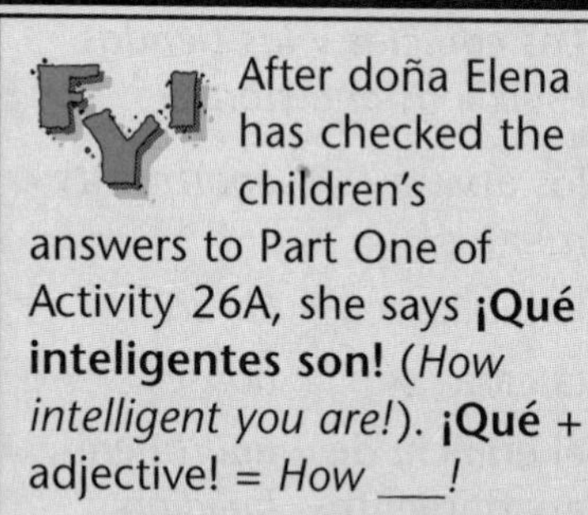

FYI After doña Elena has checked the children's answers to Part One of Activity 26A, she says **¡Qué inteligentes son!** (*How intelligent you are!*). **¡Qué + adjective!** = *How ___!*

ACTIVITY LESSON

Activity 26A: Work with buildings

Materials: Cassette player; Activity Cassette 2, Side A; Blackline Master 26A; pencils; current Month Picture; and a calendar.

Preparation: Copy and distribute Blackline Master 26A to the children. Display the current Month Picture. Make sure each child has a pencil.

Have the children complete the name and date lines on their papers, pointing to the day on a calendar and the Month Picture if necessary. Then tell them that they are going to work on Part One first. Ask what the picture represents (*a house*—**una casa**). Tell them to listen to doña Elena as she tells them what to do in Part One: label the parts of the house, using the words in the word bank (**Palabras**). Play Activity 26A, stopping the tape at the harp sound to allow children time to label the house. Once children have completed the task, tell them to correct their papers as doña Elena checks their answers to Part One. Then move on to Part Two, in which children are to listen and read each word as doña Elena says it and circle **sí** (*yes*) if the word is a type of building and **no** (*no*) if it is not. Restart the tape, playing it to the end of the activity. Then check the answers with the children.

Answers to Part One:

Children should have labeled one or more windows with **la ventana** (1), one or more roof surfaces with **el techo** (2), and the front door and/or the garage door with **la puerta** (3).

Answers to Part Two:

1. no
2. sí (or **no**, since apartments are in an apartment building)
3. sí
4. sí
5. sí
6. no
7. sí
8. sí
9. no
10. no

Activity 26B: Make a cross-cultural connection

Mention to the children that in the video, **la maestra** greeted them at her house with an expression that is used in Spanish-speaking countries. Ask them if they can recall what the expression is, giving them the English equivalent if necessary (**Mi casa es tu casa**—*My house is your house*). Tell the children that in Spanish-speaking cultures people take great pride in their homes (whether the home is very small or very large). They enjoy having guests and are very hospitable. Hosts will often tell their guests *You are in your own home* (**Estás en tu casa**). Hosts may also give their guests gifts.

Ask how guests are typically received in this country. What does one typically say when someone comes to visit? (Hi, Glad you could come, Welcome, etc.) Mention that it is not usual in the United States for hosts to give their guests gifts. It is more typical for guests, particularly those coming for a longer stay, to bring a small gift to the host (e.g., a plant or something else for the house).

Activity 26C: What kind of building do you live in?

Lead a discussion of various kinds of buildings in which people live. What kinds of buildings or structures do people live in (houseboats, tents, igloos)? Have the children seen these other kinds of structures? Let them relate their stories—where they saw the structure, what it looks like, who lives in it.

CLOSING

Tell the children that Spanish class is finished for today. In the next lesson children will learn the names of more buildings.

HERITAGE SPEAKERS

Ask heritage speakers how guests are greeted in their homes or how they are greeted when they visit their relatives or friends here and in their countries of origin. Perhaps there are other phrases they or their family members use to greet guests.

DICTIONARY

Materials: Children's copies of Blackline Master 26A; crayons, colored pencils or markers; blank paper; children's dictionary pages.

Have the children create a page for the letter **C** by drawing a picture of a house. Underneath the picture they should write **la casa**. Encourage them to be creative (e.g., perhaps they would like to draw a typical house for the year 2900 on Earth, in space, or on another planet)! Have them file the page with their other dictionary pages. Remind them to file it under **c** for **casa** (*house*), not **l** for **la** (*the*). If they already have a **C** page, be sure they order their **C** pages correctly.

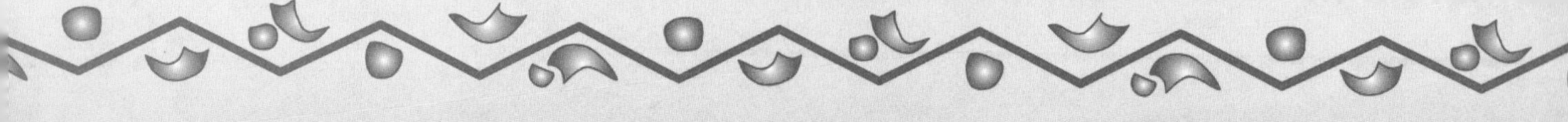

Lesson 27

Materials to gather

- VCR and Video Lesson 27 on Tape 9
- Cassette player
- Activity Cassette 2
- Song Cassette
- Overhead projector
- Overhead transparency of Blackline Master 5B ("Alphabet Rap")
- Blank overhead transparency
- Blackline Masters 27B-1 and 27B-2 (word puzzle and answers)
- Pencils
- Current Month Picture
- A calendar
- Two pieces of white construction paper
- Crayons, markers, or colored pencils
- Tape or tacks
- ***Optional materials:*** blank paper

Objectives

Language

- Comprehend continuous conversation about buildings
- Learn the words for *entrance* (**entrada**) and *exit* (**salida**)
- Learn the words for two more buildings
- Review that the letter **h** is silent in Spanish

Culture

- Sing **"Las vocales en español"** (*"The Vowels in Spanish"*) with the letter **h**

Review

- Review three parts of buildings
- Read words in Spanish
- Recognize types of buildings

Vocabulary

la cafetería	*cafeteria*
la entrada	*entrance*
la salida	*exit*
el hotel	*hotel*
el hospital	*hospital*

Warm-up

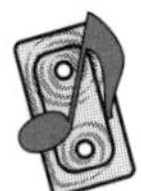

Materials: Cassette player; "Alphabet Rap" on the Song Cassette; an overhead projector; and the overhead transparency of Blackline Master 5B.

Project your overhead transparency of Blackline Master 5B. Ask a volunteer to point to the three letters the Spanish alphabet has that the English alphabet doesn't have (**ch, ll, ñ**). Then play the "Alphabet Rap" on the Song Cassette and encourage the children to sing along.

Review

Brainstorm with the children a list in English of building types for which they know the Spanish names. Write each building type they mention on the chalkboard. Then point to each word and ask them to tell you the Spanish word. Reassure them that it's all right if they can't remember the words. They will have ample opportunities to hear and practice the words.

Los edificios y las tiendas (*Buildings and stores*):

los apartamentos	*apartments*
la biblioteca	*library*
el rascacielos	*skyscraper*
la casa	*house*
el edificio de apartamentos	*apartment building*
la escuela	*school*
el restaurante	*restaurant*
el supermercado	*supermarket*
la tienda	*store*
la tienda de ropa	*clothing store*

Introduce the video

Invite the children to listen and watch as **la maestra** reminds them what's different about the letter **h** in Spanish and introduces the names of more buildings.

VIDEO LESSON

1. Greeting the children

La maestra greets the children with **Buenos días** (*Good morning*) and asks them how they are. LeeAnn says **Tengo hambre** (*I'm hungry*). **La maestra** suggests that perhaps LeeAnn can go to **la cafetería** (*cafeteria*) or **el restaurante** (*restaurant*).

See the Review section of this lesson for a list of types of buildings.

2. Practice vocabulary for parts of a building

LeeAnn and **la maestra** review the names of various buildings. **La maestra** mentions the word **el hospital**, which is a cognate for *hospital*. She mentions that buildings are **alto** (*tall*), **bajo** (*small*), **grande** (*big*), or **pequeño** (*small*). She visits the model city and asks the children to identify what structures are buildings.

¿Es un edificio?	*Is it a building?*
Sí, es un edificio porque tiene un techo, una puerta y ventanas.	*Yes, it's a building because it has a roof, a door, and windows.*

3. Introducing the words *exit* and *entrance*

LeeAnn reads the words **el techo** (*roof*), **la puerta** (*door*), and **la ventana** (*window*). **La maestra** talks about the purpose of these building parts. She introduces the words for *entrance*, the way into a building, and *exit*, the way out of a building.

la entrada	*entrance*
¿Dónde está la entrada?	*Where is the entrance?*
la salida	*exit*
¿Dónde está la salida?	*Where is the exit?*

4. Naming the buildings

La maestra reviews the names of many buildings and describes each briefly. Then she plays a game of **¿Qué edificio es?** (*What building is it?*). Children identify **el rascacielos** (*skyscraper*), **los apartamentos** (*apartments*), **la casa** (*house*), **la tienda** (*store*), **la escuela** (*school*), and **el supermercado** (*supermarket*).

CROSS-CULTURAL CONNECTIONS

Point out the roof of **el supermercado** (*supermarket*). Such red tile roofs are more typical of areas with warmer climates, such as South America or the south of Spain. In the United States they are found in warm-weather states, such as Florida, Texas, or southern California, but not in northern states, such as Michigan, Oregon, Pennsylvania, where the weather is cooler.

5. Presenting the names of two more buildings

LeeAnn identifies **el restaurante** as a cognate for *restaurant.* **La maestra** introduces two more cognates: **el hotel** (*hotel*) and **el hospital** (*hospital*). She explains that the letter **h** in Spanish is not pronounced.

6. Singing *"Las vocales en español"* ("The Vowels in Spanish")

La maestra reminds LeeAnn and the children that the letter **h** is silent in Spanish. Everyone sings the song with the letter **h** and the vowels.

Las vocales en español.	*The vowels in Spanish.*
Las vocales en español.	*The vowels in Spanish.*
A, E, I, O, U.	***A, E, I, O, U.***
La H con la A dice HA.	*The **H** with the **A** says **HA.***
La H con la E dice HE.	*The **H** with the **E** says **HE.***
Con la I dice HI.	*With the **I** it says **HI.***
Con la O dice HO.	*With the **O** it says **HO.***
La H con la U dice HU.	*The **H** with the **U** says **HU.***

7. Closing

La maestra asks LeeAnn and the children to name the buildings in which one does certain things, e.g., the building into which one goes to learn—**la escuela** (*school*). She reviews the structural parts that all buildings have in common and reviews the words **la entrada** (*entrance*) and **la salida** (*exit*). She and LeeAnn say **Adiós** (*Good-bye*) and **Hasta luego** (*See you later*).

After viewing the video, praise the children for their good listening and watching skills.

Activity Lesson

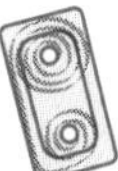

Activity 27A: Sing the vowel song with the letter *h*

Materials: Cassette player; Activity Cassette 2, Side A.

Preparation: Write the following on the chalkboard:

HA HE HI HO HU

Ask the children what is different about the pronunciation of the letter **h** in Spanish (it is silent). Tell the children they are going to practice the pronunciation of the letter **h** by singing *"The Vowels in Spanish"* (**"Las vocales en español"**). Point to the letters as they are sung. For song lyrics, see section 6 of this Video Lesson.

Activity 27B: Find the words!

Materials: Overhead projector; a blank transparency; Blackline Masters 27B-1 and 27B-2; pencils; current Month Picture; and a calendar.

Preparation: Copy and distribute Blackline Master 27B-1 to the children. Make a transparency of Blackline Master 27B-2 (the answers to the puzzle).

Tell the children to write their names and the date on the top of their pages. If they need help determining the date and how to spell the month, point to the day on the calendar and the current Month Picture.

Explain that the Spanish names of five buildings and the Spanish words for *entrance* and *exit* are hidden in the puzzle. All the words that are hidden are listed in the word bank (**Palabras**). Children are to find and circle each word. The words go from left to right and top to bottom. As they locate each word in the puzzle, they should write it on one of the lines below the puzzle. After children have completed the puzzle, check their answers by displaying your overhead transparency of Blackline Master 27B-2 and pointing out each word in the puzzle to them.

Word Search

The names for five buildings, and the words for *entrance* and *exit* are hidden in this puzzle. Find them and circle them. The words go from left to right and from top to bottom in the puzzle. Then write the words you found in the blanks below.

A	P	A	R	T	A	M	E	N	T	O	S	Y	R	R
M	S	X	H	N	A	D	A	R	Ñ	I	A	V	A	Z
C	Q	E	R	I	T	S	M	T	A	N	L	R	S	O
E	U	N	R	I	E	E	L	E	O	G	I	Z	C	O
S	I	T	O	C	A	S	A	B	O	L	D	S	A	T
P	A	R	I	N	A	C	N	I	N	E	A	N	C	S
A	R	A	E	P	Q	U	V	T	Ñ	S	B	M	I	U
Ñ	B	D	L	O	N	E	E	S	T	O	C	U	E	R
O	X	A	A	T	E	L	A	T	I	C	A	S	L	K
L	T	I	E	N	D	A	P	D	I	T	Z	I	O	V
Z	H	U	C	I	E	N	C	I	A	S	R	C	S	Ñ
Y	M	Y	T	Y	M	I	Z	N	V	M	X	A	F	O

Palabras

ENTRADA TIENDA ESCUELA
APARTAMENTOS RASCACIELOS CASA SALIDA

_______________ _______________
_______________ _______________
_______________ _______________
____

Blackline Master 27B-1

Answer Key

Word Search

The names for five buildings, and the words for *entrance* and *exit* are hidden in this puzzle. Find them and circle them. The words go from left to right and from top to bottom in the puzzle. Then write the words you found in the blanks below.

A	P	A	R	T	A	M	E	N	T	O	S	Y	R	R
M	S	X	H	N	A	D	A	R	Ñ	I	A	V	A	Z
C	Q	E	R	I	T	S	M	T	A	N	L	R	S	O
E	U	N	R	I	E	E	L	E	O	G	I	Z	C	O
S	I	T	O	C	A	S	A	B	O	L	D	S	A	T
P	A	R	I	N	A	C	N	I	N	E	A	N	C	S
A	R	A	E	P	Q	U	V	T	Ñ	S	B	M	I	U
Ñ	B	D	L	O	N	E	E	S	T	O	C	U	E	R
O	X	A	A	T	E	L	A	T	I	C	A	S	L	K
L	T	I	E	N	D	A	P	D	I	T	Z	I	O	V
Z	H	U	C	I	E	N	C	I	A	S	R	C	S	Ñ
Y	M	Y	T	Y	M	I	Z	N	V	M	X	A	F	O

Palabras

ENTRADA TIENDA ESCUELA
APARTAMENTOS RASCACIELOS CASA SALIDA

ENTRADA TIENDA
APARTAMENTOS RASCACIELOS
CASA SALIDA
ESCUELA

Blackline Master 27B-2

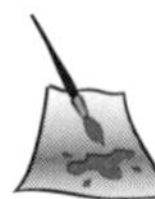

Activity 27C: Cooperative learning—Make signs

Materials: Two pieces of white construction paper; crayons, markers, or colored pencils; and tape or thumb tacks.

Preparation: Write the Spanish words for *entrance* and *exit* on the chalkboard:

ENTRADA SALIDA

Talk with the children about where they are used to seeing exit and entrance signs (movie theaters, classrooms, grocery stores). Ask them how the signs look (exit signs are often lit in red; *entrance* is often painted on the door to stores where people enter). Ask them which sign is placed inside a building (*exit*) and which sign is placed outside (*entrance*).

Pointing to the words **ENTRADA** and **SALIDA** on the chalkboard, ask the children which one means *entrance* and which one means *exit*. Divide the class into two groups. Have one group make an entrance sign for your Spanish class and one group an exit sign. Tell them to negotiate the color they want the word to be. Encourage them to be creative (using various colors for the letters, adorning them with borders, etc.) If allowed in your school, tape or tack up the completed signs on either side of the doorway to your classroom.

If You Have Time . . .

Materials: Blank paper; crayons, markers, or colored pencils.

Allow children to make their own Spanish entrance and exit signs to take home.

Closing

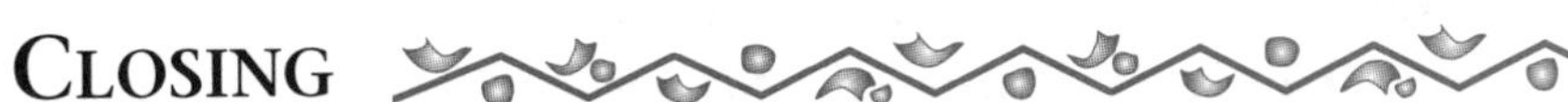

Tell the children that Spanish class is finished for today. In the next lesson they will read the story about Fredo's adventures in the music store again.

Lesson 28

Materials to gather

- VCR and Video Lesson 28 on Tape 10
- Cassette player
- Activity Cassette 2
- Song Cassette
- Overhead projector
- Blank overhead transparency
- Blackline Master 28B (money in the Hispanic world)
- Overhead transparency of Blackline Master 2B (20 Spanish-speaking countries)
- Two foreign currency rate charts from two different days of a local or national newspaper
- World map
- ***Optional materials:*** *"Las aventuras de Fredo"* (*"Fredo's Adventures"*), Book 1: **"La tienda de música"** (*"The Music Store"*); U.S. and foreign coins or bills; computer with modem, Internet access, and a web browser

Objectives

Language

- Learn to state the price of something
- Understand that **alto** and **bajo** are used to refer to prices as well as buildings and people

Culture

- Review that **maracas** are a Latin American instrument
- Understand that some Spanish words are used in English

Review

- Review vocabulary for types of buildings
- Read **"La tienda de música"** (*"The Music Store"*)
- Count from 10 to 100 by tens
- Review adjectives

Vocabulary

la tienda de zapatos	*shoe store*
el precio/los precios	*price/prices*
¿Cuánto es?	*How much is it?*
los dólares	*dollars*
alto	*high (price)*
bajo	*low (price)*

Warm-up

Write a dollar sign on the chalkboard ($). Ask the children what the symbol means (dollars) and where they see it (on price tags, in ads, anywhere the price of something is being given). Compare the cost of a very high-priced item (e.g., a house or a car) with the cost of a lower-priced item that the children are more likely to buy (e.g., a food item, a notebook). How many of the lower-priced items could they buy for the cost of the high-priced item?

Review

Materials: Cassette player; **"De diez en diez"** (*"Ten by Ten"*) on the Song Cassette, Side A.

Have the children count themselves off by tens in Spanish. Ask them if they remember Lorena's dance from ten to one hundred. Tell them you are going to play that activity on the tape now and when their number comes up, they should do a short dance. If necessary, reassure them that their dance doesn't have to be as complicated as Lorena's. They can simply twist from side to side or do jumping jacks. If anyone is very reluctant to dance, he/she could write his/her number on the chalkboard or say the number aloud after **la maestra**. For song lyrics, see song 7 in the Song Appendix.

Introduce the video

Invite the children to listen and watch as **la maestra** introduces how one talks about prices in Spanish and reviews big numbers so the children can state prices.

Los números grandes (*big numbers*):

diez	*10*
veinte	*20*
treinta	*30*
cuarenta	*40*
cincuenta	*50*
sesenta	*60*
setenta	*70*
ochenta	*80*
noventa	*90*
cien	*100*

Video Lesson

1. Greeting Winston and the children

La maestra greets Winston and the children with **Buenos días** (*Good morning*) and asks them how they are. Winston says **Tengo calor** (*I'm hot*), which prompts **la maestra** to remind him that the last time they were together he said **Tengo frío** (*I'm cold*). She asks him **¿Estás enfermo?** (*Are you sick?*).

2. Reviewing the names of buildings

La maestra talks about all the different size buildings there are—**el rascacielos** (*skyscraper*), **los apartamentos** (*apartments*), **el edificio de apartamentos** (*apartment building*), **la casa** (*house*), **la tienda** (*store*), **la escuela** (*school*), and **el supermercado** (*supermarket*).

Hay muchos edificios.	*There are many buildings.*
Hay edificios altos y grandes.	*There are tall and large buildings.*
Y hay edificios bajos.	*And there are low buildings.*
Hay edificios pequeños y hay edificios bonitos.	*There are small buildings and pretty buildings.*
El rascacielos es muy alto.	*The skyscraper is very high.*
Hay muchos apartamentos en el edificio de apartamentos.	*There are many apartments in the apartment building.*
La casa es muy bonita.	*The house is very pretty.*
La tienda es muy grande, ¿no?	*The store is very big, isn't it?*
Hay muchos maestros y muchos alumnos en la escuela.	*There are many teachers and many pupils in the school.*
Hay mucha comida en el supermercado.	*There is a lot of food in the supermarket.*
Hay frutas y carne y leche.	*There are fruits and meat and milk.*

3. Reading about Fredo's adventures

La maestra mentions different kinds of stores: **la tienda de ropa** (*clothing store*), **la tienda de zapatos** (*shoe store*), and **la tienda de música** (*music store*). The children read about Fredo's adventures in the book **"La tienda de música"** (*"The Music Store"*). For additional sentences, see the Video Lessons in Lesson 25 (section 6) and Lesson 26 (section 2).

Aquí hay ___.	*Here is ___.*
¿Toca Fredo ___?	*Does Fredo play ___?*
No, no toca ___.	*No he doesn't play ___.*

If children are having difficulty understanding the story, remind them to watch for visual cues provided by the pictures and to listen and watch for words that sound like English words. You might also mention that the background music is a hint to the location of Fredo's adventure.

4. Reviewing *los números grandes* (*big numbers*)

La maestra asks Winston **¿Qué instrumento musical es?** (*What musical instrument is it?*) and mentions that **las maracas es un instrumento musical latino** (*maracas are a Latin American musical instrument*). Showing him the price tag on the maracas, she asks **¿Cuánto cuesta?** (*How much does it cost?*). Lorena dances (**baila**) as **la maestra** asks the children **¿Qué número es?** (*What number is it?*).

diez	*ten*	sesenta	*sixty*
veinte	*twenty*	setenta	*seventy*
treinta	*thirty*	ochenta	*eighty*
cuarenta	*forty*	noventa	*ninety*
cincuenta	*fifty*	cien	*one hundred*

5. Stating prices

La maestra shows Winston several prices (**los precios**) and asks him how much they are. She explains that **alto** and **bajo** are used to refer to people and prices.

¿Es un precio bajo o es un precio alto?	*Is it a low price or a high price?*
Ochenta y nueve dólares.	*Eighty-nine dollars.*
Es alto. Es mucho dinero.	*It's high. It's a lot of money.*

6. Practicing adjectives

Showing clown pictures, **la maestra** asks the children questions about them. She reviews the adjectives and how their endings change depending on the noun they modify. She plays **¿Cómo es el payaso/la payasa?** (*What's the male/female clown like?*).

alto/alta	*tall*	delgado/delgada	*thin*
bajo/baja	*short*	feo/fea	*ugly*
gordo/gorda	*fat*	bonito/bonita	*pretty*

7. Closing

La maestra praises Winston and the children for all they know how to do. She and Winston say **Adiós** (*Good-bye*) and **Hasta luego** (*See you later*).

Encourage the children to say the numbers as Lorena dances and **la maestra** asks **¿Qué número es?** (*What number is it?*).

EN ESPAÑOL

When playing games with the children, **la maestra** often uses the phrase **Uno más** (*One more*) to indicate she has just one more question for them. She also compliments the children by saying **¡Excelente!** (*Excellent!*). Use these phrases with your class.

After viewing the video, praise the children for their good listening and watching skills.

Activity Lesson

Fredo Book Activity

Materials: Cassette player; Song Cassette, Side B; ***"Las aventuras de Fredo"*** (*"Fredo's Adventures"*), Book 1: **"La tienda de música"** (*"The Music Store"*).

Mention that reading in Spanish takes practice just as reading in English does. Ask the children to name the title of the book they read during the Video Lesson (**"La tienda de música"**). Ask a volunteer to tell the main plot of the story (Fredo goes to the music store, tries unsuccessfully to play various instruments, finally finds a guitar, which he can play, and leaves the store with the guitar). Distribute the books and go to Book 1: **"La tienda de música"** (*"The Music Store"*). Tell the children to follow along in their books as doña Elena reads the story. Play the audiotape. Once doña Elena has finished the story, ask volunteers to read one page at a time aloud.

FYI Many European countries (including Spain) have agreed to start using a common currency, the Euro, in the near future.

Activity 28A: Fredo's music store adventure

Note: If your school has ***"Las aventuras de Fredo"*** (*"Fredo's Adventures"*) books available for the children, substitute the Fredo Book Activity in the margin for this activity.

Materials: VCR; Video Lesson 28 on Tape 10.

Preparation: Recue the videotape to section 3, in which doña Elena reads the story **"La tienda de música"** (*"The Music Store"*).

Tell the children that reading in Spanish takes practice just like reading in English does. Ask them to name the title of the book they read during the Video Lesson (**"La tienda de música"**). Ask a volunteer to tell the main plot of the story (Fredo goes to the music store, tries unsuccessfully to play various instruments, finally finds a guitar, which he can play, and leaves the store with the guitar). Play section 3 of Video Lesson 28 again and tell the children to read along as doña Elena reads the story. Then rewind the videotape and ask for volunteers to read each page as you replay the story without the sound. Tell the other children to follow along.

Activity 28B: Language across the curriculum: An economics lesson

Materials: Overhead projector; a blank overhead transparency; Blackline Master 28B; and two foreign currency rate charts from two different days of a local or national newspaper; *optional:* U.S. and foreign coins or bills.

Preparation: Make a transparency of Blackline Master 28B.

Lead the children in a discussion of the currencies in the Spanish-speaking countries.

Begin by asking the children what they use to buy things in the United States (dollars, pennies, nickels, dimes, quarters). If you brought U.S. currency, display it. Explain that in other countries people use different looking coins and paper money and that each country has its own currency. If you have currency from other countries, show it to the children and tell them from what countries it comes. Project the transparency of Blackline Master 28B and read the names of the various currencies in the Spanish-speaking countries. Point out that while some countries' currencies may share the same name, their values are not the same. In Argentina something may cost 10 pesos while in Chile the same thing may cost more or fewer pesos. Explain that each currency's value changes daily in relation to the U.S. dollar. Using the currency rate charts from the newspaper, show how the rates vary and how many Mexican pesos are in one U.S. dollar.

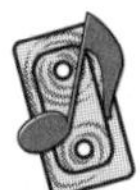

Activity 28C: Sing about the Spanish-speaking countries

Materials: Cassette player; **"La canción de geografía"** (*"The Geography Song"*) on the Song Cassette, Side A; the overhead transparencies of Blackline Master 2B and 28B; and a world map.

Project transparency 2B (Spanish-speaking countries). Ask for two volunteers to help out as the class sings *"The Geography Song"* (**"La canción de geografía"**)—one to point to the countries' names on the transparency, and one to locate the countries on the map. Play the song and encourage the children to sing along. For song lyrics, see Song 2 in the Song Appendix. Then, display your transparency of Blackline Master 28B. Ask volunteers to read each country's name and its currency while the map volunteer locates the country on the world map.

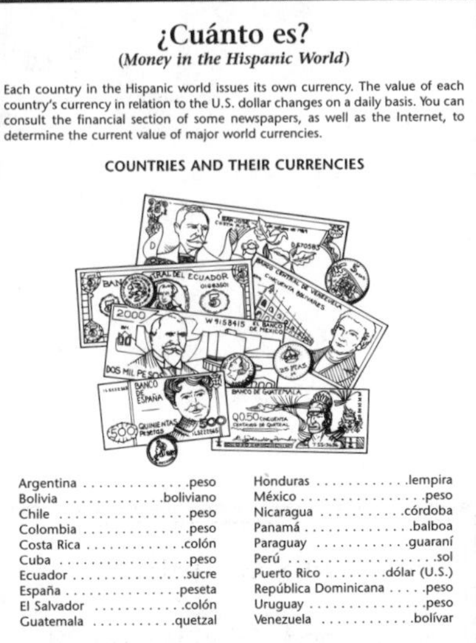

¿Cuánto es?
(Money in the Hispanic World)

Each country in the Hispanic world issues its own currency. The value of each country's currency in relation to the U.S. dollar changes on a daily basis. You can consult the financial section of some newspapers, as well as the Internet, to determine the current value of major world currencies.

COUNTRIES AND THEIR CURRENCIES

Country	Currency	Country	Currency
Argentina	peso	Honduras	lempira
Bolivia	boliviano	México	peso
Chile	peso	Nicaragua	córdoba
Colombia	peso	Panamá	balboa
Costa Rica	colón	Paraguay	guaraní
Cuba	peso	Perú	sol
Ecuador	sucre	Puerto Rico	dólar (U.S.)
España	peseta	República Dominicana	peso
El Salvador	colón	Uruguay	peso
Guatemala	quetzal	Venezuela	bolívar

Blackline Master 28B

CLOSING

Tell the children that Spanish class is finished for today. In the next lesson children will review all the new things they've learned this year.

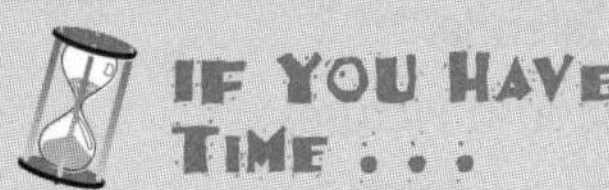

Materials: Computer with modem, connection to the Internet, and a web browser.

With your class, determine the current exchange rates for the Spanish-speaking countries by locating the information on the World Wide Web. Choose one of your web browser's search engines. Go to the "business" or "financial" section of the search engines and run a search using the keywords "currency exchange." From the brief descriptions of the various sites that come up, choose one that is likely to yield the best results and click on the underscored text.

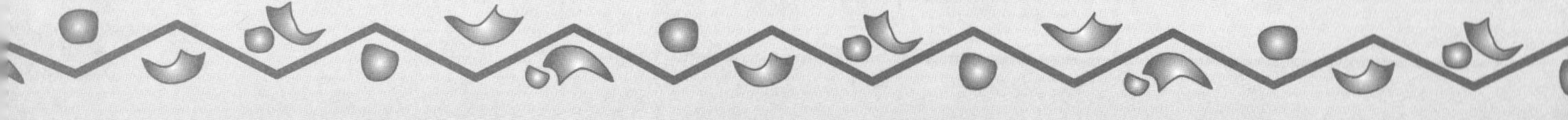

Lesson 29

Materials to gather

- VCR and Video Lesson 29 on Tape 10
- Cassette player
- Song Cassette
- Calendar
- Month Pictures
- A world map
- Overhead projector
- Blackline Master 2B (20 Spanish-speaking countries)
- Four large pieces of white posterboard
- Pencils
- Crayons, markers, or colored pencils
- Tape
- ***Optional materials:*** blank paper; children's dictionary pages

Objectives

Language

- No new language concepts are introduced in this lesson.

Culture

- Recall that the sound at the end of some adjectives changes depending on the noun being modified

Review

- Identify musical instruments
- Describe people
- Name colors
- Review the names of several parts of a building
- Review school subjects

Vocabulary

No new vocabulary is introduced in this lesson.

Warm-up

Materials: The current Month Picture; a calendar.

Greet the children and tell them it's time for Spanish class (**la clase de español**). Ask them to tell you the date in Spanish: **el** [*number*] **de** [*month*]. Assist them by pointing to the day on the calendar and the Month Picture.

Review

Write the following prices on the board. Pointing to each price, ask the children to tell you how many dollars it is. If you feel comfortable, ask **¿Cuánto es?** (*How much is it?*).

$89.00	ochenta y nueve dólares
$5.00	cinco dólares

Pointing to $89.00, ask if in comparison to the other number ($5.00) $89.00 is a high price or a low price. Again, if you feel comfortable, ask **¿Es un precio alto o un precio bajo?** (*Is it a high price or is it a low price?*). Answer: **Alto** (*High*) or **Es un precio alto** (*It's a high price*).

Introduce the video

Invite the children to listen and watch as **la maestra** reviews many things the children have learned and practiced this year.

Video Lesson

Los instrumentos musicales:

el clarinete	*clarinet*
la flauta	*flute*
la guitarra	*guitar*
la pandereta	*tambourine*
el piano	*piano*
el tambor	*drum*
la trompeta	*trumpet*
el violín	*violin*

Adjectives:

grande	*big*
mediano/ mediana	*medium*
pequeño/ pequeña	*small*
alto/alta	*tall*
bajo/baja	*short*
feo/fea	*ugly*
bonito/ bonita	*pretty*
gordo/ gorda	*fat*
delgado/ delgada	*thin*

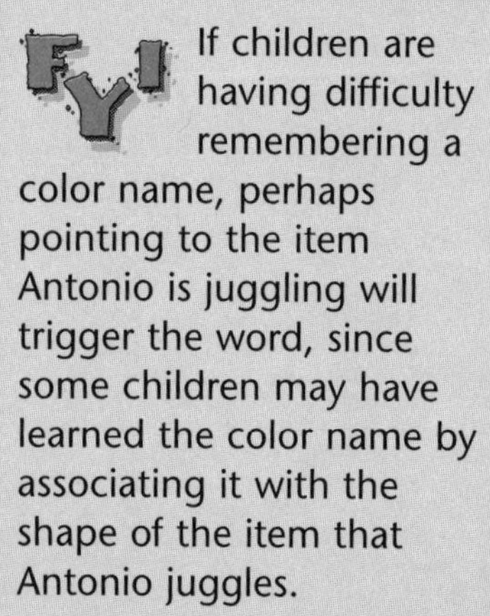

If children are having difficulty remembering a color name, perhaps pointing to the item Antonio is juggling will trigger the word, since some children may have learned the color name by associating it with the shape of the item that Antonio juggles.

1. Greeting the children

La maestra greets the children with **Buenos días** (*Good morning*) and asks them how they are. **La maestra** tells the children **Estoy muy bien porque mi amigo Kipper está aquí** (*I'm very well because my friend Kipper is here*). She greets Kipper and asks him how he is. He says **Muy contento** (*Very happy*).

2. Identifying musical instruments

Antonio mimes playing various instruments as **la maestra** asks the children **¿Qué toca?** (*What's he playing?*) and reinforces their answer **Toca** + the name of the instrument. Showing pictures of instruments, she asks **¿Qué instrumento es?** (*What instrument is it?*). She describes the instruments.

3. Describing people

La maestra asks the children **¿Cómo es el payaso/la payasa?** (*What is the* [*male/female*] *clown like?*). The children describe the clowns.

4. Reviewing adjectives for describing things

La maestra reviews the adjectives **sucio/sucia** (*dirty*) and **limpio/limpia** (*clean*). Doña Elena and Antonio demonstrate the adjectives **suave** (*soft*) and **duro/dura** (*hard*).

5. Practicing color names

Pointing to shapes of various colors, **la maestra** asks the children **¿De qué color es?** (*What color is it?*).

amarillo	*yellow*
anaranjado	*orange*
azul	*blue*
blanco	*white*
café	*brown*
gris	*gray*
morado	*purple*
negro	*black*
rojo	*red*
rosado	*pink*
verde	*green*

6. Practicing the names of buildings

La maestra plays **¿Qué edificio es?** (*What building is it?*) with the children, reviewing the names of various buildings.

7. Remembering the parts of a building

With Kipper, **la maestra** reviews structural parts buildings have in common and the function of each one—**el techo** (*roof*), **las ventanas** (*windows*), **la puerta** (*door*). She asks LeeAnn and Winston **¿Dónde está la entrada?** (*Where is the entrance?*) and **¿Dónde está la salida?** (*Where is the exit?*).

8. Naming school subjects

La maestra asks the children what class is shown in each picture.

¿Qué clase es?	*What class is it?*
Es la clase de ___.	*It's ___ class.*
la clase de arte	*art class*
la clase de ciencias	*science class*
la clase de computadoras	*computer class*
la clase de drama	*theater, drama class*
la clase de español	*Spanish class*
la clase de inglés	*English class*
la clase de matemáticas	*math class*
la clase de música	*music class*
el recreo	*recess*

9. Closing

La maestra and Kipper bid the children **Hasta luego** (*See you later*) and **Hasta pronto** (*See you soon*).

Los edificios:

los apartamentos
(*apartments*)
la biblioteca
(*library*)
la casa
(*house*)
el edificio de apartamentos
(*apartment building*)
la escuela
(*school*)
el hospital
(*hospital*)
el hotel
(*hotel*)
el rascacielos
(*skyscraper*)
el restaurante
(*restaurant*)
el supermercado
(*supermarket*)
la tienda
(*store*)
la tienda de ropa/zapatos
(*clothing/shoe store*)

After viewing the video, praise the children for their good listening and watching skills.

Activity Lesson

If your class has been preparing a production of Fredo's adventures in the music store (see Activity 25C), this would be a good point to hold the performance.

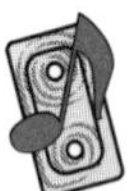

Activity 29A: Review the Spanish-speaking countries

Materials: Cassette player; "**La canción de geografía**" (*"The Geography Song"*) on the Song Cassette, Side A; an overhead projector; the overhead transparency of Blackline Master 2B; and a world map.

Mention to the children that in the Video Lesson **la maestra** reviewed much of what they have learned this year. Now they are going to review the names of all the Spanish-speaking countries by singing *"The Geography Song"* ("**La canción de geografía**"). Ask how many Spanish-speaking countries there are in the world (20). Project the transparency of Blackline Master 2B. Ask for a volunteer to point to each country on the map and another to point to the names of the countries on the transparency as you play the song. For song lyrics, see Song 2 in the Song Appendix.

Activity 29B may take more than one class period to complete.

Activity 29B: Cooperative learning—The seasons and months

Materials: Month Pictures; four large pieces of white posterboard; pencils; crayons, markers, or colored pencils; and tape.

Display the Month Pictures. Pointing to them, mention to the children that they've practiced the names of the months and seasons with **la maestra** this year. Divide the class into four groups. Assign each group one of the four seasons. Give each group a piece of posterboard and say that each group should draw and color in a picture representing their season according to the climate in your location. Encourage them to work together in planning what the picture will look like. Tell them to be sure to include the Spanish name of the season somewhere on their picture. When the pictures are complete, have the children describe them for the class. Encourage them to use the Spanish words when possible. Finally, tape the season drawings on the board and have each group set the appropriate Month Pictures under their drawing.

el invierno (*winter*): diciembre (*December*), enero (*January*), febrero (*February*)

la primavera (*spring*): marzo (*March*), abril (*April*), mayo (*May*)

el verano (*summer*): junio (*June*), julio (*July*), agosto (*August*)

el otoño (*fall*): septiembre (*September*), octubre (*October*), noviembre (*November*)

Activity 29C: Talk about feelings

Materials: Cassette player; **"¿Cómo está Lorena?"** (*"How Is Lorena?"*) on the Song Cassette, Side A.

Tell the children you are going to play the song *"How Is Lorena?"* (**"¿Cómo está Lorena?"**). They are to listen carefully for each feeling expression **la maestra** says and mime each one.

¿Cómo está Lorena? Está enojada.	*How is Lorena?* *She's angry.*
¿Cómo está Lorena? Está contenta.	*How is Lorena?* *She's happy.*
¿Cómo está Lorena? Está triste.	*How is Lorena?* *She's sad.*

Ask volunteers to mime other feeling expressions. Have the children guess what the expressions are.

Additional feeling expressions:

(Estoy) muy bien.	*(I'm) very well.*
(Estoy) muy mal.	*(I'm) very bad.*
(Estoy) así, así.	*(I'm) so-so.*
Tengo frío.	*I'm cold.*
Tengo calor.	*I'm hot.*
Tengo hambre.	*I'm hungry.*
Tengo sed.	*I'm thirsty.*
Tengo sueño.	*I'm sleepy.*
Tengo miedo.	*I'm afraid.*

Materials: Blank paper; crayons, colored pencils, or markers; and children's dictionary pages.

Have the children make a dictionary page for their favorite season. Children who have moved to your town/city from an area of the country with a different climate may wish to make their picture appropriate to the season in their former location. Be sure they write the first letter of the season name on the top of their pages (i.e., **I**; **P**; **V**; or **O**) and the name of the season at the bottom (see Activity 29B for the season names). Have them file the page with their other dictionary pages.

CLOSING

Tell the children that Spanish class is finished for today. In the next lesson LeeAnn will be a contestant on a TV game show.

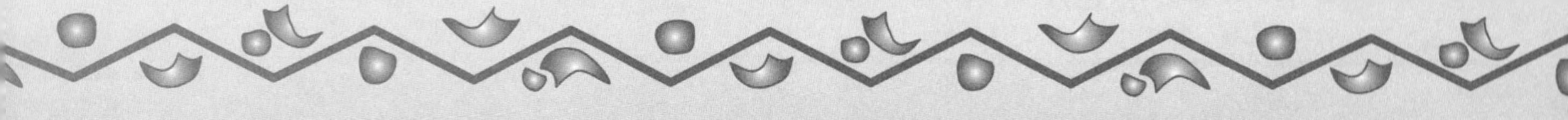

Lesson 30

Materials to gather

- VCR and Video Lesson 30 on Tape 10
- Cassette player
- Song Cassette
- Red Flashcards 1, 2, 4, 5, 25, 26, 30, and 45–58
- Your Flashcard of a CD player and CDs (from Lesson 15 Review)
- Month Pictures
- Colored paintbrushes (from Lesson 4)
- Blank paper
- Crayons or markers
- Chalk
- Children's "Alphabet Rap" papers (from Activity 5B)
- *Optional materials:* blank transparency; overhead projector; Blackline Master 5B

Objectives

Language

- Comprehend extended dialogue in a game show
- Participate in a game show

Culture

- Name the language widely spoken in the United States

Review

- Solve math problems
- Name building parts
- Name a building from its description
- Describe people
- Recognize musical instruments

Vocabulary

No new vocabulary is presented in this lesson.

Warm-up

Talk with the children about their favorite television game shows or computer games: What's the object of the game? Why do they like it? How many people can play the game? Ask what **la maestra**'s favorite show is (***"Super Repaso"***—*"Super Review"*).

Review

Have the children call out questions that they've been answering in Spanish class. For example:

¿Cómo estás tú?	*How are you?*
¿Cómo te llamas tú?	*What is your name?*
¿Cómo se llama?	*What's his/her name?*
¿Qué es esto?	*What is this?*
¿Qué mes es?	*What month is it?*
¿Qué estación es?	*What season is it?*
¿Qué tiempo hace?	*What's the weather like?*
¿Qué tiempo hace en + [*name of season*]?	*What is the weather like in ___?*
¿Cuál es la fecha?	*What is the date?*
¿De qué color es?	*What color is it?*
¿Qué número es?	*What number is it?*
¿Qué clase es?	*What class is it?*
¿Qué instrumento (musical) es?	*What [musical] instrument is it?*
¿Qué edificio es?	*What building is it?*
¿Cómo es el payaso/ la payasa?	*What is the male/ female clown like?*
¿Qué instrumento toca Fredo?	*What instrument does Fredo play?*

Introduce the video

Invite the children to listen and watch as LeeAnn plays *"Super Review"* (**"Super Repaso"**) with other pupils.

Video Lesson

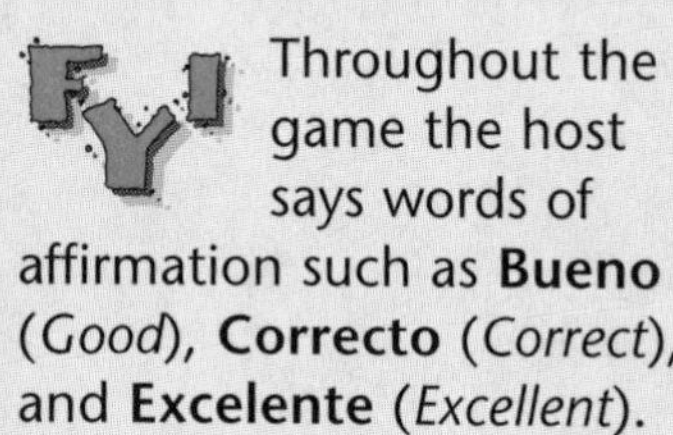

Throughout the game the host says words of affirmation such as **Bueno** (*Good*), **Correcto** (*Correct*), and **Excelente** (*Excellent*).

1. Greeting the children

Wacky-looking game show host **El profesor Correctísimo** (*Professor Most Correct*) welcomes everyone to "**Super Repaso**" ("*Super Review*") and introduces the teams: **el equipo Rojo y el equipo Verde** (*the Red team and the Green team*). The game begins with LeeAnn as a participant.

2. Playing Round One of *"Super Repaso"* (*"Super Review"*)

Questions

1. ¿Cuántos son veintisiete más catorce?
   (*How much is 27 plus 14?*)
2. Name two parts of **un edificio** (*a building*).
3. Finish this sentence: **Un edificio muy alto es** ___.
   (*A very tall building is* ___.)
4. Define the word *cognate.*
5. Complete this sentence: **La payasa es** ___.
   (*The female clown is* ___.)

The host checks the scoreboard, **¿Cuántos puntos hay?** (*How many points are there?*): **el equipo Verde—veinte puntos** (*the Green team—20 points*), **el equipo Rojo—treinta puntos** (*the Red team—30 points*).

6. ¿Qué instrumento toca Fredo?
   (*What instrument does Fredo play?*)
7. Where would you go to buy **frutas** (*fruit*), **leche** (*milk*) **y pan** (*and bread*)?
8. Give an example of a musical instrument that is a cognate.
9. ¿Cuántos son noventa y cuatro menos doce?
   (*How much is 94 minus 12?*)
10. Give the two words **en español** (*in Spanish*) for *entrance* and *exit.*

Answers:

1. cuarenta y uno (*41*)
2. la puerta (*door*), la ventana (*window*); *also* el techo (*roof*)
3. el rascacielos (*skyscraper*)
4. Words that sound similar and have the same meaning in different languages.
5. gorda (*fat*)
6. la guitarra (*guitar*)
7. el supermercado (*supermarket*)
8. el violín (*violin*)
9. ochenta y dos (*82*)
10. entrada (*entrance*) salida (*exit*)

Profesor Correctísimo checks the final points—**el equipo Verde tiene cuarenta y el equipo Rojo tiene sesenta** (*the Green team has 40 and the Red team has 60*)—and announces the winner: **El equipo Rojo gana** (*The Red team wins*). He congratulates the winning team—**¡Felicidades al equipo Rojo!** (*Congratulations to the Red team!*)—and thanks everyone for playing.

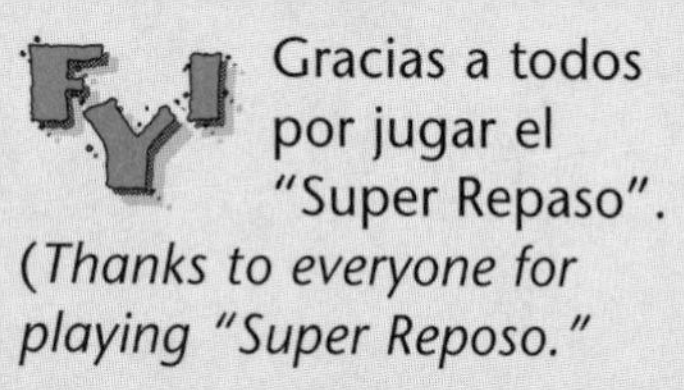

Gracias a todos por jugar el "Super Repaso". (*Thanks to everyone for playing "Super Reposo."*)

3. Taking a commercial break

La maestra says **Hola** (*Hello*) to the children and talks about the game and everything the children have learned. She encourages them to be active participants.

4. Playing Round Two of *"Super Repaso"*

El profesor Correctísimo greets the audience and contestants.

	Questions
1.	Una familia vive en la casa. Muchas familias viven en ___. (*One family lives in the house. Many families live in* ___.)
2.	Treinta y cinco más diecinueve son ___. (*35 + 19 is* ___.)
3.	Name **la parte de un edificio** (*the part of a building*) that keeps out the rain.
4.	¿Qué instrumento musical es largo y negro? (*Which musical instrument is long and black?*)
5.	¿Cuántos son ochenta y tres menos ocho? (*How much is 83 minus 8?*)
6.	Read this sentence **en español** (*in Spanish*): **Me gusta la música.** (*I like music.*)
7.	Name the opposite of **bonito** (*pretty*).
8.	Name two **instrumentos musicales** (*musical instruments*) you could buy at **la tienda de música** (*the music store*).
9.	Name the language widely spoken in the United States.
10.	Finish this sentence: **El payaso es** ___. (*The male clown is* ___.)

Answers:

1. los apartamentos (*apartments*)
2. cincuenta y cuatro (*54*)
3. el techo (*roof*)
4. el clarinete (*clarinet*)
5. setenta y cinco (*75*)
6. (student reads the sentence)
7. feo (*ugly*)
8. el clarinete y la flauta (*the clarinet and the flute*)
9. el inglés (*English*)
10. delgado (*thin*)

El profesor Correctísimo checks the scoreboard: **Los puntos para el equipo Verde—setenta puntos; el equipo Rojo—treinta puntos** (*The points for the Green team—seventy points; the Red team—thirty points*). **El equipo Verde gana** (*The Green team wins*). He thanks everyone for playing and the show is over.

5. Closing

La maestra asks the children **¿Te gusta el "Super Repaso"?** (*Do you like to play "Super Review"?*) and tells them **A mí me gusta mucho** (*I like to play a lot*). She gives the children suggestions for how they can play their own game of **"Super Repaso."**

After viewing the video, praise the children for their good listening and watching skills.

Activity Lesson 

> ***Numbers for totaling points:***
>
> | | |
> |---|---|
> | *10* | diez |
> | *20* | veinte |
> | *30* | treinta |
> | *40* | cuarenta |
> | *50* | cincuenta |

Activity 30A: Play *"Super Repaso"* (*"Super Review"*)

Materials: Red Flashcards 45, 51, and 54.

Preparation: Take down any ***Español para ti*** visuals that you have displayed. On Red Flashcard 45 cover up the picture of the easel. On 51 cover up the picture of the piano. Keep the Flashcards out of the children's sight.

Divide the class into two teams—team Purple (**el equipo Morado**) and team Green (**el equipo Verde**). Ask for a volunteer from each team to keep score on the chalkboard for his/her team. Each team should choose a spokesperson. Tell the children you will ask a question. Team members should consult and once they have an answer, the spokesperson will raise his/her hand. You will call on the spokesperson whose hand was raised first. If the answer given is incorrect, you will allow the spokesperson for the opposing team to answer the question. Each correct answer is worth 10 points (**diez puntos**).

Questions	Answers
1. (Hold up Red Flashcard 45 and ask:) What class is this?	las ciencias (*science*)
2. (Write the math problem 62 minus 7 on the chalkboard and ask:) What is the answer to this math problem?	cincuenta y cinco (55)
3. (Hold up Red Flashcard 51 and ask:) What instrument is it?	la trompeta (*trumpet*)
4. (Hold up Red Flashcard 54 and ask:) What is this building?	el edificio de apartamentos (*apartment building*)
5. If you are in a movie theater and want to leave, what sign do you look for?	la salida (*exit*)

Tell the children that this round of "**Super Repaso**" has ended. Have the scorekeepers total up the points and announce the number of points for their team in Spanish. Announce which team won.

Activity 30B: Cooperative learning—Round Two of *"Super Repaso"* (*"Super Review"*)

Materials: Red Flashcards 1, 2, 4, 5, 25, 26, 30, and 45–58; your Flashcard of a CD player and CDs; Month Pictures; colored paintbrushes; blank paper; crayons or markers; chalk.

Tell the children it's time for another game of "**Super Repaso**" (*"Super Review"*), but that this time they are going to make up the questions. Each team is to make up five questions that they will ask the other team. The questions can be in English or Spanish, but the answers must be in Spanish. Each correct answer will be worth 10 points (**diez puntos**). Put the visuals and chalk listed in the Materials at their disposal. If they need a visual to accompany a question and there isn't an appropriate one available, tell them to make one.

When each team has its questions ready, play the game. Have the teams alternate asking questions. You should keep score on the board, total the points at the end of the game, and announce which team won. If children are having difficulty formulating their questions in Spanish or you need to check an answer, consult the Topics and Language Covered section in the Front Matter of this Teacher's Manual.

Activity 30B:

Remind the children of all the things they have practiced in Spanish class this year: the numbers 1–100; color words; how to say how they feel; how to greet each other at various times of the day; the names of the seasons and months; the type of weather in each season; the names of the Spanish-speaking countries; how Spanish came to the United States; the names of school subjects and classes, pieces of clothing, musical instruments, and buildings; and many adjectives for describing people and things.

Activity 30C: Sing the "Alphabet Rap"

Materials: Cassette player; "Alphabet Rap" on the Song Cassette, Side A; children's "Alphabet Rap" papers (from Activity 5B); *optional:* a blank overhead transparency; an overhead projector; Blackline Master 5B.

Preparation: Have the children take out their "Alphabet Rap" papers. If they have misplaced them, make an overhead transparency of Blackline Master 5B and project it.

Tell the children that learning the alphabet in Spanish is key to learning how to spell, read, and write in Spanish and that they have a song that will help them remember the Spanish alphabet. Play the song, encouraging the children to sing along. Some children may find that dancing as they sing or making various letter shapes with their arms, hands, or whole bodies is helpful for remembering the lyrics.

IF YOU HAVE TIME . . .

Preparation: Write the following words (without the English) in a vertical list on the chalkboard: **rascacielos** (*skyscraper*), **trompeta** (*trumpet*), **edificio** (*edifice, building*), **apartamento** (*apartment*), **tambor** (*drum*). Ask the children to give the English equivalent of each word, writing the equivalents on the board as they provide them. Then ask them which words look and sound similar in English and Spanish. Ask them what such words are called (cognates).

CLOSING

Tell the children that Spanish class is finished for today. In the next lesson **la maestra** will do math problems with them and review the names of the days of the week.

Lesson 31

Materials to gather

- VCR and Video Lesson 31 on Tape 11
- Cassette player
- Activity Cassette 2
- Song Cassette
- Current Month Picture
- A calendar
- Blackline Master 31A ("Calendar Rap")
- Blank overhead transparency
- Overhead projector
- Blackline Master 31B (crossword puzzle; **b** and **v** with vowels)
- Pencils
- ***Optional materials:*** blank paper; crayons, markers, or colored pencils; children's dictionary pages

Objectives

Language

- Practice the names of the days of the week
- Read and answer the question **¿Dónde vives tú?** (*Where do you live?*)

Culture

- Remember that on a Spanish calendar Monday is the first day of the week
- Learn that questions in Spanish take an upside-down question mark at the beginning and a regular question mark at the end
- Review that the letters **b** and **v** sound the same in Spanish
- Sing the "Calendar Rap"

Review

- Solve addition and subtraction problems
- Sing **"Las vocales en español"** (*"The Vowels in Spanish"*) with **b** and **v**

Vocabulary

¿Qué día (de la semana) es hoy?	*What day (of the week) is today?*
lunes	*Monday*
martes	*Tuesday*
miércoles	*Wednesday*
jueves	*Thursday*
viernes	*Friday*
sábado	*Saturday*
domingo	*Sunday*
¿Dónde vives tú?	*Where do you live?*
Vivo en ___.	*I live in ___.*

Warm-up

Materials: Current Month Picture; a calendar.

Greet the children and let them know it is time for Spanish class (**la clase de español**). Ask them to tell you what the date is in Spanish: **el** [*number*] **de** [*month*]. If children need help with the number, point to it on the calendar. If they need help with the month, point to the Month Picture.

Review

Materials: A calendar.

Ask the children what day of the week it is. Review the names of the days of the week in English. Pointing to Sunday on the calendar, ask them what day of the week calendars usually begin with in the United States. Mention that this isn't so in other parts of the world.

Introduce the video

Invite the children to listen and watch as **la maestra** practices the names of the days of the week and talks about the pronunciation of the letters **b** and v.

VIDEO LESSON

1. Greeting the children

La maestra greets LeeAnn and the children with **Buenos días** (*Good morning*) and asks them how they are. She reviews the feeling expressions **Estoy muy contento/contenta** (*I'm very happy*), **Estoy enojado/enojada** (*I'm angry*), and **Tengo hambre** (*I'm hungry*). LeeAnn explains that **una chica** (*a girl*) said **Estoy enojada**.

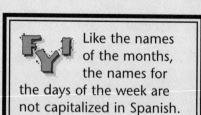

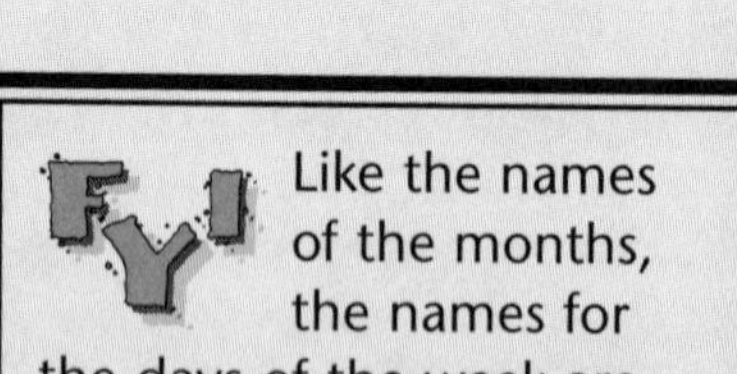
Like the names of the months, the names for the days of the week are not capitalized in Spanish.

2. Practicing the days of the week

La maestra asks the children **¿Qué día (de la semana) es hoy?** (*What day [of the week] is today?*). She reminds the children that on a Spanish calendar *Monday* (**lunes**) is the first day of the week.

lunes	*Monday*	viernes	*Friday*
martes	*Tuesday*	sábado	*Saturday*
miércoles	*Wednesday*	domingo	*Sunday*
jueves	*Thursday*		

3. Singing the "Calendar Rap"

La maestra and the children sing the "Calendar Rap."

Lunes, martes, miércoles, tres.	*Monday, Tuesday, Wednesday, three.*
Uno, dos, tres.	*One, two, three.*
Jueves, viernes, sábado, seis.	*Thursday, Friday, Saturday, six.*
Uno, dos, tres, cuatro, cinco, seis.	*One, two, three, four, five, six.*
Y domingo siete es.	*And Sunday is seven.*
Uno, dos, tres, cuatro, cinco, seis, siete.	*One, two, three, four, five, six, seven.*

4. Identifying numbers

La maestra asks the children to identify the numbers **veinte** (*twenty*), **treinta y cinco** (*thirty-five*), **cuarenta y seis** (*forty-six*), and **ochenta y nueve** (*eighty-nine*). Lorena dances to **los números grandes** (*big numbers*) as **la maestra** and the children count from ten to one hundred by tens.

diez	*ten*	sesenta	*sixty*
veinte	*twenty*	setenta	*seventy*
treinta	*thirty*	ochenta	*eighty*
cuarenta	*forty*	noventa	*ninety*
cincuenta	*fifty*	cien	*one hundred*

5. Talking about how we use numbers

LeeAnn and **la maestra** talk about ways we use numbers, e.g., **en la clase de matemáticas** (*math class*), to read prices when shopping, to measure things, and as a sports announcer at an athletic event. The children identify the numbers on football players' jerseys.

6. Solving math problems

La maestra reviews the *plus* (**más**) and *minus* (**menos**) signs. She asks the children to solve addition and subtraction problems: **seis más nueve son quince** (*six plus nine is fifteen*), **siete menos cuatro son tres** (*seven minus four is three*), and **veinticuatro menos cuatro son veinte** (*twenty-four minus four is twenty*).

7. Singing *"Las vocales en español"* (*"The Vowels in Spanish"*)

La maestra explains that words in Spanish are spelled almost exactly as they sound, but that the letters **b** and **v** sound very similar to one another. Everyone sings the song with the letter **b** and then with **v.**

Las vocales en español.	*The vowels in Spanish.*
La vocales en español.	*The vowels in Spanish.*
A, E, I, O, U.	***A, E, I, O, U.***
La B con la A dice BA.	*The **B** with the **A** says **BA.***
La B con la E dice BE.	*The **B** with the **E** says **BE.***
Con la I dice BI.	*With the **I** it says **BI.***
Con la O dice BO.	*With the **O** it says **BO.***
La B con la U dice BU.	*The **B** with the **U** says **BU.***

8. Changing the form of the verb

Showing children the question below, **la maestra** explains that questions in Spanish have an upside-down question mark at the beginning and a right-side-up question mark at the end. The children read and answer the question, changing **vives** (*you live*) to **vivo** (*I live*).

¿Dónde vives tú?	*Where do you live?*
Vivo en ___.	*I live in ___.*

9. Closing

La maestra, LeeAnn, and the children sing **"Las vocales en español"** (*"The Vowels in Spanish"*) with the letter **b** again. LeeAnn and **la maestra** say **Adiós, chicos** (*Good-bye, boys and girls*).

LANGUAGE ACROSS THE CURRICULUM

If children in your class are active in school or local team sports, ask them to bring in their team shirts. Have them describe the colors of the shirts and say the numbers in Spanish.

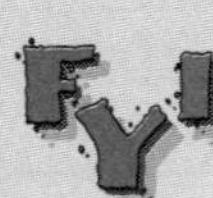

Closing: *Boy* can be **el niño** or **el chico (los chicos** in plural). *Girl* can be **la niña** or **la chica (las chicas** in plural). If referring to *boys and girls,* the masculine plural form **chicos** is used.

After viewing the video, praise the children for their good listening and watching skills.

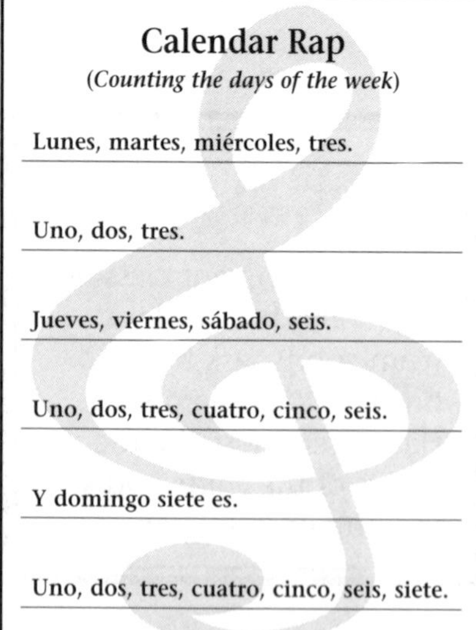
Calendar Rap
(*Counting the days of the week*)

Lunes, martes, miércoles, tres.

Uno, dos, tres.

Jueves, viernes, sábado, seis.

Uno, dos, tres, cuatro, cinco, seis.

Y domingo siete es.

Uno, dos, tres, cuatro, cinco, seis, siete.

Blackline Master 31A

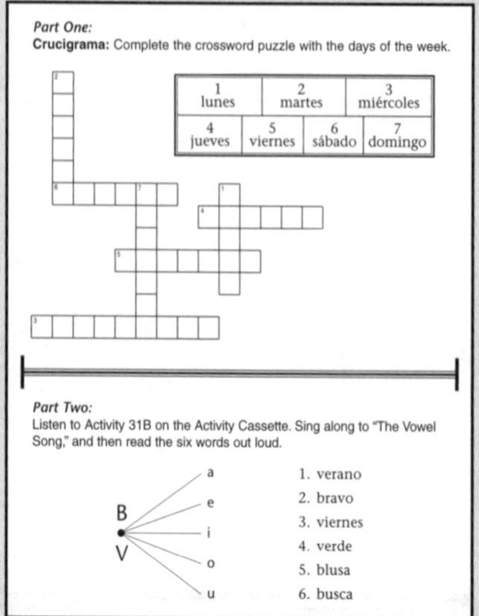
Part One:
Crucigrama: Complete the crossword puzzle with the days of the week.

1 lunes	2 martes	3 miércoles	
4 jueves	5 viernes	6 sábado	7 domingo

Part Two:
Listen to Activity 31B on the Activity Cassette. Sing along to "The Vowel Song," and then read the six words out loud.

1. verano
2. bravo
3. viernes
4. verde
5. blusa
6. busca

Blackline Master 31B

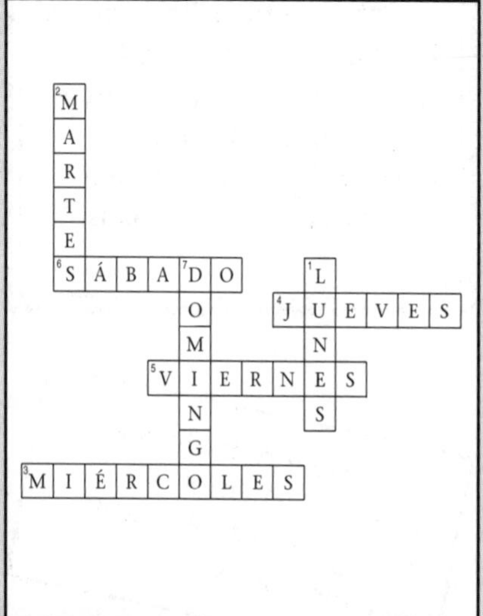

Answers to BLM 31B, Part One

ACTIVITY LESSON

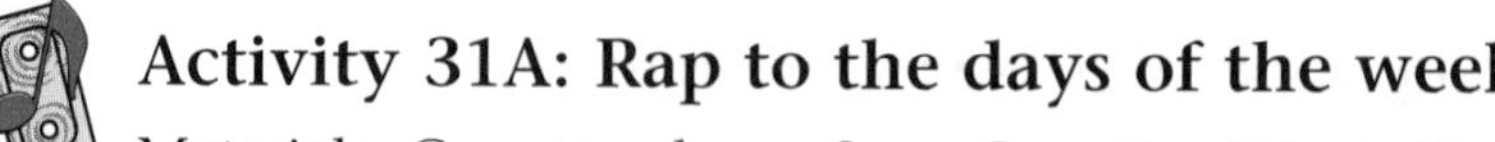

Activity 31A: Rap to the days of the week

Materials: Cassette player; Song Cassette, Side A; Blackline Master 31A; a blank overhead transparency; and an overhead projector.

Preparation: Make an overhead transparency of Blackline Master 31A. Project the transparency.

Mention that **la maestra** told the children that on Spanish calendars the week begins with Monday, whereas on calendars in the U.S. Sunday is the first day of the week. Ask them what else is different about the days of the week in Spanish and English (in English they are capitalized; in Spanish they are not). Pointing to the lyrics on the transparency, tell the children to sing along. Ask a volunteer to point to each line. If children are having difficulties, rewind the tape and play the song again. Let them know (particularly children new to ***Español para ti***) that they will learn the lyrics and the days of the week with time.

Activity 31B, Part One: Complete the puzzle

Materials: Current Month Picture; a calendar; Blackline Master 31B; and pencils.

Preparation: Display the current Month Picture. Copy and distribute Blackline Master 31B so that each child has a copy.

Have the children fill in their names and the date on the top of their papers. If they need help determining the date, point to the day on the calendar and to the current Month Picture. Then tell them to complete the crossword puzzle in Part One with the days of the week listed on their pages, according to their numbers. Remind them to be sure to include the accent marks in the words for *Wednesday* (**miércoles**) and *Saturday* (**sábado**).

Activity 31B, Part Two: Practice the letters *b* and *v*

Materials: Cassette player; Activity Cassette 2, Side A; and children's copies of Blackline Master 31B.

Be sure children have their copies of Blackline Master 31B in front of them. Direct their attention to Part Two of their papers. Tell them they are going to sing *"The Vowels in Spanish"* (**"Las vocales en español"**) with the letters **v** and **b** and then pronounce words with those letters. Play Activity 31B on the audiocassette. For song lyrics with the letter **b**, see Video Lesson section 7 of this Lesson.

Las vocales en español. (2x)	*The vowels in Spanish. (2x)*
A, E, I, O, U.	***A, E, I, O, U.***
La V con la A dice VA.	*The **V** with the **A** says **VA.***
La V con la E dice VE.	*The **V** with the **E** says **VE.***
Con la I dice VI.	*With the **I** it says **VI.***
Con la O dice VO.	*With the **O** it says **VO.***
La V con la U dice VU.	*The **V** with the **U** says **VU.***

After the children have sung both verses of *"The Vowels in Spanish,"* direct their attention to the words listed in Part Two of their papers. Have them read the words out loud. Are they pronouncing the letters **b** and **v** the same? Remind them that the letters are pronounced almost exactly the same.

1.	verano	*summer*	4.	verde	*green*
2.	bravo	*bravo*	5.	blusa	*blouse*
3.	viernes	*Friday*	6.	busca	*he* or *she looks for*

DICTIONARY

Materials: Blank paper; crayons, markers, or colored pencils; children's dictionary pages; and copies of Blackline Master 31B.

Tell the children to make two dictionary pages—one for the letter **B** and one for the letter **V**. Have them choose one word with **b** and one with **v** from the list in Part Two of Blackline Master 31B. They should enter these words on their dictionary pages and illustrate them. For *summer* (**verano**), they might draw something they really like to do in summer or illustrate the weather in that season. Once they have completed their drawings, they should file the pages with their other dictionary pages.

CLOSING

Tell the children that Spanish class is finished for today. In the next lesson they will learn a new song and visit a Mexican restaurant.

Lesson 32

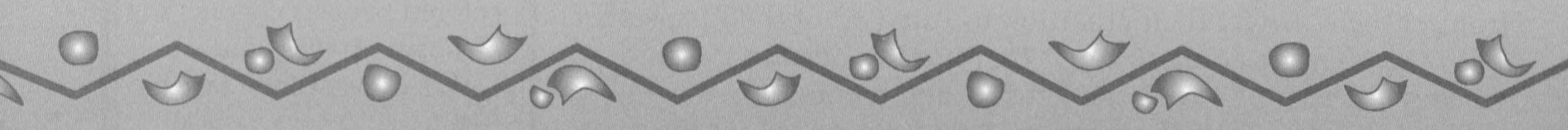

Materials to gather

- VCR and Video Lesson 32 on Tape 11
- Cassette player
- Activity Cassette 2
- ***Optional materials:*** the 11 colored paintbrushes (from Lesson 4 Review)

Objectives

Language

- Decipher **el mensaje mágico** (*the magic message*)
- Answer the question **¿Adónde vas?** (*Where are you going?*)
- Understand extended conversations about the park, the beach, the restaurant, and the house

Culture

- Realize that Spain and Mexico are two different countries
- Understand that lunch is usually the main meal of the day in Spanish-speaking countries
- Learn that the tradition of the **siesta** (*nap*) affects school and work schedules in many Spanish-speaking countries

Review

- Exchange greetings with **la maestra**

Vocabulary

la siesta	*nap*
¿Adónde vas (tú)?	*Where are you going?*
Voy a ___.	*I'm going (to) ___.*
el parque	*park*
la playa	*beach*
Llevo ___.	*I am wearing ___.*
los pantalones cortos	*shorts*
las sandalias	*sandals*
el cuarto/los cuartos	*room/rooms*
la sala	*living room*
la cocina	*kitchen*
el comedor	*dining room*
el baño	*bathroom*

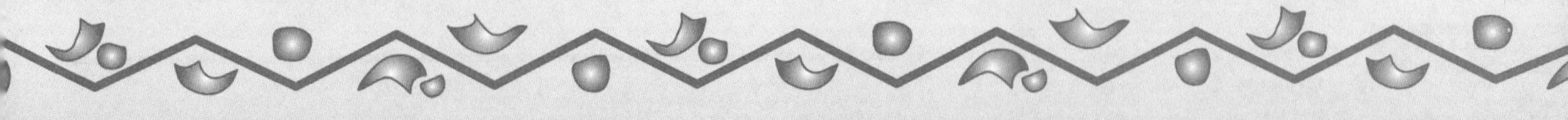

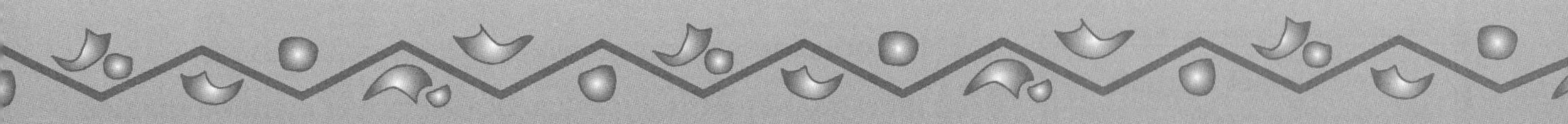

el dormitorio	*bedroom*
la silla/las sillas	*chair/chairs*
la mesa/las mesas	*table/tables*
la cama/las camas	*bed/beds*
las cortinas	*curtains*
¿Cuántas ___ hay en ___?	*How many ___ are there in ___?*
Hay ___.	*There are ___.*

Warm-up

Let the children know it is time for Spanish class (**la clase de español**). Ask the children to tell you in Spanish what day of the week it is and what the weather is like.

Days of the week:

lunes	*Monday*
martes	*Tuesday*
miércoles	*Wednesday*
jueves	*Thursday*
viernes	*Friday*
sábado	*Saturday*
domingo	*Sunday*

Weather expressions:

Hace calor.	*It's hot.*
Hace frío.	*It's cold.*
Hace sol.	*It's sunny.*
Hace viento.	*It's windy.*
Hace buen tiempo.	*It's good weather.*
Hace mal tiempo.	*It's bad weather.*
Llueve.	*It's raining.*
Nieva.	*It's snowing.*

Review

Talk with the children about places they like to go after school or on the weekend (to the park, to the swimming pool, to a friend's house, to the library, to a restaurant, to the beach).

Introduce the video

Invite the children to listen and watch as **la maestra** goes to many different places.

Children who have been through Level 2 of ***Español para ti*** may be able to say some of these phrases in Spanish: **Voy a la playa** (*I'm going to the beach*), **Voy al parque** (*I'm going to the park*), **Voy a la piscina** (*I'm going to the swimming pool*). Note: The Spanish present tense translates into the present or present progressive in English. Context usually makes clear which tense is meant.

Video Lesson

1. Greeting the children and LeeAnn

La maestra greets the children with **Buenas tardes** (*Good afternoon*) and asks them how they are. LeeAnn says **Tengo sueño** (*I'm sleepy*). **La maestra** prescribes **una siesta** (*a nap*) for LeeAnn, who thinks this is **una buena idea** (*a good idea*).

In explaining **el mensaje mágico** (*the magic message*), **la maestra** mentions **La Mano Mágica** (*The Magic Hand*)—a character used to introduce the alphabet and spelling in Level 3 of ***Español para ti.***

2. Introducing *el mensaje mágico* (*the magic message*)

La maestra presents the pedagogical device **el mensaje mágico** (*the magic message*)—the silent enactment of a phrase the children know. Antonio mimes the message, which is **Toca** (*touch*). The spoken message will be revealed at the end of the Video Lesson (**al final de la clase**).

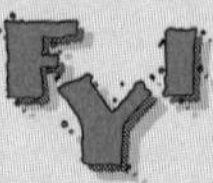

¿Dónde? means *Where?*, whereas **¿Adónde?** means *To where?*. When the preposition **a** (*to*) is followed by the masculine definite article **el** (*the*), **a** + **el** contract to **al** (*to the*).

3. Reviewing how to say where one is going

LeeAnn reads the question **¿Adónde vas?** (*Where are you going?*) and she and **la maestra** answer it. **La maestra** reviews the expressions **Voy a la casa** (*I am going home*), **Voy a la escuela** (*I am going to school*), and **Voy al parque en bicicleta** (*I am going to the park by bicycle*).

4. Going to the park

La maestra rides her bike to the park and talks about the weather.

Voy al parque en bicicleta.	*I am going to the park by bicycle.*
¿Por qué? Porque hace calor y hace sol.	*Why? Because it's hot and it's sunny.*
Es muy divertido ir al parque en bicicleta.	*It's a lot of fun to go to the park by bicycle.*

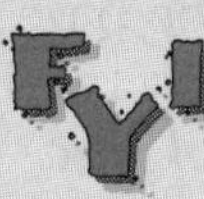

Me encanta la playa. = *I love the beach.*

5. Enjoying the beach

At the beach, **la maestra** talks about her surroundings, what she's wearing, and how much fun she's having.

Estoy aquí en la playa.	*Here I am at the beach.*
Todos se divierten en la playa.	*Everyone has a good time at the beach.*
Yo me divierto mucho en la playa porque hay arena, mucha arena.	*I have a very good time at the beach because there's sand, lots of sand.*
Aquí en la playa, en esta silla, tengo una toalla.	*Here at the beach, in this chair, I have a towel.*
Esta toalla tiene un mapa.	*This towel has a map.*
Este mapa es de España.	*This is a map of Spain.*
En España todos los niños hablan español y todos van a la playa y se divierten en la playa.	*In Spain, all the children speak Spanish and everyone goes to the beach and has lots of fun at the beach.*

6. Talking about what one does at the beach

LeeAnn and **la maestra** talk about **la ropa especial** (*special clothing*) worn at the beach—**el traje de baño** (*bathing suit*), **los pantalones cortos** (*shorts*), **las gafas** (*sunglasses*), and **las sandalias** (*sandals*). **La maestra** asks LeeAnn what she does at the beach: **¿Qué haces en la playa?** LeeAnn says **Tomo el sol** (*I sunbathe*). **La maestra** adds **Juego al volibol** (*I play volleyball*).

In the volleyball playing scene, point out that doña Elena is the dark-haired woman in the white shorts and black blouse.

7. Going to the restaurant Lindo Michoacán

When LeeAnn says **Tengo hambre** (*I'm hungry*), **la maestra** says **Vamos al restaurante** (*Let's go to the restaurant*). She explains that **España** (*Spain*) and **México** are different countries and that one wouldn't easily find a Mexican restaurant in Spain.

¿Qué edificio es?	*What building is it?*
Es un edificio muy especial.	*It's a very special building.*
¿Cómo se llama el restaurante?	*What's the name of the restaurant?*
Es un restaurante mexicano.	*It's a Mexican restaurant.*
Me gusta mucho la comida mexicana y tengo hambre.	*I like Mexican food a lot and I'm hungry.*

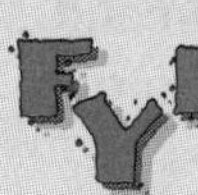

Michoacán is one of Mexico's states (**estados**). It is located in the southwestern part of the country, on the Pacific coast. You may want to have children look it up on a map.

8. Touring the home of *la maestra*

La maestra takes the children on a tour of her home. See Lesson 26, Video Lesson section 6 for statements she makes in front of her house.

En mi casa hay muchos cuartos.	*In my house there are many rooms.*
En la sala tomo el café con mis amigos.	*In the living room I drink coffee with my friends.*
¿Cuántas ___ hay en ___?	*How many ___ are there in ___?*
Hay ___.	*There are ___.*
En la cocina preparamos la comida.	*In the kitchen we prepare the food.*
Un cuarto es el baño.	*One room is the bathroom.*
Comemos en el comedor.	*We eat in the dining room.*
Duermo en el dormitorio.	*I sleep in the bedroom.*

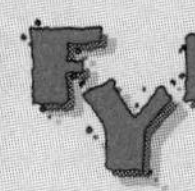

Children familiar with ***Español para ti*** will remember the house tour from Level 3. On the tour, she mentions the following household furnishings: **la silla/las sillas** (*chair/chairs*), **la mesa/las mesas** (*table/tables*), **la cama** (*bed*), **las cortinas** (*curtains*).

9. Closing

La maestra reveals **el mensaje mágico** (*the magic message*). She explains that **Toca** means *Touch* and that it means *Play* when used with a musical instrument. She and LeeAnn review the question **¿Adónde vas?** (*Where are you going?*) and answer **Voy** ___ (*I am going to* ___).

After viewing the video, praise the children for their good listening and watching skills.

Activity Lesson

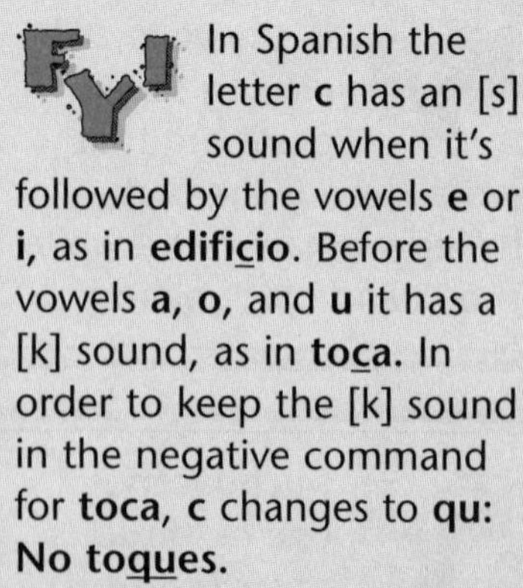

FYI In Spanish the letter **c** has an [s] sound when it's followed by the vowels **e** or **i,** as in **edificio**. Before the vowels **a, o,** and **u** it has a [k] sound, as in **toca.** In order to keep the [k] sound in the negative command for **toca, c** changes to **qu: No toques.**

Activity 32A: Practice the magic message

Materials: Cassette player; Activity Cassette 2, Side A.

Ask children what *magic message* (**el mensaje mágico**) **la maestra** said in the Video Lesson (**Toca**—*Touch* or *Play* + an instrument). Do children recall how to say the opposite (**No toques**—*Don't touch* or *Don't play* + an instrument)? Tell them to follow **la maestra**'s directions as she tells them to touch something, to play an instrument, or not to. Encourage them to mime playing any instrument she mentions. Play Activity 32A, stopping the tape at the sound of the harp. **La maestra** will tell the children **Toca tu cabeza** (*Touch your head*), **Toca la trompeta** (*Play the trumpet*), and **No toques el violín** (*Don't play the violin*).

HERITAGE SPEAKERS

Ask heritage speakers when they eat their main meal on weekends.

Activity 32B: Cross-cultural connections

Tell the children that in Spanish-speaking countries, the largest meal of the day is usually eaten in the afternoon around 2:00 P.M., with families gathering for two or three hours to eat and take **una siesta** (*a nap*). Children generally go home from school, parents return from their jobs, and shops and banks close. Because this is a time for rest and family, people refrain from visiting or phoning during this period. Ask the children how this differs from lunch time in the United States. (People generally take an hour or less for lunch and eat anywhere from noon to 2:00 P.M., dinner/supper is usually considered the main meal of the day.) Encourage the children to see the practice of eating the main meal at lunch as something positive—hours of activity follow it, which is better for the body.

Activity 32C: At the beach

Optional materials: VCR, Video Tape 11, Video Lesson 32, section 5.

Ask the children to recall the scene from the video in which **la maestra** was at the beach. If necessary, replay section 5 of the Video Lesson. Have them describe what she talked about (weather, sand, the clothing she wore). Ask them if they like to go to the ocean or lake. Do they know how to swim? Do they like to swim? Do they prefer to swim in a pool or in the ocean or in a lake?

Closing

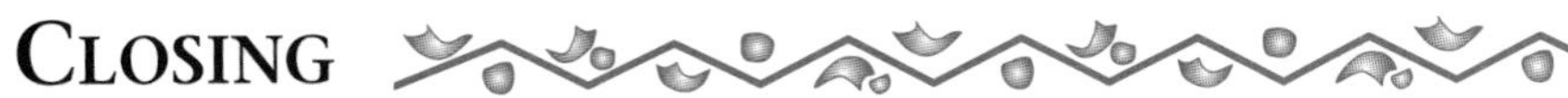

Tell the children that Spanish class is finished for today. In the next lesson they will learn a new song.

Materials: The 11 colored paintbrushes from Lesson 4.

Ask volunteers to say what they are wearing and state the color of each item. Remind them to adjust the ending on the color words **rojo** (*red*), **rosado** (*pink*), **blanco** (*white*), **negro** (*black*), **anaranjado** (*orange*), and **amarillo** (*yellow*) to match the ending on the end of the clothing word, e.g., **los pantalones son negros** (*the pants are black*). For a list of clothing, see the Vocabulary section in Lesson 11.

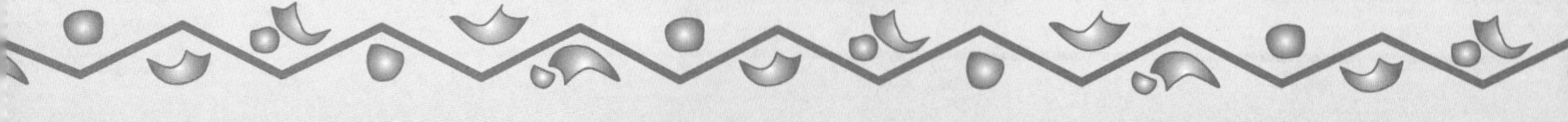

LESSON 33

Materials to gather

- VCR and Video Lesson 33 on Tape 11
- Cassette player
- Song Cassette
- Current Month Picture
- A calendar
- Red Flashcards 1, 58–63
- Pictures of a beach scene and a park
- Tape or glue
- Cardboard or a laminating machine
- Blackline Master 33A ("**¿Adónde vas?**")
- Blank overhead transparency
- Overhead projector
- Blackline Master 33B (places and sentences)
- Pencils
- ***Prepare ahead:*** beach and park Flashcards (for Review activity)

OBJECTIVES

Language

- Decipher the secret message **Busca** (*Look for*)
- Sing the new song "**¿Adónde vas?**" (*"Where Are You Going?"*)
- Learn the names of new places to go

Culture

- Understand how knowing Spanish can help in one's career

Review

- Review saying one is going to various places
- Visit the doctor
- Visit the police chief

Vocabulary

el museo	*museum*
el cine	*movie theater*
Busca ___.	*Look for ___.*

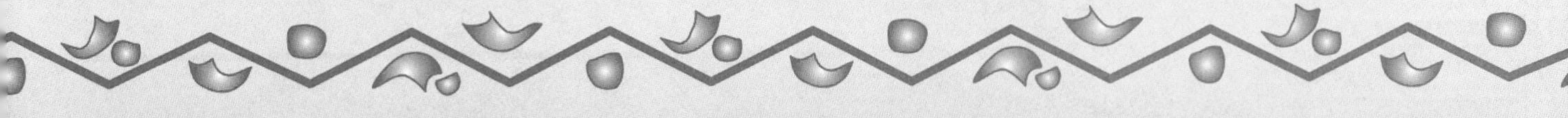

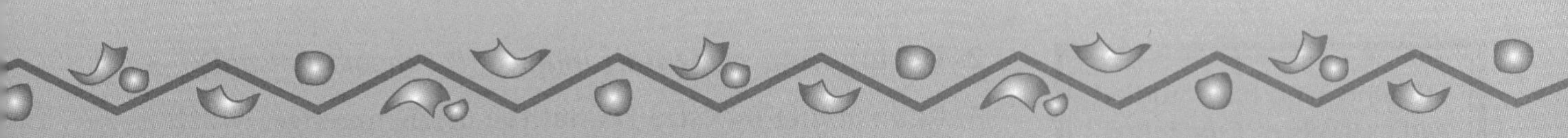

Warm-up

Materials: A calendar; current Month Picture.

Display the current Month Picture. Greet the children and ask them what the day and date are. If they need help with the date, refer them to the number of the day on the calendar and to the name of the month on the Month Picture: **el** [*number*] **de** [*month*].

Review

Materials: Red Flashcard 1; pictures of a beach scene and a park; tape or glue; and cardboard or a laminating machine.

Preparation: Make Flashcards to represent **el parque** (*park*) and **la playa** (*beach*) using pictures from travel magazines or tourist brochures. Tape or glue the pictures to cardboard or laminate them for future use.

Hold up Red Flashcard 1 and ask the children what it is (**la casa**—*house*). Then ask children how they would say they are going home (**Voy a la casa**—*I'm going home*). Do the same with your Flashcards of the beach and park:

¿Adónde vas?	*Where are you going?*
el parque / Voy al parque.	*park / I'm going to the park.*
la playa / Voy a la playa.	*beach / I'm going to the beach.*

Introduce the video

Invite the children to listen and watch as **la maestra** and doña Elena sing a new song about going places.

Days of the week:

lunes	*Monday*
martes	*Tuesday*
miércoles	*Wednesday*
jueves	*Thursday*
viernes	*Friday*
sábado	*Saturday*
domingo	*Sunday*

VIDEO LESSON

Students who have studied earlier levels of ***Español para ti*** should remember this command, but those who are new this year may not be familiar with it. If some children start to say the magic message, remind them not to tell it until the end of the lesson.

Place names:

el restaurante (*restaurant*)

el museo (*museum*)

la biblioteca (*library*)

el supermarcado (*supermarket*)

el cine (*movie theater*)

el hospital (*hospital*)

1. Greeting the children

La maestra greets the children with **Buenos días** (*Good morning*) and asks them how they are. She says **Estoy muy bien** (*I'm very well*) and reviews the expressions **Así, así** (*So-so*); **Muy mal** (*Very bad*); and **Estoy contento/contenta** (*I'm happy*).

2. Deciphering *el mensaje mágico* (*the magic message*)

Antonio and **la maestra** act out the magic message, which is **Busca** (*Look for*). The children's old friend from Levels 1–3, Rosco the wolf, peeks out of the bag.

3. Introducing more places

The children read and answer the question **¿Adónde vas?** (*Where are you going?*). **La maestra** reviews **Voy al parque** (*I'm going to the park*), **Voy a la casa** (*I'm going home*), and **Voy a la playa** (*I'm going to the beach*). She introduces more place names and has the children say they are going to each one.

Voy al restaurante.	*I'm going to the restaurant.*
Voy al museo.	*I'm going to the museum.*
Voy a la biblioteca.	*I'm going to the library.*
Voy al supermercado.	*I'm going to the supermarket.*
Voy al cine.	*I'm going to the movies.*
Voy al hospital.	*I'm going to the hospital.*

4. Learning a new song

La maestra presents the song "**¿Adónde vas?**" ("*Where Are You Going?*") and explains that adding the pronoun **tú** (*you*) is done to emphasize the word *you*.

¿Adónde vas? ¿Adónde vas tú? (2x)	*Where are you going? Where are you going? (2x)*
Voy al museo, al museo, al museo.	*I'm going to the museum, to the museum, to the museum.*
Aquí estoy.	*Here I am.*

Repeat verse with the following:

Voy al cine. Voy al cine, al cine.	*I'm going to the movies. I'm going to the movies, to the movies.*
Voy al restaurante, al restaurante.	*I'm going to the restaurant, to the restaurant.*
Voy al supermercado, al supermercado.	*I'm going to the supermarket, to the supermarket.*
Voy a la biblioteca, a la biblioteca.	*I'm going to the library, to the library.*
Voy al hospital, al hospital.	*I'm going to the hospital, to the hospital.*

5. Reviewing questions and answers

Winston asks **la maestra** where she is. She appears and asks him how he is. She reviews the following questions and answers.

¿Cómo estás?	*How are you?*
Estoy contento.	*I'm happy.*
¿Dónde estás?	*Where are you?*
Estoy aquí.	*I'm here.*
¿Adónde vas?	*Where are you going?*
Voy a la escuela.	*I'm going to school.*
Voy al hospital.	*I'm going to the hospital.*

6. Visiting the doctor's office

La maestra visits the doctor's office. **La maestra** tells LeeAnn that **la oficina del doctor está en el hospital** (*the doctor's office is in the hospital*).

Aquí estoy en la oficina del doctor.	*I'm here in the doctor's office.*
Es una oficina muy bonita.	*It's a very pretty office.*
El doctor habla español y la enfermera habla español también.	*The doctor speaks Spanish and the nurse also speaks Spanish.*
¿Está usted mal?	*Are you ill?*
¿Por qué está aquí entonces?	*Then why are you here?*
Estoy aquí para visitarle.	*I'm here to visit you.*
Tiene muchos pacientes, ¿no?	*You have many patients, don't you?*
El español es importante en su trabajo, ¿no?	*Spanish is important for your work, isn't it?*

In speaking with the doctor and police chief, **la maestra** uses the formal *you* (**usted**). **Usted** is used as an indication of respect when addressing older people and people in positions of authority. The police chief addresses LeeAnn with the familiar *you* (**tú**), but LeeAnn uses **usted** with him. **Tú** is used when addressing family members, friends, colleagues, and children. It is often not necessary to include pronouns in Spanish since the form of the verb (here: **está**) and context make it clear which form of *you* is meant.

7. Visiting the police station

LeeAnn answers the question **¿Adónde vas?** (*Where are you going?*) with **Voy a la estación de policía** (*I'm going to the police station*) because she's interested in being a police officer. LeeAnn and **la maestra** visit with **el jefe de la policía** (*police chief*).

8. Revealing *el mensaje mágico* (the magic message)

LeeAnn and the children reveal the message—**Busca** (*Look for*).

9. Closing

La maestra and LeeAnn bid the children **Adiós** (*Good-bye*).

After viewing the video, praise the children for their good listening and watching skills.

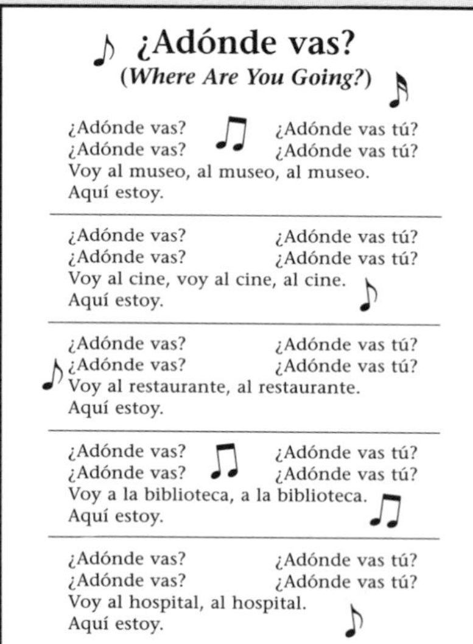

¿Adónde vas?
(*Where Are You Going?*)

¿Adónde vas? ¿Adónde vas tú?
¿Adónde vas? ¿Adónde vas tú?
Voy al museo, al museo, al museo.
Aquí estoy.

¿Adónde vas? ¿Adónde vas tú?
¿Adónde vas? ¿Adónde vas tú?
Voy al cine, voy al cine, al cine.
Aquí estoy.

¿Adónde vas? ¿Adónde vas tú?
¿Adónde vas? ¿Adónde vas tú?
Voy al restaurante, al restaurante.
Aquí estoy.

¿Adónde vas? ¿Adónde vas tú?
¿Adónde vas? ¿Adónde vas tú?
Voy a la biblioteca, a la biblioteca.
Aquí estoy.

¿Adónde vas? ¿Adónde vas tú?
¿Adónde vas? ¿Adónde vas tú?
Voy al hospital, al hospital.
Aquí estoy.

Blackline Master 33A

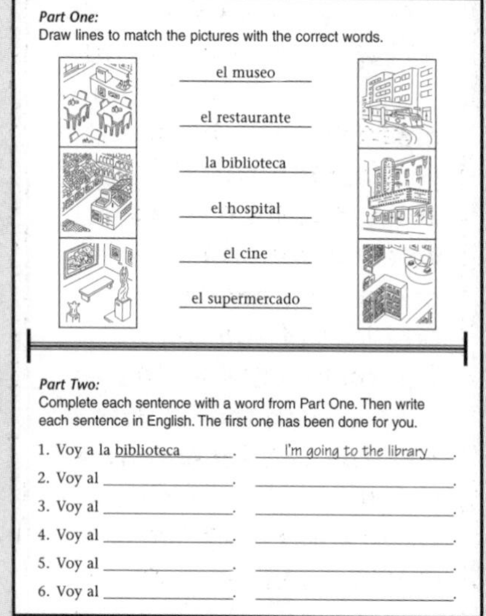

Part One:
Draw lines to match the pictures with the correct words.

el museo
el restaurante
la biblioteca
el hospital
el cine
el supermercado

Part Two:
Complete each sentence with a word from Part One. Then write each sentence in English. The first one has been done for you.

1. Voy a la biblioteca. I'm going to the library.
2. Voy al ______. ______.
3. Voy al ______. ______.
4. Voy al ______. ______.
5. Voy al ______. ______.
6. Voy al ______. ______.

Blackline Master 33B

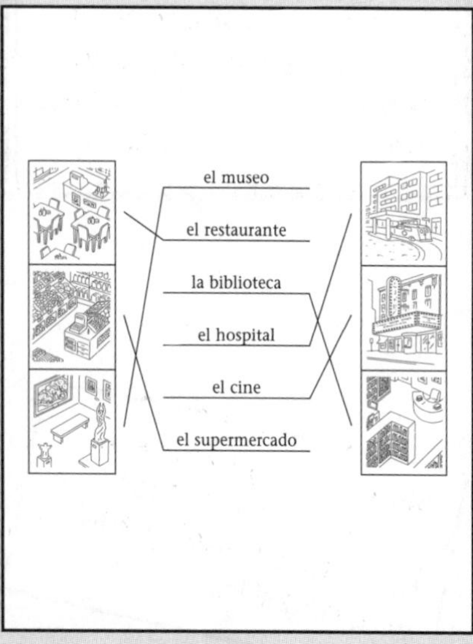

Answers to BLM 33B, Part One

Activity Lesson

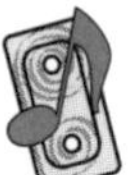

Activity 33A: Learn the song *"¿Adónde vas?"* (*"Where Are You Going?"*)

Materials: Cassette player; Song Cassette, Side A; a blank overhead transparency; Blackline Master 33A; an overhead projector; and Red Flashcards 58–63.

Preparation: Make a transparency of Blackline Master 33A. Display Red Flashcards in song order:

Red Flashcards:

#59	el museo	*museum*
#62	el cine	*movie theater*
#58	el restaurante	*restaurant*
#60	la biblioteca	*library*
#61	el supermercado	*supermarket*
#63	el hospital	*hospital*

Play the song through once and ask the children what places are mentioned in the song *"Where Are You Going?"* (**"¿Adónde vas?"**). If they need help, point to the Red Flashcards. Next, tell the children they are going to learn the song. Project the transparency. Ask one volunteer to point to each verse and a second volunteer to hold up each Red Flashcard as the children sing each verse.

Activity 33B: Write where you are going

Materials: Blackline Master 33B; pencils; a calendar; and current Month Picture.

Preparation: Copy and distribute Blackline Master 33B so that each child has one. Display the current Month Picture.

Have the children write their names and the date on the top of the page. If they need help with the date, point to the number of the day on the calendar and to the current Month Picture. Tell them to complete Part One by drawing a line from each picture to the name of each place. Check the children's answers (see the answers in the margin). Then have them complete each of the sentences in Part Two by writing in one of the place names from Part One.

Part Two Answers (the order of children's sentences may vary):

2. Voy al museo.	*I'm going to the museum.*
3. Voy al restaurante.	*I'm going to the restaurant.*
4. Voy al hospital.	*I'm going to the hospital.*
5. Voy al cine.	*I'm going to the movies.*
6. Voy al supermercado.	*I'm going to the supermarket.*

Activity 33C: Practice saying where you are going

Materials: Red Flashcards 1, 58–63; your Flashcards of a beach scene and a park (from the Review activity of this lesson).

Holding up each Flashcard, ask the children the name of each place. If you feel comfortable, ask **¿Qué es?** (*What is it?*). Also ask how they would say they are going to the place or ask **¿Adónde vas?** (*Where are you going?*).

Red Flashcards:		**¿Adónde vas?**
#1:	la casa (*house*)	Voy a la casa. (*I'm going home.*)
#58:	el restaurante (*restaurant*)	Voy al restaurante. (*I'm going to the restaurant.*)
#59:	el museo (*museum*)	Voy al museo. (*I'm going to the museum.*)
#60:	la biblioteca (*library*)	Voy a la biblioteca. (*I'm going to the library.*)
#61:	el supermercado (*supermarket*)	Voy al supermercado. (*I'm going to the supermarket.*)
#62:	el cine (*movie theater*)	Voy al cine. (*I'm going to the movies.*)
#63:	el hospital (*hospital*)	Voy al hospital. (*I'm going to the hospital.*)
Your Flashcards:		
beach:	la playa	Voy a la playa. (*I'm going to the beach.*)
park:	el parque	Voy al parque. (*I'm going to the park.*)

CLOSING

Tell the children that Spanish class is finished for today. In the next lesson **la maestra** will review the names of the places and have a new magic message for the children.

DICTIONARY

Tell the children to bring to the next class a picture of their favorite place, chosen from those they have learned (see Activity 33C). Suggest they draw a picture and remind them that if they are going to cut a picture out of a magazine or newspaper, they should ask their parents first for permission. If necessary, remind them that they are not to cut pictures out of books and magazines from the library. In a later class, they will prepare a dictionary page for the place.

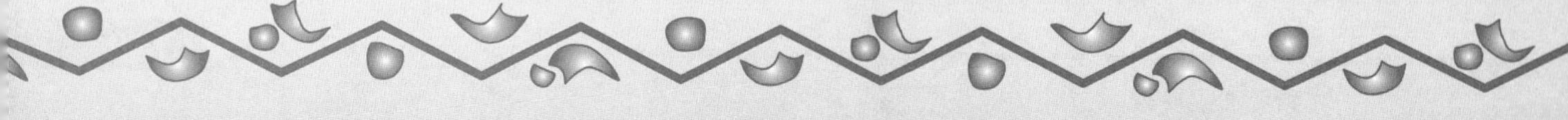

Lesson 34

Materials to gather

- VCR and Video Lesson 34 on Tape 12
- Cassette player
- Song Cassette
- Overhead transparency of Blackline Master 33A ("**¿Adónde vas?**")
- Overhead projector
- Red Flashcards 1, 58–63
- Your Flashcards of the beach and the park (from Lesson 33 Review)
- ***Optional materials:*** children's drawings or pictures from the Dictionary activity in Lesson 33; blank paper; tape or glue; children's dictionary pages

Objectives

Language

- Decipher the secret message **Salta** (*Jump*)
- Learn the difference between **Voy a** (*I'm going to*) and **Vamos a** (*We're going to*)
- Comprehend extended conversations about grocery shopping and about the library

Culture

- Recall the definition of a cognate

Review

- Practice saying where one is going
- Sing "**¿Adónde vas?**" (*"Where Are You Going?"*)
- Review saying place names

Vocabulary

Vamos a ___.	*We're going to ___. / Let's go to ___.*
Salta.	*Jump.*

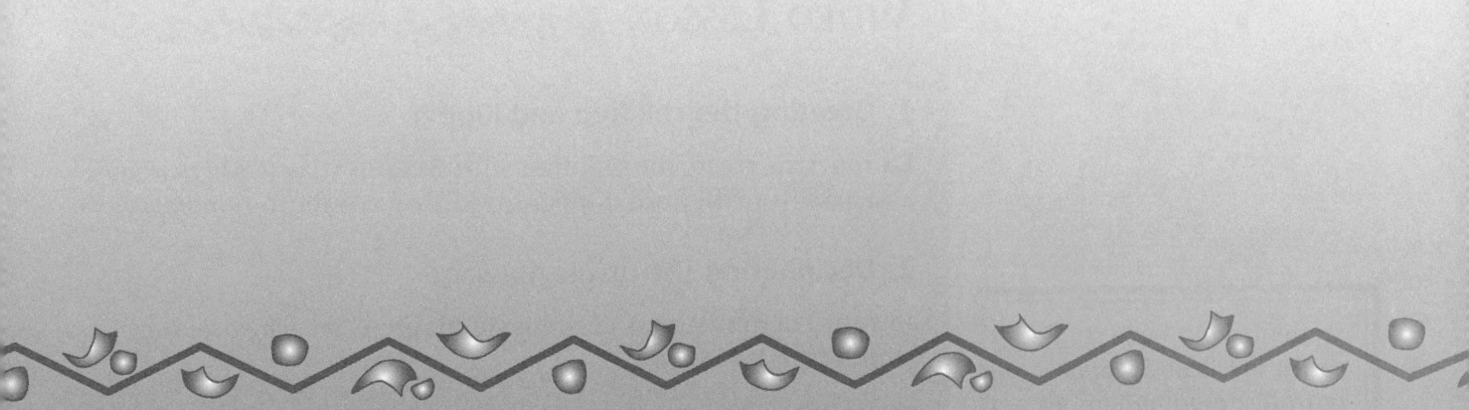

Warm-up

Greet the children and tell them it's time for Spanish class (**la clase de español**). Ask them what they've been learning to talk about in the last few lessons (where they are going).

Review

Materials: Red Flashcards 1, 58–63; your Flashcards of the beach and the park from Lesson 33.

Hold up one Flashcard at a time and ask the children how they say *I'm going to* that place. If you feel comfortable, ask **¿Adónde vas?** (*Where are you going?*).

Red Flashcards:

#1	Voy a la casa.	*I'm going home.*
#58	Voy al restaurante.	*I'm going to the restaurant.*
#59	Voy al museo.	*I'm going to the museum.*
#60	Voy a la biblioteca.	*I'm going to the library.*
#61	Voy al supermercado.	*I'm going to the supermarket.*
#62	Voy al cine.	*I'm going to the movies.*
#63	Voy al hospital.	*I'm going to the hospital.*

Your Flashcards:

beach:	Voy a la playa.	*I'm going to the beach.*
park:	Voy al parque.	*I'm going to the park.*

Introduce the video

Invite the children to listen and watch as **la maestra** goes shopping and to the library.

VIDEO LESSON

Students who have studied earlier levels of ***Español para ti*** should remember this command, but those who are new this year may not be familiar with it. Remind those children who know the answer not to reveal the magic message at this time.

Are children saying **Voy al restaurante** and **Voy a la biblioteca**? If necessary, stop the tape and replay it so they can hear the difference. For your information, the preposition **a** (*to*) and the masculine definite article **el** (*the*) contract to **al.**

You may have noticed that **la maestra** and the grocery clerk use the formal form of *you* (**usted**) with one another.

1. Greeting the children and Kipper

La maestra greets the children with **Buenos días** (*Good morning*) and asks how they are. Kipper says **Estoy contento** (*I'm happy*).

2. Deciphering the magic message

Antonio demonstrates **el mensaje mágico** (*the magic message*), which is **Salta** (*Jump*).

3. Practicing saying where one is going

La maestra shows the children Red Flashcards of places and asks **¿Adónde vas?** (*Where are you going?*). Children respond with **Voy al restaurante** (*I'm going to the restaurant*), **Voy al museo** (*I'm going to the museum*), **Voy a la biblioteca** (*I'm going to the library*), **Voy al supermercado** (*I'm going to the supermarket*), **Voy al cine** (*I'm going to the movies*), and **Voy al hospital** (*I'm going to the hospital*).

4. Singing *"¿Adónde vas?"* (*"Where Are You Going?"*)

La maestra and doña Elena sing the song.

¿Adónde vas? ¿Adónde vas tú? (2x)	*Where are you going?* *Where are you going? (2x)*
Voy al museo, al museo, al museo.	*I'm going to the museum,* *to the museum, to the museum.*
Aquí estoy.	*Here I am.*

Repeat verse with the following:

Voy al cine. ...	*I'm going to the movies. . . .*
Voy al restaurante, ...	*I'm going to the restaurant, . . .*
Voy al supermercado, ...	*I'm going to the supermarket, . . .*
Voy a la biblioteca, ...	*I'm going to the library, . . .*
Voy al hospital, ...	*I'm going to the hospital, . . .*

5. Going shopping

La maestra asks Kipper where he would go to find **frutas** (*fruits*), **carne** (*meat*), and **leche** (*milk*)—**el supermercado** (*super-market*). She goes shopping.

¿Dónde están las frutas y los vegetales?	*Where are the fruits* *and vegetables?*
Están allá.	*They're over there.*
Voy de compras en el supermercado.	*I'm going shopping in* *the supermarket.*
¿Qué compro?	*What am I buying?*
¿Y qué más?	*And what else?*
Necesito algo de tomar.	*I need something to drink.*
Aquí tenemos jugo de naranja.	*Here we have* *orange juice.*

6. Explaining the *I* and *we* forms of the verb *to go*

La maestra explains the difference between **Voy a** and **Vamos a.**

Voy a ___.	*I am going to ___.*
Vamos a ___.	*We are going (let's go) to ___.*

7. Visiting the library

La maestra visits a busy school library.

Niños, estoy en la biblioteca y tengo libros.	*Children, I am in the library and I have books.*
Los libros son muy importantes y los libros son nuestros amigos.	*Books are very important and books are our friends.*
A todos los niños les gustan los libros.	*All the children like books.*

8. Playing a choosing game

La maestra says **Vamos a jugar** (*Let's play*) and then, holding up a Red Flashcard, she asks the children if they are going to one place or another.

¿Adónde vas? ¿Al museo o al restaurante?	*Where are you going? To the museum or to the restaurant?*
Al museo.	*To the museum.*
¿Adónde vas? ¿Vas al hospital o a la biblioteca?	*Where are you going? Are you going to the hospital or to the library?*
Voy a la biblioteca.	*I'm going to the library.*
¿Adónde vas? ¿Vas al supermercado o al cine?	*Where are you going? Are you going to the supermarket or to the movies?*
Voy al cine.	*I'm going to the movies.*

9. Revealing the magic message

Antonio mimes **el mensaje mágico** (*the magic message*) and the children reveal what Antonio has mimed—**Salta** (*Jump*).

Tell the children it is okay to say the magic message when Antonio demonstrates it.

10. Closing

Holding up Red Flashcards, **la maestra** quickly practices the question **¿Adónde vas?** (*Where are you going?*) and several answers. She reviews what a cognate is, mentions that **el hospital** (*hospital*) is a cognate, and that the letter **h** in Spanish is silent. Saying **Adiós** (*Good-bye*), **la maestra** ends class.

After viewing the video, praise the children for their good listening and watching skills.

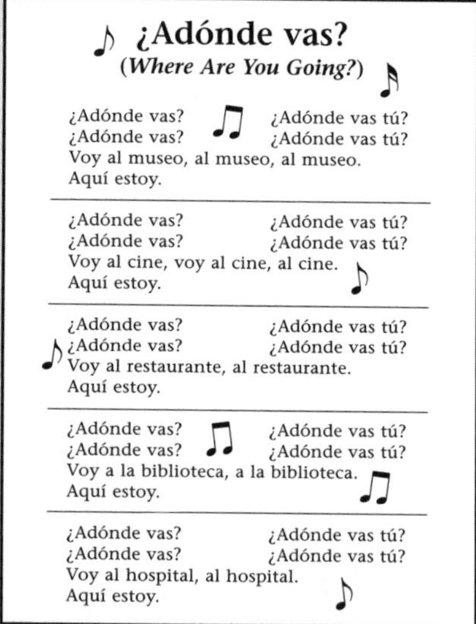
¿Adónde vas?
(Where Are You Going?)

¿Adónde vas? ¿Adónde vas tú?
¿Adónde vas? ¿Adónde vas tú?
Voy al museo, al museo, al museo.
Aquí estoy.

¿Adónde vas? ¿Adónde vas tú?
¿Adónde vas? ¿Adónde vas tú?
Voy al cine, voy al cine, al cine.
Aquí estoy.

¿Adónde vas? ¿Adónde vas tú?
¿Adónde vas? ¿Adónde vas tú?
Voy al restaurante, al restaurante.
Aquí estoy.

¿Adónde vas? ¿Adónde vas tú?
¿Adónde vas? ¿Adónde vas tú?
Voy a la biblioteca, a la biblioteca.
Aquí estoy.

¿Adónde vas? ¿Adónde vas tú?
¿Adónde vas? ¿Adónde vas tú?
Voy al hospital, al hospital.
Aquí estoy.

Blackline Master 33A

Activity 34B:
If the children have difficulty singing the song on their own, replay the Song Cassette and tell them to sing along with **la maestra** and doña Elena again. Reassure them that they'll be able to sing the song on their own with practice.

Activity Lesson

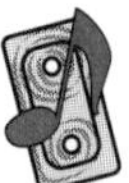

Activity 34A: Sing *"¿Adónde vas?"* (*"Where Are You Going?"*)

Materials: Cassette player; Song Cassette, Side A; the transparency of Blackline Master 33A; an overhead projector; and Red Flashcards 58–63.

Preparation: Project your transparency of Blackline Master 33A. Display the Red Flashcards in numerical order.

Tell the children they are going to sing *"Where Are You Going?"* ("**¿Adónde vas?**"). Ask one volunteer to point to each verse and a second volunteer to hold up each Red Flashcard as the children sing that verse. Let the second volunteer know that the places aren't displayed in the order they are sung. Now play the Song Cassette.

Activity 34B: Sing in two groups

Materials: The transparency of Blackline Master 33A; an overhead projector; and Red Flashcards 58–63; *optional*: cassette player; Song Cassette, Side A.

Preparation: Project the transparency. Display the Red Flashcards in song order as follows:

#59 el museo (*museum*)
#62 el cine (*movie theater*)
#58 el restaurante (*restaurant*)
#61 el supermercado (*supermarket*)
#60 la biblioteca (*library*)
#63 el hospital (*hospital*)

Divide the class into two groups. Tell them they are going to sing the song *"Where Are You Going?"* ("**¿Adónde vas?**") in two groups and without the help of **la maestra** and doña Elena! One group will sing the first two lines (**¿Adónde vas? ¿Adónde vas tú?**). The other group will sing the lines that answer that question. They will sing all six verses. Mention that the lyrics are displayed to help them and that the places are also displayed in the order that each one comes up in the song.

Activity 34C: What does that mean?

Materials: Red Flashcards 1, 58–63; your Flashcards for the beach and the park from Lesson 33.

Preparation: Display all the Flashcards. Write the following sentences on the chalkboard:

Voy a ___.	Vamos a ___.
I'm going to ___.	We're going to ___.

Pointing to the first sentence, ask the children which word means *I'm going* (**Voy**) and which word means *to* (**a**). Point to the second Spanish sentence and ask which word means *We're going* (**Vamos**) and which word means *to* (**a**). Ask volunteers to form sentences with these words and with the vocabulary for places as shown on the Flashcards.

Red Flashcards:		**Sentences:**
#1:	la casa (*house*)	Voy a la casa. (*I'm going home.*)
#58:	el restaurante (*restaurant*)	Voy al restaurante. (*I'm going to the restaurant.*)
#59:	el museo (*museum*)	Voy al museo. (*I'm going to the museum.*)
#60:	la biblioteca (*library*)	Voy a la biblioteca. (*I'm going to the library.*)
#61:	el supermercado (*supermarket*)	Voy al supermercado. (*I'm going to the supermarket.*)
#62:	el cine (*movie theater*)	Voy al cine. (*I'm going to the movies.*)
#63:	el hospital (*hospital*)	Voy al hospital. (*I'm going to the hospital.*)
Your Flashcards:		
beach:	la playa	Voy a la playa. (*I'm going to the beach.*)
park:	el parque	Voy al parque. (*I'm going to the park.*)

CLOSING

Tell the children that Spanish class is finished for today. In the next lesson they are going to learn other meanings for one of the color words.

DICTIONARY

Materials: Children's drawings or pictures from the Dictionary activity in Lesson 33; blank paper; tape or glue; children's dictionary pages; Red Flashcards 1, 58–63; and your Flashcards for the beach and park.

Preparation: Display all Flashcards. Write **Voy a ___** on the chalkboard.

Have children who brought in a magazine picture (Dictionary Activity in Lesson 33) tape it or glue it to a blank paper. Ask volunteers to hold up their pictures and say in Spanish the name of their favorite place. Have all children write the first letter of the place name on the top of their paper. Underneath have them write the place name (e.g., **el cine, la playa**) and how they would say *I'm going to* that place in Spanish (see Activity 34C). Refer them to the sentence **Voy a ___** on the chalkboard and the displayed Flashcards. Children should file their new dictionary page with their other pages.

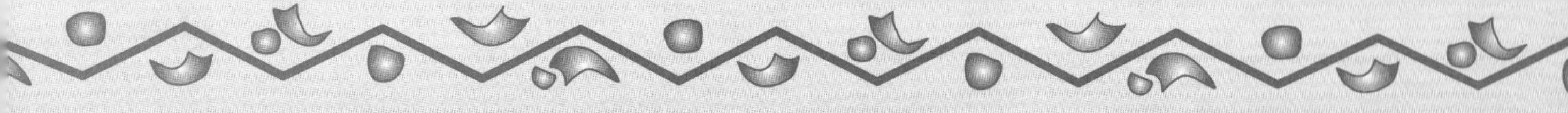

Lesson 35

Materials to gather

- VCR and Video Lesson 35 on Tape 12
- Cassette player
- Song Cassette
- Current Month Picture
- A calendar
- Blackline Master 35B (letter)
- Pencils
- Overhead transparency of Blackline Master 33A ("**¿Adónde vas?**")
- Red Flashcards 58–63
- ***Optional materials:*** ***"Las aventuras de Fredo"*** (*"Fredo's Adventures"*) books

Objectives

Language

- Decipher the secret message **Anda** (*Walk*)
- Understand another Fredo story—**"El café mágico"** (*"The Magic Café"*)
- Recognize buildings from their descriptions

Culture

- Learn that a word may have more than one meaning
- Sing "**¿Adónde vas?**" (*"Where Are You Going?"*)

Review

- Answer the question **¿Adónde vas?** (*Where are you going?*)
- Recall that a building has an entrance and an exit
- Review vocabulary for building parts
- Understand extended conversation in a visit to a Mexican restaurant

Vocabulary

Anda.	*Walk.*
el café	*coffee; café, coffee shop*
tiene	*he/she/it has*
come	*he/she/it eats*
toma	*he/she/it drinks*
el plátano/los plátanos	*banana/bananas*
la fresa/las fresas	*strawberry/strawberries*
la uva/las uvas	*grape/grapes*
el pan	*bread*
el cereal	*cereal*
la leche	*milk*

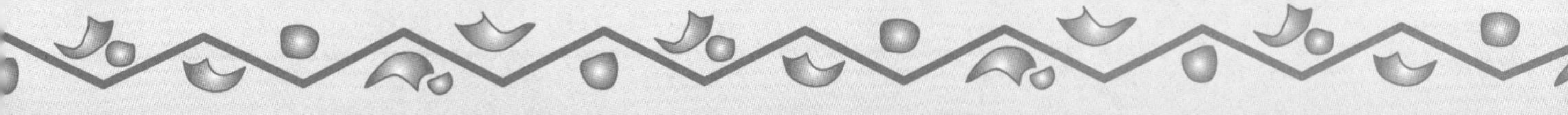

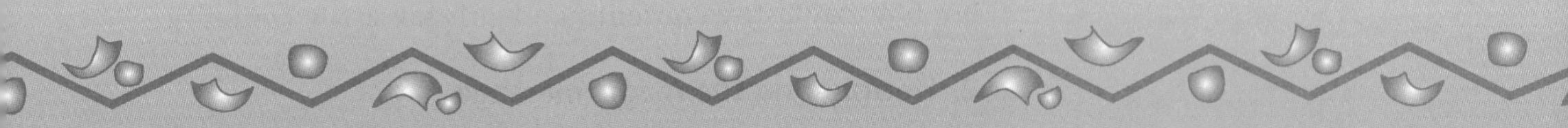

la fruta/las frutas	*fruit/fruits*
la manzana/las manzanas	*apple/apples*
el jugo/los jugos	*juice/juices*
ahora	*now*
¿Qué pasa?	*What's happening?* *What's going on?*

Warm-up

Greet the children and tell them it is time for Spanish class (**la clase de español**). Either miming or drawing figures on the chalkboard, review the following adjectives.

tall	alto/alta	*dirty*	sucio/sucia
short	bajo/baja	*clean*	limpio/limpia
thin	delgado/delgada	*ugly*	feo/fea
fat	gordo/gorda	*pretty*	bonito/bonita

Review

Ask the children what fruits they like to eat. Encourage them to use any Spanish words they may have learned in earlier years:

la fresa/las fresas	*strawberry/strawberries*
el limón/los limones	*lemon/lemons*
la manzana/las manzanas	*apple/apples*
la naranja/las naranjas	*orange/oranges*
la pera/las peras	*pear/pears*
el plátano/los plátanos	*banana/bananas*
la uva/las uvas	*grape/grapes*

Introduce the video

Invite the children to listen and watch as doña Elena reads another adventure book about Fredo in which many adjectives and fruits appear.

Remind the children to change the **o** sound to an **a** sound at the end of the adjective if it describes a female.

Heritage Speakers

Spanish-speaking children from Caribbean countries may use **la banana** rather than **el plátano** to refer to a yellow banana. The word **el plátano** is used in the Caribbean to refer to the *plantain* (a different variety of banana, which is eaten cooked). In Puerto Rico **el guineo** is used rather than **el plátano** for the yellow banana.

VIDEO LESSON

1. Greeting the children

La maestra greets the children with **Buenos días** (*Good morning*) and asks them how they are. Winston says **Estoy muy contento** (*I'm very happy*). **La maestra** reviews **Estoy triste** (*I'm sad*) and points out that both a girl and a boy say **Estoy triste**, but boys say **Estoy content<u>o</u>** and girls say **Estoy content<u>a</u>.**

2. Deciphering the magic message

La maestra tells the children **Vamos a mirar** (*Let's watch*). Antonio mimes walking. **La maestra** stops Winston from saying **el mensaje mágico** (*the magic message*). She tells him **No digas nada porque vamos a esperar hasta el fin de la lección** (*Don't say anything because we are going to wait until the end of the lesson*).

3. Practicing saying where one is going

Winston and the children read **¿Adónde vas?** (*Where are you going?*) and review answers to it.

Voy al restaurante.	*I'm going to the restaurant.*
Voy al museo.	*I'm going to the museum.*
Voy a la biblioteca.	*I'm going to the library.*
Voy al supermercado.	*I'm going to the supermarket.*
Voy al cine.	*I'm going to the movies.*
Voy al hospital.	*I'm going to the hospital.*

4. Singing *"¿Adónde vas?"* (*"Where Are You going?"*)

La maestra and doña Elena sing the song. For song lyrics, see Song 10 in the Song Appendix.

5. Singing *"¿Adónde vas?"* (*"Where Are You Going"*) *again*

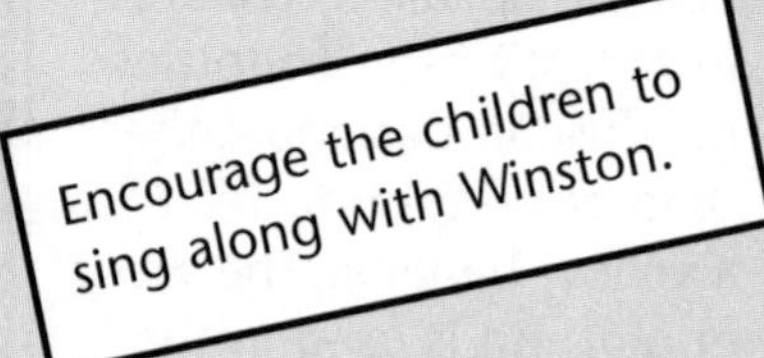

Encourage the children to
sing along with Winston.

This time **la maestra** sings the first two lines of each verse and shows the children the Red Flashcards for places. Our rather young bass, Winston, and the children sing the remaining lines of the verse. She cues the children's verses in the following order: **Voy al supermercado / Voy a la biblioteca / Voy al museo / Voy al restaurante / Voy al cine** (*I'm going to the supermarket / library / museum / restaurant / movies*).

6. Reviewing building parts vocabulary

La maestra asks LeeAnn and Winston **¿Dónde está la entrada?** Winston tells her **la puerta** (*door*). She enters through **la entrada** (*entrance*). She asks them **¿Dónde está la salida?** (*Where is the exit?*) and she exits through **la salida** (*exit*).

7. Visiting the Mexican restaurant

La maestra visits **el restaurante Lindo Michoacán**. For her statements, see Lesson 32, Video Lesson, section 7.

8. Introducing additional meanings of the word *café*

La maestra explains that the word **café** has three meanings: **café** means *brown,* **el café** means both *coffee* and *café* or *coffee shop*. She mentions that **un café es un restaurante pequeño** (*a café is a small restaurant*).

9. Reading about Fredo's adventure in the Magic Café

Doña Elena reads Book Two of ***"Las aventuras de Fredo"*** (*"Fredo's Adventures"*)—**"El café mágico"** (*"The Magic Café"*) as the children read along.

Fredo tiene hambre.	*Fredo is hungry.*
Busca un restaurante.	*He looks for a restaurant.*
Aquí está la entrada del café mágico.	*Here is the entrance to the Magic Café.*
Come un plátano.	*He eats a banana.*
¿Qué pasa?	*What's happening?*
Ahora, Fredo está alto.	*Now, Fredo is tall.*

10. Playing a game to practice the names of buildings

La maestra asks Winston and the children questions about where they would go to do various things: **el hospital** (*hospital*), **el rascacielos** (*skyscraper*), **los apartamentos** (*apartments*).

11. Revealing the magic message

Antonio performs the message. Winston and the children say the message: **Anda** (*Walk*).

12. Closing

La maestra and Winston say **Adiós** (*Good-bye*).

LANGUAGE ACROSS THE CURRICULUM

Ask the children if they can think of an English color word that has more than one meaning—*orange*. One meaning is the color orange; another meaning is the fruit.

Foods Fredo eats and how he looks:

el plátano–alto (*banana–tall*)

las fresas–bajo (*strawberries–short*)

las uvas–gordo (*grapes–fat*)

el pan–delgado (*bread–thin*)

el cereal–feo (*cereal–ugly*)

la leche–bonito (*milk–pretty*)

la manzana–sucio (*apple–dirty*)

el jugo–limpio (*juice–clean*)

After viewing the video, praise the children for their good listening and watching skills.

Activity Lesson

Activity 35A: Read "El café mágico" (*"The Magic Café"*)

Note: If your school has ***"Las aventuras de Fredo"*** (*"Fredo's Adventures"*) books available for the children, substitute the Fredo Book Activity in the margin for this activity.

Materials: VCR; Video Lesson 35 on Tape 12.

Preparation: Recue Video Lesson 35 to section 9, in which doña Elena reads the story **"El café mágico."**

Ask the children what adventure of Fredo's they've already read about (his adventures in the music store—**"La tienda de música."**) Ask them where Fredo's latest adventure took place (a café or small restaurant). Play section 9 of the video with the sound and tell the children to read along with doña Elena. Remind them to look for visual clues in the pictures and to listen and watch for words they know. Then rewind the tape to the beginning of the story and replay it without the sound. Pause the tape to give the children time to read each line of the story to themselves. Finally, do a quick comprehension check with the children (allow them to answer in English):

Questions:

1. Where does Fredo go? (to the Magic Café—**el café mágico**)
2. What does he do there? (He eats and drinks.)
3. What does he eat? (a banana—**un plátano**; strawberries—**las fresas**; grapes—**las uvas**; bread—**el pan**; cereal—**el cereal**; milk—**la leche**; an apple—**una manzana**; juice—**el jugo**).
4. What happens when he eats and drinks? (He changes shape. He turns ugly. He gets dirty. Finally, he becomes clean.)
5. Why is the café called the Magic Café? (Its food has magical qualities that make people change.)
6. Would you like to eat in such a café? (*Answers will vary.*)

Activity 35B: Write a letter!

Materials: Current Month Picture; a calendar; Blackline Master 35B; and pencils.

Preparation: Display the current Month Picture. Copy and distribute Blackline Master 35B so that each child has one.

Have children fill in their names and the date on their papers. Tell them they are going to write a letter to a new friend by using the words in the word bank (**Palabras**). Point out that they won't use all the words. For example, there are two types of places where one can live—**un apartamento** (*apartment*) and **una casa** (*house*). There are two school subjects —**el español** (*Spanish*) and **la música** (*music*) and several colors—**rojo** (*red*), **blanco** (*white*), **azul** (*blue*), and **verde** (*green*).

Fredo Book Activity

Materials: Cassette player; Song Cassette, Side B; and ***"Las aventuras de Fredo"*** (*"Fredo's Adventures"*) books.

Tell the children they are going to read another story about Fredo's adventures. Distribute the copies of ***"Las aventuras de Fredo"*** (*"Fredo's Adventures"*) among the children. Tell them to turn to Book 2 —**"El café mágico"** (*"The Magic Café"*)—and to read along silently as doña Elena reads the story. Play ***"Las aventuras de Fredo"*** Book 2, **"El café mágico"** (*"The Magic Café"*) on the Song Cassette, Side B. Then allow children time to re-read the story on their own. Use the questions in Activity 35A to check comprehension.

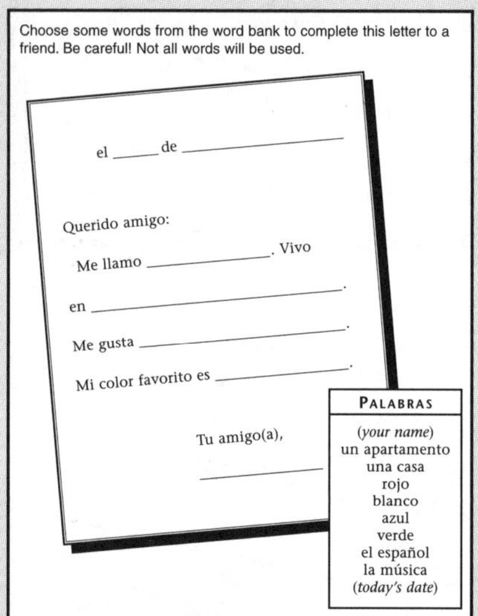

Choose some words from the word bank to complete this letter to a friend. Be careful! Not all words will be used.

el ____ de ____________

Querido amigo:

Me llamo ____________. Vivo

en ____________.

Me gusta ____________.

Mi color favorito es ____________.

Tu amigo(a),

____

Palabras

(*your name*)
un apartamento
una casa
rojo
blanco
azul
verde
el español
la música
(*today's date*)

Blackline Master 35B

Children's letters should read:

el *number* de *current month*

Querido amigo:

Me llamo *child's name*. Vivo en **un apartamento** *or* **una casa**. Me gusta **el español** *or* **la música**. Mi color favorito es **rojo, blanco, azul,** *or* **verde**.

Tu amigo(a),
child's name

English equivalent:

the number of month

Dear friend,

My name is child's name. I live in *an apartment* or *a house*. I like *Spanish* or *music*. My favorite color is *red, white, blue,* or *green*.

Your friend,
child's name

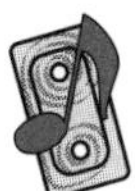

Activity 35C: Sing *"¿Adónde vas?"* (*"Where Are You Going?"*)

Materials: Cassette player; "**¿Adónde vas?**" (*"Where Are You Going?"*) on the Song Cassette, Side A; the overhead transparency of Blackline Master 33A; and Red Flashcards 58–63.

Preparation: Display the Red Flashcards in song order. Project the transparency.

Ask for a volunteer to hold up the Red Flashcard that corresponds to each verse as the children sing. Ask for another volunteer to point to each verse on the transparency. For song lyrics, see Song 10 in the Song Appendix.

If the children are willing, divide the class into two groups. Have them sing the song without the music. Assign one group the question lines of the song and the other group the *I'm going to* lines of the song. Cue the *I'm going to* lines by pointing to one of the Red Flashcards.

Closing

Tell the children that Spanish class is finished for today. In the next lesson **la maestra** will review more adjectives and vocabulary for mealtimes.

If children need help with the day, point to the number of the day on the calendar. If they need help spelling the name of the month, point to the current Month Picture.

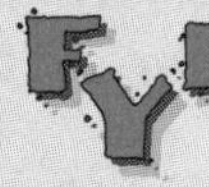

In personal letters in Spanish, the greeting is usually followed by a colon and the closing is followed by a comma.

Red Flashcards
(in song order):

#59: Voy al museo.
(*I'm going to the museum.*)

#62: Voy al cine.
(*I'm going to the movies.*)

#58: Voy al restaurante.
(*I'm going to the restaurant.*)

#61: Voy al supermercado.
(*I'm going to the supermarket.*)

#60: Voy al la biblioteca.
(*I'm going to the library.*)

#63: Voy al hospital.
(*I'm going to the hospital.*)

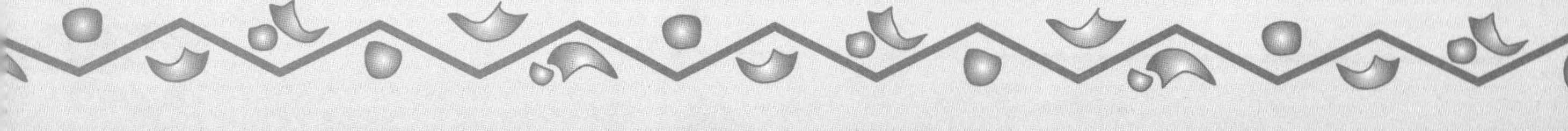

Lesson 36

> **Materials to gather**
> - VCR and Video Lesson 36 on Tape 12
> - Cassette player
> - Song Cassette
> - Overhead transparency of Blackline Master 33A ("**¿Adónde vas?**")
> - ***Optional materials:*** *"Las aventuras de Fredo"* (*"Fredo's Adventures"*) books

Objectives

Language

- Decipher the secret message **Corre** (*Run*)
- Understand an extended conversation about mealtimes

Culture

- Sing "**¿Adónde vas?**" (*"Where Are You Going?"*)

Review

- Review the meanings of the word **café**
- Read **"El café mágico"** (*"The Magic Café"*)
- Review the adjectives **duro/dura** (*hard*) and **suave** (*soft*)

Vocabulary

Corre.	*Run.*
el desayuno	*breakfast*
el almuerzo	*lunch*
la cena	*dinner*
por la mañana	*in the morning*
por la tarde	*in the afternoon*
por la noche	*in the evening*
¿Qué haces?	*What are you doing?*
como	*I eat*
tomo	*I have* (literally *I take*); *I drink*
el pan tostado	*toast*
el jugo de naranja	*orange juice*
un vaso de leche	*a glass of milk*

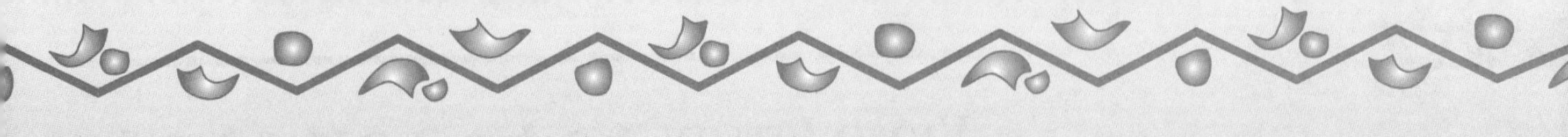

las papas	*potatoes*
el sándwich	*sandwich*
el pollo	*chicken*
el arroz	*rice*
las zanahorias	*carrots*
Buen provecho.	*Enjoy your meal.*

Warm-up

Tell the children it's time for Spanish class (**la clase de español**). Ask them which mealtime is their favorite and what they particularly like to eat at that meal.

Review

Open the classroom door from the inside and begin to walk out. Then ask the children what you were doing (leaving the room). Ask them what sign in Spanish would be above the door—**la salida** (*exit*). Next, open the classroom door from the hallway and walk in. Ask the children what you were doing (entering the room) and what Spanish sign would be above the door on the hallway side—**la entrada** (*entrance*).

Introduce the video

Invite the children to listen and watch as **la maestra** talks about what she eats at various times of the day.

Video Lesson

Students who are new to ***Español para ti*** this year may not be familiar with the command **Corre** (*Run*).

Foods Fredo eats and how he looks:

el plátano–alto (*banana–tall*)

las fresas–bajo (*strawberries–short*)

las uvas–gordo (*grapes–fat*)

el pan–delgado (*bread–thin*)

el cereal–feo (*cereal–ugly*)

la leche–bonito (*milk–pretty*)

la manzana–sucio (*apple–dirty*)

el jugo–limpio (*juice–clean*)

1. Greeting the children and Kipper

La maestra greets the children and Kipper with **Buenos días** (*Good morning*) and asks them how they are. Kipper says **Estoy muy bien** (*I'm very well*). **La maestra** tells Kipper and the children **Estoy contenta** (*I am happy*).

2. Seeing the magic message

Antonio demonstrates **el mensaje mágico** (*the magic message*), which is **Corre** (*Run*). **La maestra** asks Kipper **¿Sabes?** (*Do you know?*) but then tells him **Pero no digas** (*But don't tell*).

3. Recalling the meanings of the word *café*

La maestra asks Kipper **¿Puedes leer?** (*Are you able to read [this]?*). Kipper reads the word **el café. La maestra** reviews the meanings of **café**—*brown, coffee,* and *small restaurant* (**el restaurante pequeño**).

4. Reading *"El café mágico"* ("The Magic Café")

Doña Elena reads the book aloud while the children read along on the screen.

Fredo tiene mucha hambre.	*Fredo is very hungry.*
Come uvas.	*He eats grapes.*
¿Qué pasa?	*What's happening?*
Ahora, Fredo está gordo, muy gordo.	*Now Fredo is fat, very fat.*
¡Pobrecito!	*Poor little one!*
A Fredo le gusta la fruta.	*Fredo likes fruit.*
A Fredo no le gusta estar sucio.	*Fredo doesn't like being dirty.*
Toma jugo.	*He drinks juice.*
Aquí está la salida del café mágico.	*Here is the exit of the Magic Café.*
Y ahora, Fredo es Fredo.	*And now, Fredo is Fredo.*
El fin.	*The end.*

5. Talking about mealtimes

La maestra takes **un plátano** (*banana*), **una fresa** (*strawberry*), and **una manzana** (*apple*) out of her pockets. She talks about what she eats for breakfast, lunch, and dinner.

Por la mañana tomo el desayuno.	*In the morning I have breakfast.*
¿Qué como?	*What do I eat?*
¿Qué haces?	*What are you doing?*

Como el cereal.	*I eat cereal.*
¿Qué pones en el cereal?	*What do you put in your cereal?*
Por la tarde como el almuerzo.	*In the afternoon I eat lunch.*
Por la noche como la cena.	*In the evening I eat dinner.*
¡Buen provecho!	*Enjoy your meal!*

6. Reviewing the adjectives *suave* (soft) and *duro* (*hard*)

La maestra eats some of the same foods Fredo eats to see what will happen to her and is disappointed in the results!

Hago un experimento.	*I'm going to do an experiment.*
Cuando Fredo come el plátano, Fredo está muy alto.	*When Fredo eats the banana, Fredo is very tall.*
A ver.	*Let's see.*
No estoy alta.	*I'm not tall.*
¡Nada!	*Nothing!*
El pan es muy suave.	*The bread is very soft.*
Pero la manzana es muy dura.	*But the apple is very hard.*

Doña Elena tells Antonio to **siéntate** (*sit*) on various objects and asks him how it feels: **Es suave** (*It's soft*), **Es duro** (*It's hard*). **La maestra** asks Kipper if various foods are hard or soft. She points out that **la manzana** ends in an **a** sound so **dura** also ends in an **a** sound.

7. Saying where one is going

La maestra asks **¿Adónde vas?** (*Where are you going?*): **Voy al supermercado** (*I'm going to the supermarket*), **Voy a la biblioteca** (*I'm going to the library*), **Voy al cine** (*I'm going to the movies*), **Voy al restaurante** (*I'm going to the restaurant*), **Voy al café** (*I'm going to the coffee shop*).

8. Singing *"¿Adónde vas?"* (*"Where Are You Going?"*)

Everyone sings the song. For song lyrics, see Song 10 in the Song Appendix.

9. Revealing *el mensaje mágico* (*the magic message*)

Antonio demonstrates the message—**Corre** (*Run*).

10. Closing

Kipper and **la maestra** say **Adiós** (*Good-bye*) to the children.

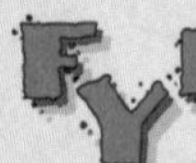

The verb **tomar** has several meanings: *to take, to have* when referring to mealtimes, and *to drink.* The word **como** means *I eat;* the word **cómo** as in **¿Cómo estás?** means *how.* Their pronunciation is the same.

Foods and beverages (in order of mention):

el cereal (*cereal*)

el pan tostado (*toast*)

el jugo de naranja (*orange juice*)

un vaso de leche (*a glass of milk*)

las papas (*potatoes*)

el sándwich (*sandwich*)

las fresas (*strawberries*)

el pollo (*chicken*)

el arroz (*rice*)

las zanahorias (*carrots*)

las uvas (*grapes*)

After viewing the video, praise the children for their good listening and watching skills.

ACTIVITY LESSON

Activity 36A: Sing *"¿Adónde vas?"* (*"Where Are You Going?"*)

Materials: Cassette player; Song Cassette, Side A; Red Flashcards 58–63; and the overhead transparency of Blackline Master 33A.

Preparation: Display Red Flashcards 58–63 in random order. Project the overhead transparency.

Tell the children they are going to sing the song about places they go. Ask for volunteers to point to the Flashcards and to the verses on the transparency as the class sings.

Activity 36B: Read *"El café mágico"* (*"The Magic Café"*)

Note: If you school has ***"Las aventuras de Fredo"*** (*"Fredo's Adventures"*) books available for the children, substitute the Fredo Book Activity in the margin for this activity.

Materials: VCR; Video Lesson 36 on Tape 12.

Preparation: Recue Video Lesson 36 to section 4, in which doña Elena reads the story **"El café mágico."**

Tell the children to read along with doña Elena as she reads *"The Magic Café"* (**"El café mágico"**). Play section 4 of the video with the sound. Remind the children to look for visual clues in the pictures and to listen and watch for words they know. Then rewind the video to the beginning of the story and replay it without the sound, pausing it at each picture. Ask volunteers to read the lines aloud.

FREDO BOOK ACTIVITY

Materials: Cassette player; Song Cassette, Side B; and ***"Las aventuras de Fredo"*** (*"Fredo's Adventures"*) books.

Tell the children they are going to read about Fredo's adventures in The Magic Café. Distribute the copies of ***"Las aventuras de Fredo"*** (*"Fredo's Adventures"*) among the children. Tell them to turn to Book 2—**"El café mágico"** (*"The Magic Café"*)—and to read along silently as doña Elena reads the story. Play ***"Las aventuras de Fredo"*** Book 2, **"El café mágico"** (*"The Magic Café"*) on the Song Cassette, Side B. Then have the class re-read the story with volunteers reading aloud.

Activity 36C: Soft (*suave*) and hard (*duro*)

Write the words **suave** and **duro** on the chalkboard. Direct the children to name in English objects that fit under each category.

CLOSING

Tell the children that Spanish class is finished for today. In the next lesson children will learn a new song.

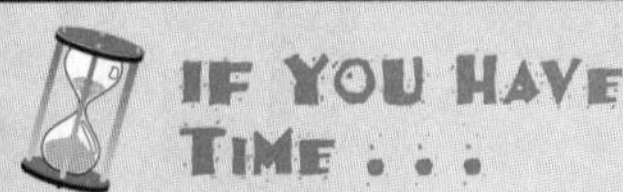

IF YOU HAVE TIME . . .

List the Spanish words for the three mealtimes on the board: **el desayuno** (*breakfast*), **el almuerzo** (*lunch*), and **la cena** (*dinner*). Have the children name in English foods for each meal. List the words under their appropriate categories.

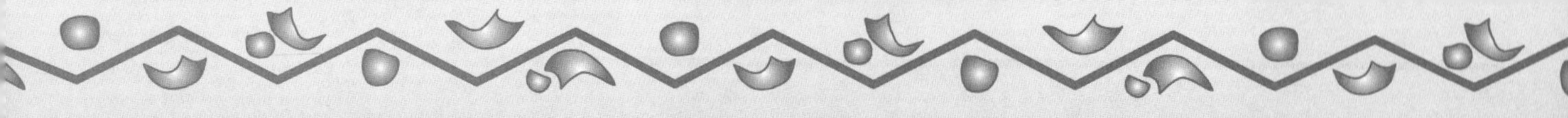

Lesson 37

Materials to gather

- VCR and Video Lesson 37 on Tape 13
- Cassette player
- Song Cassette
- Overhead projector
- A blank overhead transparency
- Blackline Master 37A-1 ("**La canción de geografía**")
- Blackline Master 37A-2 ("**En los Estados Unidos**")
- A map of the United States
- A world map
- ***Optional materials:*** a map of your state with Spanish names of towns or cities circled

Objectives

Language

- Decipher the magic message—**Muéstrame** (*Show me*)
- Sing a new song—"**En los Estados Unidos**" (*"In the United States"*)
- Learn how to say one is going to a particular country or city

Culture

- Recall the concept of opposite seasons
- Learn that many place names in the U.S. are of Spanish origin

Review

- Sing "**La canción de geografía**" (*"The Geography Song"*)
- Sing "**¿Adónde vas?**" (*"Where Are You Going?"*)

Vocabulary

los Estados Unidos	*the United States of America*
Norteamérica	*North America*
Sudamérica	*South America*
Muéstrame ___.	*Show me ___.*

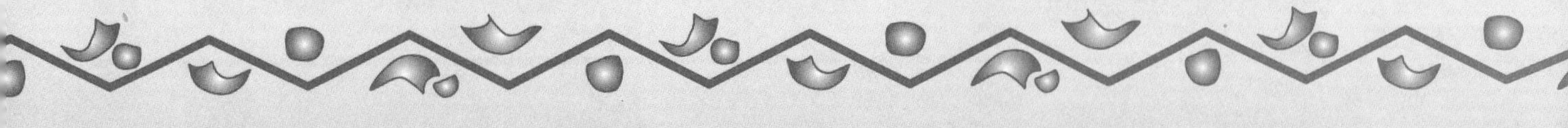

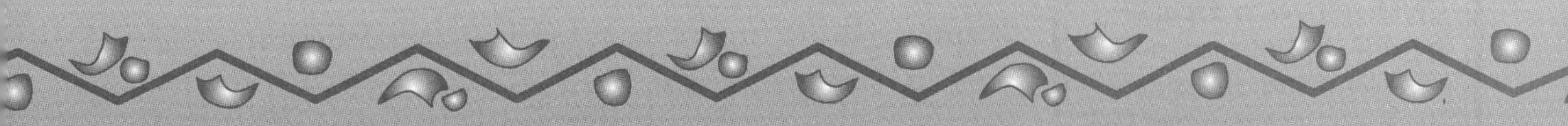

Warm-up

Talk with the children about what opportunities they have had to use their knowledge of Spanish and the Spanish-speaking cultures outside of the classroom. Have they met other people who speak Spanish and tried to talk with them in Spanish? Have they heard a Spanish song on the radio? Have they heard about a Spanish-speaking country on the television or read about one in the news?

Review

Ask a volunteer to role-play Antonio and act out the magic messages **la maestra** has presented so far. The children should call out each message.

Run.	Corre.	*Walk.*	Anda.
Jump.	Salta.	*Look for.*	Busca.
Touch.	Toca.		

Introduce the video

Invite the children to listen and watch as **la maestra** sings a new song and tells them some exciting news about her summer plans.

Video Lesson

Children new to ***Español para ti*** will not recognize the command. Reassure them that the message will be revealed at the end of the lesson.

1. Greeting the children

La maestra greets Winston and the children with **Buenos días** (*Good morning*) and asks them how they are.

2. Introducing another *mensaje mágico* (*magic message*)

Antonio demonstrates the magic message—**Muéstrame** (*Show me*).

3. Hearing about summer plans

La maestra is very excited. She pulls an airline ticket out of her *pocket* (**el bolsillo**) and exclaims **Voy a la Argentina** (*I'm going to Argentina*). Winston asks her **¿Por qué?** (*Why?*). She explains **Voy a la Argentina en el verano, en julio, para esquiar en las montañas** (*I'm going to Argentina in the summer, in July, to ski in the mountains*). She reminds Winston and the children that north of the equator it is summer in July but that south of the equator it is *winter* (**el invierno**) in July.

4. Singing the song about geography

La maestra asks Winston and the children to name **un país de habla española** (*a Spanish-speaking country*). Everyone sings **"La canción de geografía"** (*"The Geography Song"*). For the lyrics, see Song 2 in the Song Appendix.

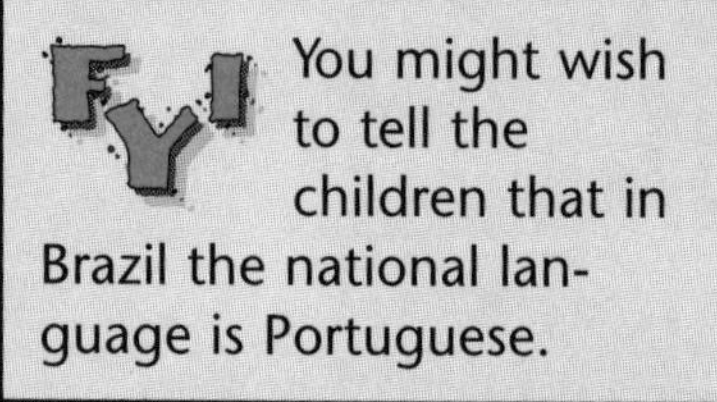

You might wish to tell the children that in Brazil the national language is Portuguese.

5. Introducing a new song

La maestra shows the children Argentina on a map of South America. She shows the children areas of the U.S. where there are many Spanish named places. She teaches the children a new song, **"En los Estados Unidos"** (*"In the United States"*).

Chorus:

En los Estados Unidos	*In the United States*
Hay ciudades pequeñas y grandes,	*There are small and large cities,*
Y algunas basan sus nombres	*And some base their names*
En la historia del mundo hispano.	*On the history of the Hispanic world.*

Los Angeles, San Diego, San Francisco,	*Los Angeles, San Diego, San Francisco,*
Las Vegas, Amarillo, Santa Fe,	*Las Vegas, Amarillo, Santa Fe,*
San Antonio, San Agustín.	*San Antonio, Saint Augustine.*
(*Repeat chorus.*)	
Orlando, Reno, El Dorado, Española,	*Orlando, Reno, El Dorado, Española,*
Buena Vista, Monterey, Mesa, Durango.	*Buena Vista, Monterey, Mesa, Durango.*
(*Repeat chorus.*)	
Los Estados Unidos, sí.	*The United States, yes.*

La maestra asks Winston **¿Dónde vives tú?** (*Where do you live?*) and answers for him **En los Estados Unidos** (*In the United States*).

6. Singing *"¿Adónde vas?"* (*"Where Are You Going?"*)

Winston asks **la maestra ¿Adónde vas?** (*Where are you going?*). She replies **Voy a la Argentina** (*I'm going to Argentina*) and explains that one uses **Voy a** + a country name, a city name, or a place name to say where one might be going. Doña Elena and **la maestra** sing the song. For the lyrics, see Song 10 in the Song Appendix. Winston asks **la maestra ¿Cómo vas?** (*How are you going?*). She tells him **Voy en avión** (*I'm going by plane*), **no voy en bicicleta** (*I'm not going by bicycle*).

7. Revealing *el mensaje mágico* (*the magic message*)

Antonio demonstrates the magic message **Muéstrame** (*Show me*) one more time.

8. Closing

La maestra mentions again that it will be winter in Argentina when she goes there in July. She and Winston say **Adiós** (*Good-bye*) to the children.

After viewing the video, praise the children for their good listening and watching skills.

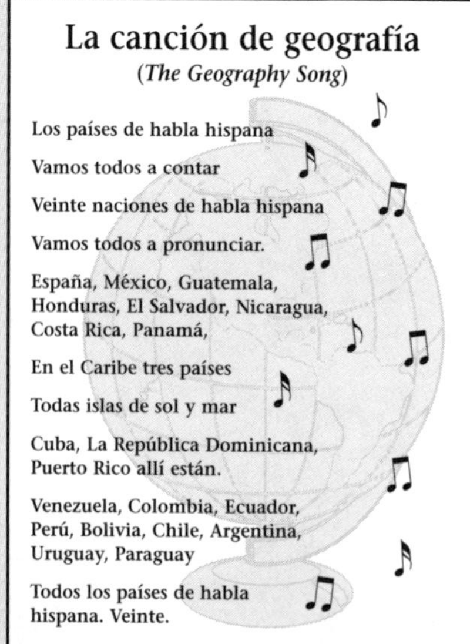

La canción de geografía
(*The Geography Song*)

Los países de habla hispana
Vamos todos a contar
Veinte naciones de habla hispana
Vamos todos a pronunciar.

España, México, Guatemala,
Honduras, El Salvador, Nicaragua,
Costa Rica, Panamá,

En el Caribe tres países
Todas islas de sol y mar

Cuba, La República Dominicana,
Puerto Rico allí están.

Venezuela, Colombia, Ecuador,
Perú, Bolivia, Chile, Argentina,
Uruguay, Paraguay

Todos los países de habla
hispana. Veinte.

Blackline Master 37A-1

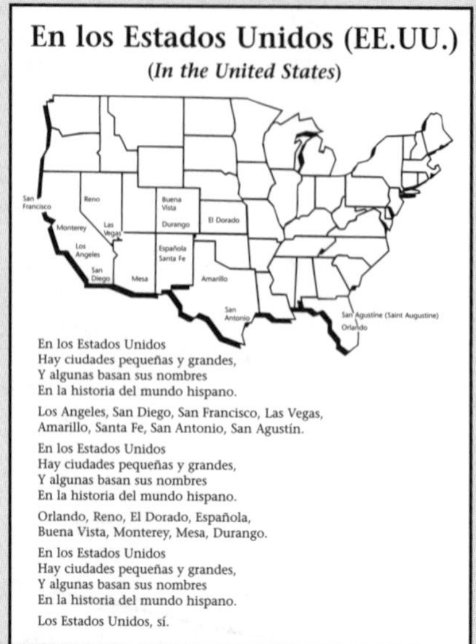

En los Estados Unidos (EE.UU.)
(*In the United States*)

En los Estados Unidos
Hay ciudades pequeñas y grandes,
Y algunas basan sus nombres
En la historia del mundo hispano.

Los Angeles, San Diego, San Francisco, Las Vegas,
Amarillo, Santa Fe, San Antonio, San Agustín.

En los Estados Unidos
Hay ciudades pequeñas y grandes,
Y algunas basan sus nombres
En la historia del mundo hispano.

Orlando, Reno, El Dorado, Española,
Buena Vista, Monterey, Mesa, Durango.

En los Estados Unidos
Hay ciudades pequeñas y grandes,
Y algunas basan sus nombres
En la historia del mundo hispano.

Los Estados Unidos, sí.

Blackline Master 37A-2

ACTIVITY LESSON

Activity 37A: Sing two songs

Materials: Cassette player; Song Cassette, Side A; a blank overhead transparency; Blackline Masters 37A-1 and 37A-2; and an overhead projector.

Preparation: Make an overhead transparency of Blackline Masters 37A-1 and 37A-2. Project the transparency of Blackline Master 37A-1 (**"La canción de geografía"**).

Tell the children to sing along with **la maestra** to **"La canción de geografía"** (*"The Geography Song"*). Point out that all the Spanish lyrics are projected and stop the tape at the end of the song. Next, project the overhead transparency of Blackline Master 37A-2 (**"En los Estados Unidos"**). Tell the children they are going to sing the new song *"In the United States"* about cities in the United States that have Spanish names. Explain that because of the history of the United States and its many explorers from Spanish-speaking areas of the world, there are many cities with Hispanic names. Play the song, pointing to each of the place names as **la maestra** sings them.

Activity 37B: U.S. cities with Spanish names

Materials: Overhead projector; the overhead transparency of Blackline Master 37A-2; a map of the United States; *optional:* a map of your state with Spanish names of towns or cities circled.

Project the overhead transparency of Blackline Master 37A-2. Pointing to the word **Amarillo** on the transparency, ask the children what the word means in English (*yellow*). Ask heritage speakers or explain what some of the other Spanish place names mean in English. For example, **Los Ángeles** (*the angels*), **San Diego** (*Saint Diego*), **San Francisco** (*Saint Francis*), **Las Vegas** (*the meadows*), **Reno** (*reindeer*), **El Dorado** (*the golden one*), **Buena Vista** (*good view*), **Monterey** (*mountain king*). Locate the cities on your U.S. map. If there are places in your state with Spanish names, e.g., Peru in Maine, point them out on a map.

Activity 37C: Locate Argentina

Materials: A world map.

Display the world map. Ask children where **la maestra** is going in July (Argentina). Help them locate it on the world map by pointing out the equator and asking them if Argentina is north or south of the equator (south). Once they have located the country, ask them what she is going to do there in July (ski). Ask what season it will be in Argentina in July (winter). Have four volunteers locate the equator on the map and talk about the concept of opposite seasons. (In North America winter is December, January, and February and it is generally cold. In South America December, January, and February are summer months and it is hot during those months. When it's winter in North America, it's summer in South America.) Encourage them to say the months and seasons in Spanish and to describe the weather in Spanish also.

La estación (*Season*):	**Norteamérica** (*North America*):	**Sudamérica** (*South America*):
el invierno (*winter*):	diciembre, enero, febrero (*December, January, February*)	junio, julio, agosto (*June, July, August*)
la primavera (*spring*):	marzo, abril, mayo (*March, April, May*)	septiembre, octubre, noviembre (*September, October, November*)
el verano (*summer*):	junio, julio, agosto (*June, July, August*)	diciembre, enero, febrero (*December, January, February*)
el otoño (*fall*):	septiembre, octubre, noviembre (*September, October, November*)	marzo, abril, mayo (*March, April, May*)

CLOSING

Tell the children that Spanish class is finished for today. In the next lesson **la maestra** will review the names of buildings.

EN ESPAÑOL

If you feel comfortable, ask questions and reinforce answers in Spanish.

¿Adónde va la maestra en julio?
(*Where is **la maestra** going in July?*)

Va a la Argentina.
(*She's going to Argentina.*)

¿Qué va hacer en Argentina?
(*What is she going to do in Argentina?*)

Va a esquiar./Esquiar.
(*She's going to ski./Ski.*)

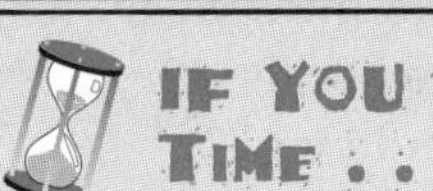

IF YOU HAVE TIME . . .

Ask the children to name your state capital. Then ask them what the capital city of the entire United States is called. Mention that each country has a capital city. On the world map, have children locate the capital city of Argentina (Buenos Aires). Point out the difference in how the capital city is marked as opposed to other major cities (different type size or style or with a star rather than a dot). For the next Spanish class, have them research the population and principal products of Argentina (population: approx. 37,673,000; products: grains, livestock products).

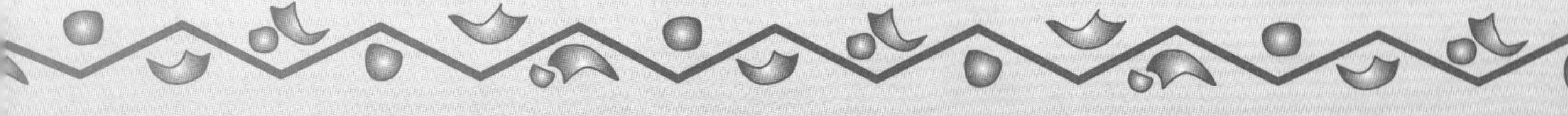

Lesson 38

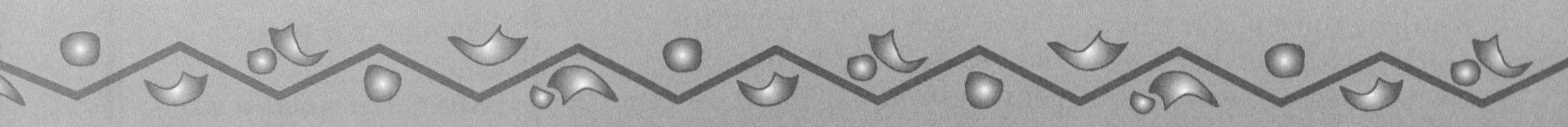

Materials to gather

- VCR and Video Lesson 38 on Tape 13
- Cassette player
- Song Cassette
- Overhead projector
- Overhead transparency of Blackline Master 33A ("**¿Adónde vas?**")
- Overhead transparency of Blackline Master 37A-2 ("**En los Estados Unidos**")
- Blackline Master 38B (three buildings)
- Pencils
- Calendar
- Current Month Picture
- U.S. or world map

Objectives

Language

- Decipher **el mensaje mágico** (*the magic message*) **Colorea** (*Color*) or **Dibuja** (*Draw*)
- Comprehend an extended conversation about San Diego
- Recall the colors and meanings of the traffic lights

Culture

- Learn how so many cities and towns in the U.S. came to have Spanish names

Review

- Sing "**En los Estados Unidos**" (*"In the United States"*)
- Practice the names of buildings
- Sing "**¿Adónde vas?**" (*"Where Are You Going?"*)

Vocabulary

EE.UU.	*abbrev. for* los Estados Unidos (*United States of America*)
la ciudad/las ciudades	*city/cities*
el pueblo/los pueblos	*town/towns*
el este	*east*
el norte	*north*
el oeste	*west*
el sur	*south*
el centro	*city center, downtown*

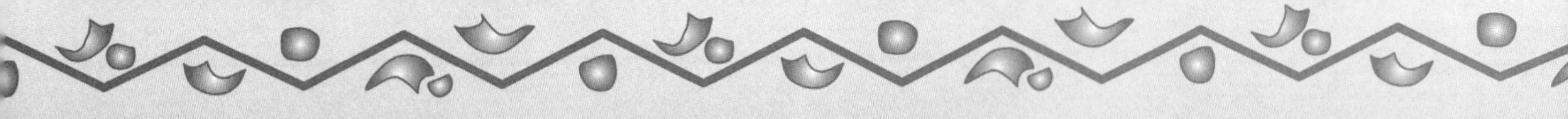

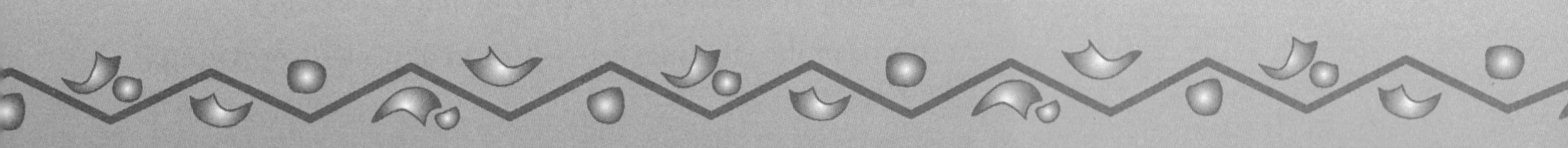

las luces del tráfico	*traffic lights*
Verde: ¡Sigue!	*Green: Go!*
Amarillo: ¡Espera!	*Yellow: Wait!, Caution!*
Rojo: ¡Alto!	*Red: Stop!*
Colorea.	*Color.*
Dibuja.	*Draw.*

Warm-up

Lead the children in a discussion of the town or city in which you live. Ask them if it is a city, a town, or a village. What kinds of buildings are located in the town or city (e.g., skyscrapers, tall buildings, short buildings, stores, houses, apartment houses)? What are the characteristics of a city (e.g., large population, lots of buildings and roads, public transportation system, many businesses)? What are the characteristics of a small town or village (few people, few buildings and roads, few businesses, more open space)?

Review

Materials: Cassette player; **"En los Estados Unidos"** (*"In the United States"*) on the Song Cassette, Side A; the overhead transparency of Blackline Master 37A-2; and an overhead projector.

Tell the children they are going to practice Spanish names of places in the United States by singing the new song **"En los Estados Unidos"** (*"In the United States"*). Point to the lyrics on the transparency as you play the song.

Introduce the video

Invite the children to listen and watch as **la maestra** explains how so many places in the United States came to have Spanish names and as she describes the city of San Diego.

En los Estados Unidos (EE.UU.)

(In the United States)

En los Estados Unidos
Hay ciudades pequeñas y grandes,
Y algunas basan sus nombres
En la historia del mundo hispano.

Los Angeles, San Diego, San Francisco, Las Vegas, Amarillo, Santa Fe, San Antonio, San Agustín.

En los Estados Unidos
Hay ciudades pequeñas y grandes,
Y algunas basan sus nombres
En la historia del mundo hispano.

Orlando, Reno, El Dorado, Española, Buena Vista, Monterey, Mesa, Durango.

En los Estados Unidos
Hay ciudades pequeñas y grandes,
Y algunas basan sus nombres
En la historia del mundo hispano.

Los Estados Unidos, sí.

Blackline Master 37A-2

VIDEO LESSON

1. Greeting the children

La maestra greets Kipper and the children with **Buenas tardes** (*Good afternoon*) and asks them how they are.

2. Viewing *el mensaje mágico* (*the magic message*)

Antonito mimes the message—**¡Colorea!** (*Color!*) or **¡Dibuja!** (*Draw!*).

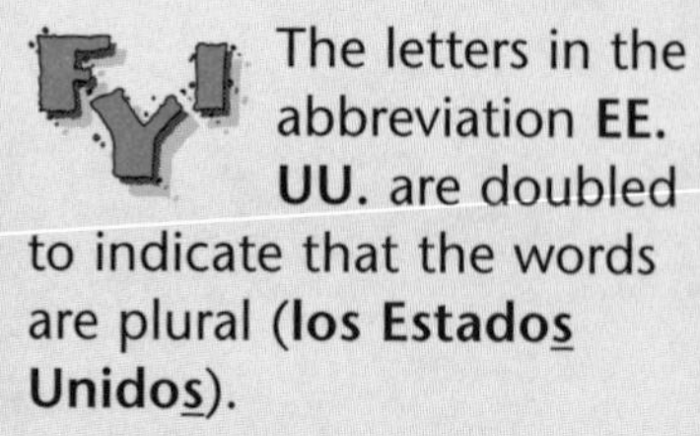

The letters in the abbreviation **EE. UU.** are doubled to indicate that the words are plural (**los Estados Unidos**).

3. Presenting how cities in the U.S. came to have Spanish names

La maestra explains that **EE. UU.** is the abbreviation for **los Estados Unidos** (*United States*). She reminds the children that many *cities* (**las ciudades**) and *towns* (**los pueblos**) in the U.S. have Spanish names because many Spaniards who settled in Mexico also settled in the Southwestern U.S. and Florida. She also mentions that many people from Puerto Rico and other parts of the Caribbean live in the Northeast U.S.

el sur	*south*	el oeste	*west*
el norte	*north*	el este	*east*

LANGUAGE ACROSS THE CURRICULUM

Locate your state on a map of the U.S. Talk with the children about what region of the country you are in—north, south, east, west, central, etc. Ask if children in the class have lived in other areas of the U.S. and have them point out the places on the map. In what regions are those places?

4. Singing *"En los Estados Unidos"* (*"In the United States"*)

La maestra sings the song with the children. For song lyrics, see song 11 in the Song Appendix.

5. Playing a game with the children

Kipper and the children answer the question **¿Qué edificio es?** (*What building is it?*) as **la maestra** shows them pictures of various buildings and parts of buildings.

el rascacielos	*skyscraper*
los apartamentos	*apartment building*
la tienda	*store*
la entrada	*entrance*
la salida	*exit*

la tienda de ropa (*clothing store*)

Es una palabra muy larga. (*It's a very long word.*)

6. Playing *¿Qué edificio es?* (*What building is it?*)

La maestra plays a game of **¿Qué edificio es?** (*What building is it?*) with the children: **el rascacielos** (*skyscraper*), **los apartamentos** (*apartment building*), **la casa** (*house*), **la tienda** (*store*), **la escuela** (*school*), **el supermercado** (*supermarket*).

As each of the building names appears on the screen in section 6, point to it in order to draw the children's attention to it.

7. Talking about San Diego

La maestra explains that one of her favorite cities, San Diego, is in the west of the U.S. (**el oeste de los Estados Unidos**). She describes the city.

Ésta es la ciudad— el centro de la ciudad.	*This is the city— the center of the city.*
Y en el centro hay muchos edificios.	*And in the center there are many buildings.*
Hay unos edificios bajos pero hay muchos edificios muy altos.	*There are some short buildings but there are many very tall buildings.*
Y los edificios más altos son los rascacielos.	*And the very tall buildings are the skyscrapers.*
Sí, qué centro más bonito.	*Yes, what a very pretty center.*

8. Singing *"¿Adónde vas?"* ("Where Are You Going?")

Kipper responds to the question **¿Adónde vas?** according to Red Flashcards: **Voy a la biblioteca** (*I'm going to the library*), **Voy al restaurante** (*I'm going to the restaurant*). Doña Elena and **la maestra** sing the song. For the lyrics, see Song 10 in the Song Appendix.

9. Introducing traffic lights

La maestra explains the colors and commands of the traffic lights.

Éstas son las luces del tráfico.	*These are the traffic lights.*
Hay tres luces del tráfico.	*There are three traffic lights.*
El verde es "¡Sigue!"	*Green is "Go!"*
Amarillo—"¡Espera!"	*Yellow—"Wait!, Caution!"*
El rojo—"¡Alto!"	*Red—"Stop!"*

10. Solving *el mensaje mágico* (the magic message)

Antonio mimes the message and the children reveal it—**Colorea** (*Color*) or **Dibuja** (*Draw*).

11. Closing

La maestra and Kipper say **Adiós** (*Good-bye*) and **Hasta luego** (*See you later*).

After viewing the video, praise the children for their good listening and watching skills.

En los Estados Unidos (EE.UU.)

(In the United States)

En los Estados Unidos
Hay ciudades pequeñas y grandes,
Y algunas basan sus nombres
En la historia del mundo hispano.

Los Angeles, San Diego, San Francisco, Las Vegas,
Amarillo, Santa Fe, San Antonio, San Agustín.

En los Estados Unidos
Hay ciudades pequeñas y grandes,
Y algunas basan sus nombres
En la historia del mundo hispano.

Orlando, Reno, El Dorado, Española,
Buena Vista, Monterey, Mesa, Durango.

En los Estados Unidos
Hay ciudades pequeñas y grandes,
Y algunas basan sus nombres
En la historia del mundo hispano.

Los Estados Unidos, sí.

Blackline Master 37A-2

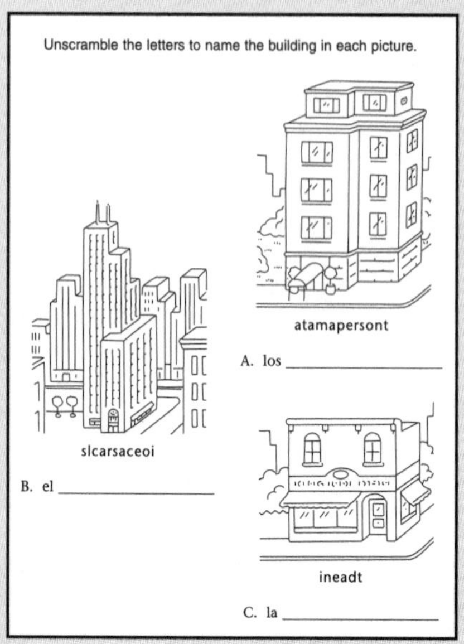

Unscramble the letters to name the building in each picture.

atamapersont

A. los ______________

slcarsaceoi

B. el ______________

ineadt

C. la ______________

Blackline Master 38B

Activity Lesson

Activity 38A: Sing two familiar songs

Materials: Cassette player; Song Cassette, Side A; the overhead transparencies of Blackline Masters 33A and 37A-2; and an overhead projector.

Project the overhead transparency of Blackline Master 33A. Tell the children they are going to sing "**¿Adónde vas?**" (*"Where Are You Going?"*) with doña Elena and **la maestra.** Divide the class into two groups—one to sing the questions and one to sing the answers. When the song ends, stop the tape. Then display the overhead transparency of Blackline Master 37A-2 and tell the children they are going to sing the song "**En los Estados Unidos**" about cities and towns in the U.S. with Spanish names. Restart the tape and encourage the children to sing along. Point to the lyrics on the transparency. For song lyrics with English equivalents, see Songs 10 and 11 in the Song Appendix.

Activity 38B: Unscramble the words

Materials: Blackline Master 38B; pencils; calendar; current Month Picture; *optional:* VCR, Video Lesson 38, section 6.

Preparation: Display the calendar and the current Month Picture. Copy Blackline Master 38B so that each child has a copy.

Ask the children what building names **la maestra** reviewed in the video (**el rascacielos**—*skyscraper,* **la casa**—*house,* **los apartamentos**—*apartment building,* **la escuela**—*school,* **la tienda**—*store,* and **el supermercado**—*supermarket*). Distribute Blackline Master 38B. Tell the children to write their names and the current date on their sheets. If they need help with the date, point to the number of the day on the calendar and then to the current Month Picture. Draw their attention to each picture on the Blackline Master and ask them what kind of building each one is. Then have them write the name of each building by unscrambling the letters. If the children have difficulty doing the activity, you may wish to replay section 6 of Video Lesson 38, pointing to each building name as it appears on the screen. Finally, write the answers below on the board so that the children can check what they've written.

a. los apartamentos (*apartment building*)
b. el rascacielos (*skyscraper*)
c. la tienda (*store*)

Activity 38C: Where do you want to go?

Materials: U.S. map or world map.

Preparation: Write the following on the board: Voy a ___.

Call on one volunteer at a time to complete the sentence (*I'm going to* ___) with the name of a country or city he/she would like to visit or that is his/her favorite.

Have the children report their findings from *If you have time . . .* in Lesson 37, Activity Lesson.

CLOSING

Tell the children that Spanish class is finished for today. In the next lesson they will practice more traffic-related vocabulary.

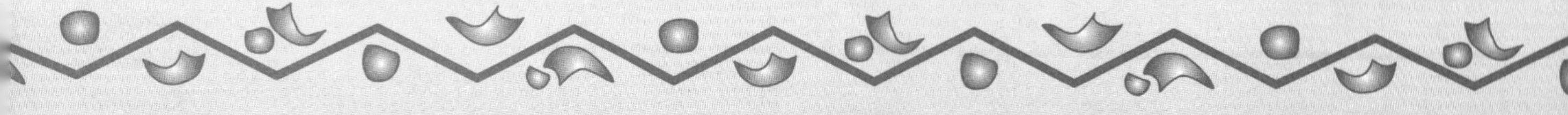

Lesson 39

Materials to gather

- VCR and Video Lesson 39 on Tape 13
- Cassette player
- Activity Cassette 2
- Red, yellow, and green paintbrushes (from Lesson 4 Review)
- Red Flashcards 58–63
- ***Optional materials:*** blank paper; yellow, red, and green markers or colored pencils for each child; children's dictionary pages; Song Cassette; overhead transparency of Blackline Master 33A ("**¿Adónde vas?**"); overhead projector

Objectives

Language

- Decipher a new **mensaje mágico** (*magic message*)—**Tengo calor** (*I'm hot*)
- Learn the names of several modes of transportation
- Say how one is going somewhere
- Sing "**¿Cómo vas?**" (*"How Are You Going?"*)

Culture

- Recognize that there is a lot of traffic in the city
- Review safety rules for crossing the street

Review

- Sing "**¿Adónde vas?**" (*"Where Are You Going?"*)
- Answer the question **¿Adónde vas?** (*Where are you going?*)

Vocabulary

el centro	*center*
rápido	*rapidly*
despacio	*slowly*
Miro a la derecha.	*I look to the right.*
Miro a la izquierda.	*I look to the left.*
Cruzo la calle.	*I cross the street.*
¿Cómo vas (tú)?	*How are you going?*
Voy en ___.	*I'm going by ___.*
el coche/los coches	*car/cars*
el camión/los camiones	*truck/trucks*
el autobús/los autobuses	*bus/buses*
la moto/las motos	*motorcycle/motorcycles*
el taxi/los taxis	*taxi/taxis*

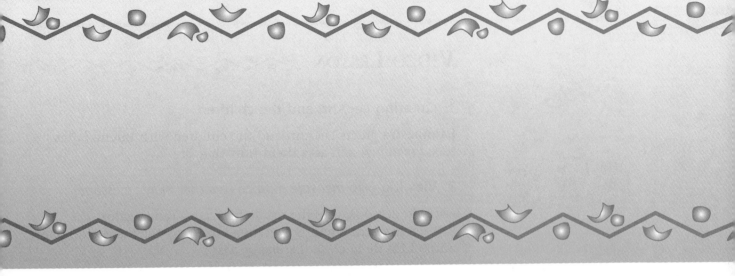

Warm-up

Let the children know it's time for Spanish class (**la clase de español**). Ask them how they get where they are going. For example, do they walk, ride their bicycles, ride in the car? Ask them to think of all the various modes of transportation that exist (e.g., bicycle, car, truck, train, bus, plane, boat, spaceship).

Review

Materials: Red, yellow, and green paintbrushes from Lesson 4.

Ask the children what they need to do when they cross the street (stop, observe a traffic light or crossing guard if present, or look to the left, look to the right, and proceed with caution). Ask them what the colors red, yellow, and green have to do with crossing the street (they indicate what the vehicle traffic is doing). Holding up the red paintbrush, ask what it means on a traffic light (*Stop!*—**¡Alto!**). Do the same for yellow (*Wait!, Caution!*—**¡Espera!**) and green (*Go!*—**¡Sigue!**).

Introduce the video

Invite the children to listen and watch as **la maestra** talks about where she is going and how she is going to get there.

VIDEO LESSON 

1. Greeting LeeAnn and the children

La maestra greets LeeAnn and the children with **Buenos días** (*Good morning*) and asks them how they are.

2. Viewing *otro mensaje mágico* (*another magic message*)

Antonio demonstrates the magic message—**Tengo calor** (*I'm hot*). **La maestra** reminds everyone not to say the magic message until **el fin de la clase** (*the end of class*).

3. Singing *"¿Adónde vas?"* (*"Where Are You Going?"*)

LeeAnn reads the question **¿Adónde vas?** (*Where are you going?*). **La maestra** gives sample answers using **Voy a** + a place name. Doña Elena and **la maestra** sing "**¿Adónde vas?**" (*"Where Are You Going?"*). For song lyrics, see Song 10 in the Song Appendix.

4. Talking about city traffic

La maestra and LeeAnn talk about buildings in a city. Standing on a busy street corner, **la maestra** describes the traffic.

Aquí está la esquina en el centro de la ciudad.	*Here is the corner in the center of the city.*
Hay mucho tráfico en la ciudad.	*There's a lot of traffic in the city.*
Hay coches. Hay camiones.	*There are cars. There are trucks.*
Hay autobuses y hay taxis.	*There are buses, and there are taxis.*

5. Presenting the words *slowly* and *rapidly*

La maestra introduces the words **rápido** (*rapidly*) and **despacio** (*slowly*).

El tráfico en el centro de la ciudad es muy rápido.	*The traffic in the center of the city is very fast.*
Ahora en el centro de la ciudad el tráfico es despacio.	*Now in the center of the city the traffic is slow.*

6. Reviewing the traffic light commands

La maestra reviews the commands indicated by **las tres luces del tráfico** (*traffic lights*).

7. Talking about street crossing safety

La maestra reminds LeeAnn and the children what to do before crossing the street.

Miro a la derecha.	*I look to the right.*
Miro a la izquierda.	*I look to the left.*
Cruzo la calle.	*I cross the street.*

Traffic light commands:

Verde: ¡Sigue! (*Green: Go!*)

Amarillo: ¡Espera! (*Yellow: Wait!*)

Rojo: ¡Alto! (*Red: Stop!*)

FYI Estoy aquí en la calle. (*Here I am in the street.*)

Voy a cruzar la calle. (*I'm going to cross the street.*)

El tráfico es un poco peligroso, entonces hay que mirar a la derecha, a la izquierda y cruzar la calle. (*The traffic is a little dangerous so one must look to the right, to the left, and cross the street.*)

8. Introducing modes of transportation

La maestra asks LeeAnn **¿Cuáles son las formas de transporte?** (*What are the forms of transportation?*): **el taxi** (*taxi*); **los coches** (*cars*); **las motos** (*motorcycles*); **los autobuses** (*buses*).

9. Presenting a new question and answer

LeeAnn reads the question **¿Cómo vas?** (*How are you going?*). She and **la maestra** answer the question in different ways.

10. Singing *"¿Cómo vas?"* ("How Are You Going?")

Singing to the **"¿Adónde vas?"** (*"Where Are You Going?"*) tune, **la maestra** and LeeAnn sing **"¿Cómo vas?"** (*"How are you Going?"*).

¿Cómo vas? ¿Cómo vas tú? (2x)	*How are you going?* *How are you going? (2x)*
Voy en moto. (2x) Yo voy.	*I'm going by motorcycle. (2x)* *I'm going.*
Voy en taxi. Voy en taxi. Voy en taxi. Yo voy.	*I'm going by taxi. I'm going by taxi. I'm going by taxi. I'm going.*
Voy en coche. (2x) Voy en coche. Yo voy.	*I'm going by car. (2x)* *I'm going by car. I'm going.*

Voy en bicicleta.
(*I'm going by bicycle.*)
Voy en moto.
(*I'm going by motorcycle.*)
Voy en taxi.
(*I'm going by taxi.*)
Voy en coche.
(*I'm going by car.*)
Voy en autobús.
(*I'm going by bus.*)

11. Taking a trip to the park

La maestra rides her bicycle to the park. She exclaims **Voy al parque en bicicleta** (*I'm going to the park by bicycle*). **¿Por qué?** (*Why?*). **Porque hace calor y hace sol** (*Because it's hot and it's sunny*). **Es muy divertido ir al parque en bicicleta** (*It's a lot of fun going to the park by bicycle*).

12. Reviewing the difference between two questions

La maestra asks LeeAnn where she's going and how she's going.

¿Adónde vas y cómo vas tú?	*Where are you going and how are you going?*
Voy al cine en taxi.	*I'm going to the movies by taxi.*
Voy al restaurante en coche.	*I'm going to the restaurant by car.*
Voy al restaurante. Voy en coche.	*I'm going to the restaurant.* *I'm going by car.*

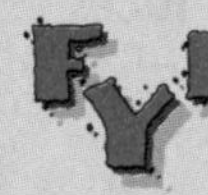

In closing, **la maestra** reviews means of transportation and also mentions **el yipi** (*jeep*).

13. Revealing *el mensaje mágico* (the magic message)

Antonio mimes the message, which the children reveal—**Tengo calor** (*I'm hot*).

14. Closing

La maestra and LeeAnn bid the children (**niños**) and teachers (**maestros**) **Adiós** (*Good-bye*).

After viewing the video, praise the children for their good listening and watching skills.

Activity Lesson

Activity 39A: Match the signal color to the command

Materials: Cassette player; Activity Cassette 2, Side A.

Preparation: Write the following words on the chalkboard:

Amarillo	¡Sigue!
Rojo	¡Espera!
Verde	¡Alto!

Point out to the children that you have written three color words on the board (**amarillo**—*yellow,* **rojo**—*red,* **verde**—*green*). Ask them what the three colors have to do with traffic (they are the colors of traffic lights). Mention that you've also written three commands on the board. Tell them to listen carefully, and when **la maestra** says a color, they should call out the traffic signal command that the color represents. **La maestra** calls out the colors as follows: **Verde: ¡Sigue!** (*Green: Go!*); **Amarillo: ¡Espera!** (*Yellow: Wait!, Caution!*); **Rojo: ¡Alto!** (*Red: Stop!*).

Activity 39B: Rapidly or slowly?

Preparation: Write the following words on the chalkboard:

rápido	despacio

Pointing to **rápido**, ask the children what it means (*rapidly, quickly*). Do the same with **despacio** (*slowly*). Mention that *rapidly* and **rápido** are cognates, i.e., they sound similar and share the same meaning. Ask the children what they like to do rapidly (run, ski, skate, do their homework, do the dishes, clean their rooms) and what they like to do slowly (read a good book, walk to school, eat ice cream, clean their rooms). List what they say under the appropriate word.

Dictionary

Materials: Blank paper; yellow, red, and green markers or colored pencils for each child; children's dictionary pages.

Ask the children to recall the order of the colored lights on a traffic signal (from top to bottom: *red*—**rojo**, *yellow*—**amarillo**, *green*—**verde**). Have the children draw a traffic light. (An example can be found in ***Español para ti,*** Level 2, Blackline Master 53A.) Next to each color light they should write the appropriate command:

red:	¡Alto!
yellow:	¡Espera!
green:	¡Sigue!

At the top of their pages have them write **las luces del tráfico** (*traffic lights*) and alphabetize the new page under **l** for **luces** (*lights*).

Activity 39C: Sing *"¿Adónde vas?"* (*"Where Are You Going?"*)

Materials: Red Flashcards 58–63; *optional:* the overhead transparency of Blackline Master 33A; an overhead projector; **"¿Adónde vas?"** (*"Where Are You Going?"*) on the Song Cassette, Side A; and a cassette player.

Preparation: Display Red Flashcards 58–63 in the following (song) order: 59, **el museo** (*museum*); 62, **el cine** (*movie theater*); 58, **el restaurante** (*restaurant*); 61, **el supermercado** (*supermarket*); 60, **la biblioteca** (*library*); and 63, **el hospital** (*hospital*).

Tell the children they are going to sing the song on their own. Divide the class into two groups—those who ask the question and those who answer. Have those who will ask begin the song. If children are having difficulty or are reluctant to sing, play the song on the Song Cassette and project the overhead transparency with the lyrics. For song lyrics, see Song 10 in the Song Appendix.

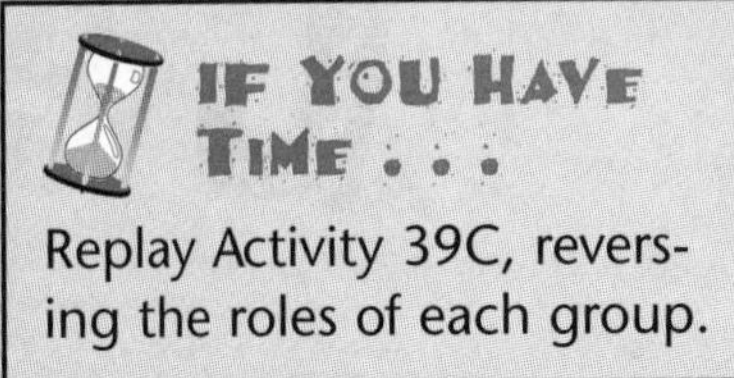

Replay Activity 39C, reversing the roles of each group.

CLOSING

Tell the children that Spanish class is finished for today. In the next lesson **la maestra** is going to introduce additional modes of transportation.

Lesson 40

> **Materials to gather**
>
> - VCR and Video Lesson 40 on Tape 14
> - Cassette player
> - Song Cassette
> - Red Flashcards 58–63
> - Blackline Master 40B (6 sentences)
> - Pencils
> - Current Month Picture
> - Calendar

Objectives

Language

- Decipher a new **mensaje mágico** (*magic message*)—**Tengo frío** (*I'm cold*)
- Understand what Spanish questions have in common
- Comprehend extended conversations about various forms of transportation
- Read sentences that include information about where and how one is going

Culture

- Review street crossing safety

Review

- Sing "**¿Adónde vas?**" (*"Where Are You Going?"*)
- Review the question **¿Cómo vas?** (*How are you going?*)

Vocabulary

el bote/los botes	*boat/boats*

Warm-up

Tell the children it's time for Spanish class (**la clase de español**). Mention that Antonio and **la maestra** have been showing them magic messages for several lessons. Ask volunteers to demonstrate one of the secret messages. Remind them not to say anything! The class should reveal each message when you tell them it's time. Have each volunteer mime the magic message two or three times. **Muéstrame** (*Show me*) may be difficult for the children to mime.

Anda.	*Walk.*	Muéstrame.	*Show me.*
Busca.	*Look for.*	Salta.	*Jump.*
Colorea.	*Color.*	Toca.	*Touch.*
Corre.	*Run.*	Tengo calor.	*I'm hot.*
Dibuja.	*Draw.*		

Review

Ask the children what **la maestra** reviewed in the last lesson about crossing the street: look to the right, look to the left, cross the street, and be careful. Ask them if they can recall the words for *right* (**la derecha**) and *left* (**la izquierda**). Ask volunteers to demonstrate crossing the street, telling the class what they are doing.

Miro a la derecha.	*I look to the right.*
Miro a la izquierda.	*I look to the left.*
Cruzo la calle.	*I cross the street.*

Children may not be able to say these phrases in Spanish yet. It is sufficient to have them describe in English what **la maestra** reviewed.

Introduce the video

Invite the children to listen and watch as **la maestra** rides a motorcycle!

Video Lesson

1. Greeting the children

La maestra greets the children with **Buenas tardes** (*Good afternoon*) and asks them how they are. She says she heard some children say **Así, así** (*So-so*) and **Tengo hambre** (*I'm hungry*). She greets Winston and asks him **¿Cómo estás?** (*How are you?*). He tells her **Muy bien** (*Fine*).

2. Presenting *el mensaje mágico* (*the magic message*)

Antonio demonstrates the message—**Tengo frío** (*I'm cold*).

3. Singing *"¿Adónde vas?"* (*"Where Are You Going?"*)

Winston reads the question **¿Adónde vas?** (*Where are you going?*). **La maestra** reviews several answers, e.g., **Voy al restaurante** (*I'm going to the restaurant*). She and doña Elena sing the song. For song lyrics, see Song 10 in the Song Appendix.

4. Talking about the similarities in questions

La maestra shows the children the questions **¿Adónde vas?** (*Where are you going?*) and **¿Cómo vas?** (*How are you going?*). She reviews what they have in common, e.g., upside-down and right side up question marks, the verb **vas**, and accent marks on the question words. She tells the children that every asking word in Spanish has an accent mark.

5. Introducing the boat as a mode of transportation

Winston and **la maestra** talk about various ways they travel.

¿Cómo vas?	*How are you going?*
Voy en ___.	*I'm going by ___.*

La maestra talks about a boat.

Aquí estoy en un bote.	*Here I am on a boat.*
Estoy en el bote y el bote está en el lago.	*I'm on the boat and the boat is on the lake.*

6. Presenting the motorcycle as a way of going somewhere

La maestra rides to school on a motorcycle.

Aquí viene la moto.	*Here comes the motorcycle.*
Es la moto de un amigo.	*It is a friend's motorcycle.*
¿Quién está en la moto?	*Who is on the motorcycle?*
Yo estoy en la moto.	*I'm on the motorcycle.*
¿Adónde vamos?	*Where are we going?*
Vamos a la escuela en la moto.	*We're going to school by motorcycle.*
Me gusta mucho ir a la escuela en la moto.	*I really like to go to school by motorcycle.*

7. Demonstrating travel by truck

La maestra drives a truck home.

Aquí está el camión.	*Here is the truck.*
Es muy grande.	*It's very large.*
¿De qué color es el camión?	*What color is the truck?*
El camión es de color gris.	*The truck is gray.*
Yo voy en camión.	*I'm going by truck.*
Voy a casa en camión.	*I'm going home by truck.*

8. Recalling street crossing safety

La maestra reminds children that they have to be careful of the forms of transportation (**las formas de transporte**) when crossing the street. She reviews street-crossing safety with the children.

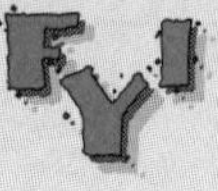

Miro a la derecha.
(*I look to the right.*)

Miro a la izquierda.
(*I look to the left.*)

Cruzo la calle.
(*I cross the street.*)

¡Cuidado!
(*Be careful!*)

9. Reviewing the words for *rapidly* and *slowly*

Showing the children and Winston film of traffic traveling at different speeds, **la maestra** reviews the words **rápido** (*rapidly*) and **despacio** (*slowly*). She tells Winston **salta rápido** (*jump rapidly*) and **salta despacio** (*jump slowly*).

10. Reading sentences

Winston and the children read several answers to the questions **¿Adónde vas?** and **¿Cómo vas?** (*Where are you going?/How are you going?*): **Voy al parque en bicicleta** (*I'm going to the park by bicycle*), **Voy al museo en taxi** (*I'm going to the museum by taxi*), **Voy al restaurante en moto** (*I'm going to the restaurant by motorcycle*), and **Voy al hospital en coche** (*I'm going to the hospital by car*).

11. Revealing *el mensaje mágico* (*the magic message*)

Antonio demonstrates the message and the children say how they would express feeling that way—**Tengo frío** (*I'm cold*).

12. Closing

Winston and **la maestra** bid the children **Hasta luego** (*See you later*) and **Hasta la vista** (*Until we meet again*).

After viewing the video, praise the children for their good listening and watching skills.

Activity Lesson

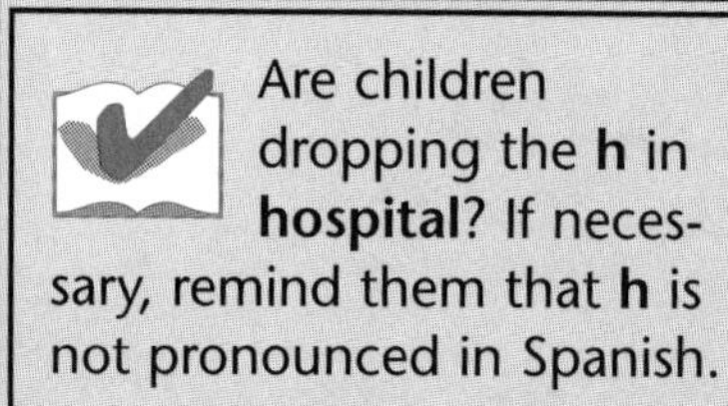

Are children dropping the **h** in **hospital**? If necessary, remind them that **h** is not pronounced in Spanish.

Complete the sentences using the pictures and words in the word bank to help you. Then, read the sentences aloud.

1. Voy en ______.
2. Voy en ______.
3. Voy en ______.
4. Voy en ______.
5. Voy en ______.
6. Voy en ______.

Palabras
camión
coche
bote
bicicleta
moto
autobús

Blackline Master 40B

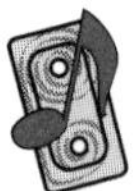

Activity 40A: Sing *"¿Adónde vas?"* (*"Where Are You Going?"*)

Materials: Cassette player; Song Cassette, Side A; and Red Flashcards 58–63.

Display the Red Flashcards in the following (song) order: 59, 62, 58, 61, 60, 63. Gesturing toward the Flashcards, tell the children they are going to sing the song about where they are going. Play the song, pointing to each Red Flashcard as they sing about each place. Encourage the children to sing along. For song lyrics, see Song 10 in the Song Appendix.

Activity 40B: Write how you are going somewhere

Materials: Blackline Master 40B; pencils; current Month Picture; and a calendar.

Preparation: Display the current Month Picture and the calendar. Copy and distribute Blackline Master 40B so that each child has a copy.

Tell the children to write their names and the date on the top of their papers. If they need help with the date, point to the number of the day on the calendar and to the current Month Picture. Remind them that they've been learning to say how they are going somewhere in Spanish. Point out that on their papers are six sentences. Ask what **Voy en** means (*I'm going by*). Have them complete each sentence using the pictures and words in the word bank. When they have finished, ask volunteers to read one sentence apiece aloud. Children should have completed the Spanish sentences as follows:

1. Voy en coche. — *I'm going by car.*
2. Voy en autobús. — *I'm going by bus.*
3. Voy en bote. — *I'm going by boat.*
4. Voy en moto. — *I'm going by motorcycle.*
5. Voy en bicicleta. — *I'm going by bicycle.*
6. Voy en camión. — *I'm going by truck.*

Activity 40C: What's the same? What's different?

Preparation: Write the following questions on the chalkboard.

¿Adónde vas? ¿Cómo vas?

Talk with the children about the similarities in the questions: they both begin with an upside-down question mark and end with a right side up question mark; they both contain the verb **vas** which means *you are going* or *are you going;* and both question asking words have an accent mark over the **o**. Ask them what is different in each question (the question asking words **¿Adónde?** and **¿Cómo?**). Ask them what each of those words means (**¿Adónde?**—*Where (to)?*, **¿Cómo?**—*How?*).

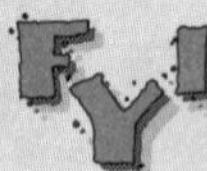

¿Adónde vas? (*Where are you going?*)

¿Cómo vas? (*How are you going?*)

CLOSING

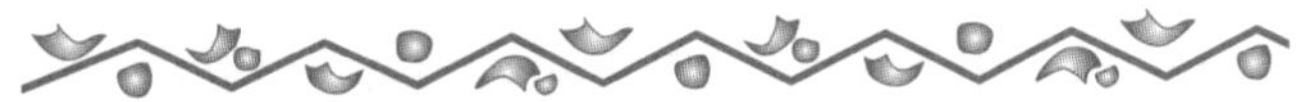

Tell the children that Spanish class is finished for today. In the next lesson **la maestra** will go more places by other forms of transportation.

IF YOU HAVE TIME . . .

Ask one volunteer at a time to sketch a picture of one of the forms of transportation they've been learning. The class should then say **Voy en** (*I'm going by*) + the form of transportation the volunteer has drawn. See Activity 40B for possible sentences.

FAMILY CONNECTION

To foster a friendly link between home and school, you may want to send out Family Letter 3 (see the Teacher's Resource Book). This letter suggests how families can be involved in their children's learning of Spanish.

Lesson 41

Materials to gather

- VCR and Video Lesson 41 on Tape 14
- Cassette player
- Activity Cassette 2
- Song Cassette
- Overhead transparency of Blackline Master 37A-1 ("**La canción de geografía**")
- Overhead projector
- Flashcards of a beach scene and a park (from Lesson 33)
- Overhead transparency of Blackline Master 37A-2 ("**En los Estados Unidos**")
- Blackline Master 41B (4 sentences)
- Pencils
- Calendar
- Current Month Picture
- Red Flashcards 58–63
- Pictures of a bicycle, boat, bus, car, jeep, motorcycle, taxi, truck
- Heavyweight white paper
- Laminating machine
- ***Prepare ahead:*** You may want to laminate the pictures of the forms of transportation, which you will need for Activity 41C.

Objectives

Language

- Figure out another **mensaje mágico** (*magic message*)—**Tengo hambre** (*I'm hungry*)
- Understand extended conversations about going places by various modes of transportation
- Read sentences

Culture

- Review that there is a lot of traffic in a city and that city traffic can be dangerous
- Review that the abbreviation for **los Estados Unidos** (*the United States*) is **EE.UU.**

Review

- Sing "**En los Estados Unidos**" (*"In the United States"*)
- Listen to extended conversations about San Diego

Vocabulary

el yipi/los yipis	*jeep/jeeps*

Warm-up

Materials: Cassette player; **"La canción de geografía"** (*"The Geography Song"*) on the Song Cassette, Side A; and the overhead transparency of Blackline Master 37A-1.

Ask children to name as many Spanish-speaking countries as they can. Then project your overhead transparency of Blackline Master 37A-1 and tell them they are going to practice naming them all by singing **"La canción de geografía"** (*"The Geography Song"*). Play the song on the Song Cassette. For song lyrics with the English equivalents, see Song 2 in the Song Appendix.

Review

Materials: Your Flashcards of the beach scene and the park.

Hold up each Flashcard and ask the children how they would say *I'm going to* + the place shown. If you feel comfortable, ask **¿Adónde vas?** (*Where are you going?*) as you hold up each Flashcard.

Voy a la playa.	*I'm going to the beach.*
Voy al parque.	*I'm going to the park.*

Introduce the video

Invite the children to listen and watch as **la maestra** goes many places and travels by various forms of transportation.

Video Lesson

1. Greeting the children

La maestra greets the children with **Buenos días** (*Good morning*) and asks them how they are. She says **¡Hola!** (*Hello!*) to Kipper and asks him how he is.

2. Deciphering *el mensaje mágico* (*the magic message*)

Antonio demonstrates another magic message—**Tengo hambre** (*I'm hungry*).

3. Answering the question *¿Adónde vas?*

Kipper reads the question **¿Adónde vas?** (*Where are you going?*) and answers with **Voy al parque** (*I'm going to the park*).

Other replies:

Voy a la biblioteca.
(*I'm going to the library.*)

Voy al museo.
(*I'm going to the museum.*)

Voy a la escuela.
(*I'm going to school.*)

Voy al centro de la ciudad.
(*I'm going downtown.*)

4. Singing *"En los Estados Unidos"* ("*In the United States*")

La maestra mentions that there are **ciudades grandes** (*large cities*), **ciudades pequeñas** (*small cities*), and cities with Spanish names. She sings **"En los Estados Unidos"** (*"In the United States"*). For song lyrics, see Song 11 in the Song Appendix.

Kipper says **Tenemos una canción** (*We have a song*).

5. Talking about San Diego

La maestra says **Yo vivo en los Estados Unidos** (*I live in the United States*). She asks Kipper **¿Vives tú en los Estados Unidos?** (*Do you live in the United States?*). He replies **Sí, vivo aquí** (*Yes, I live here*). She reviews the abbreviation for **los Estados Unidos** (EE.UU.). Finally, she describes the downtown area of San Diego. For her statements, see Lesson 38, Video Lesson, section 7.

6. Describing city traffic

La maestra talks about the traffic in the city of San Diego. For her statements, see Lesson 39, Video Lesson, section 4.

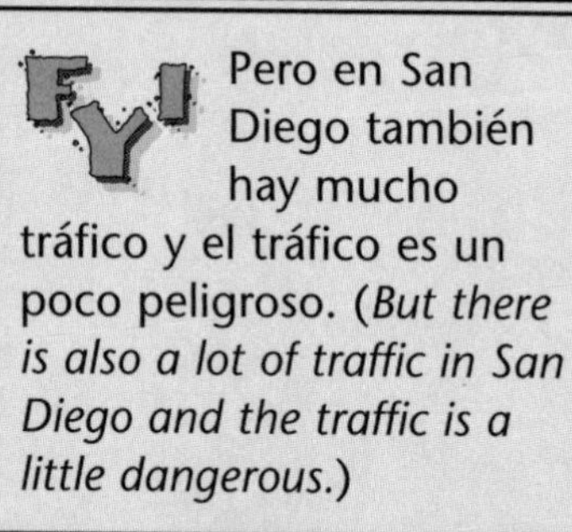

Pero en San Diego también hay mucho tráfico y el tráfico es un poco peligroso. (*But there is also a lot of traffic in San Diego and the traffic is a little dangerous.*)

7. Asking and answering the question *¿Cómo vas?* (*How are you going?*)

The children read the question **¿Adónde vas?** (*Where are you going?*). **La maestra** reminds them that they can answer with the name of a place in the city or the name of a town or city: **Voy a** ___ (*I'm going to* ___). She asks them to read the question **¿Cómo vas?** (*How are you going?*) and to answer it: **Voy en** ___ (*I'm going by* ___).

8. Presenting the taxi as a form of transportation

La maestra goes to the store in a taxi.

Aquí viene el taxi.	*Here comes the taxi.*
Aquí está el señor.	*Here is the man.*
Abre la puerta del taxi.	*He opens the door of the taxi.*
Voy a la tienda en taxi.	*I'm going to the store by taxi.*
La tienda se llama Marshalls.	*The store is called Marshalls.*

El señor es conductor del taxi.	*The man is the driver of the taxi.*
Me gusta mucho ir de compras.	*I like to shop very much.*

9. Going to the restaurant by car

La maestra describes going to the restaurant with doña Elena.

Aquí viene el coche.	*Here comes the car.*
Es el coche de mi amiga doña Elena.	*It is my friend doña Elena's car.*
Yo voy al restaurante y mi amiga doña Elena va al restaurante también.	*I'm going to the restaurant and my friend doña Elena is also going to the restaurant.*
Vamos al restaurante porque yo tengo mucha hambre.	*We're going to the restaurant because I'm very hungry.*

10. Going to the supermarket in a jeep

La maestra describes going to the supermarket in a jeep.

Me gusta mucho el yipi.	*I like the jeep a lot.*
Voy a la tienda en yipi.	*I'm going to the store by jeep.*
Estoy en la tienda.	*I'm at the store.*
Me gusta ir al supermercado en yipi.	*I like to go to the supermarket by jeep.*

Borrowed words often have variant spellings. *Jeep* in Spanish can be spelled as **jipi** or **yipi**.

11. Explaining differing word order

Kipper asks **la maestra** why she changes the word order in a sentence. She explains that the word order depends on the question you are answering.

¿Adónde vas?
(*Where are you going?*)
Voy a la tienda en yipi.
(*I'm going to the store by jeep.*)
¿Cómo vas?
(*How are you going?*)
Voy en yipi a la tienda.
(*I'm going by jeep to the store.*)

12. Reading sentences

La maestra asks the children **¿Adónde vas?** (*Where are you going?*) and **¿Cómo vas?** (*How are you going?*). The children read aloud the answers that appear on the screen.

Voy al parque en bicicleta.	*I'm going to the park by bicycle.*
Voy al museo en taxi.	*I'm going to the museum by taxi.*
Voy al restaurante en moto.	*I'm going to the restaurant by motorcycle.*
Voy al hospital en coche.	*I'm going to the hospital by car.*

13. Revealing *el mensaje mágico* (*the magic message*) and saying good-bye

Antonio demonstrates the magic message. Kipper and the children reveal the message—**Tengo hambre** (*I'm hungry*). **La maestra** and Kipper say **Adiós** (*Good-bye*) to the children.

After viewing the video, praise the children for their good listening and watching skills.

Activity Lesson

Activity 41A: Sing *"En los Estados Unidos"* (*"In the United States"*)

Materials: Cassette player; Song Cassette, Side A; the overhead transparency of Blackline Master 37A-2; and an overhead projector.

Project the transparency of Blackline Master 37A-2. Tell the children they are going to sing the song about places in the United States with Spanish names. Mention to them that the lyrics are displayed. Play the song. Ask for a volunteer to point to each city or town name as it is mentioned in the song.

Activity 41B: Let's go somewhere!

Materials: Cassette player; Activity Cassette 2, Side A; Blackline Master 41B; pencils; a calendar; and the current Month Picture.

Preparation: Copy and distribute Blackline Master 41B so that each child has a copy.

Have the children write their names and the date on the top of their papers. If they need help with the date, point to the number of the day on the calendar and to the current Month Picture. Tell the children to complete the sentences on their sheets. Let them know that all the words they need are in the word bank. After they have completed all the sentences, play Activity 41B and tell them to listen carefully. **La maestra** will instruct them to read each sentence. She will then say the sentences they should have written. Children should have completed the sentences as follows:

1. Voy al parque en bicicleta.	*I'm going to the park by bicycle.*
2. Voy al museo en taxi.	*I'm going to the museum by taxi.*
3. Voy al restaurante en moto.	*I'm going to the restaurant by motorcycle.*
4. Voy al hospital en coche.	*I'm going to the hospital by car.*

Complete each sentence using the pictures and the words in the word bank. To check your answers, you will read each sentence aloud and listen carefully as **la maestra** confirms what you've written.

1. Voy al ________ en ________.
2. Voy al ________ en ________.
3. Voy al ________ en ________.
4. Voy al ________ en ________.

PALABRAS: taxi, moto, coche, hospital, parque, bicicleta, museo, restaurante

Blackline Master 41B

Activity 41C: Cooperative learning—Where are you going and how?

Materials: Red Flashcards 58–63; your Flashcards of a beach scene and a park (from Lesson 33); pictures of a bicycle, boat, bus, car, jeep, motorcycle, taxi, truck; heavyweight paper; and a laminating machine.

Preparation: Make a Flashcard for each transportation mode by affixing the pictures to the sheets of heavyweight paper. Laminate the Flashcards and display them. Write the following questions on the chalkboard.

¿Adónde vas? ¿Cómo vas?

Have the children work in pairs. Tell them they should ask one another where they are going and how they are going there. Point out that you've written the questions on the board and displayed Flashcards of the various places and forms of transportation that they've been learning to talk about. Possible statements:

Answers to *¿Adónde vas?*	(*Where are you going?*):
Voy a la biblioteca.	*I'm going to the library.*
Voy a la casa.	*I'm going home.*
Voy al cine.	*I'm going to the movies.*
Voy a la escuela.	*I'm going to the school.*
Voy al hospital.	*I'm going to the hospital.*
Voy al museo.	*I'm going to the museum.*
Voy a la playa.	*I'm going to the beach.*
Voy al parque.	*I'm going to the park.*
Voy al restaurante.	*I'm going to the restaurant.*
Voy al supermercado.	*I'm going to the supermarket.*
Voy a la tienda.	*I'm going to the store.*

Answers to *¿Cómo vas?*	(*How are you going?*):
Voy en autobús.	*I'm going by bus.*
Voy en coche.	*I'm going by car.*
Voy en bicicleta.	*I'm going by bicycle.*
Voy en yipi.	*I'm going by jeep.*
Voy en bote.	*I'm going by boat.*
Voy en moto.	*I'm going by motorcycle.*
Voy en camión.	*I'm going by truck.*
Voy en taxi.	*I'm going by taxi.*

CLOSING

Tell the children that Spanish class is finished for today. In the next lesson **la maestra** will go to the airport. Is she leaving for her vacation in Argentina?

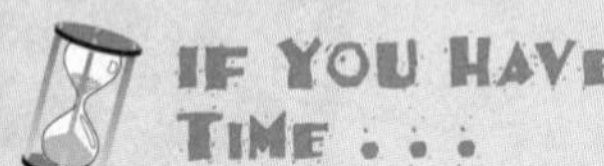

Materials: Same as in Activity 41C.

Have volunteers choose one place Flashcard and one form of transportation Flashcard and hold them up. The class should say *I'm going to* (**Voy a**) + the place name shown on the volunteer's place Flashcard and then *I'm going by* (**Voy en**) + the form of transportation shown on the volunteer's transportation form Flashcard.

Lesson 42

Materials to gather

- VCR and Video Lesson 42 on Tape 14
- Cassette player
- Activity Cassette 2
- Song Cassette
- Blackline Master 42A (two parts—transportation and places)
- Calendar
- Current Month Picture
- Red Flashcards 58–63
- Transportation Flashcards (from Activity 41C)
- Pictures of a train and an airplane
- Heavyweight white paper
- Laminating machine
- Pencils
- ***Optional materials:*** blank paper; colored pencils or markers; children's dictionary pages
- ***Prepare ahead:*** You may want to laminate the pictures of the plane and the train. They will be used with Activity 42C.

Objectives

Language

- Decipher another **mensaje mágico** (*magic message*)—**Tengo sed** (*I'm thirsty*)
- Understand the difference between two verb forms
- Combine the answers to two questions into one sentence
- Read several sentences
- Understand extended conversations about a train and a plane

Culture

- Talk about things best done slowly

Review

- Review the vocabulary **rápido** (*rapidly*) and **despacio** (*slowly*)
- Answer the questions **¿Adónde vas?** (*Where are you going?*) and **¿Cómo vas?** (*How are you going?*)
- Practice transportation vocabulary by playing **¿Cuál falta?** (*What's missing?*)

Vocabulary

¿Qué tal?	*How's it going?*
el tren/los trenes	*train/trains*
el avión/los aviones	*plane/planes*
Hago un viaje.	*I'm taking a trip.*

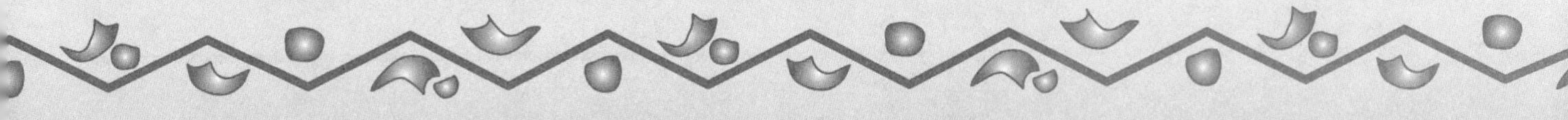

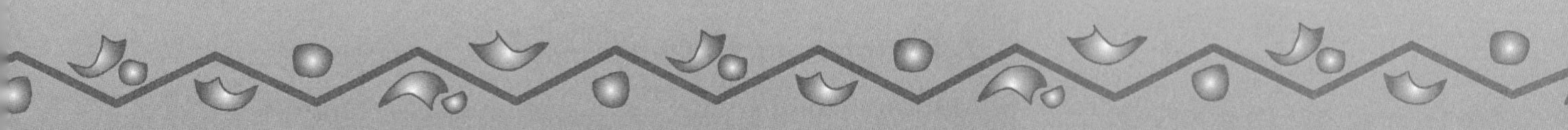

Warm-up

Materials: Your Flashcards of a car, bus, bicycle, truck, and jeep.

Display the Flashcards. Ask the children how they get to school (**la escuela**). If you feel comfortable, ask **¿Cómo vas a la escuela?** (*How do you go to school?*). Take a poll to see how many ride a bus (**el autobús**), how many come by car (**el coche**), bicycle (**la bicicleta**), truck (**el camión**) or jeep (**el yipi**), and how many walk. Depending on where you live, some children may ride a train (**el tren**) or a subway (**el metro**).

Review

Walk slowly around the room and ask the children how you are walking (**despacio**—*slowly*). Walk quickly and ask them how you are walking now (**rápido**—*rapidly*). Have the children stand in a circle. Ask for a volunteer to call out **Anda** (*Walk*) + the word for *rapidly* or *slowly*. The children should walk in a circle (one behind the other) around the room to the pace indicated by the volunteer until the volunteer tells them to walk at a different pace.

Introduce the video

Invite the children to listen and watch as **la maestra** rides by train and by plane.

EN ESPAÑOL

to walk = andar
I walk = (yo) ando
Walk! = ¡Anda!

Video Lesson

1. Greeting the children

La maestra greets the children with **Buenos días** (*Good morning*) and asks them how they are. She greets Winston and asks him **¿Cómo estás?** (*How are you?*). Winston says **¡Hola!** (*Hello!*) and asks **¿Qué tal, Maestra?** (*How's it going, Teacher?*).

2. Deciphering *el mensaje mágico* (*the magic message*)

Antonio demonstrates the magic message—**Tengo sed** (*I'm hungry*).

3. Explaining the difference between two verb forms

La maestra explains the difference between **Voy a** ___ (*I'm going to* ___) and **Vamos a** ___ (*We're going to* ___*/Let's go to*___).

4. Describing a city center

With San Diego in the background, **la maestra** describes the center of the city. For her statements, see Lesson 38, Video Lesson, section 7.

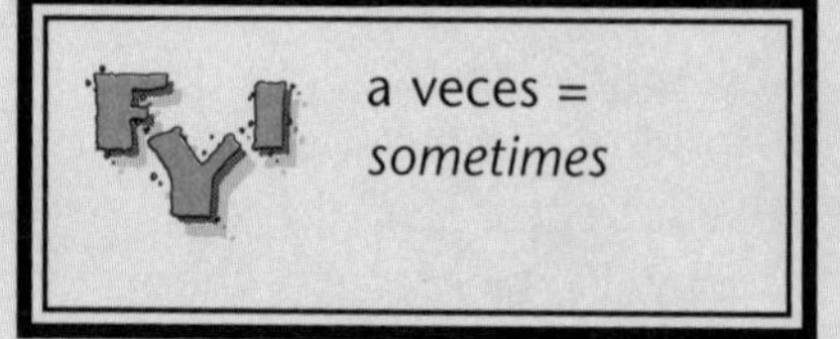

a veces = *sometimes*

5. Reviewing *rapidly* and *slowly*

La maestra describes the speed of the traffic in the city: **El tráfico en el centro de la ciudad es muy rápido** (*The traffic in the center of the city is very fast*); **Ahora el tráfico no es rápido** (*Now the traffic is not fast*); **El tráfico es despacio** (*The traffic is slow*).

6. Describing San Diego's traffic

Standing on a street corner, **la maestra** describes the traffic. For her statements, see Lesson 39, Video Lesson, section 4.

7. Reading two questions and answering them

La maestra asks the children to read the questions and give an answer. She shows them how to combine the answer to both questions with one sentence.

¿Adónde vas?	*Where are you going?*
Voy a la playa.	*I'm going to the beach.*
¿Cómo vas?	*How are you going?*
Voy en coche.	*I'm going by car.*
Voy a la playa en coche.	*I'm going to the beach by car.*
Voy en coche a la playa.	*I'm going by car to the beach.*

8. Introducing the train as a way to go somewhere

La maestra takes the train.

Estoy en la estación de los trenes.	*I'm at the train station.*
Voy de viaje.	*I'm going on a trip.*
Voy de viaje en tren.	*I'm going on a trip by train.*
Tengo mi maleta.	*I have my suitcase.*
Vamos en tren.	*Let's go by train.*

9. Presenting the plane as a form of transportation

La maestra tells the children how to say *I'm taking a trip* (**Hago un viaje**). Showing them **un boleto** (*a ticket*), she says **Este verano voy a la Argentina** (*This summer I'm going to Argentina*).

Estoy aquí con el avión.	*Here I am with the plane.*
¿Vamos en avión?	*Are we going by plane?*
¿Y quién es?	*And who is this?*
Es la piloto.	*It's the (female) pilot.*
¿Es un avión grande o pequeño?	*Is it a large or small plane?*
Es un avión pequeño.	*It's a small plane.*
Voy en avión.	*I'm going by plane.*

10. Reading sentences

Winston asks **la maestra ¿Vas en un avión pequeño a la Argentina?** (*Are you going in a small plane to Argentina?*). She tells him **No, no voy en un avión pequeño** (*No, I'm not going in a small plane*), **Voy en un avión grande** (*I'm going in a large plane*). The children read sentences.

11. Playing *¿Cuál falta?* (*What's missing?*)

La maestra tells the children **El transporte es muy importante** (*Transportation is very important*). She reviews the forms of transportation and plays a game of **¿Cuál falta?** (*What's missing?*).

12. Revealing *el mensaje mágico* (*the magic message*) and Closing

After Antonio demonstrates the message, the children reveal it—**Tengo sed** (*I'm thirsty*). **La maestra** asks Winston **¿Vamos a tomar?** (*Shall we have a drink?*). **La maestra** and Winston bid the children **Adiós** (*Good-bye*) and **Hasta la vista** (*Until we meet again*).

Voy al centro en bicicleta.
(I'm going downtown by bicycle.)
Voy en bote al lago.
(I'm going by boat on the lake.)
Voy a la escuela en yipi.
(I'm going to school by jeep.)
Voy en moto a la tienda.
(I'm going by motorcycle to the store.)

Las formas de transporte (*forms of transportation*):

el autobús	*bus*
el avión	*plane*
la bicicleta	*bicycle*
el bote	*boat*
el camión	*truck*
el coche	*car*
la moto	*motorcycle*
el taxi	*taxi*
el tren	*train*
el yipi	*jeep*

After viewing the video, praise the children for their good listening and watching skills.

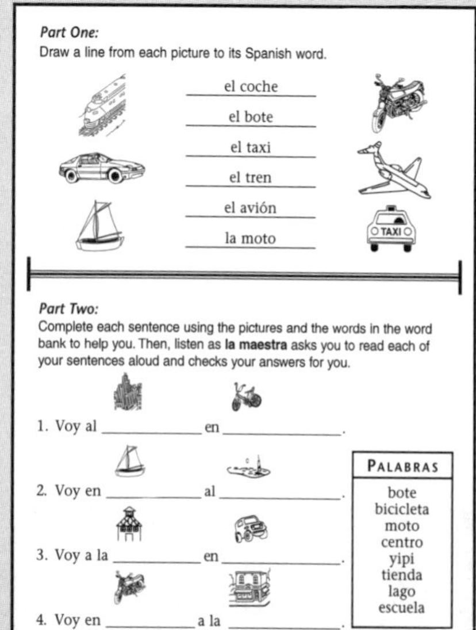

Part One:
Draw a line from each picture to its Spanish word.

el coche
el bote
el taxi
el tren
el avión
la moto

Part Two:
Complete each sentence using the pictures and the words in the word bank to help you. Then, listen as **la maestra** asks you to read each of your sentences aloud and checks your answers for you.

1. Voy al ______ en ______.
2. Voy en ______ al ______.
3. Voy a la ______ en ______.
4. Voy en ______ a la ______.

PALABRAS
bote
bicicleta
moto
centro
yipi
tienda
lago
escuela

Blackline Master 42A

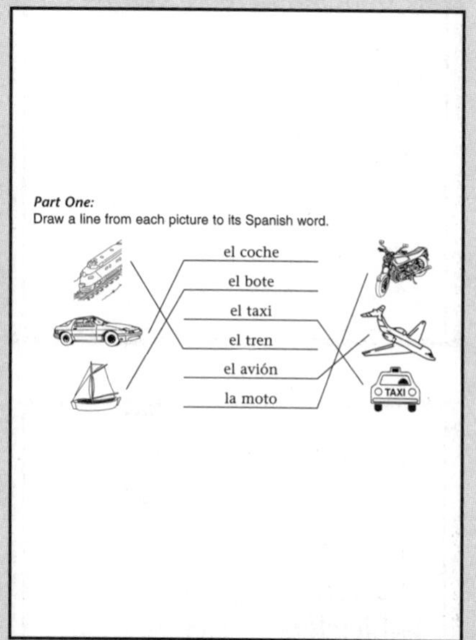

Part One:
Draw a line from each picture to its Spanish word.

el coche
el bote
el taxi
el tren
el avión
la moto

Activity 42A, Part One, Answers

ACTIVITY LESSON

Activity 42A: Practice forms of transportation

Materials: Cassette player; Activity Cassette 2, Side A; Blackline Master 42A; a calendar; the current Month Picture; and pencils.

Preparation: Copy and distribute Blackline Master 42A so that each child has one.

Have the children write their names and the date on the top of their papers. If they need help with the date, point to the number of the day on the calendar and to the current Month Picture. Draw the children's attention to Part One. Tell them to draw a line from each picture of a form of transportation to the Spanish word for it. After they have completed Part One, direct their attention to Part Two. Have them complete the sentences about where they are going and how they are getting there by using the pictures and words in the word bank. Allow the children time to do this, then play Activity 42A. **La maestra** instructs them to read each sentence and to check their answer as she reads each sentence after them.

In Part Two children should have completed their sentences as follows:

1. Voy al centro en bicicleta.	*I'm going downtown by bicycle.*
2. Voy en bote al lago.	*I'm going by boat on the lake.*
3. Voy a la escuela en yipi.	*I'm going to school by jeep.*
4. Voy en moto a la tienda.	*I'm going by motorcycle to the store.*

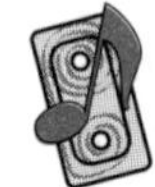

Activity 42B: Sing *"¿Adónde vas?"* (*"Where Are You Going?"*)

Materials: Cassette player; "**¿Adónde vas?**" (*"Where Are You Going?"*) on the Song Cassette, Side A; and Red Flashcards 58–63.

Display the Red Flashcards in song order: 59, 62, 58, 61, 60, 63. Gesturing toward the Flashcards, tell the children they are going to sing the song about where they are going. Ask for a volunteer to point to each of the places shown in the Red Flashcards as the place is sung about. Play the song on the Song Cassette. Encourage the children to sing. For the lyrics with English equivalents, see Song 10 in the Song Appendix.

Activity 42C: Make up a new song

Materials: Your transportation Flashcards (including those of the train and airplane).

Preparation: Prepare the Flashcards if you haven't already done so (for Activity 41C) and display them for the class. Write the following (Spanish only) on the chalkboard.

¿Cómo vas?	*How are you going?*
¿Cómo vas tú?	*How are you going?*
Voy en ___, en ___, en ___.	*I'm going by ___, by ___, by ___.*
Yo voy.	*I'm going.*

Tell the children they are going to sing a new song, using the phrases on the chalkboard and transportation Flashcards. Divide the class into two groups: one group to sing the question verse and one group to sing the reply verses. Tell the children that for each reply verse, you will hold up the Flashcard for the transportation mode they are to use in the verse. Tell them to use the tune of "**¿Adónde vas?**" (*"Where Are You Going?"*). Point to the pictures in the following order:

car:	Voy en coche, en coche, en coche.	*I'm going by car, by car, by car.*
train:	Voy en tren, en tren, en tren.	*I'm gong by train, by train, by train.*
bus:	Voy en autobús, en autobús, en autobús.	*I'm going by bus, by bus, by bus.*
bicycle:	Voy en bicicleta, en bicicleta, en bicicleta.	*I'm going by bicycle, by bicycle, by bicycle.*
truck:	Voy en camión, en camión, en camión.	*I'm going by truck, by truck, by truck.*
airplane:	Voy en avión, en avión, en avión.	*I'm going by airplane, by airplane, by airplane.*
jeep:	Voy en yipi, en yipi, en yipi.	*I'm going by jeep, by jeep, by jeep.*
boat:	Voy en bote, en bote, en bote.	*I'm going by boat, by boat, by boat.*
motorcycle:	Voy en moto, en moto, en moto.	*I'm going by motorcycle, by motorcycle, by motorcycle.*
taxi:	Voy en taxi, en taxi, en taxi.	*I'm going by taxi, by taxi, by taxi.*

Activity 42C:

If children need to be reminded of the tune, replay the first few verses of "**¿Adónde vas?**" (*"Where Are You Going?"*) on the Song Cassette, Side A.

DICTIONARY

Materials: Blank paper; colored pencils or markers; children's dictionary pages; and your transportation Flashcards.

Display the Flashcards. Give each child three pieces of blank paper and tell them to draw a picture of a form of transportation on each piece of paper. Underneath the drawing, they should write the name of the transportation form (with the definite article **el** or **la**). Above the drawing, they should write the first letter of the word. Have them file their new pages with their other dictionary pages. For a list of vocabulary for forms of transportation, see the marginal material in section 11 of this Video Lesson.

CLOSING

Tell the children that Spanish class is finished for today. In the next lesson children will read about another one of Fredo's adventures.

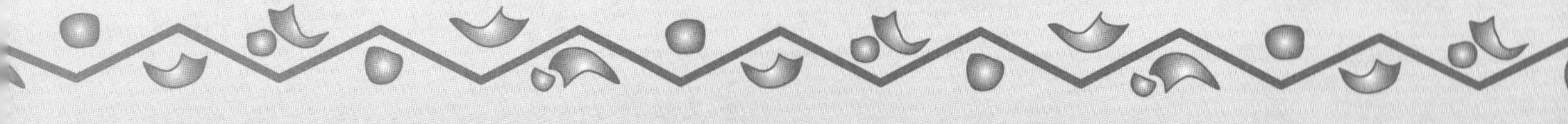

Lesson 43

> **Materials to gather**
>
> - VCR and Video Lesson 43 on Tape 15
> - Cassette player
> - Song Cassette
> - Gold Flashcards 28–33
> - Blank paper
> - Colored pencils or pens
> - ***Optional materials:*** *"Las aventuras de Fredo"* (*"Fredo's Adventures"*) books

Objectives

Language

- Read another story about Fredo's adventures
- See four forms of the verb **ir** (*to go*)
- Decipher a new **mensaje mágico** (*magic message*)—**Estoy enojado/enojada** (*I'm angry*)

Culture

- Understand the difference between various forms of the same verb

Review

- Review several feeling expressions
- Practice vocabulary for forms of transportation
- Answer two questions in one sentence

Vocabulary

Estoy aburrido/aburrida.	*I'm bored.*
Estoy cansado/cansada.	*I'm tired.*
Voy a ___ en ___.	*I'm going to ___ by ___.*

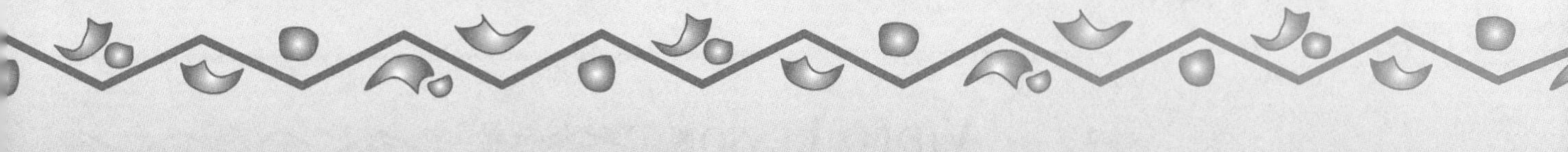

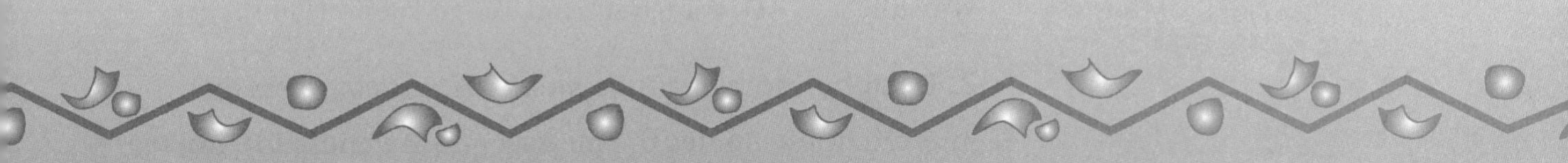

Warm-up

Materials: Gold Flashcards 28–33.

Tell the children that it's time for Spanish class (**la clase de español**) and that you have several magic messages for them. Hold up Gold Flashcard 28 and ask the children what they would say in Spanish if they felt that way (**Tengo frío**—*I'm cold*). Do the same with Gold Flashcards 29–33.

Gold Flashcards:

#28	Tengo frío.	*I'm cold.*
#29	Tengo calor.	*I'm hot.*
#30	Tengo hambre.	*I'm hungry.*
#32	Tengo sed.	*I'm thirsty.*
#33	Tengo miedo.	*I'm afraid.*

Review

Talk with the children about the books they've read this year in Spanish class. Who is the main character? (Fredo) What does he do? (**Fredo tiene aventuras**—*Fredo has adventures.*) What kinds of adventures? (**Fredo toca los instrumentos músicales en la tienda de música**—*Fredo plays musical instruments in a music store,* and he changes shape when eats various foods in the Magic Café [**el café mágico**].)

Introduce the video

Invite the children to listen and watch as **la maestra** reviews forms of transportation, and to read along as doña Elena presents another story about Fredo.

EN ESPAÑOL

If you feel comfortable, tell the children you have **unos mensajes mágicos** (*some magic messages*) and ask **¿Cómo estás?** (*How are you?*) as you hold up each Gold Flashcard.

Video Lesson

1. Greeting the children

La maestra greets the children with **Buenos días** (*Good morning*) and asks them how they are. She greets Winston with **¡Hola!** (*Hello!*) and asks him **¿Qué tal?** (*How's it going?*). Winston says **Así, así** (*So-so*) and **Tengo sueño** (*I'm sleepy*).

2. Deciphering *el mensaje mágico* (*the magic message*)

Antonio demonstrates the message—**Estoy enojado/enojada** (*I'm angry*).

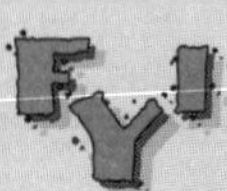

Pobrecita means *Poor little girl;* **Pobrecito** means *Poor little boy.* The endings **-ita** and **-ito** mean *little* and are terms of endearment.

3. Reviewing feeling expressions

Lorena dances as **la maestra** asks **¿Cómo está Lorena?** (*How is Lorena?*) and answers the question.

Está enojada.	*She's angry.*
Está contenta.	*She's happy.*
Está triste.	*She's sad.*

You may wish to point out that when Winston says he's bored, he uses **aburrido** whereas **la maestra** uses **aburrida.**

4. Introducing two new feeling expressions

La maestra introduces new ways of describing how one feels.

Estoy aburrido/aburrida.	*I'm bored.*
¿Estás aburrido?	*Are you bored?*
No, no estoy aburrido/aburrida.	*No, I'm not bored.*
Estoy cansado/cansada.	*I'm tired.*
¿Estás cansado/cansada?	*Are you tired?*
No, no estoy cansado/cansada.	*No, I'm not tired.*
Sí, tengo sueño.	*Yes, I'm sleepy.*

Las formas de transporte (*forms of transportation*):

el autobús	*bus*
el avión	*plane*
la bicicleta	*bicycle*
el bote	*boat*
el camión	*truck*
el coche	*car*
la moto	*motorcycle*
el taxi	*taxi*
el tren	*train*
el yipi	*jeep*

5. Playing *¿Cuál falta?* (*What's missing?*)

La maestra and Winston name several **formas de transporte** (*forms of transportation*). **La maestra** plays a game of **¿Cuál falta?** (*What's missing?*) with the children.

6. Reading several sentences

Winston reads the question **¿Adónde vas?** (*Where are you going?*) and answers **Voy a la escuela** (*I'm going to school*). He reads the question **¿Cómo vas?** (*How are you going?*) and answers it with **Voy en coche** (*I'm going by car*). **La maestra** reviews how to answer both questions in one sentence: **Voy a ___ en ___** (*I'm going to ___ by ___*). The children read the following sentences:

Voy al centro en bicicleta.	*I'm going downtown by bicycle.*
Voy en bote al lago.	*I'm going by boat on the lake.*
Voy a la escuela en yipi.	*I'm going to school by jeep.*
Voy en moto a la tienda.	*I'm going by motorcycle to the store.*

7. Introducing the difference between several forms of the same verb

La maestra shows the children four forms of the same verb that the children have heard and used.

Voy	*I go* or *I'm going*
Vamos	*We go* or *we are going;* also *Let's go*
Vas	*You go* or *you are going*
Va	*He/She goes* or *He/She is going*

8. Reading about Fredo

Doña Elena reads another adventure story about Fredo—**"En la ciudad"** (*"In the City"*).

Fredo está aburrido.	*Fredo is bored.*
¿Qué va a hacer?	*What's he going to do?*
Fredo va a la ciudad.	*Fredo goes to the city.*
¿Adónde va y cómo va?	*Where is he going and how is he going?*
Fredo va al supermercado.	*Fredo is going to the supermarket.*
Va en coche.	*He is going by car.*
Pero, el coche está en el supermercado.	*But, the car is in the supermarket.*
¡Qué extraño!	*How strange!*
¿Un coche en el supermercado?	*A car in the supermarket?*
¡Qué lástima!	*What a pity!*
Por fin, va a casa.	*Finally, he's going home.*

9. Revealing *el mensaje mágico* (*the magic message*)

Antonio demonstrates the message. After **la maestra** counts to three (**uno, dos, tres**), the children and Winston reveal **Estoy enojado** (*I'm angry*).

10. Closing

La maestra and Winston say **Adiós** (*Good-bye*) and **Hasta la vista** (*Until we meet again*) to the children.

The present tense (e.g., **voy**) in Spanish can be rendered in English in either the present tense (e.g., *I go*) or the present progressive tense (e.g., *I am going*). Context makes it clear which English form to use.

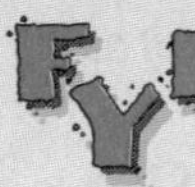

The verb forms **voy, vas, vamos,** and **va** are from the verb **ir** (*to go*).

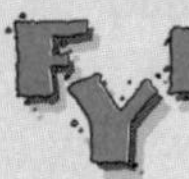

Qué has different meanings. As a question word, it means *what:* **¿Qué va a hacer?** (*What's he going to do?*). In an exclamation, it can mean *how* or *what:* **¡Qué extraño!** (*How strange!*); **¡Qué lástima!** (*What a pity!*).

When revealing the magic message, did the children remember to change the ending on **enojado?**—boys: **Estoy enojado**, girls: **Estoy enojada**.

After viewing the video, praise the children for their good listening and watching skills.

Activity Lesson

Activity 43A: Read *"En la ciudad"* (*"In the City"*)

Note: If your school has the book ***"Las aventuras de Fredo"*** (*"Fredo's Adventures"*) available for the children, substitute the Fredo Book Activity in the margin for this activity.

Materials: VCR; Video Lesson 43 on Tape 15.

Preparation: Recue Video Lesson 43 to section 8, in which doña Elena reads the story **"En la ciudad"** (*"In the City"*).

Ask the children what adventures of Fredo's they've already read about: his adventures in the music store—**"La tienda de música"** (*"The Music Store"*) and in the café—**"El café mágico"** (*"The Magic Café"*). Ask them where Fredo's latest adventure took place (in the city). Play section 8 of the video with the sound and tell the children to read along with doña Elena. Remind them to look for visual clues in the pictures and to listen and watch for words they know. Then rewind the tape to the beginning of the story and replay it without the sound. Pause the tape to give the children time to read each line of the story to themselves. Finally, do a quick comprehension check with the children:

Questions:	**Answers** (accept English):
1. Where does Fredo go?	He goes to the city. (**Va a la ciudad.**)
2. Where in the city does he go and how does he get there?	He goes to the supermarket in a car; to the beach in an upside-down plane, to the library on a motorcycle, to the restaurant in a bus, to the movies in a boat, to the museum on a bicycle, to the park in a truck, to the hospital in a jeep.
3. What's strange about how Fredo gets where he's going?	He drives the car into the supermarket. He flies the plane upside-down. He drives the motorcycle into the library and the bus into the restaurant. There is no water in the movie theater so how could he go there in a boat? He rides his bicycle into the restaurant. He hits a tree with his truck in the park. He stands upside-down while driving his jeep to the hospital.
4. Why does he do these strange things?	He's bored (**Está aburrido**).

Fredo Book Activity

Materials: Cassette player; Song Cassette, Side B; and ***"Las aventuras de Fredo"*** (*"Fredo's Adventures"*) books.

Tell the children they are going to read another story about Fredo's adventures. Distribute your copies of ***"Las aventuras de Fredo"*** (*"Fredo's Adventures"*) among the children. Tell them to turn to the third story in the book—**"En la ciudad"** (*"In the City"*)—and to read along silently as doña Elena reads the story. Play ***"Las aventuras de Fredo"*** Book 3, **"En la ciudad"** (*"In the City"*) on the Song Cassette, Side B. Then allow children time to re-read the story on their own. Use the questions in Activity 43A to check comprehension.

5. Have you gone to some of the places Fredo went to in this story? *Answers will vary.*
6. Did you get there the way he did? *Answers will vary.*

Activity 43B: A picture is worth a thousand words

Materials: Blank paper; colored pencils or pens.

Preparation: Write the following sentences (Spanish only) on the chalkboard.

Lorena está triste.	*Lorena is sad.*
Lorena está contenta.	*Lorena is happy.*
Lorena está enojada.	*Lorena is angry.*

Distribute the paper and pencils or pens among the children. As you do so, draw their attention to the three sentences you have written on the board. Ask volunteers to read each one and to demonstrate to the class how they would look if they felt that way. The class should say in English how each volunteer is feeling. Next, have the children draw three pictures of Lorena—one for each way she is feeling—and to write the appropriate sentence under each picture. Finally, have volunteers show their pictures and read their sentences.

Activity 43C: Role-play Lorena

Materials: Cassette player; "**¿Cómo está Lorena?**" (*"How Is Lorena?"*) on the Song Cassette, Side A.

Have the children stand up. Tell them they are going to role-play Lorena as **la maestra** asks the question *How is Lorena?* (**¿Cómo está Lorena?**) and then says how Lorena is feeling. Tell them to listen carefully to what **la maestra** says and then to act and dance the way Lorena is feeling.

¿Cómo está Lorena?	*How is Lorena?*
Está enojada. Enojada.	*She's angry. Angry.*
Está enojada.	*She's angry.*
¿Cómo está Lorena?	*How is Lorena?*
Está contenta. Está contenta. Contenta.	*She's happy. She's happy. Happy.*
¿Cómo está Lorena?	*How is Lorena?*
Está triste. Está triste. Triste.	*She's sad. She's sad. Sad.*

Closing

Tell the children that Spanish class is finished for today. In the next lesson the children will learn how to gesture for silence the way Spanish-speakers do.

Lesson 44

Materials to gather

- VCR and Video Lesson 44 on Tape 15
- Cassette player
- Activity Cassette 2
- Song Cassette
- Red Flashcards 58–63
- Transportation Flashcards (from Activity 41C)
- Flashcards of the park and the beach (from Lesson 33)
- ***Optional materials: "Las aventuras de Fredo"*** (*"Fredo's Adventures"*) books

Objectives

Language

- Decipher **un mensaje mágico** (*a magic message*)—**Voy a la playa** (*I'm going to the beach*)
- Learn several new exclamatory phrases
- Understand a sustained conversation with a policeman
- Comprehend sustained conversations in a restaurant

Culture

- Learn how Spanish speakers indicate one should be quiet

Review

- Read **"En la ciudad"** (*"In the City"*)

Vocabulary

¡Qué extraño!	*How strange!*
¡Qué lástima!	*What a pity!*
¡Silencio!	*Silence!*

Warm-up

If you feel comfortable, greet the children with **Hola** (*Hello*), **Buenos días** (*Good morning*), or **Buenas tardes** (*Good afternoon*). Mention that in the last lesson they learned two new expressions for how they might be feeling. Mime being tired and ask them what they would say if they felt that way (**Estoy cansado/cansada**—*I'm tired*). Mime being bored (e.g., slump in a chair, sigh, roll your head from side to side) and ask them what they would say if they felt like that (**Estoy aburrido/aburrida**—*I'm bored*). Finally, ask them to say how they are really feeling today. If you feel comfortable, ask **¿Cómo estás?** (*How are you?*).

Review

Materials: Red Flashcards 58–63; your Flashcards of the beach and park scenes; and your transportation Flashcards.

Display all the Flashcards. Lead the children in a discussion of the latest Fredo adventure story they've read. Ask them to name the places he went to and the various modes of transportation he used. Accept one-word answers. As place names and transportation modes are mentioned, point to the corresponding Flashcards.

Places:	**Transportation:**
la ciudad (*city*)	
el supermercado (*supermarket*)	el coche (*car*)
la playa (*beach*)	el avión (*airplane*)
la biblioteca (*library*)	la moto (*motorcycle*)
el restaurante (*restaurant*)	el autobús (*bus*)
el cine (*movie theater*)	el bote (*boat*)
el museo (*museum*)	la bicicleta (*bicycle*)
el parque (*park*)	el camión (*truck*)
el hospital (*hospital*)	el yipi (*jeep*)

It is not necessary for the children to remember which form of transportation Fredo used to get to each place. The purpose of the activity is to review place names and transportation vocabulary so it will be fresh in their minds when they read the book in the lesson.

Introduce the video

Invite the children to listen and watch as doña Elena reads the story about Fredo's adventures in the city and as **la maestra** visits with a motorcycle policeman.

Feeling expressions:

(Estoy) muy bien.
(*I'm very well.*)

(Estoy) así, así.
(*I'm so-so.*)

(Estoy) muy mal.
(*I'm very bad.*)

(Estoy) muy contento/contenta.
(*I'm very happy.*)

(Estoy) enojado/enojada.
(*I'm angry.*)

(Estoy) triste.
(*I'm sad.*)

Tengo frío.
(*I'm cold.*)

Tengo calor.
(*I'm hot.*)

Tengo hambre.
(*I'm hungry.*)

Tengo sed.
(*I'm thirsty.*)

Tengo miedo.
(*I'm afraid.*)

Tengo sueño.
(*I'm sleepy.*)

Tengo dolor.
(*I'm hurt.*)

Tengo catarro.
(*I have a cold.*)

Video Lesson

1. Greeting the children

La maestra greets the children with **Buenos días** (*Good morning*) and asks them **¿Cómo estás tú?** (*How are you?*). She greets LeeAnn and asks her if she knows another way to ask how one is—**¿Qué tal?** (*How's it going?*). **La maestra** reviews **Estoy cansado/cansada** (*I'm tired*) and **Estoy aburrido/aburrida** (*I'm bored*).

2. Displaying *el mensaje mágico* (*the magic message*)

LeeAnn reads the question **¿Adónde vas?** (*Where are you going?*). **La maestra** explains that anytime one wants to say one is going somewhere, one says **Voy a** + the place name. Showing a shot of a beach scene, **la maestra** asks the children how they would say they were going to that place. She reminds them **No digas nada** (*Don't say anything*) and **Espera hasta el fin de la lección** (*Wait until the end of the lesson*).

3. Reading about Fredo's adventures in the city

The children read **"En la ciudad"** (*"In the City"*) with doña Elena. For more statements from the story, see Lesson 43, Video Lesson, section 8.

¿Adónde va Fredo?	*Where is Fredo going?*
Fredo va a la playa.	*Fredo is going to the beach.*
Y ¿cómo va?	*And how is he going?*
Va en avión.	*He's going by airplane.*
Pero, el avión está al revés.	*But, the plane is upside-down.*
¿Un avión al revés?	*An upside-down airplane?*
Tiene un accidente.	*He has an accident.*

4. Introducing several exclamations

La maestra introduces the following exclamations. She also tells the children how to say *shhh* in Spanish—**¡ch!**

¡Qué lástima!	*What a pity!*
¡Qué extraño!	*How strange!*
¡Silencio!	*Silence!*

5. Talking with a policeman

La maestra visits with a motorcycle policeman.

¿Qué edificio es?	*What building is it?*
Es la estación de la policía.	*It's the police station.*
Y aquí está el coche de la policía.	*And here is the police car.*
¡Qué interesante!	*How interesting!*
Pero, aquí viene la moto.	*But, here comes the motorcycle.*
Buenos días, Maestra. ¿Cómo está usted?	*Good morning, Teacher. How are you?*
Señor policía, la moto es muy grande y muy bonita.	*Mr. Policeman, the motorcycle is very large and very pretty.*
Sí, Maestra, y rápida.	*Yes, Teacher, and very fast.*
Señor, habla muy bien en español.	*Sir, you speak Spanish very well.*
Gracias.	*Thank you.*

6. Visiting a Mexican restaurant

La maestra visits a Mexican restaurant. For her statements outside the restaurant, see Lesson 32, Video Lesson, section 7. Statements from the tour of the kitchen are below. Statements from the scene with the waiter (**el camarero**) appear in Lesson 46, Video Lesson, section 7, and the scene with the musicians (**los músicos**) appear in lesson 47, Video Lesson, section 5.

Clase, éste es mi amigo Javier.	*Class, this is my friend Javier.*
Javier es el dueño del restaurante, ¿sí?	*Javier is the owner of the restaurant, right?*
¿Quieres ver la cocina?	*Do you want to see the kitchen?*
Sí, quiero ver la cocina.	*Yes, I want to see the kitchen.*
¿Qué hacen en la cocina?	*What do they do in the kitchen?*
Preparan la comida.	*They prepare the food.*
Es el cocinero.	*He is the (male) cook.*
Es la cocinera.	*She is the (female) cook.*
Ella es la tortillera.	*She is the tortilla cook.*
La tortillera es una cocinera muy especial porque hace tortillas.	*The tortilla cook is a very special cook because she makes the tortillas.*

7. Revealing *el mensaje mágico* (*the magic message*)

After viewing the ocean scene, the children reveal the message—**Voy a la playa** (*I'm going to the beach*).

8. Closing

LeeAnn and **la maestra** bid the children **Adiós** (*Good-bye*).

CROSS-CULTURAL CONNECTIONS

When **la maestra** compliments the policeman on his ability to speak Spanish, he replies with a simple *thank you* (**gracias**). It is customary in Spanish-speaking and English-speaking cultures to say *thank you* when one has received a compliment. Also, note that **la maestra** and the policeman use the formal *you* (**usted**) in speaking to one another.

The restaurant visit is the longest scene of sustained conversation the children have viewed thus far. Remind them to look for visual clues (what people are doing or how they are gesturing) and to listen for familiar vocabulary in order to determine what's being said. In the scene, **la maestra** greets many people. The familiar language used in her greetings should help put children at ease.

After viewing the video, praise the children for their good listening and watching skills.

ACTIVITY LESSON

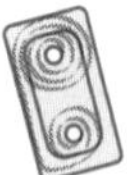

Activity 44A: Express surprise about something

Materials: Cassette player; Activity Cassette 2, Side B.

Preparation: Write the following exclamations (Spanish only) on the chalkboard.

¡Qué extraño!	*How strange!*	¡Qué grande!	*How large!*
¡Qué bonito!	*How pretty!*	¡Qué alto!	*How tall!*

Pointing to the statements on the board, tell the children that they have heard **la maestra** use these exclamations many times to express her surprise at how strange, how pretty, how big, or how tall something is. Tell them to listen carefully and to practice saying each exclamation when indicated by doña Elena. Play Activity 44A, stopping the tape at each sound of the harp to allow children time to repeat the exclamation. At the end of the taped activity, tell the children to express surprise about how big something is (¡**Qué grande**!), how strange something is (¡**Qué extraño**!), how pretty something is (¡**Qué bonito**!), and how tall something is (¡**Qué alto**!).

Activity 44B: Read *"En la ciudad"* (*"In the City"*)

Note: If your school has the book ***"Las aventuras de Fredo"*** (*"Fredo's Adventures"*) available for the children, substitute the Fredo Book Activity in the margin for this activity.

Materials: VCR; Video Lesson 44 on Tape 15.

Preparation: Recue Video Lesson 44 to section 3, in which doña Elena reads the story **"En la ciudad"** (*"In the City"*).

Tell the children to read along with doña Elena as she reads *"In the City"* (**"En la ciudad"**). Play section 8 of the video with the sound. Remind the children to look for visual clues in the pictures and to listen and watch for words they know. Then rewind the tape to the beginning of the story and replay it without the sound, pausing the tape at each line of the story. Ask volunteers to read the lines aloud.

FREDO BOOK ACTIVITY

Materials: Cassette player; Song Cassette, Side B; and ***"Las aventuras de Fredo"*** (*"Fredo's Adventures"*) books.

Tell the children they are going to read about Fredo's adventures in the city. Distribute your copies of ***"Las aventuras de Fredo"*** (*"Fredo's Adventures"*) among the children. Tell them to turn to the third story in the book—**"En la ciudad"** (*"In the City"*)—and to read along silently as doña Elena reads the story. Play ***"Las aventuras de Fredo"*** Book 3, **"En la ciudad"** (*"In the City"*) on the Song Cassette, Side B. Then have the class re-read the story with volunteers reading aloud.

Activity 44C: So many different jobs in one place!

Lead the children in a discussion of all the different jobs they saw illustrated in the restaurant scene. You might explain that it is typical for a restaurant, particularly a large restaurant, to have several cooks with each one responsible for a certain type of food (e.g., a pastry chef, an entrée chef, a salad chef). Ask them how many cooks work in the Mexican restaurant (three). Ask what a waiter or waitress does (takes orders, recommends specials, serves the food, clears away dishes). Mention that in some restaurants, several people will wait on one table, e.g., one person will take the orders, another will bring the food, and another will clear away the dishes). Ask the children what was different about the instruments the musicians in the video were playing (there was one very big guitar and one very small one). If children have been to restaurants where there are musicians playing, ask them to talk about what instruments the musicians played.

Restaurant professions:

el dueño/la dueña (*owner*)

el cocinero/la cocinera (*cook, chef*)

el camarero/la camarera (*waiter/waitress*)

el músico/la música (*musician*)

HERITAGE SPEAKERS

Ask heritage speakers if they know of any Mexican, Spanish, Chilean, Argentine, etc., restaurants in your area. Ask them to describe the decor and food of the restaurant(s). What particular dish do they like to eat? Ask them to describe a tortilla to the children.

CLOSING

Tell the children that Spanish class is finished for today. In the next lesson, the children will visit the Mexican restaurant again and review vocabulary for professions.

Lesson 45

Materials to gather

- VCR and Video Lesson 45 on Tape 15
- Blackline Masters 45A-1 and 45A-2 (word puzzle)
- Blackline Master 45B (matching game)
- Blank transparency
- Overhead projector
- Pencils
- A current calendar
- Current Month Picture
- *Optional materials:* blank paper; markers or colored pencils; and children's dictionary pages

Objectives

Language

- Decipher **un mensaje mágico** (*a magic message*)—**Siéntate** (*Sit down*)
- Comprehend sustained conversations with people about their work

Culture

- Review how Spanish can be useful for many professions in the United States

Review

- Review vocabulary for professions

Vocabulary

Siéntate.	*Sit down.*
el trabajo	*job*
trabajo	*I work*
trabaja	*he/she works*
el secretario/la secretaria	*male/female secretary*
el doctor/la doctora	*male/female doctor*
el enfermero/la enfermera	*male/female nurse*
el maestro/la maestra	*male/female teacher*
el director/la directora	*male/female principal*
el policía/la policía	*policeman/policewoman*
el dueño/la dueña	*male/female owner*
el cocinero/la cocinera	*male/female cook*
el camarero/la camarera	*waiter/waitress*
la oficina	*office*

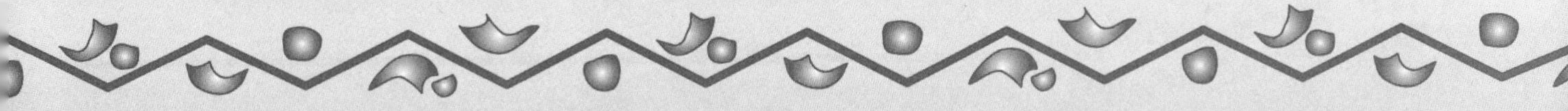

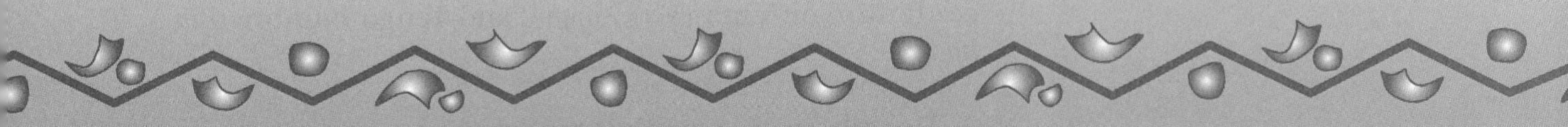

Warm-up

Ask the children to name the various professions represented in your school (e.g., principal, teachers, nurse, secretary, [music, science teacher]). If necessary, say people's names and ask what the person is or does.

Review

Ask the children to name the professions of the people **la maestra** spoke with in the last lesson, e.g., in the scene outside the police station (policeman) and in the scene in the Mexican restaurant (owner, cooks, waiter, musicians).

Some children may recall the Spanish names for the professions in Lesson 44:

el policía	*policeman*
el dueño	*male owner*
el cocinero	*male cook*
la cocinera	*female cook*
la tortillera	*female tortilla cook*
el camarero	*waiter*
los músicos	*musicians*

Introduce the video

Invite the children to listen and watch as **la maestra** visits a school and talks with several people there about what they do.

Children who have been with ***Español para ti*** for several years may recall the following professions vocabulary:

el director
(*male principal*)

la directora
(*female principal*)

el enfermero
(*male nurse*)

la enfermera
(*female nurse*)

el maestro
(*male teacher*)

la maestra
(*female teacher*)

el secretario
(*male secretary*)

la secretaria
(*female secretary*)

Video Lesson

1. Greeting the children

La maestra greets the children with **Buenos días** (*Good morning*) and asks them **¿Cómo estás?** (*How are you?*). She greets Winston and asks him **¿Qué tal?** (*How's it going?*). She reviews the feeling expressions **Muy bien** (*Very well*), **Muy contento/contenta** (*Very happy*), and **Tengo hambre** (*I'm hungry*).

2. Deciphering *el mensaje mágico* (*the magic message*)

Antonio demonstrates the magic message—**¡Siéntate!** (*Sit down!*).

3. Identifying various professions

Winston reads the word **trabajo** (*job; I work*). **La maestra** reviews vocabulary for professions.

la secretaria	*(female) secretary*
¿Dónde está la secretaria?	*Where is the (female) secretary?*
En la oficina.	*In the office.*
La secretaria trabaja en la oficina.	*The (female) secretary works in the office.*
el doctor	*(male) doctor*
¿Dónde está el doctor?	*Where is the (male) doctor?*
En el hospital.	*In the hospital.*
El doctor trabaja en el hospital.	*The (male) doctor works in the hospital.*
la policía	*policewoman*
¿Dónde está la policía?	*Where is the policewoman?*
La policía está en la calle.	*The policewoman is in the street.*

4. Visiting people who work in a school

La maestra visits with **la secretaria** (*secretary*), **la enfermera** (*nurse*), **la maestra** (*teacher*), and **la directora** (*principal*).

Ésta es la oficina de la escuela.	*This is the school office.*
¿Quién trabaja en la oficina?	*Who works in the office?*
La secretaria trabaja en la oficina.	*The (female) secretary works in the office.*
Y ella está en su escritorio.	*And she is at her desk.*
La enfermera es muy importante cuando los niños en la escuela están mal.	*The (female) nurse is very important when the children in the school are sick.*
Es la enfermera y trabaja en la oficina de la enfermera.	*It is the nurse and she works in the nurse's office.*

FYI There are two forms for *you* in Spanish—the informal **tú** and the formal **usted**. The informal **tú** is used by adults when addressing children and among close friends and adult relatives. Adults who do not know each other well use the formal **usted**, as **la maestra** and the police chief do in section 5 (**¿Cómo está usted?**—*How are you?*). Children use the formal **usted** when addressing adults as LeeAnn does with the police chief. Note that the police chief uses the informal **tú** with LeeAnn (**¿Cómo te llamas tú?**—*What is your name?*).

Los niños trabajan mucho en la clase de la maestra.	*The children work a lot in the teacher's class.*
La directora tiene una oficina muy grande y muy bonita.	*The (female) principal has a very large and very pretty office.*
La directora trabaja mucho en la escuela porque los niños son muy importantes.	*The principal works a lot in the school because the children are very important.*
Tengo que irme.	*I have to go.*

5. Talking with people who do police work

La maestra talks with **el policía** (*policeman*) about his work. For their statements, see Lesson 44, Video Lesson, section 5. LeeAnn and **la maestra** talk with **el jefe de la policía** (*police chief*) (**M** = Maestra, **J** = Jefe, **L** = LeeAnn):

M: Niños, éste es el jefe de la policía. Buenos días, señor.	*Children, this is the police chief. Good morning, sir.*
J: Buenos días.	*Good morning.*
M: ¿Cómo está usted?	*How are you?*
J: Muy bien. ¿Y usted?	*Very well. And you?*
M: Muy bien, gracias.	*Very well, thank you.*
J: ¿Y cómo te llamas tú?	*And what is your name?*
L: Me llamo LeeAnn. ¿Y usted?	*My name is LeeAnn. And you?*
J: Me llamo José Troncoso.	*My name is José Troncoso.*
L: Mucho gusto.	*Pleased to meet you.*
J: Mucho gusto.	*Pleased to meet you.*

6. Meeting people who work in a restaurant

La maestra visits with **el dueño** (*owner*) at the restaurant as well as with **el cocinero** (*male cook*), **la cocinera** (*female cook*), and **la tortillera** (*female tortilla cook*). For their statements, see Lesson 44, Video Lesson, section 6. **La maestra** mentions that **el camarero** (*waiter*) is another person who works in a restaurant.

7. Revealing *el mensaje mágico* (*the magic message*)

Antonio demonstrates the message. Then the children reveal it—¡**Siéntate**! (*Sit down!*).

8. Closing

Winston and **la maestra** bid the children **Hasta luego** (*See you later*) and **Adiós** (*Good-bye*).

Presenting episodes containing sustained conversation more than once gives the children added exposure to Spanish as it is spoken in real life, at the same time that it gives them practice in using context clues to figure out meaning. During the second viewing the children will probably understand much more of the conversation between **la maestra** and the policemen, restaurant owner, and cooks than they did during the first viewing.

After viewing the video, praise the children for their good listening and watching skills.

Word Search: Professions

The names of seven professions are hidden in this puzzle. Find them and circle them. The words go from left to right and from top to bottom in the puzzle. Use the word bank to help you. Then write the words you found in the blanks below.

E	N	F	E	R	M	E	R	O	F	G	F	Y	R	R
M	S	X	H	N	A	D	A	R	Ñ	I	U	V	W	Z
C	Q	H	D	I	E	S	M	T	A	N	T	R	Ñ	O
E	U	A	O	I	S	E	C	R	E	T	A	R	I	O
S	I	N	C	B	T	I	S	B	O	L	O	S	O	T
P	A	T	T	N	R	R	N	I	N	E	L	N	K	S
A	R	E	O	P	O	U	V	T	Ñ	S	B	M	A	U
Ñ	B	A	R	O	N	C	E	S	T	O	C	U	D	R
O	X	M	A	T	E	M	D	I	R	E	C	T	O	R
C	O	C	I	N	E	R	A	D	I	T	Z	I	E	V
Z	H	U	C	I	E	N	C	I	A	S	R	C	R	Ñ
Y	M	Y	T	Y	M	I	C	A	M	A	R	E	R	O

Palabras

MAESTRO DOCTORA DIRECTOR
ENFERMERO CAMARERO COCINERA SECRETARIO

Blackline Master 45A-1

Answer Key

Word Search: Professions

The names of seven professions are hidden in this puzzle. Find them and circle them. The words go from left to right and from top to bottom in the puzzle. Use the word bank to help you. Then write the words you found in the blanks below.

E	N	F	E	R	M	E	R	O	F	G	F	Y	R	R
M	S	X	H	N	A	D	A	R	Ñ	I	U	V	W	Z
C	Q	H	D	I	E	S	M	T	A	N	T	R	Ñ	O
E	U	A	O	I	S	E	C	R	E	T	A	R	I	O
S	I	N	C	B	T	I	S	B	O	L	O	S	O	T
P	A	T	T	N	R	R	N	I	N	E	L	N	K	S
A	R	E	O	P	O	U	V	T	Ñ	S	B	M	A	U
Ñ	B	A	R	O	N	C	E	S	T	O	C	U	D	R
O	X	M	A	T	E	M	D	I	R	E	C	T	O	R
C	O	C	I	N	E	R	A	D	I	T	Z	I	E	V
Z	H	U	C	I	E	N	C	I	A	S	R	C	R	Ñ
Y	M	Y	T	Y	M	I	C	A	M	A	R	E	R	O

Palabras

MAESTRO DOCTORA DIRECTOR
ENFERMERO CAMARERO COCINERA SECRETARIO

ENFERMERO DOCTORA
DIRECTOR CAMARERO
COCINERA MAESTRO
SECRETARIO

Blackline Master 45A-2

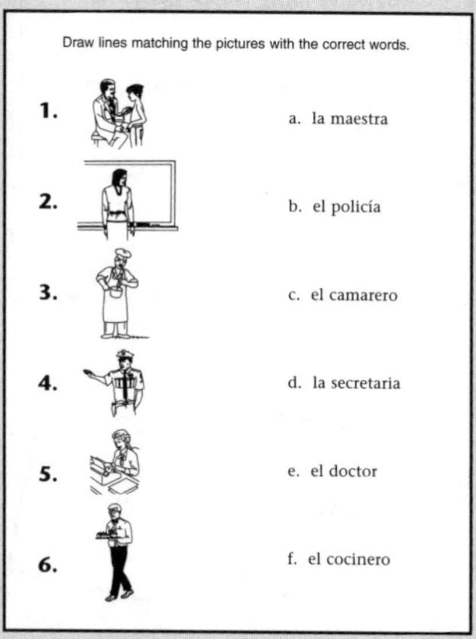

Draw lines matching the pictures with the correct words.
1.
2.
3.
4.
5.
6.
a. la maestra
b. el policía
c. el camarero
d. la secretaria
e. el doctor
f. el cocinero

Blackline Master 45B

Activity Lesson

Activity 45A: Find the hidden words

Materials: Blackline Masters 45A-1 and 45A-2; a blank transparency; an overhead projector; pencils; a current calendar; and current Month Picture.

Preparation: Make an overhead transparency of Blackline Master 45A-2. Copy and distribute Blackline Master 45A-1 so that each child has a copy. Display the current calendar and Month Picture.

Have the children fill in their names and the date on the top of the paper. If they need help with the date, point to the number of the day on the calendar and to the name of the month on the Month Picture. Tell the children that hidden in the puzzle are the words for seven professions. The words run from left to right and from top to bottom. The children should use the word bank to help them find the words. Then they should write each word they found on one of the lines below. When the children have completed the activity, project your overhead transparency of Blackline Master 45A-2 and allow children time to check their answers.

Activity 45B: Match pictures and words

Materials: Blackline Master 45B; pencils; a current calendar; and current Month Picture.

Preparation: Copy and distribute Blackline Master 45B so that each child has a copy.

Have the children fill in their names and the date on the top of the paper. Show the number of the day on the calendar and the Month Picture if they need help with the date. Draw a line from the picture of a profession on the left to the corresponding word on the right.

Children should have matched the pictures and words as follows:

1. e—el doctor (*male doctor*)
2. a—la maestra (*female teacher*)
3. f—el cocinero (*male cook*)
4. b—el policía (*male policeman*)
5. d—la secretaria (*female secretary*)
6. c—el camarero (*waiter*)

Activity 45C: What do they do?

Lead the children in a discussion of the professions of policeman, policewoman, and police chief. What does a policeman/policewoman do (patrols the streets by foot, motorcycle, or car; goes to disturbance or crime scenes; helps people)? What does a police chief do (oversees the work of the police officers and may also perform the duties of the officers)?

CLOSING

Tell the children that Spanish class is finished for today. In the next lesson **la maestra** will play several games with the children.

DICTIONARY

Materials: Blank paper; colored markers or pencils; and children's dictionary pages.

Preparation: Write the following on the chalkboard:

Boys:	Girls:
el secretario	la secretaria
el doctor	la doctora
el enfermero	la enfermera
el policía	la policía
el jefe	la jefa
el dueño	la dueña
el cocinero	la cocinera
el camarero	la camarera

Tell the children to draw a picture of their favorite profession of those listed on the board. They should write the name of the profession under the picture and the first letter of the profession name on the top of the page. Have them alphabetize their new page among their dictionary pages. For English translations, see the Vocabulary section of this lesson.

Lesson 46

Materials to gather

- VCR and Video Lesson 46 on Tape 16
- Cassette player
- Activity Cassette 2
- Number Cards 10–100 by tens
- Current calendar
- Current Month Picture
- Blackline Master 46A (numbers and professions)
- Pencils
- ***Prepare ahead:*** If possible, arrange for someone involved in one of the professions the children have been learning about in Spanish class to come and talk with them about his/her job. For example, a doctor, waiter/waitress, a cook/chef, police officer or police chief, school principal, or nurse. (See Activity 46B.)

Objectives

Language

- Decipher a new **mensaje mágico** (*magic message*)—**Toma** (*Drink*)
- Understand more of the extended conversation in the restaurant
- Learn a new question and answer

Culture

- Hear again why speaking Spanish helps the doctor

Review

- Review vocabulary for school and restaurant professions
- Play **¿Cuál falta?** (*What's missing?*) and **¿Quién es?** (*Who is it?*)

Vocabulary

¡Toma!	*Drink!*
¿Qué quieres ser?	*What do you want to be?*
Quiero ser ___.	*I want to be ___.*
la sopa	*soup*
el refresco	*soft drink*

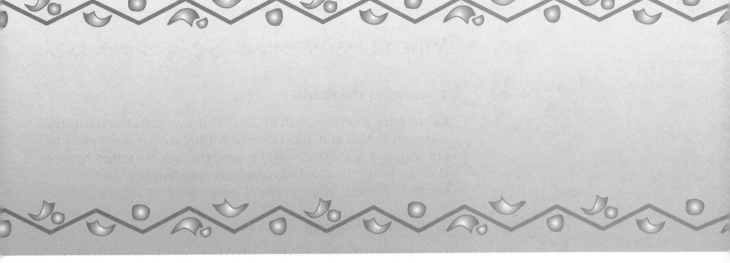

Warm-up

Mention to the children that it is time for Spanish class (**la clase de español**). Ask a volunteer to describe the weather in Spanish.

Hace calor.	*It's hot.*
Hace frío.	*It's cold.*
Hace sol.	*It's sunny.*
Llueve.	*It's raining.*
Nieva.	*It's snowing.*
Hace viento.	*It's windy.*
Hace mal tiempo.	*It's bad weather.*
Hace buen tiempo.	*It's good weather.*

Review

Materials: Number Cards 10–100 by 10s (found in the Teacher's Resource Book).

Distribute the Number Cards among the children. If there are more children than Number Cards, pair the children up and give each pair a Card. Ask for a volunteer to practice the numbers by tens with the class by calling out the numbers first in order and then randomly in Spanish. The child (or children) with the number should stand and repeat the number aloud.

Introduce the video

Invite the children to listen and watch as **la maestra** and the children talk about what profession they would like to have.

Numbers:

10	diez
20	veinte
30	treinta
40	cuarenta
50	cincuenta
60	sesenta
70	setenta
80	ochenta
90	noventa
100	cien

VIDEO LESSON

1. Greeting the children

La maestra greets LeeAnn and the children with **Buenas tardes** (*Good afternoon*) and asks them how they are—**¿Cómo estás tú?** LeeAnn says **Así, así** (*So-so*). **La maestra** says **No tengo hambre** (*I'm not hungry*) and asks LeeAnn **¿Tienes hambre?** (*Are you hungry?*). LeeAnn responds **Sí, y tengo sed** (*Yes, and I'm thirsty*).

2. Viewing *el mensaje mágico* (*the magic message*)

La maestra asks the children what they would say if they wanted to tell someone to do what Antonio demonstrates—**Toma** (*Drink*).

3. Reviewing the vocabulary for school professions

LeeAnn and **la maestra** name professions of school personnel.

School personnel:

el secretario (*male secretary*)
la secretaria (*female secretary*)
el director (*male principal*)
la directora (*female principal*)
el maestro (*male teacher*)
la maestra (*female teacher*)
el enfermero (*male nurse*)
la enfermera (*female nurse*)

4. Playing a game of *¿Cuál falta?* (*Who's missing?*)

La maestra reviews the names of school personnel. One picture at a time disappears and she asks the children **¿Cuál falta?** (*Who's missing?*).

5. Introducing a new question and answer

Winston reads the new question. He and **la maestra** give several responses.

¿Qué quieres ser?	*What do you want to be?*
Quiero ser ___.	*I want to be ___.*

6. Visiting the doctor's office

La maestra visits the doctor's office and talks with the doctor about his work and why it is important that he speaks Spanish. For their statements, see Lesson 33, Video Lesson, section 6.

7. Visiting the Mexican restaurant

After mentioning all the ways children may answer the question **¿Qué quieres ser?** (*What do you want to be?*), including **Quiero ser cocinero** (*I want to be a cook*), **la maestra** visits the Mexican restaurant. For her statements outside the restaurant, see Lesson 32, Video Lesson, section 7. For the conversation with the restaurant owner, see Lesson 44, Video Lesson, section 6. For her conversation with the musicians, see Lesson 47, Video Lesson, section 5. Statements from the conversations with doña Elena and the waiter are below.

¿Dónde está doña Elena? Siempre llega tarde.	*Where is doña Elena?* *She's always late.*
¿Dónde está el camarero?	*Where is the waiter?*
Aquí está el menú.	*Here is the menu.*

EN ESPAÑOL

Note that the definite article **el** or **la** (*the*) is not used in Spanish when stating one's profession or what one wants to be: **Quiero ser doctor** (*I want to be a doctor*), **Quiero ser maestra** (*I want to be a teacher*).

¿Qué hay para comer?	*What is there to eat?*
¿Hay sopa?	*Is there soup?*
Sí, hay sopa.	*Yes, there is soup.*
Quiero sopa, por favor.	*I want soup, please.*
¿Y para tomar?	*And to drink?*
Para mí, leche, por favor.	*For me, milk, please.*
Yo quiero un refresco.	*I want a soft drink.*

8. Practicing vocabulary for professions

Asking **¿Quién es?** (*Who is it?*), **la maestra** asks the children to identify various professions. The name of each profession appears on the screen.

La secretaria trabaja en la oficina.	*The secretary works in the office.*
La maestra trabaja en la clase.	*The teacher works in the classroom.*
La cocinera trabaja en el restaurante.	*The cook works in the restaurant.*
El camarero trabaja en el restaurante.	*The waiter works in the restaurant.*
El policía es muy importante y tiene la moto.	*The policeman is very important and has a motorcycle.*

9. Revealing *el mensaje mágico* (*the magic message*)

The children watch Antonio and then reveal that they would tell him **Toma** (*Drink*) to get him to do what he is doing.

10. Closing

La maestra reviews the new question **¿Qué quieres ser?** (*What do you want to be?*) and the answer **Quiero ser** ___ (*I want to be* ___). She and Winston say **Hasta luego** (*See you later*) and **Adiós** (*Good-bye*) to the children.

After viewing the video, praise the children for their good listening and watching skills.

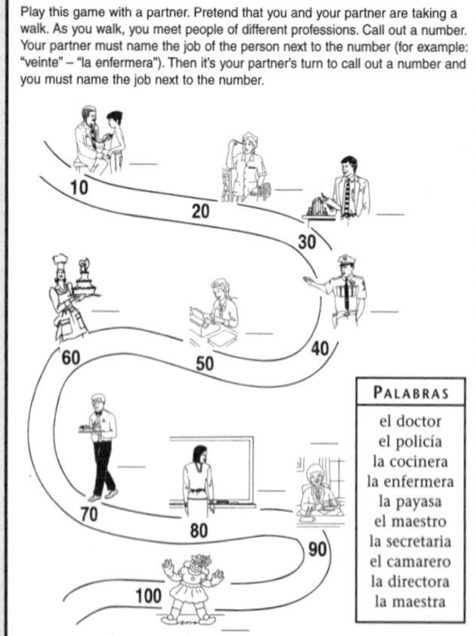
Play this game with a partner. Pretend that you and your partner are taking a walk. As you walk, you meet people of different professions. Call out a number. Your partner must name the job of the person next to the number (for example: "veinte" – "la enfermera"). Then it's your partner's turn to call out a number and you must name the job next to the number.

10 20 30 40 50 60 70 80 90 100

PALABRAS
el doctor
el policía
la cocinera
la enfermera
la payasa
el maestro
la secretaria
el camarero
la directora
la maestra

Blackline Master 46A

As **la maestra** begins the game, she asks Winston **¿Listo?** (*Ready?*).

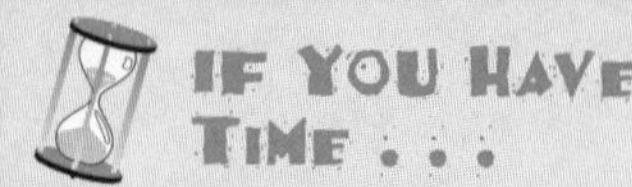

Have the children play the game in Activity 46A again, but with a different partner.

ACTIVITY LESSON

Activity 46A: Numbers and professions

Materials: Cassette player; Activity Cassette 2, Side B; a current calendar; the current Month Picture; pencils; and Blackline Master 46A.

Preparation: Copy and distribute Blackline Master 46A so that each child has a copy.

Have the children write their names and the date on the top of their copies. If they need help with the date, point to the number of the day on the calendar and to the name of the month on the Month Picture. Next, have them write the name of each profession next to the picture representing the profession. Point out that all the words for the professions are given in the word bank (**Palabras**).

Then, divide the class into pairs. Tell them to listen carefully as **la maestra** explains how they will play the game shown on their pages. **La maestra** calls out a number and Winston names the profession of the person standing by the number **la maestra** said. Once the taped activity is finished, allow children time to play the game with a partner, taking turns to call out the numbers in Spanish.

Number:		**Profession:**
10	diez	el doctor (*male doctor*)
20	veinte	la enfermera (*female nurse*)
30	treinta	el maestro (*male teacher*)
40	cuarenta	el policía (*policeman*)
50	cincuenta	la secretaria (*female secretary*)
60	sesenta	la cocinera (*female cook*)
70	setenta	el camarero (*male waiter*)
80	ochenta	la maestra (*female teacher*)
90	noventa	la directora (*female principal*)
100	cien	la payasa (*female clown*)

Activity 46B: What do you want to be?

Lead the children in a discussion about various professions, asking them what they think they would like to do when they are older and what they think is involved in the type of professions they mention. Talk about the training and education necessary to do various types of jobs.

If you were able to arrange for a professional to visit your class (see *Prepare ahead* on the first page of this lesson), have the person talk about his/her profession and training/education. Encourage the children to ask questions.

Activity 46C: Magic messages

Divide the class into groups of four or five. Remind them that a special feature in Spanish class this year has been the *magic message* (**el mensaje mágico**). Have each group determine what magic message they will mime for the class. Each group should mime its message while the other groups try to guess it. Remind the miming group that they may need to ask "How would you tell someone to do this?" (e.g., the group is standing and then sits down, thus miming the command **Siéntate**—*Sit down!*) or "What would you say if you felt this way?" (e.g., the group mimes swallowing hard, indicating **Tengo sed**—*I'm thirsty*) or "Where would you be if you went here?" (e.g., the group draws a picture of a beach and asks the question to elicit the response **la playa**—*beach*).

Possible magic messages:

Anda.	*Walk.*	Salta.	*Jump.*
Busca.	*Look for.*	Toca.	*Touch.*
Colorea.	*Color.*	Tengo calor.	*I'm hot.*
Corre.	*Run.*	Tengo frío.	*I'm cold.*
Dibuja.	*Draw.*	Tengo hambre.	*I'm hungry.*
Estoy enojado/enojada.	*I'm angry.*	Tengo sed.	*I'm thirsty.*
Muéstrame.	*Show me.*	Voy a la playa.	*I'm going to the beach.*

CLOSING

Tell the children that Spanish class is finished for today. In the next lesson Antonio and **la maestra** will have another magic message!

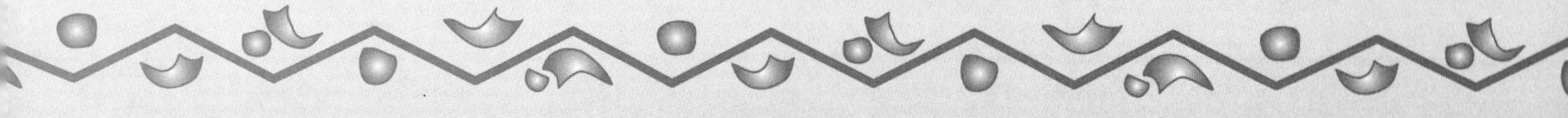

Lesson 47

Materials to gather

- VCR and Video Lesson 47 on Tape 16
- Blackline Master 47B (menu)
- Blank transparency
- Overhead projector
- One or two small tables and chairs
- One or two small pads of paper and pencils
- ***Optional materials:*** colored markers; large pieces of white paper; empty toilet paper rolls; pipe cleaners; tissue paper

Objectives

Language

- Decipher another **mensaje mágico** (*magic message*) **¡Párate!** (*Stand up!*)
- Understand more of the extended conversation in the Mexican restaurant
- Learn how to ask if something is on a menu
- Learn how to ask for a price

Culture

- Hear about two typical Mexican foods—**quesadillas** and **guacamole**

Review

- Answer several familiar questions
- Play **¿Quién es?** (*Who is it?*) with profession vocabulary

Vocabulary

¡Párate!	*Stand up!*
¿Hay ___?	*Is there/Are there ___?*
¿Cuánto cuesta?	*How much does it cost?*
¿Cuánto cuestan?	*How much do they cost?*

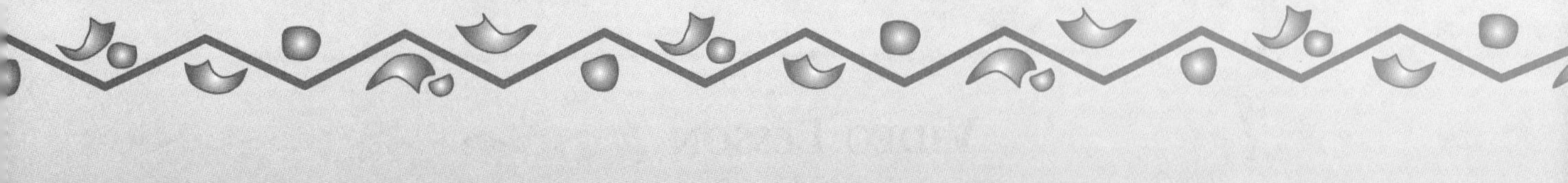

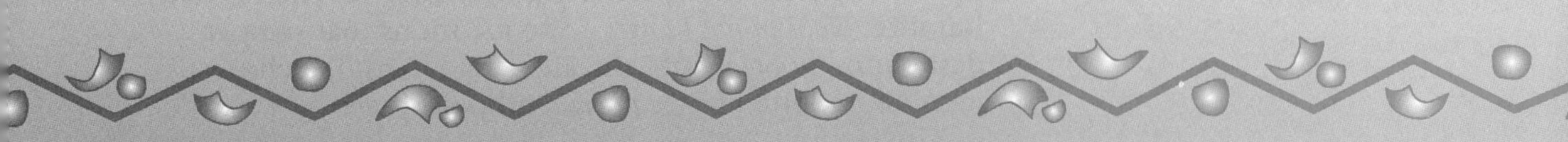

Warm-up

Tell the children it's time for Spanish class (**la clase de español**). Ask them what kind of a restaurant they visited in the last video lesson with **la maestra** (a Mexican restaurant). Who did they meet there (the owner, three cooks, a waiter, and two musicians)?

Review

Write the following numbers (without the Spanish) on the chalkboard:

4	cuatro	25	veinticinco
5	cinco	75	setenta y cinco
50	cincuenta		

Ask the children to say each number in Spanish. If you feel comfortable, ask **¿Qué número es?** (*What number is it?*).

Introduce the video

Invite the children to listen and watch as **la maestra** and Kipper introduce how to ask how much something costs and how to say the price of something.

Professions:

el dueño	*male owner*
el cocinero	*male cook*
la cocinera	*female cook*
el camarero	*waiter*
los músicos	*musicians*

Video Lesson

1. Greeting the children

La maestra greets the children with **Buenos días** (*Good morning*) and asks them how they are. She asks Kipper **¿Qué tal?** (*How's it going?*). He says **Tengo hambre** (*I'm hungry*). Kipper asks **la maestra** if she's hungry and she replies **No, no tengo hambre** (*No, I'm not hungry*). She mentions that **para el desayuno** (*for breakfast*), she ate **cereal** (*cereal*), **leche** (*milk*), **jugo de naranja** (*orange juice*), and **pan** (*bread*).

2. Viewing *el mensaje mágico* (*the magic message*)

La maestra asks the children what they would say if they were to tell someone to do the action demonstrated by Antonio—**¡Párate!** (*Stand up!*).

3. Practicing professions vocabulary

Showing Gold Flashcards of various professions, **la maestra** asks **¿Quién es?** (*Who is it?*) and **¿Dónde trabaja?** (*Where does he/she work?*) or **¿Dónde está?** (*Where is he/she?*).

La secretaria trabaja en la oficina.	*The (female) secretary works in the office.*
La directora trabaja en la escuela.	*The (female) principal works in the school.*
El doctor/el enfermero trabaja en la escuela o en el hospital.	*The (male) doctor/(male) nurse works in the school or in the hospital.*
El policía está en la calle con las luces de tráfico.	*The policeman is in the street with the traffic lights.*

4. Reviewing several questions

Kipper reads several questions and answers them. The children answer the final question.

¿Adónde vas?	*Where are you going?*
Voy a la clase.	*I'm going to class.*
¿Cómo vas?	*How are you going?*
Voy en bicicleta.	*I'm going by bicycle.*
¿Qué quieres ser?	*What do you want to be?*
Quiero ser músico.	*I want to be a musician.*

5. Visiting the Mexican restaurant

La maestra visits the Mexican restaurant. For her statements outside the restaurant, see Lesson 32, Video Lesson, section 7. For the conversation with the restaurant owner, see Lesson 44, Video Lesson, section 6. For the conversation with the waiter, see Lesson 46, Video Lesson, section 7. The conversation with the musicians follows.

Aquí vienen los músicos.	*Here come the musicians.*
Son los instrumentos musicales mexicanos.	*Those are Mexican musical instruments.*
Un guitarrón es una guitarra muy grande.	*A guitarrón is a very large guitar.*
Esto es una vihuela.	*This is a vihuela.*
Es un tipo de guitarra muy pequeña.	*It's a type of guitar that is very small.*
Me gusta la música mexicana. ¡Toquen!	*I like Mexican music. Play!*

6. Practicing professions vocabulary

La maestra and Kipper talk about all the professions represented in a restaurant. **La maestra** plays a game of **¿Quién es?** (*Who is it?*). The children identify **la secretaria** (*female secretary*), **la maestra** (*female teacher*), **la cocinera** (*female cook*), **el camarero** (*waiter*), and **el policía** (*policeman*).

7. Asking if something is on the menu and how much it costs

La maestra explains how to ask if something is on the menu and how to ask the price. She describes a **quesadilla** and **guacamole** and tells the children that every country has its own kind of foods.

¿Hay guacamole?	*Is there guacamole?*
Sí, hay ___.	*Yes, there is ___.*
No, no hay ___.	*No, there isn't ___.*
¿Cuánto cuesta?	*How much does it cost?*
Cuatro, cincuenta.	*$4.50.*
¿Hay quesadillas de maíz?	*Are there corn quesadillas?*
¿Cuánto cuestan?	*How much do they cost?*
Cinco, veinticinco.	*$5.25.*

8. Revealing *el mensaje mágico* (*the magic message*)

Antonio demonstrates the message, which is **¡Párate!** (*Stand up!*).

9. Closing

Kipper and **la maestra** say **Adiós** (*Good-bye*) and **Hasta luego** (*See you later*) to the children.

CROSS-CULTURAL CONNECTIONS

The **vihuela** is a guitar of Spanish origin. The **guitarrón** has 25 strings.

La maestra says **Hay muchos trabajos en el restaurante** (*There are many jobs in the restaurant*): **el dueño/la dueña** (*owner*), **el cocinero/la cocinera** (*cook*), **el camarero/la camarera** (*server*), **los músicos** (*musicians*).

Point out to the children that when **la maestra** reveals the answer to **¿Quién es?** (*Who is it?*), the Spanish word for the profession appears on the screen.

After viewing the video, praise the children for their good listening and watching skills.

ACTIVITY LESSON

Activity 47A: Talk about a typical menu

Lead the children in a discussion of their favorite restaurant and what the menu looks like (the menu may be printed and given to each customer or it may appear over the counter where one orders, as in a fast food restaurant). Ask how a menu is organized. What things are usually listed together (drinks, desserts, appetizers, salads, soups, main dishes)?

Activity 47B: Read a menu

Materials: Blackline Master 47B; a blank overhead transparency; and an overhead projector.

Preparation: Make a transparency of Blackline Master 47B.

Tell the children they are going to look at a typical menu from a Mexican restaurant. Project the transparency of Blackline Master 47B. Ask children to identify the categories of foods and the foods under each category (see below).

Sopas	***Soups***	**(*Price*)**
sopa de pollo	*chicken soup*	$3.00 (tres)
Comidas	***Foods/meals***	
quesadillas	*quesadillas*	$4.50 (cuatro, cincuenta)
tacos	*tacos*	$6.75 (seis, setenta y cinco)
Bebidas	***Drinks***	
jugo de naranja	*orange juice*	$1.00 (uno)
leche	*milk*	$1.25 (uno, veinticinco)
Postres	***Desserts***	
plátanos	*bananas*	$2.00 (dos)
uvas	*grapes*	$2.00 (dos)
fresas	*strawberries*	$2.00 (dos)

El menú

(*The menu*)

Sopas

sopa de pollo $3.00

Comidas

quesadillas $4.50
tacos $6.75

Bebidas

jugo de naranja $1.00
leche $1.25

Postres

plátanos $2.00
uvas $2.00
fresas $2.00

Blackline Master 47B

EN ESPAÑOL

If you feel comfortable, ask **¿Cuánto cuesta?** or **¿Cuánto cuestan?** (*How much does it/do they cost?*) if you want to ask the children for the price of each food item.

Activity 47C: Cooperative learning—Act out a restaurant scene

Materials: One or two small tables with chairs; one or two small pads of paper and pencils; and Blackline Master 47B.

Preparation: Set up the tables and chairs like a restaurant. Assign several children to be customers and one or two to be servers. Make enough copies of Blackline Master 47B so that each customer has a copy.

Ask volunteers to recall how to ask if a restaurant has something, how to ask how much it costs, and how to respond to the questions.

¿Hay ___?	*Is/Are there ___?*
¿Cuánto cuesta/cuestan?	*How much does it/do they cost?*
Sí, hay ___.	*Yes, there is/are ___.*
No, no hay ___.	*No, there isn't/aren't ___.*

Tell the customers to take their seats and to act out a scene in the restaurant in which they are asking the server questions about the menu and how much things cost. The server should take down each person's order. Encourage the children to use as much Spanish as they can.

CLOSING

Tell the children that Spanish class is finished for today. In the next lesson they will practice more of the restaurant vocabulary.

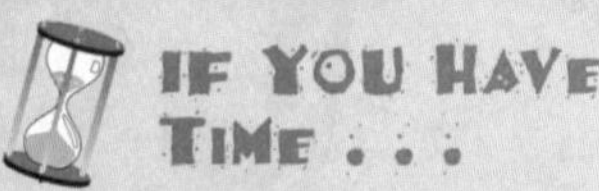

Materials: Colored markers; large pieces of white paper; empty toilet paper rolls; pipe cleaners; and tissue paper.

Make Activity 47C more elaborate. For example, have the children make colorful tablecloths using large sheets of paper and colored markers. Have others design table decorations, making vases out of toilet paper rolls and filling them with flowers made from pipe cleaners and tissue paper. Have others create their own instruments using cardboard boxes and string or borrow instruments from the music teacher. Have the children set up the restaurant and act out the scene as in Activity 47C.

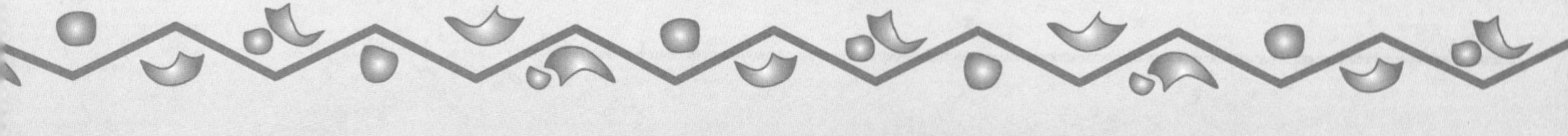

Lesson 48

Materials to gather

- VCR and Video Lesson 48 on Tape 16
- Cassette player
- Activity Cassette 2
- Overhead projector
- Overhead transparency of Blackline Master 47B (menu)
- Current Month Picture
- Current calendar

Objectives

Language

- Decipher the last **mensaje mágico** (*magic message*)—**Dame** ___ (*Give me* ___)

Culture

- Hear about some more Mexican foods

Review

- Review professions vocabulary
- Answer the question **¿Qué quieres ser?** (*What do you want to be?*)
- Review common phrases used in a restaurant
- Read **"El café mágico"** (*"The Magic Café"*)

Vocabulary

Dame ___.	*Give me ___.*
Sí, hay ___.	*Yes, there is/there are ___.*
No, no hay ___.	*No, there isn't/there aren't ___.*

Warm-up

Materials: Current Month Picture; a current calendar.

Let the children know it's time for Spanish class (**la clase de español**). Ask them to tell you the date in Spanish: **el** [*number*] **de** [*month*]. If necessary, point to the number of the day on the calendar and then to the name of the month on the Month Picture. For numbers 1–31, see Topics and Language Covered in the Front Matter of this book.

Review

Preparation: Draw two clown figures on the chalkboard: one short male clown and one tall female clown. (See Blackline Master 22A for sample clown drawings.)

Ask the children to describe each clown: **el payaso es bajo** (*the male clown is short*); **la payasa es alta** (*the female clown is tall*). Ask them what other describing words they learned this year. If necessary, mime or draw additional figures to help them remember other adjectives.

feo/fea	*ugly*	delgado/delgada	*thin*
bonito/bonita	*pretty*	pequeño/pequeña	*small*
gordo/gorda	*fat*	grande	*big*

Introduce the video

Invite the children to listen and watch as **la maestra** helps them practice the names of professions.

EN ESPAÑOL

If you feel comfortable, say **Buenos días** (*Good morning*), **Buenas tardes** (*Good afternoon*), or **Hola** (*Hello*).

VIDEO LESSON

1. Greeting the children

La maestra greets the children with **Buenos días** (*Good morning*) and asks them how they are. She asks Winston how he is; he tells her **Muy bien** (*Very well*) and she remarks **Como siempre** (*As always*).

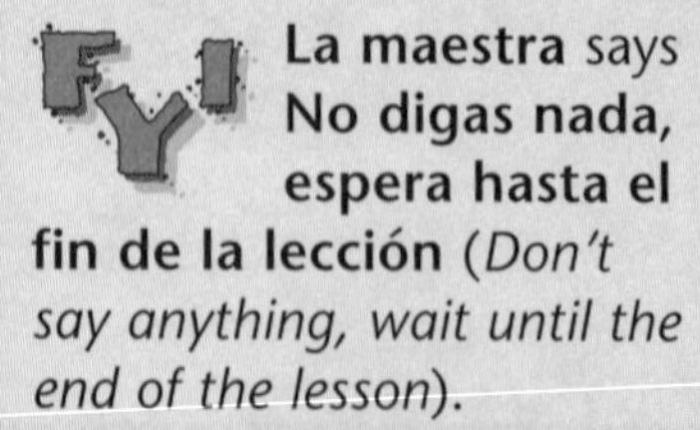

La maestra says **No digas nada, espera hasta el fin de la lección** (*Don't say anything, wait until the end of the lesson*).

2. Demonstrating *el mensaje mágico* (*the magic message*)

La maestra asks the children what they would tell someone if they wanted the person to do what Antonio does. The mime demonstrates the command **Dame** ___ (*Give me* ___).

3. Reviewing professions vocabulary

After reviewing the question **¿Qué quieres ser?** (*What do you want to be?*) and the answer **Quiero ser** ___ (*I want to be a* ___), **la maestra** describes **los trabajos** (*professions*). She asks Winston and the children to name these professions:

el camarero/la camarera	*waiter/waitress, server*
el director/la directora	*principal*
el doctor/la doctora	*doctor*
el enfermero/la enfermera	*nurse*
el/la policía	*policeman/policewoman*

4. Practicing professions vocabulary

La maestra plays a game of **¿Quién es?** (*Who is it?*) with the children, who identify **la enfermera** (*nurse*), **la directora** (*principal*), **el jefe** (*police chief*), and **el doctor** (*doctor*).

camarones = *shrimp*
filete relleno = *stuffed filet*
tacos = *tacos*

5. Reviewing common phrases used in a restaurant

Holding **el menú del restaurante mexicano** (*the menu from the Mexican restaurant*), **la maestra** and Winston describe some of the dishes and their prices.

¿Hay ___?	*Is there/Are there ___?*
Sí, hay ___.	*Yes, there is/there are ___.*
No, no hay ___.	*No, there isn't/there aren't ___.*
¿Qué hay?	*What is there/are there?*
¿Cuánto cuesta?	*How much does it cost?*

HERITAGE SPEAKERS

You might ask heritage speakers to describe their favorite kind of quesadilla or favorite taco filling. Perhaps non-heritage speakers enjoy eating Mexican food. Ask them to talk about their favorite kinds of dishes.

6. Recognizing numbers

La maestra asks **¿Qué números son?** (*What numbers are they?*). The children say the number on each football player's jersey:

dieciséis (*16*)
diecisiete (*17*)
treinta (*30*)
vienticuatro (*24*)
veintiuno (*21*)
veinte (*20*)
treinta y uno (*31*)
tres (*3*)
veinticinco (*25*)
treinta y dos (*32*)
cuarenta y cuatro (*44*)
cuarenta y uno (*41*)
treinta y cuatro (*34*)
cuarenta y dos (*42*)
treinta y cinco (*35*)
veinticinco (*25*)
cuarenta (*40*)

7. Practicing saying what one wants to be

Using Gold Flashcards of professions, **la maestra** asks the children **¿Qué quieres ser?** (*What do you want to be?*): **Quiero ser policía** (*I want to be a policeman/policewoman*), **Quiero ser doctor/doctora** (*I want to be a doctor*) or **Quiero ser enfermero/enfermera** (*I want to be a nurse*), **Quiero ser director/directora** (*I want to be a principal*), and **Quiero ser secretario/secretaria** (*I want to be a secretary*).

8. Reading about Fredo's adventures in *el café mágico* (*the Magic Café*)

La maestra tells the children that Fredo could say **Quiero ser cliente** (*I want to be a customer*). Doña Elena reads "**El café mágico**" as the children read along with her.

9. Revealing *el mensaje mágico* (*the magic message*)

Children solve the message by saying **Dame** ___ (*Give me* ___).

10. Closing

La maestra and Winston say **Hasta luego** (*See you later*) and **Hasta la vista** (*Until we meet again*) to the children.

After viewing the video, praise the children for their good listening and watching skills.

ACTIVITY LESSON

Activity 48A: What's on the menu?

Materials: Cassette player; Activity Cassette 2, Side B; your overhead transparency of Blackline Master 47B; and an overhead projector.

Preparation: Project the overhead transparency of Blackline Master 47B.

Tell the children to listen carefully as **la maestra** asks questions about what's on the menu. Stop the tape at the sound of the harp to allow children time to look for each food on the menu and answer the question. **La maestra** asks the children if soup, quesadillas, bread, and tacos are on the menu.

¿Hay ___?	*Is/Are there ___?*
Sí, hay ___.	*Yes, there is/are ___.*
No, no hay ___.	*No, there isn't/aren't ___.*

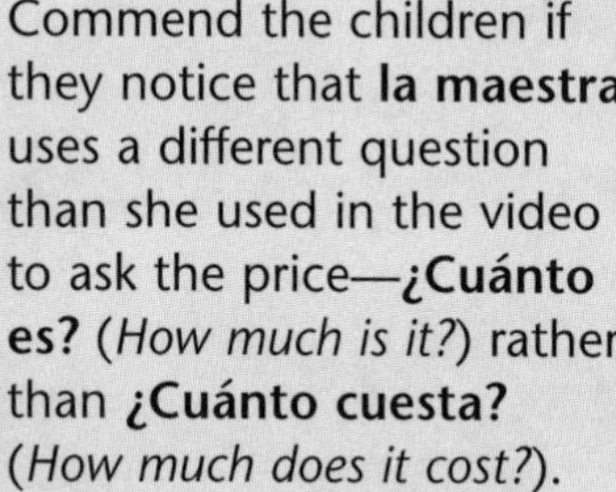

Commend the children if they notice that **la maestra** uses a different question than she used in the video to ask the price—**¿Cuánto es?** (*How much is it?*) rather than **¿Cuánto cuesta?** (*How much does it cost?*).

Activity 48B: How much does it cost?

Materials: Cassette player; Activity Cassette 2, Side B; your overhead transparency of Blackline Master 47B; and an overhead projector.

Preparation: Project the overhead transparency of Blackline Master 47B.

Pointing to the prices on the menu, remind them that the prices are in U.S. dollars. Tell the children to listen as **la maestra** asks LeeAnn how much soup, tacos, and milk cost according to the menu. Advise them to listen carefully so that they will know how to answer the questions when **la maestra** asks them. Play Activity 48B, stopping the tape at the sound of the harp so that children can locate the price of the food **la maestra** mentions and have time to state how much each item costs.

EN ESPAÑOL

The number **uno** (*one*) shortens to **un** before a masculine noun, e.g., **un dólar** (*one dollar*).

Activity 48C: More practice with prices

Preparation: Write the following prices (without the Spanish) on the chalkboard. As you point to each price, the children should say what it is.

$5.75	cinco, setenta y cinco *or* cinco dólares y setenta y cinco centavos (*cents*)
$1.15	uno, quince *or* un dólar y quince centavos
$12.98	doce, noventa y ocho *or* doce dólares y noventa y ocho centavos
$32.25	treinta y dos, veinticinco *or* treinta y dos dólares y veinticinco centavos

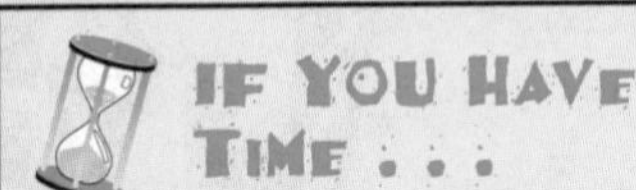

Have children work in pairs. Partners take turns writing down prices and saying them.

CLOSING

Tell the children that Spanish class is finished for today. In the next lesson they will sing some familiar songs and doña Elena will read two Fredo stories.

Lesson 49

> **Materials to gather**
>
> - VCR and Video Lesson 49 on Tape 17
> - Cassette player
> - Activity Cassette 2
> - Song Cassette
> - Overhead projector
> - Blackline Master 49B (professions game board)
> - Pennies (enough for half the class)
> - Small game piece place markers (one for each child)
> - Your overhead transparencies of Blackline Masters 1A, 5B, 10A-1, 10A-2, 15B, 31A, 33A, 37A-1, and 37A-2
> - ***Optional materials: "Las aventuras de Fredo"*** (*"Fredo's Adventures"*) books

Objectives

Language

- Recall vocabulary learned this year

Culture

- Recall the names of the twenty Spanish-speaking countries
- Remember places in the United States with Spanish names

Review

- Sing **"La canción de geografía"** (*"The Geography Song"*)
- Review three feeling expressions
- Read about Fredo's adventures in the music store and The Magic Café
- Sing the "Alphabet Rap"
- Sing **"En los Estados Unidos"** (*"In the United States"*)
- Count from 10 to 100 by tens
- Sing **"¿Adónde vas?"** (*"Where Are You Going?"*)
- Visit the Mexican restaurant

Vocabulary

No new vocabulary is introduced in this lesson.

Warm-up

Ask for a volunteer to lead the class in the opening conversation in which he/she greets the class and asks the children how they are (**V** = volunteer, **C** = class):

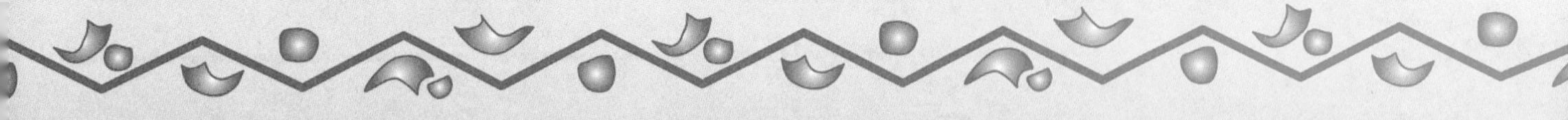

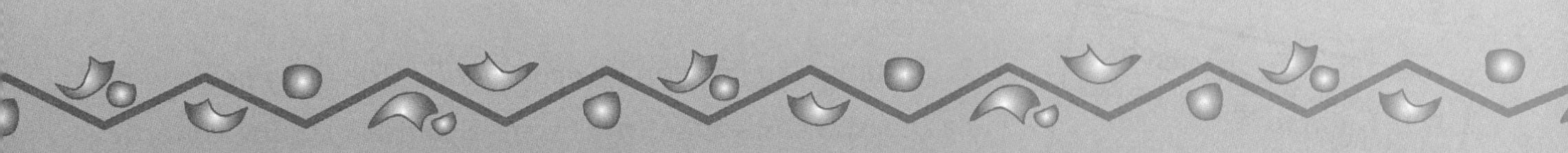

V: Buenos días (Buenas tardes), clase.	*Good morning (Good afternoon), class.*
C: Buenos días (Buenas tardes), ___.	*Good morning (Good afternoon), ___.*
V: ¿Cómo estás (tú?) *or* ¿Qué tal?	*How are you? or How's it going?*
C: Muy bien (Muy mal; Así, así), gracias. ¿Y tú?	*Very well (Very bad, (So-so), thank you. And you?*
V: Muy bien (Muy mal; Así, así), gracias.	*Very well (Very bad; So-so), thank you.*

Review

Ask the children what stories they've read about Fredo this year (his adventures in the music store, in the magic café, and in the city). Ask them what songs they've learned this year (songs about the twenty Spanish-speaking countries, places in the United States with Spanish names, and places/buildings they go to).

Fredo stories:

"La tienda de música" (*"The Music Store"*)

"El café mágico" (*"The Magic Café"*)

"En la ciudad" (*"In the City"*)

Song titles:

"La canción de geografía" (*"The Geography Song"*)

"En los Estados Unidos" (*"In the United States"*)

"¿Adónde vas?" (*"Where Are You Going?"*)

Introduce the video

Invite the children to listen and watch as **la maestra** sings many songs the children have heard this year and as doña Elena reads two stories about Fredo.

Other feeling expressions:

Muy contento/contenta.
(*Very happy.*)

Estoy triste.
(*I'm sad.*)

Estoy enojado/enojada.
(*I'm angry.*)

Tengo frío.
(*I'm cold.*)

Tengo calor.
(*I'm hot.*)

Tengo dolor.
(*I'm hurt.*)

Tengo miedo.
(*I'm afraid.*)

Tengo sed.
(*I'm thirsty.*)

Tengo sueño.
(*I'm sleepy.*)

Tengo hambre.
(*I'm hungry.*)

VIDEO LESSON

Encourage the children to sing along to the songs in this lesson.

1. Greeting the children

La maestra greets the children with **Hola, chicos** (*Hello, boys and girls*). She tells Winston, LeeAnn, and the children to relax and enjoy the lesson as she reviews much of what they have learned this year in Spanish.

2. Singing *"La canción de geografía"* ("The Geography Song")

La maestra sings about the twenty Spanish-speaking countries. For song lyrics, see Song 2 in the Song Appendix.

3. Reviewing three feeling expressions

As **la maestra** asks **¿Cómo está Lorena?** (*How is Lorena?*), Lorena dances to show the ways she feels. **La maestra** states how Lorena feels: **Está enojada** (*She's angry*), **Está contenta** (*She's happy*), and **Está triste** (*She's sad*).

4. Reviewing the names of musical instruments

Doña Elena reads **"La tienda de música"** (*"The Music Store"*)—the story about Fredo's adventures in the music store.

Mi amigo Fredo va a una tienda de música.	*My friend Fredo is going to a music store.*
Busca un instrumento musical.	*He's looking for a musical instrument.*
Aquí hay ___.	*Here is ___.*
¿Toca Fredo ___?	*Does Fredo play ___?*
No, no toca ___.	*No, he doesn't play ___.*
¿Y qué es esto?	*And what is this?*
Es ___.	*It's ___.*
Sí, toca ___.	*Yes, he plays ___.*
A Fredo le gusta la guitarra.	*Fredo likes the guitar.*
Ahora Fredo está contento y va a casa con su guitarra.	*Now Fredo is happy and he goes home with his guitar.*

Musical instruments (in story order):

la trompeta (*trumpet*)
el tambor (*drum*)
la flauta (*flute*)
el violín (*violin*)
la pandereta (*tambourine*)
el piano (*piano*)
el clarinete (*clarinet*)
la guitarra (*guitar*)

5. Reviewing the "Alphabet Rap"

Lorena dances to the "Alphabet Rap" as **la maestra** sings it. For rap lyrics, see Song 3 in the Song Appendix.

6. Singing *"En los Estados Unidos"* ("In the United States")

La maestra sings this song about places in the United States with Spanish names. For the lyrics, see Song 11 in the Song Appendix.

7. Reviewing fruit names and describing words

Doña Elena reads **"El café mágico"** (*"The Magic Café"*) about Fredo's Alice in Wonderland experiences in the Magic Café.

Fredo tiene hambre.	*Fredo is hungry.*
Busca un restaurante.	*He looks for a restaurant.*
Aquí está la entrada del café mágico.	*Here is the entrance to the Magic Café.*
Come ___.	*He eats ___.*
¿Qué pasa?	*What happens?*
Ahora Fredo está ___.	*Now Fredo is ___.*
Toma ___.	*He drinks ___.*
A Fredo le gusta la fruta.	*Fredo likes the fruit.*
A Fredo no le gusta estar sucio.	*Fredo doesn't like being dirty.*
Aquí está la salida del café mágico.	*Here is the exit from the Magic Café.*

8. Counting by tens

La maestra counts from 10 to 100 by tens as Lorena dances.

9. Reviewing building names

Doña Elena and **la maestra** sing **"¿Adónde vas?"** (*"Where Are You Going?"*). For song lyrics, see Song 10 in the Song Appendix.

10. Visiting the Mexican restaurant

La maestra and doña Elena talk with the waiter and with the musicians. For their statements, see Lesson 46, Video Lesson, section 7 and Lesson 47, Video Lesson, section 5.

Foods and adjectives
(in story order):

el plátano, alto
(*banana, tall*)

las fresas, bajo
(*strawberries, short*)

uvas, gordo
(*grapes, fat*)

el pan, delgado
(*bread, thin*)

el cereal, feo
(*cereal, ugly*)

la leche, bonito
(*milk, handsome*)

la manzana, sucio
(*apple, dirty*)

jugo, limpio
(*juice, clean*)

Numbers 10–100:

10	diez
20	veinte
30	treinta
40	cuarenta
50	cincuenta
60	sesenta
70	setenta
80	ochenta
90	noventa
100	cien

After viewing the video, praise the children for their good listening and watching skills.

Activity Lesson

Activity 49A: Read *"El café mágico"* (*"The Magic Café"*)

Note: If your school has ***"Las aventuras de Fredo"*** (*"Fredo's Adventures"*) books available for the children, substitute the Fredo Book Activity in the margin for this activity.

Materials: VCR; Video Lesson 49 on Tape 17.

Preparation: Recue Video Lesson 49 to section 7, in which doña Elena reads the story **"El café mágico."**

Tell the children to read along with doña Elena as she reads *"The Magic Café."* Play section 7 of the video with the sound. Remind the children to look for visual clues in the pictures and to listen and watch for words they know. Then rewind the tape to the beginning of the story and replay it without the sound, having the class as a whole read the story aloud with doña Elena.

If you have time, play the video a third time and have half of the class read the lines about Fredo's being hungry and what he eats and the other half the question **¿Qué pasa?** (*What happens?*) and the description of Fredo.

Activity 49B: I want to be a ___.

Materials: Cassette player; Activity Cassette 2, Side B; Blackline Master 49B; enough pennies for half of the class; small game piece place markers, one for each child.

Preparation: Copy Blackline Master 49B so that you have enough for half of the class.

Divide the class into pairs. Give each pair a copy of Blackline Master 49B, one penny, and two game piece place markers.

Explain that the Blackline Master is the game board. Review the "heads" and "tails" of the penny. Children each choose a place marker and place it on the word "Start" on their game boards. Tell them they will take turns tossing the coin and moving ahead—two spaces for "heads" and one space for "tails." For each picture they land on, they are to say *I want to be* + the name of the profession in the picture (**Quiero ser** ___). Boys should give the male name for the profession, e.g., **el maestro** (*male teacher*) and girls the female name, e.g., **la maestra** (*female teacher*). Tell them to listen as **la maestra** explains the game and reviews the names of the professions on the board game. The winner of the game is the one who gets to the "Finish" line first. Play Activity 49B. At the end of tape, allow the children several minutes to play the game.

Fredo Book Activity

Materials: Cassette player; ***"Las aventuras de Fredo"*** Book Two, **"El café mágico"** (*"The Magic Café"*) on Song Cassette, Side B; and ***"Las aventuras de Fredo"*** (*"Fredo's Adventures"*) books.

Tell the children they are going to read about Fredo's adventures in The Magic Café. Distribute your copies of ***"Las aventuras de Fredo"*** (*"Fredo's Adventures"*) among the children. Tell them to turn to the second story in the book—**"El café mágico"** (*"The Magic Café"*)—and to read along silently as doña Elena reads the story. Play the audio tape. Rewind the tape and have the class read the story aloud with doña Elena.

If you have time, play the tape a third time and have half of the class read the lines about Fredo's being hungry and what he eats and the other half the question **¿Qué pasa?** (*What happens?*) and the description of Fredo.

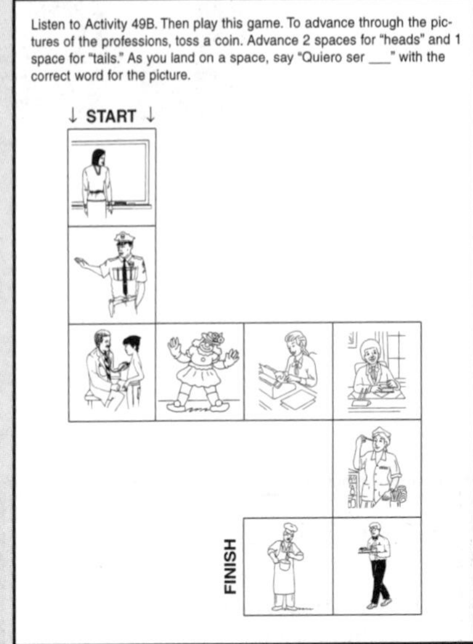

Listen to Activity 49B. Then play this game. To advance through the pictures of the professions, toss a coin. Advance 2 spaces for "heads" and 1 space for "tails." As you land on a space, say "Quiero ser ___" with the correct word for the picture.
↓ START ↓
FINISH

Blackline Master 49B

Professions shown are (from "Start" to "Finish"): **el maestro/la maestra** (*teacher*), **el policía/la policía** (*policeman/policewoman*), **el doctor/la doctora** (*doctor*), **el payaso/la payasa** (*clown*), **el secretario/la secretaria** (*secretary*), **el director/la directora** (*principal*), **el enfermero/la enfermera** (*nurse*), **el camarero/la camarera** (*waiter/waitress*), **el cocinero/la cocinera** (*cook*).

Activity 49C: Sing favorite songs

Materials: Cassette player; Song Cassette, Side A; overhead transparencies of the Blackline Masters listed below; and an overhead projector.

Ask the children which of the following songs they would like to sing. Project the lyrics and play the song on the Song Cassette. Encourage the children to sing along! For song lyrics with English equivalents, see the Song Appendix.

Song:	Blackline Master:
"Español para ti" (*"Spanish Is for You, and for Me"*)	1A
"La canción de geografía" (*"The Geography Song"*)	37A-1
"Alphabet Rap"	5B
"Months Rap"	10A-1
"Las estaciones" (*"The Seasons"*)	10A-2
"Las vocales" (*"The Vowel Tree Song"*)	15B
"Calendar Rap"	31A
"¿Adónde vas?" (*"Where Are You Going?"*)	33A
"En los Estados Unidos" (*"In the United States"*)	37A-2

CLOSING

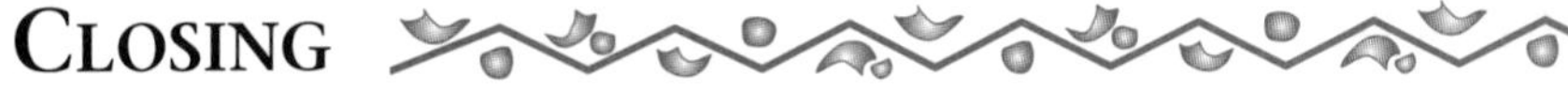

Tell the children that Spanish class is finished for today. In the next lesson children will learn a new song about colors.

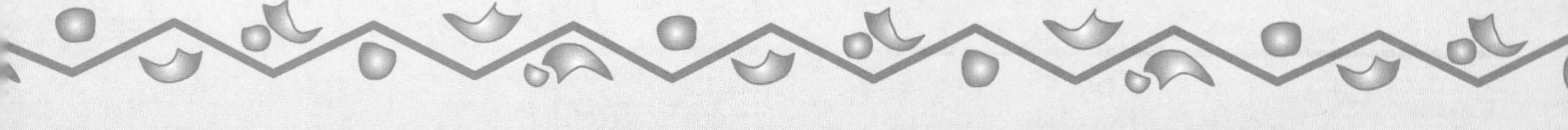

Lesson 50

Materials to gather

- VCR and Video Lesson 50 on Tape 17
- Cassette player
- Song Cassette
- Colored paintbrushes from Lesson 4 Review
- Overhead projector
- Blank transparency
- Overhead transparency of Blackline Master 31A ("Calendar Rap")
- Blackline Masters 50B-1 (word puzzle) and 50B-2 (answers)
- Blackline Master 50C (matching game)
- Pencils
- Current calendar
- Current Month Picture
- Gold Flashcards 20–27
- ***Optional materials:*** blank paper; colored markers or pencils; and children's dictionary pages

Objectives

Language

- Learn two new sentences for talking about the day of the week
- Learn the names of many animals

Culture

- Learn a Spanish children's song about colors
- Understand that llamas come from South America

Review

- Review the days of the week
- Sing the "Calendar Rap"

Vocabulary

¿Qué pasa?	*What's going on?*
Nada.	*Nothing.*
Hoy es ___.	*Today is ___.*
Mañana es ___.	*Tomorrow is ___.*
el perro	*dog*
el gato	*cat*
la gallina	*chicken*
el conejo	*rabbit*
el gallo	*rooster*
la vaca	*cow*
el cerdo	*pig*
el caballo	*horse*

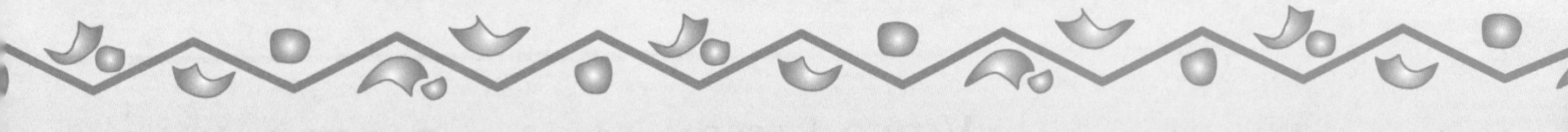

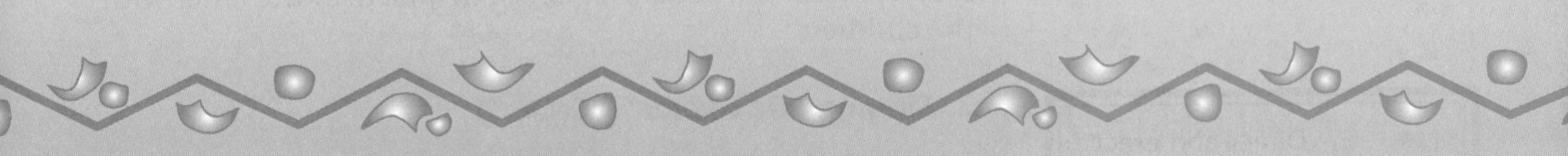

la cabra	*goat*
la llama	*llama*
la jirafa	*giraffe*
la foca	*seal*
el pato	*duck*
el elefante	*elephant*

Warm-up

Talk with the children about their favorite animals. Ask them to describe in English their pets or animals they've seen at the zoo. Children who have been through levels 1–3 of ***Español para ti*** may be able to recall the names of the following animals in Spanish:

el perro	*dog*	el gallo	*rooster*
el gato	*cat*	la vaca	*cow*
la gallina	*chicken*	el cerdo	*pig*
el conejo	*rabbit*	el caballo	*horse*

Review

Materials: Your colored paintbrushes (from Lesson 4).

Hold up one paintbrush at a time with the Spanish color word covered up. Ask the children to name the color. If you feel comfortable, ask **¿De qué color es ___?** (*What color is ___?*).

Introduce the video

Invite the children to listen and watch as **la maestra** visits a ranch and describes some of the animals there.

Colors:

amarillo	*yellow*
anaranjado	*orange*
azul	*blue*
blanco	*white*
café	*brown*
gris	*gray*
morado	*purple*
negro	*black*
rojo	*red*
rosado	*pink*
verde	*green*

Video Lesson

1. Greeting the children

La maestra greets the children with **Buenos días** (*Good morning*). She asks them how they are. She greets Winston and asks him **¿Qué tal?** (*How's it going?*) and **¿Qué pasa?** (*What's going on?*). He tells her **Nada** (*Nothing*). She practices the latter with the children.

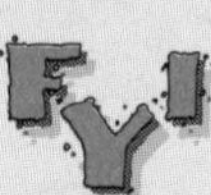

Direct and exact translations are almost never possible for songs. In translating songs, the translator tries to provide the sentiment of the song while using poetic language that fits into the rhymes and rhythms.

2. Singing *"De colores"* ("*Colors*")

La maestra sings a new song, which Spanish-speaking children learn when they are very young.

Rojo, amarillo, morado— los colores.	*Red, yellow, purple—* *the colors.*
De colores, de colores se visten los campos en la primavera.	*In colors, the countryside is* *dressed in colors in spring.*
De colores, de colores son los pajaritos que vienen de afuera.	*In colors, the little birds that* *come from afar are in colors.*
De colores, de colores es el arco iris que vemos lucir.	*In colors, the rainbow that* *we see shining is in colors.*
Y por eso los grandes amores de muchos colores me gustan a mí.	*And that is why true loves of* *many colors are pleasing to me.*
Y por eso los grandes amores de muchos colores me gustan a mí.	*And that is why true loves of* *many colors are pleasing to me.*
Los colores.	*The colors.*

Days of the week:

lunes	*Monday*
martes	*Tuesday*
miércoles	*Wednesday*
jueves	*Thursday*
viernes	*Friday*
sábado	*Saturday*
domingo	*Sunday*

3. Reviewing the days of the week

When **la maestra** asks Winston **¿Qué días de la semana estamos en la clase?** (*Which days of the week are we in class?*), he recites the first five days of the week. Then they review the days in the weekend (**el fin de semana**).

4. Singing the "Calendar Rap"

La maestra and the children sing the "Calendar Rap." For the lyrics with the English equivalents, see Activity 50A in this lesson.

5. Introducing two new sentences about days of the week

Winston and the children read new sentences: **Hoy es** ___ (*Today is* ___) and **Mañana es** ___ (*Tomorrow is* ___).

6. Presenting animals

La maestra asks Winston **¿Quiénes son tus amigos?** (*Who are your friends?*) and **¿Tienes amigos que son animales?** (*Do you have friends who are animals?*). Using Gold Flashcards, **la maestra** asks **¿Qué animal es?** (*What animal is it?*) and **¿Qué dice ___?** (*What does ___ say?*).

7. Visiting *el rancho* (*ranch*)

La maestra takes the children on a tour of a ranch. Some of her statements follow.

Este caballo se llama Tara Lynn y este caballo se llama Ginger.	*This horse is named Tara Lynn and this horse is named Ginger.*
Tara Lynn es un caballo grande y Ginger es un caballo pequeño.	*Tara Lynn is a large horse and Ginger is a small horse.*
Los animales son nuestros amigos y los caballos son muy bonitos.	*Animals are our friends and the horses are very pretty.*
¿Qué ponen las gallinas? Huevos.	*What do the chickens lay? Eggs.*
Las gallinas son muy importantes.	*Chickens are very important.*
El cerdo es muy grande y muy gordo, pero es muy simpático.	*The pig is very big and very fat, but he is very nice.*
Ahora el cerdo duerme.	*Now the pig is sleeping.*
Tiene sueño.	*He's tired.*
Y aquí estoy con una cabra.	*And here I am with a goat.*
La llama vive en Sudamérica.	*The llama lives in South America.*

8. Playing a choosing game

La maestra plays the choosing game with the children.

¿Es el perro o es el gato?	*Is it the dog or is it the cat?*
Es el gato.	*It's the cat.*

9. Introducing the names of several wild animals

La maestra introduces the names of several wild animals: **la jirafa** (*giraffe*); **el pato** (*duck*); **la foca** (*seal*); **el elefante** (*elephant*).

10. Closing

La maestra sings **"De colores"** (*"Colors"*). She and Winston bid the children **Hasta luego** (*See you later*) and **Hasta la vista** (*Until we meet again*).

Animals:

el perro	*dog*
el gato	*cat*
la gallina	*chicken*
el conejo	*rabbit*
el gallo	*rooster*
la vaca	*cow*
el cerdo	*pig*
el caballo	*horse*

CROSS-CULTURAL CONNECTIONS

Some animal sounds in Spanish vary from those in English. Rooster: **qui-qui-ri-quí** (*cock-a-doodle-doo*); dog: **guau-guau** (*bow-wow*); and horse: **ji-ji** (*neigh-neigh*).

¡Mira! (*Look!*)

After viewing the video, praise the children for their good listening and watching skills.

Activity Lesson

Activity 50A: Sing the "Calendar Rap"

Materials: Cassette player; "Calendar Rap" on Song Cassette, Side A; the overhead transparency of Blackline Master 31A; and an overhead projector.

Project the overhead transparency. Ask the children with what day of the week calendars in Spanish-speaking countries begin (**lunes**—*Monday*). Tell them they are going to practice the days of the week by singing the "Calendar Rap." Play the song, pointing to the lyrics on the transparency as the children sing.

Lunes, martes, miércoles, tres.	*Monday, Tuesday, Wednesday, three.*
Uno, dos, tres.	*One, two, three.*
Jueves, viernes, sábado, seis.	*Thursday, Friday, Saturday, six.*
Uno, dos, tres, cuatro, cinco, seis.	*One, two, three, four, five, six.*
Y domingo siete es.	*And Sunday is seven.*
Uno, dos, tres, cuatro, cinco, seis, siete.	*One, two, three, four, five, six, seven.*

Activity 50B: Find the words

Materials: Blackline Masters 50B-1 and 50B-2; a current calendar; a blank transparency; an overhead projector; the current Month Picture; and pencils.

Preparation: Make an overhead transparency of Blackline Master 50B-2. Copy and distribute Blackline Master 50B-1 so that each child has a copy.

Tell the children to write their names and the date on the top of their papers. If they need help with the date, point to the number of the day on a current calendar and then to the name of the month on the Month Picture. Explain that the names for the days of the week are hidden in the letter grid. The names run from left to right and from top to bottom. Tell them to find each name and circle it. Point out that all the days of the week appear in the word bank (**Palabras**) if they need to see how they are spelled. After they have found all the names of the days of the week, they should write the names on the lines below the grid—in Spanish calendar order from Monday to Sunday. When the children have completed the activity, project your overhead transparency of Blackline Master 50B-2 and allow children time to check their answers.

Word Search: Days of the Week

The names of the seven days of the week are hidden in this puzzle. Find them and circle them. Then write the words you found in the blanks below. The words go from left to right and from top to bottom in the puzzle. Use the word bank to help you.

E	L	F	E	R	M	M	R	O	F	G	F	Y	R	R
M	U	X	D	O	M	I	N	G	O	I	U	V	W	Z
C	N	H	D	I	E	É	M	T	Á	N	T	R	Ñ	O
E	E	A	O	I	S	R	C	J	U	E	V	E	S	O
S	S	N	C	B	T	C	S	B	O	L	O	S	O	T
P	A	T	T	N	R	O	N	I	N	E	L	N	K	S
A	R	E	O	P	O	L	V	T	Ñ	S	B	M	A	U
Ñ	B	A	R	O	N	E	E	S	M	A	R	T	E	S
O	X	M	A	T	E	S	D	I	R	E	C	T	O	R
V	I	E	R	N	E	S	O	D	I	T	Z	I	E	V
Z	H	U	C	I	É	N	C	I	A	S	R	C	R	Ñ
Y	M	Y	T	Y	M	I	C	A	S	Á	B	A	D	O

Palabras

sábado martes jueves domingo lunes viernes miércoles

Blackline Master 50B-1

Answer Key

Word Search: Days of the Week

The names of the seven days of the week are hidden in this puzzle. Find them and circle them. Then write the words you found in the blanks below. The words go from left to right and from top to bottom in the puzzle. Use the word bank to help you.

E	L	F	E	R	M	M	R	O	F	G	F	Y	R	R
M	U	X	D	O	M	I	N	G	O	I	U	V	W	Z
C	N	H	D	I	E	É	M	T	Á	N	T	R	Ñ	O
E	E	A	O	I	S	R	C	J	U	E	V	E	S	O
S	S	N	C	B	T	C	S	B	O	L	O	S	O	T
P	A	T	T	N	R	O	N	I	N	E	L	N	K	S
A	R	E	O	P	O	L	V	T	Ñ	S	B	M	A	U
Ñ	B	A	R	O	N	E	E	S	M	A	R	T	E	S
O	X	M	A	T	E	S	D	I	R	E	C	T	O	R
V	I	E	R	N	E	S	O	D	I	T	Z	I	E	V
Z	H	U	C	I	É	N	C	I	A	S	R	C	R	Ñ
Y	M	Y	T	Y	M	I	C	A	S	Á	B	A	D	O

Palabras

sábado martes jueves domingo lunes viernes miércoles

LUNES VIERNES
MARTES SÁBADO
MIÉRCOLES DOMINGO
JUEVES

Blackline Master 50B-2

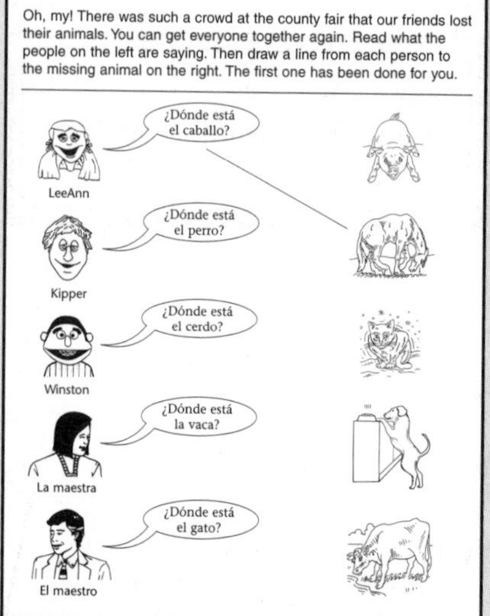

Oh, my! There was such a crowd at the county fair that our friends lost their animals. You can get everyone together again. Read what the people on the left are saying. Then draw a line from each person to the missing animal on the right. The first one has been done for you.

¿Dónde está el caballo?
LeeAnn
¿Dónde está el perro?
Kipper
¿Dónde está el cerdo?
Winston
¿Dónde está la vaca?
La maestra
¿Dónde está el gato?
El maestro

Blackline Master 50C

Activity 50C: Where is . . . ?

Materials: Gold Flashcards 20–27; Blackline Master 50C; a current calendar; the current Month Picture; and pencils.

Preparation: Copy Blackline Master 50C so that you have one copy for each child. Do not distribute them yet. Display the Gold Flashcards.

Review animal vocabulary with the children by pointing to each Gold Flashcard and asking the children to name the animal.

Gold Flashcards:

#20	el perro	*dog*	#24	el gallo	*rooster*
#21	el gato	*cat*	#25	la vaca	*cow*
#22	la gallina	*chicken*	#26	el cerdo	*pig*
#23	el conejo	*rabbit*	#27	el caballo	*horse*

Now distribute the copies of Blackline Master 50C and have the children fill in their names and the date. If they need help with the date, point to the calendar and then to the month on the current Month Picture. Tell them that each person shown on the Blackline Master is asking where an animal on the right is. Children should draw a line from the question to the appropriate animal. Ask volunteers to read each question aloud. Then allow children time to read the questions to themselves and complete the activity. Children should have drawn lines as follows: from Kipper to the dog; from Winston to the pig; from **la maestra** to the cow; from **el maestro** to the cat.

CLOSING

Tell the children that Spanish class is finished for today. In the next lesson children will hear the new song about colors again and visit a zoo.

EN ESPAÑOL

When reviewing animal names, ask **¿Qué animal es?** (*What animal is it?*) if you feel comfortable.

DICTIONARY

Materials: Gold Flashcards 20–27; blank paper; markers or colored pencils; and children's dictionary pages.

Preparation: Display Gold Flashcards 20–27 against or on the chalkboard and write the Spanish name of each animal above its picture. See Activity 50C for the animal names.

Tell the children to draw a picture of their favorite animal of those pictured in the Gold Flashcards. When they have finished their drawing, they should write the Spanish word for the animal underneath the drawing and the first letter of the animal word on the top of the page. Have children alphabetize their new page among their dictionary pages.

Lesson 51

Materials to gather

- VCR and Video Lesson 51 on Tape 17
- Cassette player
- Song Cassette
- Overhead projector
- Blank transparency
- Blackline Master 51A ("**De colores**")
- Blackline Master 51C (sentences and wild animals)
- Red Flashcards 68–75
- Colored markers or pencils in blue, red, black, yellow, orange, purple, gray, and pink (one set for each child)
- ***Optional materials:*** overhead transparency of Blackline Master 10A-1 ("Months Rap"); blank paper; colored markers or pencils; and children's dictionary pages

Objectives

Language

- Learn the names of more wild animals
- Understand a sustained conversation about animals at the San Diego Zoo

Culture

- Learn that it is important to care for all animals
- Categorize animals as domestic, farm/ranch, and wild

Review

- Sing "**De colores**" (*"Colors"*)
- Practice four color names

Vocabulary

el campo	*country(side)*
el jardín zoológico	*zoo*
¿Qué animal es?	*What animal is it?*
las jirafas	*giraffes*
el pájaro/los pájaros	*bird/birds*
las focas	*seals*
los patos	*ducks*
los elefantes	*elephants*
el pez/los peces	*fish*
el león/los leones	*lion/lions*
el tigre/los tigres	*tiger/tigers*
el gorila/los gorilas	*gorilla/gorillas*
la cebra/las cebras	*zebra/zebras*
simpático/simpática	*friendly; nice*

Warm-up

Materials: Cassette player; **"De colores"** (*"Colors"*) on the Song Cassette, Side A.

Let the children know it's time for Spanish class (**la clase de español**) by playing the new song **"De colores"** (*"Colors"*) on the Song Cassette. Encourage the children to hum along. For lyrics, see Song 12 in the Song Appendix.

Review

Materials: Red Flashcards 68–70.

Hold up Red Flashcard 68 and point to the giraffe. Ask the children to tell you the word in Spanish for the animal (**la jirafa**). Hold up Red Flashcard 69. Pointing to the seal, ask the children if they can remember what that animal is called in Spanish (**la foca**). Point to the elephant on Red Flashcard 70 and ask the same question (**el elefante**).

Introduce the video

Invite the children to listen and watch as **la maestra** and LeeAnn sing the song about colors and as **la maestra**, LeeAnn, and Kipper visit the San Diego Zoo!

EN ESPAÑOL

If you feel comfortable, ask **¿Qué animal es?** (*What animal is it?*) as you point to each animal.

VIDEO LESSON

1. Greeting the children

La maestra greets the children and LeeAnn with **Buenas tardes** (*Good afternoon*). **La maestra** says **Estoy muy contenta porque estoy en el campo** (*I'm very happy because I'm in the countryside*).

2. Singing *"De colores"* ("Colors")

La maestra explains several lines from the song before she and LeeAnn sing it.

De colores, de colores se visten los campos en la primavera.	*In colors, the countryside is dressed in colors in spring.*
De colores, de colores son los pajaritos que vienen de afuera.	*In colors, the little birds that come from afar are in colors.*
De colores, de colores es el arco iris que vemos lucir.	*In colors, the rainbow that we see shining is in colors.*
Y por eso los grandes amores de muchos colores me gustan a mí.	*And that is why true loves of many colors are pleasing to me.*
Y por eso los grandes amores de muchos colores me gustan a mí.	*And that is why true loves of many colors are pleasing to me.*

3. Practicing *los colores* (*colors*)

LeeAnn and **la maestra** describe the colors of things they are wearing: **Mi chaqueta es rosada** (*My jacket is pink*), **La camisa es roja** (*The shirt is red*). **La maestra** points to colored shapes and asks **¿De qué color es?** (*What color is it?*). As she reveals each color, the word appears on the screen: **rojo** (*red*); **morado** (*purple*); **azul** (*blue*); **anaranjado** (*orange*).

4. Reviewing the names of domestic and ranch animals

La maestra explains that domestic animals live **en la casa** (*in the house*), farm animals live **en el rancho** (*on the ranch*), and wild animals live **en el campo y en el zoológico** (*in the countryside and in the zoo*). She shows Gold Flashcards of **los animales domésticos y los animales del rancho** (*domestic animals and farm animals*) and asks the children to identify and describe the animals.

¿Qué animal es?	*What animal is it?*
Es ___.	*It's ___.*
¿De qué color es ___?	*What color is ___?*
¿Cómo es?	*What's it like?*
el cerdo	*pig*
la vaca	*cow*
el gato	*cat*
el caballo	*horse*
el perro	*dog*

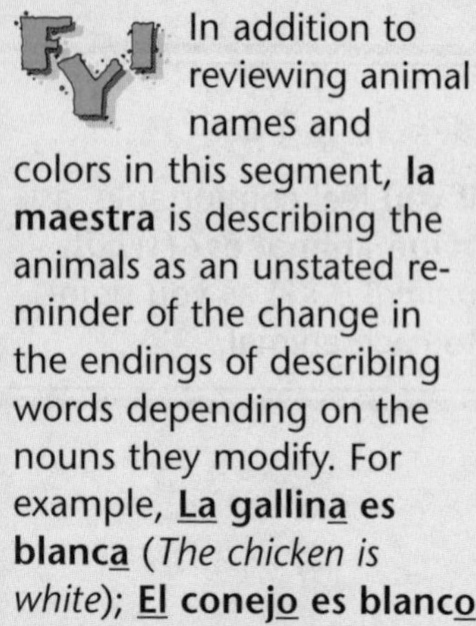

FYI In addition to reviewing animal names and colors in this segment, **la maestra** is describing the animals as an unstated reminder of the change in the endings of describing words depending on the nouns they modify. For example, **La gallina es blanca** (*The chicken is white*); **El conejo es blanco** (*The rabbit is white*).

In talking about the animals, **la maestra** also asks **¿Es grande o es pequeño?** (*Is it large or small?*) and **¿Es un animal de la casa o del rancho?** (*Is it a house animal or a ranch animal?*). Of the dog, LeeAnn says **Es feo** (*He's ugly*), but **la maestra** tells her **Es bonito** (*He's pretty*).

la gallina	*chicken*
el conejo	*rabbit*
el gallo	*rooster*

5. Reviewing wild animals and introducing new ones

La maestra reminds the children that many of the names of wild animals are cognates and thus easy to learn. She shows Red Flashcards of each animal and says the word. The children repeat after her.

la jirafa	*giraffe*	el pez	*fish*
el pájaro	*bird*	el león	*lion*
la foca	*seal*	el tigre	*tiger*
el pato	*duck*	el gorila	*gorilla*
el elefante	*elephant*	la cebra	*zebra*

6. Visiting a zoo

LeeAnn and Winston are very excited as they visit the San Diego Zoo with **la maestra.**

Aquí estoy en el jardín zoológico.	*Here I am in the zoo.*
Vamos a ver los animales.	*We are going to see the animals.*
La jirafa es muy alta y tiene un cuello muy largo.	*The giraffe is very tall and has a very long neck.*
Aquí están unos pájaros muy grandes.	*Here are some very large birds.*
La foca es negra y come mucho pescado.	*The seal is black and eats a lot of fish.*
Los patos nadan en el agua.	*The ducks swim in the water.*
El elefante es muy grande y muy gordo y tiene una nariz muy larga.	*The elephant is very large and very fat and he has a very long nose.*
El león es muy feroz y come carne.	*The lion is very ferocious and he eats meat.*
Este tigre es blanco y negro y es muy grande.	*This tiger is white and black and he is very big.*
Aquí están los gorilas. Es una familia.	*Here are the gorillas. It's a family.*
¿Es un caballo en pijama?	*Is it a horse in pajamas?*
Es la cebra y la cebra es blanca y negra.	*It's the zebra and the zebra is white and black.*

7. Closing

La maestra mentions the importance of protecting animals whether they be wild, domestic, or ranch animals. She and LeeAnn say **Adiós** (*Good-bye*), **Hasta luego** (*See you later*), and **Hasta la vista** (*Until we meet again*).

FYI **El pez** is used to refer to live fish; **el pescado** is used to refer to a fish that has been caught.

After viewing the video, praise the children for their good listening and watching skills.

ACTIVITY LESSON

Activity 51A: Sing the new song about colors

Materials: Cassette player; **"De colores"** (*"Colors"*) on the Song Cassette, Side A; Blackline Master 51A; a blank overhead transparency; and an overhead projector.

Preparation: Make an overhead transparency of Blackline Master 51A. Project the transparency.

Ask the children what season the song is about (**la primavera**—*spring*). Tell them they are going to start learning the song. (1) Tell the children to just listen the first time you play the song. (2) Then, play the song again, pointing to each line as it is sung, encouraging the children to sing along. (3) Now play the song line by line, stopping the tape after each line. The children should listen to each line and then sing it. (4) Finally, play the song straight through. Encourage the children to sing along.

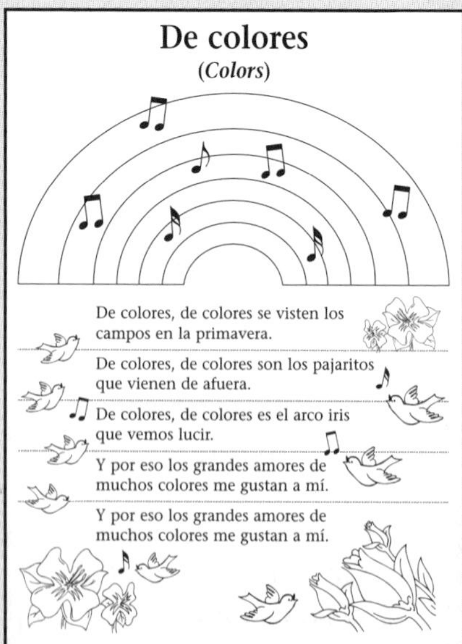

De colores
(Colors)
De colores, de colores se visten los campos en la primavera.
De colores, de colores son los pajaritos que vienen de afuera.
De colores, de colores es el arco iris que vemos lucir.
Y por eso los grandes amores de muchos colores me gustan a mí.
Y por eso los grandes amores de muchos colores me gustan a mí.

Blackline Master 51A

Activity 51B: Practice the names of the wild animals

Materials: Red Flashcards 68–75.

Review the names of the wild animals with the children. Hold up one Red Flashcard at a time and ask the children what the animal is called in Spanish. If you feel comfortable, ask **¿Qué animal es?** (*What animal is it?*).

Red Flashcards:

#68 (left)	la jirafa	*giraffe*
#68 (right)	el pájaro	*bird*
#69 (left)	la foca	*seal*
#69 (right)	el pato	*duck*
#70	el elefante	*elephant*
#71	el pez	*fish* (singular)
	los peces	*fish* (plural)
#72	el león	*lion*
#73	el tigre	*tiger*
#74	el gorila	*gorilla*
#75	la cebra	*zebra*

Materials: Red Flashcards 68–75; blank paper; colored markers or pencils; and children's dictionary pages.

Preparation: Display Red Flashcards 68–75 against or on the chalkboard and write the Spanish name of each animal above its picture. See Activity 51B for the animal names.

Tell the children to draw and color a picture of their favorite animal of those pictured in the Red Flashcards. When they have finished their drawings, they should write the Spanish word for the animal underneath the drawing and the first letter of the animal word on the top of the page. Have children alphabetize their new page among their dictionary pages.

Activity 51C: Match the sentences with the drawings and color the animals

Materials: Blackline Master 51C; colored markers or pencils in these colors: blue, red, black, yellow, orange, purple, gray, and pink (one set for each child).

Preparation: Copy and distribute Blackline Master 51C so that each child has a copy.

Point out that in the center are sentences describing the pictures on either side. Children should draw a line from each sentence to the animal it describes. Then they should color the animals according to the color stated in the sentence. **¡Qué extraño!** (*How strange!*) Once the children have colored the animals, ask volunteers to say what color each animal really should be.

Children should have matched the sentences and colored the animals as follows:

La jirafa es azul.	*The giraffe is blue.*
El elefante es rojo.	*The elephant is red.*
El pez es negro.	*The fish is black.*
La cebra es amarilla y verde.	*The zebra is yellow and green.*
El gorila es anaranjado.	*The gorilla is orange.*
El león es morado.	*The lion is purple.*
El pájaro es gris.	*The bird is gray.*
La foca es rosada.	*The seal is pink.*

¡Qué extraño! You will color these animals in strange ways. First, draw a line from the sentence to the animal. Then follow the directions and color the animals as you read about them.

La jirafa es azul.
El elefante es rojo.
El pez es negro.
La cebra es amarilla y verde.
El gorila es anaranjado.
El león es morado.
El pájaro es gris.
La foca es rosada.

Blackline Master 51C

Materials: Cassette player; the "Months Rap" on the Song Cassette; overhead transparency of Blackline Master 10A-1; and an overhead projector.

Project the transparency. Play the song and have the children sing along.

CLOSING

Tell the children that Spanish class is finished for today. In the next lesson children will read a new story about Fredo and visit the zoo again.

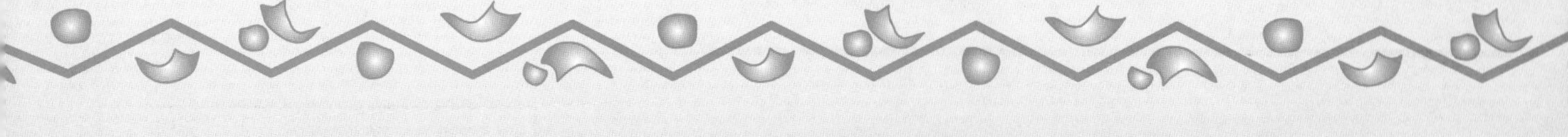

Lesson 52

Materials to gather

- VCR and Video Lesson 52 on Tape 18
- Cassette player
- Song Cassette
- Overhead projector
- Blank overhead transparency
- Overhead transparency of Blackline Master 10A-1 ("Months Rap")
- Overhead transparency of Blackline Master 51A (**"De colores"**)
- Red Flashcards 68–75
- Blackline Masters 52C (animal crossword puzzle)
- Pencils
- Current calendar
- Current Month Picture
- ***Optional materials:* "*Las aventuras de Fredo*" ("*Fredo's Adventures*") books**

Objectives

Language

- Comprehend more of the trip to the San Diego Zoo
- Read about Fredo's adventures at the zoo
- Express what animal one likes

Culture

- Sing **"De colores"** (*"Colors"*)

Review

- Sing the "Months Rap"
- Practice animal vocabulary

Vocabulary

el oso/los osos	*bear/bears*
¿Qué animal te gusta?	*What animal do you like?*
Me gusta ___.	*I like ___.*

Warm-up

Materials: Cassette player; **"De colores"** (*"Colors"*) on the Song Cassette, Side A; your overhead transparency of Blackline Master 51A; and an overhead projector

Let the children know it's time for Spanish class (**la clase de español**). Ask them what the new song they've heard in the last few lessons is about (colors, countryside, spring). Project the overhead transparency of Blackline Master 51A and play the song. Point to each line as **la maestra** sings and tell the children to follow along, singing and humming what they remember. For the lyrics with English equivalents, see Song 12 in the Song Appendix.

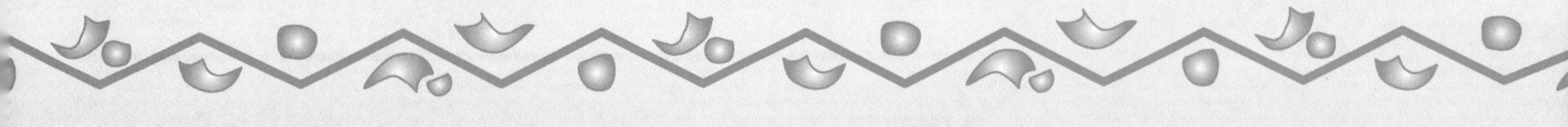

Review

Materials: Red Flashcards 68–75.

Review the names of the animals by holding up Red Flashcards one at a time and having the children call out the name of the animal. If you feel comfortable, ask **¿Qué animal es?** (*What animal is it?*) as you hold up each picture.

Red Flashcards:

#68 (left)	la jirafa	*giraffe*
#68 (right)	el pájaro	*bird*
#69 (left)	la foca	*seal*
#69 (right)	el pato	*duck*
#70	el elefante	*elephant*
#71	el pez	*fish* (singular)
	los peces	*fish* (plural)
#72	el león	*lion*
#73	el tigre	*tiger*
#74	el gorila	*gorilla*
#75	la cebra	*zebra*

Introduce the video

Invite the children to listen and watch as **la maestra** reviews the animal names with them and as doña Elena reads another Fredo adventure story.

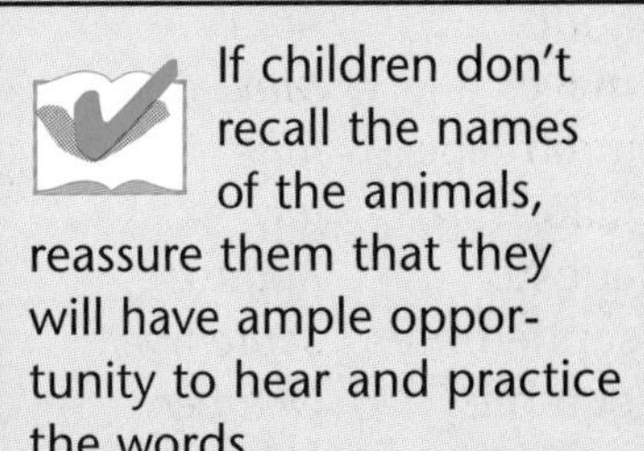

If children don't recall the names of the animals, reassure them that they will have ample opportunity to hear and practice the words.

VIDEO LESSON

Los meses del año
(*the months of the year*):

enero	*January*
febrero	*February*
marzo	*March*
abril	*April*
mayo	*May*
junio	*June*
julio	*July*
agosto	*August*
septiembre	*September*
octubre	*October*
noviembre	*November*
diciembre	*December*

1. Greeting the children

La maestra greets the children with **Buenos días** (*Good morning*) and asks them how they are. She tells them **Estoy muy bien porque estoy aquí con mi amigo Kipper** (*I'm very well because I'm here with my friend Kipper*). She asks Kipper **¿Qué pasa?** (*What's happening?*). He answers **Nada** (*Nothing*).

2. Singing the "Months Rap"

La maestra asks Kipper **¿Cuándo es tu cumpleaños?** (*When is your birthday?*), to which he replies **En marzo** (*In March*); she says that her birthday is **En enero** (*In January*). **La maestra** sings the "Months Rap." For the lyrics, see Song 4 in the Song Appendix. Showing Kipper and the children a card with the word **enero** (*January*), followed by a blank and then the word **marzo** (*March*), **la maestra** asks **¿Qué falta?** (*What's missing?*): **febrero** (*February*).

3. Visiting the San Diego Zoo

La maestra, Kipper, and LeeAnn visit the zoo. For more of their conversation, see Lesson 51, Video Lesson, section 6.

Y ésta es la entrada.	*And this is the entrance.*
Es un jardín zoológico muy grande.	*It's a very big zoo.*
Hay muchos animales en el zoológico.	*There are many animals in the zoo.*
Vamos a ver los leones y los tigres y los elefantes.	*We are going to see the lions, the tigers, and the elephants.*
Yo quiero ver las focas y los gorilas.	*I want to see the seals and the gorillas.*
Aquí están dos jirafas de la misma familia.	*Here are two giraffes of the same family.*
Aquí viven los pájaros.	*The birds live here.*
Hay patos pequeños y hay patos grandes.	*There are small ducks and big ducks.*
Es un animal enorme.	*It's an enormous animal.*
Y este tigre juega.	*And this tiger is playing.*
¡Qué grandes son los gorilas!	*How big the gorillas are!*

4. Reviewing animal vocabulary

Showing the children and Kipper Red Flashcards of animals, **la maestra** asks **¿Qué animal es?** (*What animal is it?*).

la girafa	*giraffe*	el pez	*fish*
el pájaro	*bird*	el león	*lion*
la foca	*seal*	el tigre	*tiger*
el pato	*duck*	el gorila	*gorilla*
el elefante	*elephant*	la cebra	*zebra*

5. Playing *¿Qué animal es?* (*What animal is it?*)

La maestra shows the children pictures from the trip to the zoo and asks **¿Qué animal es?** (*What animal is it?*). The name of each animal appears on the screen. **La maestra** tells the children **Me gustan los animales** (*I like animals*).

6. Reading another story about Fredo's adventures

Doña Elena reads **"En el jardín zoológico"** (*"At the Zoo"*). Some of the text follows.

Ésta es la entrada del jardín zoológico.	*This is the entrance to the zoo.*
Fredo va a visitar a sus amigos, los animales.	*Fredo is going to visit his friends, the animals.*
Fredo visita a su amigo, el elefante.	*Fredo visits his friend, the elephant.*
¿Cómo es el elefante?	*What is the elephant like?*
Es grande, gordo y gris.	*He's big, fat, and gray.*
Fredo visita a su amiga, la jirafa.	*Fredo visits his friend, the giraffe.*
¿Cómo es la jirafa?	*What is the giraffe like?*
Es alta, muy alta.	*It's tall, very tall.*
Ahora, Fredo tiene hambre y visita a su amigo, el oso.	*Now Fredo is hungry and visits his friend, the bear.*
Pero, aquí viene el guardián.	*But, here comes the zookeeper.*
El guardián está enojado.	*The zookeeper is angry.*
Aquí está la salida del jardín zoológico.	*Here is the exit to the zoo.*

Since this is the first time this story is read, you might advise the children just to listen and look at the pictures as doña Elena reads. They will understand a great deal by looking at the pictures for visual clues and listening for words they recognize.

7. Identifying animals

Showing the children Red Flashcards of animals, **la maestra** plays a choosing game: **¿Es el elefante o es el león?** (*Is it the elephant or is it the lion?*); **Es el león** (*It's the lion*).

8. Singing the song about colors

La maestra sings **"De colores"** (*"Colors"*). For song lyrics, see Song 12 in the Song Appendix.

9. Saying what animal one likes

La maestra introduces the following question and teaches the children how to answer it.

¿Qué animal te gusta?	*What animal do you like?*
Me gusta ___.	*I like ___.*

After viewing the video, praise the children for their good listening and watching skills.

10. Closing

Kipper and **la maestra** bid the children **Hasta luego** (*See you later*) and **Adiós** (*Good-bye*).

Activity Lesson

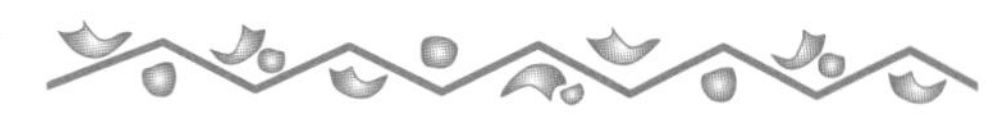

Activity 52A: Sing the "Months Rap"

Materials: Cassette player; "Months Rap" on Song Cassette, Side A; your overhead transparency of Blackline Master 10A-1; and an overhead projector.

Project the overhead transparency of Blackline Master 10A-1. Tell the children they are going to sing the rap about the months of the year. Before they rap, ask them what's different about the months in Spanish as compared to English (they aren't capitalized). Ask too what month names sound alike and share the same meaning in Spanish and English (all except **enero**—*January*). Have a volunteer point to each line of the rap as it is sung. Play the "Months Rap" on the Song Cassette and encourage the children to sing along. For the lyrics with English equivalents, see Song 4 in the Song Appendix.

Activity 52B: Read *"En el jardín zoológico"* (*"At the Zoo"*)

Note: If your school has ***"Las aventuras de Fredo"*** (*"Fredo's Adventures"*) books available for the children, substitute the Fredo Book Activity in the margin for this activity.

Materials: VCR; Video Lesson 52 on Tape 18.

Preparation: Recue Video Lesson 52 to section 6, in which doña Elena reads the story **"En el jardín zoológico"** (*"At the Zoo"*).

Ask the children what adventures of Fredo's they've already read about (his adventures in the musical instrument store—**"La tienda de música,"** in the café—**"El café mágico,"** and in the city—**"En la ciudad"**). Ask them where Fredo's latest adventure took place (in the zoo). Tell them to read along with doña Elena as she reads *"At the Zoo"* (**"En el jardín zoológico"**). Play section 6 of the video with the sound. Remind the children to look for visual clues in the pictures and to listen and watch for words they know. Then rewind the tape to the beginning of the story and replay it without the sound, pausing the tape to give the children time to read each line of the story to themselves. Finally, do a quick comprehension check with the children:

Questions:	**Answers** (accept English):
1. Where does Fredo go?	He goes to the zoo.
2. What does he do at the zoo?	He visits friends. (**Visita a sus amigos.**)
3. What friends does he visit?	the elephant (**el elefante**), the giraffe (**la jirafa**), the lion (**el león**), the seals (**las focas**), the fish (**los peces**), the duck (**el pato**), the bear (**el oso**)

Materials: Cassette player; ***"Las aventuras de Fredo"*** Book Four, **"En el jardín zoológico"** on Song Cassette, Side B; and ***"Las aventuras de Fredo"*** (*"Fredo's Adventures"*) books.

Tell the children they are going to read another story about Fredo's adventures. Distribute your copies of ***"Las aventuras de Fredo"*** (*"Fredo's Adventures"*) among the children. Tell them to turn to the fourth story in the book—**"En el jardín zoológico"** (*"At the Zoo"*)—and to read along silently as doña Elena reads the story. Play the audio tape. Then allow children time to re-read the story on their own. Use the questions in Activity 52B to check comprehension.

4. What happens when he visits his various friends? — The elephant wraps him in his trunk. Fredo climbs a ladder to talk to the giraffe. He puts his head in the lion's mouth. The seal spins him like a ball. He swims with the fish. He walks like the duck. He has a picnic with the bear.
5. What happens to Fredo at the end of the story? — The zookeeper kicks him out of the zoo.

Activity 52C: Complete the crossword puzzle

Materials: Blackline Master 52C; pencils; a current calendar; a current Month Picture; a blank overhead transparency; and an overhead projector.

Preparation: Copy and distribute Blackline Master 52C so that each child has one. Make an overhead transparency of Blackline Master 52C to use as an answer key.

First have the children write their name and the date on their papers. If they need help with the date, point to the number of the day on the calendar and then to the name of the month on the Month Picture. Tell them to complete the puzzle by using the pictures as clues. If they need help with spelling the name of each animal, point out that the animal names appear in the word bank (**Palabras**). When the children have completed the puzzle, help them check their answers, using the overhead transparency

Crucigrama

Complete the crossword puzzle for animals. Use the word bank to help you.

PALABRAS
tigre
gorila
león
cebra
elefante
pájaro
jirafa
pato
foca

Blackline Master 52C

CLOSING

Tell the children that Spanish class is finished for today. In the next lesson children will read the story about Fredo's adventures at the zoo again.

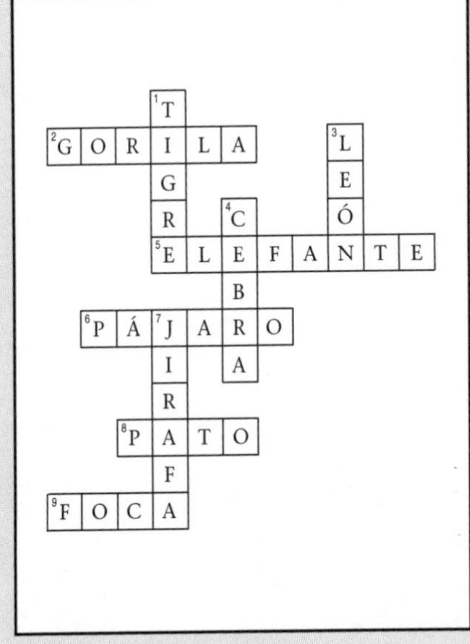

Answer Key for BLM 52C

Lesson 53

Materials to gather

- VCR and Video Lesson 53 on Tape 18
- Cassette player
- Activity Cassette 2
- Red Flashcards 58–63
- ***Optional materials:*** Song Cassette; ***"Las aventuras de Fredo"*** *("Fredo's Adventures")* books

Objectives

Language

- Comprehend more of the story about Fredo's adventures at the zoo
- Learn the name for the person who takes care of animals at the zoo

Culture

- Review that in Spanish the week starts with Monday instead of Sunday
- Review that the months in Spanish are not capitalized

Review

- Practice the days of the week and months of the year
- Use the sentences **Hoy/Mañana es** ___ (*Today/Tomorrow is* ___)
- Review animal vocabulary
- Review several forms of the verb **ir** (*to go*)
- Sing the "Calendar Rap," the "Months Rap," and "**¿Adónde vas?**" (*"Where Are You Going?"*)

Vocabulary

el guardián	*zookeeper*

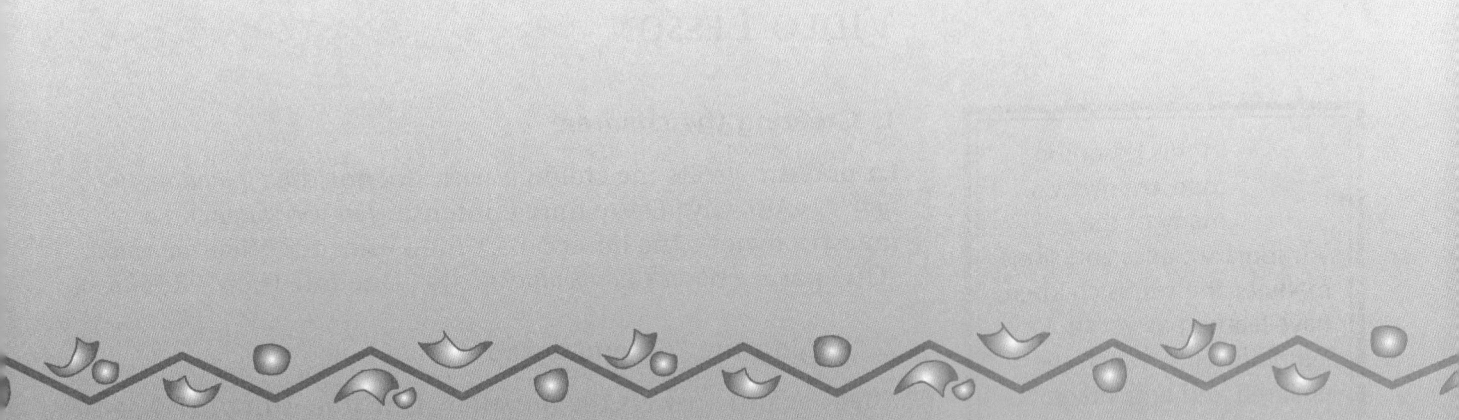

Warm-up

Greet the children. Ask what day of the week it is and what month it is. If you feel comfortable, say **Hola** (*Hello*), **Buenos días** (*Good morning*), or **Buenas tardes** (*Good afternoon*). Ask **¿Qué día es?** (*What day is it?*) and **¿Qué mes es?** (*What month is it?*).

Review

Materials: Red Flashcards 58–63.

Distribute the Flashcards among the children. Have a volunteer ask **¿Dónde está** + a place name? (*Where is* + a place name?). The child with the card showing the place the volunteer is seeking should stand and say **Aquí está** + the place name (*Here is* + the place name). For example:

¿Dónde está el restaurante?	*Where is the restaurant?*
Aquí está el restaurante.	*Here is the restaurant.*

Red Flashcards:

#58	el restaurante	*restaurant*
#59	el museo	*museum*
#60	la biblioteca	*library*
#61	el supermercado	*supermarket*
#62	el cine	*movie theater*
#63	el hospital	*hospital*

Introduce the video

Invite the children to listen and watch as **la maestra** reviews the days of the week and the months or the year, practices the names of many animals, and sings many songs.

Los meses del año
(*the months of the year*):

enero	*January*
febrero	*February*
marzo	*March*
abril	*April*
mayo	*May*
junio	*June*
julio	*July*
agosto	*August*
septiembre	*September*
octubre	*October*
noviembre	*November*
diciembre	*December*

Los días de la semana
(*the days of the week*):

lunes	*Monday*
martes	*Tuesday*
miércoles	*Wednesday*
jueves	*Thursday*
viernes	*Friday*
sábado	*Saturday*
domingo	*Sunday*

VIDEO LESSON

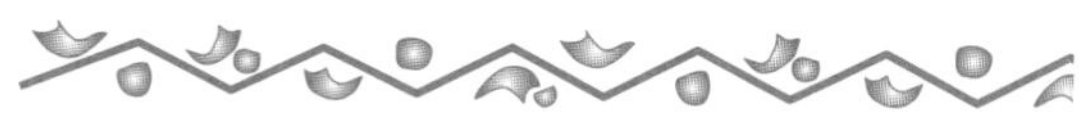

In this lesson, **la maestra** reviews many of the vocabulary topics and sings many of the songs children have learned as vocabulary-learning tools. Watch the children and encourage them to sing along. Are they able to name the days of the week? the months? Do they recognize the animals and are they able to identify them by their Spanish names?

Los animales *(animals)*:

la cebra	*zebra*
el elefante	*elephant*
la foca	*seal*
el gorila	*gorilla*
la jirafa	*giraffe*
el león	*lion*
el oso	*bear*
el pájaro	*bird*
el pato	*duck*
el pez	*fish*
el tigre	*tiger*

1. Greeting the children

La maestra greets the children with **Buenos días** (*Good morning*). LeeAnn says **Estoy muy contenta** (*I'm very happy*). **La maestra** reviews the questions **¿Cómo estás tú?** (*How are you?*), **¿Qué pasa?** (*What's happening?*), and **¿Qué tal?** (*How's it going?*).

2. Singing the "Calendar Rap"

After LeeAnn answers the question **¿Qué día es hoy?** (*What day is today?*) with **Hoy es miércoles** (*Today is Wednesday*), **la maestra** sings the "Calendar Rap." For the days of the week, see the Warm-up in this lesson. For the "Calendar Rap" lyrics, see Song 9 in the Song Appendix.

3. Introducing phrases used in talking about days of the week

LeeAnn tells **la maestra** that a Spanish calendar begins with *Monday* (**lunes**) whereas an English calendar begins with *Sunday* (**domingo**). **La maestra** introduces a new sentence referring to tomorrow.

Mañana es ___. *Tomorrow is ___.*

4. Singing the "Months Rap"

After asking **¿Qué mes es?** (*What month is it?*), **la maestra** sings the "Months Rap." For the lyrics, see Song 4 in the Song Appendix.

5. Recognizing the missing month

La maestra shows LeeAnn and the children a board with the words **abril ___ junio** (*April ___ June*). LeeAnn and the children fill in the missing month—**mayo** (*May*). LeeAnn points out that the names of the months are not capitalized in Spanish whereas they are in English.

6. Singing *"¿Adónde vas?"* (*"Where Are You Going?"*)

Doña Elena and **la maestra** sing "**¿Adónde vas?**" (*"Where Are You Going?"*). For song lyrics, see Song 10 in the Song Appendix.

7. Reviewing animal vocabulary

La maestra asks LeeAnn where she would go if she wanted to visit animals that are not domestic. LeeAnn tells her **el jardín zoológico** (*zoo*). **La maestra** shows Red Flashcards of the animals and asks the children **¿Qué animal es?** (*What animal is it?*).

8. Playing *¿Qué animal es?* (*What animal is it?*)

¡Vamos a jugar! (*Let's play!*) As pictures of zoo animals appear on the screen, **la maestra** asks the children **¿Qué animal es?** (*What animal is it?*). She describes the animals, e.g., **El oso es muy grande y también es muy fuerte** (*The bear is very big and it is also very strong*).

9. Reviewing several forms of the same verb

She reviews the difference between the verb forms **voy** (*I'm going*), **vas** (*you are going*), **va** (*he/she is going*), and **vamos** (*we are going*).

10. Reading about Fredo's adventures in the zoo

Doña Elena reads **"En el jardín zoológico"** (*"At the Zoo"*) as the children read along. **La maestra** introduces the word **el guardián** (*zookeeper*).

Fredo visita a su amigo, el león.	*Fredo visits his friend, the lion.*
¿Cómo es el león?	*What is the lion like?*
Es feroz, pero Fredo no tiene miedo.	*He's ferocious, but Fredo isn't afraid.*
¿Cómo son las focas?	*What are the seals like?*
Son bonitas y juegan con Fredo.	*They are pretty and they play with Fredo.*
¿Cómo son los peces?	*What are the fish like?*
Son pequeños y tienen muchos colores.	*They are small and they have many colors.*
Anda con el pato.	*He walks with the duck.*
Es bajo.	*It's short.*

11. Guessing what animal Antonio is miming

Antonio mimes an animal as **la maestra** asks the children **¿Qué animal es?** (*What animal is it?*): **el elefante** (*elephant*). She asks **¿De qué color es el elefante?** (*What color is the elephant?*). LeeAnn tells her **Es gris** (*It is gray*).

12. Closing

LeeAnn and **la maestra** say **Adiós** (*Good-bye*) to the children.

EN ESPAÑOL

Vamos also means *Let's go!* and *Shall we go?* Context and voice intonation should make the meaning clear.

After viewing the video, praise the children for their good listening and watching skills.

Activity Lesson

In Activity 53A, **la maestra** says **¿Adónde vas? ¿Vas al museo? ¿Vas a la escuela? No sé. Vamos a cantar.** This means *Where are you going? Are you going to the museum? Are you going to school? I don't know. Let's sing!*

Activity 53A: Sing *"¿Adónde vas?"* (*"Where Are You Going?"*)

Materials: Cassette player; Activity Cassette 2, Side B; and Red Flashcards 58–63.

Preparation: Display the Red Flashcards in song order: 59 (museum), 62 (movie theater), 58 (restaurant), 62 (supermarket), 60 (library), 63 (hospital). Write the following expressions (Spanish only) on the chalkboard:

Voy a ___.	*I'm going to ___.*
Vamos a ___.	*We are going to ___.*
Va a ___.	*He/She is going to ___.*

Tell the children they are going to sing the song in which they say where they are going. Draw their attention to the Red Flashcards, which show all the places mentioned in the song. Point out that the pictures are arranged in the order the places are sung about in the song. Play Activity 53A, pausing the tape at the end of the song to tell the children to listen carefully as **la maestra** explains when you use each of the phrases you have written on the chalkboard. If possible point to each phrase as **la maestra** talks about it. At the end of the activity, mention to the children that **voy** can mean both *I go* and *I'm going,* **vamos** both *we go* and *we are going,* and **va** both *he/she goes* and *he/she is going.*

Fredo Book Activity

Materials: Cassette player; ***"Las aventuras de Fredo"*** Book Four, **"En el jardín zoológico"** on Song Cassette, Side B; and ***"Las aventuras de Fredo"*** (*"Fredo's Adventures"*) books.

Tell the children they are going to read about Fredo's adventures in the zoo. Distribute your copies of ***"Las aventuras de Fredo"*** (*"Fredo's Adventures"*) among the children. Tell them to turn to the fourth story in the book—**"En el jardín zoológico"** (*"At the Zoo"*)—and to read along silently as doña Elena reads the story. Play the audio tape. Then have the class re-read the story with volunteers reading aloud.

Activity 53B: Read *"En el jardín zoológico"* (*"At the Zoo"*)

Note: If your school has ***"Las aventuras de Fredo"*** (*"Fredo's Adventures"*) books available for the children, substitute the Fredo Book activity in the margin for this activity.

Materials: VCR; Video Lesson 53 on Tape 18.

Preparation: Recue Video Lesson 53 to section 10, in which doña Elena reads the story **"En el jardín zoológico."**

Tell the children to read along with doña Elena as she reads *"At the Zoo"* (**"En el jardín zoológico"**). Play section 10 of the video with the sound. Remind the children to look for visual clues in the pictures and to listen and watch for words they know. Then rewind the tape to the beginning of the story and replay it without the sound, pausing the tape at each line of the story. Ask volunteers to read the lines aloud.

Activity 53C: Name that animal!

Materials: Cassette player; Activity Cassette 2, Side B.

Ask the children to imitate the sounds made by domestic and wild animals (e.g., dogs, cats, lions, ducks, even fish). Tell the children to listen carefully to the sounds on the tape and at the sound of the harp to call out the name (in Spanish) of the animal they just heard. Restart the tape for confirmation of the animal by **la maestra** and the next animal sound. Animal sounds are in this order: **el perro** (*dog*), **el gato** (*cat*), **la vaca** (*cow*), **el pato** (*duck*), **el tigre** or **el león** (*tiger* or *lion*), **el elefante** (*elephant*).

CLOSING

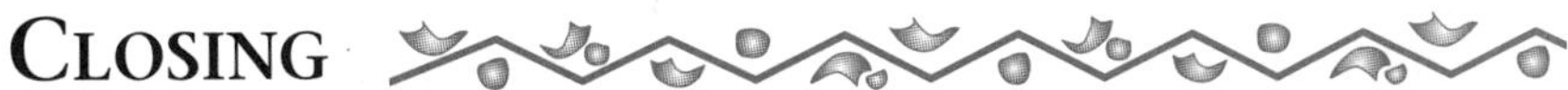

Tell the children that Spanish class is finished for today. In the next lesson children will practice the animal names again.

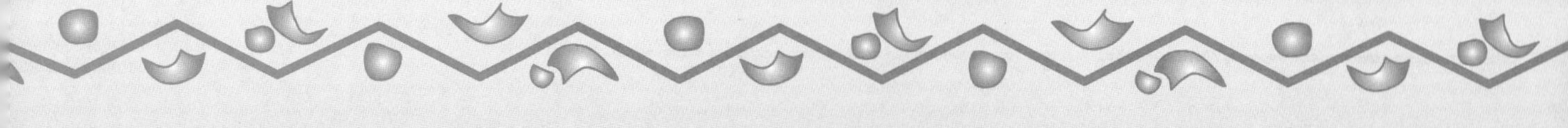

Lesson 54

> **Materials to gather**
>
> - VCR and Video Lesson 54 on Tape 18
> - Cassette player
> - Song Cassette
> - Gold Flashcards 20–27
> - Red Flashcards 68–75
> - A picture of a brown, black, or grizzly bear
> - A blank piece of paper or cardboard
> - Paste or tape
> - Laminating machine
> - Overhead projector
> - Overhead transparency of Blackline Master 51A (**"De colores"**)
> - Blackline Master 54B (path with animals)
> - Blackline Master 54C (4 strange creatures)
> - Current calendar
> - Current Month Picture
> - Pencils
> - ***Optional materials:*** blank paper; colored markers or pencils
> - ***Prepare ahead:*** bear Flashcard (for Review section)

Objectives

Language

- Understand more of the visit to the San Diego Zoo

Culture

- Learn that zoos not only care for animals but also study them

Review

- Review the vocabulary for domestic, farm, and wild animals
- Play **¿Qué animal es?** (*What animal is it?*)
- Identify animals by their sounds and actions

Vocabulary

No new vocabulary is introduced in this lesson.

Warm-up

Talk with the children about their experiences with wild animals. Perhaps it is common to see bear, deer, fox, skunks, raccoons, or other wild animals in your area. Ask the children to talk about wild animals they may have seen at a nearby zoo, in other parts of the world, or on television nature shows. Ask what wild animals are not naturally found in the United States (e.g., zebras, giraffes, gorillas).

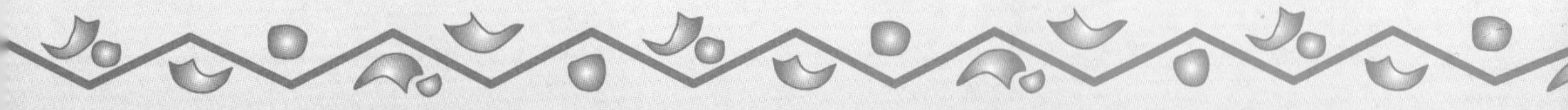

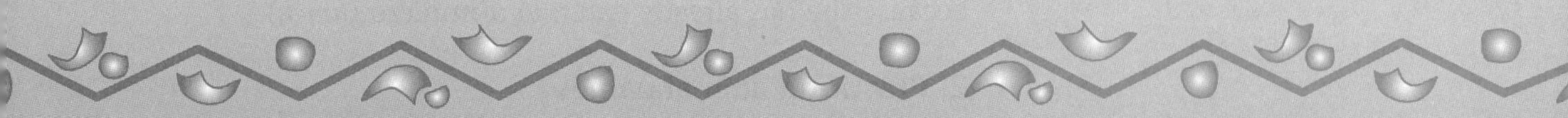

Review

Materials: Gold Flashcards 20–27; Red Flashcards 68–75; a picture of a brown, black, or grizzly bear; blank piece of paper or cardboard; paste or tape; and a laminating machine.

Preparation: Make a Flashcard of the bear by pasting or taping your picture of a bear to the piece of blank paper or cardboard. On the back of the Flashcard write **el oso** (*bear*). Laminate the Flashcard.

Practice the names of the domestic, farm, and wild animals by holding up one Flashcard at a time and asking the children to identify the animal shown. If you feel comfortable, ask **¿Qué animal es?** (*What animal is it?*).

Gold Flashcards:		**Red Flashcards:**	
#20	el perro (*dog*)	#68 (left)	la jirafa (*giraffe*)
#21	el gato (*cat*)	#68 (right)	el pájaro (*bird*)
#22	la gallina (*chicken*)	#69 (left)	la foca (*seal*)
#23	el conejo (*rabbit*)	#69 (right)	el pato (*duck*)
#24	el gallo (*rooster*)	#70	el elefante (*elephant*)
#25	la vaca (*cow*)	#71	el pez (*fish* [singular])
#26	el cerdo (*pig*)		los peces (*fish* [plural])
#27	el caballo (*horse*)	#72	el león (*lion*)
		#73	el tigre (*tiger*)
Your Flashcard:		#74	el gorila (*gorilla*)
	el oso (*bear*)	#75	la cebra (*zebra*)

Introduce the video

Invite the children to listen and watch as **la maestra** devotes the entire lesson to animals!

Heritage Speakers

Ask heritage speakers to talk about wild animals in their countries of origin. Perhaps they've seen them in their natural habitats.

Video Lesson

1. Greeting the children

La maestra greets the children with **Buenas tardes** (*Good afternoon*). Kipper says **Estoy muy contento** (*I'm very happy*). **La maestra** reviews **Estoy enojado/enojada** (*I'm angry*) and **Tengo hambre** (*I'm hungry*). She tells the children she isn't hungry because she has already eaten **el almuerzo** (*lunch*).

2. Practicing animal names

La maestra shows Kipper and the children Gold Flashcards with pictures of farm and domestic animals and asks **¿Qué animal es?** (*What animal is it?*). Children answer **Es** (*It's*) + the name of the animal.

el cerdo	*pig*	el perro	*dog*
la vaca	*cow*	la gallina	*chicken*
el gato	*cat*	el conejo	*rabbit*
el caballo	*horse*	el gallo	*rooster*

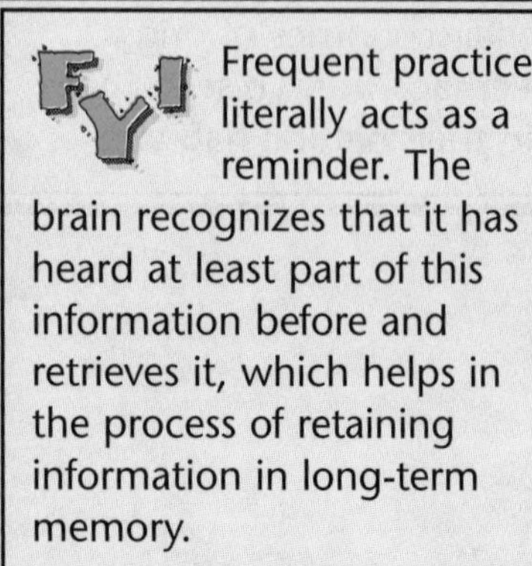

FYI Frequent practice literally acts as a reminder. The brain recognizes that it has heard at least part of this information before and retrieves it, which helps in the process of retaining information in long-term memory.

3. Playing a miming game for domestic animals

Antonio mimes the motions and sounds of several animals as **la maestra** asks **¿Qué animal es?** (*What animal is it?*). Children identify **el perro** (*dog*), **el gato** (*cat*), **la vaca** (*cow*), and **el gallo** (*rooster*).

4. Reviewing the names of zoo animals

Before moving on to **los animales del jardín zoológico** (*zoo animals*), **la maestra** points out that the animals practiced thus far are all from **el rancho** (*farm*). She shows the Red Flashcards of the animals and asks **¿Qué animal es?** (*What animal is it?*). She points out that **el gorila** (*gorilla*), **el tigre** (*tiger*), and **la cebra** (*zebra*) are cognates.

el gorila	*gorilla*	el elefante	*elephant*
el pez	*fish*	la girafa	*giraffe*
el tigre	*tiger*	el pájaro	*bird*
la foca	*seal*	la cebra	*zebra*
el pato	*duck*	el león	*lion*

5. Playing the miming game for zoo animals

Antonio mimes the actions and sounds of zoo animals: **el tigre** (*tiger*), **el gorila** (*gorilla*). **La maestra** asks Kipper which two animals sound alike—**el tigre** (*tiger*) and **el león** (*lion*).

6. Visiting the San Diego Zoo

La maestra describes the animals at the San Diego Zoo. Throughout the tour, we hear the shouts of **¡Mira! ¡Mira!** (*Look! Look!*) from our excited friends Kipper and LeeAnn. For other statements, see Lesson 51, Video Lesson, section 6, and Lesson 52, Video Lesson, section 3.

Aquí está el mapa del zoológico.	*Here is the map of the zoo.*
La jirafa alta es la mamá y la jirafa pequeña es el bebé.	*The tall giraffe is the mother and the small giraffe is the baby.*
Hay patos pequeños y hay patos grandes.	*There are small ducks and large ducks.*
Es un gato grande.	*It's a big cat.*
Aquí está otro animal.	*Here is another animal.*
Es el oso.	*It's the bear.*
El oso es café.	*The bear is brown.*

FYI Because of the variation in individual monitors, the bear may not appear to be brown. Children may say the bear is black (**negro**).

7. Playing *¿Qué animal es?* (*What animal is it?*)

La maestra says **Vamos a jugar** (*Let's play!*). She asks **¿Qué animal es?** (*What animal is it?*) using pictures of the animals from the zoo.

8. Closing

La maestra explains that a zoo takes care of animals and does research to learn how to protect animals. She and Kipper say **Adiós** (*Good-bye*) and **Hasta luego** (*See you later*) to the children.

After viewing the video, praise the children for their good listening and watching skills.

Activity Lesson 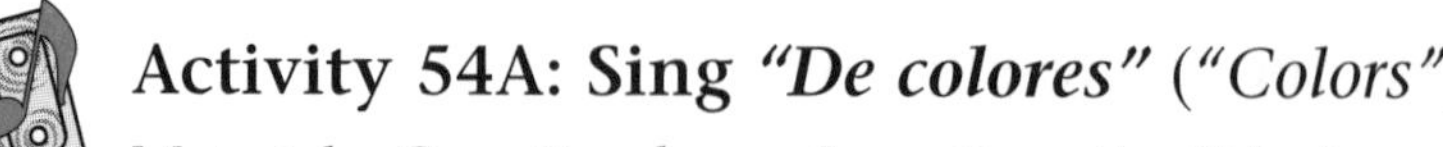

Activity 54A: Sing *"De colores"* (*"Colors"*)

Materials: Cassette player; Song Cassette, Side A; your overhead transparency of Blackline Master 51A; and an overhead projector.

Project the overhead transparency of Blackline Master 51A. Tell the children to sing along with **la maestra**. Play the song a couple of times and encourage them to try to sing a bit more of the song each time. As each line is sung, point to it on the transparency. For the lyrics with English equivalents, see Song 12 in the Song Appendix.

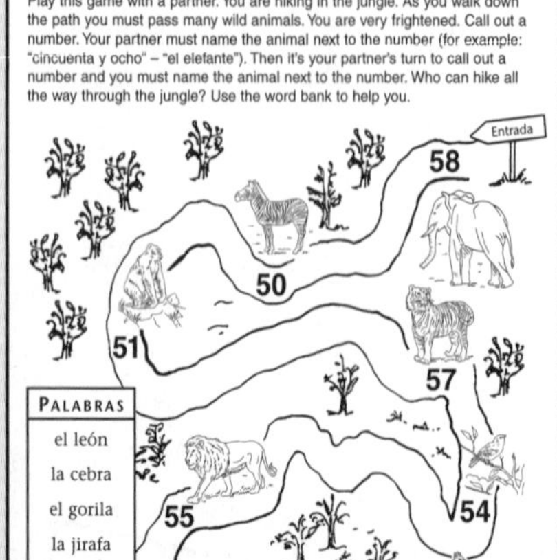

Blackline Master 54B

Activity 54B may also be played as a class activity. Make an overhead transparency of Blackline Master 54B. Divide the class into teams and assign each team a marker. The teams take turns calling out numbers and animals as you move the markers along the transparency.

Activity 54B: Cooperative learning—Hiking in the wild kingdom

Materials: Blackline Master 54B; a current calendar; and the current Month Picture.

Preparation: Copy and distribute Blackline Master 54B so that each child has a copy.

Have the children write their names and the date on their papers. If they need help with the date, point to the number of the day on the current calendar and the name of the month on the Month Picture. Next, divide the class into pairs. Tell the children they are going on a hike through the wild kingdom. Point out that they are to begin their hike at the entrance (**Entrada**) to the well worn path and that they should follow the path to the exit (**Salida**). As they hike, one partner calls out a number; the other partner calls out the name of the animal next to the number. Partners reverse roles as they proceed down the path. If they need help recalling the animal names, they should consult the word bank (**Palabras**). Children should call out the numbers and animals as follows:

58	cincuenta y ocho	el elefante	*elephant*
50	cincuenta	la cebra	*zebra*
51	cincuenta y uno	el gorila	*gorilla*
57	cincuenta y siete	el tigre	*tiger*
54	cincuenta y cuatro	el pájaro	*bird*
55	cincuenta y cinco	el león	*lion*
52	cincuenta y dos	la foca	*seal*
56	cincuenta y seis	la jirafa	*giraffe*

Activity 54C: What kind of animal is that?

Materials: Blackline Master 54C; a current calendar; the current Month Picture; and pencils.

Preparation: Copy and distribute Blackline Master 54C so that each child has one.

Have the children write their names and the date on their papers. If they need help with the date, point to the number of the day on the current calendar and the name of the month on the Month Picture. Tell the children to look closely at the animals in the pictures. What's wrong with them? (they are really two animals in one) On the lines provided in each box, children should write the names of the two animals that make up the animal pictured in the box. If they need help with spelling, point out that the name of each animal is listed in the word bank (**Palabras**). Children should have written the names as follows:

Top left:	el gorila / el león	*gorilla / lion*
Top right:	el pájaro / la cebra	*bird / zebra*
Middle:	el pez / la jirafa	*fish / giraffe*
Bottom:	el pato / el tigre	*duck / tiger*

CLOSING

Tell the children that Spanish class is finished for today. In the next lesson children will read a new Fredo adventure story.

These strange-looking animals are mixtures of two animals! Figure out which two animals make up each one and write their names in the blanks. Check the word bank for clues.

PALABRAS

el gorila
el pájaro
el pato
el león
el pez
la cebra
el tigre

Blackline Master 54C

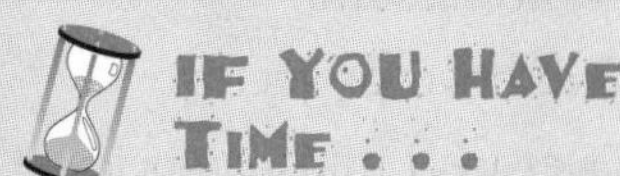

Materials: Gold Flashcards 20–27; Red Flashcards 68–75; your Flashcard of the bear; blank paper; and markers or colored pencils.

Display all the Flashcards. Have the children draw their own picture of a strange animal that is made up of two or more of the animals displayed in the Flashcards. On their pictures, they should write the name of each animal that makes up their creature. If they need help with spelling, turn the Flashcards around so they can see the animal names.

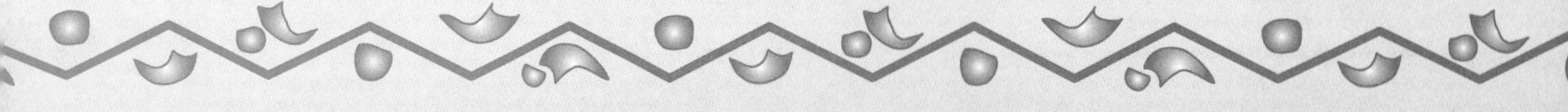

LESSON 55

Materials to gather

- VCR and Video Lesson 55 on Tape 19
- Cassette player
- Song Cassette
- Overhead projector
- Overhead transparencies of Blackline Masters 51A and 37A-2 (**"De colores"** and **"En los Estados Unidos"**)
- Blackline Master 55C (farmyard scene)
- Pencils
- Current calendar
- Current Month Picture
- ***Optional materials:*** *"Las aventuras de Fredo"* (*"Fredo's Adventures"*) books

OBJECTIVES

Language

- Use pictures and familiar vocabulary as clues to understanding a new Fredo story
- Learn two words for expressing location or position
- Answer the question **¿Dónde vive ___?** (*Where does ___ live?*)

Culture

- Sing **"De colores"** (*"Colors"*)
- Learn that **"De colores"** (*"Colors"*) is often sung at **fiestas** (*parties*)

Review

- Answer the question **¿Qué animal es?** (*What animal is it?*)
- Identify animals by their sounds and actions

Vocabulary

¿Dónde vive ___?	*Where does ___ live?*
En el rancho.	*On the farm.*
En el jardín zoológico.	*At the zoo.*
En la casa.	*At home.*
la gata	*female cat*
delante de	*in front of*
detrás de	*behind, in back of*
la concha	*shell*

Warm-up

Encourage the children to talk about their favorite animal(s). Have them describe their pets or the pets of friends or relatives that they particularly like. If there are children in the class who live on farms, ask them to talk about what animals they have on the farm.

Review

Using a book or other object, trigger children's use of prepositions that indicate position in English. For example, place a book under the desk and ask them where the book is (under the desk); place it on the desk and ask the same question (on or on top of). Continue this procedure placing the book behind, in front of, and beside something.

Introduce the video

Invite the children to listen and watch as **la maestra** introduces new words for saying where something is located.

VIDEO LESSON

Los animales (*animals*):

el caballo	*horse*
la cebra	*zebra*
el cerdo	*pig*
el conejo	*rabbit*
el elefante	*elephant*
la foca	*seal*
la gallina	*chicken*
el gallo	*rooster*
el gato	*cat*
el gorila	*gorilla*
la jirafa	*giraffe*
el león	*lion*
el oso	*bear*
el pájaro	*bird*
el pato	*duck*
el perro	*dog*
el pez	*fish* (singular)
los peces	*fish* (plural)
el tigre	*tiger*
la vaca	*cow*

1. Greeting the children

La maestra greets the children with **Buenos días** (*Good morning*). Winston says **Muy bien, gracias** (*Very well, thank you*) in response to the question **¿Cómo estás tú?** (*How are you?*). **La maestra** reviews the feeling expressions **Estoy triste** (*I'm sad*) and **Estoy contento/contenta** (*I'm happy*).

2. Singing *"De colores"* ("Colors")

La maestra sings the song that celebrates the colors in spring. Encourage the children to sing the words **De colores.** She explains that this song is sung at **fiestas** (*parties*) in Spanish-speaking countries. For song lyrics, see Song 12 in the Song Appendix.

3. Practicing animal vocabulary

La maestra explains that **los pajaritos** are *little birds*. She shows Winston and the children Gold and Red Flashcards and asks them **¿Qué animal es?** (*What animal is it?*).

4. Identifying animals by their sounds and actions

Antonio mimes the actions and sounds of **el pájaro** (*bird*), **el pato** (*duck*), **el caballo** (*horse*), and **el cerdo** (*pig*) as **la maestra** asks **¿Qué animal es?** (*What animal is it?*).

5. Talking about where animals live

La maestra asks Winston **¿Dónde vive el cerdo?** (*Where does the pig live?*) and Winston tells her **En el rancho** (*On the farm*). She asks where else animals live—**en el jardín zoológico** (*at the zoo*). She asks the children questions about where various animals live.

¿Dónde vive—en el rancho o en el jardín zoológico?	*Where does it live—on the farm or at the zoo?*
En el jardín zoológico.	*At the zoo.*
En el rancho.	*At the ranch.*

6. Reading a new Fredo adventure story

La maestra asks Winston what animals live at home—**el perro** (*dog*) and **el gato** (*cat*). She talks about Fredo's female cat (**la gata**). Doña Elena reads "**¿Dónde está Mimi?**" (*"Where Is Mimi?"*).

Aquí están Fredo y su gata.	*Here are Fredo and his cat.*
La gata se llama Mimi.	*The cat's name is Mimi.*

Fredo y Mimi están delante de la casa.	*Fredo and Mimi are in front of the house.*
Fredo busca a Mimi.	*Fredo is looking for Mimi.*
Mimi está detrás de la puerta.	*Mimi is behind the door.*
Mimi está cerca de la casa.	*Mimi is close to the house.*
Mimi está lejos de la casa.	*Mimi is far from the house.*
Mimi está arriba del refrigerador.	*Mimi is on top of the refrigerator.*
Mimi está debajo del coche.	*Mimi is under the car.*
Mimi está dentro de la chimenea.	*Mimi is inside the chimney.*
Mimi está fuera de la casa.	*Mimi is outside the house.*
Mimi está sobre la cama.	*Mimi is on the bed.*
Ahora duerme.	*Now she is sleeping.*

7. Introducing words for expressing position

La maestra introduces two prepositions that express position.

delante de	*in front of*
detrás de	*behind, in back of*

8. Showing examples of the new position expressions

Doña Elena asks the children **¿Dónde está Antonio?** (*Where is Antonio?*). He is **delante de** (*in front of*) and **detrás de la concha** (*behind the shell*). **La maestra** reviews the position phrases. Showing the children pictures from the Fredo story about Mimi, she tells the children **Fredo y Mimi están delante de la casa** (*Fredo and Mimi are in front of the house*) and **Mimi está detrás de la puerta** (*Mimi is behind the door*).

9. Singing *"En los Estados Unidos"* (*"In the United States"*)

After explaining that the word **en** (*in*) also expresses position or location, **la maestra** sings **"En los Estados Unidos"** (*"In the United States"*). For song lyrics, see Song 11 in the Song Appendix.

10. Closing

La maestra reviews the prepositions **delante de** (*in front of*), **detrás de** (*behind*), and **en** (*in*). She says **Adiós** (*Good-bye*) and **Hasta luego** (*See you later*) to the children.

After viewing the video, praise the children for their good listening and watching skills.

Activity Lesson

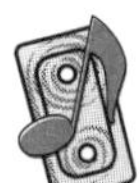

Activity 55A: Sing about colors and about the United States

Materials: Cassette player; **"En los Estados Unidos"** (*"In the United States"*) and **"De colores"** (*"Colors"*) on the Song Cassette, Side A; your overhead transparencies of Blackline Masters 37A-2 and 51A; and an overhead projector.

Display your overhead transparency of Blackline Master 37A-2 with the lyrics to the song about places in the United States with Spanish names. Ask for a volunteer to point to each line of the song as the class sings it. Play **"En los Estados Unidos"** (*"In the United States"*) on the Song Cassette.

Next project your overhead transparency of Blackline Master 51A. Play the song **"De colores"** on the Song Cassette and tell the children to sing along to the song about colors. Let them know that it's all right if they just sing the lines **De colores.** Have a volunteer point to each line of the song on the overhead transparency as the class sings. For lyrics with English equivalents, see Songs 11 and 12 in the Song Appendix.

Children may not have sung **"En los Estados Unidos"** in a while so you may need to play it a couple of times so they can refamiliarize themselves with it. If they are having difficulty with it, tell them to sing just the line **"En los Estados Unidos"** and the names of the cities.

Activity 55B: Read *"¿Dónde está Mimi?"* (*"Where Is Mimi?"*)

Note: If your school has ***"Las aventuras de Fredo"*** (*"Fredo's Adventures"*) books available for the children, substitute the Fredo Book Activity in the margin for this activity.

Materials: VCR; Video Lesson 55 on Tape 19.

Preparation: Recue Video Lesson 55 to section 6, in which doña Elena reads the story **"¿Dónde está Mimi?"**

Ask the children what adventures of Fredo's they've already read about (his adventures in the musical instrument store—**"La tienda de música,"** in the café—**"El café mágico,"** in the city—**"En la ciudad,"** and at the zoo—**"En el jardín zoológico"**). Ask them what Fredo is doing in his latest adventure (looking for his cat, Mimi). Tell them to read along with doña Elena as she reads *"Where Is Mimi?"* (**"¿Dónde está Mimi?"**). Play section 6 of the video with the sound. Remind the children to look for visual clues in the pictures and to listen and watch for words they know. Then rewind the tape to the beginning of the story and replay it without the sound, pausing the tape to give the children time to read each line of the story to themselves. Finally, do a quick comprehension check with the children:

	Questions:	**Answers** (accept English):
1.	Where is Mimi at the beginning of the story?	Mimi is in front of the house. (**Mimi está delante de la casa.**)

Fredo Book Activity

Materials: Cassette player; ***"Las aventuras de Fredo"*** Book Five, **"¿Dónde está Mimi?"** on Song Cassette, Side B; and ***"Las aventuras de Fredo"*** (*"Fredo's Adventures"*) books.

Tell the children they are going to read another story about Fredo's adventures. Distribute your copies of ***"Las aventuras de Fredo"*** (*"Fredo's Adventures"*) among the children. Tell them to turn to the fifth story in the book—**"¿Dónde está Mimi?"** (*"Where Is Mimi?"*)—and to read along silently as doña Elena reads the story. Play the audio tape. Then allow children time to re-read the story on their own. Use the questions in Activity 55B to check comprehension.

2. During the story, where is she?	behind the door (**detrás de la puerta**), close to the house (**cerca de la casa**), far from the house (**lejos de la casa**), under the car (**debajo del coche**), inside the chimney (**dentro de la chimenea**), outside the house (**fuera de la casa**), on the bed (**sobre la cama**)
3. What is she doing when Fredo finds her?	She's sleeping. (**Duerme.**)
4. Where is she at the end of the story?	In Fredo's arms./With Fredo. (**Con Fredo.**)

Activity 55C: Which animals don't belong here?

Materials: Blackline Master 55C; pencils; a current calendar; and the current Month Picture.

Preparation: Copy and distribute Blackline Master 55C so that each child has a copy.

Have the children write their names and the date on their papers. If they need help with the date, point to the number of the day on the current calendar and the name of the month on the Month Picture. Tell the children that the picture on the paper is of Mrs. Ranchera's farmyard. Mention that some animals from a zoo not far away wandered out of the zoo and into the farmyard. Children are to locate the zoo animals and write their names on the lines provided (**Animales del zoológico**) and then write the names of the farm or ranch animals (**Animales del rancho**) shown in the picture on the lines provided. Point out that all the animal words are in the word bank (**Palabras**). Children should have listed the animals as follows:

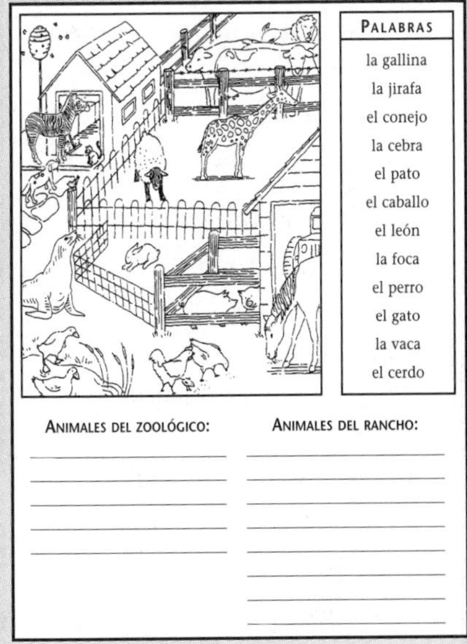

Blackline Master 55C

Animales del zoológico:		**Animales del rancho:**	
la jirafa	*giraffe*	la gallina	*chicken*
la cebra	*zebra*	el conejo	*rabbit*
el león	*lion*	el caballo	*horse*
la foca	*seal*	el perro	*dog*
el pato	*duck*	el gato	*cat*
(the duck could go on		la vaca	*cow*
either list)		el cerdo	*pig*

Closing

Tell the children that Spanish class is finished for today. In the next lesson children will learn a song about Mimi!

Lesson 56

Materials to gather

- VCR and Video Lesson 56 on Tape 19
- Cassette player
- Song Cassette
- Overhead projector
- Blank overhead transparency
- Blackline Master 56A ("**¿Dónde está Mimi?**" lyrics)
- Blackline Master 56C (sentence–picture matching game)
- Pencils
- Current calendar
- Current Month Picture
- ***Optional materials:* "*Las aventuras de Fredo*"** ("*Fredo's Adventures*") books

Objectives

Language

- Understand a conversation about dwelling places
- Learn additional location phrases
- Sing a new song **"¿Dónde está Mimi?"** (*"Where Is Mimi?"*)
- Learn hand motions to accompany the new song
- Comprehend more of the story **"¿Dónde está Mimi?"** (*"Where Is Mimi?"*)

Culture

- Hear a merengue rhythm and learn that merengue is a Latin rhythm
- Recall that samba is a Latin rhythm

Review

- Review location phrases **delante de** (*in front of*) and **detrás de** (*behind*)

Vocabulary

cerca de	*close to*
lejos de	*far from*

Warm-up

Let the children know it's time for Spanish class (**la clase de español**). Ask who has a house pet. Ask volunteers to say what kind of animal they have and then to describe the pet's favorite hiding or sleeping place. Encourage children to use the Spanish word for the animal if they know it (e.g., **el perro**—*dog;* **el gato**—*cat;* **el conejo**—*rabbit*). For a complete list of animals, see the Review section in Lesson 54.

Review

Stand in front of the desk and ask the children to tell you where you are standing in relation to the desk (**delante del escritorio**—*in front of the desk*). Stand behind the desk and ask where you are standing in relation to the desk (**detrás del escritorio**—*behind the desk*).

Introduce the video

Invite the children to listen and watch as **la maestra** teaches them a new song about Fredo's cat Mimi and where she hides!

Video Lesson

1. Greeting the children

La maestra greets the children with **Buenos días** (*Good morning*). Winston asks **la maestra ¿Qué tal?** (*What's happening?*). She asks him **¿Qué pasa?** (*How's it going?*); they both say they are **Muy bien** (*Very well*).

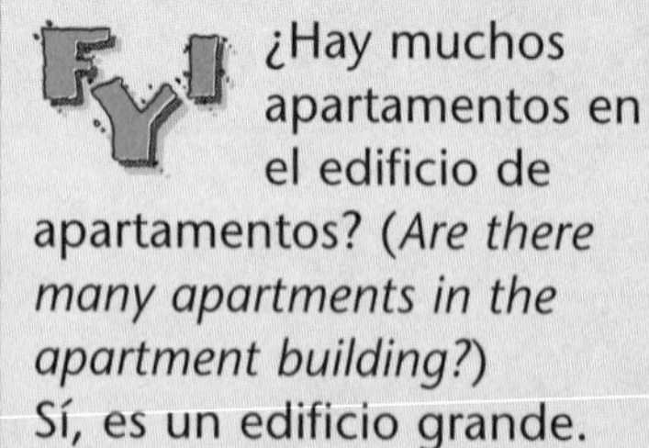

¿Hay muchos apartamentos en el edificio de apartamentos? (*Are there many apartments in the apartment building?*)
Sí, es un edificio grande. (*Yes, it's a large building.*)

2. Talking about dwellings

La maestra tells Winston **Yo vivo en una casa** (*I live in a house*) and asks him **¿Dónde vives tú?** (*Where do you live?*). He replies **Vivo en un apartamento** (*I live in an apartment*).

3. Reviewing *delante de* (in front of) and *detrás de* (behind)

Winston and the children read the location phrases **delante de** (*in front of*) and **detrás de** (*behind*). **La maestra** demonstrates the sentences **Las manos están delante** (*The hands are in front*), **Las manos están detrás** (*The hands are behind*). To practice the location phrases, doña Elena asks the children **¿Dónde está Antonio?** (*Where is Antonio?*)—**delante de la concha** (*in front of the shell*), **detrás de la concha** (*behind the shell*).

4. Introducing new location phrases

La maestra introduces two more location phrases. She demonstrates each phrase with her hands. Doña Elena asks the children **¿Dónde está Antonio?** (*Where is Antonio?*)—**cerca de la concha** (*near the shell*), **lejos de la concha** (*far from the shell*).

cerca de	*close to*
lejos de	*far from*

5. Introducing a new song

La maestra sings the first four lines of the new song and demonstrates the arm and hand movements as she does so.

Delante de, delante de, delante de	*In front of, in front of, in front of*
Detrás de, detrás de, detrás de	*Behind, behind, behind*
Cerca de, cerca de, cerca de	*Close to, close to, close to*
Lejos de, lejos de, lejos de	*Far from, far from, far from*

6. Singing the new song—"¿Dónde está Mimi?" (*"Where Is Mimi?"*)

La maestra sings the new song as pictures of Fredo and Mimi appear. For song lyrics, see Activity 56A in this lesson.

7. Choosing the correct location phrase

Pointing to pictures of Mimi, **la maestra** asks the children where Mimi is.

¿Está detrás de la casa o delante de la casa?	*Is she behind the house or in front of the house?*
Está delante de la casa.	*She's in front of the house.*
¿Está detrás o delante de la puerta?	*Is she behind or in front of the door?*
Está detrás de la puerta.	*She's behind the door.*
¿Mimi está cerca o lejos de la casa?	*Is Mimi close to or far from the house?*
Está cerca de la casa.	*She's close to the house.*
¿Está cerca o lejos de la casa?	*Is she close to or far from the house?*
Esta lejos de la casa.	*She's far from the house.*

8. Reading *"¿Dónde está Mimi?"* (*"Where Is Mimi?"*)

Doña Elena reads "**¿Dónde está Mimi?**" (*"Where Is Mimi?"*). For statements from the story, see Lesson 55, Video Lesson, section 6.

9. Practicing the first part of the new song

La maestra reassures Winston and the children that they aren't expected to understand or read every word. She explains that the new song has a merengue rhythm, which, like the samba in the "Alphabet Samba," is a Latin rhythm. **La maestra** and Winston sing the first four lines of the song. For song lyrics, see section 6 above.

10. Singing the new song again

La maestra sings "**¿Dónde está Mimi?**" (*"Where Is Mimi?"*). For song lyrics, see Activity 56A of this lesson.

11. Closing

La maestra, Winston, and the children review and practice the four location phrases they've learned thus far. Winston and **la maestra** bid the children **Adiós** (*Good-bye*) and **Hasta la vista** (*Until we meet again*).

Me gusta leer. (*I like to read.*) Me gusta cantar. (*I like to sing.*)

When **la maestra** sings the song with the pictures from the Fredo story, she adds an extra phrase to some of the lines. When she sings it without the pictures, each location phrase is sung three times only. Praise children if they notice this difference.

After viewing the video, praise the children for their good listening and watching skills.

¿Dónde está Mimi?
(Where Is Mimi?)

Mimi, ¿dónde está?
Delante de, delante de, delante de,
Detrás de, detrás de, detrás de (¡detrás de la puerta!)
Cerca de, cerca de, cerca de (¡cerca de la casa!)
Lejos de, lejos de, lejos de (¡lejos de la casa!)
Arriba de, arriba de, arriba de (¡arriba!)
Debajo de, debajo de, debajo de (¡debajo del coche!)
Dentro de, dentro de, dentro de (¡dentro!)
Fuera de, fuera de, fuera de (¡fuera de la casa!)
Ah, Mimi. Aquí está. Muy bien. Hola, Mimi. Hola.

Blackline Master 56A

Activity Lesson

Activity 56A: Sing the new song

Materials: Cassette player; **"¿Dónde está Mimi?"** (*"Where Is Mimi?"*) on the Song Cassette, Side A; a blank overhead transparency; Blackline Master 56A; and an overhead projector.

Preparation: Make an overhead transparency of Blackline Master 56A.

Tell the children they are going to sing the new song but that first they are going to practice the hand motions that go with the first four location lines. Have the children hold their hands up in front of them and shake them. Ask with what location phrase the motion goes (*in front of*—**delante de**). Next, have the children put their hands behind their backs. Ask with what phrase the motion goes (*behind*—**detrás de**). Follow the same procedure for *close to* (**cerca de**) by having them put their hands in a fist and raising them up close to their chin, and for *far from* (**lejos de**) by having them put one hand to their brow in a searching motion.

Ask a volunteer to point to each line of the song on the overhead transparency as the children sing along and make the motions they've learned thus far. Play the song. If the children are enjoying singing the song, play it again.

¿Mimi? ¿Mimi? ¿Dónde está Mimi?	*Mimi? Mimi? Where is Mimi?*
¿Dónde está?	*Where is she?*
Delante de, delante de, delante de,	*In front of, in front of, in front of,*
Detrás de, detrás de, detrás de (¡detrás de la puerta!)	*Behind, behind, behind (behind the door!)*
Cerca de, cerca de, cerca de (¡cerca de la casa!)	*Close to, close to, close to (close to the house!)*
Lejos de, lejos de, lejos de (¡lejos de la casa!)	*Far from, far from, far from (far from the house!)*
Arriba de, arriba de, arriba de (¡arriba!)	*On top of, on top of, on top of (on top of!)*
Debajo de, debajo de, debajo de (¡debajo del coche!)	*Under, under, under (under the car!)*
Dentro de, dentro de, dentro de (¡dentro!)	*Inside, inside, inside (inside!)*
Fuera de, fuera de, fuera de (¡fuera de la casa!)	*Outside, outside, outside (outside the house!)*
Ah, Mimi. Aquí está. Muy bien. Hola, Mimi. Hola.	*Ah, Mimi. Here she is. Very good. Hi, Mimi. Hi.*

Fredo Book Activity

Materials: Cassette player; ***"Las aventuras de Fredo,"*** Book Five **"¿Dónde está Mimi?"** on Song Cassette, Side B; and ***"Las aventuras de Fredo"*** (*"Fredo's Adventures"*) books.

Tell the children they are going to read about Fredo's cat, Mimi. Distribute your copies of ***"Las aventuras de Fredo"*** (*"Fredo's Adventures"*) among the children. Tell them to turn to the fifth story in the book—**"¿Dónde está Mimi?"** (*"Where Is Mimi?"*)—and to read along silently as doña Elena reads the story. Play the audio tape. Then have the class re-read the story with volunteers reading aloud.

Activity 56B: Read *"¿Dónde está Mimi?"* (*"Where Is Mimi?"*)

Note: If your school has ***"Las aventuras de Fredo"*** (*"Fredo's Adventures"*) books available for the children, substitute the Fredo Book Activity in the margin for this activity.

Materials: VCR; Video Lesson 56 on Tape 19.

Preparation: Recue Video Lesson 56 to section 8, in which doña Elena reads the story **"¿Dónde está Mimi?"**

Tell the children to read along with doña Elena as she reads *"Where Is Mimi?"* (**"¿Dónde está Mimi?"**). Play section 8 of the video with the sound. Remind the children to look for visual clues in the pictures and to listen and watch for words they know. Then rewind the tape to the beginning of the story and replay it without the sound, pausing the tape at each line of the story. Ask volunteers to read the lines aloud.

If children have difficulty pronouncing words as they read aloud, reassure them that they will hear the story again and they should listen carefully as they read along with doña Elena the next time.

Activity 56C: Match the sentences and pictures

Materials: Blackline Master 56C; pencils; a current calendar; and the current Month Picture.

Preparation: Copy and distribute Blackline Master 56C so that each child has a copy.

Have the children write their names and the date on their papers. If they need help with the date, point to the number of the day on the current calendar and the name of the month on the Month Picture. Tell them to answer the question at the top of the paper—**¿Dónde está Mimi?** (*Where is Mimi?*) by matching each sentence to the picture it describes. When they have completed that task, divide the class into pairs and have them check their answers with a partner. The partners should then take turns reading the sentences aloud to one another. Children should have matched the sentences and pictures as follows:

Sentence:	Picture:
Mimi está lejos de la casa. (*Mimi is far from the house.*)	b
Mimi está detrás de la puerta. (*Mimi is behind the door.*)	a
Mimi está cerca de la casa. (*Mimi is close to the house.*)	d
Mimi está delante de la casa. (*Mimi is in front of the house.*)	c

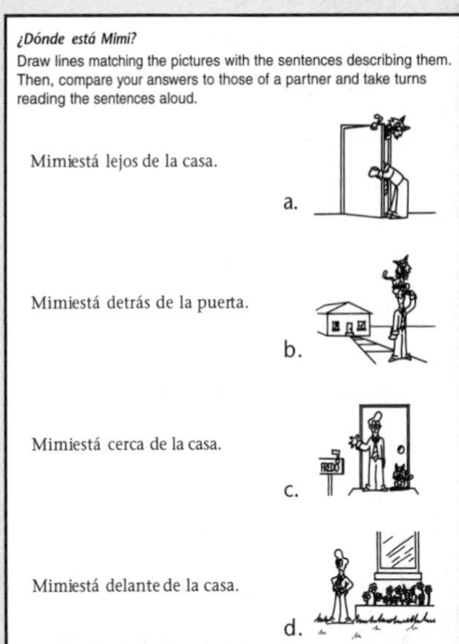

¿Dónde está Mimi?

Draw lines matching the pictures with the sentences describing them. Then, compare your answers to those of a partner and take turns reading the sentences aloud.

Mimiestá lejos de la casa. a.

Mimiestá detrás de la puerta. b.

Mimiestá cerca de la casa. c.

Mimiestá delante de la casa. d.

Blackline Master 56C

CLOSING

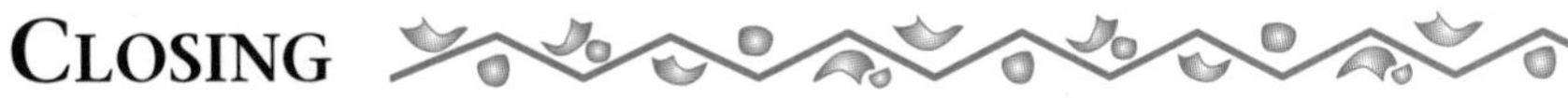

Tell the children that Spanish class is finished for today. In the next lesson children will learn more location phrases.

LESSON 57

Materials to gather

- VCR and Video Lesson 57 on Tape 19
- Cassette player
- Song Cassette
- Overhead projector
- Overhead transparency of Blackline Master 56A ("**¿Dónde está Mimi?**")
- Blackline Master 57B (clowns in various positions)
- Blank transparency
- Pencils
- Current calendar
- Current Month Picture
- World map
- Overhead transparency of Blackline Master 37A-1 ("**La canción de geografía**")
- ***Optional materials:*** blank paper; markers or colored pencils; and children's dictionary pages

OBJECTIVES

Language

- Learn additional location phrases and their hand motions

Culture

- Learn that there are often several ways of saying something
- Sing "**De colores**" (*"Colors"*)

Review

- Answer the questions **¿Qué día de la semana es?** (*What day of the week is it?*), **¿Qué mes es?** (*What month is it?*), and **¿Cuál es la fecha?** (*What is the date?*)
- Review the location phrases and their motions (**delante de**—*in front of*, **detrás de**—*behind*, **cerca de**—*close to*, and **lejos de**—*far from*)
- Sing "**¿Dónde está Mimi?**" (*"Where Is Mimi?"*)
- Answer the questions **¿Qué animal es?** (*What animal is it?*) and **¿De qué color es ___?** (*What color is ___?*)

Vocabulary

arriba de	*on top of, over, above*
debajo de	*under, underneath, below*
abajo de	*under, underneath, below*

Warm-up

Greet the children and let them know it's time for Spanish class (**la clase de español**). If you feel comfortable, greet them with **Hola** (*Hello*), **Buenos días** (*Good morning*), or **Buenas tardes** (*Good afternoon*). Ask for a volunteer to lead the class in the opening conversation. Tell the volunteer to ask *What's happening?* (**¿Qué pasa?**) rather than *How are you?* (**¿Cómo estás tú?**). Ask the class if they can recall how Kipper answered that question (**Nada**—*Nothing*) (**V** = Volunteer, **C** = class):

V: Hola (Buenos días; Buenas tardes), clase.	*Hello (Good morning; Good afternoon), class.*
C: Hola (Buenos días; Buenas tardes), ___.	*Hello (Good morning; Good afternoon), ___.*
V: ¿Qué pasa?	*What's happening?*
C: Nada.	*Nothing.*

Review

Write the following location phrases (Spanish only) on the chalkboard:

delante de (*in front of*):	extend arms frontward and shake both hands
detrás de (*behind*):	put hands behind back
cerca de (*close to*):	make hands into fists and hold them up under the chin
lejos de (*far from*):	hand at brow as if searching for someone

Make each of the motions indicated and ask the children to say the appropriate location phrase.

Introduce the video

Invite the children to listen and watch as **la maestra** introduces additional location phrases and reviews some describing words.

Video Lesson

1. Greeting the children

La maestra greets the children with **Hola** (*Hello*) and asks **¿Qué tal?** (*How's it going?*).

2. Reviewing questions and answers about the date

La maestra asks Kipper these questions. For numbers 1–31, days of the week, and months of the year, see the Topics and Language Covered at the front of the book.

¿Qué día de la semana es?	*What day of the week is it?*
Es ___.	*It's ___.*
¿Qué mes es?	*What month is it?*
Es ___.	*It's ___.*
¿Cuál es la fecha?	*What is the date?*
El [*number*] de [*month*].	*The ___ of ___.*

3. Reviewing location phrases

Holding a card with location phrases, **la maestra** asks the children and Kipper to read each phrase: **delante de** (*in front of*), **detrás de** (*behind*), **cerca de** (*close to*), **lejos de** (*far from*).

4. Singing *"¿Dónde está Mimi?"* ("Where Is Mimi?")

La maestra reviews the hand motions for each of the phrases in section 3. She sings the song about that roaming cat Mimi.

¿Mimi? ¿Mimi? ¿Dónde está Mimi?	*Mimi? Mimi? Where is Mimi?*
¿Dónde está?	*Where is she?*
Delante de, delante de, delante de,	*In front of, in front of, in front of,*
Detrás de, detrás de, detrás de (¡detrás de la puerta!)	*Behind, behind, behind (behind the door!)*
Cerca de, cerca de, cerca de (¡cerca de la casa!)	*Close to, close to, close to (close to the house!)*
Lejos de, lejos de, lejos de (¡lejos de la casa!)	*Far from, far from, far from (far from the house!)*
Arriba de, arriba de, arriba de (¡arriba!)	*On top of, on top of, on top of (on top of!)*
Debajo de, debajo de, debajo de (¡debajo del coche!)	*Under, under, under (under the car!)*
Dentro de, dentro de, dentro de (¡dentro!)	*Inside, inside, inside (inside!)*
Fuera de, fuera de, fuera de (¡fuera de la casa!)	*Outside, outside, outside (outside the house!)*
Ah, Mimi. Aquí está. Muy bien.	*Ah, Mimi. Here she is. Very good.*
Hola, Mimi. Hola.	*Hi, Mimi. Hi.*

5. Introducing additional location phrases

La maestra introduces three more location phrases. She explains that the second and third phrases have the same meaning and that in most languages there are often two ways of saying the same thing. She presents hand motions for these new phrases. Doña Elena asks the children **¿Dónde está Antonio?** (*Where is Antonio?*): **arriba de la concha** (*on top of the shell*), **abajo de la concha** (*under the shell*).

arriba de	*on top of, over, above*
abajo de / debajo de	*under, underneath of, below*

Hand motions for the new location phrases:

arriba de:
hand(s) over the head

debajo de:
hand(s) under the head

6. Practicing the new location phrases

La maestra practices the new location phrases with the children: **Mimi está arriba del refrigerador** (*Mimi is on top of the refrigerator*), **Mimi está debajo/abajo del coche** (*Mimi is under the car*).

7. Practicing two familiar questions and answers

La maestra practices two other familiar questions and answers: **¿Qué animal es?** (*What animals is it?*), **Es el elefante** (*It's the elephant*), and **¿De qué color es el elefante?** (*What color is the elephant?*), **El elefante es gris** (*The elephant is gray*).

¿Tocas "De colores" en la guitarra?
(*Do you play "Colors" on the guitar?*)

Sí, toco la guitarra y toco la trompeta.
(*Yes, I play the guitar and I play the trumpet.*)

8. Singing *"De colores"* (*"Colors"*)

La maestra sings the song **"De colores"** (*"Colors"*). For song lyrics, see Song 12 in the Song Appendix.

9. Reviewing three describing words

La maestra explains the diminutive endings **-ito** and **-ita** and reviews three describing words.

pájaro	*bird*	casa	*house*
pajarito	*little, small bird*	casita	*little, small house*

¿Cómo es la casa?	*What is the house like?*
La casa es grande/ mediana/pequeña.	*The house is large/ medium-sized/small.*

Tell the children that reading the location phrases as they appear on the screen and listening to the phrases as **la maestra** sings will help them learn to pronounce the phrases.

10. Singing *"¿Dónde está Mimi?"* (*"Where Is Mimi?"*)

After reviewing the location phrases and motions, **la maestra** sings **"¿Dónde está Mimi?"** (*"Where Is Mimi?"*) again.

11. Closing

Kipper says one location phrase at a time. **La maestra** and the children make the motions for each phrase. Kipper and **la maestra** say **Adiós** (*Good-bye*) and **Hasta luego** (*See you later*).

After viewing the video, praise the children for their good listening and watching skills.

Activity Lesson

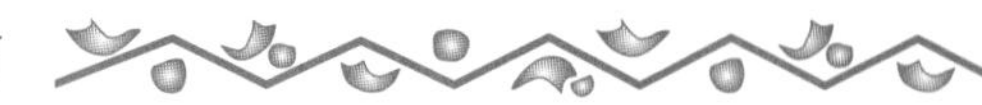

Activity 57A: Sing about Mimi!

Materials: Cassette player; **"¿Dónde está Mimi?"** (*"Where Is Mimi?"*) on the Song Cassette; your overhead transparency of Blackline Master 56A; and an overhead projector.

Preparation: Write the location phrases below (Spanish only) on the chalkboard.

Review the hand motions that go with the location phrases the children have learned. Ask a volunteer to say each location phrase. Children should make the appropriate motion.

delante de (*in front of*): extend arms frontward and shake both hands

detrás de (*behind*): put hands behind back

cerca de (*close to*): make hands into fists and hold them up under the chin

lejos de (*far from*): hand at brow as if searching for someone

arriba de (*on top of, over, above*): hand(s) over the head

debajo/abajo de (*under, underneath, below*): hand(s) under the head

Project the transparency of Blackline Master 56A and ask a volunteer to point to each line of the song as the children sing it. Children make the motions as they sing along with **la maestra**. For song lyrics with English equivalents, see Video lesson, section 4.

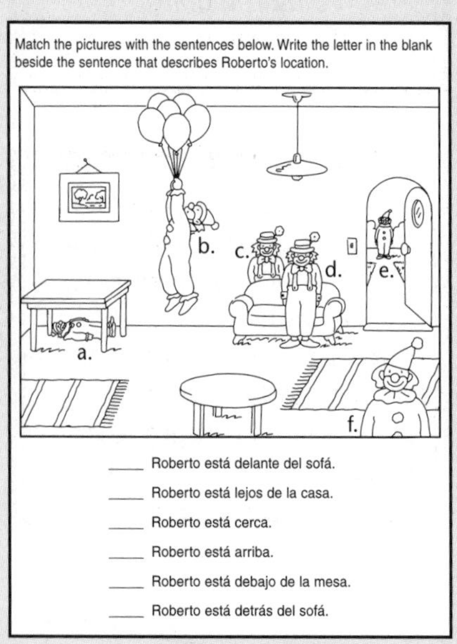

Match the pictures with the sentences below. Write the letter in the blank beside the sentence that describes Roberto's location.

____ Roberto está delante del sofá.

____ Roberto está lejos de la casa.

____ Roberto está cerca.

____ Roberto está arriba.

____ Roberto está debajo de la mesa.

____ Roberto está detrás del sofá.

Blackline Master 57B

Activity 57B: Where is Roberto, the clown? *(¿Dónde está el payaso, Roberto?)*

Materials: Blackline Master 57B; pencils; a current calendar; the current Month Picture; a blank overhead transparency; and an overhead projector.

Preparation: Copy and distribute Blackline Master 57B so that each child has a copy. Make an overhead transparency of Blackline Master 57B.

Have the children write their names and the date on their papers. If they need help with the date, point to the number of the day on the current calendar and the name of the month on the Month Picture. Tell the children that the sentences underneath the picture describe each of Roberto's locations. They are to match each sentence with the clown that the sentence describes by writing the correct letter in the blank. When the children have completed the activity, check their answers. Then ask volunteers to read each sentence aloud. As the volunteers read, point to the sentences on your overhead transparency and advise the rest of the class to read along.

Answers from top to bottom: d, e, f, b, a, c

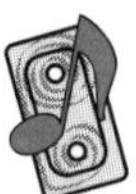

Activity 57C: Recall the 20 Spanish-speaking countries

Materials: Cassette player; **"La canción de geografía"** (*"The Geography Song"*) on the Song Cassette, Side A; a world map; your over-head transparency of Blackline Master 37A-1; and an overhead projector.

Display the map of the world. Ask the children to name as many of the twenty Spanish-speaking countries as they can. As they do so, locate them on the map or ask them to locate them on the map. Next, project the transparency with the lyrics to *"The Geography Song"* (**"La canción de geografía"**). Find the names of the countries they didn't recall in the lyrics and locate them on the map. Finally, play the song and encourage the children to sing along. Point to each country name on the transparency and have a volunteer point to the country on the map as the class sings. For song lyrics with English equivalents, see Song 2 in the Song Appendix.

CLOSING

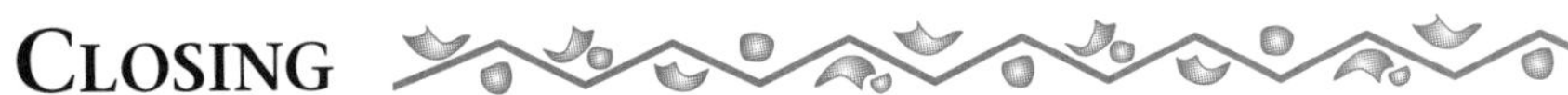

Tell the children that Spanish class is finished for today. In the next lesson children will learn two more location phrases and review the names of buildings.

DICTIONARY

Materials: Blank paper; markers or colored pencils; and children's dictionary pages.

Preparation: Write the Spanish location phrases given in Activity 57A on the chalkboard (Spanish only).

Tell the children to draw a picture of their favorite animal standing some-where in relationship to a house. The animal could be in front of the house, behind the house, far away from the house, etc. Underneath the picture, they should write the location phrase that describes where the animal is. Point out that the phrases are on the board. The new dictionary page should be filed alpha-betically by the first letter of the first word of the location phrase.

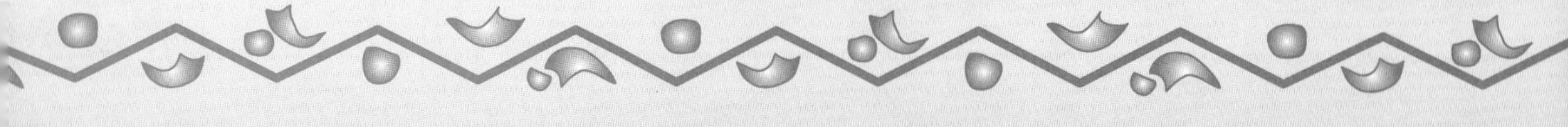

Lesson 58

Materials to gather

- VCR and Video Lesson 58 on Tape 20
- Cassette player
- Song Cassette
- Overhead projector
- Overhead transparency of Blackline Master 56A ("**¿Dónde está Mimi?**")
- Blackline Master 58B (house and yard scene)
- Pencils
- Current calendar
- Current Month Picture
- 11 colored paintbrushes (from Lesson 4 Review)
- ***Optional materials:*** children's dictionary pages; "**El alfabeto**" (found in the Teacher's Resource Book); colored construction paper; markers or colored pencils; staples and stapler or brackets; glitter; glue; stickers

Objectives

Language

- Learn two additional location phrases

Culture

- Recall that a building has an exit and an entrance

Review

- Sing "**¿Dónde está Mimi?**" (*"Where Is Mimi?"*)
- Recall the names of several buildings and building parts
- Practice the location phrases and hand-arm motions

Vocabulary

dentro de	*inside of*
fuera de	*outside of*

Warm-up

Ask for a volunteer to lead the class in the opening conversation. Tell the volunteer to ask *How's it going?* (**¿Qué tal?**) rather than *How are you?* (**¿Cómo estás tú?**). Remind the class to use **tú** (familiar *you*) when asking their classmate how he/she is (**V** = volunteer, **C** = class):

V: Hola (Buenos días; Buenas tardes), clase.	*Hello (Good morning; Good afternoon), class.*
C: Hola (Buenos días; Buenas tardes), ___.	*Hello (Good morning; Good afternoon), ___.*
V: ¿Qué tal?	*How's it going?*
C: Muy bien (Muy mal; Así, así), gracias. ¿Y tú?	*Very well (Very bad; So-so), thank you. And you?*
V: Muy bien (Muy mal; Así, así), gracias.	*Very well (Very bad; So-so), thank you.*

Review

Write the following location phrases (Spanish only) on the chalkboard:

delante de (*in front of*): extend arms frontward and shake both hands

detrás de (*behind*): put hands behind back

cerca de (*close to*): make hands into fists and hold them up under the chin

lejos de (*far from*): hand at brow as if searching for someone

arriba de (*on top of, over, above*): hand(s) over the head

debajo/abajo de (*under, underneath, below*): hand(s) under the head

Make each of the motions indicated and ask the children to say the appropriate location phrase.

Introduce the video

Invite the children to listen and watch as **la maestra** introduces how to say *inside of* and *outside of*.

EN ESPAÑOL

If you feel comfortable, greet the children with **Hola** (*Hello*), **Buenos días** (*Good morning*), or **Buenas tardes** (*Good afternoon*).

VIDEO LESSON

1. Greeting the children and LeeAnn

La maestra greets the children and LeeAnn with **Buenas tardes** (*Good afternoon*). She asks **¿Qué tal?** (*How's it going?*) and points out the difference in sound between **Buenos días** (*Good morning*) and **Buenas tardes**.

2. Reviewing and playing games with location phrases

La maestra reviews the location phrases. LeeAnn says one location phrase at a time and **la maestra** and the children make the corresponding motion. Then **la maestra** gives the motions and the children and LeeAnn say the location phrases. For motions, see the Review section of this lesson.

3. Introducing new location phrases

LeeAnn reads the new phrases. **La maestra** explains the motions. Doña Elena asks the children **¿Dónde está Antonio?** (*Where is Antonio?*)—**dentro de la concha** (*inside the shell*).

dentro de (*inside of*): fingers of one hand inside the other hand

fuera de (*outside of*): fingers of one hand placed outside of (in front of) the other hand

4. Singing *"¿Dónde está Mimi?"* (*"Where Is Mimi?"*)

La maestra points to pictures of Mimi **dentro de la chimenea** (*inside the chimney*) and **fuera de la casa** (*outside the house*). She sings **"¿Dónde está Mimi?"** (*"Where Is Mimi?"*). For song lyrics, see Song 13 in the Song Appendix.

5. Recalling two important parts of a building

La maestra reviews the words **la entrada** (*entrance*) and **la salida** (*exit*) with LeeAnn and Winston.

6. Reviewing the names of buildings

Showing LeeAnn Red Flashcards of buildings, **la maestra** reviews the names of several types of buildings. LeeAnn tells her **Vivo en un apartamento** (*I live in an apartment*). **La maestra** tells the children **Yo vivo en una casa y LeeAnn vive en un edificio de apartamentos** (*I live in a house and LeeAnn lives in an apartment building*).

¿Qué edificio es?	*What building is it?*
Es el edificio de apartamentos.	*It's the apartment building.*
Es el rascacielos.	*It's the skyscraper.*
Es el hospital.	*It's the hospital.*

7. Playing *¿Qué edificio es?* (*What building is it?*)

La maestra points to pictures of buildings and asks the children **¿Qué edificio es?** (*What building is it?*). Children identify **el rascacielos** (*skyscraper*), **los apartamentos** (*apartments*), **la casa** (*house*), **la tienda** (*store*), **la escuela** (*school*), and **el supermercado** (*supermarket*).

8. Reviewing and practicing the location phrases

After telling the children, **Un edificio muy importante en tu vida es la escuela** (*An important building in your life is the school*), **la maestra** asks them if they are **dentro de la escuela** (*inside the school*) or **fuera de la escuela** (*outside the school*). She reviews all the location phrases using the pictures of Mimi and Fredo and the motions. Doña Elena practices the location phrases with the children by asking them **¿Dónde está Antonio?** (*Where is Antonio?*) each time Antonio changes position.

9. Closing

La maestra tells the children they are learning Spanish **paso a paso** (*step-by-step*).

In section 7 of the video, each building word is revealed on the screen after the children have said the word and **la maestra** says the word several times. Point this out to children and tell them to repeat the word to themselves after **la maestra** says it the first time. Repeating and seeing the words and the pictures will help them remember the vocabulary.

After viewing the video, praise the children for their good listening and watching skills.

Activity Lesson

An alternative way of singing the song would be to have half the class singing the lyrics as the other half makes the motions.

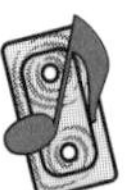

Activity 58A: Sing the song about Mimi's whereabouts

Materials: Cassette player; "**¿Dónde está Mimi?**" (*"Where Is Mimi?"*) on the Song Cassette, Side A; your overhead transparency of Blackline Master 56A; and an overhead projector.

Preparation: Write the following location phrases (Spanish only) on the chalkboard:

delante de (*in front of*): extend arms frontward and shake both hands

detrás de (*behind*): put hands behind back

cerca de (*close to*): make hands into fists and hold them up under the chin

lejos de (*far from*): hand at brow as if searching for someone

arriba de (*on top of, over, above*): hand(s) over the head

debajo/abajo de (*under, underneath, below*): hand(s) under the head

dentro de (*inside of*): fingers of one hand inside the other hand

fuera de (*outside of*): fingers of one hand placed outside of (in front of) the other hand

Review all the location phrases by making each motion and having the children say which location phrase it is. Then have a volunteer call out the location phrases one at a time in the order you've written them on the chalkboard. The children should make the motion for each phrase. Next, project your overhead transparency of Blackline Master 56A. Play the song and encourage the children to sing along and make the motions. For song lyrics with English equivalents, see Song 13 in the Song Appendix.

Here is the Espinola family. Read the descriptions in the sentences below and fill in the name of the person who is in each location described. There's only one description for each family member. The first sentence is done for you.

1. Nano está delante de la casa y delante de Rosa.
2. ______ está detrás de Nano.
3. ______ está lejos de la casa.
4. ______ está debajo del cerdo.
5. ______ está cerca del reloj.
6. ______ está sobre el techo.
7. ______ está cerca del abuelo.
8. ______ está fuera de la casa.
9. ______ está arriba del pato.

Violeta, Horacio, Lulú, María, Papá, Marco, Mamá, Rosa, Nano

Blackline Master 58B

Activity 58B: Who is where?

Materials: Blackline Master 58B; pencils; a current calendar; and the current Month Picture.

Preparation: Copy and distribute Blackline Master 58B so that each child has a copy.

Have the children write their names and the date on their papers. If they need help with the date, point to the number of the day on the current calendar and the name of the month on the Month Picture. Tell the children that for each person with a name in the picture (the grandfather bending over the sink is not named), there is a sentence describing that person. Some sentences may describe more than one person, but children should be sure when they are done that each name in the picture has been used in a sentence. Answers are:

1. Nano	4. Lulú	7. Marco
2. Rosa	5. Mamá	8. Papá
3. Horacio	6. Violeta	9. María

Activity 58C: Practice color words

Materials: Your 11 colored paintbrushes (from Lesson 4).

Review the color words quickly by holding up one paintbrush at a time with the color name covered and asking the children to identify the color in Spanish. Then have one volunteer at a time describe something (classroom objects or pieces of clothing, for example) in the classroom by its colors. The class is to guess what item the volunteer is describing. You may wish to do this in pairs or small groups.

Los colores (*colors*):

amarillo	*yellow*	morado	*purple*
anaranjado	*orange*	negro	*black*
azul	*red*	rojo	*red*
blanco	*white*	rosado	*pink*
café	*brown*	verde	*green*
gris	*gray*		

CLOSING

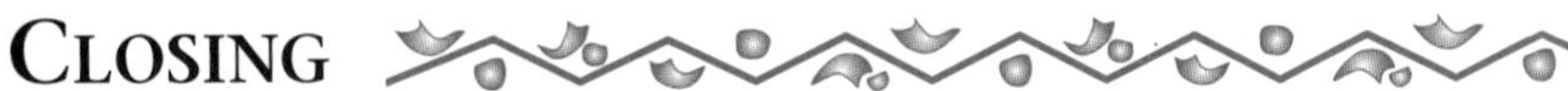

Tell the children that Spanish class is finished for today. In the next lesson children will read the story about Fredo's adventures at the zoo and sing about the wayward cat Mimi.

DICTIONARY

Materials: **"El alfabeto"** (found in the Teacher's Resource Book); colored construction paper; colored markers or pencils; staples and stapler or brackets; children's dictionary pages; *optional*: glitter, glue, stickers.

Preparation: Copy and distribute **"El alfabeto"** so that each child has one.

Have the children assemble their dictionaries. (1) Have them arrange their dictionary pages alphabetically. (2) Have them create a "contents" page. On their **"El alfabeto"** pages they should circle each letter for which they have a page in their dictionary. They should put this page on top of their other pages. (3) Provide each child with two pieces of colored construction paper—one for the front cover and one for the back. On the cover page they should write **"Mi diccionario"** and their name, grade number, and school name. Allow them to add other decorations if they wish, e.g., stickers or glitter. (4) Help them fasten their dictionaries together with staples or brackets. (5) In the next lesson, allow time for children to look at one another's dictionaries.

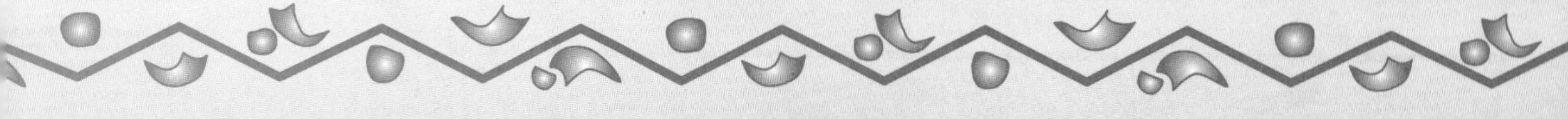

Lesson 59

Materials to gather

- VCR and Video Lesson 59 on Tape 20
- Cassette player
- Song Cassette
- Overhead projector
- Overhead transparency of Blackline Master 51A (**"De colores"**)
- Blackline Master 59B (nine sentences)
- Pencils
- Current calendar
- Current Month Picture
- ***Optional materials:*** children's dictionaries

Objectives

Language

- Comprehend more of the story **"En el jardín zoológico"** (*"At the Zoo"*)
- Understand more of the trip to the San Diego Zoo

Culture

- Hear **"Dulce canta el burro"** (*"Sweetly Sings the Donkey"*)
- Learn that animals have a function and that the function varies depending on the animal

Review

- Sing **"De colores"** (*"Colors"*)
- Read **"En el jardín zoológico"** (*"At the Zoo"*)
- Review animal names

Vocabulary

No new vocabulary is introduced in this lesson.

Warm-up

Tell the children that their Spanish lessons are almost over for this school year and that in the next two videos they will revisit some places, re-read some stories, and sing some songs again with **la maestra**. Ask what their favorite places, stories, and songs have been and what they remember most about them.

Review

Mention that one topic they learned more about this year is animals. Ask them to name as many wild and domestic animals as they can in Spanish. The following lists alphabetically all the animals children have learned in ***Español para ti***, Levels 1–4.

el burro	*donkey*	el gorila	*gorilla*
el caballo	*horse*	la jirafa	*giraffe*
la cebra	*zebra*	el león	*lion*
el cerdo	*pig*	el oso	*bear*
el conejo	*rabbit*	el pájaro	*bird*
el elefante	*elephant*	el pato	*duck*
la foca	*seal*	el perro	*dog*
la gallina	*chicken*	el pez/los peces	*fish*
el gallo	*rooster*	el tigre	*tiger*
el gato	*cat*	la vaca	*cow*

Introduce the video

Invite the children to listen and watch as Winston, LeeAnn, and Kipper all join **la maestra** for this lesson.

Video Lesson

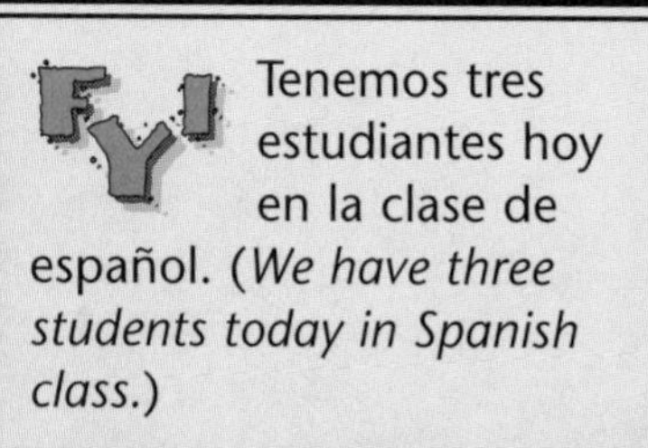

Tenemos tres estudiantes hoy en la clase de español. (*We have three students today in Spanish class.*)

Encourage the children to sing with along with **la maestra**—even if all they can sing without reading the lyrics are the words **De colores**!

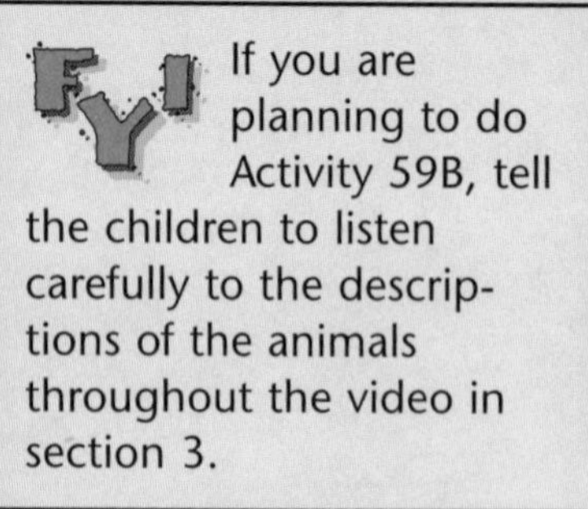

If you are planning to do Activity 59B, tell the children to listen carefully to the descriptions of the animals throughout the video in section 3.

1. Greeting the children, Winston, LeeAnn, and Kipper

La maestra greets everyone with **Buenos días** (*Good morning*). She tells the children that this lesson is devoted to relaxing and having fun.

2. Singing *"De colores"* (*"Colors"*)

La maestra says **¡Vamos a cantar!** (*Let's sing!*) and she sings the song about the colors of spring in the countryside. For song lyrics, see Song 12 in the Song Appendix.

3. Reading *"En el jardín zoológico"* (*"At the Zoo"*)

Doña Elena reads the story about Fredo's antics at the zoo. For lines from the story, see Lesson 52, Video Lesson, section 6 and Lesson 53, Video Lesson, section 10.

4. Playing *¿Qué animal es?* (*What animal is it?*)

La maestra shows the children pictures of wild animals and asks **¿Qué animal es?** (*What animal is it?*). Children name the animals.

la cebra	*zebra*	el león	*lion*
el elefante	*elephant*	el oso	*bear*
la foca	*seal*	el pájaro	*bird*
el gorila	*gorilla*	el pato	*duck*
la jirafa	*giraffe*	el tigre	*tiger*

5. Visiting the San Diego Zoo one last time

Kipper, LeeAnn, and **la maestra** visit the zoo. For their statements, see Lesson 51, Video Lesson, section 6; Lesson 52, Video Lesson, section 3; and Lesson 54, Video Lesson, section 6.

6. Playing *¿Qué animal es?* (*What animal is it?*)

La maestra asks the children **¿Qué animal es?** (*What animal is it?*) as she shows them pictures of animals at the zoo.

7. Playing another game with animal vocabulary

Antonio makes the sounds and actions of **el perro** (*dog*), **el gato** (*cat*), **la vaca** (*cow*), **el caballo** (*horse*), and **el elefante** (*elephant*). The children guess the animals when **la maestra** asks **¿Qué animal es?** (*What animal is it?*).

8. Singing a song about the donkey

After mentioning the sounds the rooster **(el gallo)** and donkey **(el burro)** make in Spanish, **la maestra** sings **"Dulce canta el burro"** (*"Sweetly Sings the Donkey"*) once through and then in a round with herself!

Dulce canta el burro	*Sweetly sings the donkey.*
Al ir a comer.	*When he comes to eat.*
Si no lo cuidamos	*If we don't take care of him,*
Él rebuznará.	*He will bray.*
Cají, cajó, cajá.	*Cají, cajó, cajá.*
Cají, cajó, cajá.	*Cají, cajó, cajá.*
Cají, cajó, cajá.	*Cají, cajó, cajá.*
Cají, cajó, cajá.	*Cají, cajó, cajá.*

9. Talking about animals

La maestra talks about the different functions of animals—as pets, for their products, and for their work. She mentions that donkeys (**los burros**) are used for work purposes on farms and ranches in South America (**Sudamérica**) and Spain (**España**).

10. Closing

La maestra, LeeAnn, Kipper, and Winston bid the children **Adiós** (*Good-bye*) and **Hasta luego** (*See you later*).

Children new to ***Español para ti*** this year may not recognize the song **"Dulce canta el burro"** (*"Sweetly Sings the Donkey"*).

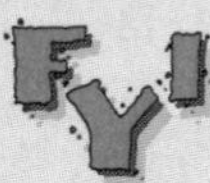

When she talks about the animals toward the end of the video lesson, **la maestra** uses the following Spanish words and sentences.

los animales domésticos
(*pets, domestic animals*)

La vaca produce la leche.
(*The cow produces milk.*)

Las gallinas producen los huevos.
(*The chickens produce eggs.*)

After viewing the video, praise the children for their good listening and watching skills.

Activity Lesson

Activity 59A: Sing the song about colors

Materials: Cassette player; **"De colores"** (*"Colors"*) on the Song Cassette; your overhead transparency of Blackline Master 51A; and an overhead projector.

Preparation: Project the overhead transparency of Blackline Master 51A.

Lead the children in a discussion of the way nature's colors in your area vary depending on the time of year. For example, in spring and summer the grass is green whereas in the fall and winter it may be brown or covered with snow. Tell the children they are going to sing the song about the colors in the countryside. For song lyrics with English equivalents, see Song 12 in the Song Appendix.

Activity 59B: What am I? (*¿Qué soy yo?*)

Materials: Blackline Master 59B; pencils; a current calendar; and the current Month Picture.

Preparation: Copy and distribute Blackline Master 59B so that each child has a copy.

Have the children write their names and the date on their papers. If they need help with the date, point to the number of the day on the current calendar and the name of the month on the Month Picture. Remind the children that during their trip to the San Diego Zoo, **la maestra** described many of the animals. Explain to the children that on the paper are nine riddles that describe the animals listed in the word bank (**Palabras**). They are to complete each riddle by writing on the line the name of the animal described. Point out that the first one has been completed for them. Ask a volunteer to read the riddle and solution for number one aloud. Allow children time to complete the activity. Then ask volunteers to read the riddles and their solutions aloud. Answers and English equivalents are as follows:

1. Soy anaranjado y negro. Soy un gato grande. Soy <u>el tigre</u>.
   (*I am orange and black. I am a large cat. I am the tiger.*)
2. Soy negro. Me gusta comer los plátanos. Soy <u>el gorila</u>.
   (*I am black. I like to eat bananas. I am the gorilla.*)
3. Soy un gato grande. Tengo mucho pelo. Me gusta comer carne. Soy <u>el león</u>.
   (*I am a big cat. I have a lot of hair. I like to eat meat. I am the lion.*)
4. Soy blanca y negra. No soy un caballo en pijama. Soy <u>la cebra</u>.
   (*I am white and black. I'm not a horse in pajamas. I'm the zebra.*)
5. Soy muy gordo. Tengo la nariz grande. Soy gris. Soy <u>el elefante</u>.
   (*I am very fat. I have a big nose. I am gray. I am the elephant.*)

¿Qué soy yo?
Figure out the names of the animals in the riddles and write their names in the blanks. Use the word bank to help you.

1. Soy anaranjado y negro. Soy un gato grande.
   Soy ______ *el tigre* ______.
2. Soy negro. Me gusta comer los plátanos.
   Soy ____________.
3. Soy un gato grande. Tengo mucho pelo.
   Me gusta comer carne.
   Soy ____________.
4. Soy blanca y negra. No soy un caballo en pijama.
   Soy ____________.
5. Soy muy gordo. Tengo la nariz grande. Soy gris.
   Soy ____________.
6. Soy pequeño. Tengo muchos colores.
   Me gusta cantar.
   Soy ____________.
7. Soy muy alta. Soy muy bonita. Tengo miedo del león.
   Soy ____________.
8. Soy un párajo. Me gusta nadar.
   Soy ____________.
9. Me gusta el agua. Como muchos peces.
   Me gusta jugar.
   Soy ____________.

Palabras
el león
la jirafa
el pájaro
el gorila
el pato
la cebra
la foca
el tigre
el elefante

Blackline Master 59B

Children new to ***Español para ti*** this year may not know the following words: in item 3 **pelo** (*hair*) and in 5 **nariz** (*nose*).

The following words may be unfamiliar to all children: in 3 **carne** (*meat*), in 8 **nadar** (*to swim*), and in 9 **agua** (*water*).

6. Soy pequeño. Tengo muchos colores. Me gusta cantar. Soy el pájaro.
   (*I am small. I have many colors. I like to sing. I am the bird.*)
7. Soy muy alta. Soy muy bonita. Tengo miedo del león. Soy la jirafa.
   (*I am very tall. I am very pretty. I am afraid of the lion. I am the giraffe.*)
8. Soy un pájaro. Me gusta nadar. Soy el pato.
   (*I am a bird. I like to swim. I am the duck.*)
9. Me gusta el agua. Como muchos peces. Me gusta jugar. Soy la foca.
   (*I like the water. I eat lots of fish. I like to play. I am the seal.*

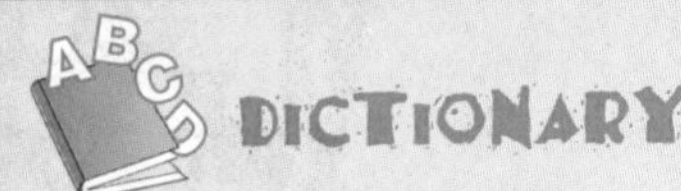

Materials: Children's dictionaries.

Ask volunteers to show the class their dictionaries, saying each word they have included and describing briefly each drawing. You may wish to have children do this in pairs.

Activity 59C: Where is ___?

Mention to the children that they've learned phrases for saying where someone is, e.g., behind, close to, on top of. Tell the children that you will position yourself in various locations and they are to describe your location in relation to the classroom object you are touching or pointing to.

Locations:	Children's responses:
stand in front of the closed classroom door, touch the door	delante de la puerta / La maestra está delante de la puerta.
stand behind the desk, touch the desk	detrás de / La maestra está detrás del escritorio.
stand close to the window, touch the window	cerca de la ventana / La maestra está cerca de la ventana.
stand far away from your desk chair, point to the chair	lejos de la silla / La maestra está lejos de la silla.
hold a book over your head	debajo/abajo del libro / La maestra está debajo/abajo del libro.
put a piece of paper on the floor, stand on it	arriba del papel / La maestra está arriba del papel.
stand outside the classroom, point toward the classroom	fuera de la clase / La maestra está fuera de la clase.
move into the classroom	dentro de la clase / La maestra está dentro de la clase.

CLOSING

Tell the children that Spanish class is finished for today. In the next lesson they will review vocabulary for mealtimes and say good-bye for the year to **la maestra**, Winston, Kipper, and LeeAnn.

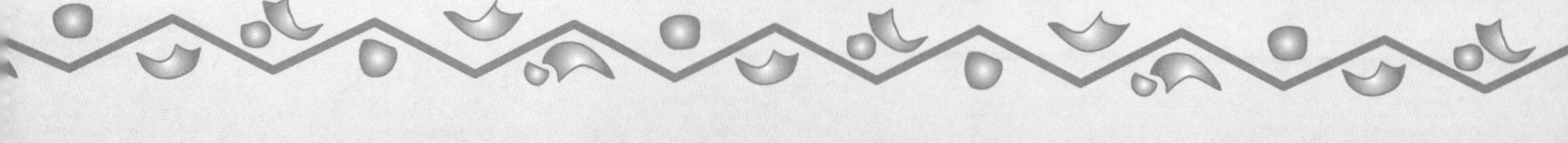

Lesson 60

Materials to gather

- VCR and Video Lesson 60 on Tape 20
- Cassette player
- Song Cassette
- Overhead projector
- Overhead transparencies you made during the year of song lyrics on Blackline Masters (for Review section)
- Blackline Master 60A (story with pictures)
- Overhead transparency of Blackline Master 56A ("**¿Dónde está Mimi?**")
- Current calendar
- Current Month Picture
- Writing paper
- Pencils or pens
- Colored markers

Objectives

Language

- Understand extended conversations about people's professions, musical instruments, and the center of San Diego

Culture

- Visit a Mexican restaurant
- Review why it's important to know Spanish

Review

- Recall vocabulary for musical instruments
- Remember vocabulary for professions
- Review vocabulary for describing a city and its buildings

Vocabulary

No new vocabulary is introduced in this lesson.

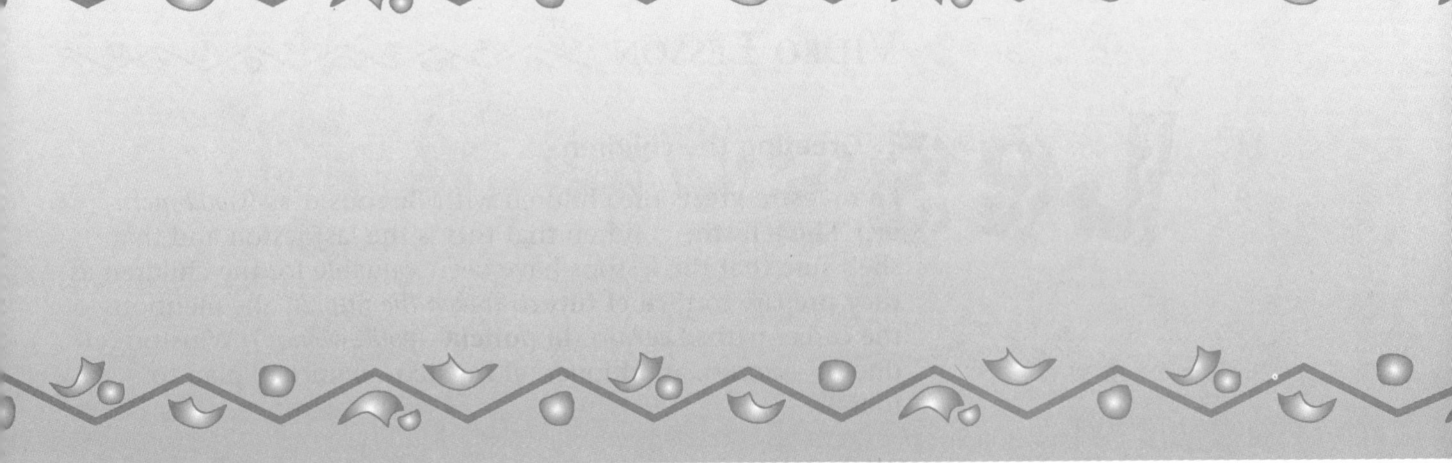

Warm-up

Remind the children that the school year is coming to a close and that summer is on the way. Encourage them to talk about their plans for summer vacation. Point out that this is their last Spanish lesson of the school year. Do they recall where **la maestra** is going on vacation (skiing in Argentina)?

Review

Materials: Cassette player; Song Cassette, Side A; and an overhead projector.

Ask the children to pick one or two of their favorite songs to sing. Let them sing the songs with the cassette; then encourage them to sing by themselves but with the lyrics displayed. A list of the Blackline Masters with lyrics is provided in the margin. For the lyrics with English equivalents, see the Song Appendix.

Introduce the video

Invite the children to listen and watch as **la maestra**, Kipper, Winston, and LeeAnn visit some of their favorite people and places.

Songs and Blackline Masters:

"Español para ti"
(1A)
"Months Rap"
(10A-1)
"Las estaciones"
(10A-2)
"Las vocales"
(15B)
"Calendar Rap"
(31A)
"¿Adónde vas?"
(33A)
"La canción de geografía"
(37A-1)
"En los Estados Unidos"
(37A-2)
"De colores"
(51A)
"¿Dónde está Mimi?"
(56A)

Video Lesson

1. Greeting the children

La maestra greets the children with **Buenos días** (*Good morning*). She tells the children that this is the last lesson and that she's sure that the lessons have been valuable for the children as they prepare to **toca el futuro** (*touch the future*). She mentions the career paths LeeAnn (**la policía**—*policewoman*), Winston (**el doctor**—*doctor*), and Kipper (**el músico**—*musician*) plan to follow.

2. Visiting the music store

La maestra looks for Kipper, LeeAnn, and Winston. After finding them, she asks them **¿Qué tal?** (*How's it going?*). She asks them if they remember visiting **la tienda de música** (*music store*). In the music store, she describes many of the instruments. For her statements, see Lesson 14, Video Lesson, section 5 and Lesson 15, Video Lesson, section 3.

3. Talking with the motorcycle policeman

LeeAnn asks **¿Vamos a la estación de la policía?** (*Are we going to the police station?*). For the conversation between **la maestra** and the policeman, see Lesson 44, Video Lesson, section 5.

4. Talking with the police chief

La maestra and LeeAnn visit with **el jefe de policía** (*police chief*). For their statements, see Lesson 45, Video Lesson, section 5.

5. Visiting the Mexican restaurant

La maestra visits the Mexican restaurant. For her statements and conversations, see Lesson 32, Video Lesson, section 7; Lesson 44, Video Lesson, section 6; Lesson 46, Video Lesson, section 7; and Lesson 47, Video Lesson, section 5.

6. Talking about *el centro de la ciudad* (*center of the city*)

Standing across the bay from the center of San Diego, a city with a Spanish name, **la maestra** describes the city. For her statements, see Lesson 38, Video Lesson, section 7.

7. Closing

La maestra thanks the children for a wonderful year and congratulates them on all they have learned **paso a paso** (*step-by-step*). She, LeeAnn, Kipper, and Winston bid the children **Adiós** (*Good-bye*) for Level 4.

After viewing the video, praise the children for their good listening and watching skills.

Here is a story that you may make serious or silly. Read the first part of each sentence. Then choose one of the pictures. Below the picture you choose, write the word that belongs to the picture in order to finish the sentence

Hoy es sábado. Hace ________ ________ ________.

Vivo en ________ ________ ________.
Quiero comer el desayuno.

Quiero comer ________ ________ ________.
Ahora estoy muy bien.

Voy a ________ ________ ________.
Ando en la calle.

Ahora tengo hambre. Voy a ________.

Blackline Master 60A

Activity Lesson

Activity 60A: Make up your own story

Materials: Blackline Master 60A; pencils; a current calendar; and the current Month Picture.

Preparation: Copy and distribute Blackline Master 60A so that each child has a copy.

Have the children write their names and the date on their papers. If they need help with the date, point to the number of the day on the current calendar and the name of the month on the Month Picture. Tell the children that **la maestra** has begun the story for them and has given them options for completing it. For each sentence in the story, she has indicated pictures with which they associate a specific word. Tell them to complete each sentence by choosing one picture and writing its corresponding word on the line. Possible completions are as follows.

> Hoy es sábado. Hace [calor, sol *or* buen tiempo / frío / mal tiempo].
> (*Today is Saturday. It's* [*hot, sunny, or good weather / cold / bad weather*].)
>
> Vivo en [una casa / un apartamento *or* un edificio de apartamentos / una chimenea].
> (*I live in* [*a house / an apartment or an apartment building / a chimney*].)
>
> Quiero comer el desayuno.
> (*I want to eat breakfast.*)
>
> Quiero comer [el pan / el cereal / un sándwich]. Ahora estoy muy bien.
> (*I want to eat* [*bread / cereal / a sandwich*]. *Now I'm very well.*)
>
> Voy a [la escuela / el jardín zoológico / el rascacielos]. Ando en la calle.
> (*I'm going to* [*school / the zoo / the skyscraper*]. *I'm walking on the street.*)
>
> Ahora tengo hambre. Voy a [casa].
> (*Now I'm hungry. I'm going* [*home*].)

Activity 60B: Sing about that crazy Mimi one last time

Materials: Cassette player; **"¿Dónde está Mimi"** (*"Where Is Mimi?"*) on the Song Cassette, Side A; your overhead transparency of Blackline Master 56A; and an overhead projector.

Preparation: Write the following location phrases (Spanish only) on the chalkboard:

> delante de (*in front of*): extend arms frontward and shake both hands
>
> detrás de (*behind*): put hands behind back
>
> cerca de (*close to*): make hands into fists and hold them up under the chin

lejos de (*far from*): hand at brow as if searching for someone

arriba de (*on top of, over, above*): hand(s) over the head

debajo/abajo de (*under, underneath, below*): hand(s) under the head

dentro de (*inside of*): fingers of one hand inside the other hand

fuera de (*outside of*): fingers of one hand placed outside of (in front of) the other hand

Mention to the children that they now know all the location phrases that come up in the song about Mimi. Review all the motions that go with the phrases by having the children make them and say the corresponding phrase. Divide the class into two groups—one group to make the motions, one to sing the lyrics. Project your overhead transparency of Blackline Master 56A. Play the song and encourage the children to either sing along or make the motions. Have the groups reverse roles and play the song again. For song lyrics with English equivalents, see Song 13 in the Song Appendix.

Activity 60C: Cooperative learning—Write a letter

Materials: Writing paper; pencils or pens; and colored markers.

Have the children work in small groups and write letters to **la maestra**, doña Elena, or to one of the puppet friends LeeAnn, Winston, or Kipper. Brainstorm a few ideas on what to mention in the letters, e.g., a favorite episode, a question about Latin music or musical instruments, how they hope to use Spanish in their futures, or an idea for what to include in future videos. Help the children draft the letters and then assign a volunteer in each group to write them. Have the other children decorate the letters. Post the final products on the bulletin board.

Encourage the children to role-play the Mexican restaurant scene from the video. Ask for volunteers to play **la maestra**, **el dueño** (*owner*), **el cocinero** (*male cook*), **la cocinera** (*female cook*), **la tortillera** (*tortilla maker*), **el camarero** (*waiter*), doña Elena, and **los músicos** (*musicians*).

CLOSING

Tell the children that Spanish class is finished until the next school year. Congratulate them on the many things they have learned and tell them that **la maestra** is looking forward to teaching them more Spanish when they meet again after vacation.

FAMILY CONNECTION

To foster a friendly link between home and school, you may want to send out Family Letter 4 (see the Teacher's Resource Book). The letter fosters understanding of what the children are learning in Spanish and suggests enrichment and practice activities outside of school. The final letter suggests ways to continue the children's interest in Spanish over the summer.

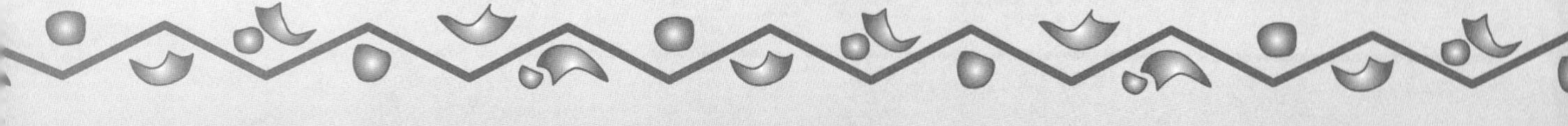

Song Appendix

The lesson where each song is first introduced is indicated in parentheses.

Song 1 (Lesson 1)

Español para ti

(*Spanish Is for You, and for Me*)

Español para ti.	*Spanish for you.*
Español para mí.	*Spanish for me.*
Para ti, para mí.	*For you, for me.*
Y así todos sentir	*And so, everyone feels*
Una nueva sensación.	*A new sensation.*

Song 2 (Lesson 2)

La canción de geografía

(*The Geography Song*)

Los países de habla hispana	*The Spanish-speaking countries*
Todos vamos a contar.	*Let's count them all.*
Veinte naciones de habla hispana	*Twenty Spanish-speaking nations*
Vamos todos a pronunciar.	*Let's pronounce them all.*
España, México, Guatemala,	*Spain, Mexico, Guatemala,*
Honduras, El Salvador, Nicaragua,	*Honduras, El Salvador, Nicaragua,*
Costa Rica, Panamá.	*Costa Rica, Panama.*
En el Caribe tres países	*In the Caribbean three countries*
Todas islas de sol y mar	*All islands of sun and sea*
Cuba, La República Dominicana,	*Cuba, Dominican Republic,*
Puerto Rico allí están.	*Puerto Rico are there.*
Venezuela, Colombia, Ecuador,	*Venezuela, Colombia, Ecuador,*
Perú, Bolivia, Chile,	*Peru, Bolivia, Chile,*
Argentina, Uruguay y Paraguay.	*Argentina, Uruguay, and Paraguay.*
Todos los países de habla hispana	*All the Spanish-speaking countries*
Veinte.	*Twenty.*

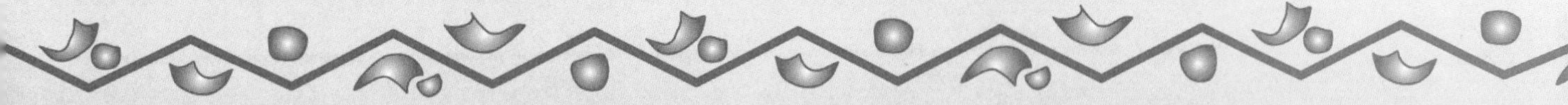

Song 3 (Lesson 5)

Alphabet Rap

a	b	c	n	ñ	o
ch	d	e	p	q	
f	g		r	s	
h	i		t	u	
j	k		v	w	x
l	ll	m	y	z	

Song 4 (Lesson 10)

Months Rap

Los meses del año son:	*The months of the year are:*
Uno, enero.	*1, January.*
Dos, febrero.	*2, February.*
Tres, marzo.	*3, March.*
Cuatro, abril.	*4, April.*
Cinco, mayo.	*5, May.*
Seis, junio.	*6, June.*
Siete, julio.	*7, July.*
Ocho, agosto.	*8, August.*
Nueve, septiembre.	*9, September.*
Diez, octubre.	*10, October.*
Once, noviembre.	*11, November.*
Doce, diciembre.	*12, December.*
Y no más.	*And no more.*

Song 5 (Lesson 10)

Las estaciones
(*The Seasons*)

En el invierno, en el invierno,	*In the winter, in the winter,*
diciembre, enero, febrero.	*December, January, February.*
La primavera, la primavera,	*The spring, the spring,*
marzo, abril y mayo.	*March, April, and May.*
En el verano, en el verano,	*In the summer, in the summer,*
junio y julio y agosto.	*June and July and August.*
Viene septiembre, octubre,	*Come September, October,*
noviembre,	*November,*
para el otoño.	*for the fall.*

Song 6 (Lesson 15)

Las vocales
(*The Vowel Tree Song*)

A, E, I, O, U (4x)
A, mapa.
E, Pepe.
I, Lili.
O, rojo.
U, cucú.
A, E, I, O, U (2x)

Song 7 (Lesson 28)

De diez en diez
(*Ten by Ten*)

Diez, diez, diez.	*Ten. (4x)*
Veinte, veinte, veinte, veinte.	*Twenty. (4x)*
Treinta, treinta, treinta, treinta.	*Thirty. (4x)*
Cuarenta, cuarenta, cuaranta.	*Forty. (3x)*
Cincuenta, cincuenta, cincuenta.	*Fifty. (3x)*
Sesenta, sesenta, sesenta.	*Sixty. (3x)*
Setenta, setenta, setenta.	*Seventy. (3x)*
Ochenta, ochenta, ochenta.	*Eighty. (3x)*
Noventa, noventa, noventa.	*Ninety. (3x)*
Cien, cien, cien.	*Hundred. (3x)*

Song 8 (Lesson 29)

¿Cómo está Lorena?

(*How Is Lorena?*)

¿Cómo está Lorena?	*How is Lorena?*
Está enojada.	*She's angry.*
¿Cómo está Lorena?	*How is Lorena?*
Está contenta.	*She's happy.*
¿Cómo está Lorena?	*How is Lorena?*
Está triste.	*She's sad.*

Song 9 (Lesson 31)

Calendar Rap

Lunes, martes, miercoles, tres.	*Monday, Tuesday, Wednesday, three.*
Uno, dos, tres.	*One, two, three.*
Jueves, viernes, sabado, seis.	*Thursday, Friday, Saturday, six.*
Uno, dos, tres, cuatro, cinco, seis.	*One, two, three, four, five, six.*
Y domingo siete es.	*And Sunday is seven.*
Uno, dos, tres, cuatro, cinco, seis, siete.	*One, two, three, four, five, six, seven.*

Song 10 (Lesson 33)

¿Adónde vas?

(*Where Are You Going?*)

¿Adónde vas? ¿Adónde vas tú?	*Where are you going? Where are you going?*
¿Adónde vas? ¿Adónde vas tú?	*Where are you going? Where are you going?*
Voy al museo, al museo, al museo.	*I'm going to the museum, to the museum, to the museum.*
Aquí estoy.	*Here I am.*

Repeat verse with the following:

Voy al cine. Voy al cine, al cine.	*I'm going to the movies. I'm going to the movies, to the movies.*
Voy al restaurante, al restaurante.	*I'm going to the restaurant, to the restaurant.*
Voy al supermercado, al supermercado.	*I'm going to the supermarket, to the supermarket.*
Voy a la biblioteca, a la biblioteca.	*I'm going to the library, to the library.*
Voy al hospital, al hospital.	*I'm going to the hospital, to the hospital.*

➤ **Song 11** (Lesson 37)

En los Estados Unidos

(*In the United States*)

Chorus:

En los Estados Unidos	*In the United States*
Hay ciudades pequeñas y grandes,	*There are small and large cities,*
Y algunas basan sus nombres	*And some base their names*
En la historia del mundo hispano.	*On the history of the Hispanic world.*
Los Angeles, San Diego, San Francisco,	*Los Angeles, San Diego, San Francisco,*
Las Vegas, Amarillo, Santa Fe,	*Las Vegas, Amarillo, Santa Fe,*
San Antonio, San Agustín.	*San Antonio, Saint Augustine.*

Repeat chorus.

Orlando, Reno, El Dorado, Española,	*Orlando, Reno, El Dorado, Española,*
Buena Vista, Monterey, Mesa, Durango.	*Buena Vista, Monterey, Mesa, Durango.*

Repeat chorus.

Los Estados Unidos, sí.	*The United States, yes.*

➤ **Song 12** (Lesson 50)

De colores

(*Colors*)

De colores, de colores se visten los	*In colors, the countryside is dressed*
campos en la primavera.	*in colors in spring.*
De colores, de colores son los pajaritos	*In colors, the little birds that come from*
que vienen de afuera.	*afar are in colors.*
De colores, de colores es el arco iris	*In colors, the rainbow that we see*
que vemos lucir.	*shining is in colors.*
Y por eso los grandes amores de	*And that is why true loves of many*
muchos colores me gustan a mí.	*colors are pleasing to me.*
Y por eso los grandes amores de	*And that is why true loves of many*
muchos colores me gustan a mí.	*colors are pleasing to me.*

Song 13 (Lesson 56)

¿Dónde está Mimi?
(*Where Is Mimi?*)

¿Mimi? ¿Mimi? ¿Dónde está Mimi?	*Mimi? Mimi? Where is Mimi?*
¿Dónde está?	*Where is she?*
Delante de, delante de, delante de,	*In front of, in front of, in front of,*
Detrás de, detrás de, detrás de (¡detrás de la puerta!)	*Behind, behind, behind* *(behind the door!)*
Cerca de, cerca de, cerca de (¡cerca de la casa!)	*Close to, close to, close to* *(close to the house!)*
Lejos de, lejos de, lejos de (¡lejos de la casa!)	*Far from, far from, far from* *(far from the house!)*
Arriba de, arriba de, arriba de (¡arriba!)	*On top of, on top of, on top of* *(on top of!)*
Debajo de, debajo de, debajo de (¡debajo del coche!)	*Under, under, under* *(under the car!)*
Dentro de, dentro de, dentro de (¡dentro!)	*Inside, inside, inside* *(inside!)*
Fuera de, fuera de, fuera de (¡fuera de la casa!)	*Outside, outside, outside* *(outside the house!)*
Ah, Mimi. Aquí está. Muy bien.	*Ah, Mimi. Here she is. Very good.*
Hola, Mimi. Hola.	*Hi, Mimi. Hi.*

Song 14 (Lesson 59)

Dulce canta el burro
(*Sweetly Sings the Donkey*)

Dulce canta el burro	*Sweetly sings the donkey*
Al ir a comer.	*When he comes to eat.*
Si no lo cuidamos	*If we don't take care of him,*
Él rebuznará.	*He will bray.*
Cají, cajó, cajá.	*Cají, cajó, cajá.*
Cají, cajó, cajá.	*Cají, cajó, cajá.*
Cají, cajó, cajá.	*Cají, cajó, cajá.*
Cají, cajó, cajá.	*Cají, cajó, cajá.*